BARRON'S

Regents Exams and Answers

United States History and Government

EUGENE V. RESNICK, B.A., M.A.
Social Studies Teacher, Midwood High School, Brooklyn, New York

JOHN MCGEEHAN, B.A., M.A., J.D.
Consultant and Writer, New York State Education Department,
Bureau of Social Studies Education, Educational Testing,
and Curriculum Development

MORRIS GALL, J.D., PH.D.
Former President, Association of Teachers of Social Studies
in the City of New York

WILLIAM STREITWIESER, B.A., M.A.
Former Social Studies Teacher, Northport High School, Northport, New York

Test-Taking Tips by
MARK WILLNER, M.A.
Chairman of Social Studies Department,
Midwood High School, Brooklyn, New York

Published by Kaplan, Inc., d/b/a Barron's Educational Series
750 Third Avenue
New York, NY 10017
www.barronseduc.com

ISBN: 978-1-5062-5415-9

Printed in Canada

10 9 8 7 6 5 4 3 2 1

Kaplan, Inc., d/b/a Barron's Educational Series print books are available at special qua
discounts to use for sales promotions, employee premiums, or educational purposes. I
more information or to purchase books, please call the Simon & Schuster special sale
department at 866-506-1949.

Contents

What the Exam Is About

If you are reading this, you are probably at the end of 11th grade and preparing to take the Regents exam in Social Studies. You probably already know that New York State requires you to take the U.S. History and Government Regents exam. Almost every 11th-grade student in New York State will be taking the same exam at the same time you are.

U.S. History and Government is part of a sequence of social studies courses you are required to take from first grade through 12th grade. The purpose of social studies is to help you understand the events and developments that shape the nation and the world you live in. In ninth and tenth grade, you studied cultures on continents other than North America because you need to understand that we live in an interdependent world. In 11th grade, you returned to a study of your own nation. Now that you are more mature and will be eligible to vote in a year or two, you should have a clear understanding of the nature of our Constitution and the workings of our government.

Students in 11th-grade social studies learn about the Constitutional foundations of American society before studying the history of the United States from after the Civil War to modern times.

WHAT IS THE U.S. HISTORY AND GOVERNMENT REGENTS EXAM LIKE?

If you took the Global Studies Regents last year, you already have some idea of what the exam is like. The U.S. History and Government Regents is divided into three parts. All parts have questions on the topics, themes, and skills covered in 11th grade.

The exam is constructed as follows:

- 50 Multiple-Choice Questions   50 minutes   55 percent of grade
- One Thematic Essay   45 minutes   15 percent of grade
- 8 Document-Based Questions
- One Document-Based Essay   60 minutes   30 percent of grade

Many students lose points because they neglect to answer some parts of questions or misread the questions. Be sure to review the following sections: "How to Use This Book" (pages 3–5) and "Test-Taking Tips" (beginning on page 6).

How to Use This Book

This book is designed to help you get the most out of your review for the Regents exam in U.S. History and Government.

TEST-TAKING TIPS

The first section, Test-Taking Tips, will help you become a *better* test taker. Be sure to read this valuable material carefully. The brief rules, many hints, and practice questions will increase your understanding and confidence in answering short-answer and essay questions. The sample answers will enable you to distinguish between a complete and well-written essay and a poor one.

Reread the Test-Taking Tips after taking two or more of the exams, and feel your assurance grow.

PREVIOUS REGENTS EXAMS AND ANSWERS

The second section contains previous Regents exams and answer analyses. The exams will serve as a content review and as a study guide to indicate what is important. By answering the multiple-choice and essay questions, you will be able to discover your weak points. You will then be able to remedy your deficiencies by carefully studying the answers provided. They are more than just model answers; additional facts and explanations have been included for a more thorough understanding of the subjects on which the questions are based. Careful study of the answers will increase your skill in interpreting the questions and in applying the facts learned.

SELF-ANALYSIS CHARTS

The Self-Analysis Charts enable you to note the content areas tested on the exam and the number of questions in each content area. You can calculate your score in each of the content areas of a test to see in which content areas you show strengths or weaknesses.

Each chart has three columns:

1. Column 1 names each topic included in the exam.
2. Column 2 lists the number of each short-answer question on that topic asked in the given exam.
3. Column 3 shows the total point value of short-answer questions on each topic. Since each correct answer is worth about $1\frac{1}{7}$ points, totals are shown to the nearest full point in each content category.

You can calculate the number of points you earned for each content category by multiplying the number of questions you got right by the point value for each question noted at the bottom of the Self-Evaluation Chart. You can calculate the percentage of questions you got right in each content category by dividing the number of points you earned by the total number of points for each category given in Column 3.

If you score lower than 75 percent on any topic, first review your class notes and textbook material; then review the model answers in the book AND the explanations of all choices for each question on that topic. Studying the explanations of the wrong choices will greatly enhance your understanding of the subject matter and alert you to possible errors. It will also be helpful to you to review additional content.

SKILLS QUESTIONS

Please note that space has been provided in the Self-Analysis Charts for you to score and compare separately your achievement on the skills questions on each exam. The skills material includes interpretation of reading passages, cartoons, charts, diagrams, graphs, and maps.

SUMMARY

1. Read the first section, Test-Taking Tips.
2. Take the first exam under test conditions.
3. Answer as many essay questions as possible.
4. Mark Part I of the exam.
5. Complete the Self-Analysis Chart for that exam.
6. Record your weak spots.
7. Answer both the Part II and Part III questions.
8. Study the answers to ALL the questions you could not answer, or answered inadequately.
9. Review your notes and text material on those topics before taking the next exam. Reread the Test-Taking Tips.

Repeat this procedure, exam by exam, and watch that mark soar.

IMPORTANT TERMS TO KNOW

The Glossary of Terms is designed to show you which terms or concepts appeared most frequently on past tests. As you review the Glossary of Terms, you will notice one, two, or three asterisks (*) preceding some of the terms defined. While all the terms are important to know, those with asterisks should be considered most crucial. One asterisk (*) denotes a term that is frequently tested; two asterisks (**) denote a term that is **very** frequently tested; and three asterisks (***) denote a term that is **most** frequently tested.

Test-Taking Tips

TAKING THE REGENTS EXAM

Although teachers and students alike find an "all or nothing" exam at the completion of the course distasteful, the Regents exam in U.S. History and Government in some ways, unfortunately, falls into this category. Without passing the Regents exam, you cannot graduate.

Although this brief section does not claim to provide a comprehensive study guide for taking the Regents, it does contain several tips to help you achieve a good grade on the U.S. History and Government Regents. They are divided into GENERAL HELPFUL TIPS and SPECIFIC HELPFUL TIPS.

GENERAL HELPFUL TIPS

TIP 1
Be confident and prepared.

SUGGESTIONS

- Review short-answer sections from previous tests.
- Use a clock or watch, and take previous exams at home under exam conditions (i.e., don't have the radio or television on).
- Get a review book (The preferred book is Barron's *Let's Review: U.S. History and Government.*)
- Visit *www.barronseduc.com* for the latest information on the Regents exams.
- Talk over the answers to questions on these tests with someone else. Use Barron's website to communicate with subject specialists.
- Finish all your homework assignments.
- Look over classroom exams that your teacher gave during the term.

- Take class notes carefully.
- Practice good study habits.
- Know that there are answers for every question.
- Be aware that the people who made up the Regents want you to pass.
- Remember that thousands of students over the last few years have taken and passed the Regents. You can pass too!
- On the night prior to the exam, lay out all the things you will need, such as clothing, pens, and admission cards.
- Go to bed early; eat wisely.
- Bring at least two pens to the exam room.
- Bring your favorite good luck charm/jewelry to the exam.
- Once you are in the exam room, arrange your things, get comfortable, be relaxed, and attend to personal needs (the bathroom).
- Keep your eyes on your own paper; do not let them wander over to anyone else's.
- Be polite in making any reasonable demands of the proctor, such as changing your seat or having window shades raised or lowered.

TIP 2

Read test instructions and questions carefully.

SUGGESTIONS

- Be familiar with the test directions ahead of time.
- Decide upon the task(s) that you have to complete.
- Know how the test will be graded.
- Know which question or questions are worth the most points.
- Give only the information that is requested.
- Underline important words and phrases.
- Ask for assistance from the proctor if you do not understand the directions.

TIP 3

Budget your test time in a balanced manner.

SUGGESTIONS

- Bring a watch or clock to the test.
- Know how much time is allowed.
- Arrive on time; leave your home earlier than usual.
- Prepare a time schedule and try to stick to it. (The suggested times for each section are 50 minutes for the 50 multiple-choice questions, 45 minutes for the one thematic essay, and 60 minutes for the document-based questions.)
- Answer the easier questions first.
- Devote more time to the harder questions and to those worth more credit.
- Don't get "hung up" on a question that is proving to be difficult; go on to another question and return later to the difficult one.
- Ask the proctor for permission to go to the bathroom, if necessary, or if only to "take a break" from sitting in the room.
- Plan to stay in the room for the entire three hours. If you finish early, read over your work—there may be some things that you omitted or that you may wish to add. You also may wish to polish your grammar, spelling, and penmanship.

TIP 4

Be "kind" to the exam grader/evaluator.

SUGGESTIONS

- Assume that you are the teacher grading/evaluating your test paper.
- Answer questions in an orderly sequence.
- Write legibly.
- Use proper grammar, spelling, and sentence structure.
- Write essay answers in ink.
- Proofread your answers prior to submitting your exam paper. Have you answered all the short-answer questions and the required number of essays?

TIP 5

Use your reasoning skills.

SUGGESTIONS

- Answer *all* questions.
- Relate (connect) the question to anything that you studied, wrote in your notebook, or heard your teacher say in class.
- Relate (connect) the question to any film you saw in class, any project you did, or to anything you may have learned from newspapers, magazines, or television.
- Decide whether your answers would be approved by your teacher.
- Look over the entire test to see whether one part of it can help you answer another part.
- Write down as many of the **16 key concepts** and the **13 enduring constitutional issues** that you remember from your U.S. History and Government classes. (Among the **concepts** are culture, diversity, empathy, and interdependence.) Try to remember the meanings of these terms. Use them in answering questions, where relevant.

TIP 6

Don't be afraid to guess.

SUGGESTIONS

- In general, go with your first answer choice.
- Eliminate obvious incorrect choices.
- If still unsure of an answer, make an educated guess.
- There is no penalty for guessing; therefore, answer ALL questions. An omitted answer gets no credit.

Let's now review the six GENERAL HELPFUL TIPS for short-answer questions:

> ### SUMMARY OF TIPS
> 1. Be confident and prepared.
> 2. Read test instructions and questions carefully.
> 3. Budget your test time in a balanced manner.
> 4. Be "kind" to the exam grader/evaluator.
> 5. Use your reasoning skills.
> 6. Don't be afraid to guess.

SPECIFIC HELPFUL TIPS FOR THE SHORT-ANSWER (MULTIPLE-CHOICE) QUESTIONS

TIP 1
Answer the easy questions first.

The best reason for using this hint is that it can build up your confidence. It also enables you to use your time more efficiently. You should answer these questions first, while skipping over and circling the numbers of the more difficult questions. You can always return to these later during the exam. Easy questions usually contain short sentences and few words. The answer can often be arrived at quickly from the information presented.

Example

The authors of the United States Constitution believed that the voice of the people should be heard frequently. Which part of the Government was instituted to respond most directly to the will of the people?

1. Senate
2. House of Representatives
3. Supreme Court
4. Presidency

(from an actual Regents exam)

The correct answer, choice 2, is obvious. It is the only choice describing a component—in fact, the only component—in the original Constitution that was chosen directly by *the will of the people*. Senators were initially chosen by state legislatures (choice 1). Supreme Court judges have always been appointed (choice 3), while the President (choice 4) is chosen via an indirect vote by the people and at times has not been reflective of *the will of the people*.

TIP 2
Consider what the questioner wants you to do, and underline key words.

Remember that the people who made up the Regents questions had specific tasks they want you to accomplish. These tasks can be understood if you read instructions carefully, underline key words, and put yourself "in their shoes." Try to figure out what they would want a student to do with a given question. Determine for yourself exactly what is being tested. Underlining helps you focus on the key ideas in the question.

Example

At times, the United States Government has passed protective tariffs to

1. encourage foreign trade
2. help the nation's manufacturers
3. reduce the cost of consumer goods
4. improve the quality of goods

(from an actual Regents exam)

By underlining *protective tariffs*, you are on your way to focusing on the thrust of this question. You are being asked to identify something done that was presumed to be beneficial to the U.S. economy at specific times in history. The correct answer, choice 2, contains the only beneficial impact that a protective tariff would have. Choices 1 and 3, although beneficial, describe consequences likely to occur with the removal of tariffs. Choice 4 has little to do with whether or not tariffs exist. Now, in the next question, underline the key words.

The Republican presidents of the 1920s generally followed a foreign policy based on

1. collective security
2. brinkmanship
3. noninvolvement
4. militarism

(from an actual Regents exam)

The key words in the stem that needed to be underlined were *Republican* and *1920s*. You would thus be led to conclude that the only relevant choice would be 3, which describes the isolationist foreign policy of the United States in the post-World War I period. All the presidents in the 1920s were Republicans and generally wanted to reduce America's involvement with other nations.

TIP 3

Look for clues among choices in the question, as well as in other questions.

By reading questions and choices carefully, you may often find words and phrases that provide clues to an answer. This hint is important because it assists you in making links and connections between various questions.

Example

Which events best support the image of the 1920s as a decade of nativist sentiment?

1. the passage of the National Origins Act and the rise of the Ku Klux Klan
2. the Scopes trial and the passage of women's suffrage
3. the Washington Naval Conference and the Kellogg-Briand Pact
4. the growth of the auto industry and the Teapot Dome affair

(from an actual Regents exam)

Choice 1 is correct. It is the only choice naming events that were connected to harsh feelings toward foreigners. That harshness was part of the thinking of Americans who had *nativist sentiments*.

Let's examine another attempt to find a clue.

In the Colonial Era, developments such as the New England town meetings and the establishment of the Virginia House of Burgesses represented

1. colonial attempts to build a strong national government
2. efforts by the British to strengthen their control over the colonies
3. steps in the growth of representative democracy
4. early social reform movements

(from an actual Regents exam)

Can you determine the right answer? Both developments were political in purpose, and both were examples of democracy. The only choice that relates to these features is 3.

TIP 4

Examine all possibilities. Beware of tricky and tempting foils (decoys).

By remembering this tip you will be careful to survey all possible responses before making a selection. A given choice, or two, may initially appear to be the correct answer. This often happens when you are asked to make a generalization about a group of people or events.

Example

A similarity between the Red Scare of the 1920s and McCarthyism in the 1950s was that during each period

1. thousands of American citizens were expelled from the United States
2. the Communist Party gained many members in the United States
3. many government employees were convicted of giving secrets to the Soviet Union
4. the civil liberties of American citizens were threatened

(from an actual Regents exam)

Choice 4 is correct; however, all the other choices certainly "sound" correct. Indeed, the other choices represent true decoys. Choices 1 and 2 are tempting, as they do have a connection with the color *Red* in *Red Scare*. Choice 1 is certainly something "scary," even though no such event ever occurred in American history.

TIP 5

Always select the broader, more encompassing choice.

This tip is most helpful when two or more choices are correct, but you conclude that one choice is broader (or more encompassing) than the other. Indeed, one choice may actually include the other or others.

Example

"Up to our own day, American history is the history of the colonization of the Great West. The existence of an area of free land, . . . and the advance of American settlement westward explain American development."

This quotation of the 1890s suggests that the American frontier

1. should be preserved for free use by all the people
2. has mirrored European values and social patterns
3. will continue indefinitely as a region to be colonized
4. has had a positive effect on the growth of the United States

(from an actual Regents exam)

Choices 1, 2, and 3 have some validity, as they have been characteristic of varying attitudes toward the frontier. However, choice 4 is the best choice. It more fully and broadly answers the question. Examine the next question and see if you can figure out the answer.

Throughout United States history, the most important aim of the country's foreign policy has been

1. participation in international organizations
2. advancement of national self-interest
3. containment of communism
4. development of military alliances

(from an actual Regents exam)

Choices 1, 3, and 4 have all characterized U.S. foreign policy at varying times in our nation's history. However, each of these policies was put forth only when we decided it helped meet what we perceived to be our national self-interest at the time. Therefore, choice 2 is the best, all-encompassing answer for this question.

TIP 6

Use a process of elimination.

This tip provides a very good way of arriving at an answer. It is particularly useful when you face a difficult question and are unsure of the best response. Also, it increases your chances of coming up with the correct answer and (1) assists in discarding *unacceptable* choices and (2) narrows the possible *acceptable* choices. (You may wish to physically cross out on the question page the choices that you decide are incorrect.)

Example

How did the personal diplomacy conducted by President Franklin D. Roosevelt during World War II affect the presidency?

1. Subsequent presidents have refused to use this unsuccessful method.
2. The president's role in shaping United States foreign policy was strengthened.
3. The president's war powers as Commander in Chief were sharply reduced.
4. Congress increased its power over the executive branch.

(from an actual Regents exam)

In wartime, a president's ability to expand his powers as a result of his role as Commander in Chief is very great. This was certainly true of Franklin D. Roosevelt during World War II. Choice 3, therefore, is clearly wrong as it states an untrue situation. Choice 4 is wrong, as Congress during wartime will usually side with the president. Choice 1 can be eliminated, as it is simply untrue. Presidents since Roosevelt have sought to increase their diplomatic powers, well aware of his precedent-setting actions. Therefore, choice 2 is correct.

See if you can use a process of elimination to figure out the right answer to this next question.

Which statement is accurate about American culture during the Great Depression?

1. The federal government provided money to support the arts.
2. Most movies featured realistic themes and unhappy endings.
3. Rock-and-roll music became popular.
4. Interest in professional sports declined.

(from an actual Regents exam)

Did you pick choice 1? Good! Choice 2 can be eliminated, as it describes the opposite of what happened—most movies had happy themes, and sought to uplift peoples' spirits. The sadness of the times also spurred people to seek some enjoyment in entertainment forms such as sporting events (choice 4). Rock-and-roll music was not to become popular until the 1950s, many years after the Great Depression.

TIP 7
Detect differences among the choices presented.

You should be careful in picking out foils and decoys, something we mentioned in Tip #4. In a similar manner, this tip helps you in choosing among general and specific answers. This is especially important when you have reduced your selections to two choices.

Example

In the 1920s, the depressed situation of United States agriculture was chiefly caused by

1. overregulation by government
2. mechanization and overproduction
3. inefficient production techniques
4. stock-market speculation

(from an actual Regents exam)

The four choices all sound like factors that would lead to economic crises but, upon closer examination, choices 1 and 3 can be ruled out, as neither was characteristic of the United States in the 1920s. There was little regulation by government, as laissez-faire was a commonly held belief. Also, while production techniques were inefficient by today's standards, they were adequate in the 1920s as they resulted in a surplus of goods. Choices 2 and 4 were indeed factors leading to the Great Depression, yet stock-market speculation, choice 4, did not significantly affect *the depressed situation of United States agriculture*. Factors that did affect this situation are described in choice 2, the correct answer.

TIP 8
Don't choose an answer that is correct in itself but incorrect as it relates to the question.

It is crucial to keep this tip in mind when evaluating a question that has attractive choices. They will appear attractive because each has an element of truth; however, you must decide which one of these has the greatest relationship to the question itself. Let's look at a question we have seen elsewhere—Tip #7.

Example

In the 1920s, the depressed situation of United States agriculture was chiefly caused by

1. overregulation by government
2. mechanization and overproduction
3. inefficient production techniques
4. stock-market speculation

(from an actual Regents exam)

As you know, the correct answer is choice 2. Yet, although choices 2 and 4 were factors leading to the Great Depression, it is only choice 2 that best relates to the question. (See the discussion for Tip #7.) Now, try the following question.

Example

Which event of the early 1900s is evidence that Upton Sinclair's novel, *The Jungle*, had an important impact on the United States?

1. adoption of reforms in public education
2. passage of legislation limiting immigration
3. adoption of the 18th Amendment establishing Prohibition
4. passage of legislation requiring federal inspection of meat

(from an actual Regents exam)

Choice 4 is the correct answer, as it describes an event relating directly to Upton Sinclair's novel. The other three choices describe events that did occur in the first third of the 20th century, but had nothing to do with the novel.

TIP 9

Look for "giveaways" and "freebies."

There are times when a test question practically gives away the answer. You can determine such rare moments by focusing on obvious words, prefixes, grammatical construction, and other revealing tips.

Example

Which New Deal program was chiefly designed to correct abuses in the stock market?

1. Federal Emergency Relief Act
2. Civilian Conservation Corps
3. Works Progress Administration
4. Securities and Exchange Commission

(from an actual Regents exam)

Choice 4 stands out as the correct answer; *securities* is a word practically synonymous with *stock market*. The New Deal programs named in choices 1, 2, and 3 had nothing to do with correcting *abuses in the stock market*.

TIP 10

Think out the answer before looking at the possible choices.

This tip helps to stimulate memory recall. As you read a question, your "intellectual radar" may pick up something that will jog loose a key thought, concept, or fact in your mind.

Example

The Great Society of Lyndon Johnson is most similar to which other presidential program?

1. Warren Harding's Return to Normalcy
2. Franklin D. Roosevelt's New Deal
3. Ronald Reagan's New Federalism
4. George Bush's Thousand Points of Light

(from an actual Regents exam)

As you were reading the question, you should have thought about some well-known president and his domestic program that aimed to improve our nation's standard of living. Choice 2 meets these criteria. Along with the Great Society program, the New Deal sought to have the federal government take an active role in promoting peoples' health and welfare. The programs identified in choices 1, 3, and 4 did not have this goal.

This tip is also useful when interpreting cartoons. As you look at a cartoon, try to guess its meaning prior to looking at the choices. Most cartoon interpretation questions will require you to decide on a title for the cartoon or to indicate the message of the cartoonist.

Example

Which aspect of the United States Government is best illustrated by the cartoon?

1. system of checks and balances
2. veto power of the president
3. congressional committee system
4. civilian control of the military

(from an actual Regents exam)

The cartoon suggests something that the Senate can do and/or has already done. It also conveys a negative thought, to judge by the torn paper in a wastebasket labeled "rejections." The correct choice is 1. Choices 2, 3, and 4 do not deal with a specific power of the Senate, even though they do describe ways by which a governmental action can be restricted.

TIP 11

Make informed and educated guesses.

If you are not sure of an answer, don't be afraid to guess. Any answer is better than no answer—you have nothing to lose, as there is no penalty for guessing. Remember that the correct answer is there, somewhere, right on the exam page, waiting for you to find it. If you've eliminated one or more options, then your chances of picking the right answer increases from one out of four to one out of three, etc. A word of caution—guessing should be used only as a last resort. Do not go into the Regents expecting to pass by guessing your way through the questions. There is no substitute for careful, diligent exam preparation long before the exam date itself.

Example

Which New Deal reforms most directly targeted the basic problem of the victims of the Dust Bowl?

1. guaranteeing workers the right to organize and bargain collectively
2. regulating the sale of stocks and bonds
3. providing farmers low-cost loans and parity payments
4. raising individual and corporate income tax rates

(from an actual Regents exam)

Choice 3 is the correct answer. It contains the word *farmers*, a clear link to the phrase *Dust Bowl*. Even if you did not recognize this phrase right away, you could certainly eliminate choices 2 and 4; they do not refer to people (*victims*). While choice 1 does refer to people (*workers*), it does not name a group that would be associated with *dust*. Let's look at another question whose answer could be arrived at by making an informed and educated guess.

The widespread use of computers had led to a national concern over

1. increased pollution of the environment
2. guarding the right of privacy
3. protection of the right to petition
4. a decline in television viewing

(from an actual Regents exam)

At first reading, this question might appear strange because you might not expect to see a question about computers on a history exam. In addition, it is possible that your teacher did not cover the subject of computers in your social studies class. Nevertheless, even if these things were true and if you don't know how to use a computer, you can still guess at the answer. Careful rereading of the question would reveal that choices 3 and 4 are not really items causing *national concern*. Choices 1 and 2 do describe issues of such concern; however, using computers has little to do with causing pollution. Since they do have the capacity to store great amounts of information about people, abuse of this capacity could cause problems affecting the right to privacy—choice 2.

Let's now review the 11 SPECIFIC HELPFUL TIPS for short-answer questions:

SUMMARY OF TIPS

1. Answer the easy questions first.
2. Consider what the questioner wants you to do, and underline key words.
3. Look for clues among choices in the question, as well as in other questions.
4. Examine all possibilities. Beware of tricky and tempting foils (decoys).
5. Always select the broader, more encompassing choice.
6. Use a process of elimination.
7. Detect differences among the choices presented.
8. Don't choose an answer that is correct in itself but incorrect as it relates to the question.
9. Look for "giveaways" and "freebies."
10. Think out the answer before looking at the possible choices.
11. Make informed and educated guesses.

In addition to these SPECIFIC HELPFUL TIPS, here are five more bonus ones:

1. Read each question twice.
2. Generally, try to go with your first inclination.
3. Avoid looking for patterns.
4. Be aware that universals (i.e., *always, never, only*) should usually be disregarded as possible correct choices.
5. Bear in mind that sometimes the essays will provide answers to the short answers.

SPECIFIC HELPFUL TIPS FOR THE ESSAY QUESTIONS

TIP 1
Understand the essay format: thematic and document-based questions.

Part II of the Regents exam consists of one thematic essay for which you will have 45 minutes to write. The thematic essay will be worth 15 percent of your score. Write a well-organized essay that includes an introduction, several paragraphs that address the task, and a conclusion. Be aware of key terms in the question, for example, *show, discuss, compare.* The thematic essay does not ask only for a recollection of facts, but rather asks the student to focus on themes and to demonstrate critical thinking. Those scoring the essay will use the following Generic Scoring Rubric:

GENERIC SCORING RUBRIC
THEMATIC ESSAY

5

- Shows a thorough understanding of the theme
- Addresses all aspects of the task
- Shows an ability to analyze, evaluate, compare, and/or contrast issues and events
- Richly supports essay with relevant facts, examples, and details
- Writes a well-developed essay, consistently demonstrating a logical and clear plan of organization
- Includes a strong introduction and conclusion

4

- Shows a good understanding of the theme
- Addresses all aspects of the task
- Shows an ability to analyze, evaluate, compare, and/or contrast issues and events
- Includes relevant facts, examples, and details, but may not support all aspects of the task evenly
- Writes a well-developed essay, demonstrating a logical and clear plan of organization
- Includes a good introduction and conclusion

3

- Presents a satisfactory understanding of the theme
- Addresses most aspects of the task or addresses all aspects in a limited way
- Is able to analyze or evaluate issues and events, but not in any depth
- Writes a satisfactorily developed essay, demonstrating a general plan of organization
- Uses some facts, examples, and details
- Restates the theme in the introduction and concludes with a simple restatement of the theme

2

- Attempts to address the theme, but uses vague and/or inaccurate information
- Develops a faulty analysis or evaluation of theme
- Writes a poorly organized essay, lacking focus and using few facts, examples, and details
- Has vague or missing introduction and/or conclusion

1

- Shows limited understanding of the theme; omits concrete examples; details are weak or nonexistent
- Lacks an analysis or evalution of the issues and events beyond stating vague and/or inaccurate facts
- Attempts to complete the task, but essay demonstrates a major weakness in organization
- Uses little or no accurate or relevant facts, details, or examples
- Has no introduction or conclusion

0

- Fails to address the theme
- Is illegible
- Blank paper

Part III of the Regents exam consists of one document-based question for which you will have 60 minutes to write. The document-based essay will be worth 30 percent of your score. The document-based question will be divided into two parts; a Part A short-answer section (15 percent) and a Part B essay (15 percent). Following the questions, approximately eight short documents will be provided. Each Part A question will address a specific document. Answer the question using the document and the author's point of view and incorporate information about the time period from which the document has been selected. The Part B essay requires you to state your position (thesis) in an introductory paragraph, then develop your argument in the body of the essay using information from most of the documents to support your position. Using outside information from your knowledge of the time period will enhance the essay. You should include a brief conclusion restating your position. As with the multiple-choice section, budget your time. Those scoring the essay will use the following Generic Scoring Rubric:

GENERIC SCORING RUBRIC
DOCUMENT-BASED QUESTION

5

- Thoroughly addresses all aspects of the task by accurately analyzing and interpreting most of the documents
- Incorporates relevant outside information
- Richly supports essay with relevant facts, examples, and details
- Writes a well-developed essay, consistently demonstrating a logical and clear plan of organization
- Uses information from the documents in the body of the essay
- Includes a strong introduction and conclusion

4

- Addresses all aspects of the task by accurately analyzing and interpreting most of the documents
- Incorporates relevant outside information
- Includes relevant facts, examples, and details, but discussion may be more descriptive than analytical
- Writes a well-developed essay, demonstrating a logical and clear plan of organization
- Includes a good introduction and conclusion

3

- Addresses most aspects of the task or addresses all aspects in a limited way; uses some of the documents
- Incorporates limited or no relevant outside information
- Uses some facts, examples, and details, but discussion is more descriptive than analytical
- Writes a satisfactorily developed essay, demonstrating a general plan of organization
- States the theme in the introduction and concludes with a simple restatement of the theme or topic

2

- Attempts to address some aspects of the task, making limited use of the documents
- Presents no relevant outside information
- Uses few facts, examples, and details; discussion simply restates contents of the documents
- Writes a poorly organized essay, lacking focus
- Has vague or missing introduction and/or conclusion

1

- Shows limited understanding of the task with vague, unclear references to the documents
- Presents no relevant outside information
- Attempts to complete the task, but essay demonstrates a major weakness in organization
- Uses little or no accurate or relevant facts, details, or examples
- Has no introduction or conclusion

0

- Fails to address the task
- Is illegible
- Blank paper

TIP 2
Go over the thematic essay before writing any answers and draw initial impressions.

Write down some ideas that come to mind, while underlining key words and phrases. This tip is valuable as it helps you retain initial ideas and thoughts about the subject matter of the question. In addition, it could provide you with some outline notes that could ultimately be used for your answer.

TIP 3
Go over the document-based question and draw initial impressions.

Go over the Historical Context section and the Task sections of the document-based question. Write down any quick notes about the time period being addressed by the question. Once again, this could provide you with some outline notes that could ultimately be used for your answer.

TIP 4
Prepare a time schedule.

This tip enables you to organize your test-taking time and allows you to focus your attention on those essays that are easiest for you. Allow sufficient time for each essay part. If there are three parts to an essay, decide how much time to allocate for each part. Write as much as you know for each part. The more you write, using as many examples as possible to answer the question, the better your chances for obtaining maximum credit. However, make adjustments according to the number of parts and to the value of each one. If you allocate 30 minutes for a three-part essay in which each part has equal worth, and then devote 20 minutes to part a, you will probably get maximum credit for part a but very little credit for parts b and c. Apportion time and values accordingly.

TIP 5
Look for key words, both in the directions and in the question itself.

By understanding key words in the directions, you are on your way to answering the question in a proper manner. The key directive words for all Regents essay questions are listed in a set of general instructions on the exam itself, between the short-answer questions and the essay questions.

The key directive words in the instructions are *discuss*, *describe*, *explain*, and *evaluate*. They are defined and these definitions should be referred to as you answer the essay question.

PART II: THEMATIC ESSAY

Directions: Write a well-organized essay that includes an introduction, several paragraphs addressing the task below, and a conclusion.

Theme: Government—Power of the Judiciary

Shortly after the formation of the new constitutional government, the Supreme Court established itself as an equal to the legislative and executive branches.

Task:

From your study of the Supreme Court under the leadership of Chief Justice John Marshall, identify two cases that strengthened the power of the Supreme Court.
For each case identified: • *Discuss* the facts of the case   • *Describe* the court's decision   • *Explain* how the decision strengthened the power of the Supreme Court and the federal government

You may use cases decided during the Marshall Court era. Some suggestions you might wish to consider are *Marbury* v. *Madison* (1803), *McCulloch* v. *Maryland* (1819), and *Gibbons* v. *Ogden* (1824).

You are *not* limited to these suggestions.

Guidelines: The key content words in the question are *judiciary, equal, strengthened, decision*. The focus of the thematic essay should be concentrating on how the Supreme Court strengthened itself with powers granted or assumed through the cases provided. It is critical that you limit your discussion after describing the facts and the decision to how the case strengthened the power of the Supreme Court.

TIP 6

Outline an answer before writing.

By following this tip, you will be able to begin organizing your essay answers in a definitive manner. You will also be able to put down important ideas quickly and clearly. Your outline can be structured in any format you wish—it will not be graded. It can be placed in your exam booklet.

Example

An example of a simple, usable outline is given on page 30. It is based on the Thematic Essay from a Regents exam.

Theme: Reform Movements in the United States

> Reform movements are intended to improve different aspects of American life. Through the actions of individuals, organizations, or the government, the goals of these reform movements have been achieved, but with varying degrees of success.

Task:

Identify **two** reform movements that have had an impact on American life and for **each**

- *Discuss* **one** major goal of the movement
- *Describe* **one** action taken by an individual, an organization, or the government in an attempt to achieve this goal
- *Evaluate* the extent to which this goal was achieved

You may use any reform movement from your study of United States history. Some suggestions you might wish to consider include the abolitionist movement, women's suffrage movement, temperance movement, progressive movement, civil rights movement, women's rights movement, and environmental movement.

You are *not* limited to these suggestions.

I. Progressive Movement
    A. Major goal
        Use the power of the government to address problems associated with the rise of industry in the United States, such as unsafe and unsanitary conditions.
    B. Action taken
        In 1906, Upton Sinclair, one of several "muckrakers," wrote *The Jungle*, a novel that exposed the dangerous and unhealthy conditions in the meatpacking industry.
    C. Level of success
        The Progressive Movement was successful in achieving its goal. In 1906 the federal government passed the Meat Inspection Act and the Pure Food and Drug Act.

II. Civil Rights Movement
    A. Major goal
        Change policies in the United States that segregated African Americans from whites in public facilities, and that limited the ability of African Americans to vote.
    B. Action taken
        In 1955, the Rev. Martin Luther King, Jr., led the African American community in Montgomery, Alabama, to boycott the bus system following the arrest of Rosa Parks for not giving up her seat to a white rider.
    C. Level of success
        The bus boycott was successful in pressuring the city of Montgomery to end its discriminatory policies in regard to bus ridership. By the mid-1960s, the movement was successful in pushing for major legislation in regard to civil rights, such as the Civil Rights Act (1964) and the Voting Rights Act (1965).

This outline is like a skeleton. A good essay will add "muscle, flesh, ligaments," etc., in complete sentences.

TIP 7

Make use of the question to compose your introductory sentence.

Directions: Write a well-organized essay that includes an introduction, several paragraphs addressing the task below, and a conclusion.

Theme: Separation of Powers

The balance of the three branches of the federal government has, historically, been in a constant state of flux.

Task:

From your study of the Reconstruction Period (1863–1876), identify two examples of the operation of checks and balances within the federal government.

For each example identified:

- *Discuss* a specific proposed action by the particular branch of government (executive, legislative, or judicial).
- *Describe* the reaction to the action by another branch of government.
- *Explain* the settlement or outcome of the debated issue.

You may use any examples from the Reconstruction Period. Some suggestions you might wish to consider are Lincoln's Proclamation of Amnesty and Reconstruction (December 1863) and Congress's Wade-Davis Bill (July 1864), President Johnson's plan of Reconstruction (May 1865) and the reaction of Congress with the passage of the Military Reconstruction Act (March 1867) and the passage by Congress of the Tenure in Office Act (March 1867), President Johnson's veto of the Act (1867), and the subsequent impeachment of President Johnson (1868).

You are *not* limited to these suggestions.

Guidelines: Once you have read the question and decided on the two examples of checks and balances, you can begin to write your answer with a topic sentence that "borrows" words from the question. Consider the following:

Example

> The Reconstruction Period (1863–1876) provides a helpful time period in United States history to discuss examples of the system of checks and balances and how the system has contributed to the flexibility of government.

TIP 8

Be sure to include sufficient details and examples in your answer.

This tip is very important and will help you to do well on an answer by letting the grader know that *you know* your material. Following this tip will show that you have explained and given support to the main ideas you have expressed. You should use it after writing your topic sentence and any other introductory statements. For the general statements you make, along with the main ideas you express, you must present any necessary, requested supporting data. This could include events, names, dates, reason, results, or other facts. As you write your essay answers, make believe that the person who will grade them is *not* a social studies teacher. Therefore, it becomes your responsibility to state *all* necessary information in a clear, logical, and supportive manner. Below is an essay question and a sample, partial answer to each of three parts.

Directions: Write a well-organized essay that includes an introduction, several paragraphs addressing the task below, and a conclusion.

Theme: Government—Power of the Judiciary

> Shortly after the formation of the new constutitional government, the Supreme Court established itself as an equal to the legislative and executive branches.

Task:

> From your study of the Supreme Court under the leadership of Chief Justice John Marshall, identify two cases which strengthened the power of the Supreme Court.
>
> For each case identified:
> - *Discuss* the facts of the case
> - *Describe* the court's decision
> - *Explain* how the decision strengthened the power of the Supreme Court and the federal government

You are *not* limited to these suggestions.

Guidelines: You may use cases decided during the Marshall Court era. Some suggestions you might wish to consider are *Marbury* v. *Madison* (1803), *McCulloch* v. *Maryland* (1819), and *Gibbons* v. *Ogden* (1824).

Example

> *Gibbons* v. *Ogden* (1824) involved competing steamboat companies navigating the waters of the Hudson River between New Jersey and New York. Because of the fact that the Hudson River made the common boundary of New York and New Jersey, the issue became one involving interstate commerce, a power delegated in the Constitution to the Congress of the United States. The Supreme Court's decision clearly defined Congress's power to regulate interstate (and foreign) commerce.

TIP 9

Use connective and linking words in your answers.

The use of such words, also called transitional words, is important when writing your essay answers. These words make your answers clearer and more logical, while helping the reader to understand the development of your ideas. The words are also useful in providing supporting data for main ideas, as well as changing from one idea to another. Here is a list of words that are often used to make connections and linkages, along with the specific purposes they serve in constructing a meaningful essay answer.

Connective and Linking Words	Purpose
1. first, second, next, last	to show sequence and order
2. because, therefore, thus, consequently, ultimately	to show cause and effect
3. for example, in other words, indeed	to emphasize something, to clarify an idea
4. however, but, yet, on the other hand, instead, still, although	to show contrast or change
5. similarly, in like manner	to show no change
6. furthermore, moreover, in addition, also, another	to note added information
7. meanwhile, presently, previously, subsequently	to show time relationship
8. finally, in conclusion, to sum up	to present a summary, to tie things together

The above suggestions would be useful when doing any kind of expository writing, whether in social studies or any other subject. Try them out on your next U.S. History and Government classroom exam, as well as when practicing essay writing with previous Regents exam essay questions.

TIP 10

If you are short of time, give an answer in outline form.

A Regents exam is three hours long; however, for any number of reasons, you may find yourself running short of time. If this happens, you should briefly, but neatly, put your answer in an outline form. (*Some* answer is better than *no* answer.) You should do this *only* as an *emergency measure*—not something you planned to do initially. For that reason, be assured that this tip is not contradicting #6. The advice in that tip was simply a guideline for you, to help in putting forth the complete essay answer that would be graded. In regard to the advice in this tip, however, the outline *is* the answer; it is what will be graded. Consequently, you should devote much care to its construction. It should follow a specific, easy-to-read style, such as the Harvard outline standard. Roman numerals, followed by capital letters and Arabic numerals, should be used. Sentences and phrases, as both topics and sub-topics, should be written in the same form and in the same tense. This is called *parallel construction*.

TIP 11

If you are uncertain about what to write, make an informed and educated guess.

If you are not sure of what to write down for an answer, don't be afraid to guess. This is the advice we gave you in Tip #11 for the short-answer questions. With the essays, as with the short answers, you have nothing to lose by making an educated guess; there is no penalty for guessing. Indeed, with the essays, you may even be able to get some extra credit—part credit is certainly better than no credit at all! You cannot afford to leave blank a 15-point question. Present whatever information you can give about an item.

A word of caution, however, as we said in Tip #11 for short answers. Guessing should be used *only* as a last resort in answering a question. Do not go into the Regents expecting to pass by guessing your way through the questions. There is no substitute for careful, diligent exam preparation long before the exam date itself.

PART III: DOCUMENT-BASED ESSAY

The following questions (Part A and Part B) are based on the accompanying documents (1–6). Some of these documents have been edited for the purpose of this exercise. The question is designed to test your ability to work with historical documents and to demonstrate knowledge of the subject matter being presented. As you analyze the documents, take into account both the source of the document and the author's point of view.

Directions: Write a well-organized essay that includes your analysis of the documents. You should include specific historical details and you may discuss documents not provided in the question.

Historical Context:
The Bill of Rights was added to the Constitution in 1791 to protect individual liberties against government abuse.

PART A

The documents below relate to issues concerning the Fourth, Fifth, Sixth, and Eighth Amendments. Examine each document carefully and then answer the questions that follow.

Document 1

> I have little patience with people who take the Bill of Rights for granted. The Bill of Rights, contained in the first ten amendments to the Constitution, is every American's guarantee of freedom.
>
>   President Harry Truman, Memoirs, Vol. II (1955)

1. What did President Truman mean by the statement "the first ten amendments . . . is every American's guarantee of freedom"?

Note: Eight documents form this segment of the actual exam. A single document is supplied as an example.

PART B

Essay Response:

Your essay should be well organized with an introductory paragraph that states your position on the question. Develop your position in the next paragraphs and then write a conclusion. In your essay, include specific historical details and refer to the specific documents you analyzed in Part A. You may include additional information from your knowledge of social studies.

Example

> The Bill of Rights was added to the Constitution in 1791 to protect individual liberties against government abuse. Assess the validity of this statement with particular attention to the areas of search, interrogation, and prosecution.

Even if you are not familiar with President Truman and the specific cases defining amendments in the areas of search, interrogation, and prosecution, you would most likely be able to respond to the question by describing protections in your own environment, perhaps the school setting. Can your locker be searched by the school principal? What steps have to be taken by the school before you can be suspended or expelled? You know more than you think!

TIP 12

Write a suitable summary statement.

A suitable summary statement shows that you have successfully developed your main ideas in your essay. In addition, composing your summary statement helps to conclude your essay in a logical manner. A summary statement can be a rephrasing of the major points asserted in the introduction to the essay. It can also present the conclusions of the essay, which contains an orderly development of ideas. Thus, the person grading your essay will be impressed with its ending.

Example

Write a well-organized essay that includes an introduction, several paragraphs addressing the task below, and a conclusion.

Theme: Science and Technology

Science and technology have brought about great changes in many areas of American life.

Task:

From your study of the 20th century, choose three major scientific/technological developments.

For each scientific/technological development chosen:

- *Identify* the scientific/technological development.
- *Describe* the effects of the scientific/technological development on American life.
- *Discuss* the extent to which the development had a positive or a negative effect on American life.

You may use any major scientific/technological developments from your study of 20th-century U.S. history. Some suggestions you may wish to consider are mass production of the automobile (1900–1930), invention of the airplane and eventual trans-Atlantic flight (1903–1927), television (1945–present), nuclear weapons (1945–present), and home use of the personal computer (1980–present).

You are *not* limited to these suggestions.

Guidelines: After selecting the examples you chose to use and presenting the required descriptions and discussions, finish with a summary statement that "returns" to the main point of the essay identified in the question. A suitable summary statement for this essay would be as follows:

Example

> Science and technology have brought about great changes in many areas of American life. The effects of the development of nuclear weapons and missile defense systems have had a negative effect on American life in the sense that they have contributed to society living in a perpetual state of fear of a nuclear holocaust. On the other hand, the home use of the personal computer has brought much of the world's information into people's homes through the Internet, therefore having a positive effect on American life.

TIP 13

Edit and proofread your writing.

You should make use of this tip after writing each essay answer to be sure that you have checked the following: legible penmanship, organization of the answer, sufficient content, and proper grammar and spelling. A sloppy and poorly written answer is not going to make a good impression on the grader. If you cannot read your own handwriting, you cannot expect a grader to be able to read it.

Below are some guidelines that will assist you in editing your answers to essay questions. Did you:

1. write an introductory topic sentence that states what the essay is about?
2. compose factual and detailed sentences that support the main ideas?
3. express a complete thought in each sentence?
4. use suitable transitional and connective words? (See Tip #9.)
5. indent the first word of each paragraph?
6. begin each sentence with a capital letter?
7. punctuate your sentences correctly?
8. spell all names and words correctly?
9. write legibly?

10. answer the question?

11. answer the question without extraneous and unwanted material?

12. write your answer in a clear manner, so that even a non-social studies teacher could understand it?

TIP 14

Refer to the sources, dates, and authors of the documents in the document-based question.

You should note important information about the document that is provided immediately following the document—specifically the author, title, publisher and date of the document. This information can give you a better understanding of the document and its reliability. Knowing the background of a document's author—such as his or her religion, gender, political affiliation, class position, race, or country of origin—might provide insight into the document's purpose or point of view. A careful analysis of sourcing information can strengthen an essay's argument.

Let's now review the 14 SPECIFIC HELPFUL TIPS for answering essay questions described above:

SUMMARY OF TIPS

1. Understand the essay format: thematic and document-based questions.
2. Go over the thematic essay before writing any answers and draw initial impressions.
3. Go over the document-based question and draw initial impressions.
4. Prepare a time schedule.
5. Look for key words, both in the directions and in the question itself.
6. Outline an answer before writing.
7. Make use of the question to compose your introductory sentence.
8. Be sure to include sufficient details and examples in your answer.
9. Use connective and linking words in your answers.
10. If you are short of time, give an answer in outline form.

11. If you are uncertain about what to write, make an informed and educated guess.
12. Write a suitable summary statement.
13. Edit and proofread your writing.
14. Refer to the sources, dates, and authors of the documents in the document-based question.

In addition to these tips, here are five more bonus ones:

1. Read each question twice.
2. Include everything in an answer that you wish to say. Don't cross-reference answers. (Don't make reference in one essay answer to something in another answer.) It is very possible that no teacher will grade more than one of your three essays.
3. Select the essays easiest for you, and not those that you feel will impress the graders.
4. Do not abbreviate. Write *and*, not &. Write *United States*, not *U.S.*
5. Write as much as you know that is relevant for the thematic essay. The more you write, the better your chances for obtaining maximum credit.

Glossary of Terms

* **Abolitionists** those who supported doing away with (abolishing) the institution of slavery.
* **abortion** the ending of a pregnancy before a live birth.

   acid rain rain, snow, or sleet containing nitric or sulphuric acid produced from the contamination of the atmosphere by smokestack and automobile emissions. It can damage plants and animals and erode stone and buildings.

* **acculturation** the modification of a people's **culture** through adaptation or borrowing from other cultures; the merging of cultures.
* **activism** belief in direct vigorous action.

   administration the management of government; the body of officials in the executive branch; the term of office of a **president**.

* **advocate** (1) to plead a case or support a particular issue; (2) one who pleads such a case or supports an issue.
* **affirmative action** public policy of incorporating women and racial and **ethnic** minorities into economic, political, and social institutions; usually applied through legislation or court orders.
* **affluent** wealthy, well-to-do.
* **aggression** unprovoked attack or act of violence.
** **agrarian** relating to agriculture or land.
* **airlift** supplying a city or region by airplane. In the Berlin Airlift of 1948–1949, the United States and allies flew food and other necessities into West Berlin because the Soviet Union had imposed a blockade on land routes.
** **ally** a person, party, or country joined with another for a common purpose.
*** **amendment** change or addition made in the **Constitution**; proposed by **Congress** or a national convention called by Congress and ratified by state legislatures or special state conventions.

° Denotes a term that has been frequently tested on past exams.
°° Denotes a term that has been very frequently tested on past exams.
°°° Denotes a term that has been most frequently tested on past exams.

amnesty a general pardon for political offenses, generally to a large group of individuals.

anarchist one who believes in the abolition of government or is opposed to organized government.

* **anarchy** the absence of government; a state of disorder or chaos.

* **Antifederalists** opponents of **ratification** of the **Constitution** in 1787 and 1788; opponents of the extension of federal power.

* **antitrust** relating to the limitation or control of monopolies, trusts, or unfair business combinations.

apartheid racial **segregation**, specifically in South Africa before 1991.

Appalachia region of the Appalachian Mountains from Alabama to New York and western New England characterized in many parts by poverty and economic underdevelopment.

* **appeasement** attempts to conciliate an aggressor by making concessions. The policy of appeasement toward Hitler in the 1930s ultimately failed to avoid war.

* **appoint** to name to an office. A president's major appointments must be confirmed by the **Senate**.

apportionment allotment of voting districts as required by law.

* **arbitration** process of settling a dispute by referring it to a third party; both sides usually agree beforehand to abide by the arbitrator's decision.

armageddon a vast, final, destructive conflict.

armistice a truce preliminary to a peace treaty.

* **Articles of Confederation** the charter of the first national government of the United States; in effect from 1781 until replaced by the **Constitution** in 1789.

assembly a gathering or body of representatives, usually of a state or locality.

* **assimilation** process of being absorbed into a group or culture.

Atlantic Charter document issued in 1941 by President Franklin Roosevelt and Prime Minister Winston Churchill outlining the mutual wartime goals of England and the United States and their principles for assuring peace after the war.

backlash strong negative reaction to a law or political event.

* **balance of power** policy aimed at securing peace by maintaining approximate military equality among countries or **blocs**.

* **balanced budget** plan for government taxes and spending in which expenses do not exceed income.

belligerent a participant in a war.

bicameral legislature law-making body made up of two houses or chambers.

** **big business** group of large profit-making corporations.

* **Big Stick policy** willingness to use military power to influence foreign affairs. It derives from Theodore Roosevelt's saying, "Walk softly, but carry a big stick."

** **Bill of Rights** first ten amendments to the **Constitution**, adopted in 1791.

bipartisan involving the cooperation of two political parties.

* **birth control** artificial or natural means of avoiding pregnancy.

** **black codes** a series of laws that sought to control and regulate the conduct of freed slaves during and after the **Reconstruction** period in the southern states. Generally, they denied blacks their basic civil rights.

* **bloc** a group of countries or voters.

Bolsheviks radical socialists and communists under the leadership of Lenin and Trotsky who came to power following the Russian Revolution in 1917.

bonus a government payment to war veterans usually based on length of service.

* **boom** period of economic expansion.

Boston Massacre incident in 1770 in which five colonists were killed in Boston when British soldiers fired on a crowd throwing rocks and snowballs; the soldiers were tried and acquitted of murder.

Boston Tea Party incident in Boston, December 16, 1773, when colonists dressed as Indians forced their way aboard merchant ships in the harbor and threw overboard their cargoes of tea so that recently imposed British taxes on it could not be collected.

bourgeoisie economic and social class between the aristocracy or the very wealthy class and the working class (the **proletariat**); the commercial or professional class; the middle class.

** **boycott** method used by unions and other political groups to force concessions from management or opponents. To boycott is to join together in refusing to deal with or buy from a party in order to influence them to negotiate or make concessions.

brain trust experts without official positions who served as advisors to President Franklin Roosevelt.

brinkmanship pushing a dangerous situation to the limit before stopping.

* **brown power** phrase describing attempts by Hispanic Americans to use their growing numbers to improve their political and economic standing.

---

* **budget** financial plan for income and expenses.
* **budget deficit** the amount by which a government's expenses exceed its revenue or income.
  bureaucracy administrative officials of government.

* **cabinet** the advisors to the **president** who also manage the principal executive departments of the U.S. government. The **cabinet** is not mentioned in the **Constitution**, but has grown and developed over time from custom and practice.
* **Camp David Accords** agreements reached in 1978 between President Sadat of Egypt and Prime Minister Begin of Israel, negotiated by President Carter at the presidential retreat in Camp David, Maryland. The accords evolved into a peace treaty between Israel and Egypt in 1979, providing for Egypt's official recognition of Israel and Israel's withdrawal from the Sinai Peninsula.
* **capital** (1) the seat or main location of a government; (2) money invested or used to return a profit.
* **capital gains tax** a tax on profits made from the sale of property or securities.
** **capital punishment** death sentence imposed by a court.
* **capitalism** economic system in which the means of production and distribution are privately owned and operated for profit.
  Carpetbaggers northerners who went to the South during the **Reconstruction** period to participate in and profit from its political reorganization.
  caucus a closed meeting of a political party.
  censorship preventing the publication of written material or the showing of a film, television program, or play because the government or a segment of society finds it objectionable.
* **census** a counting of the inhabitants of a region.
* **Central Powers** in World War I, Germany, Austro-Hungary, and their allies.
  centralized with power or authority concentrated in a central organization.
  charter written document establishing the rules under which an organization will operate; an organization's constitution.
** **checks and balances** division of powers among the three branches of the federal government so that each branch may limit actions and power of the others. *See also* **separation of powers**.
  Chicanos Americans of Mexican origin or descent.

** **citizen** person entitled to the rights and protection provided by the state or nation.

civil relating to the state, politics, or government.

** **civil disobedience** refusal to obey a law in order to draw attention to its unfairness or undesirability.

* **civil liberties** *see* **civil rights**.

*** **civil rights** the liberties and privileges of citizens, especially those guaranteed in the **Bill of Rights**.

* **civil service** system for filling government jobs through impartial and nonpolitical means, such as standardized exams. Begun by the federal government in the 1880s.

* **civilian** a person who is not a member of the military or armed forces; pertaining to matters outside the military.

clandestine secret; performed secretly.

* **clear and present danger** standard established by the Supreme Court for determining when the right of free speech may be limited or denied— "when there is a clear and present danger that they will bring about the substantive evils that [the government] has a right to prevent."

* **coalition** temporary alliance of groups or factions.

* **coinage** money made of metal; sometimes called hard money.

* **cold war** a conflict between nations short of actual military conflict; the political, diplomatic, economic, and strategic competition between the United States and the Soviet Union from 1946 until 1991.

** **collective bargaining** method by which workers negotiate as a group with their employer through their union representatives.

** **collective security** agreement among a group of nations to help each other maintain their safety and territory; usually by agreeing that an attack by a foreign power upon one nation will be considered an attack upon all.

** **colonialism** international policy based on control over dependent areas or colonies.

** **colony** a territory ruled or administered by a distant nation, usually for the benefit of the ruling nation.

* **commerce** the exchange or buying and selling of goods; business.

* **commerce among the states** business carried on across state lines, which **Congress** is given power to regulate by Article I, Section 8, of the **Constitution**.

* **committee** a group of people appointed or delegated for a particular purpose.

* **commodities** common economic goods that are bought and sold, such as agricultural products.

common law body of law formed over time by accumulation of precedents and prior decisions, as opposed to laws enacted by legislative bodies.

Common Sense a pamphlet by Thomas Paine that helped rally public support for the Revolutionary War.

commonwealth an organization of independent states; form of government of several states in the United States.

communiqué official bulletin, statement, or other communication.

*** **communism** political philosophy advocating collective ownership of property and the means of production and the abolition of the capitalist economic system.

compact theory of union doctrine held by many states' rights supporters that the **union** was a voluntary compact among the states and that states had the right to leave the union in the same manner they had chosen to enter it.

compromise a settlement in which each side makes concessions.

concession something yielded or given up, often in exchange for something else.

Confederate States the 11 southern states that seceded or officially withdrew from the Union in 1860 and 1861 to form an independent nation called the Confederate States of America. Their withdrawal was not recognized by the federal government or the remaining states. They were defeated in the Civil War and reabsorbed into the Union.

* **confirm** to approve or agree with.

*** **Congress** the legislative branch of the federal government; composed of the **Senate** and the **House of Representatives**.

conscription compulsory enrollment into the armed forces; forced military service; draft.

consensus general agreement.

* **conservation** careful management and protection, especially of natural resources.

conservative reluctant or resistant to change; favoring traditional views and values; one belonging to a conservative party or political group.

constituents the citizens represented by an elected public official; group of supporters.

*** **Constitution** the basic charter of the United States government, effective since 1789; it was written by the **Constitutional Convention** in 1787, ratified by the states in 1787–1788, and put into effect in 1789.

constitutionalism belief that government is limited by legal and political restraints and accountable to the governed.

* **Constitutional Convention** gathering of delegates from the 13 states in 1787 in Philadelphia for the purpose of revising the **Articles of**

Confederation; instead, they drafted an entirely new **Constitution** that was adopted in 1788 and put into effect in 1789.

Constitutional Republicanism elected government limited by legally defined guidelines.

* **consumer** the final buyer and user of a product.

* **consumerism** protection of the interests and rights of consumers against false advertising or faulty or dangerous products.

** **containment** policy adopted by the Western democracies after World War II to prevent the further expansion of communism and the Soviet Union.

* **Continental Congress** (1) any of several assemblies of delegates from the American colonies before the Revolution to promote cooperation on various issues; (2) the national legislative body under the **Articles of Confederation** (1781–1788).

* **convention** a meeting of political delegates.

conventional traditional or ordinary; in military affairs, it refers to forces or measures other than nuclear weapons.

* **cooperative** a corporation owned collectively by members who share in the profits and benefits. **Cooperatives** were first developed by farmers in the late 19th century to avoid high prices charged by middlemen for grain storage, transportation, and farm supplies.

corollary a proposition that follows a previous one, which it modifies or enlarges, such as the **Roosevelt Corollary** to the **Monroe Doctrine**.

* **corporation** an organization legally empowered to act as one person, including the ability to borrow and lend money, make contracts, own property, and engage in business.

* **corruption** illegal or improper practices; abuses of authority, especially in connection with bribery or theft.

coup an overturning; a coup d'état is the overthrow of a government.

craft union labor union made up of workers with the same skill or craft, such as carpenters or electricians.

credibility grounds for being believed or trusted.

Crédit Mobilier railroad construction company that cheated on government contracts and bribed congressmen during the late 1860s.

* **creditor nation** a nation that exports more than it imports, so that it is owed money by other nations.

* **cultural pluralism** the acceptance and encouragement of multiple ethnic, religious, and racial groups within one society; respect for ethnic diversity.

** **culture** the beliefs, social forms, and accumulated knowledge of a group, race, or people.

* **currency** money in circulation, especially paper money.

* **Darwinism** (1) the theories of biologist Charles Darwin, who explained the evolution of species by natural selection; (2) social theories loosely based on Darwin's work and arguing that "the survival of the fittest" meant that government should not protect the weak from exploitation by the strong.

Dayton Accord agreement to end the war in Bosnia negotiated by the presidents of Bosnia, Croatia, and Yugoslavia at Dayton, Ohio, in November 1995 with the assistance of the United States; agreement that established two autonomous regions—a Serb republic and a Muslim-Croat federation—within the nation of Bosnia and Herzegovina and provided for a multinational **United Nations** force to supervise the agreement.

debasement a reduction of value.

* **debtor nation** a nation that imports more than it exports and so owes money to other nations.

* **Declaration of Independence** document passed and signed by the **Continental Congress**, effective July 4, 1776, declaring the United States an independent and sovereign nation.

** **defense spending** government spending for military armaments, equipment, and personnel.

degradation a decline into a lower or worse condition.

* **delegate** a representative chosen to act for a group or another person.

demilitarized zone area where no military equipment or personnel may be deployed.

demobilize to discharge from military service.

Democratic Party political party that evolved out of the **Democratic Republicans** around 1820.

Democratic Republicans political party formed around 1800 by Jefferson, Madison, and others opposed to the **Federalists**.

demographic relating to the statistical study of human populations.

** **depression** an economic downturn, especially one characterized by high unemployment.

* **desegregation** the ending of **segregation**, which is the separation of whites and blacks.

despot a **sovereign** or authority without legal restraints; an absolute monarch; tyrant.

* **détente** relaxation of strained relations or tensions.
* **diplomacy** the practice of conducting relations between countries by negotiations rather than force.
** **direct election** election in which votes are cast by the people themselves rather than by their representatives.
  directive order issued by a high authority calling for specific action.
* **disarmament** giving up or reducing armed forces.
* **discrimination** partiality, **prejudice**, or distinctions in treatment; the denial of rights and advantages to minority groups.
  disenfranchise to take away the right to vote.
  dissenting opinion written statement by a member of a court disagreeing with the court's decision.
  distribution of wealth statistical measure of how the property or wealth of a nation is divided among its population.
* **diversity** variety; being made up of unlike parts.
  dollar diplomacy use of American political and military power abroad (usually in Latin America) to promote or advance the interests of American businesses.
* **domestic** having to do with the internal affairs of a country.
* **domino theory** belief in the 1950s and 1960s that the fall of one nation to communism would lead to the fall of neighboring nations.
** **due process of law** doctrine that government's power cannot be used against an individual except as prescribed by established law. Applied to the state governments by the 14th Amendment.

* **ecological** concerning the relationship between living things and the environment.
** **economy** the total system for business, production, consumption, and investment in a country.
* **Eisenhower Doctrine** statement made in 1957 by President Eisenhower that the United States would provide military and economic aid—and direct military intervention, if necessary—to nations of the Middle East if they were threatened by communist aggression.
* **elastic clause** part of the **Constitution** (Article I, Section 8) that gives the federal government the right to make laws "necessary and proper" to carry out its specific powers and functions; it has sometimes been used to expand the powers of the federal government; also known as the "necessary and proper clause."
** **election** process of choosing officers by vote.

* **electoral college** means of electing a **president** and vice president established by the **Constitution** and subsequent amendments; voters in each state choose "electors" who later meet to elect the **president** and vice president. Electors were originally free to vote for any candidate they chose, but they are currently pledged to vote for specific candidates. The number of electors from each state is equal to the number of **Representatives** and **Senators** from that state.

  emancipation the act of setting free; freeing from restraint or, especially, slavery.

* **Emancipation Proclamation** issued by President Lincoln in 1863, it declared free the slaves in the southern states in rebellion but did not affect slaves held in states loyal to the Union, such as Maryland, Kentucky, or Missouri.

* **embargo** prohibition on commerce with a nation or region, usually to apply pressure or force concessions.

* **emigrate** to leave one country or region to settle in another.

  encroachment step-by-step interference with the rights or possessions of others.

  endorsement approval or recommendation.

* **enjoin** to legally forbid or prohibit, usually by court order or **injunction**.

  Enlightenment era during the 17th and 18th centuries when reason replaced religion as a guide to politics, philosophy, and government.

* **environmentalists** persons concerned about the quality of air, water, and land and the protection of natural resources, "green" space, and plant and animal species.

  envoy a messenger or **representative**.

** **equal protection** principle that all people be treated the same under the law.

* **equality** condition of having the same rights, privileges, and advantages as all other citizens.

* **escalate** to increase the extent, level, or volume.

  espionage the act or practice of spying.

* **ethnic** belonging to a particular group identified by nationality or national origin and **culture** or customs.

* **ethnocentric** believing that one's own ethnic group is superior to others.

  evacuate to remove to a safer area.

* **evolution** change over time; an adjustment in the existing order.

*** **executive** person or office having administrative and managerial functions; in government, the branch responsible for carrying out the laws and for the conduct of national affairs—it includes the **president** and **cabinet** and the departments under their jurisdiction.

* **executive privilege** principle that an **executive** (such as the **president**) should not divulge certain sensitive or protected information.

* **expansionism** policy of adding to a country's territory, usually by seizing land from other nations.

exploitation wrongful or unethical use of someone or something for one's own benefit.

extraterritoriality right of a resident of a foreign country to be tried in the judicial system of his or her home country.

fascism political philosophy advocating **totalitarian** government power, intense **nationalism**, and military **expansionism**. Mussolini's Fascist party governed Italy from the 1920s through World War II.

* **Far East** the nations on the Pacific coast of Asia.

* **favorable balance of trade** exporting or selling more goods than are imported or bought.

*** **federal** relating to the central national government created by the **Constitution**.

Federal Housing Administration federal agency established in 1934 to insure mortgages and set construction standards.

Federal Reserve Note currency or paper money issued by the **Federal Reserve System** and representing a promissory obligation of the federal government. **Federal Reserve Notes** replaced the older gold and silver certificates, which were backed by or based upon specific reserves of gold and silver.

* **Federal Reserve System** federal agency created by Congress in 1913 to regulate the banking system. Federal Reserve banks in 12 districts supervise banking operations, lend money to banks, and issue currency; a Federal Reserve Commission sets and regulates interest rates.

** **federalism** system of government in which powers are divided between a central authority and local subdivisions.

* **Federalists** advocates of adopting the **Constitution** in 1787–1788 and of more powerful central government during the period 1789–1820. Many **Federalists** later joined the **Whig** Party.

* **feminism** movement advocating equal rights and privileges for women, including economic, political, legal, and social status.

filibuster use of delaying tactics, such as unlimited debate in the Senate, to prevent action on a legislative proposal.

* **fiscal** having to do with government revenues, expenditures, and budgets.

fission splitting or breaking up; nuclear fission refers to the splitting of an atomic nucleus to release a vast quantity of energy.

fluctuation a series of movements up and down or back and forth.

foreclosure the act of a lender taking possession of mortgaged property from a borrower who is unable to make the required payments.

* **foreign aid** assistance in the form of money or goods supplied to a foreign country.

*** **foreign policy** a nation's policy in dealing with other nations.

* **Fourteen Points** President Wilson's plan for international peace presented to **Congress** on January 22, 1918.

franchise the right to vote; **suffrage**.

* **free enterprise** the freedom of private businesses to operate without undue government interference.

** **free trade** the freedom to exchange goods with other countries, especially without **tariffs**.

* **freedman** a freed slave, usually referring to a former slave freed by virtue of the 13th Amendment.

* **freedom of religion** right of citizens to hold and practice religious beliefs without interference from government.

** **freedom of speech** right of citizens to say or write their views without regulation or reprisal from government; restricted in some cases, *see* **clear and present danger**.

* **freedom of the press** right of publishers to print material without prior approval by government; *see* **prior restraint**.

Freedom Riders civil rights advocates who traveled the South on buses to promote the desegregation of public facilities.

Free-Soil party political party before the Civil War opposed to the extension of slavery and the admission of slave states.

* **frontier** border region between two distinct areas, especially (in America) between settled and unsettled territory. In European usage, a frontier is the border between two countries.

Fugitive Slave Law federal law passed in 1850 that required northern states to return escaped slaves to their owners in the South. It was widely opposed by a variety of legal and extra-legal means.

* **fundamental rights** *see* **natural rights**.

GATT General Agreement on Tariffs and Trade signed by 132 countries to lower trade barriers.

gerrymandering drawing the boundaries of election districts to ensure the victory of one party or faction by including or excluding neighborhoods of a particular ethnic or social class.

* **global** relating to the world as a whole; international; worldwide.
* **Good Neighbor policy** policy first announced by President Franklin Roosevelt to promote friendly relations with all Latin American nations.
*** **government** the institutions and people responsible for the conduct of public affairs.

Great Compromise agreement in the **Constitutional Convention** of 1787 to have two houses of **Congress**, one (the **Senate**) to represent the states equally and the other (the **House of Representatives**) to represent the people proportionately. Also known as the Connecticut Compromise.

** **Great Depression** period from the stock market crash of 1929 until the start of World War II during which industrial production declined and **unemployment** rose to over one fourth of the labor force.

* **Great Society** collective name for various social programs of President Lyndon Johnson, including the so-called War on Poverty and programs for job training, subsidized housing, and free medical care for the poor and aged.

green revolution the increase in agricultural crop yields brought about by the use of machinery, fertilizers, pesticides, and improved seeds.

greenhouse effect belief that excessive carbon dioxide in the atmosphere caused by burning fossil fuels will create a layer in the upper atmosphere that retains heat and will cause the Earth's temperature to rise.

guerilla an active participant in a war who is not a member of the regular armed forces; a kind of warfare characterized by sabotage, harassment, and hit-and-run tactics.

* **habeas corpus** a writ or legal order directed to an official holding a person in custody, commanding the official to produce the person in court, show cause why the person has been confined, and prove that the person has not been deprived of liberty without **due process of law**.
* **Harlem Renaissance** a movement among black writers, artists, and musicians centered in Harlem, New York City, during the 1920s.

Head Start educational aid to preschool children from disadvantaged homes.

health maintenance organization (HMO) organization that provides health services such as hospitalization and doctors' fees to members who make a fixed monthly payment.

Hessians hired soldiers from the district of Hesse in Germany, employed by the British before and during the Revolutionary War.

* **heterogenous** composed of unlike parts; a society made up of different races, nationalities, or ethnic groups.

Holocaust originally, a burnt sacrificial offering; since World War II, it refers to the genocidal murders of millions of European Jews by the Nazis.

home front during a war, the area of a nation's domestic and civilian affairs.

* **Homestead Act** act passed by **Congress** in 1862 that gave 160 acres of western land to any head of a family who agreed to cultivate it for five years; it encouraged the rapid settlement of the West by giving immigrants and Easterners free land.

* **homogenous** made up of similar elements; a society consisting primarily of the same race, nationality, or **ethnic** group.

hot line direct telephone link, especially between the White House and the Kremlin, always ready for instant communication.

** **House of Representatives** the half of **Congress** composed of representatives allotted among the states according to their population.

*** **immigration** act of moving into a country where one is not a native to become a permanent resident.

* **impeach** to bring formal charges against a public official for misconduct. The **House of Representatives** has the power to impeach federal officials, and the trial is held by the **Senate**.

** **imperialism** the practice of forming and maintaining an empire; possession of foreign territories or colonies for the benefit of the home country; the policy of seeking to dominate economically, politically, or militarily weaker areas of the world.

implementation the means of accomplishing or carrying out a plan or program.

* **import quota** a limit on the amount of a commodity that can be brought into the country.

* **inauguration** a ceremonial beginning, especially the installing of an official at the beginning of a term.

* **incumbent** person currently serving in political office, especially one seeking reelection.

* **Indians** European term for the native inhabitants of the Americas; it was based on the mistaken belief that the continents were part of Asia or India.

indictment a legal action to charge someone with a crime.

* **individualism** doctrine that the rights and interests of individual persons are the most important source of values.

*** **industrialization** economic transformation of society by the development of large industries, machine production, factories, and an urban workforce.

* **Industrial Revolution** the transformation from an agricultural society to one based upon large-scale mechanized production and factory organization. It began in Europe (especially England) in the late 18th century and in America in the early 19th century.

* **infiltration** gradual entrance or buildup with the intent of taking control.

* **inflation** general and continuing rise in the price of goods, often due to the relative increase of available money and credit.

* **initiative** process for the direct involvement of voters in the making of laws; by gathering enough signatures on a petition, a group can force a legislature to consider a proposal or require it to be placed on the ballot for public vote.

* **injunction** order issued by a court directing someone to do or refrain from doing some specific act.

* **installment buying** practice of buying a product through regular monthly or weekly payments; failure to pay gives the seller the right to repossess the product.

insurgency an uprising or revolt against a government, short of actual war.

* **integration** bringing together or making as one; unification; applied especially to blacks and whites.

* **interdependent** depending on one another, such as nations that rely on each other's trade.

* **internal improvements** roads, canals, and other means to assist transportation and commerce. In the first half of the 19th century, debate concerned who should fund internal improvements: the states or the federal government.

** **internationalism** policy of cooperation among nations.

* **internment** the detainment and isolation of **ethnic** groups for purposes of national security (such as Japanese Americans during World War II); this is now widely held to have been **unconstitutional**.

interposition an argument that the states could legitimately object to acts of **Congress** if those acts exceeded **Congress**'s legitimate authority. Interposition fell short of **nullification**.

* **interpret** to explain or determine the meaning.

* **interstate** taking place across state lines; involving the citizens of more than one state.

* **Interstate Commerce Commission** established by **Congress** in 1887 to regulate railroad rates and prevent abuses by railroads; it was later expanded to have **jurisdiction** over other forms of transportation.
* **intervention** interference in the affairs of another country, including the use of force.

Intolerable Acts series of acts of **Parliament** directed against the American colonies and intended to assert British authority and increase revenues from the colonies.

invalidate to make null and void; to destroy the existence or effectiveness of, as, for example, a law.

Iran-Contra Affair an illegal conspiracy by officials of the Reagan administration to provide funding for the anticommunist Contra rebels in Nicaragua by secretly selling missiles to Iran and diverting the money to the Nicaraguans.

Iron Curtain the series of fortified borders separating Western Europe from Soviet-dominated Eastern Europe; the term was made popular by Winston Churchill.

** **isolationism** policy of keeping a nation apart from alliances or other political relations with foreign nations.

* **Jim Crow laws** laws enforcing **segregation** or control of blacks in such a way as to make them unequal.
* **joint resolution** a legislative act that is the same in both houses of **Congress**.
* **judicial activism** developing social policy through court decisions instead of through legislative action, often in response to changing values and circumstances.
* **judicial nationalism** term used to describe the **Supreme Court** under the leadership of John Marshall, when its decisions consolidated the power of the federal government by centralizing responsibility for commerce, contracts, and finance.
* **judicial restraint** the preference of a court to avoid upsetting existing law or practice.
** **judicial review** power of the **Supreme Court** to void acts of **Congress** that are found to violate the **Constitution**.
* **judiciary** the branch of government that interprets the law and tries cases; the system of courts.

jurisdiction authority of a court to interpret and apply the law; in general, the area of authority of a government.

* **Knights of Labor** early labor union, formed in 1869.

Kremlin complex of government offices in Moscow; the center of government of Russia and the Soviet Union.

* **Ku Klux Klan** secret organization founded in 1866 to intimidate freed slaves and keep them in conditions of servitude through threats and acts of violence; it later developed into a nativist organization opposed to Jews, Catholics, and immigrants, as well as African Americans.

** **laissez-faire** doctrine opposing government interference or regulation of economic matters beyond what is necessary to maintain property rights and enforce contracts. *Laissez faire* is French for "let alone" or "let be."

lame duck an official who has not been reelected and is serving out the remainder of a term.

*** **League of Nations** international organization of countries formed after World War I to promote world peace. It was supported by President Wilson, but the **Senate** refused to allow the United States to join. After World War II it was replaced by the **United Nations**.

** **legislature** a body of persons elected to make laws for a nation or state; a congress or parliament.

* **levy** to place and collect a tax; to draft persons for military service.

liberal advocating political or social views that emphasize **civil rights**, democratic reforms, and the use of government to promote social progress.

* **liberty** freedom; the power to do as one pleases.

life expectancy statistical estimate of the average lifespan of a particular population.

* **limited government** *see* **constitutionalism.**

* **line-item veto** power of an **executive** to **veto** specific expenditures without vetoing the entire bill that contains them. Congress gave the **president** a limited line-item veto in 1996.

* **lobbying** actions by private citizens or organizations seeking to influence (by legal means) the decisions of a **legislature** or **executive** department of government.

* **loose construction, loose interpretation** reading of the **Constitution** that allows broad use of the **elastic clause** and **implied powers**.

* **Louisiana Purchase** the purchase from France by the United States in 1803 for $15 million of the Louisiana Territory, stretching from New Orleans west to the Rocky Mountains, more than doubling the size of the United States.

Loyalists American colonists who remained loyal to England during the American Revolution; also known as **Tories**.

* **Magna Carta** agreement signed by King John I of England in 1215, granting certain rights (including trial by jury and **habeas corpus**) to the barons who had taken him prisoner.

majority number greater than one half of the votes cast (simple majority); a "two-thirds majority" requires at least two thirds of the votes cast.

malaise vague sense of unhappiness or discomfort.

* **Manifest Destiny** belief, held by many Americans in the 19th century, that the United States was destined to control the continent between the Atlantic and Pacific Oceans.

* **market economy** an economic system in which decisions about production and pricing are based on the actions of buyers and sellers in the marketplace; usually associated with capitalism.

* **Marshall Plan** the program of U.S. aid to Europe following World War II to help those nations recover from the extensive damage to their cities, industries, and transportation.

materialism valuing economic or material things more than spiritual or intellectual interests.

* **media** the industries of mass communication, such as television, radio, and newspapers.

mediator person who solves differences between two parties. Both sides do not usually agree beforehand to accept the decisions of the mediator, as they usually do with an arbitrator.

* **Medicaid** federal government program to pay the hospital and medical costs for those on welfare or whose incomes are very low.

* **Medicare** federal government program to pay the hospital costs of those over age 65 who pay a premium for additional coverage.

* **mercantilism** the economic policies of European nations from the 15th century until the **Industrial Revolution**, based on mercantile (commercial, trading) activities and characterized by the acquisition of colonies and the establishment of a **favorable balance of trade**. The American colonies were established under the mercantile system.

* **middle class** the members of a society having a socioeconomic position between the very wealthy and the poor.

* **migration** the movement of people from one place to another.

militancy aggressive opposition.

* **militaristic** characterized by military discipline and aggressiveness.

military-industrial complex the combined power of the Defense Department and the industries that supply it with equipment. The phrase was popularized by Eisenhower, who claimed that it worked for unnecessary increases in armaments.

militia part-time soldiers who do not belong to the regular armed forces.

** **minority** the portion of a group less than one half; an **ethnic** or racial group that is smaller than the dominant group and may be subjected to **discrimination**.

* **Miranda rights** constitutionally guaranteed rights of those accused of crimes to be informed by the police that they have a right to remain silent, a right to an attorney, and a right to be supplied with legal counsel if they cannot afford a private attorney; established by *Miranda* v. *Arizona* (1966).

Missouri Compromise an agreement in 1820 between congressional advocates and opponents of the extension of **slavery** that preserved sectional balance. It included the simultaneous admission of the slave state Missouri and the free state Maine and the prohibition of slavery in the northern parts of the **Louisiana Purchase**.

** **monopoly** the exclusive control or ownership of an industry by a single person or company.

* **Monroe Doctrine** policy announced in 1823, during the presidency of James Monroe, that the United States would oppose European attempts to extend their control of the Western Hemisphere. It became and remains a basic principle of American foreign policy.

moratorium agreement to postpone payment of a debt or other obligation.

mortgage legal instrument specifying payments to be made on a loan for the purchase of property. Failure to make payments gives the mortgager the legal right to repossess the property.

* **muckraker** journalists in the late 19th and early 20th centuries who reported on political or commercial corruption.

* **multicultural** different cultural beliefs and practices followed by different ethnic groups living in harmony within the same community.

multinational involving more than two nations.

municipality a city or local political unit.

munitions armaments and ammunition used in warfare.

NAFTA North American Free Trade Agreement (1993). An agreement ratified during President Clinton's first administration to eliminate trade barriers between the United States, Canada, and Mexico.

* **nationalism** (1) sense of pride in one's country; (2) extreme devotion to national interests.

* **National Labor Relations Board** federal agency established in 1935 to enforce laws against unfair labor practices.

* **National Origins Act** laws passed in 1921, 1924, and 1929 that limited **immigration** into the United States and established **quotas** for nations based on the number of persons from those nations living in the United States according to an earlier **census**. It was regarded as **discriminatory** because it favored immigrants from Western Europe.

native one who is connected with a place by birth; an original inhabitant as distinguished from immigrants or visitors.

** **Native Americans** descendants of the original inhabitants of the Americas.

* **nativism** in the United States, the policy of favoring native-born Americans and opposing immigrants.

* **natural rights** rights or liberties to which one is entitled as a human being.

necessary and proper clause portion of the **Constitution** granting **Congress** power to "make all Laws which shall be necessary and proper for carrying into Execution" its other powers.

** **neutrality** policy of not helping either side in a war.

* **Neutrality Acts** laws passed in 1935 and 1937 to avoid U.S. involvement in a war in Europe; they placed an embargo on arms sales to any nation engaged in war.

*** **New Deal** name adopted by President Franklin Roosevelt for the reforms and social programs instituted by his administration, beginning in 1933.

* **New Freedom** program of President Wilson to regulate banking and **currency** to influence the direction of the economy and to support stronger **antitrust** legislation.

* **New Nationalism** program of President Theodore Roosevelt during his unsuccessful campaign for the presidency in 1912. It promised greater government supervision of the economy to balance the power of **big business**.

* **19th Amendment** granted **suffrage** (the right to vote) to women; enacted in 1920.

* **nomination** proposal of a candidate for an office.

nonintervention policy of not becoming involved in the affairs of other nations.

* **nonpartisan** not based on party interests or bias.

nonsectarian not affiliated with any religious group.

* **nonviolence** principle that all violence is to be avoided; the use of peaceful means for political ends.

* **normalcy** the state of being normal; the term was applied to the era of the 1920s, following the disruptions of World War I.

* **North Atlantic Treaty Organization (NATO)** collective security military alliance formed in 1949 by the United States, Canada, and nations of Western Europe to oppose the threat posed by the Soviet Union and Warsaw Pact nations to Europe.

Northwest Territory federal administrative district west of the Allegheny Mountains, north of the Ohio River, south of the Great Lakes, and east of the Mississippi River, including the present states of Ohio, Indiana, Michigan, Illinois, and Wisconsin, and part of Minnesota. The Territory was organized by the **Continental Congress** in 1787 from lands claimed by several eastern states.

nullification argument or doctrine claiming that states could refuse to abide by acts of **Congress** if the states felt **Congress** had exceeded its enumerated powers. Used by states' rights advocates; championed by John C. Calhoun of South Carolina.

* **Nuremberg Tribunal** international military court held in Nuremberg, Germany, in 1945–46; top Nazi leaders were tried and convicted of crimes against humanity and violations of international law.

* **Open Door policy** an attempt by the United States in 1899 to preserve trade interests in China by asking European nations to respect the territorial integrity of China and to permit free access to ports they held in Asia.

ordinance a law or regulation, usually of a local municipality.

*** **organized labor** workers represented by labor unions.

original jurisdiction the first court with authority to consider and decide a case, as opposed to appellate jurisdiction.

* **overproduction** production of a commodity in excess of the demand for it; it usually results in falling prices.

* **parity** government support of prices for agricultural products to ensure that farm income keeps pace with income in other economic sectors.

* **Parliament** the legislative body of Great Britain, consisting of the House of Commons and the House of Lords.

partition division of a country into two or more separate parts.

* **Peace Corps** U.S. government agency formed by President Kennedy in 1961; it sought to assist developing countries by sending American volunteers to teach and provide technical assistance.

penal having to do with punishment; liable to be punished.

Pentagon headquarters of the U.S. armed forces, near Washington, D.C.

* **per capita** the average per person for a particular population, as in per capita income.

perjury making a false statement under oath.

* **philanthropy** literally, the love of mankind; desire to help humankind, usually through gifts or endowments to charitable institutions.

* **picketing** method of demonstration by workers or political groups, usually taking place at the employer or the offices of the opposition; it includes notifying the public of the unfairness of the employer with signs and conversation.

plea bargaining pleading guilty to a lesser charge in order to avoid standing trial for a more serious one.

* **pluralistic** type of society in which diverse **ethnic**, racial, and national groups coexist while maintaining their own cultural heritage.

* **plurality** a number of votes greater than any other candidate but less than a majority of all the votes cast.

pocket veto an automatic veto that occurs if the **president** does not sign a bill passed by **Congress** during the last ten days of its session.

pogrom organized, officially encouraged persecution or massacre of a group.

political machine combination of party and political officials who maintain themselves in office, sometimes through corrupt means.

*** **politics** the practice of government; the art of winning control of public affairs.

* **poll tax** (1) a tax paid to register or vote in elections (prohibited under the 24th Amendment). (2) a per-person or per-capita tax, not based on income or employment.

* **pollution** the contamination of the atmosphere by burning of automobile and smokestack emissions or the contamination of water by chemicals dumped into streams by factories or by fertilizers washed into water sources by rainfall.

popular sovereignty (1) doctrine in democratic forms of government that power ultimately derives from the people and that the consent of the governed is exercised through the vote; (2) in the years before the Civil War, a political position advocating that the legality of **slavery** in the western territories be decided by popular vote of the inhabitants; it was ridiculed by its opponents as "squatter sovereignty."

* **populism** movement that began in agricultural areas in the late 19th century seeking government regulation to curb excesses and exploitation by big business.

pragmatism belief in a practical (rather than an ethical or theoretical) approach to problems and affairs.

* **Preamble** introductory part, especially the opening of the **Constitution**, which begins "We the people. . . ."

precedence the right to be first or have more authority.

precedent rule or decision that serves as a guide for future actions or decisions; attorneys look for precedents to support their arguments when presenting a case in court.

* **prejudice** a preconceived opinion or judgment, usually negative, not based on fact.

preside to act as chairman.

*** **president** the chief executive officer of the federal government.

* **press** the news-gathering and publishing industry, including television, radio, magazines, and newspapers.

* **price supports** government measures to maintain the price of a commodity at an artificially set level.

prior restraint the prohibition of publication of an article, book, or story by a court order before the material is disclosed to the public. Permissable only in cases of obscenity or of **"clear and present danger."**

* **primary election** election in which members of a political party choose their candidates for the coming general elections.

* **processing tax** a tax on industries that convert raw materials into finished goods, such as cotton into cloth.

* **Progressive Era** the period roughly from 1900 to 1920, marked by political, economic, and social reform movements.

* **progressive tax** a tax that is higher for the wealthy than for the poor, such as income tax.

* **progressivism** a broad reform movement during the late 19th and early 20th centuries that sought to remedy the worst effects of industrialism and **urbanization** by imposing governmental controls on **big business**, improving social justice, and increasing direct democratic participation in politics.

* **prohibition** period from the enactment of the 18th Amendment in 1919 until its repeal by the 21st Amendment in 1933, during which the manufacture, sale, import, export, and transportation of alcoholic beverages was declared illegal.

proletariat the industrial working class, who sell their labor and do not own the means of production.

propaganda promotion of particular ideas and doctrines.

* **protective tariff** tax on imported goods intended to protect the interests of internal or domestic industries by raising the price of imports.

protectorate an area under the control and protection of a country that does not have full **sovereignty** over it.

proviso clause in a document or statute making some condition or provision.

* **purse** the power to authorize revenues and spending; in the federal government, **Congress** holds the power of the purse.

quarantine isolation of a person or country, usually to prevent spread of communicable diseases.

quartering forcibly housing soldiers in private residences.

* **quota** a maximum limit; a share or portion assigned to a group.

** **racism** belief that some races are inherently superior to others.

* **radical, radicalism** favoring extreme and fundamental changes.

*** **ratification** formal legal approval and adoption.

* **raw materials** products or resources not yet manufactured into their final state, such as many agricultural products, lumber, or ores.

rearmament rebuilding of a nation's armed forces, often with new and better weapons.

* **recall** political reform procedure for removing a public official from office before the end of a term by popular vote; it is usually initiated by a petition.

** **Reconstruction** period from 1865 through 1876, when the southern states were occupied by federal troops and under the direct control of the national government.

* **Red Scare** fears about the danger of **communist** subversion or invasion; especially after World War II, "Red Scare" tactics were used by Senator Joseph McCarthy and others for political purposes.

* **referendum** a proposal submitted to a popular vote before putting it into effect.

refinance to change the terms of a **mortgage** or loan to make it easier for the borrower to make the payments.

*** **reform** to improve or change, especially a social institution.

** **regulatory** enforcing the rules or laws.

rehabilitation restoration to a former or better condition.

* **relocation** the movement (sometimes by force) of a group of people to a new place.

* **reparations** payments imposed on nations defeated in war to help the victors recover the costs of war.

repercussion a widespread or indirect effect of an act.

** **representative** (1) a **delegate** or agent of another person or group of people; (2) a federal legislator; (3) a type of government by persons chosen from among the governed, usually by election.

* **Republican Party** political party formed in the 1840s, opposed to the extension of **slavery**; Lincoln was the first Republican elected president (in 1860).

  repudiate to disown or disavow.
* **reserved powers** powers not specifically granted to **Congress** or the federal government under the **Constitution**, and so held to be reserved to the states.
* **restraint of trade** language used in the **Sherman Antitrust Act** (1890) to describe combinations and activities of groups (businesses, labor unions) that were prohibited under the Act.
* **retaliatory** done in response to an attack or **aggression**; strong enough to deter an attack.
* **revenue** the income of governments from taxation, **tariffs**, fees, and other activities.
* **reverse discrimination** discrimination against whites or males.
* **revolution** rapid change, often accompanied by violence.
* **right to counsel** entitlement of an accused person to have an attorney present during questioning.
* **rights** individual liberties protected by the state or federal constitutions.

  Rights of Englishmen an expression of the American colonists during their struggle with England; they claimed to want only the same liberties and privileges enjoyed by British subjects in England, as established by **Magna Carta**, common law, and the English Bill of Rights, including **habeas corpus**, trial by jury, and representation in **Parliament**.
** **rights of the accused** include the Fifth Amendment guarantee against self-incrimination and the **right to counsel**; also known as **"Miranda rights,"** after the **Supreme Court** decision in the case of *Miranda* v. *Arizona* (1966).
* **Roaring Twenties** the 1920s, during which the United States returned to "normalcy" after World War I, with rapid economic expansion, changed social values, high spending for consumer goods, and the popularization of the automobile, radio, and motion pictures.
* **Roosevelt Corollary** supplement to the **Monroe Doctrine** asserted by President Theodore Roosevelt, who claimed the right of the United States to exercise international police power in the Western Hemisphere and to intervene in the affairs of Latin American nations.
* **"Rule of Reason"** term used by the **Supreme Court** in its decision in the case of *Standard Oil Co.* v. *United States* (1911), which held that only "bad" trusts were illegal.
* **ruling** an official decision.

** **SALT II** Strategic Arms Limitation Treaty signed by the United States and the Soviet Union to limit the number of bombers capable of carrying nuclear weapons; signed in 1979 as a major step in reducing the danger of nuclear war; a follow up to SALT I, which was the first step taken to slow the increase in nuclear weapons.

salutary neglect phrase describing the belief that the American colonies benefitted from lack of interest in their affairs by the British government during the period before 1763.

sanctuary place of refuge or protection.

satellite state a nation controlled by a more powerful nation.

* **Scopes trial** the trial of John T. Scopes in Dayton, Tennessee, in 1925 for violating a state law prohibiting the teaching of Darwinian evolution. The highly publicized trial featured William Jennings Bryan as prosecutor and Clarence Darrow for the defense. Scopes was found guilty and fined $100.

* **search and seizure** police power to look for and hold evidence in the investigation and prosecution of a crime; evidence from unreasonable searches or searches without probable cause may be excluded from a trial.

* **secession** withdrawal of a member from a political group; withdrawal of a state from the Union.

* **second-class citizenship** condition of having fewer or inferior rights and privileges.

* **sectionalism** development of internal divisions based on geographic and economic alliances; rivalry between different areas of the country.

* **Securities and Exchange Commission** federal agency established in 1934 to regulate the stock market and to prevent the abuses practiced during the 1920s that led to the **stock market crash** of 1929.

security safety; freedom from danger.

sedition the act of stirring up rebellion against a government.

** **segregation** the isolation or separation of one group from another, usually applied to keeping whites and blacks apart.

*** **Senate** the half of the federal legislature made up of two members from each state.

** **separate but equal** legal doctrine established by the **Supreme Court** in the case of *Plessy* v. *Ferguson* (1896) that separate accommodations for blacks and whites did not violate the 14th Amendment if the accommodations were of equal quality. Overruled by the later **Supreme Court** decision in *Brown* v. *Board of Education* (1954).

* **separation of church and state** doctrine that government may not restrict the free exercise of religious beliefs nor support any religious group or principle.

°° **separation of powers** doctrine that liberty of the people is best assured by the division of government into separate branches. *See also* **checks and balances**.

° **sexual harassment** policy or practice of compelling female employees to submit to the sexual advances of male superiors or to endure verbal or physical harassment, in violation of the Civil Rights Act of 1964.

° **sharecroppers** tenant farmers who leased and cultivated pieces of land in exchange for a percentage of the crop.

Shays' Rebellion armed insurrection in western Massachusetts in the fall of 1786 led by Captain Daniel Shays and others in protest against economic policies and foreclosures of farms for failure to pay taxes. It was suppressed by the state **militia**, but it had a significant effect on the framing of the **Constitution** the following summer.

° **Sherman Antitrust Act** passed in 1890 declaring combinations in restraint of trade to be illegal; it was passed to maintain competition in private industry and to correct abuses of companies that had gained **monopoly** power.

° **sit-in** action of protesters in occupying a public place to force concessions; especially by **civil rights** advocates seeking **desegregation** of public facilities.

°° **slavery** system of holding persons against their will for involuntary servitude; in a system of "chattel slavery" the person held could be bought or sold as property. Slavery in the United States was abolished by the 13th Amendment.

smokestack industries heavy industries that burn large amounts of fossil fuels, such as steel-making or auto manufacturing.

social contract the implied agreement among individuals in a community or between the people and their rulers.

° **socialism** political philosophy advocating ownership and operation of the means of production (such as land, mines, factories) by society as a collective whole, with all members sharing in the work and benefits. Socialist economic systems usually include government ownership and operation of industries.

° **social mobility** movement up or down the class scale within a society.

° **Social Security Act** passed in 1935 to provide an income for persons who are disabled or aged and for families without a wage earner; it has become the basic means of support for retired persons who lack private pensions from employers.

°° **social welfare** organized services for helping disadvantaged people.

° **sovereign** holding supreme authority.

* **sovereignty** the ultimate power and authority to make laws, either directly or through representatives; in a democracy, sovereignty lies in the people.

space satellite an object in space that orbits a planet or other body on a regular path.

* **special interest** group or industry that seeks to influence government for its own benefit.

* **speculation** taking extreme risks in business or investing in hopes of earning large profits.

spoils system system wherein government positions and offices are awarded to political supporters on the basis of party loyalty or service rather than qualification or merit; based on the saying "To the victor go the spoils"; the system was replaced to some extent by the **Civil Service**, beginning in the 1880s.

stability the ability to remain unchanged or permanent.

* **Stamp Act** act enacted by **Parliament** in 1765 that required a tax stamp on all printed and legal documents. It was soon repealed due to American resistance.

* **START II** Strategic Arms Reduction Treaty signed in 1993 by the United States and Russia to reduce the number of nuclear warheads held by each nation by half; a follow-up to START I in 1991, which was the first agreement for each nation to scrap some of its nuclear weapons.

statehood condition of being a state and a full member of the United States; for example, Hawaii achieved statehood in 1959.

*** **states' rights** group of doctrines holding that the states retained the power to overrule, oppose, or withdraw from the federal government if they chose.

* **stock market crash** a rapid fall in the price of **stocks**. The great crash of 1929 was caused by overspeculation that increased stock prices far above their true value; prices started to fall when knowledgeable investors began to sell their shares; that forced speculators, who had invested with borrowed money, to sell as well, and the combined rush to sell caused a panic, which drove prices even lower.

* **stocks** certificates showing shares of ownership in a **corporation**.

strict construction doctrine that the **Constitution** limits governmental powers to those explicitly stated; *contrast with* **loose construction**.

** **strike** work stoppage by labor in an attempt to force the employer to make concessions.

* **subjugation** the act of bringing under control.

subpoena official written order commanding a person to appear in court or to produce specific items.

subsidiary in business, a company that is controlled by another company.

subterranean below the surface of the earth.

subversion the undermining, overthrowing, or destroying of an established institution, such as government.

** **suffrage** the right to vote.

supremacy the highest power or authority.

supremacy clause portion of the **Constitution** declaring it "the supreme law of the land" and overriding any state or local laws in conflict with it.

*** **Supreme Court** the highest court in the federal judicial branch.

surcharge an extra charge.

synthetic artificially produced or man-made by combinations of chemicals.

* **tariff** taxes on imports into a country to collect revenues or to protect domestic industries.

* **Teapot Dome** federal oil reserve in Wyoming that was secretly and illegally leased to a financial backer of President Harding.

** **technology** applied science used in production.

temperance moderation in the consumption of alcoholic beverages; a movement supporting governmental measures to curb alcohol consumption.

Tennessee Valley Authority federal public works project established in 1933 that constructed dams and reengineered waterways to control flooding and generate electricity in seven southern states.

tenure the act or right of holding an office.

* **term limits** legislation that limits elected officials to a set number of years in office, usually eight to 12 years or two to three terms; a concept that has become popular in recent years and has been applied to elected officials in a number of states.

** **third parties** political parties existing at various times in the United States other than the two predominate political parties.

Third World the group of nations, especially in Asia and Africa, that were not aligned with either the communist **bloc** or the Western democracies.

* **three-fifths clause** clause in the **Constitution** saying that three fifths of the number of persons held as slaves be included in calculating representation in **Congress**, even though those persons were not citizens and were not entitled to vote. Superceded by the 14th Amendment.

Tories supporters of British rule during the Revolutionary War; also known as **Loyalists**. In England, the Tory party generally supported the king or conservative interests.

totalitarian characterized by the state or government having total control over the lives of citizens.

town meeting meeting of the citizens of a town as a legislative body.

* **trade deficit** the amount by which imports exceed exports; how much is owed to other nations.

* **trade gap** difference in amount between imports and exports.

treason acts that intentionally endanger the security or **sovereignty** of one's own nation; waging war against one's country or giving aid to its enemies.

triangular trade pattern of commerce pursued in the late 18th and early 19th centuries by New England merchants who carried sugar and molasses from the West Indies to New England, rum and manufactured goods from New England to Africa, and slaves from Africa to the West Indies.

* **Truman Doctrine** policy announced by President Truman in 1947, stating that the United States would provide military and economic aid to nations threatened by subversion or invasion; it was established specifically to assist Greece and Turkey, which were threatened with communist takeover.

** **trust** a combination of companies or industries established to reduce competition and increase profits.

* **turnout** the number of eligible voters who participate in an election.

tyranny absolute and arbitrary power without legal restraints.

unconditional surrender total surrender without exceptions or conditions; the phrase was made popular by Ulysses S. Grant.

* **unconstitutional** prohibited by or in opposition to the principles of the **Constitution**.

* **underclass** class of the permanently poor.

** **unemployment** being out of work; government compensation to people who have lost their jobs.

* **unicameral** of a legislature having only one house or chamber.

*** **union** (1) the political combination of the states; (2) the northern and border states that opposed **secession** during the Civil War; (3) an organization of workers seeking **collective bargaining** with their employer.

** **United Nations (UN)** international organization established in 1945 to preserve peace; currently has 185 members. Security Council made up of five permanent members (United States, Russia, China, Great Britain, and France) and ten nonpermanent members can cause military action, as it did during the Korean War and the Persian Gulf War, the deployment of peacekeeping forces to monitor cease-fire agreements, as it's done in the Middle East and Bosnia, and can impose economic sanctions, as it has done with Iraq, Yugoslavia, and South Africa.

* **universal suffrage** the right of all citizens to vote, regardless of sex, race, or economic status.
* **Unwritten Constitution** governmental practices and institutions not specifically set down in the **Constitution** but based upon custom and practice.
* **urbanization** the growth of cities and the increasing concentration of population in them.

  utilities companies that furnish electric power, water, gas, or other services without competition and are regulated by law.

  utopian advocating impossibly idealistic or impractical forms of government or society.

* **Versailles Treaty** peace treaty signed in 1919 between Germany and the Allies; it required Germany to give up its colonies, pay substantial reparations, and surrender territory to France, Poland, and Czechoslovakia.
* **veto** action by an executive official preventing the enactment of a legislative act. A veto by the **president** can be overridden by a two-thirds majority of **Congress**.

  VISTA Volunteers in Service to America, a program of President Johnson's 1964 Economic Opportunity Act.

* **war crimes** crimes against humanity; actions commited by armed forces against civilian populations during military conflicts, including genocide, murder, rape, extermination, deportation, enslavement, and persecutions on religious, racial, or political grounds; actions under jurisdiction of war crimes tribunals established under international law.
* **War on Poverty** President Johnson's domestic programs for social renovation, including the **VISTA**, Job Corps, and **Head Start** programs and the establishing of the Department of Housing and Urban Development.
* **War Powers Act** law passed in 1973 to limit the power of the **president** to use armed forces in combat without the authorization of **Congress**; it was adopted in response to the Vietnam War, in which millions of armed forces were sent to Vietnam without a declaration of war.

* **Watergate** hotel in Washington, D.C., where the Democratic National Committee headquarters were burglarized in 1972 by operatives of the Republican Committee to Reelect the President (Nixon). Attempts by the staff of the White House to cover up their links to the burglars eventually led to a widespread scandal and the resignation of President Nixon.

* **welfare** a government social support program to provide a limited income to people who are unemployable because of age or physical or mental condition or who are unemployed because they lack skills or initiative or because the economy has not created enough jobs; a program that has become more restrictive in recent years by limiting the number of people eligible to receive benefits or the number of years a person may receive benefits.

Whigs in the United States from around 1800 until the Civil War, a political party opposed to the Jeffersonian Republicans and Jacksonian Democrats. Many of its supporters later joined the **Republican Party**. In England, the Whig Party generally opposed the extension of the king's power and supported the predominance of **Parliament**.

Whiskey Rebellion armed insurrection in 1792 by settlers in western Pennsylvania and Virginia protesting federal excise tax on distilled spirits (whiskey). Suppressed by federal troops under Washington, who pardoned most of the participants.

Whitewater (1994) name of an investigation in which legal questions arose regarding Arkansas land investments made by President and Mrs. Clinton. Attorney General Janet Reno appointed Kenneth Starr as independent counsel to investigate the charges. On Wednesday, September 20, 2000, Special Prosecutor Robert Ray concluded the investigation without charging the Clintons with wrongdoing, saying there was insufficient evidence to prove they "knowingly participated in any criminal conduct."

work ethic belief in the value and moral good of productive labor.

* **World Trade Organization (WTO)** a specialized agency of the United Nations that is the most important organization supervising international trade; administers trade agreements, monitors trade policies and practices of nations, tries to settle trade disputes, and keeps track of statistics on trade.

Yalta Agreements agreements reached between Roosevelt, Churchill, and Stalin at Yalta in February 1945, regarding the organization of post-war Europe in anticipation of the defeat of Germany. The agreements divided Germany and Berlin into temporary zones of occupation and established the basis for the **United Nations**.

yellow journalism irresponsible, sensational, or misleading reporting of news.

Regents Examinations, Answers, Self-Analysis Charts, and Regents Specification Grids

Examination August 2017

United States History and Government

PART I: MULTIPLE CHOICE

Directions (1–50): For each statement or question, write in the space provided the *number* of the word or expression that, of those given, best completes the statement or answers the question.

1 Which geographic feature contributed most to the settlement of colonies along the Atlantic Coast?

(1) mountainous terrain
(2) extensive mineral deposits
(3) subtropical climate
(4) navigable rivers and harbors   1 ____

2 During the 1700s, the British government used mercantilism to

(1) profit from its colonies
(2) develop colonial manufacturing
(3) discourage colonial agriculture
(4) promote colonial trade with other nations   2 ____

3 The French and Indian War (1754–1763) was a turning point in the relationship between American colonists and the British government because the war

(1) increased French influence in North America
(2) ended Native American Indian attacks west of the Appalachian Mountains
(3) resulted in British debt and attempts to tax colonists
(4) created an alliance with Canada against the British   3 ____

4 The main reason Thomas Paine wrote *Common Sense* was to

   (1) urge adoption of the Albany Plan of Union
   (2) gain support for declaring independence from Great Britain
   (3) bring an end to the Revolutionary War
   (4) convince states to ratify the new Constitution   4 _____

   Base your answer to question 5 on the passage below and on your knowledge of social studies.

   ...That your Sex are Naturally Tyrannical is a Truth so thoroughly established as to admit of no dispute, but such of you as wish to be happy willingly give up the harsh title of Master for the more tender and endearing one of Friend. Why then, not put it out of the power of the vicious and the Lawless to use us with cruelty and indignity with impunity [exemption]. Men of Sense in all Ages abhor [hate] those customs which treat us only as the vassals of your Sex. Regard us then as Beings placed by providence under your protection and in immitation of the Supreem Being make use of that power only for our happiness....

   —Abigail Adams, Letter to John Adams, March 31, 1776

5 Which document most directly addressed the concerns expressed by Abigail Adams in this passage?

   (1) Federalist Papers
   (2) Monroe Doctrine
   (3) Declaration of Sentiments
   (4) Emancipation Proclamation   5 _____

6 The Northwest Ordinance of 1787 was important in United States history because it established a method for

   (1) admitting new states to the Union
   (2) promoting diplomatic relations with foreign nations
   (3) funding internal improvements
   (4) securing ports on the Pacific Coast   6 _____

7 Antifederalists insisted that a bill of rights be added to the Constitution in order to

(1) grant more power to Congress
(2) provide a method of settling disputes between states
(3) prevent states from denying individuals the right to vote
(4) protect individual rights from the power of the central government   7 _____

Base your answer to question 8 on the passage below and on your knowledge of social studies.

> ...An *elective despotism*, was not the government we fought for; but one which should not only be founded on free principles, but in which the powers of government should be so divided and balanced among several bodies of magistracy [governance], as that no one could transcend their legal limits, without being effectually checked and restrained by the others....
>
> —James Madison, *Federalist No. 48*, 1788

8 Which principle of the United States Constitution is supported by this passage?

(1) representative government
(2) writ of habeas corpus
(3) separation of powers
(4) due process of law   8 _____

9 The term *federalism* is best described as the

(1) division of power between the national government and state governments
(2) creation of a two-house legislature in the national government
(3) method of reviewing laws and executive actions
(4) establishment of three branches of government   9 _____

Base your answer to question 10 on the passage below and on your knowledge of social studies.

The right of citizens of the United States, who are eighteen years of age or older, to vote shall not be denied or abridged by the United States or by any State on account of age.

—United States Constitution, 26th Amendment, Section 1

10 Which factor contributed most directly to public support for this amendment?

(1) high crime rates
(2) the Vietnam War
(3) the Watergate affair
(4) increased life expectancy

10 _____

11 A presidential veto of a bill can be overridden by a

(1) majority vote of registered voters
(2) majority vote of the Supreme Court
(3) two-thirds vote of the state legislatures
(4) two-thirds vote of both houses of Congress

11 _____

12 The opening of the Erie Canal in 1825 was important to the development of the nation because it

(1) linked the industrial centers of the North and the South
(2) allowed the United States Navy to defend the Great Lakes
(3) forced the Spanish to sell Florida to the United States
(4) increased trade between the East Coast and the Midwest

12 _____

13 Before the Civil War, the collapse of the Whig Party and the formation of the Free Soil and the Republican parties showed that

(1) opposing views on slavery affected national unity
(2) Americans were united in their political views
(3) major political parties received most of their support in the South
(4) Americans were divided over the issue of unlimited coinage of silver

13 _____

14 Throughout the Civil War, an important advantage the North had over the South was that the North

  (1) had superior military leaders
  (2) had greater manufacturing capabilities
  (3) received support from Great Britain and France
  (4) used a strategy for fighting a defensive war   14 _____

15 The Compromise of 1877 brought an end to Radical Reconstruction by providing for the

  (1) resignation of President Rutherford B. Hayes
  (2) removal of federal troops from Southern states
  (3) establishment of a system of sharecropping
  (4) strict enforcement of the 14th amendment   15 _____

Base your answers to questions 16 and 17 on the charts below and on your knowledge of social studies.

Sources of Immigration to the United States

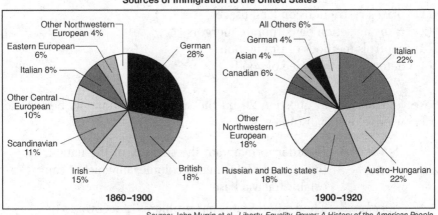

Source: John Murrin et al., *Liberty, Equality, Power: A History of the American People*, Thomson Wadsworth, 2006 (adapted)

16 Which conclusion is best supported by the information in the charts?

  (1) Immigration from the Western Hemisphere declined after 1900.
  (2) The percentage of German immigrants increased between 1860 and 1920.
  (3) Northern Europeans were not permitted to enter the United States from 1860 to 1920.
  (4) Southern and eastern Europeans made up a majority of immigrants from 1900 to 1920.   16 _____

17 What was one result of the changes in immigration patterns shown on the charts?

   (1) Restrictive immigration laws were passed.
   (2) Business increased its demand for workers.
   (3) Urban population declined.
   (4) Requirements for citizenship were eased.   17 _____

18 During the late 1800s, political machines controlled the governments of many cities by

   (1) denying voting rights to immigrants
   (2) attracting dissatisfied voters from the two major political parties
   (3) using corrupt practices and patronage
   (4) favoring civil service reform   18 _____

19 The federal government follows the economic principle of laissez-faire when it

   (1) places restrictions on land usage
   (2) takes no action on corporate mergers
   (3) controls methods of production
   (4) determines the price of goods   19 _____

Base your answer to question 20 on the speakers' statements below and on your knowledge of social studies.

   Speaker A: In order to maintain the security of the nation, the United States needs colonies in which it can establish naval bases.

   Speaker B: The United States has problems of its own to be concerned about, so we must focus our attention here at home.

   Speaker C: If the United States is to compete in a global economy, it needs to look beyond its borders for markets.

   Speaker D: Supporting an overseas empire would become an enormous burden on the American people.

20 The focus of the speakers' debate is the controversy over the

   (1) purchase of Alaska
   (2) policy of imperialism
   (3) size of the United States military
   (4) closing of the frontier   20 _____

21 **"Carnegie Donates Millions to Build Libraries"**
"Rockefeller Creates Foundation for Medical Research"

These headlines reflect the actions of Andrew Carnegie and John
D. Rockefeller as

   (1) muckrakers   (3) socialists
   (2) philanthropists   (4) conservationists   21 _____

22 The Progressive Era presidents were considered trustbusters
because they

   (1) used government power to promote business competition
   (2) supported the elimination of trade barriers
   (3) encouraged more voter participation in government
   (4) canceled treaties with other nations   22 _____

23 The primary objective of the women's movement during the first
two decades of the 20th century was to

   (1) gain property rights
   (2) promote higher education
   (3) secure full suffrage rights
   (4) win equal pay for equal work   23 _____

Base your answers to questions 24 and 25 on the cartoon below and on your knowledge of social studies.

"Touch Not a Single Bough [Branch]!"

Source: *Literary Digest,* August 9, 1919 (adapted)

24 The situation shown in this cartoon was mainly caused by the

(1) cost of paying reparations after World War I
(2) failure of President Woodrow Wilson to promote the Treaty of Versailles
(3) overwhelming public rejection of the peace terms in the Treaty of Versailles
(4) disagreement over United States participation in the League of Nations

24 _____

25 Which constitutional principle is shown in this cartoon?

(1) due process
(2) checks and balances
(3) popular sovereignty
(4) judicial review

25 _____

26 The 1920s are often called the Roaring Twenties because the decade was noted for

   (1) political reform
   (2) economic depression
   (3) social and cultural changes
   (4) ending Prohibition   26 _____

27 The Great Migration that took place between 1915 and 1930 refers to

   (1) workers who left the northeast for the south
   (2) Native American Indians who left their reservations
   (3) middle-class whites who left cities to settle in the suburbs
   (4) African Americans who left the rural south for
       northern cities   27 _____

28 Breadlines, Hoovervilles, and the Bonus Army were all direct results of

   (1) housing shortages in the 1920s
   (2) relief efforts of the New Deal
   (3) mechanization of agriculture
   (4) unemployment during the Great Depression   28 _____

29 The Fair Labor Standards Act (1938) helped American workers by

   (1) establishing health plans
   (2) legalizing strikes and boycotts
   (3) establishing a minimum wage in many industries
   (4) making labor unions accept women and
       African Americans as members   29 _____

30 Adoption of the "cash and carry" policy in 1939 and passage of the Lend-Lease Act in 1941 showed a growing commitment of the United States to

   (1) provide aid to the Allied nations
   (2) force the Japanese out of Korea
   (3) increase trade with Italy
   (4) end German violations of American territory   30 _____

31 A direct result of United States involvement in World War II was

   (1) an increase in the production of consumer goods
   (2) the entry of more women and minorities into the workplace
   (3) a decrease in industrial activity
   (4) a decrease in federal control over the economy   31 _____

32 Which event was a cause of the other three?

   (1) Congress declared war against Japan.
   (2) Japanese Americans were interned by the federal government.
   (3) The United States was attacked at Pearl Harbor.
   (4) The United States dropped an atomic bomb on both
       Hiroshima and Nagasaki.   32 _____

33 McCarthyism of the early 1950s resulted in

   (1) the end of the arms race
   (2) reduced spending on national defense
   (3) increased discrimination against returning veterans
   (4) damage to the reputations of many innocent people   33 _____

34 During the 1950s, United States foreign policy was shaped by

   (1) the principle of nonalignment
   (2) a return to pre–World War II isolationism
   (3) a willingness to compromise with communist nations
   (4) the emergence of two world superpowers   34 _____

35 The formation of the North Atlantic Treaty Organization (NATO) and the Southeast Asia Treaty Organization (SEATO) were attempts by the United States and other nations to

   (1) create mutual defense pacts
   (2) increase tariff rates between members
   (3) decrease the number of nuclear weapons
   (4) provide economic aid to poor nations   35 _____

36 In 1958, the United States government increased spending on science education and research in reaction to the

(1) creation of the Warsaw Pact
(2) launching of *Sputnik*
(3) installation of Soviet missiles in Cuba
(4) U-2 incident

36 _____

Base your answer to question 37 on the quotation below and on your knowledge of social studies.

... Believing this as I do, I have concluded that I should not permit the Presidency to become involved in the partisan divisions that are developing in this political year.

With America's sons in the fields far away, with America's future under challenge right here at home, with our hopes and the world's hopes for peace in the balance every day, I do not believe that I should devote an hour or a day of my time to any personal partisan causes or to any duties other than the awesome duties of this office—the Presidency of your country....

—President Lyndon B. Johnson, Address to the Nation,
March 31, 1968

37 What was one problem facing President Lyndon B. Johnson at the time this speech was delivered?

(1) Americans had experienced several judicial scandals.
(2) His participation in peace talks threatened the war effort.
(3) Opposition to the Vietnam War was becoming more widespread.
(4) Great Society programs forced a reduction in military spending.

37 _____

38 What was the primary method used by Dr. Martin Luther King Jr. to advance civil rights?

(1) nonviolent protest of segregation practices
(2) support for black separatism
(3) pursuit of elective public office
(4) practical education for economic gain

38 _____

Base your answers to questions 39 and 40 on the cartoon below and on your knowledge of social studies.

National-Security Blanket

Source: Herblock, *Washington Post*, May 27, 1973
(adapted)

39 Which action by President Richard Nixon is the focus of this cartoon?

 (1) recalling diplomats from Mexico
 (2) supporting tax decreases and budget cuts
 (3) attempting to hide evidence from investigators
 (4) making concessions to the Soviet Union   39 _____

40 The outcome of the events illustrated in the cartoon resulted in the

 (1) expansion of the Vietnam War into Cambodia
 (2) resignation of President Richard Nixon
 (3) growing support for environmental protection legislation
 (4) visit to Communist China by President Richard Nixon   40 _____

Base your answer to question 41 on the cartoon below and on your knowledge of social studies.

Source: Tom Toles, *Washington Post*, April 25, 2007

41 Which statement best supports the cartoonist's view in 2007 about global warming?

(1) The federal government has been slow to take action on global warming.
(2) Most people support efforts to address global warming.
(3) Dealing with global warming is too expensive.
(4) Global warming is damaging the ozone layer.　　　41 _____

42 Since the presidency of Ronald Reagan, the Republican Party has generally tried to deal with economic problems by supporting

(1) lower taxes and reduced government spending
(2) the elimination of free trade and the free-market system
(3) deficit spending and decreased military spending
(4) increased social spending and strict regulation of the stock market　　　42 _____

43 Which statement about the Hurricane Katrina disaster (2005) is an opinion rather than a fact?

   (1) The levee system in New Orleans failed.
   (2) The federal government did not do enough to aid the victims.
   (3) The federal government was criticized for its initial response to the emergency.
   (4) The Federal Emergency Management Agency (FEMA) provided housing for victims.

43 _____

Base your answer to question 44 on the cartoon below and on your knowledge of social studies.

Source: Clay Bennett, *Chattanooga Times Free Press*,
November 5, 2008

44 According to the cartoonist, one important result of the election of President Barack Obama in 2008 was that

   (1) public facilities in the South were finally integrated
   (2) the executive branch of government gained power over the legislative branch
   (3) a racial barrier in government had been broken
   (4) racial discrimination was legally eliminated in the United States

44 _____

45 The practice of yellow journalism most influenced United States entry into which war?

(1) War of 1812
(2) Spanish-American War
(3) World War II
(4) Persian Gulf War 45 _____

46 The suspension of habeas corpus during the Civil War and the passage of the USA Patriot Act during the war on terror both illustrate the national government's willingness to

(1) uphold the rights of minority citizens
(2) tolerate criticism of its wartime policies
(3) expand the power of the states to prosecute radical groups
(4) limit civil liberties when the nation is facing immediate danger 46 _____

47 The Washington Naval Conference (1921), the Kellogg-Briand Pact (1928), and the Neutrality Acts of the 1930s were all attempts by the United States to

(1) increase military spending
(2) show support for the United Nations
(3) assume a position of world leadership
(4) avoid policies likely to lead to war 47 _____

48 The baby boom following World War II resulted in the

(1) development of urban unrest in the 1950s
(2) need to increase the number of schools in the 1960s
(3) migration from cities to farms in the 1970s
(4) need to decrease the number of nursing homes in the 1980s 48 _____

49 • *Tinker* v. *Des Moines School District* (1969)
   • *New Jersey* v. *T.L.O.* (1985)
   • *Vernonia School District* v. *Acton* (1995)

Which similar issue was addressed in these Supreme Court cases?

(1) balancing the rights of students with the need of schools
   to maintain order
(2) allowing principals to determine students' constitutional rights
(3) denying public school districts the authority to allow prayer
   in schools
(4) giving state legislatures the power to fund charter schools   49 _____

50 President John F. Kennedy and President Ronald Reagan both
visited the Berlin Wall in order to

(1) assess the military strength of the Soviet Union
(2) prepare for an invasion of the Soviet Union
(3) demonstrate the commitment of the United States to
   maintain freedom in Western Europe
(4) challenge the North Atlantic Treaty Organization (NATO)
   nations that were supported by the Soviet Union   50 _____

In developing your answer to Part II, be sure to keep these general definitions in mind:

    (a) <u>describe</u> means "to illustrate something in words or tell about it"

    (b) <u>explain</u> means "to make plain or understandable; to give reasons for or causes of; to show the logical development or relationships of"

    (c) <u>discuss</u> means "to make observations about something using facts, reasoning, and argument; to present in some detail"

PART II: THEMATIC ESSAY

Directions: Write a well-organized essay that includes an introduction, several paragraphs addressing the task below, and a conclusion.

Theme: Presidential Decisions and Actions

> Throughout United States history, presidents have taken actions to address critical problems facing the nation. These actions have met with varying degrees of success.

Task:

> Select **two** presidents who took actions to address a critical problem faced by the nation and for **each**
>
> - Describe the historical circumstances that led to the problem
> - Explain an action taken by the president to address the problem
> - Discuss the extent to which this action resolved the problem

You may use any United States president who took an action to solve a critical problem facing the nation from your study of United States history. Some suggestions you might wish to consider include:

George Washington—Whiskey Rebellion
Andrew Jackson—nullification crisis
Abraham Lincoln—secession of Southern states
Franklin D. Roosevelt—Great Depression
Dwight D. Eisenhower—school integration
John F. Kennedy—Cuban missile crisis
Lyndon B. Johnson—discrimination faced by minorities
George H. W. Bush—invasion of Kuwait by Iraq
George W. Bush—attacks of September 11, 2001

You are *not* limited to these suggestions.

Guidelines:

In your essay, be sure to:

- Develop all aspects of the task
- Support the theme with relevant facts, examples, and details
- Use a logical and clear plan of organization, including an introduction and a conclusion that are beyond a restatement of the theme

In developing your answers to Part III, be sure to keep this general definition in mind:

> discuss means "to make observations about something using facts, reasoning, and argument; to present in some detail"

PART III: DOCUMENT-BASED QUESTION

This question is based on the accompanying documents. The question is designed to test your ability to work with historical documents. Some of these documents have been edited for the purposes of this question. As you analyze the documents, take into account the source of each document and any point of view that may be presented in the document. Keep in mind that the language used in a document may reflect the historical context of the time in which it was written.

Historical Context:

> During the 19th and early 20th centuries, the development of the West had political, economic, and social effects on various groups. These groups include *Native American Indians*, *women*, and *Chinese immigrants*.

Task:

> Using the information from the documents and your knowledge of United States history, answer the questions that follow each document in Part A. Your answers to the questions will help you write the Part B essay in which you will be asked to
>
> Select *two* groups mentioned in the historical context and for *each*
>
> * Discuss political, economic, *and/or* social effects of the development of the West on the group

Part A: Short-Answer Questions

Directions: Analyze the documents and answer the short-answer questions that follow each document in the space provided.

Document 1a

Buffalo hides stacked at Dodge City, Kansas, for shipment to the East, 1878

Source: National Archives (adapted)

Document 1b

"…White men had found gold in the mountains around the land of the Winding Water [in Oregon]. They stole a great many horses from us and we could not get them back because we were Indians. The white men told lies for each other. They drove off a great many of our cattle. Some white men branded our young cattle so they could claim them. We had no friends who would plead our cause before the law councils. It seemed to me that some of the white men in Wallowa [a valley in Oregon] were doing these things on purpose to get up a war. They knew we were not strong enough to fight them. I labored hard to avoid trouble and bloodshed.…"

Source: Chester Anders Fee, Chief Joseph: The Biography of a Great Indian, Wilson-Erickson

1 Based on these documents, what were **two** effects of the development of the West on Native American Indians? [2]

(1) _____

   _____

(2) _____

   _____

Document 2a

By the mid-1880s, the biggest single area in the West suitable for farming and still largely untouched by white settlement was Indian Territory. Representatives of some fifty-five tribes now called it home, but there were large tracts within it upon which no one lived.

One of these—2 million empty and unassigned acres—was called "the Oklahoma District," and the army was soon kept busy driving from it armed parties of squatters from Kansas who called themselves "Boomers." Furious lobbying eventually succeeded where invasion failed, and Congress finally voted to buy out all Indian claims to the Oklahoma District....

Source: Geoffrey C. Ward, *The West: An Illustrated History*,
Little, Brown and Company, 1996

Document 2b

Native American Indians in the West: Major Battles and Reservations

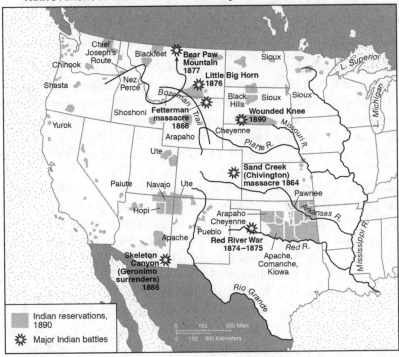

Source: Robert A. Divine et al., *America: Past and Present*,
Addison Wesley Longman, 1999 (adapted)

2 Based on these documents, what was *one* impact of westward settlement on Native American Indians? [1]

_____

_____

Document 3a

After the Battle of Wounded Knee, Commissioner of Indian Affairs Thomas Jefferson Morgan made recommendations about how to avoid future conflicts with Native American Indians.

...*Fifth*—The only possible solution of our [Native American] Indian troubles lies in the suitable education of the rising generation. So long as the Indians remain among us aliens, speaking foreign languages, unable to communicate with us except through the uncertain and often misleading medium of interpreters, so long as they are ignorant of our ways, are superstitious and fanatical, they will remain handicapped in the struggle for existence, will be an easy prey to the medicine man and the false prophet, and will be easily induced, by reason of real or imaginary wrongs, to go upon the war-path. An education that will give them the mastery of the English language, train their hands to useful industries, awaken within them ambition for civilized ways, and develop a consciousness of power to achieve honorable places for themselves, and that arouses within them an earnest and abiding patriotism, will make of them American citizens, and render future conflicts between them and the Government impossible....

Source: T.J. Morgan, *The Present Phase of the Indian Question*, 1891

Document 3b

Lakota boys are pictured when they arrived at the Carlisle Indian Industrial School in Pennsylvania, left, and three years later, right.

Source: New York Public Digital Gallery (adapted)

3 Based on these documents, what are *two* ways Native American Indians were being affected by the development of the West? [2]

(1) _____

_____

(2) _____

_____

Document 4

...By 1800 the external aspect of the landscape was changing, with the extension of cleared fields, and the gradual rebuilding of cabins over the older areas. But inside the cabins the family life still embraced the whole range of domestic manufactures. The frontier graveyards show how hard the early life was on the women of the family. The patriarch laid to rest in his family tract, beside two, three, or four wives who had preceded him, is much more common than the hardy woman who outlived her husbands. The housewife came to her new home young and raw, and found for neighbors other girls as inexperienced. She bore the children; and buried a staggering number of them, for medicine and sanitation, inadequate everywhere, were out of reach for the cabin on the border. She fed her men and raised her children, cooked their food and laid it by [stored it] for winter. She was at once butcher, packer, and baker. The family clothes showed her craftsmanship, with skins playing a large part, and homespun or knitting revealing a luxury established. When one adds to the grinding and unavoidable labor, the anguish that came from sickness and danger, the frontier woman who survived becomes an heroic character, and the children who felt her touch become the proper material from which to choose the heroes of a nation....

Source: Frederic L. Paxson, *History of the American Frontier,*
1763–1893, Houghton Mifflin, 1924

4 According to Frederic L. Paxson, what was **one** effect of westward development on frontier women living in the West? [1]

_____

_____

Document 5

It perhaps ought to be stated here, for the benefit of widows and single women over twenty-one years of age, that they are as much entitled to homesteads as men, and the women of Dakota generally avail themselves of the privilege. We can point you to young women in Dakota who carry on quite a stroke of farming now, who came here penniless a few years ago. One woman has now three hundred and twenty acres of land, paid for from her wages as servant girl, at $4.00 per week. It is the investment of what she has saved from her wages in the last two years. We, of Dakota, believe in Women's Rights, especially the right to take a homestead and manage it to their own liking....

Source: James S. Foster, Commissioner of Immigration for Dakota
Territory, *Outlines of History of the Territory of Dakota*, 1870

5 According to James S. Foster, what is **one** opportunity the development of the West offered to women? [1]

_____

_____

Document 6

This circular appeared in Kentucky's *Lexington Herald*, informing readers of the benefits of women voting in Wyoming.

WOMAN SUFFRAGE IN WYOMING.

Suffrage Circular

Women have voted in Wyoming for forty-one years on equal terms with men.

During the past thirty years there has been less divorce in Wyoming than in any state in the Union....

A smaller number of married women are working outside the home in Wyoming than in any other State in the Union.

Women teachers get equal pay for equal work in Wyoming.

There are fewer illiterate children in Wyoming than in any other State in the Union.

Young girls are better protected in Wyoming than in any State in the Union....

Source: *Lexington Herald*, May 19, 1910

6 According to this circular, what were *two* benefits of granting suffrage to women in Wyoming? [2]

(1) _____

_____

(2) _____

_____

Document 7

...A combination of push and pull factors thus triggered a wave of Chinese immigration to America. More than 20,000 Chinese arrived in the United States in 1852, quickly augmenting [increasing] the number of Chinese in California, which reached 34,933 on the eve of the Civil War. Of these Chinese, some three-fourths lived in counties where mining was the principal occupation. Most Chinese miners missed the initial rush, but they gradually took control of California placer mining. Within a decade they possessed most of the claims in the original strike region and together constituted the single largest national group of miners. Their slow start and quick dominance in California's mines formed a distinctive pattern that would be repeated throughout the mining West....

As a story of economic mobility and self-improvement, the Chinese experience on the western mining frontier was a success. To be sure, the Chinese had many disadvantages. They possessed little starting capital, they had staked no initial claims, they faced legal discrimination, and they encountered racial violence. But these disadvantages were often compensated for by advantages, including mining experience, cooperative culture, a healthy life-style, skill at aquatic management, and environmental adaptability, all of which ensured Chinese competitiveness in the American West. In 1870, several Chinese companies in Montana were listed among the territory's most profitable. For six months Chang-Ling Company with seven persons cleared $13,000 in gold. According to one 1871 account, Chinese miners took out $500,000 in gold from the Tuscarora region in Nevada. Between 1855 and 1870 more than 10 percent of the gold and silver exports through the Port of San Francisco went to China, an amount ($72,581,219) equivalent to more than $1 billion today....

Source: Liping Zhu, "No Need to Rush: The Chinese, Placer Mining, and
the Western Environment," *Montana: The Magazine of Western History*, Autumn 1999 (adapted)

7 According to Liping Zhu, what were *two* ways living in the West affected Chinese immigrants? [2]

(1) _____

_____

(2) _____

_____

Document 8a

…Besides railroad work, Chinese found opportunities elsewhere. When they learned that $8 was the going rate for a basket of laundry in San Francisco, they did it for $5 and were swamped with business. Soon scores of laundries opened, often one group working daytime, another at night. Even in smaller towns the Chinese laundry became an institution—the lone laundryman wielding his iron long hours in an isolated existence, unable to communicate with Americans, dreaming only of his hoped-for return to China.…

Source: David Lindsey, "Cathay Comes to El Dorado,"
American History Illustrated

Document 8b

…Meanwhile, in the rural regions, the Chinese were participating in the development of California's agriculture, which was turning from wheat to fruit acreage. "They were a vital factor," historian Carey McWilliams writes, "one is inclined to state *the* vital factor, in making the transition possible." Formerly farmers in the Pearl River Delta in Guangdong, the Chinese shared their agricultural experience and knowledge. They "taught their over-lords how to plant, cultivate, and harvest orchard and garden crops." Their contributions extended beyond California: Ah Bing in Oregon bred the famous Bing cherry, and Lue Gim Gong in Florida developed the frost-resis-tant orange that bore his name and that gave the state its citrus industry.…

Source: Ronald Takaki, *Strangers from a Different Shore: A History of
Asian Americans*, Little, Brown and Company, 1989 (adapted)

8 Based on these documents, what were **two** opportunities the development of the West offered to Chinese immigrants? [2]

(1) _____

_____

(2) _____

_____

Document 9

Opposition to Chinese immigration included the Workingmen's Party in the late 1870s.

> ...After being occupied during the 1850s, 1860s, and early 1870s in the placers [mines] and on major construction projects, many Chinese turned toward the cities and new industries. San Francisco was the mecca for most, for it was both the industrial capital of the Pacific Coast and the headquarters for the Chinese. The timing was unfortunate, for it brought the Chinese into conflict with the struggling labor movement that had been trying to organize itself in San Francisco during the preceding two decades, and it did so at a time when unemployment and threats to the traditionally high level of western wages made white workers angrily sensitive to the dangers of Chinese competition. A very high percentage of those workers were themselves immigrants, especially Irish and Germans—but they were white immigrants....

Source: Rodman W. Paul, *The Far West and the Great Plains in Transition, 1859–1900*, Harper & Row, 1988

9 According to Rodman W. Paul, state *one* reason for opposition to Chinese immigrants in San Francisco. [1]

_____

_____

Part B: Essay

Directions: Write a well-organized essay that includes an introduction, several paragraphs, and a conclusion. Use evidence from *at least four* documents in your essay. Support your response with relevant facts, examples, and details. Include additional outside information.

Historical Context:

> During the 19th and early 20th centuries, the development of the West had political, economic, and social effects on various groups. These groups include ***Native American Indians***, ***women***, and ***Chinese immigrants.***

Task:

> Using the information from the documents and your knowledge of United States history, write an essay in which you
>
> Select *two* groups mentioned in the historical context and for *each*
>
> - Discuss political, economic, *and/or* social effects of the development of the West on the group

Guidelines:

In your essay, be sure to:

- Develop all aspects of the task
- Incorporate information from *at least four* documents
- Incorporate relevant outside information
- Support the theme with relevant facts, examples, and details
- Use a logical and clear plan of organization, including an introduction and a conclusion that are beyond a restatement of the theme

Answers
August 2017
United States History and Government

Answer Key

PART I

1. 4	11. 4	21. 3	31. 2	41. 1
2. 1	12. 4	22. 1	32. 3	42. 1
3. 3	13. 1	23. 3	33. 4	43. 2
4. 2	14. 2	24. 4	34. 4	44. 3
5. 3	15. 2	25. 2	35. 1	45. 2
6. 1	16. 4	26. 3	36. 2	46. 4
7. 4	17. 1	27. 4	37. 3	47. 4
8. 3	18. 3	28. 4	38. 1	48. 2
9. 1	19. 2	29. 3	39. 3	49. 1
10. 2	20. 2	30. 1	40. 2	50. 3

PART II: Thematic Essay   *See* **Answers Explained** section.

PART III: Document-Based Question   *See* **Answers Explained** section.

Answers Explained

PART I (1–50)

1. **4** The geographic feature that contributed most to the settlement of colonies along the Atlantic Coast was navigable rivers and harbors. Plymouth (1620), Massachusetts Bay Colony (1630), Providence (1636), Newport (1639), and New Amsterdam (1624) were all established on protected harbors at the mouths of rivers. Jamestown (1607) was founded on the James River some 40 miles upriver from the Atlantic Ocean. The Connecticut Colony (1636) was founded on the Connecticut River, about 40 miles upriver from the Long Island Sound. Such locations allowed for trade with European countries and with the West Indies and Africa. Rivers aided agricultural development through irrigation and transportation of goods. Within a generation, as the flow of English migrants into North America increased, settlements were established inland from these initial coastal and river settlements. The push of settlers into the interior of the continent increased tensions with Native American Indians.

WRONG CHOICES EXPLAINED:

(1) Mountainous terrain did not contribute to the settlement of colonies along the Atlantic Coast. The Appalachian Mountains rise inland from the Atlantic Coast. However, they served as more of an impediment to settlement rather than an aid.

(2) Mineral deposits did not contribute to the settlement of colonies along the Atlantic Coast. Mineral deposits in the Atlantic Coast were not valuable to colonists nor were they extensively mined. The gold and silver deposits exploited by the Spanish in New Spain were not present in British North America.

(3) A subtropical climate did not contribute to the settlement of colonies along the Atlantic Coast. Subtropical climate conditions, characterized by hot and humid summers and mild winters, are generally located between 25 and 35 degrees latitude. Jamestown, Virginia, is slightly above this range, and the colonies of New England are well above it.

2. **1** During the 1700s, the British government used mercantilism to profit from its colonies. Mercantilism is the economic theory that guided the British in establishing an empire. The theory holds that only a limited amount of wealth exists in the world. Nations increase their power by increasing their share of the world's wealth. One way of acquiring wealth is by maintaining a favorable

balance of trade, with the value of exports exceeding the value of imports. Mercantilist theory suggests that governments should advance these goals by maintaining colonies so as to have a steady and inexpensive source of raw materials. The theory also holds that the colonies should not develop manufacturing but, instead, should serve as markets for goods manufactured in the ruling country. Great Britain imposed several navigation laws on the North American colonies to make sure that colonial trade occurred within the British Empire and not with Great Britain's rivals. However, some of these laws were difficult to enforce. By the 17th century, the colonies began to develop an economy independent of Great Britain.

WRONG CHOICES EXPLAINED:

(2) The British government did not use mercantilism to develop colonial manufacturing. Mercantilist theory insists that manufacturing occur primarily in the mother country so that the mother country gains the profits from producing and selling manufactured items. The role of colonies is to supply raw materials and to serve as markets for manufactured items. Several acts—such as the Wool Act (1699), the Hat Act (1732), and the Iron Act (1750)—prohibited the colonies from manufacturing these items.

(3) The British government did not use mercantilism to discourage colonial agriculture. Mercantilist theory insists that colonies develop agriculture to provide raw materials to the mother country. In this way, the mother country has a reliable and inexpensive supply of necessary raw materials. Some of these raw materials are consumed (sugar and tobacco), while others are manufactured into finished products (lumber).

(4) The British government did not use mercantilism to encourage colonial trade with other countries. British mercantilist rules insisted that certain goods could be sold only to the mother country. Parliament developed a list of "enumerated goods"—goods from the colonies that could be shipped only to Britain. These included goods that were essential for ship building, such as tar, pitch, and trees for masts. Goods that were not enumerated could be sold to other countries, but the trade had to be carried out in British ships and through British ports.

3. **3** The French and Indian War (1754–1763) was a turning point in the relationship between American colonists and the British government because the war resulted in British debt and attempts to tax colonists. In many ways, the war was a catalyst for much of the tension that culminated in the American Revolution. The French and Indian War was caused, in part, by colonial expansion into the lands beyond the Appalachian Mountains. Before the war, a few settlers crossed over the Appalachian Mountains and established farms in the Ohio River Valley. This expansion led to conflicts with the French, who had

earlier established outposts in the area, and eventually led to war with the French and their Native-American allies. The British won the war, but the war led to a massive debt for the British government. The British asserted that the colonists, who benefited from the results of the war, should help repay some of this debt. Therefore, the British enacted several taxes—the Sugar Act (1764), the Stamp Act (1765), and the Townshend Acts (1767). Many colonists asserted that only representatives elected by the colonists themselves could enact taxes on the colonies. "No taxation without representation" became the rallying cry of the colonists as protests mounted in the years leading up to the ratification of the Declaration of Independence (1776).

WRONG CHOICES EXPLAINED:

(1) The French and Indian War (1754–1763) did not result in increased French influence in North America. The opposite was true. France lost its possessions in North America and gave up its claims to disputed territory.

(2) The French and Indian War (1754–1763) did not result in an end to Native-American Indian attacks west of the Appalachian Mountains. Immediately following the war, conflicts ensued as Native American Indians faced a crisis—their French allies were displaced and British troops and colonists were expanding into areas beyond the Appalachian Mountains. Chief Pontiac, of the Ottawa people, and other Indian leaders organized resistance to British troops stationed around the Great Lakes in forts that were previously held by the French. These attacks were followed by strikes on colonial settlements along a swath of land from upstate New York to the area south of Lake Michigan and along the Appalachian frontier.

(4) The French and Indian War (1754–1763) did not result in an alliance with Canada against the British. The American colonies were still under British control, so they could not have formed alliances with other countries. In addition, Canada came under British control as a result of the French and Indian War.

4. **2** The main reason Thomas Paine wrote *Common Sense* was to gain support for declaring independence from Great Britain. Relations between Great Britain and the colonies were strained at the time Paine wrote his pamphlet. In April 1775, fighting began between opponents of Great Britain and British troops in the Massachusetts towns of Lexington and Concord. During the remainder of 1775, relations between the colonies and Great Britain worsened. In June 1775, the Battle of Bunker Hill occurred in Boston and the British parliament declared that American ships were enemy vessels. The Second Continental Congress, a body of representatives from the 13 colonies, created an army, declared war against Great Britain, and began issuing its own currency. At the same time, some members of Congress still hoped for reconciliation.

Congress sent the Olive Branch Petition to the king of England, affirming loyalty to the monarch and blaming the current problems on Parliament. Paine argued against the logic of the petition, plainly and forcefully putting the blame on the king. Paine's arguments carried the day. On July 4, 1776, the delegates to the Second Continental Congress formally ratified the Declaration of Independence.

WRONG CHOICES EXPLAINED:

(1) Thomas Paine did not write *Common Sense* in order to urge adoption of the Albany Plan of Union. Paine's 1776 pamphlet was written well after the 1754 Albany Plan of Union. The Albany Plan of Union grew out of the Albany Congress, a meeting called by Benjamin Franklin. The goal of the plan was to unite the 13 colonies in order to provide for their common defense. Franklin wanted to organize support for British forces in the French and Indian War. The plan was rejected by the colonial assemblies as well as by British authorities.

(3) Thomas Paine did not write *Common Sense* (1776) in order to bring an end to the Revolutionary War, which had started in April 1775. Paine was not arguing that the war should end. He wanted to shape the intent of the struggle and to bring more colonists to the side of supporting the move toward independence.

(4) Thomas Paine did not write *Common Sense* in order to convince states to ratify the new Constitution. Debates over the Constitution occurred over a decade after Paine's pamphlet was published. During debates over the Constitution (1787–1790), Paine strongly argued against the conservative and elitist nature of the document.

5. **3** The concerns addressed by Abigail Adams were most directly addressed by the Declaration of Sentiments. In her letter to her husband John Adams, Abigail Adams expressed hope that as John and other leaders of the patriot cause formulated a new legal framework, they would include women on an equal footing with men. Abigail Adams was not alone in her assertion of gender equality. The experience of women participating in the struggle for independence, from organizing boycotts to aiding men on the battlefield, instilled a sense of egalitarianism among many women. In addition, the rhetoric of the revolutionary era railed against tyrannical rule. Many found analogies between the tyranny of king over subject and the tyranny of husband over wife. The concerns voiced by Abigail Adams and others were not incorporated into the state and federal constitutions that were framed in the post-revolutionary era. Later, in 1848, women and their male allies met in Seneca Falls, New York, to organize a women's rights convention. The Seneca Falls Convention, which is often considered the birth of the women's rights movement, formulated the Declaration of Sentiments. The convention was organized by Lucretia Mott and Elizabeth

Cady Stanton. They argued that the laws of the country relegated women to a second-class status. Women could not vote or sit on juries. Women were not entitled to protection against physical abuse by their husbands. When women married, any property they owned became the property of their husbands. Society defined women as intellectually inferior and insisted that the proper role for women was maintaining the house and caring for children. The Declaration of Sentiments was modeled after the Declaration of Independence. The document declared that "all men and women are created equal."

WRONG CHOICES EXPLAINED:

(1) The Federalist Papers do not address the issues of gender equality raised by Abigail Adams in the passage. The Federalist Papers, written by Alexander Hamilton, John Jay, and James Madison in 1787 and 1788, were intended to win support for ratification of the Constitution. These supporters of the Constitution, who became known as Federalists, argued that the existing structure of government was inadequate for the United States. Many Federalists were alarmed at the inability of the central government established under the Articles of Confederation to raise revenue or to put down rebellions.

(2) The Monroe Doctrine does not address the issues of gender equality raised by Abigail Adams in the passage. The Monroe Doctrine, issued by President James Monroe in 1823, warned European nations to avoid further colonization of the Americas. The United States did not have the military might to enforce this pronouncement at the time. However, the Monroe Doctrine was an important statement of intent. The Monroe Doctrine and Washington's farewell address (1797) became cornerstones of America's isolationist foreign policy.

(4) The Emancipation Proclamation does not address the issues of gender equality raised by Abigail Adams in the passage. The Emancipation Proclamation was issued during the Civil War in 1862. In it, Lincoln declared that all slaves in Confederate-held territory would be freed as of January 1, 1863. Although the Emancipation Proclamation did not immediately free any slaves, it was important because it made it clear that the Civil War had become a war to liberate the slaves.

6. **1** The Northwest Ordinance of 1787 was important in United States history because it established a method for admitting new states to the Union. The act dealt with the Northwest Territory, the vast stretch of land north of the Ohio River that is between the western border of Pennsylvania and the Mississippi River. Earlier, the government established by the Articles of Confederation persuaded the various states to give up their land claims in the region. Then it passed two significant pieces of legislation. The Land Ordinance provided for an orderly system of development for the Northwest Territory. It divided up the

land and provided a plot in every town for public schools. The Northwest Ordinance spelled out the steps that these areas would have to go through in order to become states. In addition, the Northwest Ordinance banned slavery in the Northwest Territory. Although these acts are considered to be successes of the government established by the Articles of Confederation, contemporaries and historians have tended to focus on the problems of the period, such as inflation and lack of government revenues. In fact, the period is often labeled the *critical period* in the sense of a patient being in critical condition.

WRONG CHOICES EXPLAINED:

(2) The Northwest Ordinance of 1787 did not establish a method for promoting diplomatic relations with foreign nations. Diplomatic relations are carried out by the president—either personally or through his or her designated representatives. Treaties must be approved by the Senate.

(3) The Northwest Ordinance of 1787 did not establish a method for funding internal improvements. The term *internal improvements* was used in the 19th century to describe infrastructure projects, such as canals, roads, and railroads. These projects did much to expand trade, especially between the Midwest (then known as the West) and eastern cities. Most significant was the Erie Canal (completed in 1825), which connected the Hudson River in upstate New York to the Great Lakes. Public funding of such projects generated a great deal of debate among politicians.

(4) The Northwest Ordinance of 1787 did not establish a method for securing ports on the Pacific Coast. With the acquisition of the Mexican Cession (1848) following the Mexican War (1846–1848), the United States secured ports on the Pacific, including Los Angeles and San Francisco.

7. **4** Antifederalists insisted that a bill of rights be added to the Constitution in order to protect individual rights from the power of the central government. Antifederalists feared the Constitution would create an omnipotent and unaccountable government. They had vivid memories of the intrusions of the royal British government into their lives and wanted assurances that the people would have basic protections from government abuses. Eventually, many leading Antifederalists agreed to support ratification of the Constitution, which had been written in 1787, if a list of individual rights was added. This agreement led to the writing and ratification of the first ten amendments to the Constitution, known as the Bill of Rights (1791). The First Amendment protects the people from government limitations on freedom of expression and of religion. It also affirms the right of people to protest against government actions. The First Amendment also established the separation of church and state. The Second Amendment established the right to bear arms. The Fourth Amendment holds that people are to be free

from unwarranted searches by government authorities. The Fifth and Sixth Amendments list a variety of protections that people have when they are accused of crimes, such as the right to a speedy and public trial. The Eighth Amendment states that the government shall not inflict cruel and unusual punishments on people.

WRONG CHOICES EXPLAINED:
(1) The Bill of Rights, which was ratified to address the concerns of the Antifederalists, limited the power of Congress by prohibiting it from abridging certain rights. It did not grant *more* power to Congress. Antifederalists were concerned about the federal government assuming too much power.

(2) The Bill of Rights, which was ratified to address the concerns of the Antifederalists, was intended to protect the basic rights of individuals from governmental overreach. It did not settle disputes between states. The Constitution states that the Supreme Court has the power to resolve disputes between states.

(3) The Bill of Rights, which was ratified to address the concerns of the Antifederalists, was intended to protect basic rights of individuals from governmental overreach. It did not prevent states from denying individuals the right to vote. The right to vote has been extended to different groups of people with three amendments to the Constitution. The 15th Amendment (1870) prevented states from denying a citizen the vote based on that citizen's race. The 19th Amendment (1920) extended the right to vote to women. The 26th Amendment (1971) prohibited using age as a reason to deny any citizen the right to vote who is at least 18 years old.

8. **3** The passage by James Madison supports the constitutional principle of separation of powers. In the passage, Madison expressed concern about too much power being exercised by any one of the branches of government. Madison and the other framers of the Constitution created three branches of government—legislative, executive, and judicial—each with powers separate from the other two. The legislative branch creates laws. The executive branch carries out laws. The judicial branch interprets laws. The Constitution spells out the powers of each branch. After living under the British monarchy, the framers of the Constitution came to believe that a powerful government without checks was dangerous to liberty. Therefore, they created a governmental system with three branches, each with the ability to check the powers of the other two. The goal was to keep the three branches in balance.

WRONG CHOICES EXPLAINED:

(1) The passage by James Madison does not address the constitutional principle of representative government. The Constitution does call for a representative government. Congress is made up of representatives of the people. Members of the House of Representatives were to be elected by the people, while Senators were to be appointed by popularly elected state legislatures.

(2) The passage by James Madison does not address the constitutional principle of the writ of habeas corpus. The Constitution does assert that the right to obtain a writ of habeas corpus shall not be denied (except during times of rebellion or invasion). This privilege was included in the Constitution to curtail the age-old practice of tyrannical rulers throwing people into jail without formal procedures or just cause.

(4) The passage by James Madison does not address the constitutional principle of due process of law. The Constitution does spell out the procedures, known as due process, that individuals must be subjected to before they are punished. The framers of the Constitution wanted to protect people from arbitrary authority. They did not want the authorities to be able to throw people into jail indefinitely at their will.

9. **1** The term *federalism* is best described as the division of power between the national government and state governments. The Constitution created a federal system, granting powers to both the national (federal) government and the state governments. This system of divided power is different from the government established by the Articles of Confederation (1781–1788). The Articles left most power on the state level and created merely a "firm league of friendship" among the sovereign states. The federalist system is also different from the unitary system of countries such as France. In France, the central government sets policies for the entire country with very little decision-making power at the local level.

WRONG CHOICES EXPLAINED:

(2) The term *federalism* does not refer to the creation of a two-house legislature in the national government. The Great Compromise at the Constitutional Convention (1787) settled the dispute over how the states would be represented in Congress and created a two-house legislature. The dispute pitted states with larger populations against those with smaller populations. The larger states wanted representation in Congress to be based on population; the smaller states wanted an equal number of representatives for each state. The Great Compromise created the basic structure of Congress as it now exists. The plan called for a House of Representatives, in which representation would be determined by the population of each state, and a Senate, in which each state would get two members.

(3) The term *federalism* does not refer to the method of reviewing laws and executive actions. It was the Supreme Court decision in *Marbury* v. *Madison* that established the method of reviewing laws and executive actions. The 1803 case, heard under Chief Justice John Marshall, was perhaps the most important decision in the history of the Supreme Court in that it established the Supreme Court's power of judicial review. This decision strengthened the judiciary by asserting that the Supreme Court has the power to review laws and executive actions to determine whether they are consistent with the Constitution. The power of judicial review has been the main function of the Supreme Court since then.

(4) The term *federalism* does not refer to the establishment of three branches of government. The Constitution created a government with three branches, each with powers separate from the other two. The legislative branch creates laws. The executive branch carries out laws. The judicial branch interprets laws. The Constitution spells out the powers of each branch. The framers were very conscious of the problems of a government with limitless powers. Therefore, they created a governmental system with three branches, each with the ability to check the powers of the other two. The goal was to keep the three branches in balance.

10. **2** The factor that contributed most directly to public support for passage of the 26th Amendment was the Vietnam War. The 26th Amendment (1971) prohibited using age as a reason to deny any citizen the right to vote who is at least 18 years old. The amendment was ratified as many men as young as 18 were being drafted into the war in Vietnam. Proponents of the change argued that if these young men were old enough to serve in the military, they were old enough to vote. In 1964, the United States became heavily involved in the Vietnam War after Congress gave President Lyndon Johnson a blank check with the Tonkin Gulf Resolution. As the war dragged on and as the United States suffered more casualties, many Americans began to question the wisdom of American policies in Vietnam. By 1968, Johnson decided that his war policies imperiled his reelection, so he decided to not run for a second term. The following president, Richard Nixon, did not have any more success in moving the United States closer to victory in Vietnam. Many young opponents of the war pushed for ratification of the 26th Amendment, arguing that the young should have a voice in the direction of American policies.

WRONG CHOICES EXPLAINED:

(1) High crime rates did not directly contribute to public support for the constitutional amendment lowering the voting age to 18. Crime rates did climb in the 1960s and 1970s in many areas of the United States, but this development was not directly related to the push for passage of the 26th Amendment.

(3) The Watergate affair did not directly contribute to public support for the constitutional amendment lowering the voting age to 18. The Watergate scandal began in June 1972, a year after ratification of the 26th Amendment. The scandal began when five men were caught breaking into the headquarters of the Democratic Party at the Watergate Hotel in Washington, D.C. Persistent reporting drew connections between the burglars and President Richard Nixon's reelection committee and, ultimately, the White House. As Nixon's complicity in attempts to cover up the scandal became known, pressure built on the president to resign, which occurred in 1974.

(4) Increased life expectancy did not directly contribute to public support for the constitutional amendment lowering the voting age to 18. Life expectancy for both men and women in the United States has risen steadily since 1940 and is projected to continue to rise through 2080.

11. **4** A presidential veto of a bill can be overridden by a two-thirds vote of both houses of Congress. The Constitution gives the president the power to veto, or reject, legislation that he or she finds objectionable. The president vetoes a bill by returning it to Congress within ten days of having received it. The president must also submit in writing his or her objections to the bill. If the president simply does not sign the bill within those ten days, it becomes law. However, a situation might occur in which the president does not sign a bill but Congress adjourns before the ten-day period is up. In such a scenario, the bill does not become law. In that scenario, the president has carried out a pocket veto (in effect, he has put the bill into his pocket rather than returning it to Congress). In either case—a regular veto or a pocket veto—Congress has the power to override the veto with a two-thirds majority vote in both houses. In the case of a Congressional override, the bill becomes law without the president's signature.

WRONG CHOICES EXPLAINED:

(1) A majority vote of registered voters cannot override a presidential veto. There is no mechanism on a national level for voters to express either support or opposition for federal statutes. The only recourse for voters is to support or oppose candidates in state-by-state elections.

(2) A majority vote of the Supreme Court cannot override a presidential veto. The Supreme Court can undo existing legislation by a majority vote through the

process of judicial review. It can hear a case that involves an existing law. If the Supreme Court finds that the law is unconstitutional, that law is stricken from the books.

(3) A two-thirds vote of the state legislatures cannot override a presidential veto. States do not have the power to nullify federal actions. The theory that states could nullify federal actions was put forth by Thomas Jefferson and James Madison in 1796 in the Virginia and Kentucky Resolutions, which were written in response to the Alien and Sedition Acts. The theory was again put forward by John C. Calhoun and other opponents of the Tariff Act of 1828, labeled the Tariff of Abominations.

12. **4** The opening of the Erie Canal in 1825 was important to the development of the nation because it increased trade between the East Coast and the Midwest. The United States was faced with a vexing problem during its first decades. On maps, the country extended to the Mississippi River following independence and then to the Rocky Mountains following the Louisiana Purchase (1803). However, most residents of the United States resided in communities close to the Atlantic Coast, east of the Appalachian Mountains. The Erie Canal helped open up the vast landmass of the country to trade and settlement. The Erie Canal connected the Hudson River in upstate New York to the Great Lakes. The canal created an all-water route from New York City to the Midwestern communities around the Great Lakes. This connection facilitated trade between the East Coast and the Midwest. A shipment of wheat, for example, could now be transported from Chicago to New York City by an all-water route at a tenth of the cost and a fraction of the time of an overland route.

WRONG CHOICES EXPLAINED:
(1) The Erie Canal did not link the industrial centers of the North and the South. The main linkages between the North and South in the period before the Civil War were water routes on the Atlantic Ocean.

(2) The Erie Canal did not result in the United States Navy defending the Great Lakes. The canal did open up a water route between the Atlantic Ocean and the Great Lakes. However, after the War of 1812, the Great Lakes were largely demilitarized. The Rush-Bagot Treaty (ratified in 1818), which was between the United States and Great Britain, limited the number of naval vessels on the Great Lakes.

(3) The Erie Canal did not force the Spanish to sell Florida to the United States. The United States acquired Florida from Spain with the Adams-Onis Treaty (1819). That treaty occurred before the completion of the canal and is largely unrelated to developments associated with the building of the canal.

13. **1** Before the Civil War, the collapse of the Whig Party and the formation of the Free Soil and the Republican Parties showed that opposing views on slavery affected national unity. The issue of slavery became increasingly contentious in the late 1840s and 1850s. In the 1840s, both the major political parties, the Whigs and the Democrats, avoided taking strong stands on the issue of slavery. In response to the conspicuous silence on the part of the major parties on the slavery question, antislavery men in both parties founded the Free Soil Party in 1848. That party ran candidates in the presidential elections of 1848 and 1852. Those candidates garnered only 10 percent of the vote in 1848 and only 5 percent in 1852. In 1854, the Kansas-Nebraska Act intensified existing sectional divisions. The act allowed for the possibility of slavery in the territories of Kansas and Nebraska if the residents of those territories voted for it. This principle, called *popular sovereignty*, angered antislavery northerners who were assured by the Missouri Compromise (1820) that slavery would forever be prohibited from the northern half of the Louisiana Territory, which included Kansas and Nebraska. The act divided Whigs into the proslavery Cotton Whigs and the antislavery Conscience Whigs. These divisions undermined the party, which ceased to function as a national party by 1856. Meanwhile, in 1854, the modern Republican Party was born. This party was composed of many different factions—former members of the Free Soil Party, Conscience Whigs, abolitionists, and former Democrats, to name a few. Although the party was critical of slavery, it did not advocate abolition. Rather, it adopted the position that slavery should not be allowed to spread to the new territories. As the Republican Party rapidly gained strength in the North, the Democratic Party became more proslavery, with its base of support in the South. The sectional and political tensions over the slavery issue intensified and degenerated into civil war by 1861.

WRONG CHOICES EXPLAINED:

(2) The developments described in the question did not show that Americans were united in their political views. The Whig Party collapsed because of divisions over the question of slavery. The formation of the Free Soil Party and the Republican Party, both antislavery parties, also reflected division among Americans.

(3) The developments described in the question did not show that major political parties received most of their support in the South. The Republican Party received most of its support in the North. Its candidate, Abraham Lincoln, won the presidency in 1860.

(4) The developments described in the question did not show that Americans were divided over the issue of unlimited coinage of silver. The issue that divided the political parties in the 1850s was slavery. Later, in the 1890s, the issue of unlimited coinage of silver divided the major political parties. Many farmers

wanted the United States to get off the gold standard and to issue money backed by silver as well. This would increase the amount of money in circulation and would lead to inflation. Farmers supported inflationary policies so that the prices they received for their produce would increase. The issue divided the Democratic and Republican presidential candidates in the 1896 election. The Democratic candidate, William Jennings Bryan, took up the call for the unlimited coinage of silver.

14. **2** Throughout the Civil War, an important advantage the North had over the South was that the North had greater manufacturing capabilities. The Civil War spurred rapid industrialization of the North. During the war, the Union government required an enormous amount of war materials, from guns and bullets to boots and uniforms. Manufacturers rose to the occasion by rapidly modernizing production. These changes in production sped up the process of industrialization that was in its beginning stages before the war. The manufacturing capabilities of the North were only one advantage the North had over the South during the Civil War. The North also had considerably more miles of railroad tracks. Of the 30,000 miles of railroad tracks in the United States in 1861, only 9,000 were in the states that formed the Confederacy. This gave the Union the ability to resupply its troops rapidly. In addition, the North had a far greater population than that of the rebellious southern states (22 million versus six million, excluding slaves), allowing the North to recruit reinforcements for fallen soldiers. All of these advantages became significant as the war dragged on.

WRONG CHOICES EXPLAINED:

(1) The South, not the North, tended to have superior military leaders. The South had a rich military tradition. The Confederacy, therefore, had able generals and a cohort of military men to draw from.

(3) The North did not receive support from Great Britain and France. President Abraham Lincoln feared that Great Britain would form an alliance with the Confederacy in order to guarantee a steady flow of raw cotton from the plantations of the South to the textile mills of England. Lincoln's issuing of the Emancipation Proclamation (1862) was partly motivated by the desire to keep Great Britain at bay during the war. The British might decide to aid the Confederacy for economic reasons, but the British population would not condone joining the South to perpetuate slavery.

(4) The South, not the North, used a strategy for fighting a defensive war. The Confederacy did not have to invade and conquer the North in order to declare victory. The Union, on the other hand, had to fight an offensive war in southern territory in order to win.

15. **2** The Compromise of 1877 brought an end to Radical Reconstruction by providing for the removal of federal troops from southern states. The period of Reconstruction, when the United States attempted to extend democratic rights to African Americans in the South, ended after only a dozen years. However, the end did not occur all at once. Throughout the 1870s, southern conservative Democrats, who called themselves "redeemers," aggressively sought to regain power state by state. The redeemers were aided by networks of white terrorist organizations that used violence to silence African Americans and to intimidate them from participating in public life. Also, northern whites simply lost their zeal for reforming the South. However, the formal end of Reconstruction followed the disputed election of 1876. The Democratic candidate, Samuel J. Tilden, won the majority of the popular vote. However, neither he nor his Republican opponent, Rutherford B. Hayes, were able to claim enough electoral votes to be declared the winner. In three states—South Carolina, Louisiana, and Florida—the Democrats and the Republicans both claimed victory. A special electoral commission, with a Republican majority, declared Hayes the winner in the three contested states. Democrats protested, with some threatening to block Hayes's inauguration. Party leaders on both sides reached an informal agreement, known as the Compromise of 1877, which allowed Hayes to win the presidency. In return, the Republicans agreed to remove the last federal troops from the South and end Reconstruction, paving the way for rule by the Democratic Party in the South.

WRONG CHOICES EXPLAINED:
(1) The Compromise of 1877 did not provide for the resignation of President Rutherford B. Hayes. The compromise settled the disputed election of 1877. It resulted in Hayes assuming the presidency and the Republicans agreeing to end Reconstruction by pulling out the last federal troops from the South.

(3) The Compromise of 1877 did not provide for the establishment of sharecropping. The system of sharecropping developed on its own during the Reconstruction period. After the Civil War, African Americans wanted to acquire land but did not have the financial resources to do so. In this context, the sharecropping system developed. In this system, African Americans (and poor whites) would farm a few acres of a large estate and give a share, often half, of the crops to the owner as rent. In this way, African Americans were not under the direct supervision of whites. However, the system created a cycle of debt, which prevented African Americans from acquiring money and owning land.

(4) The Compromise of 1877 did not provide for the strict enforcement of the 14th Amendment. It did the opposite. The compromise ended the government's Reconstruction efforts in the South, thus effectively ending enforcement

of the 14th Amendment. In the post-Reconstruction period, the southern states developed methods of working around the equal protection guarantees of the 14th Amendment, initiating a system of Jim Crow segregation laws.

16. **4** The information in the charts supports the conclusion that southern and eastern Europeans made up the majority of immigrants from 1900 to 1920. The graph on the right indicates that between 1900 and 1920, eastern and southern Europeans made up 62 percent of immigrants coming into the United States. Eastern Europeans include people from Russia and the Baltic states as well as people from within the Austro-Hungarian empire; southern Europeans include people from Italy. The wave of immigrants from eastern and southern Europe was labeled "new immigrants." The term "new" was used by some nativists of the late 1800s and early 1900s to draw a distinction between the old immigrants and the new immigrants. These nativists came to believe that the new immigrants were somehow incapable of being assimilated into the culture of the United States. The negative feelings toward the new immigrants contributed to the passage of the quota acts of the 1920s, limiting the number of immigrants allowed into the United States.

WRONG CHOICES EXPLAINED:
(1) The information in the charts does not support the conclusion that immigration from the Western Hemisphere declined after 1900. The second chart indicates that 6 percent of immigrants into the United States were from Canada. Most of these were French Canadians who immigrated from Quebec into the states of New England. Also, immigrants from several Latin American countries made their way into the United States during the periods shown in the two charts.
(2) The information in the charts does not support the conclusion that the percentage of German immigrants increased between 1860 and 1920. The percentage of German immigrants was actually higher in the period from 1860 to 1900 (28 percent) than in the period from 1900 to 1920 (4 percent).
(3) The information in the charts does not support the conclusion that northern European immigrants were prohibited from entering the United States from 1860 to 1920. The charts do not contain information about immigration laws. There were no such laws that prohibited northern European immigrants from entering the United States.

17. **1** The changes in immigration patterns shown on the charts resulted in the passage of restrictive immigration laws. The large number of "new immigrants" into the United States—from eastern and southern Europe—led to the growth of a strong nativist (anti-immigrant) movement. Some nativists focused

on the fact that most of the new immigrants were not Protestant. Poles and Italians tended to be Catholic; Russians and Greeks tended to be Eastern Orthodox; and Jewish immigrants came from several countries in eastern Europe. Some nativists objected to the cacophony of languages heard on the streets of New York or Chicago and to the variety of food smells that filled immigrant neighborhoods. Also, some nativists argued that the new immigrants, many of whom had darker features than their English and Germanic predecessors, were a different race. Nativism rose steeply in the years after World War I, leading to the passage of the Emergency Quota Act of 1921 and the Immigration Act of 1924. These acts greatly reduced the number of immigrants allowed into the United States by establishing quotas for different nations based on the numbers of each national group present in the United States decades earlier. The first act set the quota for each nationality at 3 percent of the total number of that nationality that was present in the United States in 1910. The second act reduced the percentage to 2 percent and moved the year back to 1890.

WRONG CHOICES EXPLAINED:
  (2) The changes in immigration patterns shown in the charts did not result in the business community increasing its demand for workers. The immigrant patterns shown in the charts led to large numbers of potential laborers entering the United States.
  (3) The changes in immigration patterns shown in the charts did not result in the decline of urban populations. The large numbers of immigrants who entered the United States in the late 1800s and early 1900s tended to settle in cities, thus increasing the population of urban areas.
  (4) The changes in immigration patterns shown in the charts did not result in an easing in requirements for citizenship. The Naturalization Act of 1906 standardized procedures for becoming citizens, requiring applicants for citizenship to demonstrate competence in the English language.

  18. **3** During the late 1800s, political machines controlled the governments of many cities by using corrupt practices and patronage. Corrupt and inefficient political operations—labeled political machines—became more common in this era. Political parties on the local level created organizations whose purpose was to achieve and maintain political power. Political ideology was barely a concern in these bare-knuckled electoral contests. New York City was dominated by the Democratic Party machine, headquartered at Tammany Hall. The most famous Tammany chief was William Marcy Tweed. "Boss" Tweed and other political leaders earned a reputation for corruption. Tweed's complicated schemes included the building of a courthouse that involved millions of dollars in

kickbacks to Tammany Hall. Patronage refers to the handing out of government jobs to the friends and relatives of political leaders, regardless of their level of competency. The muckraker journalist Lincoln Steffens exposed urban corruption in *The Shame of the Cities* (1902).

WRONG CHOICES EXPLAINED:

(1) During the late 1800s, political machines did not attempt to deny voting rights to immigrants. Political machines tended to be popular with immigrant groups, particularly German and Irish immigrants.

(2) During the late 1800s, political machines did not attempt to attract voters who were dissatisfied with the two-party system. The political machines of the late 1800s were the local operations of one of the two major political parties. In most cities, the dominant political machine was associated with the Democratic Party.

(4) During the late 1800s, political machines did not favor civil service reform. Many reformers in the late 1800s and early 1900s attempted to end the corruption and patronage associated with the political machines. The political machines, therefore, were the target of these reform efforts, not the initiators of them.

19. **2** The federal government follows the economic principle of laissez-faire when it takes no action on corporate mergers. The French phrase *laissez-faire* means "to let alone." It describes a hands-off approach in regard to the relationship between the government and the economy. During the Gilded Age of the late 1800s, mergers and trusts allowed corporations to gain monopoly control over entire industries. The men who controlled the major corporations in the United States came to be known as "robber barons," a scornful title meant to call attention to their cutthroat business practices. Corporate leaders and their allies in government argued that any attempt at government intervention into the economic and social worlds would hinder economic progress and growth. Many of these corporate leaders subscribed to the ideas of Social Darwinism—the attempt to apply Charles Darwin's ideas about the natural world to social relations. Social Darwinism was popularized in the United States by William Graham Sumner, who was attracted to Darwin's ideas about competition and survival of the fittest. Social Darwinism appealed to owners of large corporations because it justified their great wealth and power and also warned against any type of regulation or reform. Critics of corporate power pushed the government to take steps to rein in these massive corporations. The government passed the Sherman Antitrust Act (1890), for instance, but that had limited success.

WRONG CHOICES EXPLAINED:

(1), (3), and (4) These choices do not describe examples of the government following the economic principle of laissez-faire. The French phrase *laissez-faire* means "to let alone." It describes a government policy that takes a hands-off approach in regard to economic activities. These choices—placing restrictions on land usage (choice 1), controlling methods of production (choice 3), and determining the price of goods (choice 4)—all involve a high degree of government intervention in economic activities.

20. **2** The focus of the speakers' debate is the controversy over the policy of imperialism. *Speakers A* and *C* support the policy of imperialism. The United States began to play a more active role in the world, especially in the Western Hemisphere, after the Spanish-American War (1898). *Speaker A* is arguing that attaining colonies is an important step for the United States to take as it expands its power in the world. The passage reflects the thinking of historian Alfred Thayer Mahan, a retired admiral, who stressed the importance of naval power in achieving and maintaining influence on the world stage. In an 1890 book, he pushed for the United States to develop a strong navy, maintain military bases and coaling stations throughout the world, and administer an overseas empire. *Speaker C* is citing the economic aspects of imperialism. He notes that new colonies could provide the United States with additional markets for its products. New markets and new sources for raw materials became increasingly important as the United States expanded its industrial sector in the late 1800s and early 1900s. *Speakers B* and *D* are opposed to the United States pursuing a policy of imperialism. *Speaker B* is arguing that United States policy should focus on helping people in the United States rather than looking abroad. *Speaker B* is responding to pro-imperialists who believe it is the burden of the "civilized" nations to "uplift" the peoples of Asia, Africa, and Latin America. *Speaker D* is noting the economic costs to the United States of maintaining an overseas empire. The most prominent anti-imperialist was the author Mark Twain, who chaired the American Anti-Imperialist League.

WRONG CHOICES EXPLAINED:

(1) The focus of the speakers' debate is not the purchase of Alaska. The United States purchased Alaska from Russia in 1867. Many Americans thought that the purchase of Alaska was a waste of money. They labeled the purchase as Seward's Folly, named for Secretary of State William H. Seward, who negotiated the deal with Russia.

(3) The focus of the speakers' debate is not the size of the United States military. Debates around the size of the American military have existed throughout American history. The debate is often presented as guns versus butter, with

policy makers weighing the merits of increasing military spending versus spending more money on civilian needs.

(4) The focus of the speakers' debate is not the closing of the frontier. In the 19th century, the frontier was the unofficial boundary line between settled and sparsely settled or unsettled lands. The frontier line shifted farther and farther west as more of the United States became settled. The 19th-century historian Frederick Jackson Turner argued, in 1893, that the existence of this frontier had been a positive factor in the development of the American character. Some public thinkers saw the closing of the frontier as a call for the United States to look for new lands and new opportunities abroad.

21. **3** The headlines reflect the actions of Andrew Carnegie and John D. Rockefeller as philanthropists. The first headline refers to Carnegie's support for libraries. Carnegie gained his wealth in the steel industry. The second headline refers to Rockefeller's support for medical research. Rockefeller gained his wealth in the oil industry. Several wealthy businessmen partook in philanthropy. Carnegie asserted in an essay entitled "Wealth" (1899) that the wealthy have a duty to live responsible, modest lives and to give back to society. This "gospel of wealth" asserted that wealthy entrepreneurs should distribute their wealth so that it could be put to good use rather than be frivolously wasted. Carnegie ended up donating the majority of his fortune to charity and public-oriented projects. Carnegie believed in a laissez-faire approach to social problems. He did not want the government interfering in the social and economic spheres. That is, in part, why Carnegie urged his fellow millionaires to take action on behalf of the community. In this way, the government would not have to.

WRONG CHOICES EXPLAINED:

(1) The headlines do not reflect the actions of muckrakers. The term *muckraker* was applied to journalists who wrote magazine articles and books that exposed wrongdoing by government officials, showed the negative side of industrialization, and let the world see a variety of social ills. Important muckrakers include Upton Sinclair, who exposed the dangerous and unhygienic conditions of the meat-packing industry in his novel *The Jungle* (1906); Ida Tarbell, who wrote a scathing history of the Standard Oil Trust in 1904; and Lincoln Steffens, whose book *The Shame of Our Cities* (1902) showed the corruption of urban political machines.

(2) The headlines do not reflect the actions of socialists. Both Carnegie and Rockefeller were capitalists, not socialists. The term *socialism* refers to a range of economic and social systems as well as political ideologies, theories, movements, and parties that seek to establish such systems. Socialist systems are characterized by some form of social ownership of the means of production— either by the government or by the workers themselves—through collective or

cooperative ownership. Socialists generally believe in some form of democratic control of the economic sphere. Eugene V. Debs, who was a leader in the labor movement, was one of the founders of the Socialist Party of America in 1901.

(4) The headlines do not reflect the actions of conservationists. Conservationists were concerned about the rapid disappearance of natural areas in the United States. Logging and mining operations were taking a toll on forested areas starting in the late 1800s. President Theodore Roosevelt (1901–1909) embraced the cause of conservationism.

22. **1** The Progressive Era presidents were considered trustbusters because they used government to promote business competition. During the late 1800s, many of the leading figures in the business community—such as John D. Rockefeller, Andrew Carnegie, and J. P. Morgan—shared the view that economic competition was inefficient and wasteful. Business leaders often created trusts (combinations of companies) in order to eliminate competition and control a particular industry. Rockefeller established the first large trust in the oil-processing industry. He often drove competitors in an area out of business by drastically reducing his prices so that smaller companies could not compete. Eventually, Rockefeller would either buy out the competition or simply drive them out of business. Once the competition was eliminated, he would raise his prices. Progressive critics and reformers, who believed that competition was important for consumers, saw the concentration of economic power in a few hands as potentially dangerous to the economy as a whole. Though the Sherman Antitrust Act (1890) was passed to limit monopolistic practices, the act was not enforced with a great deal of enthusiasm. In the Progressive Era of the early 1900s, political leaders moved more aggressively against trusts. President Theodore Roosevelt (1901–1909) made a point of using the act to pursue "bad trusts." He defined these bad trusts as ones that interfered with commerce, but they were not necessarily the biggest trusts. One of Roosevelt's first targets was the Northern Securities Company, a railroad holding company. His efforts were challenged in court. In *Northern Securities Co. v. United States* (1904), the Supreme Court upheld the power of the government to break up Northern Securities under the Sherman Antitrust Act. The case was a victory for Roosevelt. President William Howard Taft (1909–1913) expanded Roosevelt's trust-busting efforts, initiating 70 antitrust suits in his four years as president. Under Taft, the government was successful in breaking up Rockefeller's Standard Oil Trust in 1911. Later, President Woodrow Wilson strengthened the antitrust powers of the federal government with the Clayton Antitrust Act (1914).

WRONG CHOICES EXPLAINED:

(2) Trust-busting did not involve support for the elimination of trade barriers. The most common barrier to international trade is higher tariff rates. The rate of tariffs on goods coming into the United States has generated a great deal of debate in United States history. Some have argued that higher tariff rates would protect American manufacturing, while others have argued that higher tariff rates would push up retail prices for consumer goods. Progressives generally supported lower tariff rates. President Woodrow Wilson pushed for the Underwood Tariff Act, which lowered tariff rates from an average of 40 percent to 25 percent.

(3) Trust-busting did not involve encouraging more voter participation in government. Many Progressive Era reformers did encourage greater voter participation. Reformers pushed for the recall, which would allow the populace to remove elected officials before their term ended; the referendum, which would allow people to vote directly on proposed legislation; and the initiative, which would enable citizens to introduce a bill to the local or state legislature by petition.

(4) Trust-busting did not involve canceling treaties with other nations. At times, the Senate has refused to approve a treaty that the president negotiated. This occurred in 1919 when supporters of the Treaty of Versailles failed to garner two-thirds of senators to approve the treaty. Wilson pushed for approval so that the United States would be a participant in the newly formed League of Nations. However, some senators wanted to isolate the United States from world affairs and opposed membership in the League.

23. **3** The primary objective of the women's movement during the first two decades of the 20th century was to secure full suffrage rights. The right to vote was central to the women's rights movement for nearly a century before the ratification of the 19th Amendment in 1920, which prohibited states from denying citizens the right to vote based on sex. In 1848, a group of women and their male allies held a convention in Seneca Falls, New York, to publicize their cause and to organize their movement. The main product of the convention was the issuing of the Seneca Falls *Declaration of Sentiments*, modeled after the Declaration of Independence. By the end of the 19th century, suffragists won voting rights for women in several of the states. However, women were still prohibited from participating in national elections. In 1913, women held an important suffrage parade in Washington, D.C., to publicize their cause. However, it was not until the World War I period that the movement fully got the ear of President Woodrow Wilson. The suffrage movement was successful in achieving its goal with the ratification of the 19th Amendment to the Constitution in 1920.

WRONG CHOICES EXPLAINED:

(1) The agenda of the women's rights movement included extending property rights to women, but that was not the central demand of the movement in the first two decades of the 20th century. During the colonial period and during the first decades of United States history, the legal doctrine of *femme covert* applied to women. The doctrine held that wives had no independent legal or political standing. Therefore, any property or belongings that a woman might have brought into the marriage became her husband's. In the 1830s and 1840s, many states passed Married Women's Property Acts, which allowed married women to own property independent of their husbands.

(2) The agenda of the women's rights movement included promoting higher education for women, but that was not the central demand of the movement in the first two decades of the 20th century. Women's rights advocates in the 19th century pushed for expanded higher-education opportunities for women. Several teaching seminaries for women opened in the 1700s and 1800s. Oberlin College was the first coeducational college in the United States. It began accepting women in 1837.

(4) The agenda of the women's rights movement included winning equal pay for equal work, but that was not the central demand of the movement in the first two decades of the 20th century. In the 1960s, this became an important goal of the women's rights movement. The Equal Pay Act of 1963 and the Civil Rights Act of 1964 include provisions that are intended to guarantee equal pay for equal work. However, these acts have had mixed results. Women were earning approximately 60 percent of men's salaries for comparable work in the 1970s. That figure has grown to approximately 78 percent today.

24. **4** The situation in the cartoon was mainly caused by disagreements over United States participation in the League of Nations. In the cartoon, President Woodrow Wilson is depicted as protecting a tree labeled League Covenants from the Senate's ax. The cartoon was published as the Senate debated approval of the Treaty of Versailles in 1919. By approving the Treaty of Versailles, the Senate would have also made the United States a member of the League of Nations. Earlier, in his Fourteen Points document, President Wilson championed the idea of an organization composed of the world's nations. The victorious powers in Europe after World War I largely ignored Wilson's idealistic vision for a postwar world, but they agreed to create the League of Nations. Wilson pushed for Senate approval of the Treaty of Versailles so that the United States would be a participant in this new organization. However, some senators wanted to isolate the United States from world affairs and opposed membership in the League. These isolationists announced that they would vote to reject the treaty. Another group of senators, alluded to in the cartoon, took a middle position.

They would agree to vote to approve the treaty if the Senate put certain conditions on U.S. participation in the League of Nations. Wilson refused to compromise with these senators and urged his Senate allies to reject any conditions for U.S. membership in the League. Without the support of these senators in the middle, the Treaty of Versailles was rejected by the Senate. As a result, the United States did not join the League of Nations.

WRONG CHOICES EXPLAINED:
    (1) The situation in the cartoon was not caused by the cost of paying reparations after World War I. After World War I, the Treaty of Versailles (1919) demanded that Germany pay reparations for war-related damages. However, the debate in the United States over ratification of the treaty centered around participation in the League of Nations, not reparations.
    (2) The situation in the cartoon was not caused by the failure of President Woodrow Wilson to promote the Treaty of Versailles. The opposite was true. Wilson was a staunch supporter of the League. Instead, isolationist Senators opposed United States membership in the League and voted against ratification of the Treaty of Versailles.
    (3) The situation in the cartoon was not caused by the overwhelming public rejection of the peace terms in the Treaty of Versailles. It is extremely difficult to gauge public opinion accurately in the era before professional polling. Evidence points to a mixed reaction to the treaty, with a large degree of opposition. German Americans and Irish Americans were especially critical of the terms of the treaty. However, the showdown depicted in the cartoon is between the executive branch and the legislative branch, not between the government and the American people.

    25. **2** The cartoon depicts the constitutional principle of checks and balances. The cartoon shows a conflict between two branches of the federal government—the executive branch that was represented by President Woodrow Wilson protecting the tree labeled League Covenants and the legislative branch that was threatening to chop down that tree with its ax. The Constitution gives the president the power to negotiate treaties with foreign nations. However, such treaties are approved only with the "advice and consent" of two-thirds of the Senate. This ability of the legislative branch to block an initiative of the executive branch is one of several checks built into the system of governance established by the Constitution. The framers of the Constitution were very conscious of the problems of a government with limitless powers. After living under the British monarchy, they came to believe that a powerful government without checks was dangerous to liberty. Therefore, they created a governmental system with three branches, each with the ability to check the powers of the other two.

The goal was to keep the three branches in balance. Other examples of this concept include the president's ability to veto bills and the Supreme Court's ability to use the power of judicial review to strike down laws it deems unconstitutional.

WRONG CHOICES EXPLAINED:

(1) The situation depicted in the cartoon does not illustrate the constitutional principle of due process. The term *due process* refers to the formal legal proceedings that are carried out, in conformity with established rules and principles, before an individual is punished by the state. Due process rules are contained in both the Fifth Amendment and the 14th Amendment to the Constitution. The cartoon does not allude to such procedures.

(3) The situation depicted in the cartoon does not illustrate the constitutional principle of popular sovereignty. The term *popular sovereignty* literally means the power of the people to decide something. In American history, the term was used in relation to the question of whether or not slavery would exist in new states. The people of a territory would vote on the issue before the territory applied for statehood. The Kansas-Nebraska Act allowed for the possibility of slavery, under the principle of popular sovereignty, in the territories of Kansas and Nebraska—areas that had been closed to slavery by the Missouri Compromise (1820).

(4) The situation depicted in the cartoon does not illustrate the constitutional principle of judicial review. The term *judicial review* refers to the power of the Supreme Court to determine whether laws are consistent with the Constitution. If the Court determines that a particular law is unconstitutional, that law is immediately voided. This power was established in the Supreme Court's decision in the *Marbury* v. *Madison* case (1803). The cartoon does not allude to this power.

26. **3** The 1920s are often called the Roaring Twenties because the decade was noted for social and cultural changes. The decade was characterized by changing ideas concerning gender. The "new woman" of the 1920s was more engaged in public issues than in previous decades. She might have participated in the political struggles of the progressive movement and gained a new sense of confidence in public issues, especially after women achieved the right to vote in 1920. The changing image of women during the 1920s was symbolized by the popularity of the flappers and their style of dress. Flappers were independent-minded young women of the 1920s who openly defied Victorian moral codes about "proper" ladylike behavior. The decade also witnessed the development of mass culture. Radio grew from being virtually nonexistent at the beginning of the decade to becoming an extremely popular medium by the end of it. By 1923, there were almost 600 licensed radio stations. Movie attendance achieved staggering levels in the 1920s. By the end of the decade, three-fourths

of the American people (roughly 90 million) were going to the movies every week. The first talkie, *The Jazz Singer*, came out in 1927. An important cultural development was the Harlem Renaissance, which was a literary, artistic, and intellectual movement centered in the African-American neighborhood of Harlem, in New York City. A key goal of the movement was to increase pride in African-American culture by celebrating African-American life and forging a new cultural identity among African-American people. Contributions included the poetry of Langston Hughes, Claude McKay, and Countee Cullen and the jazz music of Louis Armstrong, Duke Ellington, and Bessie Smith.

WRONG CHOICES EXPLAINED:

(1) The label "Roaring Twenties" did not refer to political reform in the 1920s. In fact, the decade is not noted for political reform. The Progressive Era of the 1900s and 1910s is noted for political reform. The Progressive reform movement was a response to the economic instability, social inequality, and political corruption that began during the Gilded Age and continued into the 20th century. Progressive reformers called for greater government intervention in the economy as well as increased democratization of the political process, social justice, and conservation of natural resources.

(2) The label "Roaring Twenties" did not refer to economic depression in the 1920s. In fact, the economy was healthy for most of the 1920s. The following decade, the 1930s, experienced the Great Depression. Not everyone shared equally in the economic growth of the 1920s. The gap between the wealthy and poor increased, and farmers struggled to get by. The Great Depression began with the stock market crash of October 1929.

(4) The label "Roaring Twenties" did not refer to ending Prohibition in the 1920s. Prohibition was in effect throughout the decade; it did not end until 1933. Prohibition went into effect with the ratification of the 18th Amendment, which banned the production, transport, and sale of alcohol as of January 1, 1920. Although per capita consumption of alcohol dropped dramatically in the early 1920s, it increased as the decade progressed, possibly approaching pre-Prohibition levels by 1925. Further, the amount of lawlessness in America went up as bootleggers, speakeasies, and organized crime filled the gap left by the death of the legitimate alcoholic beverage industry.

27. **4** The Great Migration that took place between 1915 and 1930 refers to African Americans who left the rural south for northern cities. There were several important reasons for the Great Migration. One factor was the mistreatment that African Americans received in the South. Jim Crow laws, which segregated public facilities, made African Americans second-class citizens. In addition, African Americans were excluded from the political system in the

South. A series of obstacles, such as literacy tests and poll taxes, limited their ability to vote. However, the main factor that drew African Americans north was jobs. By the turn of the 20th century, the industrial revolution was in full swing in northern cities such as New York and Chicago. Factories using new mass production techniques were able, at first, to fill the jobs with local people and European immigrants. However, World War I created a labor crisis for these factories. Factories were producing goods around the clock. Even before the United States entered the war in 1917, U.S. factories were producing war goods for Great Britain. After entering the war, demand for these goods increased. In addition, European immigration to the United States dropped significantly due to the war. Finally, millions of potential factory workers were pressed into the U.S. military. Factory agents from the North frequently made recruiting trips to the South, offering immediate employment and free passage to the North.

WRONG CHOICES EXPLAINED:

(1) The Great Migration that took place between 1915 and 1930 does not refer to workers who left the Northeast for the South. Later, in the post–World War II period, many Americans abandoned the states of the Northeast and the upper Midwest and moved to the Sun Belt states of the South and the West. This migration was caused, in part, by the decline of the industrial base of the Northeast and the upper Midwest. The states of the upper Midwest, from Ohio to Wisconsin, became known as the Rust Belt as factories closed in this region.

(2) The Great Migration that took place between 1915 and 1930 does not refer to Native American Indians who left their reservations. Native-American Indian reservations are parcels of land that are managed by Native-American Indian tribes under the auspices of the federal government's Bureau of Indian Affairs. Over time, many Native Americans have left reservations to seek opportunities elsewhere. Of the 2.5 million Native American Indians in the United States, approximately one million live on reservations.

(3) The Great Migration that took place between 1915 and 1930 does not refer to middle-class whites who left cities to settle in suburbs. In the post–World War II period, many middle-class whites did make the move from city to suburb. A key motive for the move was simply a housing shortage in urban centers. Not much new housing was built during the Great Depression or during World War II. The sudden return of millions of G.I.s after World War II created a crisis. In addition, some white veterans were not pleased to return from the war to find that their neighborhoods had changed as African Americans had moved in during the war. Whether motivated by racism or concern for property values, a "white flight" out of New York, Detroit, Philadelphia, Chicago, and other major cities occurred from the late 1940s to the 1970s.

28. **4** Breadlines, Hoovervilles, and the Bonus Army were all direct results of unemployment caused by the Great Depression. The Great Depression (1929–1939) was devastating for American workers. Between 1929 and 1933, wages fell by 60 percent and unemployment tripled to over 12 million people. Breadlines formed in many cities as many unemployed people sought basic foodstuffs from charitable organizations. Hoovervilles were shantytowns occupied by homeless people. There were hundreds of Hoovervilles across the United States, occupied by hundreds of thousands of homeless people. The name "Hoovervilles" was meant to mock President Herbert Hoover. Critics held that Hoover did not take sufficient action on behalf of the nation's neediest people. Hoover was a believer in supply-side economics. This approach to the economy stressed stimulating the supply side of the economy—manufacturers, banks, and insurance corporations. The theory is that if there is growth in the supply side, there will be a general economic revival. As a result, the theory continues, the benefits of a robust economy will trickle down to everyone. The Bonus Army was a protest movement of unemployed veterans of World War I. Its main goal was to pressure the Hoover administration to support the early payment of money promised to veterans (veterans were scheduled to receive bonuses in 1945). In June 1932, a group of World War I veterans who called themselves the Bonus Expeditionary Force, or Bonus Army, marched into Washington, D.C., to demand their bonuses immediately. About 15,000 men, mostly unemployed and poor, set up an encampment in the nation's capital to demand their money.

WRONG CHOICES EXPLAINED:
   (1) Breadlines, Hoovervilles, and the Bonus Army were not the result of housing shortages in the 1920s. Significant housing shortages did not exist in the 1920s. Housing shortages in the United States occurred later, in the 1940s after World War II. Relatively few units were added to the existing housing stock during the years of the Great Depression and World War II. When hundreds of thousands of G.I.s returned from the war in 1945 and 1946, many were eager to start families in new homes, but few units were available. Eventually, the shortage was alleviated, most notably through the building of suburban developments.
   (2) Breadlines, Hoovervilles, and the Bonus Army were not the result of relief efforts of the New Deal. In many ways, the New Deal was a response to the breadlines and Hoovervilles that appeared in many cities as the devastation of the Great Depression was felt by more people. The handling of the Bonus Army protest in Washington, D.C. (1932) damaged the reputation of President Herbert Hoover and helped pave the way for the election of Franklin D. Roosevelt. Roosevelt initiated a breathtaking number of relief programs upon taking office in 1933. His New Deal efforts did not end the Great Depression, but they did alleviate the suffering of millions of individuals.

(3) Breadlines, Hoovervilles, and the Bonus Army were not the result of mechanization of agriculture. The mechanization of agriculture did frequently have negative repercussions on farmers. While mechanization reduced the hours needed for agricultural tasks, it also undermined small-scale family farms. First, mechanization increased overall production. This lowered the prices that farmers received per bushel of corn or wheat. Second, many farmers could not afford the new equipment or went into debt purchasing new equipment. However, the negative impact of mechanization was more of a rural phenomenon. The developments in the question were more urban phenomena.

29. **3** The Fair Labor Standards Act (1938) helped American workers by establishing a minimum wage in many industries. President Franklin D. Roosevelt pushed a number of New Deal programs that benefited industrial workers in a variety of ways. An important aspect of his New Deal was increasing workers' wages and therefore their purchasing power. He saw that one of the causes of the Great Depression was that workers in the 1920s were not able to purchase enough consumer goods to keep the economy growing. The act established a minimum wage that employers would be required to pay workers. Certain classes of workers were exempted from the minimum wage requirements. Workers receiving tips are generally not subject to the minimum wage unless the amount of tips received does not bring the worker's earnings up to minimum wage requirements. Also, independent contractors are not subject to minimum wage requirements. The Department of Labor has taken action against employers who have illegally classified workers as independent contractors in order to evade minimum wage requirements. Finally, certain white collar employees—professional, administrative, and executive—are exempt from the act. The Fair Labor Standards Act also established the maximum number of hours a worker may be expected to work, establishing the 40-hour week as the standard for many industries. Roosevelt said that other than the Social Security Act, the Fair Labor Standards Act was "the most far-sighted program for the benefit of workers ever adopted here or in any other country."

WRONG CHOICES EXPLAINED:
(1) The Fair Labor Standards Act did not establish health plans for workers. Employment-based health plans, offered to employees and their families, cover approximately 150 million people in the United States. Unions have frequently negotiated such health plans as one of the benefits of employment. The Affordable Care Act (2010) includes provisions to extend several protections to the health plans of employees of large businesses.
(2) The Fair Labor Standards Act did legalize strikes and boycotts. An earlier New Deal act called the Wagner Act, or National Labor Relations Act (1935),

affected workers by protecting their rights to form unions and bargain collectively. The act strengthened unions by mandating that employers bargain with unions. It also established the National Labor Relations Board to conduct elections among workers to see if they wanted to be represented by a union. The act also banned certain unfair labor practices.

(4) The Fair Labor Standards Act did not make labor unions accept women and African Americans as members. Unions have been on both sides of the question of racial justice. In the 1800s, the Knights of Labor accepted African-American members. However, the American Federation of Labor maintained racist practices well into the 20th century, keeping African-American membership to a minimum. The Congress of Industrial Organizations, organized during the Great Depression, actively courted African-American workers. After World War II, most unions removed barriers to African-American membership, making the labor movement more integrated than American society as a whole. Women were part of the labor movement from its inception in the 1830s. Many of the first industrial workers in the United States, the women of the Lowell, Massachusetts, textile mills, went out on strike in 1834 and again in 1836. Women have continued to play a central role in the labor movement in the 20th century.

30. **1** Adoption of the "cash and carry" policy in 1939 and passage of the Lend-Lease Act in 1941 showed the growing commitment of the United States to provide aid to the Allied nations. The two actions took place in the context of World War II. The war started in 1938, when Nazi Germany attacked Poland and then Great Britain and France declared war on Germany. From the onset, the United States was officially neutral in regard to World War II. However, President Franklin D. Roosevelt's sympathies were with the countries fighting against fascism. Soon after the beginning of the war, Roosevelt pushed for legislation allowing the United States to send armaments to Britain with the condition that Britain pay for the weapons first and transport them in their own ships. This cash and carry policy allowed the United States to support Britain without the risk of U.S. ships being destroyed. By mid-1940, the American public began to shift toward a more interventionist stance. The situation in Europe grew dire. Americans were shaken by the defeat of France at the hands of the Nazis in 1940. Americans saw how one of the great democratic powers was easily defeated by the Nazi war machine. With this shift in public opinion and with his victory in the presidential election of 1940, Roosevelt was ready to take more direct action. In March 1941, Congress approved his Lend-Lease Act, which allowed the United States to send armaments to Britain in American ships. The Lend-Lease Act was extended to the Soviet Union after Hitler launched an invasion of the Soviet Union in June 1941. The United States entered the war in late

1941 after Japan attacked the American naval base at Pearl Harbor, Hawaii Territory.

WRONG CHOICES EXPLAINED:

(2) Adoption of the "cash and carry" policy in 1939 and passage of the Lend-Lease Act in 1941 were not intended to force the Japanese out of Korea. In 1945, Japanese forces in Korea surrendered to American and Soviet forces. Subsequently, Korea was divided at the 38th parallel.

(3) Adoption of the "cash and carry" policy in 1939 and passage of the Lend-Lease Act in 1941 were not intended to increase trade with Italy. The United States and Italy were on opposing sides in World War II. Trade did not occur between the countries during the war.

(4) Adoption of the "cash and carry" policy in 1939 and passage of the Lend-Lease Act in 1941 were not intended to end German violations of American territory. German forces did not land on American territory during World War II.

31. **2** A direct result of United States involvement in World War II was the entry of more women and minorities into the workplace. Women and minorities were needed because factories were working around the clock producing military goods and much of the male work force was in the military. The government produced many images, usually through the Office of War Information, that showed women in industrial settings. The fictional Rosie the Riveter was often featured in this public relations campaign. These female workers were presented in a positive light—helping the nation as well as the men in combat abroad. Such a campaign was needed because prewar societal mores discouraged women from doing industrial work. The campaign was successful. By 1945, one-third of the work force was female. In addition, African Americans joined millions of other Americans in moving toward industrial centers and finding work in war-related industries. Initially, many war industries were reluctant to hire African Americans. An important African-American labor leader, A. Phillip Randolph, the president of the Brotherhood of Sleeping Car Porters, planned a public demonstration in Washington, D.C., in 1941 to protest discrimination in war-related industries. When the Roosevelt administration heard of these plans, it worked out a bargain. Roosevelt issued Executive Order 8802, banning discrimination in war-related industries. Randolph called off the march.

WRONG CHOICES EXPLAINED:

(1) United States involvement in World War II did not result in an increase in the production of consumer goods. The opposite occurred. There was a shortage of consumer goods during the war as factories converted to war-related

production. For example, from early 1942 until the end of the war in 1945, American factories produced no new automobiles.

(3) United States involvement in World War II did not result in a decrease in industrial activity. The opposite is true. Factories were running around the clock to produce weaponry to aid the American military and its allies. The increase in industrial activity quickly brought the Great Depression of the 1930s to an end.

(4) United States involvement in World War II did not result in a decrease in federal control over the economy. The opposite is true. A variety of federal agencies regulated economic activity to ensure that the needs of the military were met. These agencies included the War Production Board, the National War Labor Board, and the Office of Economic Stabilization.

32. **3** The attack on the United States naval base at Pearl Harbor, Hawaii Territory, by Japanese forces caused the other three events in the question. In the days after the attack in December 1941, Congress declared war against Japan (mentioned in choice 1). In 1942, the federal government began the internment of Japanese Americans (mentioned in choice 2). The internment was initially authorized when President Franklin D. Roosevelt issued Executive Order 9066. The order allowed the government to remove 120,000 Japanese Americans, two-thirds of them citizens, from west coast states and relocate them to camps throughout the West. Most of their property was confiscated by the government. In the case of *Korematsu* v. *United States* (1944), the Supreme Court ruled that the relocation was acceptable on the grounds of national security. The *Korematsu* decision is one of several rulings by the Supreme Court that have curtailed civil liberties in times of war. In 1945, the United States dropped two atomic bombs on Japanese cities, one on Hiroshima and one on Nagasaki (mentioned in choice 4). Soon after, Japan surrendered, thus ending World War II. Earlier in 1945, the last two battles between the United States and Japan, at Iwo Jima and Okinawa, were extremely costly. After those battles, the United States was faced with the daunting task of forcing Japan to surrender. The American people and the American military were preparing for what seemed inevitable—a long and bloody attack on the Japanese home islands. In the meantime, scientists in the United States had recently completed and tested a devastating new weapon—the atomic bomb. It was in this context that President Truman decided to drop this powerful bomb. At the time, the decision to drop the atomic bomb did not generate much public debate. The atomic bombing swiftly ended a bloody conflict that consumed 50 million lives. However, in the decades since the war, some Americans have raised questions about Truman's decision. Critics argue that it was morally wrong for the United States to have targeted civilian populations and that the Japanese were ready to surrender anyway. Many stand by the decision to drop the bomb. It is not clear that the

Japanese were on the verge of surrendering. Some members of the Japanese military argued against surrendering even after the second bomb was dropped.

WRONG CHOICES EXPLAINED:

(1), (2), and (4) These choices were not the cause of the other developments mentioned in the question. All three of these choices describe developments that occurred after the United States was attacked at Pearl Harbor (mentioned in choice 3).

33. **4** McCarthyism of the early 1950s resulted in damage to the reputations of many innocent people. The anticommunist movement of the 1950s came to be known as McCarthyism. It was named for Senator Joseph McCarthy, who became the central figure in this movement. McCarthy gained prominence when he announced that he had a list of names of State Department employees who were members of the Communist Party (1950). This and similar claims, mostly baseless, created a name for McCarthy and set the stage for a host of measures to halt this perceived threat. An atmosphere reminiscent of the Salem witch trials of the 1690s pervaded America as wild accusations became more common. Fears of communist spying on the United States intensified when the Soviet Union first tested an atomic bomb (1949). The government accused two members of the Communist Party, Ethel and Julius Rosenberg, of passing secrets of the nuclear bomb to the Soviet Union. The Rosenbergs insisted on their innocence. However, they were found guilty and were sent to the electric chair (1953). Congress investigated suspected communist sympathizers in different sectors of society. Congress especially targeted the entertainment industry, fearing that communists would subtly get their message out through television and movies. The Hollywood 10 was a group of ten prominent figures who refused to cooperate with the House Un-American Activities Committee (1947); they were jailed for contempt and subsequently blacklisted. The most intense period of McCarthyism was over by 1954. By that time, the Korean War had ended and McCarthy himself was discredited for making baseless accusations against members of the military. The hearings on these accusations, known as the Army-McCarthy hearings, were widely seen on the new medium of television (1954), demonstrating to the American public the reckless nature of McCarthy's accusations.

WRONG CHOICES EXPLAINED:

(1) McCarthyism of the early 1950s did not result in the end of the arms race. The arms race intensified in the 1950s as both the United States and the Soviet Union developed and expanded nuclear arms programs. McCarthyism served to heighten Cold War fears in the United States and created a political climate that was more amenable to sharp increases in the military budget.

(2) McCarthyism of the early 1950s did not result in reduced spending on national defense. The defense budget increased in the 1950s as both the United States and the Soviet Union expanded nuclear arms programs as well as conventional forces. McCarthyism served to heighten Cold War fears in the United States and created a political climate that was more amenable to sharp increases in the military budget.

(3) McCarthyism of the early 1950s did not result in increased discrimination against returning veterans. Veterans returning from World War II and the Korean War did not, for the most part, experience discrimination based on their prior military service. Later, in the 1960s and 1970s, some veterans of the Vietnam War experienced hostility from members of the public who were opposed to the war.

34. **4** During the 1950s, United States foreign policy was shaped by the emergence of two world superpowers. The two superpowers that emerged following World War II were the Soviet Union and the United States. The United States became increasingly concerned about the growing power of the Soviet Union after World War II and put forth a policy of attempting to prevent the expansion of communism, known as containment. President Harry S. Truman articulated this goal, which has come to be known as the Truman Doctrine, in a speech to Congress in 1947. The rivalry between the two superpowers became known as the Cold War. Truman put the idea of containment into practice in 1947 by providing $400 million in military aid to Greece and Turkey to prevent those countries from becoming communist. Another example of the containment policy was the Berlin Airlift. In 1948, before the status of Berlin was settled, the Soviet Union decided it would prevent any food or other supplies from entering the western sector of the city. The goal of this action was for the Soviet Union to block the influence of the United States and its western allies in Berlin. Ultimately, the Soviet Union hoped to make all of Berlin part of what would become East Germany. Truman decided to send thousands of planes filled with supplies into the western sector of Berlin in an action known as the Berlin Airlift. The Berlin Airlift prevented people living in the western sector of Berlin from starving and prevented the Soviet Union from taking over the city. The formation of the North Atlantic Treaty Organization (NATO) was also part of the Cold War strategy of containment. NATO was created in 1949 by the United States and its allies to challenge the growing power of the Soviet Union. The members of NATO pledged that they would view an attack on any one member as an attack on all members.

WRONG CHOICES EXPLAINED:

(1) United States foreign policy in the 1950s was not shaped by the principle of nonalignment. The nonaligned countries during the Cold War period (1945–1991) were those nations that did not ally themselves with either the United States or the Soviet Union. These countries formalized their status with the organization of the Non-Aligned Movement in 1956. The nations that initiated the movement were Yugoslavia, India, Indonesia, Egypt, and Ghana.

(2) United States foreign policy in the 1950s was not shaped by a return to pre–World War II isolationism. After World War I, the United States retreated to a policy of isolationism. However, after World War II, the United States became engaged in challenging the Soviet Union and participating in a Cold War between the two nations.

(3) United States foreign policy in the 1950s was not shaped by a willingness to compromise with communist nations. During the 1950s, the United States challenged the power of the Soviet Union and other communist nations. The United States engaged in the Korean War (1950–1953) and bolstered its military to challenge the Soviet Union. Later, under President Richard Nixon (1969–1974), the United States pursued a policy of *détente*, which involved a willingness to compromise with communist nations.

35. **1** The formation of the North Atlantic Treaty Organization (NATO) and the Southeast Asia Treaty Organization (SEATO) were attempts by the United States and other nations to create mutual defense pacts. The United States demonstrated its commitment to protect Western Europe when it participated in the founding of NATO in 1949. The members of NATO vowed to resist collectively any aggressive actions by the Soviet Union. This marked the first time that the United States joined a peacetime alliance. Five years later, SEATO was created (1954), during the administration of President Dwight D. Eisenhower, in order to challenge further communist advances in Southeast Asia. United States participation in NATO and SEATO were designed to check the power of the Soviet Union. The United States and the Soviet Union emerged at the end of World War II as rival superpowers in the Cold War. The Soviet Union occupied the nations of Eastern Europe after the war. The United States was worried that the Soviet Union would try to push into Western Europe and later into Asia. In order to block any further aggression by the Soviet Union, Truman issued the Truman Doctrine, in which he said that the goal of the United States would be to contain communism. Toward this end, the United States extended military aid to Greece and Turkey (1947) and economic aid to the war-ravaged nations of Western Europe in the form of the Marshall Plan (1948). These moves, along with participation in NATO and SEATO, represented a clear break

with the pre–World War II position of the United States. The United States made it clear even in peacetime that the country would be involved in world affairs.

WRONG CHOICES EXPLAINED:

(2) The goals of the North Atlantic Treaty Organization (NATO) and the Southeast Asia Treaty Organization (SEATO) did not include increasing tariff rates among members. These organizations were focused on mutual defense, not trade. Later, the United States participated in the North American Free Trade Agreement (1993) and the World Trade Organization (1995), which were focused on trade. The goal of both of these entities was to reduce tariff rates among participants.

(3) The goals of the North Atlantic Treaty Organization (NATO) and the Southeast Asia Treaty Organization (SEATO) did not include decreasing the number of nuclear weapons. These organizations were focused on mutual defense, not arms reduction. Later, the United States and the Soviet Union participated in the Strategic Arms Limitation Talks (SALT), which led to two arms control agreements in 1972.

(4) The goals of the North Atlantic Treaty Organization (NATO) and the Southeast Asia Treaty Organization (SEATO) did not include providing economic aid to poor nations. The United States has consistently extended economic aid to many developing nations over the years. Under President John F. Kennedy (1961–1963), the United States expanded foreign aid with the creation of the Peace Corps to assist underdeveloped countries in Africa, Latin America, and Asia. Kennedy also created the Agency for International Development to coordinate aid to foreign countries and the Alliance for Progress, which was a series of development projects in Latin America.

36. **2** In 1958, the United States government increased spending on science education and research in reaction to the launching of *Sputnik*. When the Soviet Union launched the unmanned satellite *Sputnik* into space in 1957, many Americans were caught off guard. Before the launch, America had assumed that it was technologically superior to the Soviet Union. In addition, the launching of *Sputnik* was troubling for the United States because government officials realized that the same type of rocket that launched the satellite could also be used to deliver atomic weapons quickly to any place on Earth. The launching of *Sputnik* led the American government to devote more resources to teaching science and math to young people. Local school districts made greater efforts to identify gifted students and create accelerated programs for them. In addition, districts began receiving matching funds for math, science, and foreign language instruction from

the federal government. The launching of *Sputnik* also initiated a space race with the Soviet Union. In 1969, the United States was the first nation to land a man on the moon.

WRONG CHOICES EXPLAINED:

(1) The increase in United States government spending on science education and research in 1958 was not a reaction to the creation of the Warsaw Pact. The Warsaw Pact was a military alliance that the Soviet Union created in 1955 with the communist nations of eastern and central Europe. The creation of the Warsaw Pact did not point to a gap in science education and research between the Soviet Union and the United States, as many believed that the launch of *Sputnik* did.

(3) The increase in United States government spending on science education and research in 1958 was not a reaction to the installation of Soviet missiles in Cuba. The attempt by the Soviet Union to install nuclear missiles in Cuba was discovered in 1962, four years after the initiatives referred to in the question. President John F. Kennedy saw these missiles, which were in close proximity to the United States, as an unacceptable provocation and ordered Soviet Premier Nikita Khrushchev to halt the operation and dismantle the bases. Khrushchev insisted on the right of the Soviet Union to install the missiles. For about a week, the world stood on the brink of nuclear war. Finally, a deal was reached in which the Soviet Union would abandon its Cuban missile program and the United States would quietly remove its missiles from Turkey.

(4) The increase in United States government spending on science education and research in 1958 was not a reaction to the U-2 incident. That event occurred in 1960, two years after the initiatives referred to in the question. The incident involved a U-2 American spy plane being shot down over Soviet air space. At first, the United States insisted that the plane was a weather aircraft. However, this story did not hold up to scrutiny after the Soviet Union produced the pilot of the plane, alive, along with photographs taken of Soviet military installations.

37. **3** A problem facing President Lyndon B. Johnson at the time he delivered the speech excerpted in the question (1968) was that opposition to the Vietnam War was becoming more widespread. In the speech, Johnson is announcing that he would not seek reelection. He asserts that he would focus on "America's sons in the fields far away," not on "personal partisan causes." The war in Vietnam had become increasingly contentious by 1968. The United States became heavily involved in Vietnam after Congress gave President Lyndon Johnson a blank check with the Tonkin Gulf Resolution in 1964. The United States feared that South Vietnam would become a communist nation as North Vietnam had. Over

the next several years, Johnson sent hundreds of thousands of troops to Vietnam, reinstituted the draft, and began aerial bombardment of Vietnam. Despite the presence of over half a million United States troops and the firepower of the U.S. military, President Johnson was not able to declare victory over the communist rebels in South Vietnam. As the war dragged on and as the United States suffered more casualties, many Americans began to question the wisdom of American policies in Vietnam. Some thought the war was more of a civil war that the United States should not be part of. Many young men began to oppose the war because they feared they might be drafted. Finally, many Americans grew to oppose the war after seeing unsettling images on television news programs. Families saw American soldiers burn down Vietnamese villages. They saw body bags coming back to the United States. They saw Vietnamese children burned by napalm. All of these images contributed to the growing antiwar movement in the United States. By 1968, Johnson decided that his war policies imperiled his reelection, so he decided to not run for a second term.

WRONG CHOICES EXPLAINED:

(1) President Lyndon Johnson's decision to not run for reelection was related to widespread opposition to the Vietnam War, not to judicial scandals. During Johnson's administration, the most prominent scandal involving the judiciary involved Abe Fortas, a justice on the Supreme Court. Accusations of ethics violations forced Fortas to resign from the Court in 1969.

(2) President Lyndon Johnson's decision to not run for reelection was related to widespread opposition to the Vietnam War, not to his participation in peace talks. Johnson initiated peace talks in 1968. In the following decades, evidence has emerged indicating that the Republican candidate for the presidency in 1968, Richard Nixon, used surrogates to pressure the government of South Vietnam to stall the peace talks. Nixon feared that successful peace talks in 1968 could bolster the campaign of the Democratic candidate for president, Hubert Humphrey. These efforts, and other factors, were successful in scuttling Johnson's efforts at a substantive agreement to end the fighting in Vietnam.

(4) President Lyndon Johnson's decision to not run for reelection was related to widespread opposition to the Vietnam War, not to a shifting of money from the Vietnam War to Great Society programs. The opposite was closer to the truth. Increased spending on the Vietnam War took resources away from Great Society programs, undermining their effectiveness. Dr. Martin Luther King, Jr., said at a conference in 1967, "The promises of the Great Society have been shot down on the battlefields of Vietnam."

38. **1** The primary method used by Dr. Martin Luther King, Jr., to advance civil rights was nonviolent protest of segregation practices. King drew on several religious, philosophical, and political traditions in developing his approach to social change. King's insistence on nonviolence had deep roots. Many Christians cite the biblical injunction to turn the other cheek if struck. Pacifism is especially strong in the Quaker tradition. King also gained inspiration from Mahatma Gandhi's campaign to resist British authority in India in the first half of the 20th century. Gandhi taught that to resort to violence was to stoop to the moral level of the oppressor. King also emphasized civil disobedience—the philosophical principle that asserts it is one's right, indeed one's responsibility, to resist unjust laws. Earlier in American history, that principle was articulated by the transcendentalist thinker Henry David Thoreau in his essay *Resistance to Civil Government (Civil Disobedience)* (1849). King was a central figure in the civil rights movement of the 1950s and 1960s. The high point of the movement might have been the march on Washington in 1963, where King gave his "I Have a Dream" speech. The movement culminated in the Civil Rights Act of 1964, which banned segregation in public facilities, and the Voting Rights Act of 1965, which removed barriers to African Americans voting.

WRONG CHOICES EXPLAINED:

(2) While working to advance civil rights, Dr. Martin Luther King, Jr., did not support black separatism. A central demand of the civil rights movement was that Jim Crow segregation laws be eliminated. King envisioned an integrated society, where people are judged "by the content of their character," not by "the color of their skin." Some activists who addressed the issue of social justice for African Americans did not emphasize separatism. Malcolm X, for example, advocated that African Americans organize among themselves, separate from whites. After making a pilgrimage to Mecca in 1964 and seeing Muslims of different races interacting as equals, Malcolm X revised his views about black separatism.

(3) While working to advance civil rights, Dr. Martin Luther King, Jr., did not pursue elective public office. King was generally nonpartisan. At different times, he was critical of both of the two main political parties. By 1964, when President Lyndon Johnson pushed strongly for the passage of the Civil Rights Act, King worked closely with Johnson and let the public know that he supported Johnson's reelection. However, King never ran for public office.

(4) While working to advance civil rights, Dr. Martin Luther King, Jr., did not advocate practical education for economic gain. Earlier, Booker T. Washington founded the Tuskegee Institute (1881) to teach vocational skills to African

Americans. Washington emphasized educational and economic progress for African Americans, rather than political equality and civil rights.

39. **3** The focus of this cartoon is President Richard Nixon attempting to hide evidence from investigators. In the cartoon, Nixon is depicted as hiding behind an American flag, implying that his pronouncements about national security should not be taken at face value. Instead, they are designed to distract the American public from the real issue at hand—rampant corruption within the Nixon administration. Nixon is attempting to use the flag as a "national security blanket" to cover up illegal activities, including "faked cables," "stolen files," the use of a cash slush fund, and eavesdropping on opponents. The most prominent scandal of the Nixon administration was the Watergate affair, which involved spies breaking into the headquarters of the Democratic National Committee at the Watergate Hotel in Washington, D.C. These spies were caught by local police. Their arrest led to investigations, hearings, and legal proceedings that ultimately led to the resignation of President Nixon.

WRONG CHOICES EXPLAINED:

(1) The focus of the cartoon is not President Richard Nixon recalling diplomats from Mexico. Nixon did not take such an action. The money bag labeled "Mexico" refers to a large private contribution to Nixon's Committee to Reelect the President (CRP). The money was part of a fundraising blitz in the spring of 1972, right before the implementation of a new campaign finance disclosure law. The contribution being referred to was funneled through a bank in Mexico to hide the source of the money. The source of the money was later discovered after some of the money was found in the account of one of the Watergate burglars.

(2) The focus of the cartoon is not President Richard Nixon supporting tax decreases and budget cuts. Nixon did not take such actions. The federal budget grew during each year of Nixon's presidency, and there were no significant decreases in tax rates under President Nixon. Later, President Ronald Reagan (1981–1989) signed legislation cutting taxes, although the federal budget grew for most of the years of his presidency.

(4) The focus of the cartoon is not President Richard Nixon making concessions to the Soviet Union. Nixon took steps to improve relations with the Soviet Union. In 1972, Nixon held meetings with Soviet leaders in Moscow. Improved relations with the Soviet Union spurred ongoing talks between the superpowers about their nuclear arsenals. This easing of tensions in the Cold War is known as *détente*, the French word for loosening or relaxing.

40. **2** The outcome of the events illustrated in the cartoon resulted in the resignation of President Richard Nixon. Nixon's web of illegal acts began to unwind in June 1972 when five men were caught breaking into the headquarters of the Democratic National Committee at the Watergate Hotel in Washington, D.C. Persistent reporting by Carl Bernstein and Bob Woodward of the *Washington Post* drew connections between the burglars, Nixon's reelection committee, and ultimately the White House. When it became known that Nixon taped conversations in the White House Oval Office, investigators demanded that the tapes be turned over. Nixon argued that executive privilege allowed him to keep the tapes. In *United States* v. *Nixon* (1974), the Supreme Court ordered Nixon to turn over the tapes. Nixon told a press conference in November 1973, "I am not a crook." However, less than a month after the Supreme Court decision in 1974, Nixon resigned. The next president, Gerald Ford, issued a blanket pardon of Nixon in 1974 so that Nixon would not be brought before the justice system.

WRONG CHOICES EXPLAINED:

(1) The events illustrated in the cartoon did not result in the expansion of the Vietnam War into Cambodia. By the time this cartoon was drawn (1973), Nixon had already expanded the war into Cambodia. In 1969, Nixon began a secret bombing campaign in Cambodia. In 1970, he ordered an invasion of that country. Widening the war to Cambodia led to a renewed intensity of the American antiwar movement in the spring of 1970.

(3) The events illustrated in the cartoon did not result in growing support for environmental legislation. Public support for environmental legislation had been building for a decade before the events illustrated in the cartoon. The movement was inspired partly by Rachel Carson's book *Silent Spring* (1962), which detailed the harmful effects of toxic chemicals. Earth Day, which started in 1970, also created awareness about environmental concerns. President Nixon signed legislation to create the Environmental Protection Agency (EPA) in 1970. He approved amendments to the 1963 Clean Air Act (also in 1970) that established regulatory and enforcement mechanisms.

(4) The events illustrated in the cartoon did not result in the visit to Communist China by President Richard Nixon. By the time this cartoon was drawn (1973), Nixon had already visited China. His trip to Beijing in 1972 was part of President Nixon's policy of *détente*, a policy of reducing Cold War tensions and establishing warmer relations between the communist world and the United States. Nixon's strong anticommunist credentials enabled him to open relations with communist nations without being accused of being soft on communism. Nixon became the first American president to visit Communist China. Later in 1972, he held meetings with Soviet leaders in Moscow.

41. **1** The cartoonist's view about global warming is that the federal government has been slow to take action on global warming. The cartoon creates a satirical version of the instructions listed on a fire alarm. Typical instructions on a fire alarm read, "In case of fire, break glass, pull fire alarm." These straightforward instructions are reimagined to describe the government's approach to dealing with global warming. The government's approach to global warming is depicted as indecisive, overly cautious, and unproductive. The instructions require that "everyone...agrees" that a crisis exists and that skeptics be brought in to cast doubt on the gravity of the situation. The upshot of the instructions is that political leaders have hindered taking significant steps to address global warming, citing a host of excuses that, in the cartoonist's view, are misguided and petty ("think about who is going to clean up the broken glass"). Since the early 1980s, scientists have become aware of a trend toward warmer global temperatures. Many became convinced that this warming trend was caused by trapped greenhouse gases, which, in turn, were caused by human activities, primarily the burning of fossil fuels. In the 1990s and 2000s, a virtual consensus emerged in the scientific community around the connection between global warming and the emissions generated by the burning of fossil fuels. Calls were made to limit the human activities linked to global warming. The 1992 Earth Summit in Brazil led to the adoption by most of the countries in the world of the United Nations Framework Convention on Climate Change. The 1997 Kyoto Protocols set binding obligations on industrialized countries to reduce the emission of greenhouse gases. President George W. Bush (2001–2009), who was in office at the time the cartoon was published (2007), did much to undermine measures that had been taken or were under consideration in regard to protecting the environment. First, he would not implement the Kyoto global climate change treaty. The Kyoto Protocol was adopted by 165 countries in 2001 but did not have the participation of the United States and Australia. In rejecting the protocol, Bush also cast doubt on the science that demonstrated an urgent need to deal with climate change. In the subsequent years, this casting of doubt on the science related to global warming has been adopted by many Republicans as part of their rationale to resist steps toward a more sustainable future.

WRONG CHOICES EXPLAINED:
(2) The cartoonist is not making the point that most people support efforts to address global warming. The cartoon is commenting on the response of the government to global warming, not on public opinion in regard to global warming. In polls since the 1990s, a growing majority of Americans indicate that they are "worried" or "concerned" about global warming. (This figure was approximately 65 percent in Pew and Gallup polls in 2016.) Polls also indicate that a majority of Americans support policies that address global warming.

(3) The cartoonist is not making the point that dealing with global warming is too expensive. One of the items in the instructions reads, "Realize that calling the fire dept. isn't free, you know." However, this line is meant to mock government officials who come up with a variety of excuses to avoid taking action on global warming. The cartoonist is not arguing that such actions are too expensive.

(4) The cartoonist is not making the point that global warming is damaging the ozone layer. There is no mention of damage to the ozone layer in the cartoon. The ozone layer is a region of Earth's stratosphere with a relatively high concentration of the gas ozone. The ozone layer shields Earth by absorbing most of the sun's ultraviolet radiation. Damage has been done to the ozone layer in two ways. First, the overall percentage of ozone in the ozone layer has declined. Second, holes in the ozone layer have opened around Earth's poles. The main cause of these two phenomena is man-made chemicals, such as chlorofluorocarbons (CFCs), being released into the atmosphere.

42. **1** Since the presidency of Ronald Reagan, the Republican Party has generally tried to deal with economic problems by supporting lower taxes and reduced government spending. President Reagan advanced a series of economic initiatives that bear the name Reaganomics. Reagan supported economic policies that favored big business. He based this on a belief in the effectiveness of supply-side economics. This approach to the economy stressed stimulating the supply side of the economy, such as manufacturers, banks, and insurance corporations. The idea is that if there is growth in the supply side, there will be general economic growth and the benefits of that growth will reach everyone. The alternative approach is to stimulate the demand side, which are consumers. Demand-side economics emphasizes government policies designed to increase workers' wages and expands social programs such as welfare and unemployment benefits. As a believer in supply-side economics, Reagan implemented policies that he thought would stimulate business. Reagan cut taxes for corporations and greatly reduced regulations on industry. He also cut spending on social programs to reduce government spending. By cutting corporate taxes and taxes on wealthy individuals, he cut government revenues. However, at the same time, Reagan increased spending on armaments. This combination of increased spending and decreased revenues led to a doubling of the national debt from around $900 billion in 1980 to over $2 trillion in 1986. Reagan's pro-business economic policies had mixed results. A large debt is a problem because it requires large interest payments. By 1988, the interest on the national debt reached 14 percent of total annual government expenditures. This huge debt has hindered economic growth to some degree since and forced future administrations to make difficult decisions in regard to keeping the debt under control.

WRONG CHOICES EXPLAINED:

(2) The elimination of free trade and the free-market system have not been part of the Republican Party's agenda since the Reagan administration (1981–1989). Leaders in both political parties have supported policies to bolster free trade by endorsing international agreements to lower or eliminate tariffs. Neither political party endorses eliminating the free-market system. Socialists and communists embrace the idea of replacing free-market capitalism with an alternative system.

(3) Deficit spending and decreased military spending have not been part of the Republican Party's agenda since the Reagan administration (1981–1989). Republicans have pushed for a fiscally conservative approach to spending and working toward a balanced budget. They have also supported increasing the size of the military budget. Occasionally, these two goals have come into conflict with one another.

(4) Increased social spending and stricter regulation of the stock market have not been part of the Republican Party's agenda since the Reagan administration (1981–1989). Republicans have pushed for decreases in spending on social programs and have worked to reduce regulations on the stock market and the banking industry.

43. **2** The statement, "The federal government did not do enough to aid the victims [of Hurricane Katrina]," is an opinion rather than a fact. In August 2005, Hurricane Katrina brought catastrophic damage to the Gulf Coast, resulting in more than 1800 deaths and millions left homeless, mostly in the city of New Orleans. The hardest-hit parts of the city were African American and impoverished. Many Americans were critical of the government for being ill-prepared to handle such a crisis and for not doing enough to help the people of New Orleans (as noted in choice 2). Within the federal government, it appeared that the various agencies were not communicating with one another and did not grasp the magnitude of the situation. The head of the Federal Emergency Management Agency (FEMA), Michael Brown, testified that he informed White House officials on August 29 that the levees had breached and the city was flooding (as noted in choice 1). However, the Bush administration stated that they did not hear of the breach until August 30. In a radio interview, Homeland Security Secretary Michael Chertoff dismissed reports that thousands of individuals had taken refuge in the New Orleans Convention Center. President George W. Bush's pronouncement that FEMA Chief Michael Brown was doing a "heck of a job" seemed to be further evidence of the president's inability to grasp the gravity of the situation. Eventually, FEMA was able to provide housing to approximately 114,000 households in trailers (as noted in choice 4). The mishandling of the crisis damaged President Bush's approval ratings.

WRONG CHOICES EXPLAINED:

(1), (3), and (4) These are all incorrect choices because they are all indisputable facts. The correct choice (2), by contrast, presents an evaluation of the federal government's response to Hurricane Katrina and therefore is an opinion.

44. **3** According to the cartoonist, one important result of the election of President Barack Obama in 2008 was that a racial barrier in government had been broken. The cartoon alludes to photographs of water fountains in the South before passage of the 1964 Civil Rights Act. Water fountains often had signs above them saying "Whites Only" or "White Only." Sometimes water fountains would sit near one another, one labeled "White" and the other labeled "Colored." The practice of having separate water fountains was part of the system of Jim Crow segregation. This system developed after the Reconstruction period (1865–1877) in the southern states of the United States, creating separate facilities for African Americans and white people. These included separate waiting rooms at train stations, separate entrances to public buildings, and separate schools. In many cases, African Americans were simply barred from certain public facilities. The legal foundation of separate facilities was called into question in the *Brown* v. *Board of Education of Topeka* case (1954) when the Supreme Court asserted that segregation in public schools was inherently unfair and detrimental to African-American students. Later, the Civil Rights Act (1964) barred discrimination in all public facilities. Even with the dismantling of segregation, the idea of an African American successfully running for the presidency seemed unlikely to many Americans. However, the symbolic "Whites Only" sign on the presidency came down in 2008. Barack Obama first fended off a strong challenge to the Democratic nomination by Senator Hillary Clinton. Clinton's bid for the nomination, if successful, could have resulted in a different historic milestone—the first female president in the United States. In the general election, the Democratic Party was aided by an unpopular sitting Republican president, George W. Bush, and by an unfocused campaign by Republican Senator John McCain. The McCain campaign failed to articulate a consistent message. Obama and his running mate, Senator Joe Biden of Delaware, were able to cement support in traditionally blue (Democratic-leaning) states and successfully challenged McCain in traditionally red (Republican-leaning) states such as North Carolina, Virginia, and Indiana. Obama garnered 53 percent of the popular vote and won 365 electoral votes to McCain's 173.

WRONG CHOICES EXPLAINED:
(1) The cartoonist is not asserting that the election of President Barack Obama in 2008 resulted in the integration of public facilities in the South. The Civil Rights Act of 1964 prohibited segregation in public facilities. The allusion to "Whites Only" water fountains is meant to illustrate the fall of one last historically all-white institution—the presidency.

(2) The cartoonist is not asserting that the election of President Barack Obama in 2008 resulted in the executive branch of government gaining power over the legislative branch. The cartoonist is not commenting on the distribution of power within the government. The basic system of checks and balances remained in place following the 2008 presidential elections.

(4) The cartoonist is not asserting that the election of President Barack Obama in 2008 resulted in the legal elimination of racial discrimination in the United States. The Civil Rights Act of 1964 banned racial discrimination in public facilities. Laws that existed before the 2008 election also prohibited racial discrimination in housing and employment. It is very difficult, however, to eliminate all forms of racial discrimination in society completely.

45. **2** The practice of yellow journalism most influenced United States entry into the Spanish-American War. Yellow journalism refers to the sensationalistic, irresponsible coverage of events in the media. Yellow journalists created support for the Spanish-American War by writing articles about the sinking of the United States battleship *Maine*. In 1898, the *Maine* exploded and sunk in the harbor of Havana, Cuba. Many in the United States thought that the destruction of the ship was the work of Spain, especially after American newspapers bluntly accused Spain of the crime despite the scarcity of evidence. The coverage of the sinking of the *Maine* was one of several causes of the war. Spain controlled Cuba at the time, but a Cuban independence movement was trying to break its ties to Spain. Many Americans wanted the United States to intervene on Cuba's side in this struggle. Some Americans saw parallels between the Cuban struggle for independence from Spain and America's struggle for independence from Great Britain. Also, some American businessmen were angered by the interruption of the sugar harvest by the fighting between Cuban rebels and Spanish forces. American newspapers breathlessly followed events in Cuba, with lurid accounts of Spanish wrongdoing. The Spanish-American War was brief. American forces landed in Cuba on June 22, 1898, and Spain surrendered on July 17. Fighting in the Philippines, which was also a Spanish possession, lasted just days. The United States and Spain negotiated the Treaty of Paris (1898) following the war. In the treaty, Spain agreed to cede the Philippines, Puerto Rico, and Guam to the United States; the United States agreed to pay Spain $20 million for these possessions.

WRONG CHOICES EXPLAINED:

(1) Yellow journalism did not play a significant role in the United States entry into the War of 1812. Newspapers carried news of the events leading up to the war. However, these accounts are not seen as important factors in the U.S. declaration of war against Great Britain. The War of 1812 had many causes, including the British impressment of American sailors and British assistance to Native American Indian tribes in the Great Lakes region.

(3) Yellow journalism did not play a significant role in the United States entry into World War II. Newspapers, magazines, radio stations, and theatrical newsreels all carried news of events leading up to the United States entrance into World War II. However, these accounts are not seen as important factors in the U.S. declaration of war against the Axis powers in 1941. Many Americans hoped that the United States would intervene in the war earlier. The event that brought the United States into the war was the Japanese attack on the United States naval base at Pearl Harbor, Hawaii Territory.

(4) Yellow journalism did not play a significant role in the United States entry into the Persian Gulf War. Traditional forms of media, as well as cable news and the Internet, all carried news of events leading up to the United States declaration of war against Iraq. However, these accounts are not seen as important factors in the beginning of the Persian Gulf War in 1991. Tensions developed in 1990 when Iraqi leader Saddam Hussein sent the Iraqi military into Kuwait to occupy that country. Operation Desert Storm initiated by President George H. W. Bush was the name given to the efforts of the United States–led coalition in the Persian Gulf War in 1991. The goal of Operation Desert Storm was to remove Iraqi forces from Kuwait. The operation was successful. Hussein was quickly forced to withdraw his troops.

46. **4** The suspension of habeas corpus during the Civil War and the passage of the USA Patriot Act during the war on terror both illustrate the national government's willingness to limit civil liberties when the nation is facing immediate danger. The writ of habeas corpus was suspended by President Abraham Lincoln during the Civil War. In 1863, he authorized the arrest without due process of people he thought were aiding the Southern cause. By the end of the war, over 14,000 people had been arrested under Lincoln's wartime provisions. Most of those arrested, however, were people actively aiding the Southern side in the Civil War. The Democratic Party, the party of the Southern slaveholders, still operated openly in the North during the war, running a vigorous campaign for president against Lincoln in 1864. The USA Patriot Act was passed by Congress less than two months after the September 2001 terrorist attacks. It greatly expanded the government's authority in the fight against terrorism. The law gave federal authorities greater authority to subject political organizations to

surveillance and to conduct secret searches of phone, Internet, medical, banking, and student records with minimal judicial oversight. Also, the act gives greater powers to law authorities to investigate American citizens *without* probable cause; authorities can assert that such investigations are for "intelligence purposes." Finally, the USA Patriot Act allows for the incarceration of noncitizens for indefinite periods on mere suspicion with no right of counsel, habeas corpus, or opportunities to appear before public tribunals. Some critics have argued that it gives the government too much power to circumvent the Constitution.

WRONG CHOICES EXPLAINED:

(1) The suspension of habeas corpus during the Civil War and the passage of the USA Patriot Act during the war on terror do not illustrate the national government's willingness to uphold the rights of minority citizens. The national government has taken actions to protect the rights of minority citizens, such as the Civil Rights Act of 1964 and the Americans with Disabilities Act of 1990. However, the two actions mentioned in the question limited the rights of people.

(2) The suspension of habeas corpus during the Civil War and the passage of the USA Patriot Act during the war on terror do not illustrate the national government's willingness to tolerate criticism of wartime policies. The national government has frequently tolerated criticism of wartime policies, as it did during the Vietnam War. However, the two actions mentioned in the question limited certain rights during wartime.

(3) The suspension of habeas corpus during the Civil War and the passage of the USA Patriot Act during the war on terror do not illustrate the national government's willingness to expand the power of the states to prosecute radical groups. Both acts expanded the powers of the national government, not state governments.

47. **4** The Washington Naval Conference (1921), the Kellogg-Briand Pact (1928), and the Neutrality Acts of the 1930s were all attempts by the United States to avoid policies likely to lead to war. The presidents of the 1920s attempted to isolate the United States from world affairs and to reduce spending on war munitions. President Warren Harding successfully pressed for a reduction of naval power among Britain, France, Japan, Italy, and the United States at the Washington Naval Conference in 1921. Later, President Calvin Coolidge continued to pursue an isolationist foreign policy and helped to negotiate the Kellogg-Briand Pact (1928). The United States was one of 63 nations to sign the pact, which renounced war in principle. Because the pact was negotiated outside of the League of Nations, it was unenforceable, rendering it meaningless. Isolationism continued to hold sway into the 1930s, even as the world was becoming increasingly dangerous with the rise of fascism in Europe and a

militarist government in Japan. In the Neutrality Acts of 1935–1937, Congress made it clear that neither the United States government nor private U.S. firms were to trade with belligerent nations. President Franklin Roosevelt grew frustrated with these acts because they did not make a distinction between aggressors and victims in the conflicts of the 1930s. A later Neutrality Act (1939) allowed the United States to supply the opponents of fascism with materials on a cash and carry basis.

WRONG CHOICES EXPLAINED:

(1) The Washington Naval Conference (1921), the Kellogg-Briand Pact (1928), and the Neutrality Acts of the 1930s were not attempts by the United States to increase military spending. The opposite is true. The three items were designed to avoid the possibility of war and to reduce military expenditures.

(2) The Washington Naval Conference (1921), the Kellogg-Briand Pact (1928), and the Neutrality Acts of the 1930s were not attempts by the United States to show support for the United Nations. The three items all occurred before the founding of the United Nations (1945).

(3) The Washington Naval Conference (1921), the Kellogg-Briand Pact (1928), and the Neutrality Acts of the 1930s were not attempts by the United States to assume a position of world leadership. The three items were all expressions of isolationism, reflecting a desire among U.S. political leaders to withdraw from world affairs.

48. **2** The baby boom following World War II resulted in the need to increase the number of schools in the 1960s. For several years before 1946, birth rates in the United States remained relatively low. Couples tended to have fewer children during the lean years of the Great Depression. The dislocation and physical separation caused by World War II kept the birth rate even lower. However, when the war ended, returning veterans quickly got down to the business of starting families. The spike in birth rates from 1946 through the early 1960s produced a baby boom that has had lasting repercussions in American society. The baby boom required states to spend more money on constructing and operating new schools in the 1950s and 1960s. In addition, these young families needed housing. The baby boom contributed to the growth of suburban communities outside of major cities in the 1950s and 1960s. The Servicemen's Readjustment Act (1944), more commonly known as the G.I. Bill, provided low-interest loans for veterans to purchase homes. Developers often bought large tracts of land to build hundreds of houses. To save time and money, these developments included many houses that each had identical plans. The most famous suburban developer was William Levitt. Levittown, on Long Island, New York, became synonymous with these mass-produced communities.

WRONG CHOICES EXPLAINED:

(1) The baby boom following World War II did not result in the development of urban unrest in the 1950s. Urban unrest is more associated with the 1960s as major riots occurred in African-American neighborhoods in several cities in the United States (Watts, Los Angeles in 1965; Detroit and Newark in 1967; Washington, D.C., Baltimore, and Chicago in 1968). Some urban unrest occurred in the 1950s and was often associated with clashes over civil rights, but this was not the result of the baby boom.

(3) The baby boom following World War II did not result in the migration from cities to farms in the 1970s. There was not a major migration from cities to farms in the 1970s. Some members of the counterculture formed rural communes in the 1960s and 1970s, but this trend was counterbalanced by the decline of the family farm.

(4) The baby boom following World War II did not result in the need to decrease the number of nursing homes in the 1980s. As the baby boomers, born between 1946 and 1964, approach old age in the coming years, the need for nursing homes will increase.

49. **1** The Supreme Court cases of *Tinker* v. *Des Moines* (1969), *New Jersey* v. *T.L.O.* (1985), and *Vernonia School District* v. *Acton* (1995) addressed the issue of balancing the rights of students with the need of schools to maintain order. In the case of *Tinker* v. *Des Moines* (1969), the Court ruled that a school board prohibition against students wearing black armbands in protest of the war in Vietnam was unconstitutional. The Court ruled that students in school had the right to free speech, including symbolic speech, as long as their actions did not interfere with the educational process. The Court said, "Students do not shed their constitutional rights at the schoolhouse gate." The Supreme Court moved in a different direction in *New Jersey* v. *T.L.O.* (1985) and *Vernonia School District* v. *Acton* (1995). Both cases established limits on a student's right to privacy and demonstrated that students in school do not always enjoy the same constitutional liberties that adults do. The case of *New Jersey* v. *T.L.O.* deals with the legality of searching students without search warrants. T.L.O. is the initials of a female student in a New Jersey high school whose bag was searched by school officials. In the search, evidence was found implicating her in both taking and selling marijuana. T.L.O. was convicted of delinquency charges. She appealed to the Supreme Court, arguing that the school's search of her bag was illegal because the school did not have a warrant and therefore violated the Fourth Amendment. The Supreme Court ruled that the search was permissible, noting that school officials may balance a student's expectation of privacy with the school's need to maintain discipline and security. The case of *Vernonia School*

District v. *Acton* upheld the random drug testing of students. Opponents challenged random drug testing on the grounds that it amounted to a search without a warrant. The Supreme Court acknowledged that the drug tests amounted to a search but ruled that a school could conduct them. The Court ruled that school districts have a legitimate interest in preventing teenage drug use.

WRONG CHOICES EXPLAINED:

(2) The three cases listed in the question do not address the issue of allowing principals to determine students' constitutional rights. It is the Constitution itself as well as Supreme Court decisions that determine individuals' constitutional rights. It is the job of principals and other school officials to establish policies that are consistent with the Constitution and Supreme Court decisions. States, districts, and schools may afford students additional rights, but they may not abridge established constitutional rights.

(3) The three cases listed in the question do not address the issue of denying public school districts the authority to allow prayer in school. Schools districts do not have the authority to mandate prayer in school. In the case of *Engel* v. *Vitale* (1962), the Supreme Court ruled that the Regents' Prayer, a state-mandated prayer that was recited by public school children in New York State, was unconstitutional because it violated the doctrine of separation of church and state. Schools districts may set aside spaces within a school for students to engage in private prayer.

(4) The three cases listed in the question do not address the issue of giving state legislatures the power to fund charter schools. State legislatures have the power to fund charter schools. In the future, the Supreme Court may examine whether states may allow religious institutions to establish publicly funded charter schools.

50. **3** President John F. Kennedy and President Ronald Reagan both visited the Berlin Wall in order to demonstrate the commitment of the United States to maintain freedom in Western Europe. The communist government of East Germany built the Berlin Wall in 1961 to encircle West Berlin completely and to separate it from East Germany. Berlin was divided when Germany was divided into East Germany and West Germany in 1949. Berlin was located completely within East German territory, so West Berlin was physically separate from the rest of West Germany. Before construction of the wall, many residents of East Germany escaped to the west through West Berlin. Two years later, in 1963, President John F. Kennedy visited West Berlin to express solidarity with the city's residents. He visited Checkpoint Charlie, one of the eight crossings in the wall. During the visit, Kennedy delivered a famous speech at a square that was later renamed John-F.-Kennedy-Platz. Kennedy critiqued the communist system and delivered the line *"Ich bin ein Berliner,"* which means in English, "I too am a

Berliner." Later, in the 1980s, President Reagan visited West Berlin several times. His most noted speech made in West Berlin occurred in June 1987 when he encouraged Soviet leader Mikhail Gorbachev to allow more openness in the communist world. Specifically, Reagan implored the Soviet leader, "Mr. Gorbachev, tear down this wall!" The speech was given at the historic Brandenburg Gate, which became part of the Berlin Wall when the wall was erected. The gate was another one of the eight crossings in the Berlin Wall. In 1989, communist governments began to collapse in Eastern Europe. It was clear that Soviet leader Mikhail Gorbachev would not try to halt this development as previous Soviet leaders had. The iconic image of this movement was the collapse of the Berlin Wall in November 1989. The wall had become a symbol of the rift between the communist bloc countries and the western democratic countries. By 1991, the Soviet Union itself collapsed, ending communism in Europe.

WRONG CHOICES EXPLAINED:

(1) The visits to the Berlin Wall by President John F. Kennedy and President Ronald Reagan were not meant to assess the military strength of the Soviet Union. Specialists in the Pentagon, the State Department, the Central Intelligence Agency, and other agencies worked diligently at assessing the Soviet Union's military capabilities.

(2) The visits to the Berlin Wall by President John F. Kennedy and President Ronald Reagan were not meant to prepare for an invasion of the Soviet Union. Such an invasion never occurred. It would have led to a third world war.

(4) The visits to the Berlin Wall by President John F. Kennedy and President Ronald Reagan were not meant to challenge the North Atlantic Treaty Organization (NATO) nations that were supported by the Soviet Union. In fact, no such nations existed. During the Cold War, NATO stood united in opposition to the Soviet Union and the Warsaw Pact nations.

PART II: THEMATIC ESSAY

Presidential Decisions and Actions

Over time, various United States presidents have been confronted with crucial issues and problems that demanded immediate attention. Presidents have frequently had to make important decisions to act in these circumstances. Some of these presidential actions have been more successful than others. Two successful presidential actions were President George Washington's response to the Whiskey Rebellion and President Dwight D. Eisenhower's response to the crisis in Little Rock, Arkansas, over school desegregation.

In 1794, farmers in western Pennsylvania rose in protest over a federal excise tax on whiskey. The historical circumstances that led to the protest can be traced back several years. In 1791, Secretary of the Treasury Alexander Hamilton proposed a broad, ambitious financial program to establish the United States on sound financial ground. First, he pushed for the creation of a national bank, which would hold the government's tax revenues and act as a stabilizing force on the economy. President Washington signed the bank into law in 1791. Hamilton also proposed an elaborate and controversial plan to deal with the new nation's substantial debt. He insisted that debts carried over from the war years be paid back, or funded, at full value. In addition, Hamilton insisted that the government assume, or agree to pay back, state debts incurred during the war. To provide revenue for these measures, Hamilton also proposed new taxes.

The most prominent, and controversial, of these taxes was an excise tax, or sales tax, on whiskey. This tax hit grain farmers especially hard. These hardscrabble farmers in remote rural areas were barely making ends meet. Distilling grain into whiskey allowed these farmers to increase their meager profits. Transporting bushels of grain over primitive roads to population centers was prohibitively expensive; distilling it down to whiskey made it easier to transport. The grain farmers of western Pennsylvania felt that they could not shoulder this substantial tax. In 1794, farmers took action. Fifty men gathered and marched to the home of the local tax collector. From there, the gathering swelled to 7000 men who then marched to Pittsburgh. At this point, the federal government took action. Washington nationalized nearly 13,000 militiamen into the army and marched them himself to Pennsylvania to suppress the rebellion and ensure that the laws of the land were followed.

The action was successful in that it both put down the rebellion and established federal authority. Alexander Hamilton and George Washington had vivid memories of Shays' Rebellion, which occurred less than a decade earlier. They were determined that the current rebellion would not get out of control, as had Shays' Rebellion. Washington made it clear that a strong national government would not tolerate unlawful challenges to its authority.

In the 1950s, another challenge to federal authority prompted a president to take a strong stand. In 1957 in Little Rock, Arkansas, President Dwight D. Eisenhower called in army paratroopers to enforce federal desegregation mandates in the face of resistance by Arkansas state authorities as well as by protesters who were resisting integration. The historical circumstances that led to Eisenhower's action include the landmark *Brown v. Board of Education of Topeka* decision in 1954. This decision declared segregated schools inherently unfair and ordered states and communities to take measures to undo this system. Segregation of public facilities had long been the rule in the South. White southerners created the system of Jim Crow segregation to put African Americans into a second-class status. In the 1950s, activists challenged segregation, winning a major victory in the *Brown* decision.

The school board in Little Rock, Arkansas, decided to begin the desegregation of Central High School at the start of the 1957 school year by admitting nine African-American students. The plan developed without much controversy. However, just before the beginning of the school year, Arkansas governor Orville Faubus decided to send the National Guard to block the school and not permit the nine African-American students to enter the building. The news of Faubus's action prompted a large crowd of pro-segregation whites to come to the school. Faubus instigated a mob to enforce white supremacy in Little Rock.

At this point, the federal government acted. President Dwight D. Eisenhower was not a strong supporter of the civil rights movement, but he was alarmed to see the Arkansas governor directly challenge federal authority. At first, Eisenhower urged the governor to comply with the segregation plan. Governor Faubus gave Eisenhower his word that he would withdraw the National Guard troops from the school. However, Faubus made no provisions for the safety of the nine African-American students. The students had to confront an angry mob of white people with only a small contingent of local police to protect the students. At that point, President Eisenhower decided to send in federal troops to guarantee the safety of the students and to ensure that Little Rock High School would comply with the *Brown* decision. Some of the troops remained at the school for the entire school year. Eisenhower's decision led to a backlash among white Arkansans. The school board ended up closing Central High School for the entire next year. However, the action was ultimately successful. Central High School reopened in 1959 and by the 1960s became increasingly more integrated. In a larger sense, the action was successful in demonstrating the resolve of the federal government to enforce African-American civil rights in the face of massive resistance by opponents of desegregation.

Both President Washington and President Eisenhower took decisive actions in regard to crises. President Washington was eager to assert the power of the federal government in maintaining law and order. President Eisenhower was reluctant to use the power of the federal government to intervene in a state issue. However, both decided to use the military to subdue challenges to the rule of law and to ensure that similar challenges did not happen in the future.

PART III: DOCUMENT-BASED QUESTION

Part A: Short Answer

Document 1a and Document 1b

1(1) Based on the two documents, one effect of the development of the West on Native American Indians was the destruction of the buffalo, which many Native American Indians depended upon.

1(2) Based on the two documents, another effect of the development of the West on Native American Indians was that many of their horses and cattle were often stolen by white settlers.

These answers receive full credit because they state two effects of the development of the West on Native American Indians.

Document 2a and Document 2b

2 One impact of westward settlement on Native American Indians was that they lost lands that had been set aside for them.

This answer receives full credit because it states one impact of westward settlement on Native American Indians.

Document 3a and Document 3b

3(1) Based on these documents, one way Native American Indians were being affected by the development of the West was that their culture was demeaned by white society as "superstitious and fanatical."

3(2) Based on these documents, another way Native American Indians were being affected by the development of the West was that Native American Indian children attending the Carlisle Indian Industrial School were forced to stop wearing traditional clothes and began to dress like whites.

These answers receive full credit because they state two ways Native American Indians were being affected by the development of the West.

Document 4

4 According to Frederic L. Paxson, one effect of westward development on frontier women living in the West was that they had to work very hard in difficult conditions to provide for the varied necessities of life for their families.

This answer receives full credit because it states one effect of westward development on frontier women living in the West.

Document 5

5 According to James S. Foster, one opportunity the development of the West offered to women was that it made land available for single women to obtain a homestead and to engage in farming.

This answer receives full credit because it states one opportunity the development of the West offered to women.

Document 6

6(1) According to the circular, one benefit of granting suffrage to women in Wyoming was that women teachers were getting paid at the same rate as male teachers.

6(2) According to the circular, another benefit of granting suffrage to women in Wyoming was that young girls were safer in Wyoming than they were in any of the other states in the United States.

These answers receive full credit because they state two benefits of granting suffrage to women in Wyoming.

Document 7

7(1) According to Liping Zhu, one way living in the West affected Chinese immigrants was that they were very successful in mining operations, establishing several very profitable mining operations.

7(2) According to Liping Zhu, another way living in the West affected Chinese immigrants was that they experienced legal discrimination and ethnic violence.

These answers receive full credit because they state two ways living in the West affected Chinese immigrants.

Document 8a and Document 8b

8(1) Based on the two documents, one opportunity the development of the West offered to Chinese immigrants was starting successful laundry businesses.

8(2) Based on the two documents, another opportunity the development of the West offered to Chinese immigrants was purchasing land and developing successful agricultural enterprises.

These answers receive full credit because they state two opportunities the development of the West offered to Chinese immigrants.

Document 9

9 According to Rodman W. Paul, one reason for opposition to Chinese immigration in San Francisco was that Chinese immigrants competed for jobs with white immigrant groups that had previously moved to the region.

This answer receives full credit because it states one reason for opposition to Chinese immigration in San Francisco.

Part B: Document-Based Essay

The development of the West in the late 19th and early 20th centuries was profoundly important for the United States as a whole. Two particular groups that were affected by the development of the West were women and Chinese immigrants. Both groups experienced political, economic, and social changes in the growing region of the West. For both groups, the West provided challenges as well as opportunities. Women worked extremely hard on the western frontier but were also able to achieve economic and political progress. Chinese immigrants suffered discrimination and violence in the West but were also able to achieve a great deal of economic success.

In the late 19th and early 20th centuries, hundreds of thousands of settlers made their way to the West. A variety of economic opportunities drew people to the West, including building railroads, mining, logging, farming, and ranching. Migrants to the West hoped to achieve a degree of self-sufficiency and independence. The Homestead Act of 1862 also drew settlers to the West. The act granted people up to 160 acres as an enticement for moving west. The populations of Minnesota, the Dakotas, Kansas, and Nebraska all grew dramatically between the end of the Civil War and 1900: from 300,000 to five million.

Life on the frontier demanded great physical efforts by both men and women. In more settled communities back east, middle-class women of the 19th century were expected to play a secondary, domestic role. Men were expected to compete in the rough-and-tumble public realm of business and politics. Women, though, were expected to tend to the children and create a moral, Christian setting in the home to aid the children's development. In the West, women had far greater responsibilities. They were expected to grow, store, and prepare food. Women were expected to be the "butcher, packer, and baker." Further, they were expected to create all of the family's clothing—to knit, to sew, and to treat animal pelts. Women, of course, bore children. The demands of frontier life and of childbirth, in conditions that were rudimentary and often unsanitary, took their toll on women. Women often died much earlier in life than men did. Grave markers from the frontier era often indicate that the adult male in a family was often buried with a second, third, or fourth wife. (Document 4)

The West in the late 19th century was physically demanding and often dangerous to the health of women, but it also offered opportunities for them. Under the Homestead Act, widowed and unmarried women over the age of 21 could apply for homesteads. An 1870 account of life in the Dakota Territory by the territory's Commissioner of Immigration notes approvingly the large number of women who acquired their own homesteads. The account points to women who came to the territory penniless and eventually became successful farmers. (Document 5)

The importance of women's contributions to the success of homesteads in the West—either as part of a family unit or on their own—bolstered arguments for greater political equality for women. "We, of Dakota, believe in Women's Rights," the Commissioner of Immigration for the Dakota Territory asserted in 1870. (Document 5) A 1910 description of the benefits of women voting in Wyoming noted that 41 years earlier, in 1869, Wyoming had granted women full voting rights. (Document 6) Other states in the West followed suit—Colorado in 1893 and both Utah and Idaho in 1896. Women not only attained the vote in western states, but they shaped politics in those states as well. In Wyoming, for instance, female voters helped assure that the principle of "equal pay for equal work" was applied to female and male teachers in the state. Wyoming also had a lower rate of illiteracy than other states and less divorce than other states. (Document 6) The spread of woman's suffrage in the West paved the way for the ratification of the 19th Amendment in 1920, preventing any state from denying the vote to women.

Chinese immigrants also settled in the West. Chinese immigrants were initially drawn to North America by the gold rush in California in 1849. By 1852, more than 20,000 Chinese immigrants had moved to the United States. By 1860, over 34,000 lived in California alone. The initial rush of gold seekers partook in placer mining—looking for pieces of gold in streambeds and near the surface, as opposed to hard rock mining, which extracts veins of precious minerals from solid rock well beneath the surface. Placer mining generally requires little initial capital. By 1860, Chinese immigrants had most of the placer mining claims in California. They continued to have success and by the 1870s, owned several prominent mining companies throughout the West. (Document 7)

In addition to mining, Chinese immigrants experienced success in several other fields. Thousands of Chinese workers helped complete the first transcontinental railroad in 1869, representing 90 percent of the workforce. In addition to railroad work, Chinese immigrants gravitated to the laundry business. The Chinese laundry became an "institution" in San Francisco and in small towns throughout the West. Chinese laundries were able to offer services at lower prices than were standard at the time, charging $5 instead of $8 to do a basket of laundry. (Document 8a) Chinese immigrants also excelled at agriculture. Many Chinese immigrants had worked in agriculture in the Pearl River Delta in China. They brought knowledge of agricultural techniques with them to America. They were a "vital factor" in shifting the agricultural base of California from wheat to fruit. (Document 8b)

Chinese immigrants faced a great deal of discrimination and outright hostility. Many Chinese abandoned placer mining as the industry became more large scale and industrial. They moved to cities to seek work there. The timing of this move was "unfortunate." When the economy suffered a major downturn in the 1870s following the Panic of 1873, many Californians singled out the Chinese population as the cause of the crisis. Many labeled Chinese residents as coolie labor and insisted that their presence in California depressed wages. The Workingmen's Party was formed in 1876 to argue for legislation excluding Chinese immigrants from the United States. (Document 9) This activism, coming as Reconstruction was ending in the South, proved to be successful. Federal naturalization laws, which were altered after the Civil War to accommodate African Americans, denied citizenship to Asian immigrants. The 1882 Chinese Exclusion Act excluded most Chinese from entrance into the United States. It represents the only instance in which legislation has explicitly denied a particular national group entrance into the United States.

The development of the western portion of the United States affected different groups in dramatically different ways. Mexicans who had lived in the area of the Mexican Cession (1848) were often dispossessed of their land by white settlers. In addition, Native-American Indian lands were greatly reduced. In 1867, Congress passed legislation to force Native American Indians onto reservations and make them wards of the government until they learned "to walk on the white man's road." Native Americans resisted this effort, and a series of bloody battles ensued between Native American Indians and U.S. troops. By 1890, the last resistance was subdued when the military defeated the Sioux at Wounded Knee Creek, South Dakota. Women and Chinese immigrants both faced hardships, but they also found opportunities in the West. Both married and single women were able to assume a greater degree of independence and political power than they had in the East. Chinese immigrants to the West faced hostility and discrimination, but they also found economic opportunity in a number of pursuits. The development of the West greatly altered the political, social, and economic lives of a wide variety of people.

Topic	Question Numbers	Number of Points
American political history	6, 13, 14, 15, 18, 36, 39, 40 44, 46	12
Political theory	5, 9	2
Economic theory/policy	2, 19, 21, 22, 29, 42	7
Constitutional principles	7, 8, 10, 11, 25, 49	7
American foreign policy	3, 20, 24, 30, 31, 32, 34, 35, 37, 45, 47, 50	14
American studies— the American people	4, 16, 17, 23, 28, 33, 38, 43, 48	12
Social/cultural developments	26	1
Geography	1, 12, 41	4
Skills questions included in the above content areas		
Reading comprehension	5, 8, 10, 20, 21, 37, 49	
Graph/table interpretation	16, 17	
Cartoon/image interpretation	24, 25, 39, 40, 41, 44	
Cause-effect relationship	32	
Distinguishing fact from opinion	43	

PART I

Multiple-Choice Questions by Standard

Standard	Question Numbers
1—United States and New York History	3, 4, 10, 13, 14, 15, 17, 18, 20, 24, 26, 28, 31, 32, 33, 36, 37, 39, 41, 43, 45, 47
2—World History	30, 34, 35, 50
3—Geography	1, 12, 16, 27, 48
4—Economics	2, 19, 21, 22, 29, 42
5—Civics, Citizenship, and Government	5, 6, 7, 8, 9, 11, 23, 25, 38, 40, 44, 46, 49

Parts II and III by Theme and Standard

	Theme	Standards
Thematic Essay	Presidential Decisions and Actions; Constitutional Principles; Government; Foreign Policy; Diversity; Citizenship	Standards 1, 2, 3, 4, and 5: US and NY History; World History; Geography; Economics; Civics, Citizenship, and Government
Document-based Essay	Places and Regions; Immigration and Migration; Environment; Citizenship; Government; Foreign Policy; Diversity	Standards 1, 3, 4, and 5: US and NY History; Geography; Economics; Civics, Citizenship, and Government

Examination June 2018
United States History and Government

PART I: MULTIPLE CHOICE

Directions (1–50): For each statement or question, write in the space provided the *number* of the word or expression that, of those given, best completes the statement or answers the question.

1 What was a main reason large plantations developed in the South during the colonial period?

(1) British laws promoted the growth of slavery in the South.
(2) Cotton could only be grown in wetlands.
(3) Southern mountains led to the development of isolated, self-sufficient farms.
(4) The climate in the South provided longer growing seasons.   1 ____

2 In the 1780s, the national government under the Articles of Confederation established its authority in the Northwest Territory by

(1) providing a system for the formation of new states
(2) settling the border dispute with Mexico
(3) extending the nation's border to the Rocky Mountains
(4) rejecting Native American Indian claims of sovereignty   2 ____

3 A fundamental principle of a republican form of government is that

(1) hereditary rulers are the legitimate possessors of political power
(2) legislation must be passed by the elected representatives of the people
(3) laws should be created directly by the citizens
(4) governments are not responsible for protecting individual rights   3 _____

4 What was a major argument used by the Antifederalists to oppose ratifying the Constitution?

(1) Congress was given the power to tax exports.
(2) The executive branch lacked the power to maintain order.
(3) The proposed Constitution contained no bill of rights.
(4) Only the national government could coin money.   4 _____

5 The judicial branch of government can check the legislative branch of government by

(1) vetoing bills passed by Congress
(2) declaring laws unconstitutional
(3) calling special sessions of Congress
(4) reducing congressional budgets   5 _____

6 "…Because finally, 'the equal right of every citizen to the free exercise of his Religion according to the dictates of conscience' is held by the same tenure with all our other rights. If we recur to [go to] its origin, it is equally the gift of nature; …"

— James Madison

The belief expressed in this statement was put into law by the

(1) signing of the Mayflower Compact
(2) creation of the Articles of Confederation
(3) establishment of a federal system of government
(4) addition of the first amendment to the United States Constitution   6 _____

7 "…To make all Laws which shall be necessary and proper for carrying into Execution the foregoing Powers, and all other Powers vested by this Constitution in the Government of the United States, or in any Department or Officer thereof."

— Article I, Section 8,
United States Constitution

This clause was used by Secretary of the Treasury Alexander Hamilton to justify

(1) establishing the Bank of the United States
(2) creating a federal postal system
(3) sending troops to end the Whiskey Rebellion
(4) imposing an embargo on trade with Great Britain   7 ____

Base your answers to questions 8 and 9 on the map below and on your knowledge of social studies.

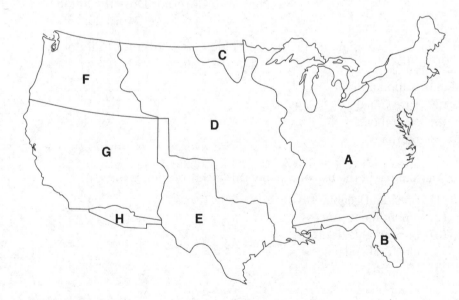

8 Which two areas of the map made up the United States in 1803 as a result of the Louisiana Purchase?

(1) *A* and *B*
(2) *A* and *D*
(3) *B* and *D*
(4) *E* and *G*   8 ____

9 Which of these areas was acquired as a result of the Mexican-American War?

(1) A
(2) B
(3) F
(4) G

9 _____

Base your answer to question 10 on the quotation below and on your knowledge of social studies.

"...As a bond of union between the Atlantic and the western states, it may prevent the dismemberment of the American empire. As an organ of communication between the Hudson, the Mississippi, the St. Lawrence, the great lakes of the north and west, and their tributary rivers, it will create the greatest inland trade ever witnessed...."

— New York Governor DeWitt Clinton,
April 26, 1824

10 Which development in transportation is Governor Clinton describing?

(1) National Road
(2) Erie Canal
(3) steamboats
(4) railroads

10 _____

11 An example of the use of the unwritten constitution is the

(1) president's cabinet
(2) amendment process
(3) bicameral legislature
(4) electoral college

11 _____

Base your answer to question 12 on the chart below and on your knowledge of social studies.

Resources of the North and South, 1861

Resources	North		South	
	Number (approximate)	Percent of National Total	Number (approximate)	Percent of National Total
Farmland	105,817,694 acres	65%	56,832,154 acres	35%
Railroad Track	21,847 miles	71%	8,947 miles	29%
Value of Manufactured Goods	$1,794,417,000	92%	$155,531,281	8%
Factories	119,500	85%	20,631	15%
Workers in Industry	1,198,000	92%	110,721	8%
Population	22,340,000 (includes 432,720 enslaved persons)	63%	9,103,332 (includes 3,521,043 enslaved persons)	37%

Source: James West Davidson et al., *The American Nation*, Prentice Hall, 2000; 1860 Census, U.S. Census Bureau (adapted)

12 Which generalization is supported by the information in the chart?

(1) The South exported more manufactured goods than the North.

(2) The North would have more difficulty supplying an army than the South.

(3) The North had greater economic strength than the South.

(4) The South would be better able to transport an army than the North.

12 _____

Base your answer to question 13 on the poster below and on your knowledge of social studies.

TO COLORED MEN!

FREEDOM,
Protection, Pay, and a Call to Military Duty!

Source: National Archives

13 Which government action most directly prompted the publication of this poster?

(1) issuance of the Emancipation Proclamation
(2) passage of the Kansas-Nebraska Act
(3) rejection of the Wilmot Proviso
(4) adoption of the Missouri Compromise

13 _____

14 At the start of the Civil War, President Abraham Lincoln stated that the major reason for fighting the war was to

(1) break the South's economic ties to Great Britain
(2) uphold the Constitution by preserving the Union
(3) enforce the terms of the Compromise of 1850
(4) punish the Confederate states for leaving the Union

14 _____

15 Passage of the Homestead Act in 1862 encouraged settlement of the Great Plains by

(1) providing free land to farmers
(2) removing barriers to Asian immigration
(3) supplying land to build transcontinental railroads
(4) placing Native American Indians on reservations

15 _____

16 Which heading best completes the partial outline below?

> I. _____
>
> A. Freedmen's Bureau
> B. Passage of the 14th amendment
> C. Military occupation of the South

  (1) Development of States Rights
  (2) Results of Manifest Destiny
  (3) Elements of Reconstruction
  (4) Limits on Civil Rights   16 _____

17 Between 1865 and 1900, how did the growth of industry affect American society?

  (1) Trade with other nations declined.
  (2) Business leaders called for lower tariffs.
  (3) The urban population increased.
  (4) Corporations supported the growth of labor unions.   17 _____

18 The federal government reacted to the Supreme Court's ruling in *Wabash, St. Louis & Pacific Railway Co.* v. *Illinois* (1886) by

  (1) passing the Interstate Commerce Act
  (2) weakening the influence of banks over big business
  (3) abandoning the government's attempts to break up monopolies
  (4) encouraging railroad employees to form unions   18 _____

19 In the late 1800s, the corporation became an important form of business organization primarily because it

  (1) had closer ties with its employees
  (2) could raise large amounts of investment capital
  (3) made better quality products
  (4) called for conservation of natural resources   19 _____

Base your answer to question 20 on the passage below and on your knowledge of social studies.

…The object of the amendment was undoubtedly to enforce the absolute equality of the two races before the law, but, in the nature of things, it could not have been intended to abolish distinctions based upon color, or to enforce social, as distinguished from political, equality, or a commingling of the two races upon terms unsatisfactory to either. Laws permitting, and even requiring, their separation in places where they are liable to be brought into contact do not necessarily imply the inferiority of either race to the other, and have been generally, if not universally, recognized as within the competency of the state legislatures in the exercise of their police power. The most common instance of this is connected with the establishment of separate schools for white and colored [African American] children, which has been held to be a valid exercise of the legislative power even by courts of States where the political rights of the colored race have been longest and most earnestly enforced.…

— United States Supreme Court, 1896

20 In this 1896 decision, the Supreme Court upheld the constitutionality of

(1) the Three-fifths Compromise
(2) Jim Crow laws
(3) affirmative action programs
(4) racial integration   20 _____

Base your answer to question 21 on the cartoon below and on your knowledge of social studies.

The News Reaches Bogota

Source: W. A. Rogers, *New York Herald*, December 1903

21 The foreign policy illustrated in this cartoon was used by the United States to

(1) punish Mexico for siding with Germany in World War I
(2) enforce the Monroe Doctrine against Great Britain
(3) secure control of land for the Panama Canal Zone
(4) announce the Open Door policy

21 _____

Base your answer to question 22 on the poster below and on your knowledge of social studies.

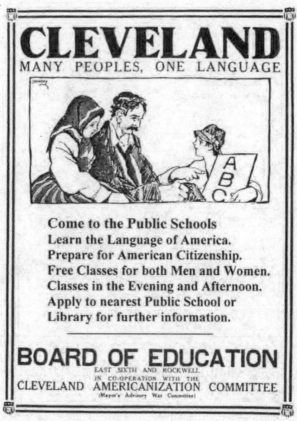

Source: J. H. Donahey, Smithsonian National Museum of American History, 1917 (adapted)

22 This 1917 poster indicates that one important educational goal for new immigrants during this time period was

(1) teaching them to read and write in their native language
(2) promoting religious tolerance
(3) ensuring the preservation of their native cultures
(4) promoting the English language as a method of assimilation   22 ____

23 The United States became directly involved in World War I as a result of Germany's

(1) negotiation of an alliance with Russia
(2) threat to spread the war to the Middle East
(3) resumption of unrestricted submarine warfare
(4) acquisition of new African colonies   23 _____

24 Progressivism was an early 20th-century movement that promoted

(1) limited war to spread social justice to other countries
(2) increased immigration to diversify the nation's population
(3) colonialism to increase United States power throughout the world
(4) government actions to correct political, economic, and social problems   24 _____

25 Which government action is directly related to the "clear and present danger" doctrine established in *Schenck* v. *United States* (1919)?

(1) limiting the first amendment rights of antiwar protesters
(2) rejecting membership in the League of Nations
(3) banning immigration from western Europe
(4) passage of the Prohibition amendment   25 _____

26 Hosting the Washington Naval Disarmament Conference (1921) and signing the Kellogg-Briand Pact (1928) were efforts by the United States to

(1) form new military alliances
(2) increase its military preparedness
(3) avoid future wars
(4) collect payment for war debts   26 _____

27 The Harlem Renaissance of the 1920s is best known for

(1) ending racial segregation in public facilities
(2) promoting the cultural creativity of African Americans
(3) encouraging passage of new voting rights legislation
(4) supporting legislation to eliminate the Ku Klux Klan   27 _____

28 Which factor best accounts for the affordability of Ford Model T automobiles in the 1920s?

(1) the efficiencies created by the assembly line
(2) the expertise of individual craftsmanship
(3) strong support from labor unions
(4) low taxes and government subsidies

28 _____

Base your answers to questions 29 and 30 on the statements below and on your knowledge of social studies.

...The ever-growing complexity of modern life, with its train of evermore perplexing and difficult problems, is a challenge to our individual characters and to our devotion to our ideals. The resourcefulness of America when challenged has never failed. Success is not gained by leaning upon government to solve all the problems before us. That way leads to enervation [lessening] of will and destruction of character. Victory over this depression and over our other difficulties will be won by the resolution of our people to fight their own battles in their own communities, by stimulating their ingenuity to solve their own problems, by taking new courage to be masters of their own destiny in the struggle of life....

— President Herbert Hoover,
February 12, 1931

...I am prepared under my constitutional duty to recommend the measures that a stricken Nation in the midst of a stricken world may require. These measures, or such other measures as the Congress may build out of its experience and wisdom, I shall seek, within my constitutional authority, to bring to speedy adoption....

— President Franklin D. Roosevelt,
March 4, 1933

29 Which idea would best be supported by President Hoover's statement?

(1) rugged individualism
(2) unemployment insurance
(3) deficit spending
(4) collective bargaining

29 _____

30 These statements illustrate a difference in opinion between the two presidents over

   (1) granting subsidies to big business
   (2) promoting free-trade policies in the Western Hemisphere
   (3) regulating supply and demand
   (4) expanding the federal government's role in the economy   30 _____

31 Which problem did Franklin D. Roosevelt address *first* in his presidency?

   (1) ending the Red Scare
   (2) standing up to dictators in Europe
   (3) bringing stability to the banking system
   (4) approving bonus payments to World War I veterans   31 _____

32 **"National Defense at Any Expense, but Keep Our Boys at Home."**

This 1941 slogan of the America First Committee promoted

   (1) globalism
   (2) protective tariffs
   (3) isolationism
   (4) reduced military spending   32 _____

Base your answers to questions 33 and 34 on the cartoon below and on your knowledge of social studies.

And He Doesn't Mean Maybe!

Source: Jim Berryman, *Washington Evening Star*, January 1943 (adapted)

33 What is the main idea of the cartoon?

(1) United States factories will not be able to manufacture military supplies in sufficient quantities.

(2) The federal government will most likely need to seize ownership of manufacturing plants.

(3) President Franklin D. Roosevelt expects other nations to supply the same amount of armaments as the United States.

(4) President Franklin D. Roosevelt is determined to supply the United States military and its allies with whatever it takes to defeat the Axis powers.

33 _____

34 One major result of the production efforts described in the cartoon was that

(1) the high unemployment of the Great Depression was greatly reduced
(2) most companies that produced military supplies went out of business after the war
(3) critics claimed that President Franklin D. Roosevelt was abusing his treaty-making power
(4) the military had difficulty enlisting soldiers because the men were working in the munitions factories

34 ____

Base your answer to question 35 on the newspaper headlines below and on your knowledge of social studies.

Source: *Pittsburgh Courier*, April 19, 1947 (adapted)

35 Which conclusion can be drawn from an examination of these 1947 newspaper headlines concerning Jackie Robinson?

(1) Robinson's integration of major league baseball was an important event in the history of civil rights.

(2) Robinson went on to organize the civil rights movement.

(3) Sports fans overwhelmingly encouraged the desegregation of public accommodations.

(4) Robinson's major league debut had no impact on race relations in the United States.

35 _____

"...From Stettin in the Baltic to Trieste in the Adriatic, an iron curtain has descended across the Continent...."

— Winston Churchill, March 5, 1946

36 With this observation, Winston Churchill warned the United States that Europe was threatened by

(1) an embargo of its Middle East oil supplies
(2) the growth of fascism in Great Britain
(3) the expansion of communism in Eastern Europe
(4) a nuclear attack by the Soviet Union   36 _____

37 The North Atlantic Treaty Organization (NATO) and the Warsaw Pact are examples of

(1) dollar diplomacy
(2) Lend-Lease
(3) mutual defense
(4) Manifest Destiny   37 _____

38 Belief in the domino theory by presidents Dwight D. Eisenhower, John F. Kennedy, and Lyndon B. Johnson directly influenced their decisions to

(1) reject the policy of collective security
(2) support a return to neutrality
(3) end the Berlin airlift
(4) increase United States military involvement in Vietnam   38 _____

39 The War on Poverty was an attempt by President Lyndon B. Johnson to

(1) send medical aid to African nations
(2) strengthen the Peace Corps
(3) decrease the number of immigrants from Latin America
(4) raise the standard of living for many Americans   39 _____

Base your answer to question 40 on the passage below and on your knowledge of social studies.

...You express a great deal of anxiety over our willingness to break laws. This is certainly a legitimate concern. Since we so diligently urge people to obey the Supreme Court's decision of 1954 outlawing segregation in the public schools, it is rather strange and paradoxical to find us consciously breaking laws. One may well ask, "how can you advocate breaking some laws and obeying others?" The answer is found in the fact that there are two types of laws: There are *just* and there are *unjust* laws. I would agree with Saint Augustine that "An unjust law is no law at all." ...

— Martin Luther King Jr.
"Letter from Birmingham Jail," April 16, 1963

40 Which approach best represents the argument made in the passage?

(1) civil disobedience
(2) armed resistance
(3) Black Power
(4) containment

40 _____

41 A main goal of President Richard Nixon's policy of détente was to

(1) sponsor free elections in North Korea
(2) negotiate an end to the Arab-Israeli conflict
(3) end diplomatic relations with China
(4) reduce tensions between the United States and the Soviet Union

41 _____

42 Which charges led to President Bill Clinton's impeachment?

(1) excessive use of the pardon power
(2) perjury and obstruction of justice
(3) illegal use of campaign funds
(4) misuse of war powers and deficit spending

42 _____

43 One way in which Social Security, Medicare, and Medicaid are similar is that they are all

  (1) programs that provide aid to education
  (2) examples of social welfare programs
  (3) attempts to balance the federal budget
  (4) aspects of public works projects   43 _____

Base your answer to question 44 on the cartoon below and on your knowledge of social studies.

Source: Jim Morin, *Miami Herald*, July 21, 2006

44 This cartoonist is critical of the leadership of President George W. Bush and Vice President Richard B. Cheney for

  (1) supporting the clear-cutting of forests
  (2) overusing the presidential veto power
  (3) weakening the system of checks and balances
  (4) waging the war in Iraq   44 _____

45 Which presidential action was most consistent with the ideas presented by President George Washington in his Farewell Address?

  (1) President James Monroe's proclamation of the Monroe Doctrine in 1823

  (2) President James Polk's policy toward Mexico in 1846

  (3) President William McKinley's request for a declaration of war against Spain in 1898

  (4) President George H. W. Bush's decision to engage in the Persian Gulf War in 1990   45 _____

46 The Populist movement of the 1890s and the civil rights movement of the 1950s and 1960s are similar in that both movements were attempts to

  (1) restrict the power of the executive branch

  (2) solve the problems brought about by industrialization

  (3) improve the lives of groups who were oppressed

  (4) require state governments to promote racial equality   46 _____

Base your answer to question 47 on the cartoon below and on your knowledge of social studies.

"You Read Books, Eh?"

Source: Herblock, *Washington Post* (adapted)

47 The tactics illustrated in the cartoon were most closely associated with

(1) isolationists supporting neutrality policies during the 1930s
(2) government leaders investigating communist activities after World War II
(3) increased federal spending for education during the 1960s
(4) Congress promoting increased security after the September 11, 2001 attacks

47 _____

48 "Flappers" in the 1920s, "beatniks" in the 1950s, and "hippies" in the 1960s are all examples of

(1) political groups who wanted to limit individual civil rights
(2) citizens who wanted to return to simpler lifestyles
(3) writers who supported United States foreign policy goals
(4) individuals who disagreed with traditional societal values   48 _____

49 The Great Depression and the economic crisis known as the Great Recession (December 2007– June 2009) were similar in that both led to

(1) a surplus in the federal budget
(2) a decrease in federal support for unemployment insurance
(3) a limit on the power of the Federal Reserve System
(4) an expansion of the federal government's role in stabilizing the economy   49 _____

Base your answer to question 50 on the map below and on your knowledge of social studies.

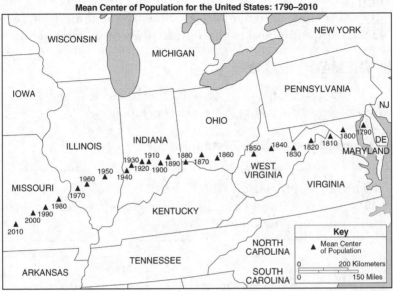

Mean Center of Population for the United States: 1790–2010

Source: U.S. Department of Commerce, Economics and Statistics Administration, U.S. Census Bureau (adapted)

50 What has been the principal cause of the population changes shown on the map?

(1) employment opportunities in northeastern states
(2) continued westward migration
(3) enactment of immigration quotas
(4) movement from farms to cities   50 _____

In developing your answer to Part II, be sure to keep these general definitions in mind:

(a) <u>describe</u> means "to illustrate something in words or tell about it"
(b) <u>discuss</u> means "to make observations about something using facts, reasoning, and argument; to present in some detail"

PART II: THEMATIC ESSAY

Directions: Write a well-organized essay that includes an introduction, several paragraphs addressing the task below, and a conclusion.

Theme: Geography—Territorial Acquisition

> Throughout the nation's history, the United States has expanded through the acquisition of new territories. These acquisitions have had both positive and negative effects on the United States.

Task:

> Select *two* territories acquired by the United States and for *each*
>
> • Describe the historical circumstances that led the United States to acquire the territory
> • Discuss *positive and/or negative* effects of the acquisition of the territory on the United States

You may use any territory acquired by the United States since 1776 from your study of United States history. Some suggestions you might wish to consider include the Ohio River valley (1783), the Louisiana Territory (1803), Florida (1819), Texas (1845), the Oregon Territory (1846), California (1848), Alaska (1867), Hawaii (1898), Puerto Rico (1899), and the Philippines (1899).

You are *not* limited to these suggestions.

Guidelines:

In your essay, be sure to:

• Develop all aspects of the task
• Support the theme with relevant facts, examples, and details
• Use a logical and clear plan of organization, including an introduction and a conclusion that are beyond a restatement of the theme

In developing your answers to Part III, be sure to keep these general definitions in mind:

(c) <u>describe</u> means "to illustrate something in words or tell about it"

(d) <u>discuss</u> means "to make observations about something using facts, reasoning, and argument; to present in some detail"

PART III: DOCUMENT-BASED QUESTION

This question is based on the accompanying documents. The question is designed to test your ability to work with historical documents. Some of these documents have been edited for the purposes of this question. As you analyze the documents, take into account the source of each document and any point of view that may be presented in the document. Keep in mind that the language used in a document may reflect the historical context of the time in which it was written.

Historical Context:

Throughout United States history, individuals have used written works as a way to focus attention on issues facing American society. These written works have had a significant influence on the United States and American society. These written works include **Common Sense** by **Thomas Paine**, **Uncle Tom's Cabin** by **Harriet Beecher Stowe**, and **The Jungle** by **Upton Sinclair**.

Task:

Using the information from the documents and your knowledge of United States history, answer the questions that follow each document in Part A. Your answers to the questions will help you write the Part B essay in which you will be asked to

Choose **two** written works mentioned in the historical context and for **each**

- Describe the historical circumstances surrounding the issue addressed by the author
- Discuss the influence of the written work on the United States and/or on American society

Part A: Short-Answer Questions

Directions: Analyze the documents and answer the short-answer questions that follow each document in the space provided.

Document 1

In 1768 John Dickinson of Pennsylvania argued for a new colonial theory which limited the power of Parliament over the colonies.

> ...Then events in due course pushed the colonial theory [of limited Parliamentary power] to a final stage. Thomas Paine's *Common Sense*, appearing in January 1776, tore every shred of authority from both King and Parliament. The two years or so preceding had piled crisis upon crisis. The Bostonians had sunk the tea; Parliament had retorted with the Intolerable Acts; the First Continental Congress had instituted a program of intercolonial economic resistance; war had erupted on Lexington Green; and an American army under the Second Congress had shut up [surrounded] General Gage and his regulars in Boston. In stirring and violent rhetoric the English-born Paine, who had recently settled in Philadelphia with a heart full of rancor for his native land, addressed the emotions as well as the minds of his readers. The "period of debate is closed," he concluded, "'TIS TIME TO PART." Although a half year was to elapse before Congress complied, Paine's trumpet call was a mighty factor in influencing the public as well as the delegates themselves to adopt the fateful step. No other work written in America, save perhaps *Uncle Tom's Cabin*, has ever had such crucial repercussions....

Source: Arthur M. Schlesinger, *The Birth of the Nation*, Houghton Mifflin, 1968

1 According to Arthur M. Schlesinger, what were *two* events that motivated Thomas Paine to write *Common Sense*? [2]

(1) _____

(2) _____

Document 2

> ... Paine published *Common Sense* in Philadelphia, and his Forester essays* first appeared in that city's newspapers. His friends also chose Philadelphia newspapers, and so did his political enemies. But since the controversy involved the "continent," *Common Sense* was reprinted in all the major American cities and the minor ones as well. Of course the debate spread, drawing in big men, John Adams, for example, and small ones as well. Within a few months over 100,000 copies of *Common Sense* had appeared, and the debates between independence and reconciliation dominated the newspapers.
>
> A part of the common sense offered by Thomas Paine was the observation that Britain's old enemies in Europe would be more likely to provide support to the colonies if they declared their independence. No European power wanted to meddle in an internal dispute which might be settled by Britain and her colonies joining forces, as they had in the past, against an external enemy. Declaring independence would reassure Europe, reassure in particular France, the nation that some in Congress looked to for money and arms....

Source: Robert Middlekauff, *The Glorious Cause: The American Revolution,*
1763–1789, Oxford University Press, 2005 (adapted)

2 According to Robert Middlekauff, what is **one** way Thomas Paine's *Common Sense* promoted support for independence? [1]

_____

_____

Document 3

...There is an exaltation, an excitement, about *Common Sense* that conveys the very uncommon sense of adventure Americans felt as they moved toward independence. With it would come new perils, but also new opportunities, new freedoms. They knew they were on the threshold of a great experience not only for themselves but perhaps for the whole world. "The cause of America," Paine told them, "is in a great measure the cause of all mankind." And they believed him.

On May 15, 1776, the Virginia House of Burgesses voted to instruct its delegates in Congress to propose independence, and on the same day the Congress adopted a resolution sponsored by John Adams, advising the various colonies to assume complete powers of government within themselves. On June 7 Richard Henry Lee, following the instructions of his Virginia constituents, moved a resolution formally declaring the colonies independent. On July 2 this resolution was adopted and two days later the famous declaration to the world, drafted by Thomas Jefferson....

Source: Edmund S. Morgan, *The Birth of the Republic, 1763–89,*
Fourth Edition, The University of Chicago Press, 2013

3 According to Edmund S. Morgan, what was *one* effect of Thomas Paine's *Common Sense*? [1]

_____

_____

Document 4

...Among the provisions of the Compromise of 1850 were the end of the slave trade, but not slavery, in Washington D.C., and the creation of a new, stricter, Fugitive Slave Law. Helping runaways had been illegal since 1793, but the 1850 law required that everyone, law enforcers and ordinary citizens, help catch fugitives. Those who refused to assist slave-catchers, or aided fugitives, could be fined up to $1,000 and jailed for six months.

It also eliminated what little legal protection fugitives once had. Before 1850, some northern states had required slave-catchers to appear before an elected judge and be tried by a jury which would determine the validity of a claim. After the 1850 Fugitive Slave Law, anyone could be taken from the street, accused of being a fugitive from slavery, and taken before a federally appointed commissioner who received $5 for every fugitive released and $10 for every one sent south. Free blacks and anti-slavery groups argued the system bribed commissioners to send kidnapped people into slavery, and obliged citizens to participate in the slavery system.

[Harriet Beecher] Stowe was furious. She believed the country was requiring her complicity in a system she thought was unjust and immoral. Living in Brunswick, ME [Maine] while Calvin Stowe taught at Bowdoin College, Stowe disobeyed the law by hiding runaways. When she shared her frustrations and feelings of powerlessness with her family, her sister-in-law Isabella Porter Beecher suggested she do more: "...if I could use a pen as you can, Hatty, I would write something that would make this whole nation feel what an accursed thing slavery is."

Moved by the letter, Stowe swore she would "if [she] lived."...

Source: Harriet Beecher Stowe Center, 2011

4 Based on this document, why was Harriet Beecher Stowe concerned about the new Fugitive Slave Law? [1]

_____

_____

Document 5a

This poster was an advertisement for Harriet Beecher Stowe's *Uncle Tom's Cabin*.

Source: The Authentic History Center

Document 5b

...Stowe is often credited with influencing the country to think differently about slavery. But what do we know about how Stowe influenced Lincoln?

A decade earlier, *Uncle Tom's Cabin* (1852) had been a publishing and propaganda phenomenon. Using stories to illustrate the human impact of slavery, Stowe's blistering pen lit the world on fire. The statistics remain record-breaking: 10,000 copies sold in the first week; a million and a half British copies in a year. The book was so successful it was immediately dramatized for the stage, where it became a theatrical icon. Massachusetts Senator Charles Sumner, leader of the radical Republicans, said, "Had there been no *Uncle Tom's Cabin*, there would have been no Lincoln in the White House."...

But pro-slavery critics charged that Stowe had made it all up and that slavery was a humane system. So Stowe wrote a nonfiction retort, *The Key to Uncle Tom's Cabin* (1853), compiling the real-life evidence that had informed her fictional stories....

Source: Katherine Kane,
"Lincoln and *The Key to Uncle Tom's Cabin*,"
Connecticut Explored, Winter 2012/2013

5 Based on these documents, what is **one** reason Southern slave owners were concerned about the publication of *Uncle Tom's Cabin*? [1]

_____

_____

Document 6

...It is not possible to measure precisely the political influence of *Uncle Tom's Cabin*. One can quantify its sales but cannot point to votes that it changed or laws that it inspired. Yet few contemporaries doubted its power. "Never was there such a literary *coup-de-main* [sudden attack] as this," said Henry Wadsworth Longfellow. In England, Lord Palmerston, who as prime minister a decade later would face a decision whether to intervene on behalf of the South in the Civil War, read *Uncle Tom's Cabin* three times and admired it not so much for the story as "for the statesmanship of it." As Abraham Lincoln was grappling with the problem of slavery in the summer of 1862, he borrowed from the Library of Congress *A Key to Uncle Tom's Cabin*, a subsequent volume by Stowe containing documentation on which she had based the novel. When Lincoln met the author later that year, he reportedly greeted her with the words: "So you're the little woman who wrote the book that made this great war."

Uncle Tom's Cabin struck a raw nerve in the South. Despite efforts to ban it, copies sold so fast in Charleston and elsewhere that booksellers could not keep up with the demand. The vehemence of southern denunciations of Mrs. Stowe's "falsehoods" and "distortions" was perhaps the best gauge of how close they hit home. "There never before was anything so detestable or so monstrous among women as this," declared the *New Orleans Crescent*. The editor of the *Southern Literary Messenger* instructed his book reviewer: "I would have the review as hot as hellfire, blasting and searing the reputation of the vile wretch in petticoats who could write such a volume." Within two years proslavery writers had answered *Uncle Tom's Cabin* with at least fifteen novels whose thesis that slaves were better off than free workers in the North was capsulized by the title of one of them: *Uncle Robin in His Cabin in Virginia and Tom Without One in Boston*. A decade later during the Civil War a South Carolina diarist with doubts of her own about slavery reflected the obsession of southerners with *Uncle Tom's Cabin* by using it as a constant benchmark to measure the realities of life in the South....

Source: James M. McPherson, *Battle Cry of Freedom: The Civil War Era*,
Oxford University Press, 1988 (adapted)

6 According to James M. McPherson, what were *two* effects of the
   publication of *Uncle Tom's Cabin*? [2]

   (1) _____

   (2) _____

Document 7

...The freedom of big business seemed limitless. Drug companies sold patent medicines containing heroin, morphine, and cocaine that promised to cure all sorts of diseases, but actually cured none of them. Food companies sold children's candy colored with toxic heavy metals. Cheap margarine was routinely marketed as butter. Crude mixtures of apple scraps, glucose, timothy seeds, and food coloring made from coal tar were sold as strawberry jam. In the age of the great trusts, the gulf between the wealthy and the poor became enormous. Robber barons built their homes in imitation of European palaces, while millions of American workers lived in urban slums.

Upton Sinclair was moved by these injustices. During the fall of 1904 he left his home in New Jersey and traveled to Chicago, intending to write a novel about the plight of the city's meatpacking workers. The beef trust controlled the industry with an iron fist. It had recently crushed a strike by union members who were seeking a pay raise of less than three cents an hour. The meatpacking industry seemed to embody everything that was wrong with American society, operating largely in secret, wielding unchecked power, threatening the health of workers and consumers. As Sinclair later argued in *The Jungle,* the beef trust was "the incarnation [representation] of blind and insensate [insensitive] greed...the Great Butcher.... the spirit of capitalism made flesh."...

Source: Eric Schlosser, Foreword to Upton Sinclair's *The Jungle*, Penguin Books, 2006

7 According to Eric Schlosser, what were **two** issues that concerned Upton Sinclair? [2]

(1) _____

(2) _____

Document 8a

... Upton Sinclair wrote "The Jungle" as a labor exposé. He hoped that the book, which was billed as "the 'Uncle Tom's Cabin' of wage slavery," would lead to improvements for the people to whom he dedicated it, "the workingmen of America." But readers of "The Jungle" were less appalled by Sinclair's accounts of horrific working conditions than by what they learned about their food. "I aimed at the public's heart," he famously declared, "and by accident I hit it in the stomach."...

When "The Jungle" was published, the public reaction was instantaneous. Outraged readers deluged President Theodore Roosevelt with letters. Roosevelt was ambivalent, but he invited Sinclair to the White House for lunch, and promised to send his labor commissioner and assistant Treasury secretary to Chicago to investigate....

Source: Adam Cohen, "100 Years Later, the Food Industry Is Still 'The Jungle'," *New York Times*, January 2, 2007

Document 8b

... By the spring of 1906, both meat inspection and pure food and drugs legislation had many supporters. This was not a simple, black-and-white fight between the public on one side and big business on the other. But the pure food and drugs issue encouraged a broad range of Americans to think of their identities as consumers, as people who were imperiled by rotten meat or adulterated drugs. Physicians, federal experts, and women's groups supported legislation. State officials, assiduously [persistently] courted by Harvey Wiley [a pioneer consumer activist], agreed that federal supervision was necessary. So did Westerners, angry at the "foreign" corporations from the East and Midwest. So, too, did more than a few of those corporations. Pabst, H. J. Heinz, and other producers, setting individualism aside, recognized the benefits of federal regulation: Washington's supervision could bring order and stability to the business; it could protect the big companies from state supervision; it could make the business too expensive for potential competitors. At the least, regulation could rescue the corporations from their public predicament in 1906. Roosevelt's investigators had largely confirmed the essentials of *The Jungle*; the meatpackers were unable to discredit Sinclair's account. Under the circumstances, a crucial group of food and drug producers accepted the inevitability of regulation and tried to shape the legislation to protect their interests as much as possible....

Source: Michael McGerr, *A Fierce Discontent: The Rise and Fall of the Progressive Movement in America, 1870–1920*, Oxford University Press, 2005

8 Based on these documents, what were **two** effects of the publication of *The Jungle*? [2]

(1) _____

(2) _____

Document 9

Upton Sinclair was present when President Lyndon B. Johnson signed legislation amending the Meat Inspection Act.

...."A man was wrapping pork shoulders. He dropped one in the sawdust, picked it up and wiped it off with a dirty, sour rag.... Beef was being broken on an open dock, by a dirt road, in 95-degree weather. There were flies in the meat. Drums of bones and meat scraps were covered with maggots."

What I just read to you was not from "The Jungle." It did not happen 60 years ago when Upton Sinclair was writing his book. It happened in July 1967. It was written by a United States Federal Government inspector after a visit to one of our great, modern packing plants....

This is an intolerable condition in the 20th century in a modern nation that prides itself on reputed leadership of the world. I have been urging and I have been asking for a strong meat inspection bill since 1964.

The Wholesome Meat Act of 1967—which has been brought to me by the good work of the Congress—will give something priceless, I think, to American housewives. It will give them assurance that the meat that they put on the dinner table for their husbands and their children is pure; that it has been packed and it has been processed in a sanitary plant....

This Wholesome Meat Act is a landmark, we think, in consumer protection. It helps every American—by assuring him that the meat his family consumes has been inspected with their health and their safety in mind....

Mr. Sinclair, we are so glad to have you here in the East Room with many of the distinguished Members of the Congress and people who are interested in this wholesome meat legislation.

This bill really crowns the crusade that you, yourself, began some 60 years ago.

We salute you, sir, and we thank you....

Source: President Lyndon B. Johnson, Remarks Upon
Signing Bill Amending the Meat Inspection Act, December 15, 1967

9 According to President Lyndon B. Johnson, what is the continuing influence of Upton Sinclair's *The Jungle*? [1]

_____

_____

Part B: Essay

Directions: Write a well-organized essay that includes an introduction, several paragraphs, and a conclusion. Use evidence from *at least* **four** documents in your essay. Support your response with relevant facts, examples, and details. Include additional outside information.

Historical Context:

> Throughout United States history, individuals have used written works as a way to focus attention on issues facing American society. These written works have had a significant influence on the United States and American society. These written works include **Common Sense by Thomas Paine**, *Uncle Tom's Cabin* **by Harriet Beecher Stowe**, and *The Jungle* **by Upton Sinclair**.

Task:

> Using the information from the documents and your knowledge of United States history, write an essay in which you
>
> Choose *two* written works mentioned in the historical context and for *each*
>
> - Describe the historical circumstances surrounding the issue addressed by the author
> - Discuss the influence of the written work on the United States and/or on American society

Guidelines:

In your essay, be sure to:

- Develop all aspects of the task
- Incorporate information from *at least* **four** documents
- Incorporate relevant outside information
- Support the theme with relevant facts, examples, and details
- Use a logical and clear plan of organization, including an introduction and a conclusion that are beyond a restatement of the theme

Answers
June 2018
United States History and Government

Answer Key

PART I

1. 4	11. 1	21. 3	31. 3	41. 4
2. 1	12. 3	22. 4	32. 3	42. 2
3. 2	13. 1	23. 3	33. 4	43. 2
4. 3	14. 2	24. 4	34. 1	44. 3
5. 2	15. 1	25. 1	35. 1	45. 1
6. 4	16. 3	26. 3	36. 3	46. 3
7. 1	17. 3	27. 2	37. 3	47. 2
8. 2	18. 1	28. 1	38. 4	48. 4
9. 4	19. 2	29. 1	39. 4	49. 4
10. 2	20. 2	30. 4	40. 1	50. 2

PART II: Thematic Essay   *See* **Answers Explained** section.

PART III: Document-Based Question   *See* **Answers Explained** section.

Answers Explained

PART I (1–50)

1. **4** A main reason large plantations developed in the South during the colonial period was that the climate of the South provided longer growing seasons. The growing season is the part of the year during which local weather conditions, such as rainfall and temperature, permit normal plant growth. Although each plant or crop has a specific growing season, the growing season of a region is usually defined as the number of days between the last frost in the spring and the first frost in the fall. The fertile soul, relatively flat land, and long growing season of the coastal regions of the South made the area ideal for large tobacco, rice, and indigo plantations. (Cotton did not become a major crop in the United States until the 1790s.) These large plantations lent themselves to the slave system of labor. In contrast, the hilly, rocky soil and shorter growing season of the northern colonies proved more suitable for smaller-scale agriculture and a more mixed economy. The smaller farms of the northern colonies were generally worked by the owner of the property and his family, with, perhaps, more people hired for planting and harvesting.

WRONG CHOICES EXPLAINED:

(1) British laws in the colonial period permitted slavery throughout the colonies. However, local geographic factors—fertile soul, relatively flat land, and a long growing season—favored the development of large plantations and slavery in the South rather than in the North.

(2) Wetlands, which are land areas saturated with water for at least part of the year, are not conducive to agriculture. Wetlands do play important roles in regard to water purification and the prevention of coastal flooding. They exist through the coastal areas of the United States.

(3) Large plantations developed in the areas of the South that were near the coast, not in the mountainous interior sections of the South. The strip of relatively flat, well-irrigated land adjacent to the coast was more favorable to large-scale agriculture. The more hilly, interior region of the South saw the development of smaller-scale farms and focused more on meeting the food needs of the local population rather than on producing staple crops.

2. **1** In the 1780s, the national government under the Articles of Confederation established its authority in the Northwest Territory by providing a system for the formation of new states. The Northwest Ordinance of 1787

provided a method for the creation of new states. It stipulated that when a territory reached 60,000 free inhabitants, it would be eligible for statehood. The law was passed during the Articles of Confederation period (1781–1788). Dealing with the land of the Northwest Territory was one of the major successes of the government under the Articles. The method for creating new states continued to be used after the Articles were replaced by the Constitution in 1789. The national government under the Articles of Confederation is often cited for its inability to resolve difficult issues. However, its actions in regard to western lands are generally seen as effective measures.

WRONG CHOICES EXPLAINED:

(2) The national government under the Articles of Confederation did not address a border dispute with Mexico. At the time that the Articles of Confederation were replaced by the Constitution (1789), the United States extended to the Mississippi River. There was no border between the United States and Mexico at that time. Later, a border dispute between the United States and Mexico contributed to the Mexican-American War (1846–1848).

(3) The national government under the Articles of Confederation did not extend the nation's border to the Rocky Mountains. At the time that the Articles of Confederation were in place (1781–1789), the United States extended to the Mississippi River. Only after the acquisition of the Louisiana Territory (1803) and the Mexican Cession (1848) did the Rocky Mountains become part of the United States.

(4) The national government under the Articles of Confederation did not directly address the issue of Native American Indian claims of sovereignty in the Northwest Territory. Settlers and Native American Indians clashed in the Northwest Territory during the 1780s, but there was no final resolution of land claims by Native American Indians.

3. **2** A fundamental principal of a republican form of government is that legislation must be passed by elected representatives of the people. In a republican form of government, the act of governing is a public affair. The Latin phrase *res publica*, from which the word "republic" is derived, means "public affair" or "public matter." Throughout history, most governments have been seen as the private concern of the rulers. In a monarchy, for example, power is often passed to an heir within the family of the monarch. A common characteristic of many republics is that elected representatives, who are supposed to reflect the will of the public, have the power to pass legislation. From its founding, the United States has adopted a republican form of government, as have the states within the United States.

WRONG CHOICES EXPLAINED:

(1) A republican form of government does not include the principle that hereditary rulers are the legitimate possessors of political power. Monarchies, on the other hand, are typically based on hereditary rulers. The United Kingdom has a constitutional monarchy. The oldest continuing hereditary monarchy is the Japanese monarchy.

(3) A republican form of government does not include the principle that laws should be created directly by the citizens. Direct democracy—in which citizens meet face-to-face to make decisions about their communities—is not widespread in the United States. The town meetings of colonial New England embodied the concept of direct democracy. Republican forms of government generally include elected representatives who have the power to pass legislation.

(4) A republican form of government does not include the principle that governments have no responsibility for protecting individual rights. Republican forms of government are generally built around a social contract in which the people agree to follow the rules of the government and the government is obligated to protect people's individual rights. This idea was put forth by John Locke in his *Two Treatises on Government*, written in the early 1690s, and in the Declaration of Independence (1776).

4. **3** A major argument used by the Antifederalists to oppose ratifying the Constitution was that the proposed Constitution contained no bill of rights. When the newly written Constitution was submitted to the states for ratification in 1787, many Americans were concerned that it would create a powerful central government that would take away the rights and liberties of the people. The Constitution itself does not devote much attention to individual rights. The opponents of the Constitution, labeled *Antifederalists*, demanded a list of individual rights that the government would not be allowed to take away. Many Antifederalists in the various states refused to support ratification of the Constitution unless such a list was added. Supporters of the Constitution, known as *Federalists*, promised to add such a list if the Antifederalists agreed to support ratification. This agreement led to the writing and ratification of the first ten amendments to the Constitution, known as the Bill of Rights.

WRONG CHOICES EXPLAINED:

(1) The Antifederalists did not express concern that Congress was given the power to tax exports. In fact, the Constitution specifically forbids Congress from taxing exports. This provision was especially important to southern states, which relied heavily on the export of various staple crops.

(2) The Antifederalists did not argue that the executive branch lacked the power to maintain order. In fact, they argued the opposite. They were concerned with the expanded powers of the executive branch in the proposed Constitution.

(4) The Antifederalists did not take issue with the fact that the Constitution stipulated that only the national government could coin money. Although Antifederalists argued that state governments should retain significant powers, they did not argue against the national government having the power to coin money.

5. **2** The judicial branch of government can check the legislative branch of government by declaring laws unconstitutional. This power, called judicial review, is one of many checks built into the system of governance in the United States. The framers of the Constitution were very conscious of the problems of a government with limitless powers. After living under the British monarchy, they came to believe that a powerful government without checks was dangerous to liberty. Therefore, the framers created a governmental system with three branches, each with the ability to check the powers of the other two. The goal was to keep the three branches in balance. Examples of this concept of checks and balances are the president's ability to veto (or reject) bills passed by Congress, the Senate's power to approve or reject presidential nominees for Supreme Court justices and ambassadors, and the Senate's power to reject or approve treaties. The primary power of the judicial branch in this system of checks and balances is judicial review. This power was established by the Supreme Court in the case of *Marbury* v. *Madison* (1803). The decision, arguably the Supreme Court's most important, established the Court's power to review laws and determine if they are consistent with the Constitution. Laws declared unconstitutional by the Court are immediately disallowed.

WRONG CHOICES EXPLAINED:
(1) The judicial branch does not have the power to veto bills passed by Congress. The vetoing of bills passed by Congress is an example of a governmental check—but it is a power of the president, not of the judiciary.

(3) The judicial branch does not have the power to call special sessions of Congress. The calling of special sessions of Congress, which occurs during periods when Congress is adjourned, is an example of a governmental check—but it is a power of the president, not of the judiciary.

(4) The judicial branch does not have the power to reduce congressional budgets. Congress has the power to establish the annual budget of the government. The president initially submits a budget request to Congress. The two branches of Congress then work out the details of the budget and write appropriations bills. Next, the two branches vote on the bills and then reconcile differences

that may exist between the House and Senate bills. Finally, these bills are presented to the president for approval.

6. **4** The belief expressed in the statement in the question was put into law by the addition of the First Amendment to the Constitution. The statement by James Madison asserts the importance of citizens having the "free exercise" of religion. Madison states that this right is no less important than any other right. The First Amendment addresses religion in two ways. First, the establishment clause prohibits the creation of an official religion in the United States. This is the basis of the separation of church and state. The First Amendment also asserts that Congress shall not prohibit the "free exercise" of religion. In other words, Congress cannot pass laws that impinge upon people's religious beliefs. In practice, it is difficult to pin down the exact meaning of this constitutional principle. The Supreme Court has been called upon over the years to attempt to interpret the principle. In *Reynolds* v. *United States* (1878), for example, the Court upheld a federal law banning polygamy, a practice common among some Mormons at the time. The Court asserted that it was permissible to ban practices, such as polygamy and human sacrifice, but that it was impermissible for the government to interfere with mere religious beliefs and opinions. Later, in *West Virginia State Board of Education* v. *Barnette* (1943), the Court upheld the rights of Jehovah's Witnesses not to salute the flag. In the 1960s, the Warren Court continued the trend toward a more expansive view of the free exercise clause. In *Sherbert* v. *Verner* (1963), the Court held that states must have a "compelling interest" to refuse to accommodate religiously motivated conduct. The case involved a Seventh-day Adventist who was denied unemployment benefits after having been fired for refusing to work on Saturdays.

WRONG CHOICES EXPLAINED:
(1) The principle of free religious exercise, advocated by James Madison in the statement in the question, was not put into law by the signing of the Mayflower Compact. The Mayflower Compact (1620) was signed over a century before Madison's birth and did not call for free religious exercise. Its references to God and Christianity presume a strict adherence to Puritan separatism, not to the free exercise of religion. The document was written and signed by the Pilgrims on board the *Mayflower* before it touched land at Plymouth, Massachusetts, in 1620. To give themselves a sense of legitimacy in an area in which they had no legal status, the Pilgrims agreed in this document to set up a government and obey its laws.
(2) The principle of free religious exercise, advocated by James Madison in the statement in the question, was not put into law by the creation of the Articles of Confederation. The Articles essentially put into writing the governing

structure that had evolved during the American Revolution. An important principle of the Articles was to preserve the independence and sovereignty of the states. The Articles did not make any provisions for the protection of religious freedom.

(3) The principle of free religious exercise, advocated by James Madison in the statement in the question, was not put into law by the establishment of a federal system of government. The term *federalism* describes the relationship among the state governments and the national government. In the governing system developed in the Constitution, powers are shared by the national government and the states. The goal is that excessive power is not concentrated in either level of government. The establishment of this system did not include provisions for the protection of religious freedom.

7. **1** Secretary of the Treasury Alexander Hamilton used the clause of the Constitution excerpted in the question to justify establishing the Bank of the United States. The clause, known as the necessary and proper clause, or the elastic clause, expands the powers of Congress. During the constitutional convention, the delegates were aware of the importance of creating a document that could meet the needs of a changing society. To meet this goal, they included the elastic clause, which stretched the powers of Congress by allowing it to "make all laws necessary and proper...." However, the definition of "necessary and proper" soon became a matter of much debate. Alexander Hamilton pushed for the creation of a national bank. This national bank would be 20 percent publicly controlled and 80 percent privately controlled. Hamilton thought it was important to have wealthy investors financially and psychologically invested in the new government. Though the power to create a national bank was not granted to Congress in the Constitution, Hamilton argued that it was permissible under the elastic clause. Thomas Jefferson argued that the creation of a national bank was not "necessary and proper." Hamilton won this debate, and a national bank was created in 1791. It existed until 1811.

WRONG CHOICES EXPLAINED:

(2) Alexander Hamilton did not use the elastic clause to justify creating the federal postal system. Congressional legislation created the postal system. The Constitution explicitly grants Congress the power to create a postal system; the elastic clause was not invoked in this situation.

(3) Alexander Hamilton did not use the elastic clause to justify sending troops to end the Whiskey Rebellion. The Constitution explicitly grants the president the power to suppress armed insurrections; the elastic clause was not invoked in this situation. President George Washington first obtained certification from a Supreme Court justice that local authorities were incapable of suppressing the

rebellion. Historians have debated the appropriateness of the federal government's response to the Whiskey Rebellion, but the actions were within the powers of the executive.

(4) Alexander Hamilton did not use the elastic clause to justify imposing an embargo on trade with Great Britain. Such an embargo was enacted under the administration of President Thomas Jefferson with the Embargo Act (1807) and the Non-Intercourse Act (1809). The Commerce Clause of the Constitution explicitly grants Congress the power to regulate trade with foreign countries.

8. **2** The two areas of the map that made up the United States as a result of the Louisiana Purchase were *A* and *D*. Area *A* is the original territory of the United States as established by the Treaty of Paris in 1783. The treaty established the Mississippi River as the western boundary of the United States. In 1803, the purchase of the Louisiana Territory, area *D*, enlarged the territory of the United States and pushed the western boundary beyond the Mississippi River. During the administration of President Thomas Jefferson, the United States purchased the Louisiana Territory from France for $15 million. The purchase nearly doubled the size of the United States and gave the United States control of the Mississippi River and the port city of New Orleans. New Orleans became increasingly important as pioneers in the late 1700s and early 1800s crossed over the Appalachian Mountains, settled in the Mississippi and Ohio River Valleys, and established farms there.

WRONG CHOICES EXPLAINED:
(1), (3), and (4) Only choice 2 consists of two areas that comprised the United States in 1803. The other three choices contain one or two areas that were acquired later. Area *B*, which is included in choices 1 and 3, consists of Florida and parts of modern-day Louisiana, Mississippi, and Alabama. It was acquired after 1803. The United States acquired the land from Spain in 1819 with the Adams-Onis Treaty. Area *E*, which is included in choice 3, is Texas. It was acquired after 1803. Texas had become independent from Mexico in 1836 and was annexed by the United States in 1845, soon after the victory of the expansionist James K. Polk in the presidential election of 1844. Area *G*, which is included in choice 4, is the Mexican Cession. It was acquired after 1803. This area was acquired as a result of the Mexican-American War. After the annexation of Texas by the United States in 1845, the United States and Mexico disagreed over the southern border of Texas. Skirmishes in the disputed area led to war between Mexico and the United States. The United States won the war, which lasted from 1846 to 1848, and acquired the Mexican Cession.

9. **4** Area *G* was acquired as a result of the Mexican-American War. The push toward the Pacific Ocean generated a desire among many Americans to obtain Mexican territory. Americans had been settling in the Mexican territory of Texas as far back as the 1820s. In 1836, Texans fought for and won independence from Mexico. Texas then became the Lone Star Republic. Many Texans were eager for their Lone Star Republic to join the United States. However, concern about the expansion of slavery put the issue of Texas annexation on the back burner until the election of the expansionist President James Polk in 1844. Even before he took office, the outgoing President John Tyler saw Polk's victory as a mandate for Texas annexation and pushed annexation through Congress. Texas joined the United States as the 15th slave state in 1845. Conflict between the United States and Mexico soon ensued. The two countries disagreed over the southern border of Texas. Mexico said it was at the Nueces River. The United States insisted it was at the Rio Grande, 150 miles to the south. In 1846, Polk sent troops into this disputed territory. Skirmishes in the disputed area led to war between Mexico and the United States. The United States won the war, which lasted from 1846 to 1848, and acquired the huge territory that comprised the northern provinces of Mexico, known as the Mexican Cession. These lands included the gold deposits discovered in California in 1849 and the lush agricultural land along the west coast.

WRONG CHOICES EXPLAINED:

(1) Area *A* is the original territory of the United States as established by the Treaty of Paris in 1783. The treaty established the Mississippi River as the western boundary of the United States.

(2) Area *B* consists of Florida and parts of modern-day Louisiana, Mississippi, and Alabama. It was granted by Spain to the United States in the Adams-Onis Treaty of 1819. The western portion of the Florida panhandle had been acquired earlier, with the Louisiana Purchase. This portion was later incorporated into the states of Alabama, Mississippi, and Louisiana.

(3) Area *F* is the Oregon Territory, which was incorporated into the United States in 1848 following the resolution of a border dispute with Great Britain. The two nations agreed that the border would be along the 49th parallel. The Oregon Territory included the entire future states of Oregon, Washington, and Idaho as well as parts of Montana and Wyoming.

10. **2** Governor DeWitt Clinton is describing the Erie Canal. Governor Clinton championed the project and successfully pushed the legislature of New York State to provide financial support. The Erie Canal (completed in 1825) provided an important link between the Atlantic Ocean and the Great Lakes. The United States was faced with a vexing problem during its first decades. On paper, the country extended to the Mississippi River following the American

Revolutionary War (1775–1783) and then to the Rocky Mountains following the Louisiana Purchase (1803). However, most residents of the United States resided in communities close to the Atlantic Coast, east of the Appalachian Mountains. The Erie Canal helped open up the vast landmass of the country to settlement by United States residents. The canal created an all-water route from New York City to the midwestern communities around the Great Lakes. This connection facilitated settlement and trade between the Atlantic Coast and the Midwest, creating, in the words of Governor Clinton, the "greatest inland trade ever witnessed." A shipment of wheat, for example, could now be transported from Chicago to New York City by an all-water route at a tenth of the cost and in a fraction of the time than when using an overland route.

WRONG CHOICES EXPLAINED:

(1) Governor DeWitt Clinton is not describing the National Road. The National Road, also known as the Cumberland Road, stretched from Maryland into the Ohio River Valley. Construction took place from 1811 to 1853. Clinton's description notes connecting the Hudson River with the St. Lawrence River and the Great Lakes—and, ultimately, with the Mississippi River. These points were not connected by the National Road.

(3) Governor DeWitt Clinton is not describing steamboats. Steamboats— developed by several people, including Robert Fulton (1807)—were used on the Erie Canal. However, Clinton is describing a specific transportation project, not a mode of transportation.

(4) Governor DeWitt Clinton is not describing railroads. In many ways, railroads rendered canals, such as the Erie Canal, far less efficient for transporting goods. The first railroad tracks in the United States were laid in 1829 by the Baltimore and Ohio Railroad. By 1860, railroads connected the far reaches of the country east of the Mississippi River and beyond. Clinton is describing a specific transportation project, not a mode of transportation.

11. **1** An example of the unwritten constitution is the president's cabinet. The unwritten constitution refers to those traditions and practices that have become part of the American political system but are not mentioned in the Constitution. Many of these practices date back to the administration of President George Washington. President Washington regularly convened a cabinet, comprised of the heads of government departments, to advise him. Additional elements of the unwritten constitution include the development of political parties, a practice unforeseen by most of the founding fathers and not mentioned in the Constitution. Congressional committees are not mentioned in the Constitution, yet the committee system has become instrumental in the functioning of Congress. Occasionally, a practice goes from being part of the unwritten

constitution to being part of the written Constitution. President Washington set a precedent of serving for no more than two terms. This tradition, however, became law with the ratification of the 22nd Amendment (1951), ratified after President Franklin D. Roosevelt broke tradition and won the presidency four times.

WRONG CHOICES EXPLAINED:

(2) The amendment process is not an example of the use of the unwritten constitution. It is spelled out in the written Constitution. First, a constitutional amendment can be proposed, either by Congress (by two-third majorities in both houses) or by a national convention. Then three-fourths of the states must approve an amendment for it to be ratified. The state-by-state approval process can occur by the consent of the state legislatures or by state ratifying conventions. Twenty-seven amendments have been added to the Constitution.

(3) The bicameral legislature is not an example of the use of the unwritten constitution. It is spelled out in the written Constitution. A two-house, or bicameral, legislature was the result of the Great Compromise at the Constitutional Convention of 1787. The compromise settled a dispute between the large states and the small states over how the states would be represented in Congress. The Great Compromise called for a House of Representatives, in which representation would be determined by the population of each state, and a Senate, in which each state would get two members.

(4) The electoral college is not an example of the use of the unwritten constitution. It is spelled out in the written Constitution. The president is officially chosen by the electoral college. The number of electors for each state is equal to the number of members of Congress from that state. The Constitution allows each state to establish a method for appointing electors. Currently, all states use the popular vote to appoint electors. In all the states except for Maine and Nebraska, whichever candidate wins the popular vote in a particular state gets all the electoral votes for that state. Maine and Nebraska voters select one elector within each congressional district; two additional electors are awarded based on the statewide popular vote. Presently, there are 538 electoral votes. A candidate must win the majority, or 270 votes, to be declared the "president elect."

12. **3** The information in the chart supports the generalization that the North had greater economic strength than the South. The chart compares acres of farmland, miles of railroad track, industrial capacity, and population of the North and the South as the Civil War was beginning in 1861. The contrast in industrial capacity—the value of manufactured goods, the number of factories, and the number of industrial workers—is striking. The North dominates each category by 85 percent or more. The greater industrial capacity of the North allowed the

United States government to procure far more weapons and ammunition than the breakaway southern states. Furthermore, the advantage that the northern states had in regard to miles of railroad tracks—71 percent compared to 29 percent—allowed the Union to move goods and people more quickly and efficiently. The difference in farmland between the two regions is less extreme—the North had 65 percent of farmland to the South's 35 percent. However, these numbers obscure the fact that a large percentage of southern farmland was devoted to cotton production. All told, the North was far better prepared to feed its soldiers than was the South. Finally, the difference in population proved to give the Union side a major advantage. If slaves are excluded from the totals of each region, the North had about 22 million free people compared to less than six million free people in the South. These figures became increasingly important as the Civil War dragged on for nearly four years. The northern states were better able to reinforce the ranks of the United States army than the southern states were able to sustain the Confederate army. All the factors in the chart help explain the victory of the Union army over Confederate forces.

WRONG CHOICES EXPLAINED:

(1) The information in the chart does not support the generalization that the South exported more manufactured goods than the North. The chart does not include statistics about exports. The chart does indicate that the overall manufacturing capacity of the South was far less than that of the North. Further, the Union was successfully in blockading South ports, thereby greatly reducing Southern exports (mainly cotton).

(2) The information in the chart does not support the generalization that the North would have had more difficulty supplying an army than the South. The information in the chart indicates the opposite. The North had more acres under cultivation, allowing for greater food production. Also, the North had greater industrial production, allowing for greater production of weaponry and ammunition. Finally, the extensive railroad network of the North would allow these goods to reach the army more easily.

(4) The information in the chart does not support the generalization that the South would be better able to transport an army than the North. The information in the chart suggests the opposite. Of the national total, 71 percent of railroad tracks were in the North, suggesting that the North would be better able to transport an army than the South.

13. **1** The publication of the poster was most directly prompted by the issuance of the Emancipation Proclamation. Perhaps President Abraham Lincoln's greatest achievement during the Civil War was playing a key role in the liberation of the slaves. Lincoln was partly motivated by the desire to keep Great Britain at bay

during the Civil War. Great Britain might have aided the Confederacy to ensure the steady flow of southern cotton, but it would not have joined the South to continue slavery. However, Lincoln did not achieve this historic goal on his own. Abolitionists, Radical Republicans, and, of course, the slaves themselves all contributed to the effort to put the issue of liberation on the wartime agenda. Lincoln was able to convince a reluctant country that ending slavery was consistent with the most basic American values. By the summer of 1862, Lincoln had come to believe that the time was right for moving forward in regard to emancipation. He waited until the Union had achieved a victory on the battlefield. The Battle of Antietam in September 1862 was enough of a Union victory to prompt the president to issue the Emancipation Proclamation. The edict ordered the freeing of all slaves in rebel-held territory as of January 1, 1863. The order exempted slaves in the loyal border states and even in Union-held areas of Confederate states. Of course, orders from the United States government did not hold any weight for Confederate leaders. So the Emancipation Proclamation did not actually free any slaves. However, the order clearly changed the goals and tenor of the war. It made clear that this was as much a war for the liberation of the slaves as it was a war to preserve the Union. The proclamation also authorized the recruiting of African Americans for service in the army. Secretary of War Edwin M. Stanton began to take action to recruit African-American troops. In January 1863, he instructed the governor of Massachusetts to begin raising an African-American regiment. The 54th Regiment Massachusetts Volunteer Infantry, led by Colonel Robert Gould Shaw, was the first African-American regiment. By the end of the Civil War in April 1865, the United States Army had organized approximately 175 African-American units; these troops constituted about one-tenth of the manpower of the army.

WRONG CHOICES EXPLAINED:

(2) The publication of the poster was not prompted by the passage of the Kansas-Nebraska Act. This 1854 act allowed for the possibility of slavery, under the principle of popular sovereignty, in the territories of Kansas and Nebraska—areas that had been closed to slavery by the Missouri Compromise (1820). Violence erupted in Bleeding Kansas as pro-slavery and antislavery men fought for control of the territory. The call to "military duty" in the poster was not extended to African-American men during the violence in Kansas.

(3) The publication of the poster was not prompted by the rejection of the Wilmot Proviso. Following the beginning of the Mexican-American War (1846–1848), Congressman David Wilmot and other northern politicians tried, unsuccessfully, to ban slavery in territories that might be gained in the war by putting forth the Wilmot Proviso (1846). The Mexican-American War was already in progress when the proviso was proposed and rejected. Its rejection did not lead to calls for African-American men to participate in military duty.

(4) The publication of the poster was not prompted by the adoption of the Missouri Compromise. The Missouri Compromise (1820) maintained the balance between free and slave states. Controversy arose between the slave-holding states and the free states in 1820 when Missouri applied for statehood as a slave state. The admission of Missouri would have upset the balance between free and slave states. A compromise was reached that allowed for the admission of two new states—Missouri as a slave state and Maine as a free state. It also divided the remaining area of the Louisiana Territory at 36° 30′ north latitude. North of that line, slavery was not permitted (except in Missouri). South of that line, it was permitted. The compromise did not lead to military action not to call for African-American men to participate in "military duty."

14. **2** At the start of the Civil War, President Abraham Lincoln stated that the major reason for fighting the Civil War was to uphold the Constitution by preserving the Union. Lincoln had been opposed to the institution of slavery his entire life. As he ran for president in 1860, he promised to block the expansion of slavery to new territories in the West. However, he said that the Constitution prohibited him from interfering with slavery where it already existed. As the war progressed, Lincoln slowly began to change his views in regard to the relationship between the federal government and slavery. He began to see that the institution of slavery was a major strength of the Southern economy. Further, abolitionists, Radical Republicans, and, of course, the slaves themselves all contributed to the effort to put the issue of liberation on the wartime agenda. At first, Lincoln was reluctant to take action against slavery for fear of pushing the border states toward secession. When Congress passed the Confiscation Acts in 1861 and 1862, Lincoln was opposed to them. However, he did not veto them. These acts were framed as military measures. The first declared that any slaves pressed into working for the Confederacy could be taken as "contraband of war," meaning "confiscated property." The second act allowed for the seizure of the slaves owned by Confederate officials. In the summer of 1862, Lincoln wrote a letter to Horace Greeley, editor of the *New-York Tribune*, that shows his evolving views. Lincoln reiterated that his "paramount object" in the Civil War was "to save the Union." However, he also stated that if "I could save the Union without freeing any slave I would do it, and if I could save it by freeing all the slaves I would do it." Here he acknowledged that "freeing all the slaves" was a possible course of action. Soon after, in September 1862, he issued the Emancipation Proclamation, which went into effect on January 1, 1863. This document changed the direction and objective of the war. It also made clear that the future existence of slavery would be determined by the outcome of the war.

WRONG CHOICES EXPLAINED:

(1) Lincoln did not state that the major reason for fighting the Civil War was to break the South's economic ties to Great Britain. He implemented a naval blockade during the war to prevent trade between the Confederacy and Great Britain. However, this was part of the strategy to defeat the Confederacy and to maintain the Union.

(3) Lincoln did not state that the major reason for fighting the Civil War was to enforce the terms of the Compromise of 1850. The compromise grew out of the controversy around California's application for statehood as a free state. When Southern senators objected to the admission of an additional free state, Senate negotiators worked out a series of measures that became known as the Compromise of 1850. The most important elements of the compromise were the admittance of California as a free state, which pleased northern politicians, and a more stringent Fugitive Slave Law, which pleased southern politicians. Enforcing the Fugitive Slave Law was controversial. However, it was not Lincoln's primary objective in fighting the Civil War; maintaining the Union was.

(4) Lincoln did not state that the major reason for fighting the Civil War was to punish the Confederate states for leaving the Union. Lincoln insisted that the Confederate states had not actually left the Union. He held the position that the states were in rebellion and that his goal, as president, was to suppress the rebellion and maintain the Union. Toward the end of the war, he pushed for more lenient terms for Reconstruction. In his Second Inaugural Address, Lincoln said that "[w]ith malice toward none, with charity for all," he hoped to "bind up the nation's wounds." This generous attitude toward the rebellious South did not reflect a desire to punish those states.

15. **1** Passage of the Homestead Act in 1862 encouraged settlement of the Great Plains by providing free land to farmers. By the time of the Civil War, the government wanted to encourage settlement in the huge area of relatively flat land between the Mississippi River and the Rocky Mountains known as the Great Plains. Much of this area has rich soil and a long growing season. With the absence of Democrats from Congress during the Civil War, the Republicans were able to pass several pieces of legislation that reflected their vision of America. Hundreds of thousands of people applied for and were granted homesteads. Many of these homesteaders did not have extensive farming skills and went bankrupt. Increasingly by the late 1800s, it became difficult for small farmers, even competent ones, to compete with large-scale agricultural operations.

WRONG CHOICES EXPLAINED:

(2) The Homestead Act did not remove barriers to Asian immigrants. Later, in 1882, Congress passed the Chinese Exclusion Act, which excluded most Chinese from entering the United States. This act represents the only instance in which legislation has explicitly denied a particular national group entrance into the United States.

(3) The Homestead Act did not supply land to build transcontinental railroads. The Pacific [Transcontinental] Railroad Act (1862) supplied land to railroad companies. The act encouraged expansion of the railroad network by giving railroad companies wide swaths of land. These generous land grants totaled more than 180 million acres, an area equal to the size of Texas. Completion of the first transcontinental railroad at Promontory Summit, Utah, in 1869 was a milestone in the development of a network of railroad lines that connected the far reaches of the country.

(4) The Homestead Act did not place Native American Indians on reservations. After the Civil War, starting in 1867, the government attempted to solve the "Indian problem" through peaceful means, rather than through more warfare. The center of this policy was pushing Native American Indians onto reservations—confined areas that were set aside by the government. This policy made Native American Indians wards of the government until they learned "to walk on the white man's road." Often the lands set aside for reservations were incapable of sustaining crops, reducing the inhabitants to utter poverty. Many tribal groups resisted being put onto reservations.

16. **3** The heading, "Elements of Reconstruction" best completes the partial outline. Reconstruction occurred from 1865 to 1877, following the Civil War. It was the period in which attempts were made to address the political, social, and economic legacies of slavery and to solve the problems arising from the readmission of the 11 secessionist states to the Union. Reconstruction began even before the Civil War ended, when President Abraham Lincoln announced his Proclamation of Amnesty and Reconstruction (1863). Lincoln and his successor, President Andrew Johnson, controlled the first phase of Reconstruction. Their goal was to reunite the country quickly and easily and to establish functioning governments in the southern states. During this first phase of Reconstruction, Congress created the Freedman's Bureau (outline entry A) in 1865 to help freedmen and freedwomen adjust to life after slavery. The bureau provided freedmen and freedwomen with job training, emergency food, and help finding housing. President Johnson tried to abolish the bureau in 1866 but was blocked by Congress. The bureau was finally abolished in 1872. Starting in 1867, the Radical Republicans in Congress took over control of Reconstruction. This second phase of Reconstruction involved more sweeping changes in the South, including the military occupation of the rebellious southern

states (outline entry C) and assurances that African Americans in the South would finally get some basic rights. This phase of Reconstruction also witnessed the ratification of the 14th Amendment (outline entry B). The modest gains for African Americans were short-lived. Reconstruction came to an end as part of a compromise to settle the disputed presidential election of 1876.

WRONG CHOICES EXPLAINED:

(1) The heading "Development of States Rights" does not complete the partial outline in the question. An outline with that heading would include subheadings such as "The Virginia and Kentucky Resolutions (1798)" and "The South Carolina Exposition and Protest (1828)."

(2) The heading "Results of Manifest Destiny" does not complete the partial outline in the question. An outline with that heading would include subheadings such as "Texas annexation (1845)" and "the Mexican Cession (1848)."

(4) The heading "Limits on Civil Rights" does not complete the partial outline in the question. An outline with that heading would include subheadings such as "Enactment of Jim Crow laws in the 1880s and 1890s" and "The Supreme Court decision in *Plessy* v. *Ferguson* (1896)."

17. **3** Between 1865 and 1900, one effect of the growth of industry in the United States was an increase in the urban population. Cities grew rapidly in the second half of the 1800s due to large-scale immigration as well as rapid industrialization. Between 1865 and 1900, the number of Americans who lived in cities jumped from 6.2 million to over 30 million, which amounted to a shift in the urban population from 20 percent of the total population to 40 percent. This rapid urbanization offered people many opportunities but also brought several problems. Corrupt and inefficient political operations—labeled political machines—became more common in this era. New York City was dominated by the Democratic Party machine, headquartered at Tammany Hall. The most famous Tammany chief was "Boss" William Marcy Tweed. The muckraker journalist Lincoln Steffens exposed urban corruption in *The Shame of the Cities* (1902). Another problem in this era was the proliferation of substandard tenement housing. The wretched living conditions that workers often experienced in tenements were documented in Jacob Riis's book *How the Other Half Lives* (1890).

WRONG CHOICES EXPLAINED:

(1) The growth of industry between 1865 and 1900 did not lead to a decline in trade with other nations. The opposite occurred. Trade with other nations increased as American industrial firms imported greater amounts of raw materials and exported finished products.

(2) The growth of industry between 1865 and 1900 did not lead to a call for lower tariff rates by business leaders. The opposite occurred. American business leaders in the late 19th century called for higher tariff rates on imported goods. This raised prices on imported goods and made American-made products comparably more affordable.

(4) The growth of industry between 1865 and 1900 did not lead corporations to support the growth of labor unions. The opposite occurred. Corporations took steps to limit the influence of unions. These steps included locking out unionized workers, hiring replacement workers (known as "scabs"), forcing workers to sign "yellow dog" contracts (in which the worker agreed to not join a union), and using armed guards to break strikes.

18. **1** The federal government reacted to the Supreme Court's ruling in *Wabash, St. Louis & Pacific Railroad* v. *Illinois* (1886) by passing the Interstate Commerce Act. The Wabash case arose as a result of efforts to regulate railroad rates. Starting in the 1870s, groups organized to promote the interests of farmers, such as the Grange, became concerned about the power and the abuses of large railroad companies. Railroads often overcharged small-scale farmers. The Grange successfully pushed for laws in several states in the 1870s and 1880s to limit abusive practices by railroads. However in the 1886 *Wabash* case, the Supreme Court ruled that Illinois could not regulate railroad rates on rail lines that crossed state boundaries, citing the interstate commerce clause of the Constitution. In response, the federal government created the Interstate Commerce Commission (ICC), the first federal regulatory agency. However, the ICC was chronically underfunded and was, therefore, largely ineffective.

WRONG CHOICES EXPLAINED:

(2) The federal government did not react to the Supreme Court's ruling in *Wabash, St. Louis & Pacific Railroad* v. *Illinois* (1886) by weakening the influence of banks over big business. During the late 1800s, the federal government made no attempts to regulate the banking industry. Later, during the Great Depression of the 1930s, the federal government passed legislation to regulate the banking industry. The Glass-Steagall Act (1933), which was part of President Franklin D. Roosevelt's New Deal, limited how banks could invest their assets and also created the Federal Deposit Insurance Corporation.

(3) The federal government did not react to the Supreme Court's ruling in *Wabash, St. Louis & Pacific Railroad* v. *Illinois* (1886) by abandoning attempts to break up monopolies. During the late 1800s, the federal government first enacted antitrust legislation. In 1890, the federal government passed the Sherman Antitrust Act to break up monopolies. However, the act was used with

limited success. Later, President Woodrow Wilson strengthened the antitrust powers of the federal government with the Clayton Antitrust Act (1914).

(4) The federal government did not react to the Supreme Court's ruling in *Wabash, St. Louis & Pacific Railroad* v. *Illinois* (1886) by encouraging railroad employees to form unions. During the late 1800s, federal government policies and actions tended to side with management over employees in regard to workplace conflicts. In the aftermath of the Pullman Strike (1894), for example, the Supreme Court upheld an injunction issued by the federal government against the strike. The Court ruled in the case *In re Debs* that the government had the right to ensure that interstate commerce not be interrupted and that the United States mail be delivered.

19. **2** In the late 1800s, the corporation became an important form of business organization primarily because it could raise large amounts of investment capital. Individuals must obtain a corporate charter from the state in order to function as a corporation. A corporate model of ownership is different from when a company is owned by a single proprietor or by a small group of proprietors. In the corporate model, individuals may invest in shares in the company that are traded on the open market. These shareholders are, in effect, partial owners of the corporation. In the late 1700s and early 1800s, corporate charters were granted to individuals but mainly on a temporary basis and mainly for a public-oriented purpose, such as building a bridge or a road. After 1810, states began rewriting incorporation laws, allowing for the chartering of businesses. Incorporation encouraged investment into the company and protected the individual investors from liability laws.

WRONG CHOICES EXPLAINED:

(1) Corporations do not necessarily have closer ties with their employees than do companies owned by a sole proprietor. The opposite is often true. Employees tend to have closer ties with the proprietor of a firm than with the members of a board of trustees. Corporate charters allow for the rapid growth of companies and a more impersonal form of management.

(3) Corporations do not necessarily make better quality products than do companies owned by a sole proprietor. The opposite is often true. Quality is determined by a variety of factors. The rise of corporations went hand in hand with the spread of mass-production techniques. Frequently, the products made in large mass-production facilities were inferior to the handmade products made by smaller firms.

(4) Corporations do not necessarily issue calls for conservation of natural resources. The opposite is often true. The growth of large production operations, facilitated by the spread of the corporate model, used increasingly large amounts of natural resources and often caused damage to the natural environment.

20. **2** In the 1896 decision cited in the question, the Supreme Court upheld the constitutionality of Jim Crow laws. The excerpt is from the decision in *Plessy v. Ferguson*. The decision stated that segregation was acceptable as long as the facilities for both races were of equal quality—hence "separate, but equal." In the case, the Supreme Court decided that racial segregation did not violate the equal protection provision of the 14th Amendment. It stated, "Laws permitting ... separation" of the races "do not necessarily imply the inferiority" of either race. The decision was a setback for those who sought an end to the Jim Crow system of racial segregation in the South. Jim Crow laws were state and local ordinances that first appeared after Reconstruction ended (1877). Typical laws called for separate schools or separate train cars for African Americans. Opponents of racial segregation argued that Jim Crow laws violated the 14th Amendment (1868), which was alluded to in the first sentence of the excerpt. These opponents stated that Jim Crow laws relegated African Americans to inferior public accommodations and had the effect of making African Americans second-class citizens. The 14th Amendment, ratified during Reconstruction, stated that no person shall be denied "equal protection of the laws." However, the Court disagreed. The "separate but equal" doctrine allowed for the continuation of the Jim Crow system until the 1950s and 1960s. The beginning of the end to the system came with the *Brown* v. *the Board of Education of Topeka* decision of 1954.

WRONG CHOICES EXPLAINED:

(1) In the 1896 decision cited in the question, the Supreme Court was not upholding the constitutionality of the Three-fifths Compromise. The compromise, arrived at during the Constitutional Convention (1787), settled the issue of how slaves would be counted when figuring out a state's representation in the House of Representatives. The Three-fifths Compromise stipulated that slaves, labeled "other persons" in the Constitution, would be counted as three-fifths of a person in the census. This compromise, however, was a moot point by 1896 because slavery had ended with the ratification of the 13th Amendment (1865).

(3) In the 1896 decision cited in the question, the Supreme Court was not upholding the constitutionality of the affirmative action programs. Affirmative action programs were not proposed until well after 1896. They began in the mid-1960s primarily as a way to increase economic and educational opportunities for minorities. The movement for affirmative action occurred after the civil rights movement successfully pushed for an end to legal segregation. In many ways, affirmative action was the next step in the struggle for civil rights. The impact of the *Plessy* decision was to uphold racial discrimination, not to rectify it.

(4) In the 1896 decision cited in the question, the Supreme Court was not upholding the constitutionality of racial integration. The decision did the

opposite; it upheld the constitutionality of racial segregation. Later, the Supreme Court did rule that segregation was unconstitutional. The landmark *Brown* v. Board of Education of Topeka decision (1954) declared segregated schools to be inherently unfair and ordered states and communities to take measures to undo this system.

21. **3** The foreign policy illustrated in the cartoon was used by the United States to secure control of land for the Panama Canal Zone. The building of the Panama Canal was a major goal of President Theodore Roosevelt, who is featured in the cartoon. The United States had recently obtained Puerto Rico, the Philippines, and other colonies after the Spanish-American War (1898). Traveling from the east coast of the United States or the Caribbean Sea to the Philippines or other Pacific Ocean possessions took a great deal of time and effort. Merchant ships and naval ships had to travel around the southern tip of South America to reach the Pacific Ocean. Roosevelt used unorthodox means to obtain land for the canal. Before 1903, Panama was a region of Colombia. When Colombia refused the U.S. offer of $10 million to build a canal, American investors, with the backing of President Roosevelt and the U.S. military, instigated a "rebellion" in Panama against Colombia. Panama became an independent country and immediately reached a deal with the United States to build a canal. This deal is alluded to in the cartoon by the "New Treaty" flag. The cartoon depicts President Roosevelt as tossing dirt onto Bogota, the Colombian capital. The cartoonist approvingly describes the dirt tossed by the president as being symbolic of "The News Reaches Bogota." The president himself was equally unapologetic about American actions in regard to Colombia; he later boasted that he "took Panama."

WRONG CHOICES EXPLAINED:

(1) The foreign policy illustrated in the cartoon did not result in the United States punishing Mexico for siding with Germany in World War I. There was some concern about Mexico joining Germany in World War I after the United States became aware of the Zimmerman note (1917), in which German foreign secretary Arthur Zimmerman indicated that Germany would help Mexico regain territory it had lost to the United States if Mexico joined the war on Germany's side. However, Mexico stayed out of World War I. The references to Bogota, rather than to Mexico City, indicate the subject of the cartoon is the Panama Canal, not Mexican foreign policy.

(2) The foreign policy illustrated in the cartoon did not result in the United States enforcing the Monroe Doctrine against Great Britain. The major purpose of the Monroe Doctrine (1823) was to limit European influence in the Western

Hemisphere. President Monroe was alarmed at threats by the Holy Alliance of Russia, Prussia, and Austria to restore Spain's lost American colonies. He also opposed a decree by the Russian czar that claimed all the Pacific northwest above the 51st parallel. By 1903, the United States did not have reason to be concerned about British actions in the Western Hemisphere.

(4) The foreign policy illustrated in the cartoon did not result in the United States announcing the Open Door policy. The Open Door policy was put forth by President William McKinley's Secretary of State John Hay (1899) in regard to China. Earlier, the major European powers had established spheres of influence in China. Each European power declared that it had exclusive trading privileges in its sphere of influence. Since the United States did not have a sphere of influence in China, the United States asserted that all of China should be open to trade with all nations. The European nations begrudgingly accepted this concept. The references to Bogota, rather than to Beijing (or Peking, as it was spelled in English at the time), indicate that the cartoon refers to the Panama Canal, not the Open Door Policy.

22. **4** The 1917 poster indicates that one important educational goal for new immigrants during that time period was promoting the English language as a method of assimilation. The poster was published by the Cleveland Americanization Committee. Such committees were part of a large-scale, nationwide Americanization movement in the 1910s. The movement was successful in pressuring over 30 states to pass laws requiring programs to assimilate immigrants. The movement focused on the learning of English and on exposure to particular American cultural values. In addition, the movement frequently condemned expressions of "foreign" cultural practices. Although some participants in the movement were motivated by a desire to help newly arrived immigrants, the movement was widely seen as xenophobic. Many supporters of Americanization also pushed for laws restricting the flow of immigrants into the United States, leading to the passage of the Emergency Quota Act of 1921 and the Immigration Act of 1924. Immigrants themselves were of different minds in regard to attempts at assimilation. Many embraced the cultural ways of their new land, but many also sought to retain elements of their native cultures and a sense of ethnic solidarity. In New York, Chicago, and other large cities, foreign language papers emerged, such as the Yiddish-language *Jewish Daily Forward* and the Italian-language *Il Progresso Italo-Americano*. Neighborhoods in New York became increasingly defined by ethnicity, such as Little Italy and the Jewish Lower East Side. Immigrant groups established savings institutions, insurance programs, choruses, political organizations, and summer camps.

WRONG CHOICES EXPLAINED:

(1) The 1917 poster does not indicate that an important educational goal for new immigrants during that time period was teaching them to read and write in their native language. The Americanization movement focused on the opposite—teaching immigrants to read and write in English. The movement often called for the suppression of foreign languages in schools.

(2) The 1917 poster does not indicate that an important educational goal for new immigrants during that time period was promoting religious tolerance. The poster does not allude to religion. Some individuals in the Americanization movement promoted Protestantism and denigrated Catholicism, Judaism, and other religions.

(3) The 1917 poster does not indicate that an important educational goal for new immigrants during that time period was ensuring the preservation of their native cultures. The Americanization movement encouraged immigrants to abandon their native cultures. Many immigrants preserved elements of their native culture despite the prodding of the Americanization movement.

23. **3** The United States became directly involved in World War I as a result of Germany's resumption of unrestricted submarine warfare. When World War I began in 1914, President Woodrow Wilson initially assumed that the United States could stay neutral and maintain commercial ties with nations on both sides of the conflict. However, Great Britain successfully blocked American ships from reaching Germany. Out of necessity, American trade shifted to Great Britain exclusively. Germany responded by warning that American ships in the waters off of Great Britain would be subject to attack by U-boats, or submarines. The sinking of the British ocean liner *Lusitania* infuriated many Americans (128 Americans were among the dead). Germany, however, wanted to keep the United States out of the war and agreed in the Sussex Pledge (1916) to make no surprise submarine attacks on American ships. The United States took advantage of this pledge and traded extensively with Great Britain. In 1917, Germany rescinded the Sussex Pledge and declared that it would resume unrestricted submarine warfare. Soon after, the United States declared war on Germany.

WRONG CHOICES EXPLAINED:

(1) The entrance of the United States into World War I in 1917 was not prompted by Germany's negotiation of an alliance with Russia. Such an alliance did not occur. Russia and Germany fought on opposite sides in the war until Russia withdrew from the war. Russian forces, fighting under the provisional government, were defeated in July 1917. After the Bolsheviks took power in November 1917, Vladimir Lenin withdrew Russia from the war. Russia and Germany signed the

Treaty of Brest-Litovsk in March 1918, but they did not form an alliance. These events occurred after the United States had entered the war (April 1917).

(2) The entrance of the United States into World War I in 1917 was not prompted by Germany's threat to spread the war to the Middle East. Fighting did occur in the Middle East as early as 1914. The main combatant in the Middle East on the side of the Central Powers was the Ottoman Empire. The British, Russians, and French were the main combatants on the side of the Allied Powers.

(4) The entrance of the United States into World War I in 1917 was not prompted by Germany's acquisition of new African colonies. Germany had established colonies in Africa before World War I, mostly in the 1880s. It did not acquire new colonies during World War I.

24. **4** Progressivism was an early 20th-century movement that promoted government actions to correct political, economic, and social problems. Progressivism existed at the grassroots level as well as in the corridors of power. The movement claimed many legislative victories and ultimately influenced both the New Deal and 20th-century liberalism. In the political realm, Progressives hoped to expand democratic participation and limit the power of corrupt and inefficient political machines. They pushed for states to adopt the initiative, referendum, and recall to increase the power of voters over the political process. The initiative would enable citizens to introduce a bill to the local or state legislature by petition. The referendum would allow people to vote directly on proposed legislation. The recall would allow the populace to remove elected officials before their term ended. In the economic realm, Progressives challenged the abuses of unbridled capitalism. Reformers were successful in pushing Congress to pass the Keating-Owens Act (1916), which regulated child labor, but the act was struck down by the Supreme Court two years later. Progressive reformers also challenged the practices and shear power of large monopolies and trusts in various industries. The Clayton Antitrust Act (1914) was part of the agenda of Progressive reformers. In the social realm, Progressives pushed for legislation on the state and local level to regulate housing conditions. Also, many Progressives addressed what they perceived as the problem of excessive drinking of alcoholic beverages. They were successful in pushing for the 18th Amendment (1919), which banned the production, transport, and sale of alcohol as of January 1, 1920.

WRONG CHOICES EXPLAINED:

(1) Progressivism did not promote limited war to spread social justice to other countries. Progressives were divided on whether or not to support American intervention in World War I. Some did believe that America could use the war to spread democracy. However, World War I was not a limited war, nor was military engagement central to the Progressive agenda.

(2) Progressivism did not promote increased immigration to diversify the nation's population. Some Progressives formed alliances with working-class immigrant communities. However, many were active in the Nativist movement, which sought to limit immigration into the United States. This movement was successful in pushing for passage of the Emergency Quota Act of 1921 and the Immigration Act of 1924.

(3) Progressivism did not promote colonialism to increase American power in the world. Progressives were divided on whether or not to support American colonialism. Some saw it as a way to bring "civilization" and "uplift" to the peoples of the world. Others saw it as an expression of power and domination over other peoples.

25. **1** The Supreme Court gave its approval to limiting the First Amendment rights of antiwar protestors by establishing the "clear and present danger" doctrine in *Schenck* v. *United States* (1919). The decision in the *Schenck* case upheld the Espionage and Sedition Acts passed during World War I to put limits on public expressions of antiwar sentiment. Charles Schenck and other members of the Socialist Party were arrested for printing and distributing flyers opposing the war and for urging young men to resist the draft. The Supreme Court argued that freedom of speech is not absolute and that the government is justified in limiting certain forms of speech during wartime. The Court argued that certain utterances pose a "clear and present danger." By analogy, the Court asserted that one is not allowed to shout "Fire!" falsely in a crowded theater.

WRONG CHOICES EXPLAINED:

(2) The "clear and present danger" doctrine, established by the Supreme Court in *Schenck* v. *United States* (1919), is not related to rejecting membership in the League of Nations. The United States did reject membership in the League of Nations when the Senate failed to ratify the Treaty of Versailles in 1920. President Woodrow Wilson pushed for the United States to approve the treaty. However, some senators wanted to isolate the United States from world affairs and opposed membership in the League. These isolationists were numerous enough to prevent the Senate from reaching the two-thirds vote necessary to ratify treaties.

(3) The "clear and present danger" doctrine, established by the Supreme Court in *Schenck* v. *United States* (1919), is not related to banning immigration from western Europe. In the 1920s, the United States did pass legislation greatly reducing the number of immigrants allowed into the country. The Emergency Quota Act (1921) and the National Origins Act (1924) established immigration quotas for different nations based on the number of each national group present in the United States decades earlier.

(4) The "clear and present danger" doctrine, established by the Supreme Court in *Schenck* v. *United States* (1919), is not related to passage of the Prohibition amendment. Prohibition, which was the outlawing of the production, sale, and consumption of alcoholic beverages, became the law of the land with the ratification of the 18th Amendment to the Constitution in 1919. It ended when the 21st Amendment (1933) repealed Prohibition.

26. **3** Hosting the Washington Naval Disarmament Conference (1921) and signing the Kellogg-Briand Pact (1928) were efforts by the United States to avoid future wars. The presidents of the 1920s attempted to isolate the United States from world affairs and to reduce spending on war munitions. President Warren Harding successfully pressed for a reduction of naval power among Britain, France, Japan, Italy, and the United States at the Washington Naval Conference in 1921. Later, President Calvin Coolidge continued to pursue an isolationist foreign policy and helped to negotiate the Kellogg-Briand Pact (1928). The United States was one of 63 nations to sign the pact, which renounced war in principle. Because the pact was negotiated outside of the League of Nations, it was unenforceable, rendering it meaningless.

WRONG CHOICES EXPLAINED:
(1) Hosting the Washington Naval Disarmament Conference (1921) and signing the Kellogg-Briand Pact (1928) were not efforts by the United States to form new military alliances. Both actions required cooperation among nations, but neither resulted in the formation of a new military alliance. The actions were expressions of isolationism; forming a military alliance would have been an expression of engagement in world affairs.

(2) Hosting the Washington Naval Disarmament Conference (1921) and signing the Kellogg-Briand Pact (1928) were not efforts by the United States to increase its military preparedness. Both actions were driven by a desire to reduce military budgets by reducing the risk of war.

(4) Hosting the Washington Naval Disarmament Conference (1921) and signing the Kellogg-Briand Pact (1928) were not efforts by the United States to collect payment for war debts. The Dawes Plan of 1924 was an effort by the United States to collect payment for war debts. The Treaty of Versailles (1919) stipulated that Germany be punished by having to pay war reparations to the victorious European powers. Under the Dawes Plan, the United States extended loans to Germany so that Germany could pay war reparations to Great Britain and France. Great Britain and France would then have funds to retire wartime debts to the United States.

27. **2** The Harlem Renaissance of the 1920s is best known for promoting the cultural creativity of African Americans. The Harlem Renaissance was a literary, artistic, and intellectual movement that celebrated African-American life and forged a new cultural identity among African-American people. The movement was centered in the African-American neighborhood of Harlem, in New York City. Contributions included the poetry of Langston Hughes, Claude McKay, and Countee Cullen and the jazz music of Louis Armstrong, Duke Ellington, and Bessie Smith. Some of Hughes' important poems include "Harlem," "The Negro Speaks of Rivers," and "I, Too, Sing America." Duke Ellington was a composer, pianist and bandleader who was perhaps the most important figure in 20th-century jazz. Some of his most important compositions are "Mood Indigo," "Don't Get Around Much Anymore," and "Take the A Train."

WRONG CHOICES EXPLAINED:

(1) The Harlem Renaissance was not focused on ending racial segregation in public facilities. Much of Harlem Renaissance art was political in nature, but the movement was more creative than political. The civil rights movement, which reached its peak in the 1950s and 1960s, challenged the Jim Crow system of racial segregation. The events in the movement include the Supreme Court decision in *Brown* v. *Board of Education of Topeka* (1954), the Montgomery bus boycott in 1956, the lunch counter sit-ins in 1960, the Freedom Rides in 1962, and the March on Washington in 1963.

(3) The Harlem Renaissance was not focused on encouraging passage of new voting rights legislation. Much of Harlem Renaissance art was political in nature, but the movement was more creative than political. The civil rights movement, which reached its peak in the 1950s and 1960s, pushed for voting rights for African Americans. A major march to raise awareness of the issue of voting rights was scheduled for March 1965. The participants began in Selma, Alabama, and marched 54 miles to Montgomery, Alabama. Unfortunately, the police acted violently against the marchers. The incident, known as "Bloody Sunday," was broadcast on national television and aroused indignation among many Americans. It was in this context that President Lyndon Johnson pushed Congress to pass the Voting Rights Act of 1965.

(4) The Harlem Renaissance was not focused on supporting legislation to eliminate the Ku Klux Klan. Much of the Harlem Renaissance art was political in nature, but the movement was more creative than political. Earlier, in 1870 and 1871, Congress passed three Enforcement Acts that protected the basic rights of African Americans. These acts, also known as the Ku Klux Klan Acts, specifically targeted the Klan for using violence and terrorism to prevent African Americans from exercising their rights as citizens. By 1872, the Klan had largely been defeated. The actions of the federal government reduced racial violence throughout the South.

In the 20th century, racial violence increased. A new Ku Klux Klan was born (1915) and, by the 1920s, was a genuine mass movement. However, the federal government did not take action against the organization this time.

28. **1** The efficiencies created by the assembly line best account for the affordability of Ford Model T automobiles in the 1920s. In 1913, Henry Ford opened a plant with a continuous conveyor belt. The belt moved the chassis of the car from worker to worker so that each did a small task in the process of assembling the final product. This mass production technique reduced the price of Ford's Model T car and also dealt a blow to the skilled mechanics who previously built automobiles. Unskilled assembly line workers gradually replaced skilled craft workers in American industry. The production and consumption of mass-produced goods stoked the American economy for much of the 1920s. New products captured the public's imagination, and new production techniques increased industrial output. If the quality of work deteriorated for factory workers in the 1920s, the availability of consumer goods to average workers greatly increased. Cars, radios, toasters, health and beauty aids, and other consumer goods filled the shelves of stores. Eventually, consumption of mass-produced goods just could not keep up with production. Manufacturers made the logical decision of beginning layoffs. Of course, unemployed workers had even less ability to purchase goods. Thus, a spiral of economic problems began that resulted in the Great Depression of the 1930s.

WRONG CHOICES EXPLAINED:
   (2) The affordability of Model T Fords in the 1920s is unrelated to the expertise of individual craftsmanship. The main factor in the reduction in price of Ford automobiles—the use of the assembly line and mass production techniques—undermined individual craftsmanship and rendered trained mechanics obsolete.
   (3) The affordability of Model T Fords in the 1920s is unrelated to strong support from labor unions. Henry Ford was strongly antiunion. Ford used unskilled workers in the assembly line process rather than trained mechanics. These unskilled workers were easier to replace and, therefore, more difficult to organize into a union. Ford was the last major car manufacturer to sign a contract with the United Auto Workers (1941).
   (4) The affordability of Model T Fords in the 1920s is unrelated to low taxes and government subsidies. Taxes for corporations were reduced in the 1920s, but this was not the primary reason for the affordability of the Model T. The tax rate was uniform throughout the automobile industry. Instead, it was Ford's mass-produced cars that initiated the trend toward lower prices. The government did not advance subsidies to the Ford Corporation in the 1920s.

29. **1** The idea of rugged individualism would best be supported by President Hoover's statement. Hoover was arguing against expanding the role of government in the economy. He asserted that government intervention would result in the "destruction of character." Rather, he urged people to rely on themselves and on their communities to triumph over economic difficulties and to become "masters of their own destiny." Hoover reflected a laissez-faire approach to the economy, which asserts that government interference in the economy should be as limited as possible. The French phrase *laissez-faire* means "to let alone." Throughout much of the history of the United States, Americans were suspicious of government intervention into the economy. However, by the 20th century, the country began to face serious economic problems that called into question the laissez-faire doctrine. In the early decades of the 20th century, progressive reformers pushed for greater government involvement in the economy to reign in capitalism—to break up monopolies, to regulate the food production industry, to help the poor, and to create peace between owners and workers. Hoover, and the other Republican presidents of the 1920s, sought to return to a laissez-faire approach. When the economy spiraled out of control starting in 1929 and millions of American were afflicted by poverty, hunger, and unemployment, Hoover still argued for "rugged individualism." Hoover did implement the far-reaching Reconstruction Finance Corporation (1932), which provided needed funds to key components of the economy. By the election of 1932, many Americans came to believe that Hoover did not do enough to help ordinary Americans. He lost the election to the Democratic candidate, Franklin D. Roosevelt.

WRONG CHOICES EXPLAINED:

(2) President Hoover's statement did not support the idea of unemployment insurance. Hoover was arguing against such government programs—against "leaning upon government to solve all the problems before us." Unemployment insurance is a government program that provides temporary cash payments to people who become unemployed through no fault of their own. During the Great Depression, Wisconsin created such a program (1932) before President Franklin D. Roosevelt enacted the first federal unemployment insurance program as part of the Social Security Act (1935).

(3) President Hoover's statement did not support the idea of deficit spending. Hoover was arguing against expanding the role of the federal government. Limiting government spending would decrease, not increase, the federal deficit. On the other hand, President Franklin D. Roosevelt's set of government programs, known as the New Deal, increased the federal deficit. Roosevelt, who took office in 1933, was influenced by the thinking of economist John Maynard Keynes. Keynes argued

that deficit spending by the government was acceptable, and even desirable, as a means of increasing overall demand and stimulating economic activity.

(4) President Hoover's statement did not support the idea of collective bargaining. Collective bargaining refers to the act of all the workers in a shop negotiating together, through a union, for better wages, better conditions, and shorter hours. The Republican presidents of the 1920s generally supported anti-union policies. Later, President Franklin D. Roosevelt (1933–1945) pushed for passage of the Wagner Act (1935), which defined "collective bargaining" as a legal right of workers in the United States. Roosevelt encouraged workers to join unions so that their wages and "purchasing power" would rise.

30. **4** The two statements illustrate a difference of opinion between the two presidents over expanding the federal government's roles in the economy. The context of both statements is the Great Depression. The Great Depression was the most devastating economic downturn in American history. Between 1929 and 1933, wages fell by 60 percent and unemployment tripled to over 12 million people. With no safety net in place, families were forced out of their homes. President Herbert Hoover (1929–1933) expressed skepticism about the usefulness of government intervention during this economic crisis. He urged people to "fight their own battles" and to be "masters of their own destiny." He was arguing for a laissez-faire, or a hands-off, approach in regard to economic policy. President Franklin D. Roosevelt (1933–1945), on the other hand, was arguing for an expansion of the role of the government in the economy. He proposed a set of programs, known as the New Deal, to address the economic crisis of the 1930s. The Roosevelt administration provided direct relief, or what would be known as welfare today, to millions of families. In addition, the New Deal included jobs programs such as the Civilian Conservation Corps (1933), which focused on young men, and the vast Works Progress Administration (1935) or WPA, which consisted of a myriad of public projects. The WPA built schools, installed sewer lines, wrote guidebooks, and produced theatrical productions. Also, the New Deal addressed the welfare of retired people and people with disabilities by creating the Social Security system in 1935.

WRONG CHOICES EXPLAINED:
(1) The two statements do not discuss granting subsidies to big business. Throughout history, the government has extended subsidies to big business in a variety of ways. Such subsidies included land grants to railroad companies in the late 1800s. More recently, subsidies included tax breaks, tax loopholes, bailouts, regulatory decisions, and direct cash subsidies. Supporters of such measures argued that these subsidies promoted economic growth; opponents argued that they were wasteful and amounted to "corporate welfare."

(2) The two statements do not discuss promoting free-trade policies in the Western Hemisphere. Later, President Bill Clinton promoted free-trade policies in the Western Hemisphere. The North America Free Trade Agreement (NAFTA), which was ratified by Congress in 1993, eliminated all trade barriers and tariffs among the United States, Canada, and Mexico. NAFTA was the subject of much controversy when it was promoted by Clinton. Free trade supporters promised global prosperity as more nations participated in the global economy. Opponents worried that nations would no longer be able to implement environmental regulations, ensure workers' rights, or protect fledging industries from foreign competition.

(3) The two statements do not discuss regulating supply and demand. President Hoover's business-friendly economic policies are often labeled supply-side economics. The theory is that if there is growth in the supply side—in regard to manufacturers, banks, and insurance companies—there will be a general economic revival and the benefits of a robust economy will trickle down to everyone. The alternative approach is to stimulate the demand side—consumers. Demand-side economics emphasize government policies designed to increase workers' wages and benefits, such as welfare and unemployment benefits. President Roosevelt tended to favor demand-side policies.

31. **3** One of the first problems President Franklin D. Roosevelt addressed was bringing stability to the banking system. When Roosevelt took office in 1933, many people had lost confidence in the banking system and had withdrawn their money in fears that their bank might fold. With thousands of people withdrawing their money at the same time, many banks actually did fold, turning their fear into a self-fulfilling prophecy. The Emergency Banking Act (1933), which was passed during Roosevelt's first week in office, closed down the banking system in the United States for four days. During this "bank holiday," the Federal Reserve Bank guaranteed that it would supply banks with currency when they reopened. This action restored people's faith in the banking system and stopped the runs on banks that were destabilizing the system. Later in 1933, Roosevelt signed the Glass-Steagall Act, which created the Federal Deposit Insurance Corporation (FDIC). The FDIC insures deposits so that if a bank does fold, people will not lose their savings.

WRONG CHOICES EXPLAINED:

(1) Ending the Red Scare was not a problem addressed by President Franklin D. Roosevelt. The Red Scare of the post–World War I era was a crusade against suspected communists, anarchists, labor leaders, and other radicals. The Bolshevik Revolution in Russia in 1917, the backlash against the large strike wave of 1919, and the virulent strain of patriotism unleashed by World War I all

set the groundwork for the Red Scare. Anticommunist sentiment continued to exist in the United States during Roosevelt's time in office (and beyond), but the most intense phase of the Red Scare was over by 1920.

(2) Standing up to dictators in Europe was not a problem addressed by President Franklin D. Roosevelt in his fist months in office in 1933. Throughout much of the 1930s, Roosevelt focused his administration's energy on the Great Depression. In addition, isolationist sentiment remained strong in the United States despite the rise of aggressive, dictatorial regimes in Germany and Italy. In the Neutrality Acts of 1935 to 1937, Congress made clear that neither the United States government nor private U.S. firms were to trade with belligerent nations. Roosevelt grew frustrated with these acts because they did not make a distinction between aggressors and victims in the conflicts of the 1930s. A later Neutrality Act (1939) allowed the United States to supply the opponents of fascism with materials on a cash-and-carry basis.

(4) Approving bonus payments to World War I veterans was not a problem addressed by President Franklin D. Roosevelt in his first months in office in 1933. The payment of bonuses was a contentious issue during the administration of Herbert Hoover (1929–1933). In June 1932, during the depths of the Great Depression, a group of World War I veterans, who called themselves the Bonus Expeditionary Force (BEF), or Bonus Army, marched into Washington, D.C. to demand a bonus that they had been promised for their service in the military. About 50,000 men, mostly unemployed and poor, set up an encampment in the nation's capital to demand their money. The handling of the Bonus Marchers—which included aggressively dismantling the encampment—seemed to reinforce many people's perception of President Hoover that he did not have the interests of ordinary Americans at heart. In 1935, Congress overrode President Roosevelt's veto and paid the veterans their bonus nine years early.

32. **3** The 1941 slogan by the America First Committee, "National Defense at Any Expense, but Keep Our Boys at Home," promoted isolationism. Throughout the 1930s, isolationists pushed for American neutrality in regard to the aggressive actions of Germany, Italy, and Japan. Many Americans remembered the horrors of World War I. In addition, the Senate's Nye committee (1934–1937) uncovered evidence that certain American corporations greatly profited from World War I. Americans wondered if the so-called merchants of death had pushed the country into World War I. Once World War II began, many Americans came to understand the gravity of the situation and began to side with the nations fighting against fascism. With this shift in public opinion and with his victory in the presidential election of 1940, President Franklin D. Roosevelt was ready to take more direct action. In March 1941, Congress approved his Lend-Lease Act, which allowed the United States to ship armaments to Britain in American ships. Although officially neutral,

the United States was moving steadily toward intervening on the side of Great Britain. The public, however, was not unified in its support of intervention. Isolationists, such as the renowned aviator Charles Lindbergh, continued to argue against any U.S. steps toward helping Britain. He was a leader of the America First Committee and, historians argue, a Nazi sympathizer. Even as late as 1941, many Americans still clearly had major reservations about America entering World War II. Debates about intervention ended abruptly on December 7, 1941. Japanese planes attacked the U.S. base at Pearl Harbor, Hawaii. Almost immediately, the United States entered World War II. With American involvement in World War II, the isolationist position was largely silenced.

WRONG CHOICES EXPLAINED:

(1) The America First Committee slogan, "National Defense at Any Expense, but Keep Our Boys at Home," did not promote globalism. As World War II began, the committee urged the United States to pursue an isolationist policy and stay out of the war. Globalism involves the opposite sentiment—greater involvement in global issues.

(2) The America First Committee slogan, "National Defense at Any Expense, but Keep Our Boys at Home," did not promote protective tariffs. Isolationists often support higher tariff rates, but the slogan does not refer to trade or tariffs.

(4) The America First Committee slogan, "National Defense at Any Expense, but Keep Our Boys at Home," did not promote reduced military spending. Although the committee was isolationist, it did endorse military expenditures. The slogan argues for "national defense at any expense."

33. **4** The main idea of the cartoon is that President Franklin D. Roosevelt is determined to supply the United States military and its allies with whatever it takes to defeat the Axis powers. In a 1940 speech, Roosevelt pledged that the United States would become the "arsenal for democracy" in the fight against fascism and militarism. To meet this pledge and reiterated by Roosevelt in the cartoon, the United States would have to step up its production of war-related materials dramatically and rapidly. In 1942, Roosevelt created the War Production Board, and later the Office of War Mobilization, to oversee the conversion from civilian industry to war production. Almost overnight, the persistent unemployment of the 1930s ended. After the United States entered the war in December 1941, the country faced the opposite problem—labor shortages. With millions of men and hundreds of thousands of women in the armed forces, the Roosevelt administration took several important steps to ensure a sufficient supply of factory workers. The government made a concerted effort to recruit women to participate in the war effort. Many recruiting posters were produced by the government, usually through the Office of War Information, showing women in industrial settings. The fictional

Rosie the Riveter character was often featured in this public relations campaign. Female workers were presented in a positive light—helping the nation as well as the men in combat abroad. Such a campaign was needed because prewar societal mores discouraged women from doing industrial work. During the Great Depression of the 1930s, women were encouraged to leave the job market so that there would be enough jobs available for male "breadwinners." The World War II recruiting campaign was successful. By 1945, one-third of the work force was female.

WRONG CHOICES EXPLAINED:

(1) The cartoon is not asserting that United States factories will not be able to manufacture military supplies in sufficient quantities. President Roosevelt says, "They're going to get it," in regard to military equipment for the United States military and its allies. The cartoon echoes Roosevelt's resolve; it says, "And he doesn't mean maybe!"

(2) The cartoon is not asserting that the federal government will most likely need to seize ownership of manufacturing plants. The cartoon doesn't allude to government seizures of factories. The government organized the conversion from civilian industry to war production with the War Production Board, and later the Office of War Mobilization. However, manufacturing plants stayed in private hands.

(3) The cartoon is not asserting that President Franklin D. Roosevelt expects other nations to supply the same amount of armaments as the United States. The cartoon focuses on Roosevelt's vow to supply the allies with armaments; it does not allude to the contributions of other nations.

34. **1** One major result of the production efforts described in the cartoon was that the high unemployment of the Great Depression was greatly reduced. In many ways, World War II, rather than the New Deal, ended the Great Depression. Unemployment fell from over 14 percent in 1940 to less than 2 percent for the last three years of the war—1943 to 1945. The United States began producing military equipment and ammunition when World War II started in 1939. War production spiked after the United States became involved in the war in late 1941. America's gross national product (GNP), which measures the total value of all goods produced and services provided by a country during a given year, rose steadily during the war years.

WRONG CHOICES EXPLAINED:

(2) The production efforts described in the cartoon did not result in producers of war-related materials going out of business after World War II. The United States successfully made the transition from a wartime economy to

a peacetime economy. Factories efficiently converted to the production of consumer goods, fueling robust economic growth in the 1950s and 1960s.

(3) The production efforts described in the cartoon did not result in critics claiming that president Franklin D. Roosevelt was abusing his treaty-making power. The production of war-related materials did not require the signing of a treaty. Further, the steps that Roosevelt took in regard to World War II, including the cash-and-carry policy, the Lend-Lease Act (1941), and the declaration of war all took place with the endorsement of Congress.

(4) The production efforts described in the cartoon did not result in the military having difficulty enlisting soldiers because the men were working in the munitions factories. A substantial number of men and women volunteered to participate in World War II. Over six million men and women enlisted in the armed services during the war. This accounts for almost 40 percent of the personnel in the armed services; the other 60 percent were drafted.

35. **1** The 1947 newspaper headlines concerning Jackie Robinson indicate that Robinson's integration of major league baseball was an important event in the history of civil rights. Robinson was the first African American to play major league baseball in the modern era. He began his major league career with the Brooklyn Dodgers in 1947. The headlines are generally positive in regard to Robinson's debut in major league baseball. One headline notes that the crowd of 26,000 cheered for Robinson when he scored a run. Another called the event "historic." Robinson met with a great deal of racist anger during his first year in major league baseball. Players on the St. Louis Cardinals threatened to go on strike if Robinson took the field for the Dodgers. In a famous incident during the 1948 season, fans in Cincinnati booed Robinson and shouted racist epithets at him before a game. In the face of this abuse, Robinson's teammate Pee Wee Reese put his arm around Robinson on the field in an act of solidarity. In the 1950s, Robinson publicly supported the civil rights movement and urged President Dwight D. Eisenhower to take action to resolve the crisis around the desegregation of public schools in Little Rock, Arkansas, in 1957.

WRONG CHOICES EXPLAINED:

(2) The 1947 headlines do not indicate that Jackie Robinson went on to organize the civil rights movement. Robinson supported the civil rights movement. He wrote a letter to President Dwight D. Eisenhower during the crisis over the integration of public schools in Little Rock, Arkansas, in 1957, urging the president to take action in defense of integration. However, Robinson was not an organizer of the movement.

(3) The 1947 headlines do not indicate that sports fans overwhelmingly encouraged the desegregation of public facilities. The headlines show that many

fans supported Robinson. However, they do not indicate either support or opposition to the broader issue of the desegregation of public facilities.

(4) The 1947 headlines do not indicate that Robinson's major league debut had no impact on race relations in the United States. One headline describes Robinson's debut as "historic." The extensive coverage of the event on the front page of the paper reflects the significance the paper placed on Robinson's debut in the major leagues.

36. **3** Winston Churchill's observation that an "iron curtain" had fallen across Europe warned the United States that Europe was threatened by the expansion of communism in Eastern Europe. This 1946 speech was one of several events that indicated that a Cold War had begun between the United States and the Soviet Union. In the following year, 1947, President Harry Truman announced that the United States would commit itself to containing communist expansion in Europe. Following World War II, the United States became increasingly alarmed with the expansionistic actions of the Soviet Union. The Soviet Red Army had pushed German troops out of Eastern Europe during the war, but Soviet troops did not evacuate this region once Germany surrendered. The Soviet Red Army stayed in Hungary, Romania, Bulgaria, Czechoslovakia, Poland, and the newly created East Germany. The Soviet Union installed communist regimes in those countries. The United States was alarmed at these moves but was unwilling to begin a third world war to push out the Soviets. However, the United States was determined not to tolerate the establishment of communist regimes beyond the "iron curtain." The term "containment" was coined after World War II to describe this policy. Truman put the idea of containment into practice in 1947 by providing $400 million in military aid to Greece and Turkey to prevent those countries from becoming communist. Other elements in the containment strategy were the Marshall Plan (1948), the Berlin Airlift (1948–1949), and the Korean War (1950–1953).

WRONG CHOICES EXPLAINED:

(1) The "iron curtain" speech by Winston Churchill was not intended to warn the United States that Europe was threatened by an embargo of its Middle East oil supplies. Much later, in 1973, the Organization of Petroleum Exporting Countries (OPEC), comprised of the Arab oil-producing nations, cut off oil exports to the United States and increased the price of oil. These moves were in retaliation for the United States' support for Israel in the 1973 Yom Kippur War between Israel and its Arab neighbors.

(2) The "iron curtain" speech by Winston Churchill was not intended to warn the United States that Europe was threatened by the growth of fascism in Great Britain. Fascist movements existed in the 1930s and 1940s in Great Britain, but

these movements represented a minority of the British population. Such fringe movements continued to exist after the war, as they did in many of the democracies of Western Europe as well as in the United States.

(4) The "iron curtain" speech by Winston Churchill was not intended to warn the United States that Europe was threatened by a nuclear attack by the Soviet Union. The United States had a monopoly on nuclear weapons at the time of Churchill's speech (1946). The Soviet Union did not successfully test a nuclear weapon until 1951.

37. **3** The North Atlantic Treaty Organization (NATO) and the Warsaw Pact are examples of mutual defense. The United States and the Soviet Union emerged at the end of World War II as rival superpowers in the Cold War. The Soviet Union occupied the nations of Eastern Europe after the war. The United Stated was worried that the Soviet Union would try to push into Western Europe. The leader of the Soviet Union, Joseph Stalin, insisted that he wanted to have only friendly nations on the border of the Soviet Union. In order to block any further aggression by the Soviet Union, Truman issued the Truman Doctrine, in which he said that the goal of the United States would be to contain communism. Toward this end, the United States extended military aid to Greece and Turkey (1947) and economic aid to the war-ravaged nations of Western Europe in the form of the Marshall Plan (1948). In 1948, the United States decided to challenge the Soviet blockade of West Berlin. In addition, the United States was one of the founding members of NATO in 1949. This marked the first time that the United States joined a peacetime alliance. The idea of mutual defense means that members of NATO view an attack on any one member as an attack on all members. In response, the Soviet Union organized the Warsaw Pact in 1955, a mutual defense alliance between the Soviet Union and the communist nations of Eastern and Central Europe.

WRONG CHOICES EXPLAINED:
(1) The North Atlantic Treaty Organization and the Warsaw Pact are not examples of dollar diplomacy. Dollar diplomacy describes the policy, put forth by President William Howard Taft (1909–1913), of protecting the United States' commercial interests in the Caribbean rather than pursuing strategic military goals.

(2) The North Atlantic Treaty Organization and the Warsaw Pact are not examples of Lend-Lease. The Lend-Lease Act (March 1941) was a measure initiated by President Franklin D. Roosevelt to extend military aid to Great Britain during World War II before the United States entered the conflict. Later in 1941, the United States entered the conflict following the Japanese attack on American territory—the naval base at Pearl Harbor, Hawaii (December 1941).

(4) The North Atlantic Treaty Organization and the Warsaw Pact are not examples of manifest destiny. The term *manifest destiny* was coined in an 1845 newspaper article. It captured the fervor of the westward expansion movement, implying that it was God's plan that the United States take over and settle the entire continent. Americans who did settle out West were probably driven more by economic factors, such as cheap land or precious metals, than by a desire to fulfill God's plan.

38. **4** Belief in the domino theory by presidents Dwight D. Eisenhower, John F. Kennedy, and Lyndon B. Johnson directly influenced their decisions to increase United States military involvement in Vietnam. The domino theory asserts that when a nation becomes communist, its neighbors will be more likely to become communist. The name of the theory alludes to the game of lining up dominos in a row so that when the first one is pushed over, the next ones in the row will each be knocked over as well. The theory presumes that communism is imposed on a country from the outside—that communism does not develop as a result of internal conditions. The United States' interest in Vietnam began under President Eisenhower in the 1950s when it sent military advisors and assistance to the government of South Vietnam after Vietnam was divided in 1954. The United States feared that South Vietnam would become a communist nation, as had North Vietnam. President Kennedy continued supporting the government of South Vietnam. The United States became heavily involved in the Vietnam War after Congress gave President Johnson a blank check with the Tonkin Gulf Resolution (1964). Despite the presence of over half a million United States troops and the firepower of the U.S. military, President Johnson was not able to declare victory over the communist rebels in South Vietnam. As the war dragged on and as the United States suffered more casualties, many Americans began to question the wisdom of American policies in Vietnam. United States involvement in Vietnam continued until 1973 when President Richard Nixon withdrew the last American troops. In 1975, the government of South Vietnam became communist.

WRONG CHOICES EXPLAINED:
    (1), (2), and (3) According to the domino theory, communist movements do not emerge as responses to conditions within a country. Rather, communism is forced upon a country by a neighboring country. If this is the case, as U.S. policy makers believed during the Cold War, the United States had a responsibility to act as a countervailing force and to block communist aggression. That approach meant that the United States would be more active in global affairs. During the entirety of the Cold War, the United States led the charge against the expansion of communism. It would not, therefore, have abandoned the North Atlantic Treaty Organization (NATO) and not rejected the ideas of collective security, as

in choice 1. The United States would not have supported a return to neutrality, as in choice 2. Finally, the United States would not have abandoned Berlin to communist aggression by ending the Berlin airlift, as in choice 3.

39. **4** The War on Poverty was an attempt by President Lyndon B. Johnson to raise the standard of living for many Americans. The War on Poverty, which was part of Johnson's Great Society agenda, refers to a series of domestic programs that Johnson pushed through Congress in 1964 and 1965. The War on Poverty included the creation of Medicare to provide health insurance for the elderly and of Medicaid to provide health insurance for welfare recipients. Johnson sought to improve education for poor students with the Head Start program, which created preschool programs, and with the Elementary and Secondary Education Act. Other initiatives included creating welfare programs, expanding civil rights for African Americans, and building public housing projects. The programs had limited success. The cycle of poverty proved to be too difficult to break in a short period of time. In addition, the Vietnam War became increasingly costly, diverting billions of dollars that could have been used for antipoverty programs.

WRONG CHOICES EXPLAINED:

(1) President Lyndon Johnson's War on Poverty was not an attempt to send medical aid to African nations. The United States provided extensive foreign aid to the developing world during the Cold War. Much of United States foreign aid came under the umbrella of the newly created United States Agency for International Development (USAID), which started in 1961. The War on Poverty, however, focused on poverty in the United States.

(2) President Lyndon Johnson's War on Poverty was not an attempt to strengthen the Peace Corps. The Peace Corps was created in 1961 by President John F. Kennedy (1961–1963) in order to give support to developing nations in fields such as education, agriculture, and health care. The program depended on volunteers, often recent college graduates, to work on development projects in poor countries. The War on Poverty, however, focused on poverty in the United States.

(3) President Lyndon Johnson's War on Poverty was not an attempt to decrease the number of immigrants from Latin America. Johnson expanded opportunities for immigrants to enter the United States with the passage of the Immigration and Nationality Act of 1965 (also known as the Hart-Celler Act), which was part of the Great Society agenda. The act changed American immigration policy that had been in place since the 1920s. It abolished the national quota system and replaced that system with overall limits on immigration into the United States. The War on Poverty, however, focused on poverty in the United States.

40. **1** In the "Letter from Birmingham Jail," Martin Luther King, Jr., was arguing for civil disobedience. King drew on several religious, philosophical, and political traditions in developing his approach to social change. Civil disobedience is a philosophical principle that asserts that it is one's right, indeed, one's responsibility to resist unjust laws. Earlier in American history, the principle was articulated by the transcendentalist thinker Henry David Thoreau in his 1849 essay *Resistance to Civil Government (Civil Disobedience)*. King also stressed the importance of nonviolence and pacifism, which have deep roots. Many Christians cite the biblical injunction to "turn the other cheek" if struck. Pacifism is especially strong in the Quaker tradition. King also gained inspiration from Mahatma Gandhi's campaign to resist British authority in India in the first half of the 20th century. Gandhi taught that to resort to violence was to stoop to the moral level of the oppressor. King was a central figure in the civil rights movement of the 1950s and 1960s. In 1963, his organization, the Southern Christian Leadership Conference, decided to launch a major campaign in Birmingham, Alabama, to protest racial segregation. The public safety commissioner of Birmingham, Eugene "Bull" Connor, would not tolerate public demonstrations. He used fire hoses, police dogs, and brutal force to put down the campaign. During the Birmingham campaign, King was arrested and wrote his famous "Letter from Birmingham Jail," a response to a call by white clergy members to allow the legal system to address the issue of racial injustice. King insisted that the black community had waited long enough for change to happen. The campaign proved to be a turning point in the push for federal legislation, including the Civil Rights Act (1964).

WRONG CHOICES EXPLAINED:

(2) In the "Letter from Birmingham Jail," Martin Luther King, Jr., was not arguing for armed resistance. The passage makes no reference to either violence or weaponry. Rather, King discussed the reason that civil rights activists were violating unjust laws.

(3) In the "Letter from Birmingham Jail," Martin Luther King, Jr., was not arguing for Black Power. Later in the 1960s, some advocates for civil rights adopted the call for Black Power. The Black Panther Party, which formed in 1966, grew out of the Black Power movement and embraced self-defense and militant rhetoric. Initially, the Back Panthers focused on community organizing. However, their activities grew increasingly confrontational.

(4) In the "Letter from Birmingham Jail," Martin Luther King, Jr., was not arguing for containment. Containment refers to the goal of preventing the expansion of communism during the Cold War (approximately 1945–1991). President Harry S. Truman articulated this goal, also known as the Truman Doctrine, in a speech to Congress in 1947.

41. **4** A main goal of President Richard Nixon's policy of détente was to reduce tensions between the United States and the Soviet Union. *Détente* is the French word for "loosening." It refers to an easing of tensions in the Cold War and to a warming of relations between the United States and the Soviet Union. It may seem ironic that Richard Nixon, a man who made a name for himself as a strong anticommunist, was responsible for the policy of détente. After all, as a congressman, Nixon pursued suspected Soviet spy Alger Hiss (1950). However, Nixon's anticommunist credentials enabled him to open relations with communist nations without being accused of being "soft on communism." In 1972, Nixon became the first United States president to visit Communist China. Later in 1972, he held meetings with Soviet leaders in Moscow. The meetings produced several agreements, including an agreement to limit antiballistic missile systems (ABMs).

WRONG CHOICES EXPLAINED:

(1) Sponsoring free elections in North Korea was not a goal of President Richard Nixon's détente policy. Currently, the Korean peninsula is divided into North Korea and South Korea at the 38th parallel. Korea was divided into two occupation zones after World War II, one controlled by the United States and one controlled by the Soviet Union. The two sides were unable to agree on a unification plan. By 1948, two separate nations were established with a border at the 38th parallel. North Korea has always been run in an authoritarian manner by the communist Workers' Party of Korea. It does not hold free elections, nor has this been a demand of the United States.

(2) Negotiating an end to the Arab-Israeli conflict was not a goal of President Richard Nixon's détente policy. The United States has made attempts to ease Arab-Israeli tensions. Since the founding of Israel in 1948, tensions have existed in the Middle East. In 1977, Egyptian President Anwar Sadat and Israeli Prime Minister Menachem Begin met with President Jimmy Carter at the Camp David presidential retreat in Maryland for 13 days and emerged with the basis for a peace treaty. The treaty resulted in an end to hostilities between Israel and Egypt, but tensions continued to exist between Israel and its other neighbors. The most serious tension since the Camp David Accords has been between Israel and Palestinians.

(3) Ending diplomatic relations with China was not a goal of President Richard Nixon's détente policy. Nixon began the process of restoring diplomatic relations between the two countries. The United States ended relations with China after China had become a communist country in 1949. With his trip to Beijing in 1972, Nixon became the first American president to visit Communist China. In 1973, both nations established liaison offices in the other country. This was a first step toward establishing formal diplomatic relations, which occurred in 1979.

42. **2** Charges of perjury and obstruction of justice led to President Bill Clinton's impeachment. The impeachment of President Clinton represents an important turning point in the deterioration of relations between the two main political parties. The proceedings also demonstrate the growing strength of the more conservative elements within the Republican Party. Republicans doggedly pursued evidence of scandal relating to President Clinton. During President Clinton's first term, Kenneth Starr was appointed as an independent counsel to investigate the participation of Bill and Hillary Clinton in a failed and fraudulent real estate project in Arkansas that dated back to 1978, when Bill Clinton was governor. Starr pursued this Whitewater case relentlessly but never tied the Clintons to the fraud. President Clinton, however, was not able to avoid implication in a more salacious scandal. Clinton was publicly accused of having a sexual affair with a White House intern named Monica Lewinsky. Clinton denied the accusations publicly and also before a federal grand jury. When Clinton was later forced to admit the affair, Congressional Republicans felt they had evidence of impeachable crimes—committing perjury to a grand jury and obstructing justice. Clinton was impeached by the House of Representatives in 1998. Impeachment is the act of bringing charges against a federal official; it is parallel to indictment in the criminal court system. After impeachment by the House, the Senate conducts a trial based on the charges listed in the "articles of impeachment." Clinton was found "not guilty" by the Senate (two-thirds are needed for conviction). Many Americans disapproved of his personal misconduct but also resented the attempt by Republicans to remove the president from office.

WRONG CHOICES EXPLAINED:
(1) The impeachment of President Bill Clinton did not stem from charges of excessive use of the pardon power. The Constitution gives the president the power to pardon individuals found guilty in federal criminal proceedings. The Constitution does not place a limit on the number of pardons a president may issue, so "excessive" use of the pardon power would not be considered an impeachable offense.

(3) The impeachment of President Bill Clinton did not stem from charges of illegal use of campaign funds. Federal campaign regulations stipulate that a candidate or an elected official cannot use campaign funds for personal purposes, unrelated to getting elected. Campaign funds cannot be treated as a personal piggy bank. Clinton was not accused of improperly using campaign funds.

(4) The impeachment of President Bill Clinton did not stem from charges of the misuse of war powers and deficit spending. During the Vietnam War, members of Congress accused President Richard Nixon of the misuse of war powers by conducting secret bombing campaigns in Cambodia (1969–1973).

The president may seek congressional approval for military actions and may take actions unilaterally in times of emergency. The degree of latitude given the president is open to interpretation and debate. In the aftermath of the bombing of Cambodia, Congress passed the War Powers Resolution (1973), which placed checks on the president's ability to use military force without congressional approval. Deficit spending is defined as the amount by which government spending exceeds revenue over a particular period of time. Although deficit spending is subject to disagreement among economists and politicians, it is not a crime.

43. **2** One way in which Social Security, Medicare, and Medicaid are similar is that they are all examples of social welfare programs. The Social Security system was one of several programs that comprised the New Deal, which was President Franklin D. Roosevelt's (1933–1945) agenda to address the poverty and dislocation caused by the Great Depression of the 1930s. The Social Security system addressed the welfare of retired people and people with disabilities. Working people pay into the system during their working years and then receive monthly payments once they reach the age of 65. Medicare and Medicaid were part of President Lyndon B. Johnson's War on Poverty, which was a series of domestic programs that Johnson pushed through Congress in 1964 and 1965. The War on Poverty was a key component of President Johnson's Great Society agenda. Medicare provides health insurance for the elderly, and Medicaid provides health insurance to low-income people. Other initiatives included creating additional welfare programs, expanding civil rights for African Americans, and building public housing projects. The programs had mixed results. Medicare and Medicaid have proved to be highly successful, but the cycle of poverty proved to be too difficult to break in a short period of time. Both the New Deal and the War on Poverty expanded social welfare programs.

WRONG CHOICES EXPLAINED:

(1) Social Security, Medicare, and Medicaid are not programs that provide aid to education. As part of the Great Society, President Lyndon Johnson sought to improve education for poor students with the Head Start program (1965), which created preschool programs, and with the Elementary and Secondary Education Act (1965).

(3) Social Security, Medicare, and Medicaid are not programs that attempt to balance the federal budget. The Social Security system is funded primarily through payroll taxes. People pay into the system when they are working, and they draw from the system when they retire. Social Security does not, for the most part, draw from the general fund. Therefore, it does not have an impact on the budget. Medicare is funded by the Social Security system; Medicaid draws its funds from the general fund.

(4) Social Security, Medicare, and Medicaid are not programs that create public works projects. President Franklin D. Roosevelt's New Deal did create several public works programs to put the unemployed to work. Most notable were the Civilian Conservation Corps (1933), which targeted young men to improve parks and to do conservation work, and the Works Progress Administration (1935), which created millions of jobs in a variety of fields, including building roads and painting murals.

44. **3** The cartoonist is critical of the leadership of President George W. Bush and Vice President Dick Cheney for weakening the system of checks and balances. In the system of checks and balances, each of the three branches of government—the executive, the legislative, and the judicial—has the ability to limit, or check, the powers of the other two. The goal is to create balance among the three branches, with no branch able to dominate the other two. Examples include the president's ability to veto bills passed by Congress and the Senate's ability to approve or reject Supreme Court nominees. The cartoon depicts the three branches of government as three actual branches on a tree. Bush, dressed as a king, and Cheney sit on one branch—the executive branch. The other two branches are missing in the cartoon; they have been cut by Cheney. The implication is that Bush and Cheney have amassed greater power in the executive branch and have severely undermined the powers of the other two branches.

WRONG CHOICES EXPLAINED:
(1) The cartoon does not allude to the clear-cutting of forests. The cutting of tree branches in the cartoon is meant metaphorically; the branches symbolize the branches of government. Logging companies have often cut every tree in an area, causing erosion and ecological disruption. The practice has been roundly condemned by environmental groups. Currently, logging companies are encouraged to manage forests by cutting only certain trees and leaving others for future years.

(2) The cartoon alludes to the relationship among the three branches of government. It does not specifically refer to presidential vetoes. The Constitution grants the president the power to issue vetoes. President Bush did not overuse the power. He issued his very first veto, after five years in office, just two days before the cartoon was published, in July 2006. Bush vetoed the Stem Cell Research Enhancement Act, which would have provided federal funding for embryonic stem cell research. That veto might have prompted the cartoon, but the cartoon focused on the system of checks and balances.

(4) The cartoon does not allude to the war in Iraq. President George W. Bush did initiate war in Iraq. Operation Iraqi Freedom (2003–2011) was the attempt by the United States to remove Saddam Hussein from office and create a less belligerent and more democratic government in Iraq. President George W. Bush insisted that Hussein was developing weapons of mass destruction that

could be used against the United States and its allies. U.S. forces failed to find evidence of such weapons. Defeating the Iraqi army and removing Saddam Hussein from office was relatively easy. However, creating stability in Iraq proved to be an elusive goal. Attacks by insurgents continued, both against U.S. forces and between different factions within Iraq, until most American forces had withdrawn from Iraq by 2011.

45. **1** President James Monroe's proclamation of the Monroe Doctrine was most consistent with the ideas presented by George Washington in his Farewell Address. President Washington is closely identified with the idea of neutrality. He issued the 1793 Neutrality Act. In his Farewell Address, Washington urged the United States to avoid "permanent alliances" with foreign powers. He did not want the newly independent nation, which was on precarious footing, to be drawn into the seemingly endless conflicts of Europe. The particular circumstances of the 1793 Neutrality Act grew out of the French Revolution, which began in 1789. Americans were divided over France's revolution. The debates took on greater significance after France and Great Britain went to war in 1793. Many Americans felt that the United States had an obligation to help France because France had helped the United States in the American Revolution. A treaty between the two countries (1778) committed the United States to help France if it were under attack. Others argued that the United States should stay out. After all, the treaty was made with a French government that no longer existed, and the French Revolution had devolved from a democratic movement into a bloodbath. The latter position won Washington's support. His calls for neutrality have been invoked by isolationists throughout American history. In 1823, President James Monroe issued the Monroe Doctrine with the intent of preventing European powers from taking over Latin-American nations. Monroe was alarmed by the threats made by the Holy Alliance of Russia, Prussia, and Austria to restore Spain's lost American colonies. He also opposed a decree by the Russian czar that claimed all the Pacific Northwest north of the 51st parallel. Although both problems worked themselves out, Monroe issued a statement warning European nations not to attempt to set up colonies in the Americas. Both Washington and Monroe took steps to avoid conflicts with European nations. The Monroe Doctrine and Washington's Farewell Address became cornerstones of America's isolationist foreign policy.

WRONG CHOICES EXPLAINED:
(2) President James Polk's policy toward Mexico in 1846 was not consistent with the ideas presented by President George Washington in his Farewell Address. President Washington argued for neutrality. President Polk, on the other hand, pushed for United States to declare war on a foreign power.

The Mexican-American War (1846–1848) grew out of the annexation of Texas (1845). The United States and Mexico disagreed over the southern border of Texas. Skirmishes in the disputed area led to war between the two countries. The United States won the war and acquired the huge territory that comprised the northern provinces of Mexico, known as the Mexican Cession.

(3) President William McKinley's request for a declaration of war against Spain in 1898 was not consistent with the ideas presented by President George Washington in his Farewell Address. President Washington argued for neutrality and avoidance of "entanglements" with Europe. President McKinley, on the other hand, pushed for the United States to declare war on a European power. The Spanish-American War had several causes—concern over American sugar investments in Cuba, sympathy for the Cuban people in their struggle for independence from Spain, the sinking of the American ship the USS *Maine* in the Havana harbor, and sensationalistic "yellow journalism." In the Treaty of Paris, which ended the Spanish-American War, Spain ceded Puerto Rico, Guam, and the Philippines to the United States.

(4) President George H.W. Bush's decision to engage in the Persian Gulf War in 1990 was not consistent with the ideas presented by President George Washington in his Farewell Address. President Washington argued for neutrality and avoidance of alliances. President Bush pushed for war against Iraq and organized a coalition of nations to join the United States. In 1990, Iraqi leader Saddam Hussein sent the Iraqi military into Kuwait to occupy that country. The goal of Operation Desert Storm was to remove Iraqi forces from Kuwait. The operation was successful. Hussein was quickly forced to withdraw his troops. The United States suffered relatively few casualties.

46. **3** The Populist movement of the 1890s and the civil rights movement of the 1950s and 1960s are similar in that both were attempts to improve the lives of groups who were oppressed. The Populist movement was a political insurgency by small-scale farmers in the late 1800s. The Populists grew angry at the concentration of wealth and power by eastern industrialists. By the late 1800s, it became increasingly difficult for small farmers to compete with large-scale agricultural operations. Expensive machinery replaced handheld tools. Although mechanization reduced the man-hours needed for agricultural tasks, it worked to undermine small-scale, family farms. Populists followed in the footsteps of the Granger movement (founded in 1867) by pushing for regulation of railroad companies, which often overcharged small-scale farmers. They also supported a national income tax so that those with higher incomes would pay more than the poor. Populists also supported increasing the amount of money in circulation. Farmers supported inflationary policies so that the prices they received for their

produce would increase. The civil rights movement focused on the oppression of African Americans. By the 1950s and 1960s, a massive movement had developed in the United States to challenge the Jim Crow system. The civil rights movement gained strength after the Supreme Court, in the case of *Brown* v. *Board of Education of Topeka* (1954), declared that segregation in schools had no place in America. In the years following the *Brown* decision occurred the Montgomery bus boycott in 1955 and 1956, the lunch counter sit-ins in 1960, the Freedom Rides in 1962, and a whole host of other civil rights activities. The high point of the movement might have been the March on Washington in 1963, where Martin Luther King, Jr., gave his "I Have a Dream" speech. It was in this context that the movement achieved significant victories. The Civil Rights Act of 1964 banned segregation in public facilities, and the Voting Rights Act of 1965 removed barriers to African Americans voting.

WRONG CHOICES EXPLAINED:

(1) Neither the Populist movement of the 1890s nor the civil rights movement of the 1950s and 1960s sought to restrict the power of the executive branch. On several occasions, the civil rights movement called on the president to take executive action to ensure that civil rights court decisions and orders were enforced. For example in 1957, when violence erupted in Little Rock, Arkansas, in response to the desegregation of Central High School, President Eisenhower sent in federal troops to guarantee the safety of the students and to ensure that Little Rock would comply with the Supreme Court decision in *Brown* v. *Board of Education of Topeka* (1954).

(2) Neither the Populist movement of the 1890s nor the civil rights movement of the 1950s and 1960s focused exclusively on solving the problems brought about by industrialization. The Populist movement did seek to check the power of industrial corporations. However, the focus of the movement was more on problems faced by farmers than by factory workers. The focus of the civil rights movement was more on political reform than on solving problems brought about by industrialization.

(4) The civil rights movement of the 1950s and 1960s focused on racial equality. The movement did not focus exclusively on pressuring states to change their policies. Much of the focus was on pressuring the three branches of the federal government to promote racial equality. Earlier, the Populist movement did not embrace racial equality. Many of its members reflected prevailing white supremacist ideas. Some white southern Populists saw that they would have more power as a biracial movement, but racist attitudes in the South prevented the formation of such a movement. In response, African-American tenant farmers and sharecroppers in the South formed the Colored Farmers Alliance in 1886. The organization had 1.2 million members at its height.

47. **2** The tactics illustrated in the cartoon were most closely associated with government leaders investigating communist activities after World War II. The cartoon is mocking the government's tactics of investigating individuals during the late 1940s and 1950s. The cartoon is depicting a teacher who appears to be guilty of nothing more than having a world map on the wall that includes the Soviet Union and displaying an image of Thomas Jefferson. The investigators are about to alter the world map by simply cutting out the Soviet Union. Perhaps the investigators in the cartoon perceived Jefferson's words from the Declaration of Independence—that "all men are created equal"—to be subversive during the Jim Crow era. A central figure in the anticommunist movement was Senator Joseph McCarthy. In 1950, he announced that he had a list of "known communists" who had infiltrated the State Department. This and similar claims, which were mostly baseless, created a name for McCarthy and set the stage for a host of measures to halt this perceived threat. Congress established committees to investigate Communist Party infiltration in different sectors of society. Congress especially targeted the entertainment industry, fearing that communists would subtly get their message out through television and movies. Loyalty oaths became commonplace for public sector employees, such as teachers. The movement drew on a long history of anti-intellectualism in the United States; the cartoon notes that one of the teacher's "crimes" is that she "reads books." The movement began to lessen in intensity by the mid-1950s. McCarthy himself went too far, accusing members of the military establishment of being communists. The Senate voted to censure him in 1954, thus ending the worst excesses of what many people referred to as a witch hunt.

WRONG CHOICES EXPLAINED:
(1) The cartoon is not associated with isolationists supporting neutrality during the 1930s. The references to the Soviet Union and "anti-subversive" committees indicate that the cartoon is commenting on anticommunism in the 1950s. Isolationism—entailing a retreat from world affairs—was strong in the 1920s and 1930s. The policy of isolationism led to the Senate rejecting the Treaty of Versailles. Approval of the treaty by the Senate would have made the United States a member of the League of Nations. Isolationist sentiment in the 1920s also led to the enactment of legislation that dramatically restricted immigration into the United States.

(3) The cartoon is not associated with increased federal spending for education in the 1960s. The purpose of the cartoon is to depict overzealous anticommunist investigators, who were searching for nonexistent evidence in garbage cans and among school supplies. Schools did struggle to gain sufficient funds in the 1950s and 1960s as the baby boom generation began to enter public schools. Schools receive the vast majority of their funds from local government, not from

the federal government. However, Great Society initiatives such as the Head Start (1965) program, which created preschool programs, and the Elementary and Secondary Education Act (1965), expanded the role of the federal government in public education.

(4) The cartoon is not associated with Congress promoting increased security after the September 11, 2001, attacks. The references to the Soviet Union and "anti-subversive" committees indicate that the cartoon is commenting on anti-communism in the 1950s. The United States did take measures to promote increased security after the 2001 terrorist attacks. The Transportation Security Administration (TSA) was created after the attacks and immediately increased security at airports. In 2003, the TSA was folded into the Department of Homeland Security. The department also absorbed the Immigration and Naturalization Service. The TSA is a cabinet level department, with the responsibility of protecting the United States from terrorist attacks and natural disasters.

48. **4** "Flappers" in the 1920s, "beatniks" in the 1950s, and "hippies" in the 1960s are all examples of individuals who disagreed with traditional societal values. All three groups challenged mainstream cultural norms. The decade of the 1920s saw many women challenging traditional gender norms. The "new woman" of the 1920s was more engaged in public issues. She might have participated in the political struggles of the progressive movement and gained a new sense of confidence in public issues, especially after women achieved the right to vote in 1920. The changing image of women during the 1920s was symbolized by the popularity of the flappers and their style of dress. Flappers openly defied Victorian moral codes about "proper" ladylike behavior. In the 1950s, beatniks challenged an increasingly homogenous mass culture. They rejected some of the central pillars of postwar culture—conformity, the suburban lifestyle, the consumer society, and patriotism. The values and norms of the beatniks are evident in the beat literary movement. The most important text of the beat movement is *On the Road*, by Jack Kerouac (1957). Initially written on a scroll—a stream of consciousness screed—the book depicts a life of spontaneity and freedom. Also important is Allen Ginsberg's book of poems, *Howl* (1956), which ripped apart the foundations of Cold War American society. The beatniks of the 1950s influenced the hippie movement. This countercultural movement became visible in the late 1960s in neighborhoods such as San Francisco's Haight-Ashbury and New York's Lower East Side. A variety of activities came to be associated with the hippie movement—urban and rural communal living, a do-it-yourself approach to the varied tasks of life, mystic spiritual experiences, drug use, experimental music, and avant-garde art. Taking inspiration from sit-ins of the civil rights movement, the counterculture organized be-ins—gatherings of young people in San Francisco's Golden Gate Park or New York's Central Park.

WRONG CHOICES EXPLAINED:

(1) "Flappers" in the 1920s, "beatniks" in the 1950s, and "hippies" in the 1960s are not examples of political groups that wanted to limit individual rights. The opposite is closer to the truth. Although none of the three cultural movements was explicitly political, many flappers supported the cause of women's rights, and many beatniks and hippies supported the civil rights movement and other movements for change.

(2) "Flappers" in the 1920s and "beatniks" in the 1950s are not examples of citizens who wanted to return to simpler lifestyles. Some hippies in the 1960s did attempt to simplify their lives. Many moved to rural communes, grew their own food, created their own art and music, and produced various products (bread, soap, ceramics) by hand.

(3) "Flappers" in the 1920s, "beatniks" in the 1950s, and "hippies" in the 1960s are not examples of writers who supported United States foreign policy goals. The opposite is closer to the truth. Many beatniks in the 1950s were critical of the nuclear arms race. In the 1960s, many hippies participated in the large-scale anti–Vietnam War movement.

49. **4** The Great Depression and the economic crisis known as the Great Recession (December 2007–June 2009) were similar in that both led to an expansion of the federal government's role in stabilizing the economy. The Great Depression was the most severe economic downturn in American history. President Franklin D. Roosevelt (1933–1945) greatly expanded the role of the federal government with the New Deal, which was the set of programs proposed by the administration to address the poverty and dislocation caused by the Great Depression. Roosevelt's initiatives were unprecedented in their scope and direction. The Roosevelt administration provided direct relief, or what would be known as welfare today, to millions of impoverished families. In addition, the New Deal created jobs programs such as Civilian Conservation Corps (1933), which focused on young men, and the vast Works Progress Administration (1935), which consisted of a myriad of public projects. In addition, the New Deal addressed the welfare of the aged by creating the Social Security system in 1935. The Great Recession of December 2007–June 2009, which resulted from the bursting of the housing bubble, from problems in the automobile industry, and from the collapse of major financial institutions, was the worst economic crisis since the Great Depression. Presidents George W. Bush and Barack Obama again expended the role of the federal government to respond to the economic crisis. In 2008, President George W. Bush initiated a $17.4 bailout of Generals Motors and Chrysler; the Obama administration continued this program. The bailout was successful. The American automobile industry recovered and paid back most of the money that was used in the bailout. President Obama also enacted a major

stimulus bill—the American Recovery and Reinvestment Act (2009). The act provided almost $800 billion to state and local governments to be used for infrastructure projects, schools, and hospitals. Finally, the Obama administration pushed for measures to add regulations to the financial industry in order to rein in some of the risky practices that led to the recession of 2008. The Dodd-Frank Wall Street Reform and Consumer Protection Act was designed to regulate financial markets and to protect consumers.

WRONG CHOICES EXPLAINED:

(1) The Great Depression and the economic crisis known as the Great Recession (December 2007–June 2009) did not lead to a surplus in the federal budget. Economic crises tend to lead to budget deficits. If unemployment is high, fewer people are paying income tax, thus reducing government revenue. Further, the government often creates programs to soften the blow of the economic downturn—as it did during both the Great Depression and the Great Recession. Such programs draw money from the federal budget. Declining revenues and rising expenditures lead to budget deficits.

(2) The Great Depression and the economic crisis known as the Great Recession (December 2007–June 2009) did not lead to a decrease in support for unemployment insurance. High unemployment during both periods led to an increase in support for unemployment insurance. Unemployment insurance was created during the Great Depression. The establishment of federal unemployment insurance was part of the Social Security Act of 1935. Unemployment insurance is a joint federal-state venture. Employers pay payroll taxes to the government, which can then extend unemployment benefits to workers if they lose their job through no fault of their own.

(3) The Great Depression and the economic crisis known as the Great Recession (December 2007–June 2009) did not lead to a limit on the power of the Federal Reserve System. In both cases, the Federal Reserve Bank (the Fed) implemented policies intended to stem the crises. If the economy is sluggish the Fed will attempt to stimulate economic growth by increasing the money supply. An important mechanism for regulating the money supply is raising or lowering the interest rates at which the Fed loans money to other banks. Other banks follow suit, raising or lowering the interest rates at which they loan money to the public. By lowering interest rates, the Fed stimulates economic activity, making it more attractive for people to borrow money to make major purchases and thus putting more money into circulation.

50. **2** The principal cause of the population changes shown on the map is continued westward expansion. The small triangles on the map depict the mean center of population at different points in United States history. To understand the

concept of the mean center of population, first imagine the United States as represented by a rigid and flat surface. Next, imagine identical weights being placed onto this plane, with each weight representing a person living in the U.S. If each and every person living in the United States was represented by a weight, the mean center of population would be the point that would keep the plane in perfect balance. Therefore if people moved farther west, the mean center of population would have to move west as well to keep the plane in balance. The mean center of the United States has done just that over the nation's history. In 1790, it was in the far eastern section of the United States (Maryland). This indicates that the eastern portion of the country contained the vast majority of the population. The mean center moved to the Midwest (Missouri) by 2010, indicating the continued westward movement of people. Several factors have contributed to the western migration of people. In the 19th century, many Americans thought of westward expansion as a divinely sanctioned march, that it was the manifest destiny of the United States to take over the entire continent. The government encouraged westward expansion with the Homestead Act (1862), which provided free land in the West to settlers who were willing to farm it. Hundreds of thousands of people applied for and were granted homesteads. The expansion of railroads into the west, leading to the completion of a transcontinental railroad in 1869, also encouraged white settlement in the Great Plains region. This movement was especially damaging for the Native American Indians of the West who were driven off their lands and relegated to several western reservations. The westward march continued in the 20th century. Americans have been drawn by the climate and economic opportunities offered by Sun Belt states, such as Arizona, Nevada, and California.

WRONG CHOICES EXPLAINED:

(1) The population changes shown on the map were not caused by employment opportunities in the northeastern states. The map shows the continued trend of westward migration. If employment opportunities in the northeastern states led to a reversal of that trend, the mean center of population would have moved east.

(3) The population changes shown on the map were not caused by the enactment of immigration quotas. The immigration quota acts of the 1920s—the Emergency Quota Act (1921) and the National Origins Act (1924)—greatly reduced immigration into the United States. However, these acts did not have an impact on migration patterns within the United States.

(4) The population changes shown on the map were not caused by movement from farms to cities. The trend of Americans moving from rural communities to urban communities was strong during the late 1800s. Between 1860 and 1900, the number of Americans who lived in cities jumped from 6.2 million to over 30

million, which amounted to a shift in the urban population from 20 percent of the total population to 40 percent. By 1920, census data indicated that, for the first time, more Americans lived in cities than in the countryside. However, the movement of people from rural areas in states such as Iowa or Kansas to urban centers such as New York or Philadelphia was offset by a general movement of the population in a western direction, including to cities in California.

PART II: THEMATIC ESSAY

Geography—Territorial Acquisitions

The physical size of the United States has grown dramatically over the course of its history. Colonists initially lived on or near the Atlantic Coast. Slowly, they moved into the interior of the continent, crossing the Appalachian Mountains and moving westward toward the Mississippi River. When the United States officially received its independence from Great Britain in 1783, its western boundary extended to the Mississippi River. In less than a century, the nation extended all the way to the Pacific Ocean. By the end of the 19th century, the United States had acquired possessions in the Caribbean, the Pacific, and Asia. The United States acquired new territory by a variety of methods. These acquisitions have had both positive and negative effects on the United States. This essay focuses on two territorial acquisitions, California (1848) and Puerto Rico (1899).

The United States acquired California as a result of the Mexican-American War. The war took place in the context of the American quest to spread over the North American continent. Many Americans came to believe that it was the nation's manifest destiny to extend all the way to the Pacific. The term captured the fervor of the westward expansion movement, implying that it was God's plan for the United States to take over and settle the entire continent. Americans who did settle out West were probably driven more by economic factors, such as cheap land or precious metals, than by a desire to fulfill a divine plan.

The push toward the Pacific Ocean generated interest in Mexican territory among many Americans. Americans had been settling in the Mexican territory of Texas as far back as the 1820s. In 1836, Texans fought for and won independence from Mexico, becoming the Lone Star Republic. Many Texans were eager for their Lone Star Republic to join the United States. However, concern about the expansion of slavery put the issue of Texas annexation on the back burner until the election of the expansionist President James Polk in 1844. Texas joined the United States as the 15th slave state in 1844. Conflict between the United States and Mexico soon ensued. The two countries disagreed over the southern border of Texas. Mexico said it was at the Nueces River. Polk insisted it was at the Rio Grande, 150 miles to the south. In 1846, Polk sent troops into this disputed territory. Skirmishes in the disputed area led to war between Mexico and the United States. Ultimately, the United States prevailed and acquired the huge territory that comprised the northern provinces of Mexico, which is known as the Mexican Cession. The war strengthened the United States, greatly increasing its territorial holdings. These lands included the territory that would soon become the state of California.

The acquisition of California immediately had both positive and negative effects on the United States. On the positive side, gold was discovered in California soon after it was acquired by the United States. As word spread, thousands of people came to California to try to strike it rich. A large percentage of the 300,000 people who migrated to California came in 1849, thus their nickname "forty-niners." The gold rush drew immigrants from all over—from eastern cities, from Canada, from Europe, from Latin America, and from China. By 1852, 20,000 Chinese immigrants had moved to the United States. By 1860, over 34,000 lived in California alone. California quickly became a thriving, multiethnic territory. California also became a center for American trade. In 1852, President Millard Fillmore, who was determined to open Japan to American trade, sent two naval expeditions to Japan. They were each led by Commodore Matthew C. Perry. By 1854, Perry was able to secure a trade treaty with Japan. The lucrative trade with Asia went through California ports. Soon after the American Civil War, completion of the first transcontinental railroad connected California with the population centers in the East and the Midwest. California continued to grow and continued to generate wealth for the United States.

On the negative side, California's application for statehood into the United States intensified sectional tensions in the United States. By 1850, California had enough people to form a state. Californians wrote up a constitution to submit to Congress in which slavery would be illegal. Southern senators objected to the admission of an additional free state. Senate negotiators worked out a series of measures to resolve this extremely contentious problem. These measures became known as the Compromise of 1850. The most important elements of the compromise were the admittance of California as a free state, which pleased northern politicians, and a more stringent Fugitive Slave Law, which pleased southern politicians. Many northerners grew alarmed at the enforcement of the Fugitive Slave Law. Previously, the majority of northerners could ignore the brutality of the slave system. Following 1850, though, slave catchers brought the system to the streets of northern cities. In response, many northern states passed "personal liberty laws" that offered protection to fugitives. Many whites and free African Americans in northern cities even formed vigilance committees to prevent the slave catchers from carrying out their orders. The tensions that intensified following the Compromise of 1850 continued throughout the decade and contributed to the Civil War.

Fifty years after the acquisition of California, the United States acquired Puerto Rico. The context for the acquisition of Puerto Rico was the rise of imperialism among the wealthy nations of the world. The scramble to imperialize Africa and Asia began among the European powers—Great Britain, France, Belgium, and Germany. By the 1890s, many American policy makers were pushing the United States to adopt an imperialist foreign policy. Imperialist ventures were motivated by a particular cultural set of ideas that created a racial hierarchy. Mainstream thinking in the United States in the late 1800s posited the superiority of the descendants of the Anglo-Saxon people and the inferiority of the nonwhite peoples of the world. This racist notion led some white Americans to feel it was the duty of the "civilized" peoples of the world to uplift the less fortunate. The push to uplift the peoples of the world was made clear in Rudyard Kipling's famous poem "The White Man's Burden" (1899). Josiah Strong, a Protestant clergyman, echoed Kipling's sentiment. Strong argued that the Anglo-Saxon race had a responsibility to "civilize and Christianize" the world.

The ideology of "The White Man's Burden" and developments in Cuba in the 1890s set the stage for the Spanish-American War and for the acquisition of Puerto Rico. A Cuban independence movement was trying to break Cuba's ties to Spain. The Spanish governor of Cuba used brutal tactics to suppress the rebellion. Many Americans wanted the United States to intervene on Cuba's side in its struggle against Spanish rule. Some Americans saw parallels between the Cuban struggle for independence from Spain and America's struggle for independence from Great Britain. Also, some American businessmen were angered by the interruption of the sugar harvest by the fighting between Cuban rebels and Spanish forces. Events in Cuba were brought to the attention of ordinary Americans through sensationalistic accounts in mass-produced and mass-distributed newspapers (nicknamed yellow journalism). Finally, the destruction of a United States warship, the USS *Maine*, in the harbor of Havana, Cuba, led to calls for war. Many in the United States thought that the destruction of the ship was the work of Spain. All of these factors combined to propel the U.S. into war with Spain in 1898.

The United States won the Spanish-American War and, as a result, acquired an empire. The United States and Spain negotiated the Treaty of Paris (signed in 1898 and ratified in 1899) following the war. In the treaty, Spain agreed to cede the Philippines, Puerto Rico, and Guam to the United States. The United States agreed to pay Spain $20 million for these possessions. The acquisition of Puerto Rico had both positive and negative effects for the United States.

On the negative side, the United States struggled to maintain its democratic ideals while simultaneously maintaining an empire. The United States was born in an anticolonial war, defeating the British to gain its independence. For much of its history, Americans stood in solidarity with other nations challenging European rule. Many Americans felt a kinship with Simón Bolívar as he led independence movements in the Spanish-held colonies of South America in the first decades of the 19th century. Bolívar himself was grateful to the United States for issuing the Monroe Doctrine in 1823, warning the European powers to keep their hands off the Americas. Many Americans, therefore, felt betrayed when the United States joined the European powers in pursuing an empire. In 1898, as the Treaty of Paris was debated in the Senate, a group of these critics of American imperialism formed the American Anti-Imperialist League. The league included American author Mark Twain, who was the vice president of the league from 1901 to 1910 and who wrote some of the league's more scathing condemnations of imperialism. Further, it became increasingly clear that the native people who lived in Puerto Rico and other American possessions would not enjoy the same constitutional rights as American citizens. The Supreme Court declared in a series of cases in 1901 that the United States was not obligated to grant its colonial subjects constitutional rights. The decisions for these Insular Cases were based on the racist assumptions that the colonial subjects were of an inferior race and that the colonial power had the responsibility to uplift these peoples before granting them autonomy.

On the positive side, American economic interests grew as a result of the acquisition of Puerto Rico. Puerto Rico became a major producer of American sugar in the first decades of the 20th century. Puerto Rico gained a greater degree of autonomy after the United States passed the Jones-Shafroth Act in 1917. The act also granted citizenship to Puerto Ricans born in 1898 or after. Since Puerto Ricans have become United States citizens, waves of migrants have moved from Puerto Rico to the United States. Puerto Ricans created vital neighborhoods in American cities such as New York City, filling entry-level jobs as generations of immigrants had done before them. Puerto Ricans have also made major contributions to the culture of the United States, from Puerto Rican astronaut Joseph Michael Acaba to baseball player Roberto Clemente to singer and actress Rita Moreno.

Territorial acquisitions have had both positive and negative effects on the United States. On the one hand, they have contributed to the wealth and power of the United States. The vast lands of the United States have provided ample living space for a growing population to reside in and have been a source of abundant natural resources. At the same time, these acquisitions have sometimes challenged basic American ideals of democracy and self-rule.

PART III: DOCUMENT-BASED QUESTION

Part A: Short Answer

Document 1

1 (1) According to Arthur M. Schlesinger, one event that motivated Thomas Paine to write *Common Sense* was that the British Parliament had passed the Intolerable Acts.

1 (2) According to Arthur M. Schlesinger, another event that motivated Thomas Paine to write "Common Sense" was that fighting had erupted in Lexington, Massachusetts.

These answers receive full credit because they state two events that motivated Thomas Paine to write Common Sense.

Document 2

2 According to Robert Middlekauff, one way that Thomas Paine's *Common Sense* promoted support for independence was that it was widely reprinted throughout the colonies and generated a great deal of debate.

This answer receives full credit because it states one way that Thomas Paine's Common Sense promoted support for independence.

Document 3

3 According to Edmund S. Morgan, one effect of Thomas Paine's *Common Sense* was that more and more delegates to the Second Continental Congress came to support independence. By July 1776, independence-minded delegates were in the majority and voted for declaring independence.

This answer receives full credit because it states one effect of Thomas Paine's Common Sense.

Document 4

4 Based on the document, Harriet Beecher Stowe was concerned about the new Fugitive Slave Law because she believed it forced all Americans, including northerners, to be complicit in the slave system.

This answer receives full credit because it states one reason Harriet Beecher Stowe was concerned about the new Fugitive Slave Law.

Document 5a and Document 5b

5 Based on the documents, Southern slave owners were concerned about the publication of *Uncle Tom's Cabin* because its antislavery massage was read by a large number of Americans. It had become a publishing "phenomenon."

This answer receives full credit because it states one reason Southern slave owners were concerned about the publication of Uncle Tom's Cabin.

Document 6

6 (1) According to James McPherson, one effect of the publication of *Uncle Tom's Cabin* was that it encouraged important leaders, including the British Prime Minister and President Abraham Lincoln, to think more deeply about the "problem of slavery."

6 (2) According to James McPherson, another effect of the publication of *Uncle Tom's Cabin* was that it set off a vehement campaign among southern defenders of slavery to both defend the institution of slavery and to denounce the book's "falsehoods" and "distortions."

These answers receive full credit because they state two effects of the publication of Uncle Tom's Cabin.

Document 7

7 (1) According to Eric Schlosser, one issue that concerned Upton Sinclair was that the food and drug industries were unregulated and regularly sold unhealthy and fraudulent products to the public.

7 (2) According to Eric Schlosser, another issue that concerned Upton Sinclair was that a small number of millionaire "robber barons" lived like European aristocrats while their workers could afford to live only in wretched slums.

These answers receive full credit because they state two issues that concerned Upton Sinclair.

Document 8a and Document 8b

8 (1) Based on the documents, one effect of the publication of *The Jungle* was that readers became concerned about the unhygienic conditions of the meat-packing industry and demanded that President Theodore Roosevelt take action.

8 (2) Based on the documents, another effect of the publication of *The Jungle* was that the federal government passed the Meat Inspection Act and the Pure Food and Drug Act to regulate the meat processing industry.

These answers receive full credit because they state two effects of the publication of The Jungle.

Document 9

9 According to President Lyndon B. Johnson, one continuing influence of Upton Sinclair's *The Jungle* was that the government continued its role in regulating the meat-processing industry; Congress had just passed the Wholesome Meat Act of 1967.

This answer receives full credit because it states one continuing influence that President Lyndon B. Johnson thinks Upton Sinclair's The Jungle *has had.*

Part B: Document-Based Essay

At different points in United States history, the publication of a particular book has dramatically altered the direction of society. The written word can have a powerful effect on history. Two significant written works that dramatically impacted society were *Common Sense* by Thomas Paine and *The Jungle* by Upton Sinclair. The first challenged American colonists to rethink their relationship with Great Britain; the second encouraged Americans to think about the way food is processed in the United States.

Thomas Paine's pamphlet *Common Sense*, written in January 1776, played an important role in convincing many Americans that the 13 North American colonies should declare independence from Great Britain. Relations between the colonies and Great Britain had been deteriorating for several years leading up to the publication of the pamphlet. The beginning of the tensions can be traced to the aftermath of the French and Indian War. After that war, which lasted from 1754 to 1763, the British government enacted a series of measures that many colonists found objectionable, including new taxes to defray the costs of the war. The Stamp Act of 1765 provoked the most intense opposition. Many colonists asserted that only representatives elected by them could enact taxes on the colonies. "No taxation without representation" became the rallying cry of the colonists. A series of taxes by the British and protests by the colonists continued over the next several years. Relations reached a boiling point after a violent standoff that led to British troops firing on a crowd of colonists (1770). The Boston Massacre intensified colonial resentment of the British presence.

In 1773, the British passed the Tea Act, which eliminated British tariffs from tea sold in the colonies by the British East India Company. This act actually lowered tea prices in Boston. However, it angered many colonists, who accused the British of doing special favors for a large company. The colonists responded by dumping cases of tea into Boston Harbor. The British responded to the Boston Tea Party by imposing a series of punitive measures known as the Intolerable Acts (1774). In April 1775, fighting began between patriots and British troops on "Lexington Green." During the rest of 1775, relations between the colonies and Great Britain worsened. The Second Continental Congress, a body of representatives from the 13 colonies, created an army and "shut up General Gage" in the Battle of Bunker Hill in Boston. (Document 1) At the same time, some members of the congress still hoped for reconciliation. Congress sent the Olive Branch Petition to the king of Great Britain, affirming loyalty to the monarch and blaming the current problems on Parliament. (King George III rejected the petition.)

It was in this context that Paine wrote *Common Sense*. He wrote about the logic of the Olive Branch Petition. Paine plainly and forcefully concluded that the period of negotiations and debate was over; "'Tis Time to Part," he concluded. The work, according to historian Arthur Schlesinger, had "crucial repercussions." (Document 1) The pamphlet was soon reproduced in newspapers throughout the colonies. Soon after publication, "over 100,000 copies" of the pamphlet were distributed in major cities and minor towns. (Document 2) He put the blame on the king, not on missteps by parliament. Paine argued that the 13 colonies would thrive if they were free of their ties to Great Britain. Paine not only argued that declaring independence made logical and moral sense, but he also argued that the colonies would more likely get support from Great Britain's rivals in Europe if they declared independence. A foreign power would not likely get involved in the internal struggles of another nation. However, they might aid an independent nation in a war against Great Britain. (Document 2)

Paine's arguments carried the day. The excitement of his prose and the forcefulness of his arguments captured the "sense of adventure" many Americans felt at the time, according to historian Edmund S. Morgan. Paine convinced Americans that their struggle for independence was "the cause of all mankind." (Document 3) Things moved quickly in the spring and summer of 1776. The Virginia House of Burgesses voted to instruct their delegates to the Second Continental Congress to support an independence resolution. By June, Richard Henry Lee of Virginia put forth a resolution to declare independence in Congress. On July 2, the delegates formally declared independence. (Document 3) On July 4, the delegates ratified the wording of the final draft of the Declaration of Independence, began signing the document (a treasonous act), and started distributing it throughout the colonies.

In the early 20th century, another publication, *The Jungle* by Upton Sinclair, also shook up the public and challenged the prevailing order. The 1906 book shined a spotlight on the unsanitary and dangerous conditions in the meatpacking industry. The book was written in the context of the rapid expansion of industry in the late 19th century. At that time, many substandard products were made available to the public. In the mad dash to maximize profits in a growing economy, producers cut corners, adulterated food, did not test their products, and routinely ignored even the most basic health and safety precautions. Food was tainted with chemicals. Drug companies sold unproved concoctions that "promised to cure all sorts of diseases" but were largely ineffective. (Document 7) Government officials either looked the other way or did not think it was within their purview to address these issues. As corporations amassed great profits for their owners, the public suffered. These shoddy production practices were brought to light by crusading journalists who worked to expose the underside of industrial production. These crusaders, known as muckrakers, used photography, mass circulation magazines, and indignant language to let the world know of these practices.

Upton Sinclair fell within this tradition of muckraking journalists. After reading about the practices of the meatpacking industry, he became "moved by these injustices." He traveled to Chicago to investigate the condition of the meatpackers. He saw firsthand the power of the beef trust over its workers, how the industry was easily able to defeat a strike by the union. The power dynamics of the meat industry represented, for Sinclair, "everything that was wrong" with industrial capitalism. (Document 7) Sinclair's research led to the publication of a stirring novel in 1906 called *The Jungle*. The book follows a Lithuanian immigrant family through the stockyards of Chicago and exposes the conditions in the meatpacking industry. Though the book is a novel, it was thoroughly researched and well written. We see the horrible conditions that existed in this industry. Meat that spoiled was brought back to the plant, doused in bleach, and flavored with spices. Workers were not provided facilities to wash their hands. Rat droppings were swept into the hopper and mixed into the sausage meat. The conditions of the meatpacking industry were thoroughly unsanitary and dangerous. Though he hoped to draw attention to the workers in the meatpacking industry, the public was more moved by the disgusting processes involved in meat processing. As Sinclair said, "I aimed at the public's heart and by accident I hit it in the stomach." (Document 8a)

President Theodore Roosevelt, after he was "deluged" with letters from the public, was moved to take action. His first action was to create an investigative commission to examine the practices of the meatpacking industry. (Document 8a) Calls for action came from many sectors of American society. Certainly, consumers were concerned. Consumer advocate Harvey Wiley lobbied for the federal government to take a more supervisory role in the meatpacking industry. Even members of the business community realized that federal action was necessary. Some owners of big businesses hoped that federal inspection would "bring order and stability" to what had become a disreputable industry. (Document 8b) In the wake of the investigative work of the federal government, Roosevelt was able to persuade Congress to take action. In 1906, Congress passed the Meat Inspection Act and the Pure Food and Drug Act, which established the Food and Drug Administration.

The impact of these actions was immediate and sweeping. By the end of 1906, meat processors were announcing that their products were in strict compliance with the provisions of the Pure Food and Drug Act. The push for safe food was not fleeting. Sixty years later, during the administration of Lyndon B. Johnson, additional food safety laws were passed to strengthen the earlier laws. The Wholesome Meat Act of 1967 continued the push of the 1906 Meat Inspection Act. President Johnson, upon signing the bill, said that consumers could rest assured that their meat was "pure" and "processed in a sanitary plant." Johnson invited an elderly Upton Sinclair to the signing ceremony to stress the impact of *The Jungle* decades after its publication. (Document 9)

Both Paine and Sinclair used the power of the written word to bring attention to matters of public concern, to convince people to rethink long-held convictions, and to move officials to take decisive action.

Topic	Question Numbers	Number of Points
American political history	2, 14, 16, 33, 39, 42, 43, 47	10
Political theory	3	1
Economic theory/policy	12, 17, 18, 19, 28, 29, 30, 31, 34, 49	12
Constitutional principles	4, 5, 6, 7, 11, 20, 25, 44	10
American foreign policy	21, 23, 26, 32, 36, 37, 38, 41, 45	11
American studies—the American people	13, 15, 22, 24, 35, 40, 46, 48, 50	11
Social/cultural developments	27	1
Geography	1, 8, 9, 10	5
Skills questions included in the above content area		
Reading comprehension	6, 7, 10, 20, 29, 30, 32, 36, 40	
Cartoon/image interpretation	13, 21, 22, 33, 34, 35, 44, 47	
Graph/table interpretation	12	
Map interpretation	8, 9, 50	
Outlining skills	16	

PART I

Multiple-Choice Questions by Standard

Standard	Question Numbers
1—United States and New York History	7, 10, 11, 14, 15, 16, 21, 22, 24, 26, 27, 29, 30, 32, 33, 35, 38, 39, 42, 45, 48
2—World History	23, 36, 37, 41
3—Geography	1, 8, 9, 50
4—Economics	12, 17, 18, 19, 28, 31, 34, 43, 49
5—Civics, Citizenship, and Government	2, 3, 4, 5, 6, 13, 20, 25, 40, 44, 46, 47

Parts II and III by Theme and Standard

	Theme	Standards
Thematic Essay	Places and Regions; Presidential Decisions and Actions; Diversity; Foreign Policy	Standards 1, 2, 3, 4, and 5: United States and New York History; World History; Geography; Economics; Civics, Citizenship, and Government
Document-Based Essay	Constitutional Principles; Civic Values; Citizenship; Government; Reform Movements; Presidential Decisions and Actions; Change; Culture and Intellectual Life	Standards 1, 2, 3, 4, and 5: United States and New York History; World History; Geography; Economics; Civics, Citizenship, and Government

Examination August 2018
United States History and Government

PART I: MULTIPLE CHOICE

Directions (1–50): For each statement or question, write in the space provided the *number* of the word or expression that, of those given, best completes the statement or answers the question.

1 The geography of the Atlantic Coastal Plain most influenced the southern economy during the period from 1620 to 1865 because it

(1) promoted a plantation system of agriculture
(2) led to diversified manufacturing
(3) encouraged development of the railroad industry
(4) resulted in widespread mining of coal   1 _____

2 Which event during the Colonial Era most influenced the concept of freedom of the press?

(1) passage of the Navigation Acts
(2) trial of John Peter Zenger
(3) creation of the Albany Plan of Union
(4) establishment of the House of Burgesses   2 _____

3 The social contract theory as applied to the Declaration of Independence most directly reflects the ideas of

(1) John Locke   (3) Baron de Montesquieu
(2) Thomas Hobbes   (4) Adam Smith   3 _____

4 A principal reason for calling the Constitutional Convention of 1787 was to

(1) strengthen the central government
(2) settle land disputes with Canada
(3) increase the power of the states
(4) weaken the system of checks and balances   4 _____

5 One reason Antifederalist governors of New York and Virginia opposed ratification of the United States Constitution was because it would

(1) force them to abandon western land claims
(2) weaken the powers of state governments
(3) strengthen slavery
(4) make the amendment process more difficult   5 _____

6 Political parties, the president's cabinet, and national nominating conventions are considered examples of

(1) delegated powers   (3) the elastic clause
(2) separation of powers   (4) the unwritten constitution   6 _____

7 Thomas Jefferson used a loose interpretation of the United States Constitution when he

(1) negotiated the purchase of the Louisiana Territory from France in 1803
(2) asked Congress to increase the size of the United States Navy
(3) ran for a second term as president
(4) opposed the reelection of John Adams in 1800   7 _____

8 Between 1820 and 1850, Southern lawmakers consistently opposed protective tariffs because these tariffs

(1) decreased trade between the states
(2) harmed American shipping
(3) increased the cost of imports
(4) weakened national security   8 _____

9 In the 1840s, westward expansion was justified by a belief in

 (1) laissez-faire   (3) cultural pluralism

 (2) popular sovereignty   (4) Manifest Destiny   9 _____

10 Which reform movement is most closely associated with William Lloyd Garrison, Frederick Douglass, and Harriet Beecher Stowe?

 (1) abolitionist   (3) Populist

 (2) labor   (4) Progressive   10 _____

Base your answers to questions 11 and 12 on the statements below and on your knowledge of social studies.

Speaker A: The political union created by the Constitution of the United States is not a temporary compact of the states but rather an unbreakable bond created by the people of the nation.

Speaker B: The reserved powers are clearly indicated and protected in both the original Constitution and in the 10th amendment of the Bill of Rights.

Speaker C: Liberty is best preserved in the hands of the government closest to the people. Union is desirable only if it preserves our liberty.

Speaker D: Nullification! Secession! What miserable words—words that threaten the continuance of both our liberty and our Union.

11 Which two speakers express the greatest support for the concept of States rights?

 (1) *A* and *B*   (3) *B* and *C*

 (2) *A* and *D*   (4) *C* and *D*   11 _____

12 The political opinions expressed in these statements relate most directly to the start of which war?

 (1) Revolutionary War   (3) Mexican-American War

 (2) War of 1812   (4) Civil War   12 _____

13 Passage of the Kansas-Nebraska Act (1854) was criticized by Northern newspapers because it

(1) limited settlement in those territories
(2) repealed the 36°30' line of the Missouri Compromise
(3) upheld the Supreme Court decision in *Gibbons v. Ogden*
(4) admitted Maine to the Union as a free state   13 _____

14 After the Civil War, the most common occupations for freedmen were

(1) sharecroppers and tenant farmers
(2) factory owners and teachers
(3) skilled artisans and mechanics
(4) miners and soldiers   14 _____

15 Which geographic factor presented a major problem for settlers on the Great Plains?

(1) limited rainfall   (3) mountainous terrain
(2) dense forests   (4) frequent flooding   15 _____

Base your answer to question 16 on the graphic organizer below and on your knowledge of social studies.

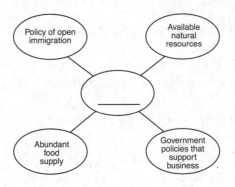

16 Which title is most appropriate for this graphic organizer?

(1) Rise of Labor Unions
(2) Innovations and Technology
(3) Vertical Integration of Business
(4) Factors Contributing to Industrialization   16 _____

17 In the United States, third parties have been influential because they have often

(1) outspent their political opponents
(2) provided the presidential candidate of the major parties
(3) suggested reforms later adopted by the two major parties
(4) elected majorities in both Congress and state legislatures

17 _____

18 One purpose of the Chinese Exclusion Act (1882) was to

(1) speed construction of the western railroads
(2) encourage settlement of the Pacific Coast
(3) expand the civil rights of immigrants
(4) protect the jobs of American workers

18 _____

19 The Interstate Commerce Act of 1887 and the Sherman Antitrust Act of 1890 were passed by Congress to

(1) help regulate the money supply
(2) promote investment in manufacturing
(3) control business practices that limited competition
(4) limit the hours of working women

19 _____

20 Which demographic change resulted from the economic developments of the late 1800s?

(1) an increase in African American migration from the North to the South
(2) an increase in the number of people living in urban areas
(3) a decrease in the number of immigrants coming to the United States
(4) a decrease in the number of factory workers in the Northeast

20 _____

21 Between 1900 and 1930, United States relations with Latin America were characterized by repeated United States efforts to

  (1) encourage the redistribution of land to the poor
  (2) deny economic aid to developing nations
  (3) limit the influence of communist dictators
  (4) control the internal affairs of many nations in the region   21 _____

22 President Theodore Roosevelt earned a reputation as a trustbuster because he

  (1) favored the conservation of natural resources
  (2) used court actions to break up business monopolies
  (3) sided with labor unions against big business
  (4) opposed the efforts of consumer advocates   22 _____

23 One way in which Ida Tarbell, Upton Sinclair, and Jacob Riis were similar is that each sought to

  (1) end racial discrimination
  (2) control illegal immigration
  (3) limit government regulations
  (4) expose economic and social abuses   23 _____

24 The purpose of the initiative, referendum, and recall was to

  (1) eliminate the two-party system
  (2) limit participation in state elections
  (3) increase citizen influence in government
  (4) strengthen the power of political machines   24 _____

Base your answer to question 25 on the photograph below and on your knowledge of social studies.

Bibb Mill No. 1, Macon, Ga.

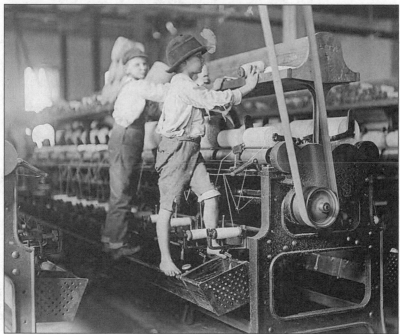

Source: Lewis Hine, January 19, 1909

25 Which conclusion is most clearly supported by this photograph?

(1) Textile manufacturing was not important to the national economy.

(2) State and federal governments did not adequately regulate child labor.

(3) American factories were less productive than factories in other countries.

(4) Strict federal safety standards were enforced in factories across the nation.

25 _____

26 During the 1920s, Congress established a quota system for immigration in order to

  (1) ensure that the United States would have enough factory workers

  (2) keep migrant workers out of the country

  (3) reduce immigration from southern and eastern Europe

  (4) assist refugees from war-torn countries   26 _____

27 Which event is an example of nativism in the 1920s?

  (1) the trial of Sacco and Vanzetti

  (2) the verdict in the Scopes trial

  (3) the Teapot Dome scandal

  (4) the stock market crash   27 _____

28 • They are suffering because they have little control over the prices for what they produce.

  • They have worldwide competition.

  • They have difficulty organizing to protect themselves.

  • They pay high prices for capital goods.

Which group's economic situation in the 1920s is most accurately described in these statements?

  (1) farmers   (3) manufacturers

  (2) railroad companies   (4) factory workers   28 _____

Base your answers to questions 29 and 30 on the cartoon below and on your knowledge of social studies.

"Yes, You Remembered Me"

Source: C. D. Batchelor, *New York Daily News*, October 11, 1936

29 The main idea of this political cartoon from the 1930s is that President Franklin D. Roosevelt

(1) continued the laissez-faire policies of earlier presidents
(2) supported business over labor
(3) favored government ownership of major industries
(4) extended help to those in need   29 _____

30 The New Deal attempted to carry out the theme of the cartoon by

(1) restricting labor union membership
(2) loaning money to foreign countries
(3) funding many public works projects
(4) banning the sale of stocks and bonds   30 _____

31 The defeat of President Franklin D. Roosevelt's "court packing" plan by Congress is an example of

(1) federalism
(3) due process
(2) checks and balances
(4) the amendment process

31 _____

Base your answer to question 32 on the excerpt from the letter below and on your knowledge of social studies.

. . . This new phenomenon [nuclear chain reaction] would also lead to the construction of bombs, and it is conceivable—though much less certain—that extremely powerful bombs of a new type may thus be constructed. . . .

Yours very truly,
Albert Einstein

— Letter to President Franklin D. Roosevelt from Albert Einstein, August 2, 1939

32 The administration of President Franklin D. Roosevelt reacted to the information contained in this letter by

(1) declaring war on the Axis powers
(2) creating the Manhattan Project
(3) proposing the Lend-Lease plan
(4) initiating the D-Day invasion of Europe

32 _____

33 The internment of Japanese Americans during World War II primarily affected those Japanese Americans who lived

(1) in the Ohio River valley
(2) along the Gulf Coast
(3) on the West Coast
(4) near the Rio Grande border with Mexico

33 _____

34 After World War II, one important outcome of the passage of the Servicemen's Readjustment Act of 1944 (GI Bill) was that it

(1) allowed women to serve in combat positions
(2) limited suburban growth
(3) provided funds for new military bases
(4) created educational and housing assistance for veterans

34 _____

35 What was the primary reason for the creation of both the Truman Doctrine and the Marshall Plan?

(1) to reward the Chinese for their role in the Allied victory over Japan
(2) the fear of Soviet communist expansion throughout Europe
(3) the need to support colonial independence movements in the developing world
(4) the protection of vital United States interests in Middle East oil fields

35 _____

36 The United States responded to the Berlin blockade in 1948 by

(1) boycotting German-made imports
(2) building the Berlin Wall
(3) stopping all traffic leaving Berlin
(4) airlifting food and supplies into Berlin

36 _____

37 A major significance of the Korean War (1950–1953) is that for the first time

(1) an atomic bomb was used in warfare
(2) Asian and United States troops fought against each other
(3) the United Nations used military force to oppose aggression
(4) the Soviet Union and the United States supported the same side

37 _____

38 **"All Federal Employees Required to Take Loyalty Oath"**
   "Army-McCarthy Hearings Begin" "Rosenbergs Convicted"

   These newspaper headlines from the decade following World
   War II are all connected to the

   (1) war crimes trials in Japan
   (2) passage of civil rights legislation in the United States
   (3) fear of communism in the United States
   (4) debate over economic aid to Europe   38 _____

39 In 1962, President John F. Kennedy responded to the discovery of
   nuclear missiles in Cuba by

   (1) ordering a naval quarantine of Cuba
   (2) capturing strategic locations in Cuba
   (3) threatening to invade the Soviet Union
   (4) prohibiting travel to the southeastern United States   39 _____

40 During the 1960s, the actions of Cesar Chavez led to improved
   conditions for

   (1) coal miners
   (2) migrant farm workers
   (3) autoworkers
   (4) health care workers   40 _____

41 Which phrase best completes the heading of the partial outline
   below?

   I. Native American Indian _____
       A. Occupation of Alcatraz
       B. Wounded Knee (1973)
       C. Formation of American Indian
          Movement (AIM)

   (1) Protests Against the Vietnam War
   (2) Demands for Equality
   (3) Attempts to Culturally Assimilate
   (4) Support for the War on Poverty   41 _____

42 Which document is the result of President Jimmy Carter's efforts to increase stability in the Middle East?

(1) Camp David Accords   (3) Panama Canal Treaty
(2) Nuclear Test Ban Treaty   (4) Paris Peace Accords   42 _____

43 What was the reason the Equal Rights Amendment did not become part of the United States Constitution?

(1) President Ronald Reagan vetoed it.
(2) Three-fourths of the states did not ratify it.
(3) The National Organization for Women (NOW) did not support it.
(4) The Supreme Court ruled it was unconstitutional.   43 _____

44 Which combination of factors contributed most directly to the severe recession in the United States economy in 2008?

(1) immigration restrictions and lack of skilled workers
(2) cuts in defense spending and social welfare programs
(3) excessive use of credit and bank speculation in the mortgage market
(4) tight monetary policy and overregulation of banks   44 _____

Base your answer to question 45 on the cartoon below and on your knowledge of social studies.

Source: Walt Handelsman, *Newsday*, April 26, 2006

45 The main idea of this cartoon is that public approval of the president in 2006 was directly linked to the

(1) cost of gasoline in the United States
(2) success in stopping human rights abuses abroad
(3) ability to restrict the flow of illegal drugs
(4) amount of the budget surplus   45 _____

Base your answer to question 46 on the cartoon below and on your knowledge of social studies.

Source: Jim Morin, *Miami Herald*, May 10, 2015

46 The main idea of this cartoon is that telephone surveillance by the National Security Administration (NSA)

(1) has been troubled by technical difficulties

(2) violates some of the protections of the United States Constitution

(3) is legal because it protects the privacy of Internet users

(4) increases hacking of top-secret government information   46 _____

47 The Alien and Sedition Acts of 1798 were similar to the Espionage and Sedition Acts passed during World War I because they both

   (1) provided for the draft of men into the military

   (2) gave the government greater control over the production of goods

   (3) tried to restrict criticism of and opposition to government policies

   (4) attempted to justify United States involvement in a foreign war   47 _____

48 Which set of events in United States history is most closely associated with westward expansion?

   (1) passage of the Indian Removal Act of 1830 and the Compromise of 1877

   (2) issuing the Emancipation Proclamation of 1863 and creation of the Federal Reserve System in 1913

   (3) passage of the Agricultural Adjustment Act of 1933 and creation of the Tennesee Valley Authority in 1933

   (4) passage of the Homestead Act of 1862 and opening of the transcontinental railroad in 1869   48 _____

49 The National Association for the Advancement of Colored People (NAACP), the Congress of Racial Equality (CORE), and the Southern Christian Leadership Conference (SCLC) are all associated with which movement?

   (1) temperance   (3) civil rights

   (2) abolition   (4) environmentalism   49 _____

Base your answer to question 50 on the cartoon below and on your knowledge of social studies.

Trying to Close the Gap

Source: Art Bimrose, *Portland Oregonian* (adapted)

50 Which action was an attempt to close the "gap" referred to in the cartoon?

(1) signing the Yalta Agreement
(2) passing the Gulf of Tonkin Resolution
(3) proposing the Strategic Defense Initiative (SDI)
(4) agreeing to the Strategic Arms Limitation Treaty (SALT)

50 _____

In developing your answer to Part II, be sure to keep these general definitions in mind:
- (a) <u>describe</u> means "to illustrate something in words or tell about it"
- (b) <u>explain</u> means "to make plain or understandable; to give reasons for or causes of; to show the logical development or relationships of "
- (c) <u>discuss</u> means "to make observations about something using facts, reasoning, and argument; to present in some detail"

PART II: THEMATIC ESSAY

Directions: Write a well-organized essay that includes an introduction, several paragraphs addressing the task below, and a conclusion.

Theme: Supreme Court Decisions

> The United States Supreme Court has issued decisions that have defined the constitutional rights of individuals and groups of people. These decisions by the Court have had a great impact on the nation.

Task:

> Select *two* United States Supreme Court cases and for *each*
>
> - Describe the historical circumstances surrounding the case
> - Explain the Court's decision
> - Discuss the impact of the Court's decision on the United States or on American society

You may use any appropriate Supreme Court case from your study of United States history. Some suggestions you might wish to consider include *Worcester v. Georgia* (1832), *Dred Scott v. Sanford* (1857), *Plessy v. Ferguson* (1896), *Korematsu v. United States* (1944), *Brown v. Board of Education of Topeka* (1954), *Engel v. Vitale* (1962), *Miranda v. Arizona* (1966), *Roe v. Wade* (1973), and *New Jersey v. T.L.O.* (1985).

You are *not* limited to these suggestions.

Guidelines:

In your essay, be sure to:

- Develop all aspects of the task
- Support the theme with relevant facts, examples, and details
- Use a logical and clear plan of organization, including an introduction and a conclusion that are beyond a restatement of the theme

In developing your answers to Part III, be sure to keep these general definitions in mind:
- (a) <u>describe</u> means "to illustrate something in words or tell about it"
- (b) <u>explain</u> means "to make plain or understandable; to give reasons for or causes of; to show the logical development or relationships of "
- (c) <u>discuss</u> means "to make observations about something using facts, reasoning, and argument; to present in some detail"

PART III: DOCUMENT-BASED QUESTION

This question is based on the accompanying documents. The question is designed to test your ability to work with historical documents. Some of these documents have been edited for the purposes of this question. As you analyze the documents, take into account the source of each document and any point of view that may be presented in the document. Keep in mind that the language used in a document may reflect the historical context of the time in which it was written.

Historical Context:

Under the Constitution, Congress has the power to support the armed forces and to declare war, but only the president is authorized to act as commander in chief. Throughout United States history, the president has used his power as commander in chief to respond to many foreign crises. These crises include the **Mexican-American War (1846–1848)** during the presidency of James K. Polk, the **Vietnam War (1964–1975)** during the presidency of Lyndon B. Johnson, and the **Persian Gulf War (1990–1991)** during the presidency of George H. W. Bush.

Task:

Using the information from the documents and your knowledge of United States history, answer the questions that follow each document in Part A. Your answers to the questions will help you write the Part B essay in which you will be asked to

Select **two** foreign crises listed in the historical context and for **each**

- Describe the historical circumstances that led to the crisis
- Explain an action taken by the president to respond to the crisis
- Discuss an effect of the president's action on the United States and/or on American society

Part A: Short-Answer Questions

Directions: Analyze the documents and answer the short-answer questions that follow each document in the space provided.

Document 1

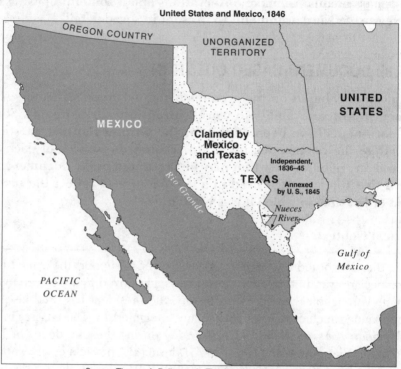

United States and Mexico, 1846

Source: Thomas A. Bailey et al., *The American Pageant*, Houghton Mifflin (adapted)

1 Based on the information provided by this map, state **one** cause of the conflict between the United States and Mexico in 1846. [1]

_____

_____

Document 2

> . . . In my message at the commencement of the present session I informed you that upon the earnest appeal both of the Congress and convention of Texas I had ordered an efficient military force to take a position "between the Nueces and the Del Norte [Rio Grande]." This had become necessary to meet a threatened invasion of Texas by the Mexican forces, for which extensive military preparations had been made. The invasion was threatened solely because Texas had determined, in accordance with a solemn resolution of the Congress of the United States [March 1, 1845], to annex herself to our Union, and under these circumstances it was plainly our duty to extend our protection over her citizens and soil. . . .

Source: President James K. Polk, *War Message*, May 11, 1846 (adapted)

2 Based on this document, what action did President James K. Polk take in 1846 regarding Texas?   [1]

_____

_____

Document 3a

. . . It was a peculiarity of nineteenth-century politics that more than a year elapsed between the election of a Congress and its initial meeting. The Thirtieth Congress, elected in 1846, assembled in December 1847 to confront the complex questions arising from the Mexican War. Although Democrats in the Senate outnumbered their opponents by almost two to one, the Whig party enjoyed a narrow margin in the House—the only time in his entire legislative career that Lincoln found himself in the majority. Both parties, however, were internally divided, especially on the question of the future expansion of slavery. In August 1846, just as the previous Congress drew to a close, Congressman David Wilmot of Pennsylvania had proposed an amendment to an appropriation bill requiring that slavery be prohibited in any territory acquired from Mexico. The Wilmot Proviso, which passed the House but failed in the Senate, split both parties along sectional lines and ushered in a new era in which the slavery issue moved to the center stage of American politics. . . .

Source: Eric Foner, *The Fiery Trial: Abraham Lincoln and American Slavery,*
W. W. Norton & Company, 2010

3a According to Eric Foner, what issue did the Wilmot Proviso attempt to address? [1]

_____

_____

Document 3b

United States Acquisitions from Mexico, 1848

Source: *Historical Maps on File*, Facts on File, 2002 (adapted)

3*b* Based on the information provided by this map, what was *one* effect of the Mexican-American War on the United States in 1848? [1]

_____

_____

Document 4

WHY ARE WE IN VIET-NAM?

... Why are these realities our concern? Why are we in South Viet-Nam?

We are there because we have a promise to keep. Since 1954 every American President has offered support to the people of South Viet-Nam. We have helped to build, and we have helped to defend. Thus, over many years, we have made a national pledge to help South Viet-Nam defend its independence.

And I intend to keep that promise.

To dishonor that pledge, to abandon this small and brave nation to its enemies, and to the terror that must follow, would be an unforgivable wrong.

We are also there to strengthen world order. Around the globe, from Berlin to Thailand, are people whose well-being rests, in part, on the belief that they can count on us if they are attacked. To leave Viet-Nam to its fate would shake the confidence of all these people in the value of an American commitment and in the value of America's word. The result would be increased unrest and instability, and even wider war. ...

Source: "Peace Without Conquest," President Lyndon B. Johnson,
Address at Johns Hopkins University, April 7, 1965

4 Based on this document, state *one* reason President Lyndon B. Johnson believed the United States should continue to assist South Vietnam. [1]

_____

_____

Document 5a

> . . . What are our goals in that war-strained land?
>
> First, we intend to convince the Communists that we cannot be defeated by force of arms or by superior power. They are not easily convinced. In recent months they have greatly increased their fighting forces and their attacks and the number of incidents.
>
> I have asked the Commanding General, General Westmoreland, what more he needs to meet this mounting aggression. He has told me. We will meet his needs.
>
> I have today ordered to Viet-Nam the Air Mobile Division and certain other forces which will raise our fighting strength from 75,000 to 125,000 men almost immediately. Additional forces will be needed later, and they will be sent as requested.
>
> This will make it necessary to increase our active fighting forces by raising the monthly draft call from 17,000 over a period of time to 35,000 per month, and for us to step up our campaign for voluntary enlistments. . . .

Source: President Lyndon B. Johnson, "Why We Are in Viet-Nam,"
News Conference, July 28, 1965 (adapted)

5*a* Based on this document, what was **one** action President Lyndon B. Johnson took in 1965 regarding Vietnam?   [1]

_____

_____

Document 5b

Allied Troop Levels in Vietnam, 1959–1969

Year	United States	South Vietnam	Australia	Korea	New Zealand	Philippines	Thailand
1959	760	243,000	--	--	--	--	--
1960	900	243,000	--	--	--	--	--
1961	3,205	243,000	--	--	--	--	--
1962	11,300	243,000	--	--	--	--	--
1963	16,300	243,000	--	--	--	--	--
1964	23,300	514,000	198	200	30	20	--
1965	184,300	642,500	1,560	20,620	120	70	20
1966	385,300	735,900	4,530	25,570	160	2,060	240
1967	485,600	798,700	6,820	47,830	530	2,020	2,200
1968	536,100	820,000	7,660	50,000	520	1,580	6,000
1969	475,200	897,000	7,670	48,870	550	190	11,570

Source: Church Committee Report on Diem Coup–1963, Vietnam,
War Statistics and Facts 1, 25thaviation.org (adapted)

5b Based on the information in this chart, what was **one** effect of the
actions taken by President Lyndon B. Johnson in 1965? [1]

_____

_____

Document 6a

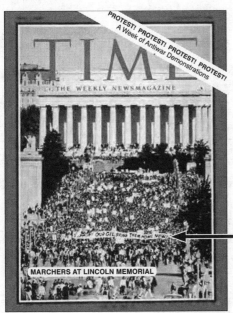

"Support Our GIs, Bring Them Home Now!"

MARCHERS AT LINCOLN MEMORIAL

Source: *Time*, October 27, 1967 (adapted)

Document 6b

> . . . With America's sons in the fields far away, with America's future under challenge right here at home, with our hopes and the world's hopes for peace in the balance every day, I do not believe that I should devote an hour or a day of my time to any personal partisan causes or to any duties other than the awesome duties of this office—the Presidency of your country.
>
> Accordingly, I shall not seek, and I will not accept, the nomination of my party for another term as your President. . . .

Source: President Lyndon B. Johnson, Address to the Nation Announcing Steps to Limit the War in Vietnam and Reporting His Decision Not to Seek Reelection, March 31, 1968

6 Based on these documents, state *two* effects of the Vietnam War on the United States.   [2]

(1) _____

_____

(2) _____

_____

Document 7a

> ### Iraq Deploys Troops Near Kuwait Border Amid Dispute on Oil
>
> WASHINGTON, July 23—American military officials are closely watching a new deployment of thousands of troops by Iraq along its border with Kuwait, where recent tensions appear to be escalating into a flaunting of strength by the two Persian Gulf countries, Pentagon officials said tonight. . . .

Source: *New York Times*, July 24, 1990

Document 7b

> ### IRAQ ARMY INVADES CAPITAL OF KUWAIT IN FIERCE FIGHTING
> ### EMERGENCY U.N. SESSION
>
> #### Casualties Are Called Heavy—Emir's Palace Besieged as Explosions Jolt City
>
> WASHINGTON, Thursday, August 2—Iraqi troops crossed the Kuwait border today and penetrated deeply into the country and into Kuwait's capital city, senior Administration officials said late Wednesday. . . .

Source: *New York Times*, August 2, 1990

Document 7c

Iraq's Naked Aggression

Without warrant or warning, Iraq has struck brutally at tiny Kuwait, a brazen [bold] challenge to world law. Iraq stands condemned by a unanimous U.N. Security Council and major Western oil purchasers. President [George H. W.] Bush's taste for bluntness stands him in good stead: "Naked aggression" is the correct term for President Saddam Hussein's grab at a vulnerable, oil-rich neighbor. . . .

Source: *New York Times*, August 3, 1990

7 Based on these documents, what was *one* cause of the Persian Gulf War? [1]

_____

_____

Document 8

Just 2 hours ago, allied air forces began an attack on military targets in Iraq and Kuwait. These attacks continue as I speak. Ground forces are not engaged.

This conflict started August 2d [1990] when the dictator of Iraq invaded a small and helpless neighbor. Kuwait—a member of the Arab League and a member of the United Nations—was crushed; its people, brutalized. Five months ago, Saddam Hussein started this cruel war against Kuwait. Tonight, the battle has been joined.

This military action, taken in accord with United Nations resolutions and with the consent of the United States Congress, follows months of constant

President George H. W. Bush

and virtually endless diplomatic activity on the part of the United Nations, the United States, and many, many other countries. Arab leaders sought what became known as an Arab solution, only to conclude that Saddam Hussein was unwilling to leave Kuwait. Others traveled to Baghdad in a variety of efforts to restore peace and justice. Our Secretary of State, James Baker, held an historic meeting in Geneva, only to be totally rebuffed. This past weekend, in a last-ditch effort, the Secretary-General of the United Nations went to the Middle East with peace in his heart—his second such mission. And he came back from Baghdad with no progress at all in getting Saddam Hussein to withdraw from Kuwait.

Now the 28 countries with forces in the Gulf area have exhausted all reasonable efforts to reach a peaceful resolution—have no choice but to drive Saddam from Kuwait by force. We will not fail. . . .

Source: President George H. W. Bush, Address to the Nation Announcing Allied Military Action in the Persian Gulf, January 16, 1991

8 Based on this document, what was **one** action taken by President George H. W. Bush in response to Iraq's 1990 invasion of Kuwait? [1]

_____

_____

Document 9a

NEWS of success in the ground war has sent America's hardcore peace activists into retreat and prompted citizens from coast to coast to proclaim that, after two decades, the country is finally purging the "Vietnam syndrome".

While families of servicemen waited anxiously, a sense of pride sometimes approaching glee infused the talk on the streets and on the air waves all day on Sunday and early yesterday. Again and again, people voiced the same view: after all the sneering and humiliation of recent years, America has proved it has the will and the might to fight and win a war. . . .

Spot opinion polls yesterday showed that well over 80 per cent of the population supported President Bush's decision to launch the ground war, and 75 per cent believed they should keep fighting until President Saddam Hussein is removed.

Commentators and historians are pointing out that Iraq is reaping all the anger pent up through years of humiliation since the debacle and retreat from Vietnam in the early 1970s. USA Today, the popular national newspaper, said the ground war "held the promise of completion, a chance to get past the anguish of Vietnam, and this time to do it right". . . .

Source: *The Times*, London, February 26, 1991

Document 9b

. . . Tonight the Kuwaiti flag once again flies above the capital of a free and sovereign nation. And the American flag flies above our Embassy.

Seven months ago, America and the world drew a line in the sand. We declared that the aggression against Kuwait would not stand. And tonight, America and the world have kept their word.

This is not a time of euphoria, certainly not a time to gloat. But it is a time of pride: pride in our troops; pride in the friends who stood with us in the crisis; pride in our nation and the people whose strength and resolve made victory quick, decisive, and just. And soon we will open wide our arms to welcome back home to America our magnificent fighting forces. . . .

Source: President George H. W. Bush, Address to the Nation on the Suspension of Allied Offensive Combat Operations in the Persian Gulf, February 27, 1991

9 Based on these documents, what were *two* effects of the Persian Gulf War on the United States?   [2]

(1) _____

_____

(2) _____

_____

Part B: Essay

Directions: Write a well-organized essay that includes an introduction, several paragraphs, and a conclusion. Use evidence from *at least four* documents in the body of the essay. Support your response with relevant facts, examples, and details. Include additional outside information.

Historical Context:

Under the Constitution, Congress has the power to support the armed forces and to declare war, but only the president is authorized to act as commander in chief. Throughout United States history, the president has used his power as commander in chief to respond to many foreign crises. These crises include the *Mexican-American War (1846–1848)* during the presidency of James K. Polk, the *Vietnam War (1964–1975)* during the presidency of Lyndon B. Johnson, and the *Persian Gulf War (1990–1991)* during the presidency of George H. W. Bush.

Task:

Using information from the documents and your knowledge of United States history, write an essay in which you

Select *two* foreign crises listed in the historical context and for *each*

- Describe the historical circumstances that led to the crisis
- Explain an action taken by the president to respond to the crisis
- Discuss an effect of the president's action on the United States and/or on American society

Guidelines:

In your essay, be sure to

- Develop all aspects of the task
- Incorporate information from *at least four* documents
- Incorporate relevant outside information
- Support the theme with relevant facts, examples, and details
- Use a logical and clear plan of organization, including an introduction and a conclusion that are beyond a restatement of the theme

Answers
August 2018
United States History and Government

Answer Key

PART I

1. 1	**11.** 3	**21.** 4	**31.** 2	**41.** 2
2. 2	**12.** 4	**22.** 2	**32.** 2	**42.** 1
3. 1	**13.** 2	**23.** 4	**33.** 3	**43.** 2
4. 1	**14.** 1	**24.** 3	**34.** 4	**44.** 3
5. 2	**15.** 1	**25.** 2	**35.** 2	**45.** 1
6. 4	**16.** 4	**26.** 3	**36.** 4	**46.** 2
7. 1	**17.** 3	**27.** 1	**37.** 3	**47.** 3
8. 3	**18.** 4	**28.** 1	**38.** 3	**48.** 4
9. 4	**19.** 3	**29.** 4	**39.** 1	**49.** 3
10. 1	**20.** 2	**30.** 3	**40.** 2	**50.** 4

PART II: Thematic Essay   *See* **Answers Explained** section.

PART III: Document-Based Question   *See* **Answers Explained** section.

Answers Explained

PART I (1–50)

1. **1** The geography of the Atlantic Coastal Plain most influenced the southern economy during the period from 1620 to 1865 because it promoted a plantation system of agriculture. The fertile soil, relatively flat land, and long growing season of the coastal regions of the South made the area ideal for large tobacco, rice, and indigo plantations. (Cotton did not become a major crop in the United States until the 1790s). While each plant or crop has a specific growing season, the growing season of a region is usually defined as the number of days between the last frost in the spring and the first frost in the fall. These large plantations lent themselves to the slave system of labor. In contrast, the hilly, rocky soil and shorter growing season of the northern colonies proved more suitable for smaller-scale agriculture and a more mixed economy. The smaller farms of the northern colonies were generally worked by the owner of the property and his family, with, perhaps, more people hired for planting and harvesting.

WRONG CHOICES EXPLAINED:

(2) The southern economy during the period from 1620 to 1865 was not known for developing a diversified manufacturing sector. Manufacturing operations began in the United States in the first half of the 19th century. An early factory complex—textile mills in Lowell, Massachusetts—opened in 1814. However, these early factories were concentrated in the northern states. A strong northern manufacturing sector aided Union forces in the Civil War. Even after the Civil War, the South was slow to industrialize.

(3) The southern economy during the period from 1620 to 1865 was not known for developing a strong railroad industry. The first section of railroad line, built and operated by the Baltimore and Ohio Railroad, opened in 1830. Railroad lines rapidly expanded in the following decades, but most of this development occurred in the northern states. By the time of the Civil War, the states of the Union had 22,000 miles of railroad tracks, compared to 9,500 miles in the states of the Confederacy.

(4) The southern economy during the period from 1620 to 1865 was not known for widespread coal mining. Coal mining increased in the United States every decade of the 1800s. However, most of this mining occurred in the northern states, most notably Pennsylvania. A smattering of coal mining operations existed in the South during the Civil War, but these were inland, not in the Atlantic Coastal Plain.

2. **2** The trial of John Peter Zenger was the event that most influenced the concept of freedom of the press during the colonial period. In 1734, Zenger, a New York City newspaper publisher, was arrested and charged with seditious libel for printing articles critical of the royal governor. His lawyer argued that he had the right to print such articles because they were truthful. The jury acquitted Zenger. In the wake of the case, more newspaper publishers were willing to print articles critical of royal authorities. The concept of freedom of the press is one of several protections enshrined in the First Amendment of the Constitution.

WRONG CHOICES EXPLAINED:

(1) The passage of the Navigation Acts is not associated with the concept of freedom of speech. The Navigation Acts were part of Great Britain's mercantilist approach to its North American colonies. The goal of the acts was to define the colonies as suppliers of raw materials to Britain and as markets for British manufactured items. Toward this end, Parliament developed a list of "enumerated goods"—goods from the colonies that could only be shipped to Britain. The enumeration of these goods was a double-edged sword; the colonies could not always get the highest price for their goods, but they had a consistent market for them. Several of the acts—such as the Wool Act (1699), the Hat Act (1732), and the Iron Act (1750)—set restrictions on colonial production of these manufactured items. In this way, Parliament gave an advantage to manufacturers in Britain.

(3) The creation of the Albany Plan of Union is not associated with the concept of freedom of speech. The Albany Plan of Union grew out of the Albany Congress, a 1754 meeting called by Benjamin Franklin. The goal of the plan was to unite the 13 colonies in order to provide for common defense and support for British forces in the French and Indian War. The plan was rejected by the colonial assemblies, as well as by British authorities, but it established the precedent of intercolonial cooperation.

(4) The establishment of the House of Burgesses is not associated with the concept of freedom of speech. The House of Burgesses was created by the Virginia Company in 1619. The company had founded the colony of Virginia in 1607 as a profit-generating venture. The company saw the need for some sort of body to govern the inhabitants of the colony and created this representative assembly. All free adult men could vote for representatives. Later, this was limited to wealthy men. After Virginia came under the jurisdiction of the crown instead of the Virginia Company (1624), the king allowed the House of Burgesses to continue. It is seen as an early example of representative government.

3. **1** The social contract theory as applied to the Declaration of Independence most directly reflects the ideas of John Locke. Locke was one of the main intellectual influences in the writing of the Declaration of Independence. He wrote *Two Treatises on Government* in the early 1690s to defend England's Glorious Revolution (1688) and to challenge Thomas Hobbes's defense of an absolutist monarchy. The body of the Declaration of Independence is a list of grievances against the king of Great Britain, but the eloquent preamble contains key elements of Locke's social contract theory. The basic idea of the theory is that people surrender some of their freedoms to the rules established by the government and the government is obligated to protect people's natural rights. Conversely, if a government violates people's natural rights, the people have the right "to alter or abolish it."

WRONG CHOICES EXPLAINED:

(2) The social contract theory as applied to the Declaration of Independence does not reflect the ideas of Thomas Hobbes. Hobbes defended an absolutist monarchy. He believed that humans were driven by selfish motives and that the natural state of humanity was a state of war. Therefore, he believed an absolute ruler was necessary in order to maintain peace and security.

(3) The social contract theory as applied to the Declaration of Independence does not reflect the ideas of Baron de Montesquieu. Montesquieu promoted the idea of separation of powers in government. He praised the English system for preventing the king from exercising absolute power. Power was separated with the king having certain powers and Parliament having certain powers. This principle was adopted by the framers of the United States Constitution. The Constitution separates power into three branches—the executive, the legislative, and the judicial. All three branches are given certain powers and each has the ability to limit, or check, the powers of the other two. The goal is to create balance among the three branches, with no branch able to dominate the other two. This principle is known as *checks and balances*.

(4) The social contract theory as applied to the Declaration of Independence does not reflect the ideas of Adam Smith (1723–1790). Smith's ideas provide the basis of classical free market economic theory. He argued that self-interest and competitiveness stimulated economic growth and prosperity.

4. **1** A principal reason for calling the Constitutional Convention of 1787 was to strengthen the central government. At the time, the United States government was based on the Articles of Confederation (1781–1788). The national government under the Articles of Confederation lacked many powers; most power remained with the state governments. The framers of this first American government created a "firm league of friendship" among the states, rather than a strong, centralized

government. Before 1776, they had lived under a powerful, distant authority and did not want to repeat that experience. Also, many of these early leaders were fiercely loyal to their states and did not want to see state power superseded. Funding the government proved to be a major problem. As written, the Articles did not give the national government the power to levy taxes. A proposal to alter the document and allow the national government to collect import duties was blocked by Rhode Island and New York, states with major ports. Concerns about the weaknesses of the government under the Articles of Confederation seemed to be borne out by Shays' Rebellion (1786–1787). This revolt of Massachusetts farmers who felt cheated by the state's economic policies was eventually put down by state armed forces. The delegates at the Constitutional Convention in Philadelphia (1787) believed that a stronger national government was needed to quickly put down any future disturbances.

WRONG CHOICES EXPLAINED:

(2) The Constitutional Convention was not called in order to settle land disputes with Canada. The United States had several conflicts with Great Britain over the border between the U.S. and British-ruled Canada. In the Webster-Ashburton Treaty (1842), the United States settled a dispute with Great Britain over the border between Maine and Canada. The treaty split the disputed territory and also settled a dispute over the border between the Minnesota territory and Canada. In 1846, the Polk administration reached a compromise with Great Britain over control of Oregon, establishing the border at the 49th parallel. That line is the current boundary between the western United States and Canada.

(3) The Constitutional Convention was not called in order to increase the power of the states. A major goal of the Constitutional Convention was to do the opposite—to decrease the power of the states and to increase the power of the central government. The government under the Articles of Confederation (1781–1788) was envisioned as a "firm league of friendship" among the states, rather than a strong, centralized government. The experience of living under the British government led to a distrust of a powerful, distant authority. Eventually, many political leaders saw the limits of this type of government and pushed for a Constitutional Convention to create a stronger central government.

(4) The Constitutional Convention was not called in order to weaken the system of checks and balances. The Constitutional Convention voted to create a central government with three branches—the legislative, the executive, and the judicial. In the Constitution, all three branches are given certain powers and each has the ability to limit, or check, the powers of the other two. The goal is to create balance among the three branches, with no branch able to dominate the other two. Thus, the principle known as *checks and balances* is central to the structure of the Constitution.

5. **2** One reason Antifederalist governors of New York and Virginia opposed ratification of the United States Constitution was because it would weaken the powers of state governments. Antifederalists feared the Constitution would create an omnipotent and unaccountable national government. Under the Articles of Confederation, which governed the United States in the 1780s before the ratification of the Constitution, the states retained major powers and the national government was given very limited powers. A central goal of the Constitution was to change this situation by giving the national government far more power and declaring it the "supreme law of the land." The Antifederalists were distrustful of distant authority. The 13 colonies had just emerged from under the thumb of the British Empire, so many colonists were eager to see power exercised locally. Eventually, many leading Antifederalists agreed to support ratification of the Constitution if a list of individual rights was added. This agreement led to the writing and ratification of the first ten amendments to the Constitution, known as the Bill of Rights.

WRONG CHOICES EXPLAINED:

(1) Antifederalist reasons for opposing the Constitution did not include forcing states to abandon western land claims. In fact, the issue of competing claims to the lands west of the established states had already been settled. Earlier, the Second Continental Congress had convinced states to give up their land claims as a condition for ratifying the Articles of Confederation. Maryland was the last state to agree to give up its western land claims (1781). These western lands then fell under the auspices of the national government until residents petitioned for territorial status and then statehood.

(3) Antifederalist reasons for opposing the Constitution did not include strengthening slavery. The Constitution recognized the institution of slavery and created regulations around the implementation of slavery. The Three-Fifths Compromise, for example, settled the issue of how slaves would be counted in the census (which would determine representation in the House of Representatives). The Fugitive Slave Clause required that slaves who escaped to another state be returned to their owners in the state from which they escaped. On the other hand, the Constitution did not include the words *slaves* or *slavery*, reflecting the unease of many of the framers of the Constitution with the institution of slavery. However, the issue of slavery was not central to the concerns of the Antifederalists.

(4) Antifederalist reasons for opposing the Constitution did not include making the amendment process more difficult. The process for amending the Constitution is not easy. First, an amendment can be proposed by Congress (by two-third majorities in both houses) or by a national convention.

Then, three-fourths of the states must approve an amendment for it to be ratified. The state-by-state approval process can occur by the consent of the state legislatures or by state ratifying conventions. However, the process for amending the Articles of Confederation—requiring unanimity among all the states— had also been difficult. In any case, the issue of the amendment process was not central to the concerns of the Antifederalists.

6. **4** Political parties, the president's cabinet, and national nominating conventions are considered examples of the unwritten constitution. The unwritten constitution refers to those traditions and practices that have become part of the American political system, but were not mentioned in the Constitution. Many of these practices date back to the administration of George Washington. Washington's administration witnessed the development of political parties, a practice unforeseen by most of the founding fathers. For most of the nation's history, two major rival parties have existed. The political parties serve to focus debate in Congress, as members of Congress tend to support their party's position. The president is, by virtue of his office, the most prominent public voice of his party, and therefore acts as its leader (although each party has a formal leader). President Washington also first regularly convened a cabinet, a group of advisors to the president that is comprised of the heads of major government departments. There are currently 15 cabinet-level departments, including the Department of Defense, the State Department, and the Department of the Interior. There are additional cabinet members who are not department heads. Cabinet members are nominated by the president and confirmed by the Senate. Political parties began holding national nominating conventions in the 1830s. Before that, members of Congress met as party caucuses to select presidential nominees for each party.

WRONG CHOICES EXPLAINED:
   (1) Political parties, the president's cabinet, and national nominating conventions are not examples of delegated powers. Delegated powers are those powers given (or delegated) to the national government by the Constitution. State powers, on the other hand, are called reserved powers, in that they are held on to (or reserved) by the states. Powers held by both the federal and the state governments are called concurrent powers. Delegated powers include declaring war, entering treaties, coining money, establishing import duties and tariffs, and regulating commerce between states.
   (2) Political parties, the president's cabinet, and national nominating conventions are not examples of separation of powers. Separation of powers describes a basic feature of the governing structure created by the Constitution. The framers of the Constitution created three branches of government, each with powers

separate from the other two. The legislative branch creates laws, the executive branch carries out laws, and the judicial branch interprets laws. The Constitution spells out the powers of each branch. The framers were very conscious of the problems of a government with limitless powers. After living under the British monarchy, they came to believe that a powerful government without checks was dangerous to liberty. Therefore, they created a governmental system with three branches, each with the ability to check the powers of the other two. The goal was to keep the three branches in balance.

(3) Political parties, the president's cabinet, and national nominating conventions are not examples of the elastic clause. The elastic clause to the Constitution, also known as the *necessary and proper clause*, addressed the concerns of some of the framers of the Constitution that Congress would not have the latitude to effectively carry out its powers. They feared that by listing specific powers, the Constitution might be seen as denying Congress additional powers to address unforeseen circumstances. They, therefore, pushed for the elastic clause, which stretched the powers of Congress by allowing it to "make all laws necessary and proper" in regard to carrying out its functions. Antifederalists were especially critical of the elastic clause, fearing that it would grant Congress limitless powers.

7. **1** Thomas Jefferson used a loose interpretation of the United States Constitution when he negotiated the purchase of the Louisiana Territory from France in 1803. The Louisiana Purchase initially presented a dilemma for President Jefferson. Previously, he had held a strict constructionist view of the Constitution. This view, also referred to as a strict interpretation of the Constitution, held that governmental officials should follow exactly what was stated and allowed for in the document. For example, in the 1790s he opposed the creation of a national bank, arguing that Congress was not granted the power to create such an institution. Secretary of the Treasury Alexander Hamilton countered this argument by invoking the elastic clause, asserting that the creation of a national bank was permissible under the Constitution. Later, Jefferson set aside his strict constructionist view of the Constitution when the Louisiana Territory became available to the United States. The territory was long held by France until France ceded it to Spain in 1763 following the French and Indian War. France then regained the territory in 1801. The ambitious French leader Napoleon Bonaparte quickly decided that it was in France's best interest to sell the Louisiana Territory at a reasonable price in order to attain cash to fund war with Great Britain. In 1803, American negotiators quickly agreed to a price of $15 million. Jefferson realized that the purchase of such land was not allowed for in the Constitution, but if he waited for a constitutional amendment specifically allowing Congress to acquire new

lands, Napoleon could rescind his offer. So Jefferson violated his long-held strict constructionist view and quickly presented the offer to Congress, which appropriated the money. For $15 million, the United States bought this vast expanse of land and nearly doubled its size. This flat area west of the Mississippi would become the most important agricultural region in the United States. In addition, the United States gained full control of the port of New Orleans and the Mississippi River.

WRONG CHOICES EXPLAINED:

(2) A president would not have to use a loose interpretation of the Constitution in order to ask Congress to increase the size of the United States Navy. The Constitution explicitly gives the president the power to suggest to Congress "such measures as he shall judge necessary." The powers of Congress include the power "to provide and maintain a Navy." Further, President Jefferson did not move to increase the size of the Navy. He took steps to reduce the size of both the navy and army. He argued that both could be reduced during times of peace.

(3) A president would not have to use a loose interpretation of the Constitution in order to run for a second term as president. The Constitution does not prohibit a president from running for a second term. President Jefferson ran for and was elected to a second term, just as President George Washington had done earlier.

(4) A president, or any individual, would not have to use a loose interpretation of the Constitution in order to oppose the election of another individual to office. The First Amendment to the Constitution protects freedom of speech, and the Constitution allows for an individual to oppose a sitting president and to run for the office of the presidency. Jefferson did just that in 1800. He opposed President John Adams in the election and was elected to be the third president of the United States.

8. **3** Between 1820 and 1850, southern lawmakers consistently opposed protective tariffs because these tariffs increased the cost of imports. Tariff rates divided northerners and southerners in the first half of the 19th century. Northern manufacturing interests supported the higher tariff rates, which would increase the price of imported goods and, therefore, make American-made goods more desirable for consumers. Such tariffs were labeled "protective" because they would protect American manufacturers from foreign competition. Southern cotton farmers, who supplied much of Great Britain's cotton, feared that high tariffs would cause a drop in international trade and would make imported items more expensive. The conflict over tariffs came to a head

following the passage of the Tariff Act of 1828. Labeled the "Tariff of Abominations" by its critics, the act set extraordinarily high tariffs on imported goods. John C. Calhoun and a group of South Carolina politicians took a strong stand against the Tariff Act and insisted on the states' right to nullify an unjust law. Ultimately, a compromise was reached, resulting in lower tariff rates.

WRONG CHOICES EXPLAINED:

(1) Southern lawmakers did not oppose protective tariffs on the grounds that they would decrease trade between the states. Protective tariffs targeted imports from foreign countries, not trade within the states. If anything, protective tariffs would encourage trade between the states.

(2) Southern lawmakers did not oppose protective tariffs on the grounds that they would harm American shipping. Shipping operations were more concentrated in northern port cities, such as Boston and New York. The southern economy was more focused on agriculture.

(4) Southern lawmakers did not oppose protective tariffs on the grounds that they would weaken national security. The revenue from tariffs went to the federal government. Increasing federal revenues would not result in a weakening of national security. If anything, more money would be available for national security.

9. **4** In the 1840s, westward expansion was justified by a belief in Manifest Destiny. The term *Manifest Destiny* was coined in an 1845 newspaper article. It captured the fervor of the westward expansion movement, implying that it was God's plan that the United States take over and settle the entire continent. Americans who did settle out West were probably driven more by economic factors, such as cheap land or precious metals, than they were by a desire to fulfill God's plan. The history of the settlement of West includes many noteworthy episodes: Texas independence from Mexico (1836), the opening of the Oregon Trail (1841), the Mexican War (1846–1848), the Mormon exodus to Utah (1847), and the California gold rush (1849). This movement was especially damaging for the Native Americans of the West who were driven off their land and relegated to several western reservations.

WRONG CHOICES EXPLAINED:

(1) Westward expansion was not justified by a belief in laissez-faire. The French phrase *laissez-faire* means "to leave alone." It describes a government policy that would take a hands-off approach in regard to economic activities. Territorial expansion occurred as a result of actions taken by the federal government—such as carrying out military engagements and negotiating treaties.

(2) Westward expansion was not justified by a belief in popular sovereignty. Popular sovereignty referred to letting the people of a particular territory decide whether or not to allow slavery in that territory. The principle was applied to the newly created Kansas and Nebraska Territories under the Kansas-Nebraska Act (1854). Violence soon erupted in "Bleeding Kansas" as proslavery and antislavery men fought for control of the state. The principle was intended to settle disputes over slavery in new territories, but it was not used to justify westward expansion.

(3) Westward expansion was not justified by a belief in cultural pluralism. *Cultural pluralism* is a term used to describe a social order in which smaller ethnic and racial groups participate in the dominant mainstream society, but still maintain their unique cultural identities. The concept implies acceptance by the broader society of the values and practices of the smaller groups. The idea of cultural pluralism came into wide usage in the early decades of the 20th century, both as a description of contemporary society and as a societal goal. The idea stood in contrast to the conception of the United States as a "melting pot," in which different ethnic groups lose their unique cultural traits as they assimilate into mainstream culture. Westward expansion was often accompanied by a belief in the superiority of mainstream American culture and institutions.

10. **1** William Lloyd Garrison, Frederick Douglass, and Harriet Beecher Stowe are closely associated with the abolitionist movement. Antislavery sentiment has existed in American society as long as slavery has existed. Most obviously, African Americans—both free and enslaved—opposed the existence of slavery. Small numbers of white Americans, from the 1600s onward, opposed slavery. Many believers in Enlightenment thought condemned slavery on humanistic grounds, while Quakers and some Evangelical Christians argued that slavery was inconsistent with Christian teachings. During the era of the American Revolution, more white Americans, including some slave-holders, began to see slavery as inconsistent with the democratic values of the revolution. Starting in the 1830s, in the wake of the Second Great Awakening, a broader movement for the abolition of slavery began to form. William Lloyd Garrison was a key figure in the movement. He called for the immediate abolition of slavery, in contrast to many other white activists who advocated a more gradual approach to ending slavery. He also asserted that there should be no compensation to slave owners and that freed slaves were entitled to the same rights as white people. He started a newspaper called *The Liberator* in 1831 to prod the public into challenging the institution of slavery. Starting in the 1840s, the towering figure in the abolitionist movement was Frederick Douglass. Douglass was born into slavery (1818) and escaped to the North in 1838. He had learned to read and write and soon

became a powerful speaker in the antislavery movement. Douglass's autobiography, *Narrative of the Life of Frederick Douglass*, written in 1845, became a best-seller. One of the most well-known and important antislavery speeches is Douglass's July 5, 1852, address to the Rochester Anti-Slavery Sewing Society, "What to the slave is the 4th of July?" The speech is critical of the United States for not abiding by its founding principles. He asserts that it is preposterous to expect enslaved African Americans to celebrate the birth of American freedom when they themselves are still oppressed. Douglass remained an important figure before, during, and after the Civil War, until his death in 1895. Harriet Beecher Stowe brought antislavery sentiment into the homes of many northerners with the publication of her best-selling novel, *Uncle Tom's Cabin*. The novel depicted, in graphic detail, the brutality of slavery. For many northerners, slavery now had a human face. The novel outraged southern supporters of slavery, who attempted to ban it.

WRONG CHOICES EXPLAINED:

(2) William Lloyd Garrison, Frederick Douglass, and Harriet Beecher Stowe are not associated with the labor movement. A large-scale union movement developed in the gilded age of the post–Civil War period. A significant early union was the Knights of Labor, founded in 1869. This union welcomed all members, regardless of race, sex, or level of skill. The Knights had a broad agenda that included not only improvements in wages and hours for their workers, but also social reforms such as an end to child labor and better safety rules. A second early union was the American Federation of Labor (1886). One of its founders and its first leader was a cigar-maker named Samuel Gompers. The AFL differed from the Knights of Labor in that it included only skilled workers, the "aristocracy of labor." Further, the AFL did not engage in any sort of political activities for broader social reform.

(3) William Lloyd Garrison, Frederick Douglass, and Harriet Beecher Stowe are not associated with the Populist movement. The Populist movement became a formidable force in the 1890s. The Populists grew angry at the concentration of wealth and power by eastern industrialists. They supported a national income tax so that those with higher incomes would pay more than the poor. The Populist Party, organized in 1892, wanted the United States to get off the gold standard and to issue money backed by silver as well. This would increase the amount of money in circulation and would lead to inflation. Farmers supported inflationary policies so that the prices they received for their produce would increase.

(4) William Lloyd Garrison, Frederick Douglass, and Harriet Beecher Stowe are not associated with the Progressive movement. The Progressive movement was a response to the economic instability, social inequality, and political

corruption that had begun during the gilded age of the post–Civil War period and continued into the 20th century. Progressive reformers, who were most active in the 1900s and 1910s, called for greater government intervention in the economy, as well as social justice measures, increased democratization of the political process, and conservation of natural resources.

11. **3** Speakers B and C express the greatest support for the concept of states' rights. The concept of states' rights describes the idea that states would retain certain rights even though the national government was supreme. The issue of states' rights became closely identified with the defense of slavery. Defenders of slavery in the South felt that the institution had sufficiently broad support among white southerners, but they feared that northern political leaders might use the power of the federal government to limit or abolish slavery. Hence, they firmly embraced the right of states to resist or nullify federal edicts. Speaker B is arguing that states' rights are clearly protected in the Constitution. The original Constitution acknowledges that states will still retain certain rights. The Tenth Amendment makes the concept of states' rights more explicit. It states that the federal government has certain powers. These powers include powers expressly stated, as well those that are implied. All remaining powers, the Tenth Amendment states, are "reserved to the States respectively, or to the people" (unless the Constitution specifically prohibits them). Speaker C goes further, opening up the possibility of secession. The speaker argues that "liberty" can only be ensured if power is maintained on the state level—"closest to the people." When the federal government attempts to limit this liberty, then "union" is no longer desirable and secession is called for. The extent of these states' rights, known as reserved powers, became the subject of much debate between the time of the ratification of the Constitution and the Civil War.

WRONG CHOICES EXPLAINED:
(1), (2), and (4) All three of these choices are incorrect because they contain either Speaker A or Speaker D, or both. Speaker A and Speaker D both express support for federal power, not states' rights. Speaker A argues that the Constitution is not a temporary measure created by the states. If it were, then states would have the right to leave the union if they so desired. Rather, the Constitution was created by the people and cannot be undone by individual states. The preamble states, "We the people . . . do ordain and establish this Constitution," not "We the states. . ." Speaker D roundly rejects both nullification and secession. Nullification is the theory that a state could declare an objectionable federal law or action null and void within that state. The speaker is arguing that nullification and secession would threaten liberty and the very existence of the United States.

12. **4** The political opinions expressed in the statements relate most directly to the start of the Civil War. On the eve of the Civil War, southern political leaders asserted the most drastic of states' rights—the right to secede. Seven southern states announced their intent to secede in the three months after the 1860 presidential election because they believed that President-elect Abraham Lincoln would undermine or abolish slavery. Four more southern states followed suit and announced their intent to secede after Lincoln was inaugurated. Lincoln made clear that he believed secession was unconstitutional and that it was not among the rights of the states. In his First Inaugural Address, he stated that, according to the Constitution, "the Union of these States is perpetual." Therefore, he added, "no State, upon its own mere motion, can lawfully get out of the Union." The southern states announced the formation of the Confederate States of America. Lincoln continued to insist that secession was illegal. The question of secession—and, indeed, of slavery—was settled by the victory of the Union army over the rebellious states of the South. Since then, it is clear that states' right do not include the right to secede.

WRONG CHOICES EXPLAINED:
(1) The political opinions expressed in the statements, relating to the issue of states' rights, are not related to the start of the Revolutionary War. The Revolutionary War grew out of tensions between Great Britain and 13 of its North American colonies. These 13 colonies grew increasingly frustrated with British colonial policies in the aftermath of the French and Indian War (1754–1763). As Great Britain attempted to assert greater control over its empire, the colonies began to protest and resist. Fighting broke out in the Massachusetts towns of Lexington and Concord in 1775. The colonies formally declared their independence from Great Britain in July 1776. Fighting continued in North America into 1781; the Treaty of Paris formally ended the war in 1783.

(2) The political opinions expressed in the statements, relating to the issue of states' rights, are not related to the start of the War of 1812. This war grew out of tensions between the United States and Great Britain. The United States grew increasingly resentful of British impressment of American sailors and of British assistance to Native American tribes in the Great Lakes region. The Treaty of Ghent (1815) ended the War of 1812 roughly where it had begun. The United States and Great Britain agreed to stop fighting, give back any territory seized in the war, and recognize the boundary between the United States and Canada that had been established before the war.

(3) The political opinions expressed in the statements, relating to the issue of states' rights, are not related to the start of the Mexican-American War. This war grew out of the desire of the United States to expand its territory. Americans had

been settling in the Mexican territory of Texas as far back as the 1820s. In 1836, Texans fought for and won independence from Mexico; Texas joined the United States in 1845. Conflict between the United States and Mexico soon ensued. The two countries disagreed over the southern border of Texas. President James K. Polk sent troops into this disputed territory. Skirmishes in the disputed area led to war between Mexico and the United States. The United States won the war, which lasted from 1846 to 1848, and acquired the huge territory that comprised the northern provinces of Mexico, which is known as the Mexican Cession.

13. **2** Passage of the Kansas-Nebraska Act (1854) was criticized by northern newspapers because it repealed the 36°30′ line of the Missouri Compromise. The Kansas-Nebraska Act allowed for the possibility of slavery in the territories of Kansas and Nebraska—areas that had been closed to slavery by the Missouri Compromise (1820). The act mandated that the question of slavery in these territories be decided by popular sovereignty. Popular sovereignty called for settlers in new territories to vote on the issue of slavery. Many northerners were angry at the act and at the sponsor of the act, Senator Stephen A. Douglas, for making additional territory open to the possibility of slavery. The act divided Whigs—between proslavery "Cotton Whigs" and antislavery "Conscience Whigs." These divisions undermined the party, which ceased to function as a national party by 1856. In addition, violence erupted in Kansas as proslavery and antislavery men fought for control of the state. "Bleeding Kansas" can be seen as a dress rehearsal for the Civil War. The question of slavery in Kansas was unresolved when the Civil War began. After southern secession, Kansas quickly joined the Union as a free state in 1861.

WRONG CHOICES EXPLAINED:
(1) The Kansas-Nebraska Act did not limit settlement in those territories. The act was designed to encourage settlement by creating a pathway for these areas to attain territorial status and then to become states. In practice, the act resulted in a flood of proslavery and antislavery men into the territory who both hoped to influence the status of slavery in the territories.

(3) The Kansas-Nebraska Act did not uphold the Supreme Court decision in *Gibbons v. Ogden*. The case of *Gibbons v. Ogden* (1824) took place earlier and did not deal with the issue of slavery. In this case, the Supreme Court invalidated a monopoly on ferry transportation between New York and New Jersey that had been issued by New York, and asserted that only the federal government could regulate interstate trade.

(4) The Kansas-Nebraska Act did not admit Maine to the Union as a free state. Maine was admitted as part of the Missouri Compromise (1820). The compromise settled a controversy that arose between the slave-holding states

and the free states in 1820 when Missouri applied for statehood as a slave state. The admission of Missouri would have upset that balance between slave-holding states and free states. The compromise allowed for the admission of two new states—Missouri as a slave state and Maine as a free state. It also divided the remaining area of the Louisiana Territory at 36°30' north latitude. Above that line, slavery was not permitted (except for in Missouri); below the line, it was permitted. The compromise was repealed by the Kansas-Nebraska Act.

14. **1** After the Civil War, the most common occupations for freedmen were sharecroppers and tenant farmers. The Civil War disrupted the agricultural system in the South by ending slavery. It was not immediately clear what would replace it. White landowners needed African American laborers to work the cotton fields. The landowners wanted to hire groups of African American laborers, to be directed by white overseers. African Americans were resistant to this setup because it reminded them too much of the slave system. However, African Americans could not become landowners themselves, because they lacked the financial resources. Out of this impasse grew the sharecropping system. In the sharecropping system, African Americans (and poor whites) would farm a few acres of a large estate and give a share, often half, of the crops to the owner as rent. In this way, African Americans were not under the direct supervision of whites. After paying back loans for seed money and the use of tools, sharecroppers were left with very little, if anything. The system created a cycle of debt, which prevented African Americans from acquiring money and owning land. Tenant farming was considered a step up on the agricultural ladder (with actual ownership of land being the highest rung). Tenant farmers often had their own tools, animals, and a small amount of capital. They rented land to farm from a landowner, but usually paid with cash instead of a share of the crop.

WRONG CHOICES EXPLAINED:
(2) After the Civil War, factory owners and teachers were not common occupations for freedmen. Some African Americans became teachers in schools that served the African American population, but the vast majority of freedmen continued to work in agriculture. Very few former slaves would have accumulated enough capital in the post–Civil War period to own a factory.

(3) After the Civil War, skilled artisans and mechanics were not common occupations for freedmen. Some African Americans performed skilled craft work, but the vast majority of freedmen continued to work in agriculture.

(4) After the Civil War, miners and soldiers were not common occupations for freedmen. Some African Americans, including freedmen, ventured west and became miners. In addition, several regiments of African American troops were formed after the Civil War. These soldiers, known as Buffalo Soldiers, participated in wars against Native Americans and in the Spanish American War

(1898), and they continued to exist into the 20th century. The regiments included freedmen, as well as African Americans who had not been enslaved. However, the vast majority of freedmen continued to work in agriculture.

15. **1** A major problem for settlers on the Great Plains was limited rainfall. The Great Plains is the vast area that lies west of the Mississippi River and east of the Rocky Mountains. It includes the present-day states of Kansas, Nebraska, North Dakota, and South Dakota, as well as parts of the states of Colorado, Iowa, Minnesota, Montana, New Mexico, Oklahoma, Texas, and Wyoming. Today, the region produces a large portion of the country's agricultural products. Before being converted to farmland, the Great Plains was known for its extensive grasslands. The rainfall of the region is generally limited. The western section (roughly west of the 100th meridian) receives less than 20 inches of rainfall per year, while the eastern area receives more than 20 inches per year. Despite limited rainfall, the region has a long growing season and rich soil. The government encouraged development of the region by passing the Homestead Act (1862), which provided free land in the region to settlers who were willing to farm it. Hundreds of thousands of people applied for and were granted homesteads. The expansion of railroads into the West, leading to the completion of a transcontinental railroad in 1869, also encouraged white settlement in the Great Plains. The railroads provided an economic lifeline for these new settlers. Freight trains brought crops and cattle from the Great Plains states to cities such as Chicago. This increased economic activity led to Native Americans being pushed off their land. The railroads also brought sportsmen out west who shot at buffalo herds from their passing train cars. While these buffalo were sport for white travelers, they were a means of sustenance for many Plains Indians. These factors all led to the decline of the Plains Indians.

WRONG CHOICES EXPLAINED:

(2) The Great Plains region is not characterized by dense forests. Dense forests are common in much of the interior of the East Coast region, the area around the Great Lakes, and the Pacific Northwest.

(3) The Great Plains region is not characterized by mountainous terrain. The Great Plains are relatively flat, with the exception of the Ozark Mountain range. Major ranges in the United States include the Appalachian Mountains, in the interior of the East Coast region, and the Rocky Mountains, west of the Great Plains. A series of mountain ranges, including the Sierra Nevada Mountains, stretch along the West Coast.

(4) The Great Plains region is not characterized by frequent flooding. Areas adjacent to rivers, such as the Mississippi River and its tributaries, are prone to flooding. The city of New Orleans, along the banks of the Mississippi River, is prone to flooding. Severe flooding occurred in the city, much of which sits below sea level, in the wake of Hurricane Katrina in 2005, leading to over 1,400 deaths.

16. **4** The most appropriate title for the graphic organizer is "Factors Leading to Industrialization." The graphic organizer contains four important factors that contributed to the rapid industrialization of the United States in the decades after the Civil War. A policy of open immigration helped provide the workforce for this industrial era. The large wave of immigrants who came to the United States between 1880 and 1920 was essential to the industrialization of the United States. An estimated 20 million people—from Russia, Italy, Poland, the Balkan region, China, and elsewhere—immigrated to the United States, most settling in industrial cities such as New York, Pittsburgh, and Chicago. The label "new immigrants" was applied to these groups. In addition, the United States has an abundance of natural resources that contributed to industrial growth. Anthracite and bituminous coal, important fuel for industrial processes, was readily available in western Pennsylvania and West Virginia. The first oil well was established in 1859 by Edwin Drake in Pennsylvania. Later in the century, the demand for oil increased as it came to be refined into gasoline, a fuel for automobiles. Another factor that contributed to industrial growth was an abundant food supply. The farms of the Great Plains were able to supply wheat and corn to the growing urban population in the late 1800s. Dairy and vegetable farms, in areas adjacent to the industrial centers, also were important in supplying the industrial workforce. Finally, government policies supported industrial growth. For instance, the government encouraged the building of railroads by passing the Pacific (Transcontinental) Railroad Act (1862). The act encouraged the expansion of the railroad network by giving railroad companies wide swaths of federally owned land. These generous land grants totaled more than 180 million acres, an area equal to the size of Texas. Further, Supreme Court decisions favored big business. In *Santa Clara County v. Union Pacific Railway* (1886), for example, the Court established the concept of "corporate personhood" and shielded corporations from onerous regulation.

WRONG CHOICES EXPLAINED:
(1) "Rise of Labor Unions" would not be an appropriate title for the graphic organizer. A graphic organizer with that title might include items such as "the birth of the Knights of Labor," "the creation of the American Federation of Labor," and "workers resist long hours and low wages."

(2) "Innovations and Technology" would not be an appropriate title for the graphic organizer. A graphic organizer with that title might include items such as "Bessemer process," "vulcanization of rubber," and "generating electrical current."

(3) "Vertical Integration of Business" would not be an appropriate title for the graphic organizer. A graphic organizer with that title might include items such as "control of the supply chain," "Andrew Carnegie buys railroad and iron mine to enhance steel production," and "establishment of distribution network."

17. **3** In the United States, third parties have been influential because they have often suggested reforms later adopted by the two major parties. In the United States, third parties have had a difficult time attracting votes. For example, in the electoral college system, used to elect the president, the winner of each state takes *all* the electoral votes of that state. Therefore, people tend to vote for one of the major candidates; they fear that a vote for a third-party candidate will aid the candidate they find least desirable. If the United States had a proportional representation system, in which parties received seats in government in proportion to the percentage of the national vote they received, people might be more likely to vote for third-party candidates. That said, several third parties have been influential in terms of pushing the two major parties to adopt certain reforms. For example, in the late 1840s, the Free Soil Party was established to oppose the expansion of slavery. Though the party was not successful, its approach to slavery helped shape the formation of the Republican Party in 1856. In the 1890s, the People's (Populist) Party put forth a comprehensive platform of reforms that were seen as radical at the time. The Populist Party grew out of anger that many farmers had at the concentration of wealth and power by eastern industrialists. Some of their ideas were not adopted—such as government ownership of banks. However, their proposal to create a national income tax—one in which those with higher incomes would pay more than the poor—was adopted with the ratification of the 16th Amendment (1913). In addition, the Populists supported the direct election of senators to make officials more accountable to the public. This became reality with the ratification of the 17th Amendment (1913).

WRONG CHOICES EXPLAINED:

(1) In the history of U.S. elections, third parties have been influential, but not by outspending their political opponents. Third parties have generally had only a fraction of the financial resources of the two major political parties.

(2) In the history of U.S. elections, third parties have been influential, but not by providing the presidential candidates of the major parties. Generally, the candidates of the major parties are individuals who have been active in those parties, not people from third parties.

(4) In the history of U.S. elections, third parties have been influential, but not by electing majorities in both Congress and state legislatures. Third parties have at different times been successful in electing members of Congress, but they have never come close to electing majorities in Congress or in state legislatures. In their most successful electoral year (1892), the Populist Party sent to Congress 11 (out of 356) representatives and 3 (out of 88) senators.

18. **4** One purpose of the Chinese Exclusion Act (1882) was to protect the jobs of American workers. The act was mainly a response to economic- and race-based opposition to immigrants in the western United States. In the 1800s, many Chinese people immigrated to the United States. The California gold rush (1848–1855) and the building of transcontinental railroad lines attracted many Chinese immigrants to the West. Nativist, or anti-immigrant, sentiment developed in the United States alongside the growing number of immigrants. Chinese and Japanese immigrants were especially targeted by nativists. Racist assumptions of the time held that Asian immigrants would never fully assimilate into the United States and that they would take jobs away from Americans. The Chinese Exclusion Act was the only instance of legislation that prohibited a particular nationality from entering the country.

WRONG CHOICES EXPLAINED:
(1) The purpose of the Chinese Exclusion Act (1882) was not to speed the construction of western railroads. The act had the opposite effect. Many Chinese immigrants worked on western railroad construction. The Chinese Exclusion Act, which cut off immigration from China, made it more difficult to find new workers for construction of the railroads.

(2) The purpose of the Chinese Exclusion Act (1882) was not to encourage settlement of the Pacific Coast. Before passage of the act, many Chinese individuals and families moved to the United States and settled along the Pacific Coast. The Chinese Exclusion Act cut off immigration from China, reducing a source of settlers to the Pacific Coast.

(3) The purpose of the Chinese Exclusion Act (1882) was not to expand the civil rights of immigrants. The act grew out of nativist resentment of immigrants. This nativist movement sought to restrict the civil rights of Chinese immigrants, as well as cut off the flow of new immigrants from China.

19. **3** The Interstate Commerce Act of 1887 and the Sherman Antitrust Act of 1890 were passed by Congress to control business practices that limited competition. During the gilded age of the late 1800s, corporations and trusts came to dominate entire industries. The men who controlled the major industries in

the United States came to be known as *robber barons*, a scornful title meant to call attention to their cutthroat business activities and their attempts to control the government. These robber barons often created trusts (combinations of companies) in order to eliminate competition and control a particular industry. The formation of trusts in several industries was seen as harmful to the interests of consumers. John D. Rockefeller established the first large trust in the oil processing industry. Critics of corporate power pushed the government to take steps to reign in these massive corporations. However, their efforts often did not end up having the desired effect. After the Supreme Court ruled in the *Wabash v. Illinois* case (1886) that states could not regulate railroads because they cross state lines, the federal government created the Interstate Commerce Commission to regulate railroads. But the ICC was chronically underfunded and was, therefore, ineffective. The Sherman Antitrust Act was designed to break up trusts. The act had limited success. At first, only a few trusts were challenged. Ironically, the act was used with equal vigor against unions, on the grounds that they were illegal formations that interfered with free trade. In the case of *United States v. E.C. Knight Company* (1895), the Supreme Court greatly limited the scope of the act by making a distinction between trade (which would be subject to the act) and manufacturing (which would not).

WRONG CHOICES EXPLAINED:

(1) The intent of the Interstate Commerce Act (1887) and the Sherman Antitrust Act (1890) was to control business practices that limited competition, not to regulate the money supply. The Federal Reserve Bank was created in 1913 in order to regulate the money supply. If the economy is sluggish, the Fed will attempt to stimulate economic growth by taking steps to increase the amount of money in circulation. If inflation occurs, the Fed will attempt to slow down economic activity by taking steps to restrict the amount of money in circulation. The most important mechanism for regulating the money supply is raising or lowering the interest rate at which the Fed loans money to other banks.

(2) The intent of the Interstate Commerce Act (1887) and the Sherman Antitrust Act (1890) was to control business practices that limited competition, not to promote investment in manufacturing. At a different time in American history, the federal government has encouraged domestic manufacturing by raising tariff rates on imported manufactured items.

(4) The intent of the Interstate Commerce Act (1887) and the Sherman Antitrust Act (1890) was to control business practices that limited competition, not to limit the hours of working women. Several states passed laws during the Progressive Era to limit the hours of working women. An Oregon law limiting the number of hours that women could work was challenged in the courts and upheld by the Supreme Court. In *Muller v. Oregon* (1908), the Court cited the

supposed physical limitations of women and the threat to their health that long workdays posed. The case specifically cited women's role as child bearers.

20. **2** The economic developments of the late 1800s resulted in an increase in the number of people living in urban areas. In the last decades of the 1800s, the United States experienced rapid industrialization. New large-scale factories, no longer dependent on rapid-flowing rivers for power, were built in urban areas. The need for new workers in cities drew immigrants from abroad and migrants from rural areas of the United States. Between 1860 and 1900, the number of Americans who lived in cities jumped from 6.2 million to over 30 million, which amounted to a shift in the urban population from 20 percent of the total population to 40 percent. This rapid urbanization offered people many opportunities, but also brought several problems. Corrupt and inefficient political operations— labeled political machines—became more common in this era. New York City was dominated by the Democratic Party machine, headquartered at Tammany Hall. The most famous Tammany chief was "Boss" William Marcy Tweed. The muckraker journalist Lincoln Steffens exposed urban corruption in *The Shame of the Cities* (1902). Another problem in this era was the proliferation of substandard tenement housing. The wretched conditions that workers often experienced in tenements were documented in Jacob Riis's book of photography and writing, *How the Other Half Lives* (1890). A third problem faced by cities in the late 1800s was an increase in crime. Gang activities, ethnic rivalries, pickpockets, barroom fights, and other criminal activities contributed to this increase in crime.

WRONG CHOICES EXPLAINED:

(1) Economic developments of the late 1800s did not result in an increase in African American migration from the North to the South. The rapid industrialization of the United States drew migrants to the North; it did not lead to an exodus from the North. Later, in the 1910s and 1920s, the United States witnessed the Great Migration of African Americans from the rural South to the urban North.

(3) Economic developments of the late 1800s did not result in a decrease in the number of immigrants coming into the United States. The rapid industrialization of the United States led to an increase in immigration from abroad. An estimated 20 million people immigrated to the United States, most settling in industrial cities such as New York, Pittsburgh, and Chicago.

(4) Economic developments of the late 1800s did not result in a decrease in the number of factory workers in the Northeast. The rapid industrialization of the United States led to an increase in the number of factory workers in the Northeast. Northeastern cities such as Philadelphia, Newark, New York, Rochester, New Haven, and Boston were all centers of industry during this period.

21. **4** Between 1900 and 1930, U.S. relations with Latin America were characterized by repeated efforts by the United States to control the affairs of many nations in the region. President Theodore Roosevelt (1901–1909) is often associated with the efforts by the United States to play a more aggressive role in Latin America. His foreign-policy approach is neatly summed up in his famous adage that the United States should "speak softly, but carry a big stick" when dealing with other nations (Roosevelt borrowed the phrase from an African proverb). The "big stick" implied the threat of military force. He envisioned the United States acting as the world's policeman, punishing wrongdoers. He asserted that the "civilized nations" had a duty to police the "backward" countries of the world. This assertion of American might is known as the Roosevelt Corollary to the Monroe Doctrine. President William Howard Taft (1909–1913) continued to pursue an aggressive foreign policy, but he put more emphasis on expanding and securing American commercial interests than on pursuing the global strategic goals that Roosevelt had championed. Taft's foreign policy has come to be known as "dollar diplomacy." Roosevelt, Taft, and their successors repeatedly interfered in the internal affairs of countries in Latin America throughout the period 1900 to 1930. For example, United States military interventions in Cuba occurred four times (1898–1902, 1906–1909, 1912, and 1917–1922), in Nicaragua three times (1909–1910, 1912–1925, and 1926–1933), in the Dominican Republic four times (1903, 1904, 1914, and 1916–1924), and in Honduras seven times (1903, 1907, 1911, 1912, 1919, 1924, and 1925).

WRONG CHOICES EXPLAINED:
(1) Between 1900 and 1930, U.S. relations with Latin America were not characterized by efforts to encourage the redistribution of land to the poor. In fact, the United States frequently intervened in Latin America to block efforts by Latin American leaders to redistribute land. The United States wanted land to stay in the hands of large-scale wealthy landowners, such as the United States–based United Fruit Company.

(2) Between 1900 and 1930, U.S. relations with Latin America were not characterized by efforts to deny economic aid to developing nations. The United States was willing to extend foreign aid to developing nations if the governments of those nations worked to secure American economic and strategic goals.

(3) Between 1900 and 1930, U.S. relations with Latin America were not characterized by efforts to limit the influence of communist dictators. U.S. opposition to communist governments is associated with the Cold War, a period of hostility between the United States and the Soviet Union that lasted from the end of World War II (1945) to the collapse of the Soviet Union (1991).

22. **2** President Theodore Roosevelt earned a reputation as a trustbuster because he used court actions to break up business monopolies. With the American economy growing by leaps and bounds in the 19th century, the presidents of the late 19th century did not challenge the doctrine of laissez-faire. The French phrase *laissez-faire* means "to let alone"; it describes a government policy that would take a hands-off approach in regard to economic activities. However, by the 20th century, the country began to face serious economic problems that called into question laissez-faire principles. President Roosevelt (1901–1909) saw the concentration of economic power in a few hands as potentially dangerous to the economy as a whole. Though the Sherman Antitrust Act (1890) was passed to limit monopolistic practices, the act was not enforced with a great deal of enthusiasm. Roosevelt made a point of using the act to pursue "bad trusts"—ones that interfered with commerce—not necessarily the biggest trusts. One of his first targets was the Northern Securities Company, a railroad holding company. His efforts were challenged in court. In *Northern Securities Co. v. United States* (1904), the Supreme Court upheld the power of the government to break up Northern Securities under the Sherman Antitrust Act. The case was a victory for Roosevelt. His efforts at challenging monopolies earned him his reputation as a trustbuster.

WRONG CHOICES EXPLAINED:
(1) President Theodore Roosevelt earned his reputation as a trustbuster by challenging monopolies, not because he favored conservation of natural resources. He did, in fact, pursue policies to conserve natural resources. Roosevelt, an avid outdoorsman, set aside millions of acres as protected areas. These areas include six national parks.

(3) President Theodore Roosevelt earned his reputation as a trustbuster by challenging monopolies, not because he sided with labor unions against big business. Roosevelt saw himself as a neutral arbitrator in regard to disputes between labor and big business, not as an advocate for labor unions. His most prominent action in regard to labor unions was helping to end the anthracite coal strike in 1902. He pressured the owners of the coal operations to accept arbitration by a government committee. The arbitration resulted in an end to the strike. The striking workers won a wage increase, but not union recognition.

(4) President Theodore Roosevelt earned his reputation as a trustbuster by challenging monopolies, not because he opposed the efforts of consumer advocates. In fact, Roosevelt pushed for legislation to protect consumers. Following publication of Upton Sinclair's novel, *The Jungle* (1906), which exposed the underside of meatpacking industry, Roosevelt signed the Meat Inspection Act (1906) and the Pure Food and Drug Act (also 1906), which established the Food and Drug Administration.

23. **4** One way in which Ida Tarbell, Upton Sinclair, and Jacob Riis were similar is that each sought to expose economic and social abuses. All three are considered *muckrakers*—journalists who wrote magazine articles and books that exposed wrongdoing by government officials, showed the negative side of industrialization, and let the world see a variety of social ills. Ida Tarbell's book, *The History of the Standard Oil Company* (1904), exposed the ruthlessness of John D. Rockefeller's oil company. Her book contributed to the government breaking up the Standard Oil Trust in 1911. Upton Sinclair exposed the underside of the meat-packing industry in the novel *The Jungle* (1906). The story follows a Lithuanian immigrant family through the stockyards of Chicago. The public uproar that followed the publication of the book led Congress to pass the Meat Inspection Act (1906) and the Pure Food and Drug Act (also 1906), which established the Food and Drug Administration. The photographs of Jacob Riis chronicled the living conditions of the urban poor. Riis was born in Denmark and immigrated to the United States in 1870. He worked as a police reporter but became interested in photographing the conditions of the urban poor. He turned his photographs of the poor in New York into the book *How the Other Half Lives* (1890). The book became influential in making middle-class people aware of the poverty that existed in the United States. These muckraking books inspired a generation of progressive reformers to push the government to intervene in these problems. A whole host of reforms were implemented by progressive reformers and their allies in the 1900s and 1910s.

WRONG CHOICES EXPLAINED:

(1) Ida Tarbell, Upton Sinclair, and Jacob Riis did not seek to end racial discrimination. Most white Progressive Era reformers turned a blind eye to the problems of race in the United States. However, African American reformers took the lead in challenging racial discrimination. For instance, Ida B. Wells, an African American muckraking journalist, challenged the mistreatment of African Americans in the country and exposed the horrors of lynching.

(2) Ida Tarbell, Upton Sinclair, and Jacob Riis did not seek to control illegal immigration. During the Progressive Era, there were few legal restrictions on immigration, so the issue of "illegal immigration" was not publicly debated. Nativists were successful in blocking immigration from China (with the Chinese Exclusion Act of 1882) and Japan (with the Gentlemen's Agreement of 1907). However, it was not until the 1920s, with the passage of the Emergency Quota Act (1921) and the National Origins Act (1924), that immigration was greatly restricted.

(3) Ida Tarbell, Upton Sinclair, and Jacob Riis did not seek to limit government regulations. They did the opposite. By exposing the negative side of industrialization and urbanization, muckraking journalists joined the call for greater government intervention into the economy.

24. **3** The purpose of the initiative, referendum, and recall was to increase citizen influence in government. All three items attempted to expand democracy and increase the power of citizens in state and local government. Progressive reformers in the first two decades of the 20th century were concerned that government was being taken over by corrupt and inefficient political machines. The muckraker journalist Lincoln Steffens exposed the underside of American municipal politics and the influence of wealthy businessmen in *The Shame of the Cities* (1902). Reformers hoped that by expanding democracy, the power of these political machines would be lessened. The initiative would enable citizens to introduce a bill to the local or state legislature by petition. The referendum would allow people to vote directly on proposed legislation. The recall would allow the populace to remove elected officials before their term ended.

WRONG CHOICES EXPLAINED:
(1) The purpose of the initiative, referendum, and recall was not to eliminate the two-party system. The three items were all designed to increase citizen participation in the political process. They did not address the number of political parties that participated in elections.

(2) The purpose of the initiative, referendum, and recall was not to limit participation in state elections. The three items were all designed to increase citizen participation in the political process, not to limit it.

(4) The purpose of the initiative, referendum, and recall was not to strengthen the power of political machines. Reformers hoped to limit the power of the corrupt, entrenched, inefficient political operations—labeled political machines—which controlled many municipal governments. They thought that one way to challenge the power of these political machines was to increase citizen participation through measures such as the initiative, referendum, and recall.

25. **2** The photograph supports the conclusion that state and federal governments did not adequately regulate child labor. Lewis Hine and other Progressive Era photographers sought to raise awareness of the prevalence of child labor in the United States. Because wages for working-class men remained relatively low, families often had to supplement their incomes with wages of children and women. In turn, the influx of women and children into the labor

force depressed overall wages. From the 1870s until World War I, child labor grew each decade. By 1900, children aged 10 to 15 years old made up 18 percent of the industrial workforce. In 1916, Congress addressed the issue of child labor and passed the Keating-Owen Child Labor Act. Using its power to regulate interstate commerce, Congress prohibited the sale across state lines of goods produced by factories that employed children under the age of 14. Less than a year later, in the case of *Hammer v. Dagenhart* (1917), the Supreme Court shot down the act. The Court asserted that the goods being regulated were not inherently "immoral," as prostitution or liquor might be. Therefore, what was being addressed by the law was manufacturing practices, and manufacturing practices were subject to state, not federal, law. Later, the Fair Labor Standards Act (1938), passed as part of President Franklin D. Roosevelt's New Deal, included strict limits on child labor.

WRONG CHOICES EXPLAINED:

(1) The photograph, of two children working in an industrial setting, would not support the conclusion that textile manufacturing was not important to the national economy. Documents containing statistics for the various categories of industrial production in the United States might shed light on the relative importance of textile manufacturing in the national economy. Such statistics could include profitability, income, or number of workers employed in different types of industrial production.

(3) The photograph, of two children working in an industrial setting, would not support the conclusion that American factories were less productive than factories in other countries. Documents containing statistics on the productivity of the industrial sector in the United States and in other countries might shed light on the relative productivity of American factories.

(4) The photograph, of two children working in an industrial setting, would not support the conclusion that strict federal safety standards were enforced in factories across the nation. In the photograph, there are not any obvious indications of safety standards being enforced. The fact that one of the children is barefoot indicates a lack of safety measures. At the time, the federal government had not yet passed safety standards for industrial operations. Such federal guidelines would not be passed until the 1930s, when New Deal legislation addressed conditions in factories.

26. **3** During the 1920s, Congress established a quota system for immigration in order to reduce immigration from southern and eastern Europe. Anti-immigrant sentiment ran very high in the 1920s. The United States had experienced a large wave of immigration in the decades leading up to World War I.

Between 1880 and 1920, an estimated 20 million people, from Russia, Italy, Poland, the Balkan region, and elsewhere, immigrated to the United States. Nativists feared that white Anglo-Saxon Americans were committing "race suicide" by allowing "inferior" races to enter America in large numbers. This anti-immigrant sentiment led to the passage of legislation that greatly reduced the number of immigrants allowed into the United States. The Emergency Quota Act (1921) and the National Origins Act (1924) set quotas for new immigrants based on nationality. The first act set the quota for each nationality at 3 percent of the total number of that nationality that was present in the United States in 1910. The second act reduced the quota to 2 percent and moved the year back to 1890. This had the effect of setting very low quotas for many of the "new immigrants"—from eastern and southern Europe. The acts did not set any limits on immigrants from within the Western Hemisphere.

WRONG CHOICES EXPLAINED:

(1) Congress's reason for establishing the quota system in the 1920s was to reduce immigration from southern and eastern Europe, not to ensure that the United States would have enough factory workers. In fact, the quota system reduced the number of potential factory workers in the United States by greatly reducing the number of immigrants allowed into the country.

(2) Congress's reason for establishing the quota system in the 1920s was to reduce immigration from southern and eastern Europe, not to keep migrant workers out of the country. Migrant farmers are seasonal farm workers who move from place to place, as crops in different locations are ready for harvest. Many migrant farmers in the 1920s, and since then, were foreign-born workers—from Mexico and other countries in Central America and the Caribbean. The quota system did not set limits on immigrants from within the Western Hemisphere so that migrant farmers from Mexico and other countries in the Western Hemisphere would not be affected by the quota laws.

(4) Congress's reason for establishing the quota system in the 1920s was to reduce immigration from southern and eastern Europe, not to assist refugees from war-torn countries. In the post–World War II period, the United States has played an important role in accepting refugees fleeing persecution or war. The U.S. took in hundreds of thousands of Europeans displaced by World War II and resettled refugees escaping from Communist regimes in Europe and Asia during the Cold War. More recently, the United States has greatly reduced the number of refugees it has allowed into the country from war-torn countries, most notably from Syria.

27. **1** The trial of Sacco and Vanzetti is an example of nativism in the 1920s. Nicola Sacco and Bartolomeo Vanzetti were accused of robbing and killing a payroll clerk in Massachusetts in 1920. The evidence against them was sketchy and the judge was openly hostile to the two men, who were not only immigrants but also anarchists. The trial illustrated the intolerance that many Americans had toward immigrants in the 1920s. After they were found guilty, many Americans protested the verdict and wondered if an immigrant, especially with radical ideas, could get a fair trial in the United States. Despite widespread protests, the two men were executed in 1927. Anti-immigrant sentiment ran very high in the 1920s. The United States passed the Emergency Quota Act (1921) and the National Origins Act (1924), both of which greatly reduced the number of new immigrants allowed into the United States. These acts set quotas for new immigrants based on nationality.

WRONG CHOICES EXPLAINED:
(2) The verdict in the Scopes trial is not an example of nativism. The trial did not involve immigrants or anti-immigrant sentiment. The 1925 Scopes trial involved the teaching of evolution in public schools. John Scopes, a Tennessee biology teacher, was arrested for violating a state law forbidding the teaching of evolution. The case turned into a national spectacle, with the famous lawyers Clarence Darrow representing Scopes and William Jennings Bryan representing the state. The trial pitted rural, traditional, and religious values against science. It is one of several important events that highlighted cultural divisions in the 1920s.

(3) The Teapot Dome scandal is not an example of nativism. The scandal did not involve immigrants or anti-immigrant sentiment. The 1922 Teapot Dome scandal occurred during the presidency of Warren Harding. Harding's Secretary of the Interior accepted bribes from oil companies in exchange for leasing them the rights to drill for oil on publicly held land in Teapot Dome, Wyoming. Although Harding was not directly implicated in the scandal, it was emblematic of a culture of corruption that existed in his administration and of the pro-business attitude of the Republican presidents of the 1920s.

(4) The stock market crash is not an example of nativism. The crash did not involve immigrants or anti-immigrant sentiment. The 1929 stock market crash led to the start of the Great Depression. In late October 1929, stock prices plummeted as investors lost confidence in the market and went on a selling frenzy. When the market finally bottomed out, the Dow Jones Industrial Average, the major indicator of stock market trends, had fallen 89 percent from its peak. The crash of the stock market is attributed to excessive speculation on the part of the public.

28. **1** The statements describe the economic situation faced by farmers in the 1920s. Throughout the 1920s, the agricultural sector lagged behind the rest of the economy. Prices farmers received for major commodities (wheat, corn, soy beans, milk) fell steeply in the 1920s. Farmers were increasingly at the mercy of middlemen and commodity brokers who set prices for farm goods (as noted in the first statement). The problems in the agriculture sector went back to the previous decade. Farmers had put more acres under cultivation during World War I to meet increased demand for agricultural products. By the 1920s, Europe was back on its feet, yet American farmers did not cut back on production. In addition, American farmers now had to compete with European producers on the global market (as noted in the second statement). Because of the decentralized nature of farming, it was difficult for farmers to organize associations or cooperatives to protect their interests (as noted in the third statement). In addition, farmers felt pressure to put a great deal of money in implements to mechanize production (as noted in the fourth statement). This push toward mechanization and expansion left the farmers of the 1920s in a cycle of debt, overproduction, and falling commodity prices. Increased tariff rates and an isolationist foreign policy further reduced the international market for American agricultural goods.

WRONG CHOICES EXPLAINED:
(2) The statements describe the economic situation of farmers in the 1920s, not of railroad companies. Railroad companies generally did well in the 1920s (at least until the late 1920s), as production and consumption of goods expanded, along with the necessity of transporting them. After the 1920s, railroad companies would begin to feel intense competition from trucks and automobiles. During the 1930s, many smaller railroad companies went out of business, and by the 1940s, the remaining ones had to consolidate their lines or face bankruptcy.

(3) The statements describe the economic situation of farmers in the 1920s, not of manufacturers. The manufacturing sector generally did well in the 1920s (at least until the late 1920s), as production and consumption of goods expanded. Manufacturers used mass-production techniques to produce an abundance of goods. New methods of advertising and distributing goods spurred a growth in consumption as well. However, the manufacturing sector began to slow down by the late 1920s, as consumption failed to keep up with production.

(4) The statements describe the economic situation of farmers in the 1920s, not of factory workers. The economic situation of factory workers was a mixed bag in the 1920s. On the one hand, jobs were plentiful in the manufacturing sector for most of the decade. Factories expanded production and needed unskilled and semi-skilled workers to operate machines. However, wages were stagnant in the 1920s. A weak union movement and pro-business government

policies contributed to keeping wages low. By the end of the decade, low wages contributed to sagging sales of manufactured goods, as consumption could not keep pace with production.

29. **4** The main idea of the political cartoon from the 1930s is that President Franklin D. Roosevelt extended help to those in need. By the time that Roosevelt was elected president in 1932, the Great Depression had been going on for three years. The limited response of President Herbert Hoover (1929–1933) to the Great Depression, coupled with his handling of the Bonus March protest in 1932 (which resulted in the deaths of two World War I veterans who were demanding early payment of their government bonuses), set the stage for the election of Roosevelt. Though Roosevelt was from an affluent background, he was able to convey to the public a sense of empathy and personal warmth. In a speech during the 1932 campaign for president, Roosevelt stated that he would promote government plans that are intended to help the "forgotten man." The 1936 cartoon asserts that Roosevelt had followed through with his promise. Upon taking office, Roosevelt moved the federal government in a new direction by asserting that it should take some responsibility for the welfare of the people. The Roosevelt administration developed a series of programs known collectively as the New Deal. Previously, people received assistance in times of need from churches, settlement houses, and other private charities. However, the levels of poverty and unemployment during the Great Depression were unprecedented. Roosevelt believed that the government needed to take action. The New Deal provided relief to individuals through a variety of agencies.

WRONG CHOICES EXPLAINED:
(1) The cartoon is not asserting that President Franklin D. Roosevelt continued the laissez-faire policies of earlier presidents. The French phrase *laissez-faire* means "to leave alone." It describes a government policy that would take a hands-off approach in regard to economic activities. When the Great Depression struck the United States in the 1930s, Franklin D. Roosevelt argued more forcefully that the government must abandon a laissez-faire approach and play an activist role in the economy. Upon taking office, he initiated a sweeping array of programs known as the New Deal.

(2) The cartoon is not asserting that President Franklin D. Roosevelt supported business over labor. Roosevelt favored policies that encouraged the formation of labor unions. Previously, government policies had generally favored business over labor. Roosevelt, however, believed that a major problem facing the economy was low wages for workers. He argued that if workers' wages increased, they would be able to purchase consumer goods. If more consumer

goods were purchased, then manufacturers would need to produce more and would hire more workers. He pushed for the Wagner Act (1935) to strengthen unions by mandating that employers bargain with their unions. This act established the National Labor Relations Board to conduct elections among workers to see if they wanted to be represented by a union. It also banned certain unfair labor practices.

(3) The cartoon is not asserting that President Franklin D. Roosevelt favored government ownership of major industries. While many of Roosevelt's critics labeled his policies "creeping socialism," Roosevelt did not challenge the basic tenets of the capitalist system, including private ownership of the means of production. Roosevelt's policies included the regulation of banks, industrial practices, and the stock market, but he did not advocate government ownership of industry.

30. **3** The New Deal attempted to carry out the theme of the cartoon—remembering "the forgotten man"—by funding many public works projects. During the depths of the Great Depression in the 1930s, President Franklin D. Roosevelt pushed for a series of reforms to address both the causes and effects of the economic crisis. Roosevelt and his advisors drew on progressive ideas in the creation of the New Deal. The administration created a series of public works agencies to address the problem of high unemployment, which hovered between 10 and 25 percent of working-age Americans. The Civilian Conservation Corps (1933), for example, provided outdoor jobs for young men. Later, Roosevelt created the Works Progress Administration (1935), one of the largest New Deal program. The WPA was a vast program of government projects that hired millions of unemployed workers. Individuals hired by the agency, for example, built schools, maintained highways, installed sewer lines, wrote guidebooks, and produced theatrical productions. At its peak in 1938, over three million people worked for the WPA; over eight million people in total worked for it by the time it was shuttered in 1943.

WRONG CHOICES EXPLAINED:

(1) The New Deal did not attempt to help "the forgotten man" by restricting labor union membership. The approach of the New Deal was the opposite; it sought to increase union membership. President Franklin D. Roosevelt believed that if workers were in unions, they would have greater purchasing power, which would, in turn, improve the overall economic situation. He pushed for the Wagner Act (1935) to strengthen unions by mandating that employers bargain with their unions. This act established the National Labor Relations Board to conduct elections among workers to see if they wanted to be represented by a union. It also banned certain unfair labor practices.

(2) The New Deal did not attempt to help "the forgotten man" by loaning money to foreign countries. The costs of the New Deal prevented the New Deal from expanding loan programs to other nations. In addition, expanding loans to foreign nations would not be seen as remembering "the forgotten man."

(4) The New Deal did not attempt to help "the forgotten man" by banning the sale of stocks and bonds. While it is true that reckless investment behavior led to the stock market crash of October 1929 (which signaled the beginning of the Great Depression), President Franklin D. Roosevelt did not attempt to ban the sale of stocks and bonds. Rather, Roosevelt sought to establish regulatory oversight of the stock market by signing legislation creating the Securities and Exchange Commission in 1934.

31. **2** The defeat of President Franklin D. Roosevelt's "court packing" plan by Congress is an example of checks and balances. By 1937, Roosevelt had grown increasingly frustrated with the conservative approach of the Supreme Court. It shot down the National Recovery Act in *Schechter v. United States* (1935) and the Agricultural Adjustment Act in *Butler v. United States* (1936). In 1937, he announced a plan to increase the number of justices on the Supreme Court to as many as 15. He said that some of the older justices had difficulty keeping up with the heavy workload. However, it was clear that the intent of his "court packing" plan was to create a Supreme Court friendlier to his New Deal programs. The Senate rejected Roosevelt's "court packing" plan in 1937 because the plan would have threatened the principle of checks and balances by making the Supreme Court a rubber stamp for New Deal legislation. Soon, however, openings on the Court allowed Roosevelt to appoint new justices and influence the direction of the Court.

WRONG CHOICES EXPLAINED:

(1) The defeat of President Franklin D. Roosevelt's "court packing" plan by Congress is not an example of federalism. Federalism describes the relationship between the national government and state governments. While the word itself implies a loose league of states, in the American context federalism gives the strong national government supremacy over the state governments. This system of divided power is different from the unitary system of countries such as France. In France, the central government sets policies for the entire country with very little decision-making power on the local level.

(3) The defeat of President Franklin D. Roosevelt's "court packing" plan by Congress is not an example of due process. *Due process* refers to procedures that people go through after they are arrested for committing a crime. These procedures must be consistent with the Constitution and apply equally to all citizens. Many of the due process guidelines are contained in several of the amendments

to the Constitution. The framers of the Constitution wanted to protect people from arbitrary authority.

(4) The defeat of President Franklin D. Roosevelt's "court packing" plan by Congress is not an example of the amendment process. The process for amending the Constitution is cumbersome. First, a constitutional amendment can be proposed, either by Congress (by two-third majorities in both houses) or by a national convention. Then, three-fourths of the states must approve an amendment for it to be ratified. The state-by-state approval process can occur by the consent of the state legislatures or by state ratifying conventions. Twenty-seven amendments have been added to the Constitution.

32. **2** The administration of President Franklin D. Roosevelt reacted to the information contained in the letter by creating the Manhattan Project. In the letter, Albert Einstein is warning Roosevelt of the potential for nuclear chain reactions to be harnessed and used in an "extremely powerful" bomb. In the context of World War II, Roosevelt decided that harnessing atomic power could be crucial to winning the war. He was especially concerned that scientists in Nazi Germany would beat the United States in developing an atomic bomb. He, therefore, allocated funding for the Manhattan Project, the secret project to develop the atomic bomb. The project, which began in 1941 in an office building in New York City, involved several sites around the country, but the final assembly of the atomic bomb occurred in Los Alamos, New Mexico. The bomb was ready by July 1945, as the United States was preparing for a final attack on Japan. After issuing an ultimatum to Japan, the United States dropped the atomic bomb on the Japanese city of Hiroshima on August 6, 1945. After the United States dropped a second atomic bomb on the city of Nagasaki, Japan surrendered, ending World War II.

WRONG CHOICES EXPLAINED:
(1) The information in the letter from Albert Einstein—about the possibility of harnessing atomic power for an "extremely powerful bomb"—did not lead President Franklin D. Roosevelt to declare war on the Axis powers. The president did declare war on the Axis powers, in December 1941, but that was in response to the Japanese sneak attack on the U.S. naval base at Pearl Harbor, Hawaii.

(3) The information in the letter from Albert Einstein—about the possibility of harnessing atomic power for an "extremely powerful bomb"—did not lead President Franklin D. Roosevelt to propose the Lend-Lease Act. The president did propose the Lend-Lease Act, in March 1941, but that was in response to the desperate situation that Great Britain faced in battling Nazi Germany. In 1940,

France had fallen to the Nazis, leaving Great Britain the only major power to fight against Hitler's war machine in Western Europe. The Lend-Lease Act allowed the United States to ship armaments to Great Britain in American ships. Though officially neutral in World War II at that point, the United States was moving steadily toward intervening on the side of Great Britain.

(4) The information in the letter from Albert Einstein—about the possibility of harnessing atomic power for an "extremely powerful bomb"—did not lead President Franklin D. Roosevelt to initiate the D-Day invasion of Europe. The president did initiate the D-Day invasion of Europe, in June 1944, but that was in response to the difficulties the Allies had in defeating the Nazis in Western Europe. The goal of the D-Day invasion was for British and American troops to break through German coastal defenses and begin pushing Nazi forces out of occupied Western Europe and bring an end to the war in Europe. Soviet forces were, at the same time, waging war on German forces in Eastern Europe. Germany finally surrendered in May 1945.

33. **3** The internment of Japanese Americans during World War II primarily affected those Japanese Americans who lived on the West Coast. In 1942, President Roosevelt issued Executive Order 9066, authorizing the government to remove 120,000 Japanese Americans, two-thirds of them citizens, from West Coast states and relocate them to camps in the interior of the country. The order allowed the military to designate certain areas "military areas" from which "any or all persons may be excluded." The West Coast, which contained the vast majority of Japanese Americans, was designated a military area. (Hawaii, which was not yet a state, contained 150,000 people of Japanese descent, but only a small number of them were interned.) Most of their property was confiscated by the government. In the case of *Korematsu v. United States* (1944), the Supreme Court ruled that the relocation was acceptable on the grounds of national security. Much later, in 1988, the United States government publicly apologized to the surviving victims and extended $20,000 in reparations to each one. The *Korematsu* decision is one of several rulings by the Supreme Court that have curtailed civil liberties in times of war.

WRONG CHOICES EXPLAINED:

(1), (2), and (4) Executive Order 9066, authorizing the internment of Japanese Americans during World War II, did not affect Japanese Americans who lived in the Ohio River valley (choice 1), along the Gulf Coast (choice 2), or near the Rio Grande border with Mexico (choice 4). It was the West Coast that was designated a "military area," with certain residents subject to exclusion. At the time, the vast majority of Japanese Americans lived on the West Coast.

34. **4** After World War II, one important outcome of the passage of the Serviceman's Readjustment Act of 1944 (GI Bill) was that it created educational and housing assistance for veterans. The GI Bill provided cash payments for tuition and living expenses to attend college. In addition, the bill provided low-interest loans for veterans to purchase homes, as well as to start businesses. The intent of the GI Bill was to help the veterans of World War II adjust to life during peacetime. The program was very successful. It helped millions of veterans advance economically. A college education and home ownership have been seen as key components of entrance into the middle class. The generous benefits extended to World War II veterans can be seen in contrast to the sparse benefits extended to World War I veterans. World War I veterans staged a major protest in 1932, the Bonus March, to pressure the government to provide them with bonuses that had been promised them.

WRONG CHOICES EXPLAINED:
(1) The GI Bill was not intended to allow women to serve in combat positions. Women were not allowed to be used in combat roles during World War II. It was not until the Persian Gulf War in 1991 that significant numbers of women served in combat roles.

(2) The GI Bill was not intended to limit suburban growth. The GI Bill had the opposite effect. Much of the housing assistance to veterans was used to purchase houses in the suburbs.

(3) The GI Bill was not intended to fund new military bases. The United States did expand its military presence in the world after World War II, but this was not the function of the GI Bill. As the Cold War intensified after World War II, the United States established military bases throughout the world.

35. **2** The primary reason for the creation of both the Truman Doctrine and the Marshall Plan was the fear of Soviet communist expansion throughout Europe. The two items are important events in the history of the Cold War. After World War II, the wartime ally of the United States, the Soviet Union, became its rival. The Cold War lasted from the end of World War II (1945) to the collapse of the Soviet Union (1991). At times, the conflict was nothing more than a rivalry; at other times, the two nations were at the brink of war. Tensions intensified immediately following World War II when the Soviet Union left its troops in the nations of Eastern Europe, turning these nations into Soviet satellites. The United States was worried that the Soviet Union would try to push into Western Europe. The leader of the Soviet Union, Joseph Stalin, insisted that he only wanted to have allied nations on the border of the Soviet Union. In order to block any further aggression by the Soviet Union, Truman issued the Truman Doctrine (1947), in which he said that the goal of the United States

would be to contain communism. Toward this end, the United States extended military aid to Greece and Turkey. The United States created the Marshall Plan in order to help Europe's economic recovery. The Marshall Plan (1948) extended billions of dollars to war-torn Western Europe after the war. It was designed to strengthen the western democracies so that they would not turn to communism.

WRONG CHOICES EXPLAINED:

(1) The reason for the creation of the Truman Doctrine and the Marshall Plan was not to reward the Chinese for their role in the Allied victory over Japan. The United States and China fought together as allies during the war. After World War II, ongoing hostilities between the Chinese government and the Chinese Communist Party exploded into open civil war. The United States supported the government, which was run by the Kuomintang (Nationalist Party). The Communist Party, led by Mao Zedong, emerged victorious in 1949.

(3) The reason for the creation of the Truman Doctrine and the Marshall Plan was not to support the development of colonial independence movements. The United States frequently opposed independence movements in the developing world during the Cold War if it thought that an independent government might side with the Soviet Union. For example, in 1960, the United States approved of, and may have played a role in, the ouster of the first democratically elected leader of the Republic of the Congo, Patrice Lumumba. Lumumba had played an important role in the transformation of the Congo from a colony of Belgium into an independent republic, and he served as the first prime minister of the Republic of the Congo.

(4) The reason for the creation of the Truman Doctrine and the Marshall Plan was not to protect vital United States interests in Middle East oil fields, though the United States did seek to protect these interests. Following a conflict in Egypt over control of the Suez Canal (1956–1957), President Dwight D. Eisenhower took a more active role in protecting the oil interests of the United States. In a 1957 speech, he pledged that the United States would support any Middle Eastern countries threatened by "any nation controlled by international communism." The Eisenhower Doctrine was invoked in 1958 when a rebel movement emerged in Lebanon; U.S. Marines were quickly dispatched to support the Lebanese president.

36. **4** The United States responded to the Berlin Blockade in 1948 by airlifting food and supplies into Berlin. After World War II, Germany was divided by the Allied powers—the United States, France, Great Britain, and the Soviet Union. The city of Berlin, which was deep in the Soviet-occupied sector of Germany, was divided as well, with the western portion of the city occupied by the Western Allies

and the eastern portion occupied by the Soviet Union. In 1948, before the future status of Berlin was settled, the Soviet Union decided it would prevent any food or other supplies from entering the western portion of the city. The goal was for the Soviet Union to block the United States and its Western Allies from maintaining their presence in Berlin. Ultimately, the Soviet Union hoped to make all of Berlin part of what would become East Germany. The United States did not stand by idly when it learned of the Berlin blockade. President Harry Truman decided to send thousands of planes, filled with supplies, into the western sector of Berlin, in an action known as the Berlin Airlift. The Berlin Airlift prevented the western sector of Berlin from starving and prevented the Soviet Union from taking over the city. In 1949, the countries of West Germany and East Germany were formally established, and the city of West Berlin was officially established as part of West Germany. The Berlin airlift was one of the early American interventions in the Cold War.

WRONG CHOICES EXPLAINED:

(1) The United States did not respond to the Berlin Blockade in 1948 by boycotting German-made products. The United States continued to trade with the sectors of Germany occupied by the Western Allies during the Berlin Blockade, although the German economy was just getting on its feet following the destruction of World War II. The United States did not trade with the Soviet Union and its allies in Eastern Europe.

(2) The United States did not respond to the Berlin Blockade in 1948 by building the Berlin Wall. The communist government of East Germany built the Berlin Wall in 1961 to completely encircle West Berlin and separate it from East Germany. Berlin had been divided when Germany was divided into East Germany and West Germany in 1949. Berlin was located completely within East German territory, so West Berlin was physically separate from the rest of West Germany. Before construction of the wall, many residents of East Germany escaped to the west through West Berlin.

(3) The United States did not respond to the Berlin Blockade in 1948 by stopping all traffic leaving Berlin. Making such a move would not help solve the crisis created by the Berlin Blockade. The people of the western section of Berlin would starve if supplies were not airlifted into the city.

37. **3** A major significance of the Korean War (1950–1953) is that for the first time the United Nations used military force to oppose aggression. Although the United States played the leading role in military operations, the U.S. and its allies acted under the auspices of the United Nations. The United Nations was created mainly to work for international peace, following the carnage of World War II. Many world leaders, as well as ordinary citizens, pushed for an international

organization that could resolve conflicts and maintain peace. The United Nations formed in 1945, complete with a Security Council and peacekeeping troops. It continues to function as an international organization. The origins of the Korean War date back to the immediate aftermath of World War II. Korea had been divided into two occupation zones after World War II, one controlled by the United States and one controlled by the Soviet Union. The two sides were unable to agree on a unification plan, and by 1948 two separate nations were established with a border at the 38th parallel. In June 1950, North Korean troops invaded South Korea. President Harry S. Truman decided to commit troops to support South Korea, and he managed to secure United Nations sponsorship. United Nations forces, led by U.S. General Douglas MacArthur, pushed the North Korean troops back to the 38th parallel and then marched into North Korea. When UN troops got to within 40 miles of the border of North Korea and China, China sent 150,000 troops over the Yalu River to push back the UN forces. After intense fighting, the two sides settled into positions on either side of the 38th parallel. By 1953, an armistice was reached accepting a divided Korea.

WRONG CHOICES EXPLAINED:
(1) The events of the Korean War (1950–1953) did not include the use of an atomic bomb. Atomic bombs had been used earlier, in 1945, at the end of World War II. The United States dropped an atomic bomb on the Japanese city of Hiroshima in August 1945. After the United States dropped a second atomic bomb on the city of Nagasaki, Japan surrendered, ending World War II.
(2) During the Korean War (1950–1953), Asian and U.S. troops fought against each other, but not for the first time. During World War II (1941–1945), troops from Japan and from the United States fought against each other.
(4) During the Korean War (1950–1953), the Soviet Union and the United States did not support the same side. Earlier, during World War II (1939–1945), the two countries were on the same side, but during the Korean War, the United States supported South Korea and UN forces, while the Soviet Union supported North Korea and China.

38. **3** The three newspaper headlines from the decade following World War II are all connected to the fear of communism in the United States. The fear of communism in the late 1940s and 1950s occurred in the context of the Cold War—a period of hostility between the United States and the Soviet Union that lasted from the end of World War II (1945) to the collapse of the Soviet Union (1991). In 1947, President Harry S. Truman felt compelled to take action against the perceived threat of domestic communism by signing Executive Order 9835, designed to root out communist influence in the federal government. The order mandated that federal employees take a loyalty oath (alluded to in the first headline). Despite

Truman's actions in regard to fears of domestic communism, Republicans consistently accused him and the Democratic Party of being "soft on communism." This accusation was aggressively taken up by Senator Joseph McCarthy, who became the central figure in the movement that became known as *McCarthyism*. McCarthy gained prominence when he announced that he had a list of names of State Department employees who were members of the Communist Party (1950). An atmosphere reminiscent of the Salem witch trials of the 1690s pervaded America, as wild accusations became more common. Fears of communist spying intensified when the Soviet Union first tested an atomic bomb (1949). The government accused two members of the Communist Party, Ethel and Julius Rosenberg, of passing secrets of the nuclear bomb to the Soviet Union. The Rosenbergs insisted on their innocence, but were found guilty and were sent to the electric chair (1953) (alluded to in the third headline). The most intense period of the anti-communist movement ended by 1954. The Korean War had ended and McCarthy himself was discredited for making baseless accusations against members of the military. The hearings on these accusations, known as the Army-McCarthy hearings (1954), were widely seen on the new medium of television (alluded to in the second headline). A key moment in these hearings occurred when a lawyer for the Army, Joseph Welch, directly challenged McCarthy's tactics. McCarthy had publicly condemned a young lawyer who worked under Welch for previously working with the National Lawyers Guild, an organization that the government claimed was a front organization for the Communist Party. Welch came to the defense of the young lawyer, saying to McCarthy, "Have you no sense of decency, sir?" The hearings demonstrated to the American public the reckless nature of McCarthy's accusations.

WRONG CHOICES EXPLAINED:

(1) The three headlines are not connected to war crimes trials in Japan. The Allies did conduct war crimes trials against Japanese officials and members of the military after World War II. The war crimes committed by Japan occurred during World War II (1937–1945) and in fighting between Japan and China that predated the beginning of World War II. The war crimes included massacres, human experimentation, starvation, and forced labor. Historians estimate that these war crimes were responsible for the deaths of between three and 14 million civilians and prisoners of war. Ultimately, almost 6,000 Japanese officials and military personnel were tried, with over 900 executed.

(2) The three headlines are not connected with passage of civil rights legislation in the United States. The United States did pass important civil rights legislation in the 1960s. The Civil Rights Acts of 1964, banning racial discrimination in public places, and the Voting Rights Act of 1965 were important milestones in the struggle for African American equality.

(4) The three headlines are not connected with debate over economic aid to Europe. In the period after World War II, the United States implemented the Marshall Plan (1948) to extend billions of dollars to war-torn Western Europe after World War II. It was, in part, designed to strengthen the western democracies so that they would not turn to communism. The Marshall Plan was part of the United States policy of containment.

39. **1** In 1962, President John F. Kennedy responded to the discovery of nuclear missiles in Cuba by ordering a naval quarantine of Cuba. The discovery of missile sites in Cuba, by a U.S. U-2 plane, began a tense episode in the history of the Cold War called the Cuban Missile Crisis. President Kennedy felt that the missiles, in such close proximity to the United States, amounted to an unacceptable provocation and ordered Soviet Premier Nikita Khrushchev to halt the operation and dismantle the bases. Khrushchev insisted on the right of the Soviet Union to install the missiles. For about a week, the world stood on the brink of nuclear war. Finally, a deal was reached in which the Soviet Union would abandon its Cuban missile program. In exchange, the United States publicly promised to not attack Cuba; privately, it agreed to remove missiles from Turkey.

WRONG CHOICES EXPLAINED:

(2) President John F. Kennedy did not capture strategic locations in Cuba in response to the discovery of nuclear missiles in Cuba. Earlier, the United States did attempt to organize an invasion of Cuba, but this was unrelated to the discovery of nuclear missiles. The Bay of Pigs invasion was planned under the Eisenhower administration and implemented by President Kennedy. The plan called for the United States to train, arm, and aid a group of Cuban exiles opposed to the Communist government of Fidel Castro. The exiles landed at the Bay of Pigs in Cuba in April 1961, but were quickly captured by Cuban forces.

(3) President John F. Kennedy did not threaten to invade the Soviet Union in response to the discovery of nuclear missiles in Cuba. No such invasion was contemplated during the Cold War. American political leaders realized that such an invasion would bring about a third world war and massive devastation on both sides.

(4) President John F. Kennedy did not prohibit travel to the southeastern United States in response to the discovery of nuclear missiles in Cuba. The United States did implement an embargo and a travel ban to Cuba starting in 1963. In 2014, President Barack Obama rolled back restrictions on traveling to Cuba. More recently, President Donald Trump has undone some of the Obama-era rules, making it more difficult to travel on one's own in Cuba.

40. **2** During the 1960s, the actions of Cesar Chavez led to improved conditions for migrant farm workers. In the 1960s, Chavez was one of the organizers of United Farm Workers (UFW). The UFW organized strikes and boycotts of farm products to advance the cause of migrant farm workers' rights. The organization had mixed results. It brought the plight of farm workers into the public eye. In the 1960s, a strike in Texas organized by the UFW demanded the establishment of a minimum wage of $1.25 for migrant farm laborers. The strike was ultimately unsuccessful, but the UWF campaign in Texas led to Senate hearings on the conditions migrant farmers labored in. In the 1970s, Chavez initiated a series of high-profile actions focused on the grape and lettuce fields of California, tended to primarily by Chicano (Mexican-American) laborers. The UFW won union recognition for many of these workers and organized a nationwide boycott of grapes.

WRONG CHOICES EXPLAINED:

(1) The actions of Cesar Chavez did not address conditions for coal miners. Unionized coal miners are represented by the United Mine Workers, founded in 1890. In the late 1890s, the union won recognition in the soft-coal (bituminous coal) mines of the Midwest. It organized a large strike in 1902 against the hard-coal (anthracite coal) operations in Pennsylvania. After the intervention of President Theodore Roosevelt, the strike resulted in a pay increase for the miners but not in union recognition. By the 1930s, the UMW grew to over 800,000 members. Today, it is a shadow of its former self, with around 70,000 members.

(3) The actions of Cesar Chavez did not address conditions of autoworkers. Unionized autoworkers are represented by the United Automobile Workers, founded in 1935 as part of the newly formed Congress of Industrial Organizations. In the late 1930s and early 1940s, it was successful in gaining union recognition for workers at the "big three" automobile makers—General Motors, Chrysler, and Ford. Its high-profile sit-down strikes in 1936 and 1937 at the General Motors plant in Flint, Michigan, were milestones in its successful unionization of the automobile industry. By the 1970s, membership was over 1.5 million. The union has declined in the decades since, as American car makers have shifted operations abroad and foreign-based automobile production facilities in the United States have resisted unionization. In addition, automation of production facilities has reduced the number of workers in the auto industry.

(4) The actions of Cesar Chavez did not address conditions of health care workers. Unionized health care workers are represented by several unions. The largest health care workers' union is the Service Employees International Union.

41. **2** The heading for the partial outline should read, "Native American Indian Demands for Equality." The three items in the outline are all important events in struggle for civil rights for Native Americans. In the 1960s, Native American activists, inspired by the example set by the civil rights movement, protested for greater equality and justice. The American Indian Movement was founded in 1968 (alluded to in item C in the outline). The movement insisted on greater autonomy on reservation lands and the return of lands that it claimed had been illegally seized. The movement had a strong presence among urban Native Americans as well as among Native Americans who lived on reservations. The following year, the movement made headlines when several dozen activists seized control of Alcatraz Island, in San Francisco Bay, claiming the land that housed the former prison belonged to the first inhabitants of the area—Native American Indians (alluded to in item A in the outline). The occupation of Alcatraz Island lasted 19 months, until 1971.

In response to protests by the American Indian Movement, the administration of President Richard Nixon promised to extend greater self-determination to tribal councils and greater federal aid. However, the movement continued to press for more fundamental change. A major event occurred in 1973 when members of AIM occupied the town of Wounded Knee, South Dakota (alluded to in item B in the outline), the site of a massacre of the Sioux by federal troops in 1890. The occupation grew partially out of political conflicts within the Oglala Sioux tribe. The main impetus of the action was to pressure the federal government to honor treaties with Native Americans and to renegotiate certain treaties. The occupation, which involved the exchange of gunfire on both sides and garnered a great deal of publicity, lasted nearly three months.

WRONG CHOICES EXPLAINED:
(1) The partial outline does not deal with protests by Native Americans against the Vietnam War. Protests against the war in Vietnam occurred around the same time, in the late 1960s and early 1970s. However, the focus of the protests in the outline was demands for equality for Native American Indians.
(3) The partial outline does not deal with attempts by Native Americans to culturally assimilate. In fact, the American Indian Movement resisted the push toward assimilation. It encouraged a revitalization of traditional Native American cultural practices.
(4) The partial outline does not deal with attempts by Native Americans to support the War on Poverty. The War on Poverty, which was part of President Lyndon Johnson's Great Society agenda, refers to a series of domestic programs passed by Congress in 1964 and 1965. The enactment of the War on Poverty measures occurred before the items in the outline. Further, although the

American Indian Movement addressed poverty on reservations, it argued that federal anti-poverty programs did not address the needs of Native Americans.

42. **1** President Jimmy Carter's efforts to increase stability in the Middle East resulted in the Camp David Accords. The Camp David Accords are considered one of the few triumphs for President Carter's troubled presidency. Since the founding of Israel in 1948, tensions have existed in the Middle East. The Arab nations refused to recognize Israel's right to exist. Four wars occurred between Israel and its neighbors between 1948 and 1973. In 1977, Egyptian President Anwar Sadat broke with the other leaders of the Arab world and flew to Israel to meet with Israeli Prime Minister Menachem Begin. Negotiations ensued between the two leaders, but they were unable to come up with a peace treaty. Carter invited the two leaders to the presidential retreat at Camp David in Maryland. The three men met for 13 days and emerged with the basis for a peace treaty. The treaty resulted in an end to hostilities between Israel and Egypt, but tensions continued to exist between Israel and its other neighbors. The most serious tensions since the Camp David Accords have been between Israelis and Palestinians. Palestinians in the West Bank have been resentful of Israel's occupation and settlement of that area after the 1967 Six-Day War.

WRONG CHOICES EXPLAINED:
    (2) The Nuclear Test Ban Treaty does not address efforts to increase stability in the Middle East. In the early 1960s, President John F. Kennedy made attempts to ease tensions between the Soviet Union and the United States. The calls for greater cooperation grew more intense in the aftermath of the Cuban Missile Crisis (1962). The following year, the United States, the Soviet Union, and Great Britain signed the Nuclear Test Ban Treaty (1963). The ban on testing nuclear weapons exempted underground tests.
    (3) The Panama Canal Treaty does not address efforts to increase stability in the Middle East. The Panama Canal Treaty is one of two treaties negotiated by President Jimmy Carter and signed by the United States and Panama in 1977. The treaties were ratified by the United States Senate in 1978. In the Panama Canal Treaty, the United States agreed to turn over the Canal Zone to Panama by the end of 1999 (which occurred as agreed upon).
    (4) The Paris Peace Accords do not address efforts to increase stability in the Middle East. The Paris Peace Accords (1973) established an end to the Vietnam War. The treaty included the governments of North Vietnam, South Vietnam, and the United States, as well as South Vietnamese rebels. The negotiations led to a withdrawal of American forces from Vietnam, but the accords were never ratified by the United States Senate. Soon after American forces withdrew,

fighting broke out again. By 1975, the government of South Vietnam collapsed, and Vietnam was reunited as a communist-run country.

43. **2** The reason the Equal Rights Amendment did not become part of the United States Constitution was that three-fourths of the states did not ratify it. The process for an amendment to become part of the Constitution is arduous. First, an amendment can be proposed by Congress (by two-third majorities in both houses) or by a national convention. Then, three-fourths of the states must approve an amendment for it to be ratified. The state-by-state approval process can occur by the consent of the state legislatures or by state ratifying conventions. The Equal Rights Amendment, proposed in 1972, would have prohibited the abridgement of "equality of rights under the law . . . on account of sex" either by the federal government or by the state governments. The push to ratify the amendment grew out of the efforts of the women's liberation movement, which developed in the 1960s to challenge inequities in the job market, representations of women in the media, violence against women, and an ingrained set of social values. The push led to a conservative backlash against the proposal. Conservatives argued that passage of the amendment would destroy the American family. The movement against the proposal was led by conservative activist Phyllis Schlafly. She organized a strong coalition, urging "positive women" to embrace femininity. The amendment was approved by both the House and the Senate but failed to get the required 38 states to ratify it, even after the deadline for ratification had been moved forward to 1982. It, therefore, did not become part of the Constitution.

WRONG CHOICES EXPLAINED:
(1) The reason that the Equal Rights Amendment did not become part of the Constitution was not that President Ronald Reagan vetoed it. The president is not directly involved in amending the Constitution. The president may argue in favor of or against a particular amendment, but he or she cannot introduce, ratify, or veto an amendment. The Constitution leaves that role to Congress and the states.

(3) The reason that the Equal Rights Amendment did not become part of the Constitution was not opposition from the National Organization of Women (NOW). The organization, founded in 1966, was strongly in favor of the amendment.

(4) The reason that the Equal Rights Amendment did not become part of the Constitution was not that the Supreme Court ruled that it was unconstitutional. The Supreme Court does not have the power to rule that an amendment is unconstitutional. Rather it reviews governmental acts to determine if they are consistent with the Constitution. This power is called judicial review.

44. **3** Excessive use of credit and bank speculation in the mortgage market were important contributing factors to the severe recession in the U.S. economy in 2008. Many economists cite the crisis in the housing market as an important cause of the Great Recession of 2008–2009. In the 2000s, lending institutions had been devising new methods of making money borrowing cheaper and easier, leading to the excessive use of credit. Many of these practices became widespread after Congress repealed most of the provisions of the 1933 Glass-Steagall Act in 1999, removing regulatory constraints on the banking industry. Banks lured first-time home buyers to take out mortgages for home purchases that were beyond their means. Banks, for instance, offered adjustable rate mortgages in which initial low rates would later jump to higher rates. These risky loans—characterized by high interest rates and less than favorable terms—were referred to as *subprime mortgages* because they were extended to people whose ability to repay and whose credit rating was less than prime. By 2008, almost 30 percent of mortgages were rated as subprime. To make this situation worse, banks would speculate in this shaky mortgage market. Lenders would sell these subprime mortgages to investment banks and other Wall Street financial institutions. In turn, Wall Street would bundle these mortgages into stock offerings. Finally, pension funds, mutual funds, foreign banks, and individuals invested in these offerings. Therefore, the risk entailed in the original mortgages was spread throughout the financial world and to many individuals whose financial health was, in some way, tied to the stock market. In 2007, the housing bubble burst as the real estate market weakened and interest rates increased. Many subprime borrowers found themselves "underwater"—that is, the market value of their home sank below the amount they owed on their mortgage. In many such situations, individuals could neither sell their homes nor afford to pay their monthly mortgage payments. Their only option was to walk away from their home and default on their loan, leading to widespread foreclosures.

WRONG CHOICES EXPLAINED:
(1) The severe recession in the United States of 2008 was not caused by immigration restrictions and lack of skilled workers. Immigration laws had not changed significantly in the lead-up to the Great Recession. Further, newly arrived immigrants tend to fill jobs as unskilled workers, rather than skilled workers.

(2) The severe recession in the United States of 2008 was not caused by cuts in defense spending and social welfare spending. Under President George W. Bush (2001–2009), spending on both domestic programs and on the military increased, with military spending increasing at a more rapid rate.

(4) The severe recession in the United States of 2008 was not caused by tight monetary policy and overregulation of banks. The opposite was true. Lending institutions made credit readily available, and the government rolled

back regulations on the banking industry that had been in place since the 1930s. Both of these factors—easy access to credit and unregulated, risky banking practices—are seen as important causes of the Great Recession.

45. **1** The main idea of the cartoon is that approval of the president in 2006 was directly linked to the cost of gasoline in the United States. The sign in front of the White House, labeled "Approval Rating," resembles a sign at a gas station indicating the price of a gallon of gasoline. When stations advertise their prices, they include nine-tenths of a cent at the end of the price, presumably so consumers will think the price is a penny cheaper than it actually is. The implication of the sign is that President George W. Bush had a low approval rating, and that an important reason for that was that gasoline prices had increased. Approval ratings for President George W. Bush steadily dropped from a high of over 90 percent following the terrorist attacks of 2001 to lows that hovered between around 30 and 40 percent from 2006 to 2008. At the time of publication of the cartoon, Bush's approval rating had dipped to around 31 percent and gasoline prices had risen to over three dollars in many areas. Changes in the price of a gallon of gasoline are determined by a number of factors—the price of a barrel of crude oil (which is subject to speculation and price swings), demand, changes in taxes and regulations, and relations with oil-producing countries. Some of these factors are within the president's control; many are not.

WRONG CHOICES EXPLAINED:

(2) The main idea of the cartoon is not that public approval of the president in 2006 was directly linked to success in stopping human rights abuses abroad. The cartoon is focused on the importance of the price of gasoline in determining presidential popularity. At different times, presidents have focused on policies designed to reduce human rights abuses abroad. President Jimmy Carter (1977–1981), for example, made this a priority of his administration. He took steps to tie foreign aid to the human rights records of recipient countries.

(3) The main idea of the cartoon is not that public approval of the president in 2006 was directly linked to ability to restrict the flow of illegal drugs. The cartoon is focused on the importance of the price of gasoline in determining presidential popularity. President Ronald Reagan (1981–1989) is often associated with the "war on drugs." In regard to the illegal flow of drugs into the United States, the Reagan administration grew increasingly frustrated with Panamanian President Manuel Noriega for a variety of reason, including his involvement with international drug trafficking. Reagan's successor, George H.W. Bush, initiated an invasion of Panama, which removed Noriega from office.

(4) The main idea of the cartoon is not that public approval of the president in 2006 was directly linked to the amount of the budget surplus. The cartoon is

focused on the importance of the price of gasoline in determining presidential popularity. Under President George W. Bush, there was a budget surplus in his first year in office (2001). This was the fourth year in a row of surpluses. After tax cuts and spending increases, there were budget deficits for the remaining years of his presidency.

46. **2** The main idea of the cartoon is that telephone surveillance by the National Security Agency violates some of the protections of the United States Constitution. The NSA employee in the cartoon is depicted saying to a colleague that he is having trouble listening in on a particular telephone conversation because of background noise. He attributes the background noise to static caused by a technical glitch. The viewer sees that the background noise is actually the framers of the Constitution complaining loudly that the whole program violates the Constitution. Debates between law-enforcement officials and privacy advocates have focused on how accessible data—culled from individuals' telecommunications activities—should be to officials.

This debate made front-page news in 2013 when a former contractor with the NSA, Edward Snowden, exposed a clandestine program known as PRISM, which permitted the agency to conduct warrantless mass data mining of phone, Internet, and other communications—including, under certain circumstances, those of United States citizens—as part of counterterrorism efforts. PRISM was first enabled by President Bush when he signed the Protect America Act into law in 2007; in 2012, President Barack Obama renewed PRISM. While in Hong Kong, Snowden met with three journalists and made available to them thousands of classified NSA documents. Subsequent articles in *The Guardian* and *The Washington Post* brought the program, and Snowden himself, to international attention. In May 2015, immediately prior to the publication of the cartoon, an appeals court ruled that the Patriot Act did not authorize the NSA to collect Americans' calling records in bulk. In June 2015, President Obama reauthorized provisions of the Patriot Act, putting some restrictions on the NSA's ability to collect bulk telecommunication data on U.S. citizens.

WRONG CHOICES EXPLAINED:

(1) The cartoon is not arguing that telephone surveillance by the National Security Agency has been troubled by technical difficulties. The men in the background are the framers of the Constitution challenging the constitutionality of the agency's PRISM program of warrantless surveillance of telecommunications data. They are not technicians or repair workers raising concerns about technical difficulties of the program.

(3) The cartoon is not arguing that telephone surveillance by the National Security Agency is legal because it protects the privacy of Internet users. The men in the background, the framers of the Constitution, are raising concerns about the constitutionality of the agency's PRISM program of warrantless surveillance of telecommunications data. They are not asserting that the program is legal. Indeed, the program did not protect the privacy of Internet users.

(4) The cartoon is not arguing that telephone surveillance by the National Security Agency increases hacking of top-secret government information. A goal of the agency's surveillance program was to identify attempts at cyberterrorism, including hacking of government information. Whether that goal was achieved is unknown, but one would not argue that the program *increased* hacking.

47. **3** The Alien and Sedition Acts of 1798 were similar to the Espionage and Sedition Acts passed during World War I because they both tried to restrict criticism of and opposition to government policies. Debates and conflicts over the proper balance between individual liberty and order have occurred throughout American history. The Alien and Sedition Acts (1798), comprised of four acts, were passed by a Federalist-dominated Congress in order to limit criticism from the opposition Republican Party during the undeclared Quasi-War with France (1798–1800). The Sedition Act made it a crime to defame the president or Congress. The broad wording of the Sedition Act seemed to challenge the free speech guarantees of the recently ratified First Amendment. The Espionage Act (1917) and Sedition Act (1918) made it a crime to interfere with the World War I draft or with the sales of war bonds, as well as to say anything "disloyal" in regard to the war effort. The Supreme Court decision in *Schenck v. United States* (1919) upheld the Espionage Act. Charles Schenck and other members of the Socialist Party had been arrested for printing and distributing flyers opposing the war and urging young men to resist the draft. The Supreme Court argued that freedom of speech is not absolute and that the government is justified in limiting certain forms of speech during wartime and other national emergencies. The Court argued that certain utterances pose a "clear and present danger." By analogy, the Court reasoned that one is not allowed to falsely shout "Fire!" in a crowded theater.

WRONG CHOICES EXPLAINED:

(1) Neither the Alien and Sedition Acts of 1798 nor the Espionage and Sedition Acts passed during World War I provided for the draft of men into the military. Drafting individuals into the military has a long history in the United States. A draft law was passed during the Civil War, but only a small percentage of men in the Union army were drafted. The Selective Service Act (1917) was passed to fill the ranks of the army during World War I. The Selective Training

and Service Act (1940) was passed in 1940, even before the United States officially entered World War II. The Selective Service Act of 1948 created the
Selective Service System, which has been in operation until the present day. It
was used to draft soldiers for the Korean War (1950–1953) and for the Vietnam
War (1955–1975).

(2) Neither the Alien and Sedition Acts of 1798 nor the Espionage and
Sedition Acts passed during World War I gave the government greater control
over the production of goods. During World War I, the federal government
played a greater role in regulating and guiding economic activity, through agencies such as the War Industries Board and the National War Labor Board.
During World War II, agencies such as the War Production Board and the
Office of Economic Stabilization gave the government greater control over
production.

(4) Neither the Alien and Sedition Acts of 1798 nor the Espionage and
Sedition Acts passed during World War I attempted to justify United States
involvement in a foreign war. During World War I, the Committee on Public
Information organized pro-war propaganda; the United States also embarked on
a major propaganda campaign during World War II. The Office of War
Information (1942–1945) put out a steady stream of posters and radio broadcasts, along with news releases.

48. **4** The events most closely associated with westward expansion are the
passage of the Homestead Act of 1862 and the opening of the transcontinental
railroad in 1869. The Homestead Act attempted to promote westward expansion by providing free land to settlers. By the time of the Civil War, the government wanted to encourage settlement in the huge area of relatively flat land
between the Mississippi River and the Rocky Mountains known as the Great
Plains. Much of this area has rich soil and a long growing season. Hundreds of
thousands of people applied for and were granted homesteads. The Homestead
Act reflected the "free labor" ideal of the Republicans. With the absence of
Democrats from Congress during the Civil War, the Republican Party was able
to pass several pieces of legislation that reflected their vision of America. This
legislation included the Pacific Railroad Act (1862), which extended government bonds and tracts of land to companies engaged in building transcontinental railroads. The government ended up granting 130 million acres of federally
held land to railroad companies. Individual states sweetened the pot for railroad construction by extending another 50 million acres to railroad companies.
These generous land grants totaled more than 180 million acres, an area equal
to the size of Texas. The first transcontinental railroad was completed in 1869.
By the end of the 19th century, four additional transcontinental lines were
completed.

WRONG CHOICES EXPLAINED:

(1) The passage of the Indian Removal Act of 1830 is associated with westward expansion, but the Compromise of 1877 is not. The Indian Removal Act authorized the president to negotiate with Native American tribes, including the Chickasaw, Choctaw, Creek, Seminole, and original Cherokee people, who lived in several southern states. Those who refused to leave their land were forced off. The forced removal of Native Americans in the 1830s and 1840s is known as the Trail of Tears. The motivation for the act was to open up land for white farmers to expand westward into the interior of the South.

(2) Neither the issuing of the Emancipation Proclamation (1863) nor the creation of the Federal Reserve System (1913) is associated with westward expansion. The Emancipation Proclamation was issued by President Abraham Lincoln during the Civil War. The document declared that as of January 1, 1863, slaves in Confederate-held territory would be free. Of course, United States laws were not enforceable in Confederate-held territory, but the Emancipation Proclamation had the important effect of turning the Civil War into a war for the liberation of the enslaved population of the South. The Federal Reserve System was created to control the money supply. The Federal Reserve Bank, which is part privately controlled and part publicly controlled, was created by legislation in 1913 during the administration of President Woodrow Wilson. One of its main functions is to regulate economic growth by regulating the supply of money.

(3) Neither the passage of the Agricultural Adjustment Act (1933) nor the creation of the Tennessee Valley Authority (1933) is associated with westward expansion. Both are part of the New Deal, President Franklin D. Roosevelt's legislative agenda designed to address the economic problems associated with the Great Depression. The Agricultural Adjustment Act extended subsidies to farmers. In effect, it paid farmers to not grow certain crops, so as to reduce surpluses and push up prices for farm commodities. In this way, farm incomes, which had taken a battering during the Great Depression, would rise. The Tennessee Valley Authority (TVA) was a set of development projects in the Tennessee River area of the South. The region was especially hard hit by the Great Depression. Even before the depression, poverty was pervasive; most homes in the region were without electricity. The TVA included major infrastructure projects, including electricity-generating dams along the Tennessee River.

49. **3** The National Association for the Advancement of Colored People (NAACP), the Congress of Racial Equality (CORE), and the Southern Christian Leadership Conference (SCLC) are all associated with the civil rights movement. The movement was perhaps the most important reform movement of the 20th century. The goal of the movement was to challenge racist practices and

create a more just society. Although its origins date to the early years of the century, if not earlier, the movement was most active between 1954 and 1968. The civil rights movement gained strength after the Supreme Court, in the case of *Brown v. Board of Education of Topeka* (1954), declared that segregation in schools had no place in America. In the years following the Brown decision, there was the Montgomery bus boycott in 1956, the lunch counter sit-ins in 1960, the Freedom Rides in 1962, and a whole host of other activities. The high point of the movement might have been the March on Washington in 1963, where Martin Luther King Jr. gave his "I Have A Dream" speech. The Civil Rights Act (1964) and the Voting Rights Act (1965) represent the crowning achievements of the movement.

The NAACP was formed in 1909. The leadership for the organization had first met in 1905 on the Canadian side of Niagara Falls, where they formed the Niagara movement. The Niagara movement and the NAACP were both led by W.E.B. Du Bois. Du Bois's call for full political equality and civil rights for African Americans was in marked contrast to the more accommodating approach of Booker T. Washington. CORE was founded in Chicago, Illinois, in 1942. The group was inspired, in part, by Mahatma Gandhi's teachings on nonviolent resistance; Gandhi was active at the time in the struggle against British rule of India. CORE was pacifist and believed that nonviolent civil disobedience could successfully be used by African Americans to challenge the Jim Crow system of segregation in the United States. In 1961, CORE organized a series of Freedom Rides through the South—bus rides with African American, as well as white passengers that challenged local codes against integrated buses. The SCLC, a key organization in the civil rights movement, was founded by Martin Luther King Jr. and approximately 60 other African American ministers and religious leaders in 1957. The SCLC consisted of a central board, which set the agenda of the organization, and local groups—churches and community groups—that affiliated with the national group.

WRONG CHOICES EXPLAINED:
(1) The NAACP, CORE, and the SCLC are not associated with the temperance movement. The temperance movement, against the consumption of alcoholic beverages, was the largest reform movement throughout the 19th century and into the 20th century. Some activists encouraged abstinence from drinking alcoholic beverages. Others pushed for laws limiting or prohibiting the sale of alcoholic beverages. The movement achieved major success with the passage of the 18th Amendment (1919), which prohibited the production, importation, transportation, and sale of alcoholic beverages. The prohibition period lasted from 1920 to 1933.

(2) The NAACP, CORE, and the SCLC are not associated with the abolition movement. The abolition movement challenged one of the most profound injustices in American history—slavery. Starting in the 1830s, William Lloyd Garrison was a key figure in the movement for the immediate and uncompensated abolition of slavery. Antislavery sentiment existed before that, but most antislavery groups advocated a more gradual approach to ending slavery. Starting in the 1840s, the towering figure in the abolitionist movement was Frederick Douglass.

(4) The NAACP, CORE, and the SCLC are not associated with the environmental movement. The environmental movement of the 1960s and 1970s pushed ecological concerns into public consciousness. The first Earth Day occurred in 1970. Also in 1970, President Richard Nixon created the Environmental Protection Agency. That same year, Nixon signed the Clean Air Act. The movement still exists, encouraging conservation of resources and raising awareness about the perils of global warming.

50. **4** The action that tried to close the "gap" referred to in the cartoon was agreeing to the Strategic Arms Limitation Treaty (SALT). In the cartoon, there is a gap between "disarmament efforts" and the "arms race." In other words, efforts by the Soviet Union and the United States to negotiate a reduction in nuclear arsenals were faltering as the race to build increasingly powerful nuclear weapons was advancing. By the 1960s, many Americans had become increasingly fearful of the massive nuclear arsenals that both the United States and the Soviet Union had developed. These weapons programs were also a drain on the resources of both countries. Starting in 1969, the two nations began negotiations to limit future weapons production. The United States and the Soviet Union signed the Strategic Arms Limitation Treaty (SALT) in 1972. This treaty called for a slight curb in the production of nuclear weapons. The treaty was part of the broader policy of détente—a warming of relations between the Soviet Union and the United States. The policy was initiated by Nixon. His strong anti-communist credentials enabled him to open relations with communist nations without being accused of being "soft on communism." In 1972, Nixon became the first American president to visit Communist China, and later that year he held meetings with Soviet leaders in Moscow.

WRONG CHOICES EXPLAINED:
(1) The Yalta Agreement did not deal with disarmament efforts or the nuclear arms race. The Yalta Conference (1945), held as World War II was coming to an end, was the most significant, and last, meeting of Prime Minister Winston Churchill of the United Kingdom, Soviet leader Joseph Stalin, and President

Franklin D. Roosevelt. In the Yalta Agreement, the "big three" agreed to divide Germany into four military zones of occupation (the fourth zone would be occupied by France). In 1949, two countries were formed out of Germany. West Germany, allied with the United States, was formed from the military zones occupied by the United States, the United Kingdom, and France. East Germany, a communist country, was formed from the military zone occupied by the Soviet Union.

(2) The Gulf of Tonkin Resolution (1964) did not deal with disarmament efforts or the nuclear arms race. The resolution provided congressional support for escalating military action in Vietnam. The United States became heavily involved in the Vietnam War after Congress gave President Lyndon Johnson a blank check with the resolution. In August 1964, Johnson announced that American destroyers had been fired upon in the Gulf of Tonkin, off the coast of North Vietnam. Later, reports questioned the accuracy of the announcement, but the incident led Congress to give Johnson the ability to escalate American military involvement in Vietnam. The Gulf of Tonkin Resolution can be considered the beginning of the war in Vietnam.

(3) The Strategic Defense Initiative (proposed in 1984) can be seen as part of the nuclear arms race, but it would not be considered a disarmament effort. The Strategic Defense Initiative, dubbed Star Wars by critics, was a proposal to create a missile defense system to protect the United States from attack by nuclear weapons. Such a system was never put into effect, but aspects of it are still being researched.

PART II: THEMATIC ESSAY

Supreme Court Decisions

Throughout American history, key Supreme Court decisions have greatly impacted individuals and groups of people. The Court has the ability to define constitutional rights. Some decisions have expanded constitutional rights, while others have restricted them. Two significant decisions, both from the second half of the 20th century, *Korematsu v. United States* (1944) and *Roe v. Wade* (1973) greatly impacted the definition of constitutional rights for Americans—with the first decision restricting them and the second decision expanding them.

In the case of *Korematsu v. United States*, the Supreme Court upheld Executive Order 9066, issued by President Franklin D. Roosevelt in 1942, just weeks after the attack by Japan on Pearl Harbor, which brought the United States into World War II. The order authorized the government to remove 120,000 Japanese American people, two-thirds of them citizens, from their homes in West

Coast states and relocate them to camps far from to the coastal cities. The order cited the possibility of "espionage" or "sabotage." It asserted that the relocation was necessary for the "successful prosecution" of the war against Japan.

The main circumstance surrounding the decision was American involvement in World War II. The United States again did not enter the conflict immediately. After German leader Adolf Hitler attacked Poland in 1939 and began World War II, the United States remained neutral. Though President Franklin D. Roosevelt sympathized with the opponents of Fascism and Nazism, isolationists argued strongly against United States intervention. The debate ended abruptly in December 1941 when Japan attacked the U.S. naval base at Pearl Harbor, Hawaii. This attack stunned many Americans and made them bitter toward Japan. Because the United States was attacked by Japan and because of American strategic interests in Asia, the primary focus of the U.S. military was Japan. The conflict between the two nations had ramifications on the home front. Japanese immigrants—*Issei* in Japanese—and native-born Americans of Japanese ancestry—*Nisei*—were increasingly looked at with anger and suspicion. It was in the context of this heightened suspicion of Japanese Americans that President Franklin D. Roosevelt issued Executive Order 9066.

Another important circumstance surrounding the decision was a history of racism in the United States toward Asians. Racist assumptions at the time held that Asian immigrants would never fully assimilate into the United States. The gold rush in California and the building of the transcontinental railroad attracted many Chinese immigrants to the West. The Chinese Exclusion Act (1882) was the only instance of legislation prohibiting a particular nationality from entering the country. In the late 1800s, many Japanese people immigrated to the West Coast of the United States. In California, these Japanese immigrants often suffered discrimination. Many white Californians harbored resentment toward their new neighbors. In the early years of the 20th century, California passed legislation ordering "orientals" to be segregated from white students in the public-school system. When Japan protested, President Theodore Roosevelt and Japanese leaders negotiated the Gentlemen's Agreement, in which Roosevelt agreed to reverse this legislation and Japan agreed to limit the number of emigrants coming into the United States. However, on the eve of World War II, anti-Japanese sentiment still existed in California and elsewhere in the United States. This anti-Asian racism predisposed white Californians to suspect their Japanese neighbors of espionage and sabotage as World War II began.

The circumstance surrounding the Korematsu case was the arrest of Fred Korematsu, a Japanese American who had refused to cooperate with the relocation order and had gone into hiding in the Oakland area. He went so far as to undergo plastic surgery on his eyelids in an unsuccessful attempt to appear less like a Japanese person. He changed his name to Clyde Sarah and claimed to be of Spanish and Hawaiian heritage. His attempts to "pass," however, came to naught. He was arrested in May 1942. Soon after, the local chapter of the American Civil Liberties Union heard about the case and asked him if they could use his case as a test of the constitutionality of Executive Order 9066. The case, *Korematsu v. United States*, made its way to the Supreme Court by 1944. The Supreme Court upheld his arrest and the relocation order. The majority decision held that the relocation was acceptable on the grounds of national security. However, the decision was not unanimous. Justice Robert Jackson asserted that the order was unconstitutional. Korematsu was a citizen of the United States, born in California; he was singled out only because he was "born of different racial stock" than white Americans. Jackson argued that that fact was not enough to incarcerate an American citizen.

The impact of the Court's decision on American society was widely felt. The internment of Japanese Americans continued throughout World War II. Much later, in 1988, the United States government publicly apologized to the surviving victims and extended $20,000 in reparations to each one. However, an important precedent of the case continues to reverberate in American society—that the government has the right to set aside constitutional protections and curtail civil liberties in times of war. This was evident with the passage of the Patriot Act in 2001, following the terrorist attacks of September 11. The Patriot Act allows for the use of National Security Letters, or NSLs, by the FBI. These NSLs allow the FBI to search telephone, email, and financial records without a court order, raising constitutional concerns for many people.

While the Court limited individual and group rights in the Korematsu case, it expanded them in the case of *Roe v. Wade* in 1973. The case dealt with the issue of a woman's right to an abortion. The act of inducing the termination of a pregnancy has occurred throughout recorded human history. In early U.S. history, abortion techniques were generally illegal after the moment of "quickening"— when the mother could feel movement of the fetus. By 1900, most states had passed laws making abortion illegal altogether, except in cases of rape or if the health of the mother was at stake. However, abortions continued and, starting in the 1930s, safer techniques were developed.

The historical circumstances of the *Roe v. Wade* case can be traced back to the 1960s. In that decade, women's rights activists and health professionals began to push for states to decriminalize or legalize abortion. Some supporters of legalized abortion stressed the issue of safety. Pushing abortions to "back alley" clinics, they argued, encouraged the use of unsafe and unregulated procedures. Others argued that the decision should be made by the woman, not by politicians. By 1973, 20 states had made abortion legal under certain circumstances (which varied from state to state). The immediate circumstance surrounding the case involved a Texas woman, known at the time by the alias Jane Roe, who sued the state of Texas for prohibiting abortions in all cases, except in cases where the life of the woman was threatened.

The case, *Roe v. Wade*, went to the Supreme Court in 1973. The Court's decision struck down state statues that prohibited or severely limited abortions. The Court declared that states shall not prohibit women from having an abortion during the first two trimesters of pregnancy. The Supreme Court reasoned that the Constitution guaranteed people the right to privacy. Abortion, they argued, was a decision that should be left to the woman with the advice of her physician. This decision echoed the reasoning of an earlier decision, *Griswold v. Connecticut* (1965), in which the Court ruled that laws forbidding the use of birth control devices were unconstitutional.

The *Roe v. Wade* decision has profoundly affected the United States. It is estimated that 50 million abortions have been performed in the United States since 1973. Opponents of the decision argue that abortion is equivalent to terminating a human life. More broadly, they argue that the prevalence of abortion undermines people's appreciation of life—that many Americans have lost sight of the sacredness of every human life. Proponents of the decision argue that women now have greater control over their reproductive lives and have the ability to make the very personal decision about whether to carry a pregnancy to term or not. Politically, the legalization of abortion in the United States has been central to the rise of the New Right. The issue propelled cultural conservatives from the margins to the mainstream of the American political arena. The issue propelled evangelical Protestants to put aside their long-held suspicions of Catholicism and to create a broad Christian conservative movement. Abortion remains one of the most contentious issues in American politics.

PART III: DOCUMENT-BASED QUESTION

Part A: Short Answer

Document 1

1 Based on the information provided in the map, one cause of the conflict between the United States and Mexico was a dispute over the border between the two countries; the United States asserted it was at the Rio Grande, while Mexico asserted it was at the Nueces River.

> *This answer receives full credit because it states one cause of the conflict between the United States and Mexico.*

Document 2

2 Based on the document, one action President James K. Polk took in regard to Texas was to send troops to the area between the Nueces River and the Del Norte (Rio Grande).

This answer receives full credit because it states one action President James K. Polk took in regard to Texas.

Document 3a

3a According to Eric Foner, the issue that the Wilmot Proviso attempted to address was whether territory acquired from Mexico would allow slavery or not.

This answer receives full credit because it states the issue that the Wilmot Proviso attempted to address.

Document 3b

3b Based on the information provided by the map, one effect of the Mexican-American War on the United States in 1848 was that it acquired a large piece of territory from Mexico. This was known as the Mexican Cession.

This answer receives full credit because it states one effect of the Mexican-American War on the United States in 1848.

Document 4

4 Based on the document, one reason President Lyndon B. Johnson believed the United States should continue to assist Vietnam was to strengthen world order by letting countries of the world see that they could count on the United States to support them if attacked.

This answer receives full credit because it states one reason President Lyndon B. Johnson believed the United States should continue to assist Vietnam.

Document 5a

5a Based on the document, one action President Lyndon B. Johnson took in 1965 regarding Vietnam was increasing the monthly draft call from 17,000 men to 35,000 men.

This answer receives full credit because it states one action President Lyndon B. Johnson took in 1965 regarding Vietnam.

Document 5b

5b Based on the information in the charts, one effect of the actions taken by President Lyndon B. Johnson in 1965 was an increase in United States troops from 23,300 in 1964 to 184,000 in 1965.

This answer receives full credit because it states one effect of the actions taken by President Lyndon B. Johnson in 1965.

Document 6a and Document 6b

6(1) Based on the documents, one effect of the Vietnam War on the United States was the development of a large-scale protest movement against American involvement in Vietnam.

6(2) Based on the documents, another effect of the Vietnam War on the United States was that President Lyndon B. Johnson decided not to run for an additional term as president.

These answers receive full credit because they state two effects of the Vietnam War on the United States.

Document 7a, Document 7b, and Document 7c

7 Based on the documents, one cause of the Persian Gulf War was that Iraqi troops engaged in "naked aggression," crossing the border and invading the neighboring country of Kuwait.

This answer receives full credit because it states one cause of the Persian Gulf War.

Document 8

8 Based on the document, one action taken by President George H.W. Bush in response to Iraq's 1990 invasion of Kuwait was to create a coalition of 28 countries, including the United States, and to use the military force of these countries to drive Iraqi troops out of Kuwait.

This answer receives full credit because it states one action taken by President George H.W. Bush in response to Iraq's 1990 invasion of Kuwait.

Document 9a and Document 9b

9(1) Based on the documents, one effect of the Persian Gulf War on the United States was to send peace activists "into retreat" and to rid the general public of its aversion to American overseas military involvements, conquering the so-called "Vietnam Syndrome."

9(2) Based on the documents, another effect of the Persian Gulf War on the United States was to instill in the country a sense of pride because the military accomplished its goal and demonstrated to the world that the United States keeps its promises.

These answers receive full credit because they state two effects of the Persian Gulf War on the United States.

Part B: Document-Based Essay

The Constitution bestows upon the president the title commander in chief. This title gives the president a great deal of latitude in dealing with international crises. While it is true that Congress has the power to declare war and to allocate money for military actions, presidents have frequently taken actions unilaterally. It is understandable that presidents would take actions on their own. An attack on the United States would very likely require an immediate and decisive response; there would not be time to wait for Congress to convene and to debate the proper response to such a crisis. However, on different occasions, critics have accused presidents of abusing their powers and taking actions in an arbitrary and misguided manner. Presidential actions in the Mexican-American War (1846–1848) and in the Vietnam War (1964–1975) generated a great deal of debate and contention, and ultimately had major impacts on the United States.

The Mexican War occurred during the years 1846 to 1848. The historical circumstances that led to the conflict date back to Americans moving into the Mexican province of Texas. As early as the 1820s, white Americans began moving into the Mexican territory of Texas. Many of these settlers were southern whites who hoped to duplicate the plantation model from the Old South. Initially, Mexico was eager to attract settlers to its northern frontier. Led by Stephen Austin, settlers were attracted to Texas because there was an abundance of affordable land that could be used for cotton cultivation. By the 1820s, tensions began to develop between the Texas settlers and the Mexican government. Texans routinely flouted Mexican law—most notably in practicing slavery, which was banned in Mexico. In 1835, the Texans rebelled against Mexico. At first, they suffered a major setback at the Alamo in San Antonio, a former mission where they had taken refuge. Weeks later, the rebels regrouped and emerged victorious. Texans won independence from Mexico, establishing the independent Lone Star Republic in 1836. Most Texans were eager for their Lone Star Republic to join the United States. However, many Whig Party politicians opposed Texas annexation because they feared that it would create new tensions around the issue of slavery. Texas was finally annexed in 1845, soon after the victory of the expansionist James K. Polk in the presidential election of 1844.

When Polk took office, he set his sights beyond Texas—he wanted to acquire the remainder of Mexico's northern provinces, including California, on the Pacific coast. Toward this end, he antagonized Mexico by claiming land that the Mexican government (and many Americans) believed was actually part of Mexico. He said that the border between Texas and Mexico was at the Rio Grande rather than at the Nueces River. (Document 1) He further antagonized Mexico by sending "an efficient military force" into the disputed territory. He claimed that this action was necessary to repel a planned invasion by Mexico. He asserted that Mexico was determined to get revenge on the United States for annexing Texas. (Document 2)

The conflict with Mexico generated a great deal of debate in the United States. Many Americans, such as the Whig congressman Abraham Lincoln, argued that Polk's rationale for sending troops to the disputed territory was bogus. He wrote that Congress should not allow Polk to wage war simply because Polk felt that another nation was about to wage war on the United States. To do so, Lincoln argued, would be giving Polk limitless power to wage war. Other Americans were concerned that the acquisition of new territory would open the possibility of expanding slavery. In Congress, Representative David Wilmot of Pennsylvania put forth an amendment to an appropriations bill that would have prohibited the expansion of slavery to territories acquired from Mexico. The Wilmot Proviso passed the House (where the populous northern states were able to exert greater power), but it failed in the Senate (where each state has equal representation). (Document 3a)

The effects of the Mexican War on the United States were profound. As Polk had hoped, the United States acquired Mexico's northern provinces, as part of the Treaty of Guadalupe Hidalgo (1848) following the American victory in the Mexican War. The Mexican Cession includes the present-day states of California, Nevada, and Utah, as well as portions of present-day Arizona, New Mexico, Wyoming, and Colorado. (Document 3b) More importantly, the acquisition of new territory brought the question of slavery to the forefront of political debates. Soon after the acquisition of the Mexican Cession, gold was discovered in California (1848). As word spread, thousands of people came to California to try to strike it rich. By 1850, California had enough people to form a state. Californians wrote up a constitution, in which slavery would be illegal, to submit to Congress. Southern senators objected to the admission of an additional free state. Senate negotiators worked out a series of measures that became known as the Compromise of 1850. The most important elements of the compromise were the admittance of California as a free state, which pleased northern politicians, and a more stringent Fugitive Slave Law, which pleased southern politicians. The compromise proved to be a temporary solution to a deeply troubling issue. The two-party system of Democrats and Whigs collapsed, to be replaced by sectional parties. (Document 3a) By the end of the 1850s, the question of slavery so dominated public debates that the country seemed ready to break apart. It did exactly that in the months following the election of Abraham Lincoln in 1860. The secession of most of the slave-holding states led to Civil War in 1861.

A century after the conclusion of the Civil War, the United States began a large-scale intervention in a conflict on the other side of the globe. The Vietnam War, which lasted from 1955 to 1975, greatly impacted the United States and ultimately undid the presidency of Lyndon Johnson.

The roots of conflict in Vietnam stretch back to the period of French imperialism in Indochina. From the mid-19th century to the mid-20th century, Vietnam was a colony of France. It was then occupied by Japan during World War II. After the war, many Vietnamese hoped to finally be free of foreign control, but France reoccupied it. A war for independence, led by Ho Chi Minh, began in 1946. In 1954, French forces were defeated and withdrew from the region, leaving Vietnam divided at the 17th parallel between a communist-controlled North Vietnam, and a western-allied South Vietnam. A rebel movement, known as the Vietcong, continued to press its cause in South Vietnam. It was at this point that the United States became involved in the conflict. President Dwight Eisenhower cited the domino theory as a rationale for American involvement in Vietnam. The theory asserts that when a nation becomes communist, its neighbors will be more likely to become communist. Years later (in 1965), President Johnson cited this long history of support for South Vietnam as a reason for continuing involvement in Vietnam. He saw continued involvement as a key to maintaining "world order." (Document 4)

President Johnson took decisive action in regard to Vietnam in 1965. In August 1964, Johnson announced that American destroyers had been fired upon in the Gulf of Tonkin, off the coast of North Vietnam. Later, reports questioned the accuracy of the announcement, but the incident led Congress to give Johnson the ability to escalate American military involvement in Vietnam. The Gulf of Tonkin Resolution can be considered the beginning of the war in Vietnam. Soon after, Johnson increased the number of troops in Vietnam to 125,000, and he increased the monthly draft call to 35,000. (Document 5a) In the following years, Johnson continued to increase American troop strength in Vietnam—to 385,300 in 1966, 485,600 in 1967, and 536,100 in 1968. (Document 5b)

The effects of President Johnson's actions in regard to Vietnam were felt deeply in American society. The war divided Americans as no previous war had. President Johnson was not able to impose military censorship on the media. As such, it became known as a "living room war" because images from Vietnam were regularly broadcast on the evening news. Families saw American soldiers burn down Vietnamese villages. They saw body bags coming back to the United States. They saw children burned by napalm. All of these images contributed to the growing antiwar movement in the United States. Also, after President Lyndon Johnson had reinstated the military draft in order to meet the personnel needs of the Vietnam War (Document 5a), the possibility of being drafted led many young people to oppose the war. Protests against the war grew large and more intense. A massive demonstration at the Lincoln Memorial in October 1967 capped a year of major protests organized by the National Mobilization Committee to End the War in Vietnam (Document 6a). The demonstrations against the Vietnam War deeply shook the political establishment, dividing Democrats into pro-hawk and pro-dove factions. It also intensified divisions within American society around ideology, culture, politics, age, race, and gender. Ultimately, the war undid the Johnson presidency; in March 1968, he announced that he would not seek reelection. (Document 6b)

Presidential actions initiated both the Mexican-American War and the Vietnam War. In both cases, the actions taken by the president generated a great deal of debate. Critics wondered aloud if the circumstances around each conflict justified the actions taken by the U.S. president. Ultimately, both conflicts led to profound changes in American society. The Mexican-American War led to a reopening of the debate over the expansion of slavery—a debate that ended in the Civil War. The Vietnam War led to major divisions in American society that continued to be felt well beyond the end of the war.

Topic	Question Numbers	*Number of Points
American political history	11, 12, 13, 17, 18, 22, 24, 31, 38, 45, 47, 48	14
Political theory	3	1
Economic theory/policy	8, 16, 19, 28, 29, 30, 44	8
Constitutional principles	2, 4, 5, 6, 7, 43, 46	8
American foreign policy	21, 32, 35, 36, 37, 39, 42, 50	10
American studies—the American people	9, 10, 14, 20, 23, 25, 26, 27, 33, 34, 40, 41, 49	16
Geography	1,15	2
Skills questions included in the above content area		
Reading comprehension	11, 12, 28, 32, 38	
Cartoon/image interpretation	25, 29, 30, 45, 46, 50	
Outlining skills	16, 41	

*Note: The 50 questions in Part I are worth a total of 60 percent of the exam. Since each correct answer is worth 60/50 or 1.2 points, totals are shown to the nearest full point in each content category.

PART I

Multiple-Choice Questions by Standard

Standard	Question Numbers
1—United States and New York History	7, 9, 10, 12, 13, 14, 17, 18, 21, 23, 25, 26, 27, 29, 32, 33, 38, 40, 43, 45, 50
2—World History	35, 36, 37, 39, 42
3—Geography	1, 15, 20, 48
4—Economics	8, 16, 19, 22, 28, 30, 34, 44
5—Civics, Citizenship, and Government	2, 3, 4, 5, 6, 11, 24, 31, 41, 46, 47, 49

Parts II and III by Theme and Standard

	Theme	Standards
Thematic Essay	Supreme Court Decisions; Constitutional Principles; Civic Values; Citizenship; Individuals, Groups, Institutions	Standards 1 and 5: United States and New York History; Civics, Citizenship, and Government
Document-Based Essay	Presidential Decisions and Actions; Foreign Policy; Places and Regions; Constitutional Principles; Interdependence	Standards 1, 2, 3, and 5: United States and New York History; World History; Geography; Civics, Citizenship, and Government

Examination June 2019
United States History and Government

PART I: MULTIPLE CHOICE

Directions (1–50): For each statement or question, write in the space provided the *number* of the word or expression that, of those given, best completes the statement or answers the question.

1 In colonial America, the Magna Carta, the English Bill of Rights, and the writings of John Locke contributed to the

  (1) diversity of religious beliefs among the colonists
  (2) political ideals and practices of the colonists
  (3) economic relationships between the colonists and the mother country
  (4) demands of colonists to end the slave trade and the practice of slavery   1 _____

2 Before 1763, most American colonists settled near the Atlantic Coast or rivers because

  (1) port cities could be more easily defended in times of war
  (2) valleys were less fertile
  (3) English colonists were only allowed to settle in these locations
  (4) navigable water offered easier access to trade and employment   2 _____

3 One way in which the Declaration of Independence and the original United States Constitution are similar is that both promote the idea of

  (1) the consent of the governed
  (2) equal rights for women
  (3) voting rights for all adult citizens
  (4) judicial review of unjust laws   3 _____

4 The main purpose of the *Federalist Papers* was to

  (1) discourage the creation of political parties
  (2) support the candidacy of George Washington
  (3) urge ratification of the Constitution
  (4) advocate independence from Great Britain   4 _____

5 ". . . Constitutions should consist only of general provisions: The reason is, that they must necessarily be permanent, and that they cannot calculate for the possible changes of things. . . ."

                            — Alexander Hamilton, 1788

Which provision of the United States Constitution best supports the idea expressed in this quotation?

  (1) eminent domain
  (2) electoral college
  (3) separation of powers
  (4) elastic clause   5 _____

6 The main objection to the adoption of the United States Constitution was based primarily on the belief that

  (1) the number of new states admitted to the Union should be limited
  (2) individual freedoms could be restricted by a strong central government
  (3) a separate judiciary would make the government ineffective
  (4) slave populations gave the South too much power   6 _____

7 Which viewpoint of the framers of the United States Constitution is demonstrated by the use of the electoral college to select the president?

  (1) distrust of the average citizen's judgment
  (2) belief that political parties strengthen the campaign process
  (3) desire to end property qualifications for voting
  (4) commitment to universal suffrage   7 _____

Base your answer to question 8 on the diagram below and on your knowledge of social studies.

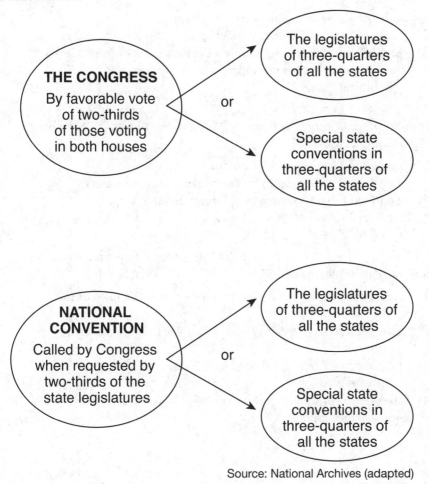

Source: National Archives (adapted)

8 What is the best title for this diagram?

  (1) Methods of Amending the Constitution
  (2) Procedures of the Executive Branch
  (3) Process of Nominating Presidential Candidates
  (4) Admission of New States to the Union   8 _____

9 The United States wanted to acquire New Orleans in 1803 in order to

  (1) end British influence in North America
  (2) promote the growth of manufacturing in the region
  (3) establish a military base to defend against attacks from Mexico
  (4) secure a port that would improve the transportation of agricultural goods

9 _____

10 The Supreme Court decision in *Gibbons* v. *Ogden* (1824) is important because it

  (1) banned the importation of manufactured goods
  (2) encouraged state investment in internal improvements
  (3) expanded federal control over interstate commerce
  (4) permitted taxes on exported goods

10 _____

11 Under Chief Justice John Marshall (1801–1835), Supreme Court decisions generally upheld Alexander Hamilton's belief that

  (1) a national debt would violate the economic principles of the Constitution
  (2) states should have more economic power than the federal government
  (3) the power of Congress should be greater than the power of the president
  (4) a loose interpretation of the Constitution could be used to increase federal power

11 _____

Base your answer to question 12 on the passage below and on your knowledge of social studies.

. . . I am not a Know-Nothing. That is certain. How could I be? How can any one who abhors the oppression of negroes [African Americans], be in favor of degrading classes of white people? Our progress in degeneracy appears to me to be pretty rapid. As a nation, we began by declaring that *"all men are created equal."* We now practically read it "all men are created equal, *except negroes."* When the Know-Nothings get control, it will read "all men are created equal, except negroes, *and foreigners, and catholics."* When it comes to this I should prefer emigrating to some country where they make no pretence of loving liberty—to Russia, for instance, where despotism can be taken pure, and without the base alloy of hypocracy. . . .

— Abraham Lincoln, letter to Joshua Speed,
August 24, 1855

12 In this 1855 letter, Abraham Lincoln opposed the Know-Nothing party because it

   (1) supported the policy of imperialism
   (2) favored unrestricted immigration
   (3) promoted resentment against minority groups
   (4) wanted equal rights for all people   12 _____

13 The Supreme Court's decision in *Dred Scott* v. *Sandford* was nullified by the passage of the

   (1) Kansas-Nebraska Act
   (2) 13th and 14th amendments
   (3) Compromise of 1850
   (4) Reconstruction Act   13 _____

14 The Civil War directly affected the Northern economy by

(1) causing a severe depression
(2) destroying much of its farmland
(3) greatly expanding the canal system
(4) stimulating the growth of factories

14 _____

15 Rapid industrialization during the late 1800s contributed to

(1) a decline in the membership of the American Federation of Labor (AFL)
(2) a reduction in government regulation of railroads
(3) a rise in the number of family farms
(4) an increase in immigration to the United States

15 _____

16 Which factor aided the building of transcontinental railroads?

(1) The federal government provided free land to the railroad companies.
(2) The railroads established fair rates for customers.
(3) Congress repealed antitrust laws against the railroads.
(4) The Supreme Court approved public ownership of the railroad industry.

16 _____

17 Which tactics were used by big business during the late 1800s to limit the power of labor unions?

(1) strikebreakers and lockouts
(2) picketing and walkouts
(3) collective bargaining and mediation
(4) wage increases and shorter hours

17 _____

18 Which constitutional right was the central focus in *Plessy* v. *Ferguson* (1896)?

(1) freedom of assembly guaranteed by the first amendment
(2) due process of the law in the fifth amendment
(3) equal protection of the law under the 14th amendment
(4) equal voting rights guaranteed by the 15th amendment

18 _____

Base your answer to question 19 on the cartoon below and on your knowledge of social studies.

The Monster Monopoly

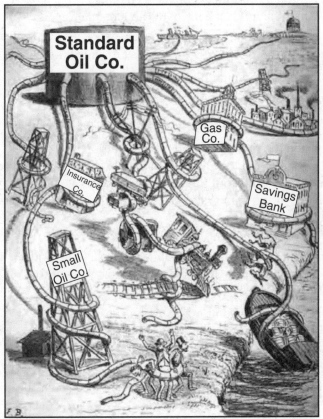

Source: Frank Beard, *Judge,* July 19, 1884 (adapted)

19 What is being criticized in this cartoon?

    (1) environmental damage   (3) oil exploration

    (2) business consolidation   (4) federal tax laws   19 _____

20 Which event was a result of the Spanish-American War?

    (1) Cuba was divided into spheres of influence.
    (2) Puerto Rico became a possession of the United States.
    (3) The Philippines became a Spanish colony.
    (4) The United States lost control of the Panama Canal.   20 _____

21 • Chinese Exclusion Act (1882)

    • Gentlemen's Agreement (1907)

    • Emergency Quota Act (1921)

These federal actions demonstrate that Americans have

    (1) supported the principle of open immigration
    (2) provided immigrants equal access to jobs and social programs
    (3) forced immigrants to settle in designated areas
    (4) favored limiting immigration at different times in the
        nation's history   21 _____

22 In the early 20th century, muckraking authors Upton Sinclair and Ida Tarbell primarily criticized the federal government for

    (1) wasting money on foreign wars
    (2) ignoring abuses committed by big business
    (3) excessive regulation of the steel industry
    (4) overspending on social welfare programs   22 _____

23 During the Progressive Era, voters were given more opportunities to select political party candidates through

    (1) direct primary elections
    (2) term limits on elected officials
    (3) initiative and recall
    (4) public funding of elections   23 _____

24 Theodore Roosevelt's Square Deal and Woodrow Wilson's New Freedom shared the goal of

    (1) achieving equal rights for minority groups
    (2) protecting the interests of big business
    (3) strengthening federal regulatory power over large
        corporations
    (4) instituting laissez-faire policies   24 _____

25 The Federal Reserve System was created in 1913 to

   (1) balance the budget
   (2) control the money supply
   (3) insure savings account deposits
   (4) regulate the stock market   25 _____

Base your answer to question 26 on these statements by President Woodrow Wilson and on your knowledge of social studies.

"... The United States must be neutral in fact as well as in name..."

         — message to U.S. Senate, 1914

"... America can not be an ostrich with its head in the sand...."

         — address in Des Moines, Iowa, 1916

"... The world must be made safe for democracy...."

         — address to Congress asking for a declaration of war,
         April 2, 1917

26 What do these statements demonstrate about President Wilson during the three years before the United States entered World War I?

   (1) He gradually changed his foreign policy goals.
   (2) He eagerly became involved in a war.
   (3) He abused the principle of separation of powers.
   (4) He was consistent in his policy of strict neutrality.   26 _____

27 President Warren Harding's call for a "return to normalcy" meant the United States should

(1) limit the number of exports
(2) reduce its role in world affairs
(3) expand efforts to end racial discrimination
(4) support woman's suffrage

27 _____

28 Which heading best completes the partial outline below?

I. _____

    A. Overproduction
    B. Underconsumption
    C. Buying on margin
    D. Unequal distribution of wealth

(1) Causes of the Industrial Revolution
(2) Causes of World War I
(3) Causes of the Great Depression
(4) Causes of World War II

28 _____

Base your answer to question 29 on the graph below and on your knowledge of social studies.

Source: *Historical Statistics of the United States, Colonial Times to 1970* (adapted)

29 Which conclusion is most clearly supported by the information provided on the graph?

(1) Deficit spending ended unemployment.
(2) World War II increased unemployment.
(3) New Deal programs only partially relieved unemployment.
(4) Unemployment after the New Deal was the same as before the stock market crash. 29 _____

30 During the 1930s, poor land management and severe drought conditions across parts of the Midwest resulted in the

(1) establishment of the United States Department of Agriculture
(2) creation of wheat surpluses
(3) decreased support for conservation
(4) development of the Dust Bowl conditions on the Great Plains 30 _____

31 During the 1930s, United States neutrality legislation was primarily designed to

(1) provide military and economic aid to Italy and Japan
(2) give the United States time to plan an attack against Germany
(3) protect American lives and property in Latin America
(4) avoid foreign policy mistakes that led to involvement in World War I 31 _____

Base your answers to questions 32 and 33 on the song lyrics below and on your knowledge of social studies.

That's Why We're Voting For Roosevelt

Herbie Hoover promised us "Two chickens in each pot,"
Breadlines and Depression were the only things we got.
I lost my job, my bank blew up, and I was on the spot.
That's why I'm voting for Roosevelt.

Hooray! Hooray! Herb Hoover's gone away,
Hooray! Hooray! I hope he's gone to stay.
For now I'm back to work and get my three squares ev'ry day.
That's why I'm voting for Roosevelt. . . .

Wall Street sure is kicking for they know they're on the pan.
Franklin D. in Washington upset their little plan,
And now the one on top is that poor once forgotten man,
That's why we're voting for Roosevelt.

Hooray! Hooray! He banished all our fear.
Hooray! Hooray! Our banks are in the clear.
He brought us back prosperity, he gave us back our beer,
That's why I'm voting for Roosevelt.

— Thomas O'Dowd, 1936

32 Which group would most likely have agreed with the lyrics of this song?

  (1) Prohibition advocates   (3) New Deal supporters
  (2) Republican Party leaders   (4) Supply-side economists   32 _____

33 According to the song lyrics, people supported Franklin D. Roosevelt primarily because he

  (1) implemented economic relief and recovery programs
  (2) favored a national suffrage amendment
  (3) continued Herbert Hoover's economic policies
  (4) reduced federal income taxes   33 _____

Base your answer to question 34 on the cartoon below and on your knowledge of social studies.

NEVER SATISFIED

Source: Vaughn Shoemaker, *Chicago News,* April 27, 1937 (adapted)

34 This cartoon is critical of President Franklin D. Roosevelt's efforts to

(1) force Congress to reduce government waste
(2) convince the Supreme Court to pass a constitutional amendment to balance the budget
(3) reverse the effects of the Great Depression
(4) increase his power over the Supreme Court

34 _____

Base your answers to questions 35 and 36 on the poster below and on your knowledge of social studies.

Source: Office of Price Administration, 1943

35 The poster indicates that rationing during World War II was a

   (1) policy to encourage small-business owners

   (2) way of assuring that only the wealthy could buy certain products

   (3) necessity caused by farm failures during the Great Depression

   (4) program that was to be applied equally to all Americans   35 _____

36 What was a major reason for wartime rationing?

   (1) ensuring that troops were adequately supplied

   (2) restricting lower-priced food imports

   (3) providing jobs for the unemployed

   (4) preventing currency deflation   36 _____

37 What would be the most appropriate heading for the partial outline below?

> I. _____
>
>   A. Treatment of Japanese Americans
>   B. Segregation of African Americans in the armed forces
>   C. United States reactions to the Nazi Holocaust
>   D. Use of the atomic bomb

   (1) Issues of Morality during World War II
   (2) Domestic Policies during World War II
   (3) Economic Problems during World War II
   (4) Reasons for the Success of the Allies during World War II   37 _____

Base your answer to question 38 on the graph below and on your knowledge of social studies.

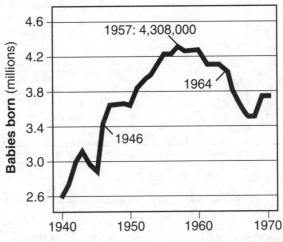

Source: *The NYSTROM Atlas of United States History,*
2000 (adapted)

38 What is the best title for this graph for the years 1946–1964?

   (1) The Graying of America
   (2) The Growth of the Middle Class
   (3) The Baby Boom Generation
   (4) From Suburbs to Cities   38 _____

Base your answers to questions 39 and 40 on the map below and on your knowledge of social studies.

Cuban Missile Crisis, 1962

Source: Gary B. Nash and Carter Smith, *Atlas of American History,* Facts on File, 2007 (adapted)

39 What was the immediate cause of the action taken by the United States that is shown on the map?

(1) Cuban refugees lobbied President Dwight Eisenhower to overthrow Fidel Castro.

(2) The Soviet Union built nuclear missile launch sites within range of United States cities.

(3) United States military bases in the Caribbean were closed by Cuban armed forces.

(4) Puerto Rican citizens asked Congress to assist them in repelling communist advances.

39 _____

40 One positive outcome of the situation shown on the map was that the United States and Soviet Union increased

    (1) communication between the two nations to avert war
    (2) military control of their Latin American colonies
    (3) cooperative humanitarian efforts in Caribbean nations suffering from natural disasters
    (4) joint efforts to end the cruel practices of Cuba's leaders   40 _____

41 The main reason President John F. Kennedy proposed the establishment of the Peace Corps was to

    (1) promote trade with Africa
    (2) combat drug use in American cities
    (3) gain support from immigrant voters
    (4) improve conditions in developing nations   41 _____

42 What was an outcome of the Watergate affair during the administration of President Richard Nixon?

    (1) Presidential powers were expanded.
    (2) Respect for the office of the president declined.
    (3) The Supreme Court cleared President Nixon of all charges.
    (4) Congress refused to take action against President Nixon.   42 _____

43 The goal of the War Powers Act of 1973 was to

    (1) allow the president to declare war without congressional approval
    (2) give Congress the sole power to authorize the use of military force
    (3) limit the president's power to use military force without congressional approval
    (4) require a declaration of war for all uses of military forces   43 _____

44 ". . . The United States, together with the United Nations, exhausted every means at our disposal to bring this crisis to a peaceful end. However, Saddam [Hussein] clearly felt that by stalling and threatening and defying the United Nations, he could weaken the forces arrayed against him. . . ."

— President George H. W. Bush, address to the nation,
January 16, 1991

President George H. W. Bush used this statement to defend

(1) taking military action to liberate Kuwait from Iraqi aggression
(2) providing foreign aid to Israel
(3) supporting Egypt against attacks by terrorists
(4) using United States troops as peacekeepers in Bosnia   44 _____

Base your answer to question 45 on the cartoon below and on your knowledge of social studies.

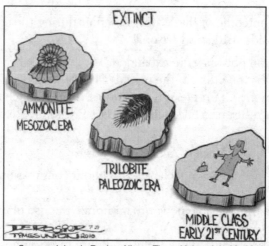

Source: John de Rosier, *Albany Times Union*, July 29, 2010

45 Which combination of factors has led to the problem shown in the cartoon?

(1) lower medical costs and high interest rates
(2) business monopolies and depletion of natural resources
(3) consumer debt and nearly stagnant wages
(4) population migration and the graying of America   45 _____

46 One way in which the goals of the Know-Nothing Party in the 1850s and the response to the Red Scare of 1919 were similar is that both

(1) called for equal rights for women and African Americans
(2) sought to limit immigration to the United States
(3) supported the overseas expansion of the United States
(4) attempted to limit the influence of big business on American politics

46 _____

47 Which term most accurately describes United States foreign policy during the Cold War?

(1) containment   (3) Big Stick
(2) nonalignment   (4) Open Door

47 _____

Base your answer to question 48 on the chart below and on your knowledge of social studies.

Action	Reaction
President Andrew Johnson disobeys the Tenure of Office Act. →	Congress impeaches Johnson and he remains in office by one vote.
Congress passes the National Industrial Recovery Act (NIRA). →	The Supreme Court declares the NIRA unconstitutional in *Schechter Poultry Corporation* v. *United States.*

48 Which aspect of governmental power is best illustrated by both examples in the chart?

(1) federalism   (3) States rights
(2) checks and balances   (4) judicial review

48 _____

49 Which economic policy argues that government should limit, as much as possible, any interference in the economy?

   (1) socialism   (3) mercantilism

   (2) laissez-faire   (4) protectionism   49 _____

50 W. E. B. Du Bois, Jackie Robinson, and James Meredith are considered pioneers in the area of

   (1) labor relations

   (2) educational reform

   (3) civil rights

   (4) environmental protection   50 _____

In developing your answer to Part II, be sure to keep these general definitions in mind:

(a) <u>describe</u> means "to illustrate something in words or tell about it"

(b) <u>discuss</u> means "to make observations about something using facts, reasoning, and argument; to present in some detail"

PART II: THEMATIC ESSAY

Directions: Write a well-organized essay that includes an introduction, several paragraphs addressing the task below, and a conclusion.

Theme: Westward Movement of the Frontier

> Throughout the nation's history, the United States has expanded through the acquisition of new territories. These acquisitions have had both positive and negative effects on the United States.

Task:

> Select *two* events that significantly influenced the westward movement of the frontier and for *each*
>
> - Describe the historical circumstances surrounding the event
> - Discuss the *positive **and/or** negative* effects of the event on the settlement of the West

You may use any event that significantly influenced the westward movement of the frontier from your study of United States history. Some events you might wish to consider include:

Signing of the Treaty of Paris (1783)

Discovery of gold in California (1848)

Creation of the reservation system (1800s)

Passage of the Homestead Act (1862)

Purchase of the Louisiana Territory (1803)

Purchase of Alaska (1867)

Opening of the Erie Canal (1825)

Completion of the transcontinental railroad (1869)

War with Mexico (1846–1848)

You are not limited to these suggestions.

Guidelines:

In your essay, be sure to:

- Develop all aspects of the task
- Discuss *at least* **two** effects for each event
- Support the theme with relevant facts, examples, and details
- Use a logical and clear plan of organization, including an introduction and a conclusion that are beyond a restatement of the theme

In developing your answers to Part III, be sure to keep these general definitions in mind:
- (a) <u>describe</u> means "to illustrate something in words or tell about it"
- (b) <u>discuss</u> means "to make observations about something using facts, reasoning, and argument; to present in some detail"

PART III: DOCUMENT-BASED QUESTION

This question is based on the accompanying documents. The question is designed to test your ability to work with historical documents. Some of these documents have been edited for the purposes of this question. As you analyze the documents, take into account the source of each document and any point of view that may be presented in the document. Keep in mind that the language and images used in a document may reflect the historical context of the time in which it was created.

Historical Context:

> In the decades following World War II, significant domestic and foreign policy issues led to political and social tensions in the United States. These issues motivated individuals and groups to organize protest movements to bring about change. Protest movements such as the *civil rights movement,* the *anti–Vietnam War movement,* and the *environmental movement* met with varying degrees of success.

Task:

> Using the information from the documents and your knowledge of United States history, answer the questions that follow each document in Part A. Your answers to the questions will help you write the Part B essay in which you will be asked to
>
> Choose *two* protest movements mentioned in the historical context and for *each*
> - Describe the historical circumstances surrounding the protest movement
> - Discuss the extent to which the protest movement was successful

Part A: *Short-Answer Questions*

Directions: Analyze the documents and answer the short-answer questions that follow each document in the space provided.

Document 1a

"AND REMEMBER, NOTHING CAN BE ACCOMPLISHED BY TAKING TO THE STREETS"

Source: Herblock, *Washington Post*, September 6, 1963 (adapted)

Document 1b

If You Miss Me At the Back of the Bus

> If you miss me at the back of the bus you can't find me nowhere come on over to the front of the bus I'll be riding up there. . . .
>
> If you miss me on the picket line you can't find me nowhere come on over to the city jail I'll be rooming over there. . . .
>
> If you miss me in the cotton fields you can't find me nowhere come on over to the courthouse I'll be voting right there. . . .

Source: recorded by Pete Seeger, 1963, written by Carver Neblett

1 Based on these documents, state *one* form of discrimination African Americans experienced in the 1960s. [1]

_____

_____

Document 2

. . . In its regional breadth, the uprising resembled the sit-in movement of 1960. But the 1963 demonstrations [after Birmingham] were more widespread, involved much larger numbers, and drew in people of all ages and backgrounds. To list the places where black people engaged in nonviolent protests would be to name virtually every town and city in the South: about 115 communities experienced 930 demonstrations of one kind or another. The number of people arrested topped 20,000, four times as many as in 1960.

The 1963 surge of nonviolent direct action made the maintenance of segregation in public accommodations untenable [unable to continue]. Black people knew that if segregation could be cracked in Birmingham, it could be cracked anywhere. Birmingham exposed the vulnerability of the South's political regime, and black people seized the opportunity to attack it. In city after city, under the relentless pressure of demonstrations, whites sat down to negotiate. During a single three-week period after Birmingham, the Justice Department noted that 143 cities had acceded [agreed] to some degree of integration. By year's end the number exceeded three hundred. Many cities set up biracial committees that enabled blacks to press for further desegregation. . . .

Source: Adam Fairclough, *Better Day Coming: Blacks and Equality, 1890–2000,* Viking Penguin, 2001

2 According to Adam Fairclough, what was *one* effect of the 1963 demonstrations in Birmingham, Alabama? [1]

_____

_____

Document 3

. . . In far too many ways American Negroes have been another nation: deprived of freedom, crippled by hatred, the doors of opportunity closed to hope.

In our time change has come to this Nation, too. The American Negro, acting with impressive restraint, has peacefully protested and marched, entered the courtrooms and the seats of government, demanding a justice that has long been denied. The voice of the Negro was the call to action. But it is a tribute to America that, once aroused, the courts and the Congress, the President and most of the people, have been the allies of progress.

Thus we have seen the high court of the country declare that discrimination based on race was repugnant [disagreeable] to the Constitution, and therefore void. We have seen in 1957, and 1960, and again in 1964, the first civil rights legislation in this Nation in almost an entire century. . . .

The voting rights bill will be* the latest, and among the most important, in a long series of victories. But this victory—as Winston Churchill said of another triumph for freedom—"is not the end. It is not even the beginning of the end. But it is, perhaps, the end of the beginning."

That beginning is freedom; and the barriers to that freedom are tumbling down. Freedom is the right to share, share fully and equally, in American society—to vote, to hold a job, to enter a public place, to go to school. It is the right to be treated in every part of our national life as a person equal in dignity and promise to all others.

But freedom is not enough. You do not wipe away the scars of centuries by saying: Now you are free to go where you want, and do as you desire, and choose the leaders you please. . . .

This is the next and the more profound stage of the battle for civil rights. We seek not just freedom but opportunity. We seek not just legal equity but human ability, not just equality as a right and a theory but equality as a fact and equality as a result.

For the task is to give 20 million Negroes the same chance as every other American to learn and grow, to work and share in society, to develop their abilities—physical, mental and spiritual, and to pursue their individual happiness. . . .

Source: Lyndon B. Johnson, Commencement Address at Howard University, June 4, 1965

*The Voting Rights Act was signed into law on August 6, 1965.

3*a* According to President Lyndon B. Johnson, what is *one* achievement of the civil rights movement?   [1]

_____

_____

b According to President Lyndon B. Johnson, what is *one* remaining goal for the civil rights movement?   [1]

_____

_____

Document 4

... As the U.S. commitment increased, so did the number of bombs dropped on the North, the volume of North Vietnamese coming into the South, the fervor of the protest movement, the billion dollar military grants, and the number of casualties. Johnson's pledge to fight communism in Southeast Asia had degenerated into what anti-war folk singer Pete Seeger labeled "the Big Muddy." And yet, the refrain of that song said, "the old fool says to push on." Tempers on both sides flared as the body counts increased, and each night's TV broadcasts introduced American viewers to faraway hell holes where their sons, brothers, friends, and husbands were stepping on land mines, perishing in Vietcong mantraps, and being cut down in hand-to-hand combat. The week of September 18–24 brought with it a grim statistic: 142 U.S. soldiers killed, 825 wounded, 3 missing—the war's highest toll in 1966. ...

Every time American troops won a small victory or held a strategic position, the President's advisers used the occasion to press for more troops and more money. These were vital, they repeatedly declared, to consolidate our gains and increase our advantages. The monthly draft was doubled several times, up to 46,000 a month in October 1966, as General Westmoreland constantly increased his call for troops. He had almost a half-million men in combat by April 1967. By the following year, he told the President, he would need almost 700,000. With that number, he said, we could win the war in two years. The "light at the end of the tunnel," which President Johnson optimistically referred to in his news broadcasts, had dimmed considerably since his earlier predictions. ...

Source: Toby Goldstein, *Waking from the Dream: America in the Sixties,* Julian Messner, 1988

4 According to Toby Goldstein, what were *two* reasons for the development of the anti–Vietnam War movement? [2]

(1) _____

_____

(2) _____

_____

Document 5

> American protest against the war in Vietnam was begun and sustained by American citizens who believed that in a representative democracy, individuals can make themselves heard and, more, can affect public policy.
>
> To us, the antiwar movement during the Vietnam era is important not because it stopped the war, which it may or may not have done; rather, it is important because it existed. It is a reminder to Americans that times come when citizens can and, indeed, must challenge their government's authority. . . .
>
> Every war has had its opponents. There was a sizable antiwar sentiment in Great Britain during the South African War (1899–1902), and in America there has always been during every war a small protest movement—most notably, until Vietnam, during the Mexican War in 1846–48 and the Philippine Insurrection in 1899–1901. But the Vietnam War was different: increasingly unpopular, undeclared and therefore in the opinion of many citizens illegal and unconstitutional as well, it was the most frustrating war in American history, and the ugliest, and the longest. The movement opposing it had years in which to grow. . . .

Source: Nancy Zaroulis and Gerald Sullivan, *Who Spoke Up?: American Protest Against the War In Vietnam, 1963–1975,* Holt, Rinehart and Winston, 1984

5 According to Nancy Zaroulis and Gerald Sullivan, what was **one** reason for protest against the Vietnam War?   [1]

_____

_____

Document 6

. . . The impact of the antiwar protests remains one of the most controversial issues raised by the war. The obvious manifestations [displays] of dissent in the United States probably encouraged Hanoi's will to hold out for victory, although there is nothing to suggest that the North Vietnamese would have been more compromising in the absence of the movement. Antiwar protest did not turn the American people against the war, as some critics have argued. The effectiveness of the movement was limited by the divisions within its own ranks. Public opinion polls make abundantly clear, moreover, that a majority of Americans found the antiwar movement, particularly its radical and "hippie" elements, more obnoxious than the war itself. In a perverse sort of way, the protest may even have strengthened support for a war that was not in itself popular. The impact of the movement was much more limited and subtle. It forced Vietnam onto the public consciousness and challenged the rationale of the war and indeed of a generation of Cold War foreign policies. It limited Johnson's military options and may have headed off any tendency toward more drastic escalation. Perhaps most important, the disturbances and divisions set off by the antiwar movement caused fatigue and anxiety among the policymakers and the public, and thus eventually encouraged efforts to find a way out of the war. . . .

Source: George C. Herring, *America's Longest War:*
The United States and Vietnam, 1950–1975, Alfred A. Knopf, 1986 (adapted)

6*a* According to George C. Herring, what was ***one*** way the anti–
Vietnam War movement was ***not*** successful?   [1]

_____

_____

b According to George C. Herring, what was ***one*** way the anti–
Vietnam War movement was successful?   [1]

_____

_____

Document 7

. . . For the first time in the history of the world, every human being is now subjected to contact with dangerous chemicals, from the moment of conception until death. In the less than two decades of their use, the synthetic pesticides have been so thoroughly distributed throughout the animate and inanimate world that they occur virtually everywhere. They have been recovered from most of the major river systems and even from streams of groundwater flowing unseen through the earth. Residues of these chemicals linger in soil to which they may have been applied a dozen years before. They have entered and lodged in the bodies of fish, birds, reptiles, and domestic and wild animals so universally that scientists carrying on animal experiments find it almost impossible to locate subjects free from such contamination. They have been found in fish in remote mountain lakes, in earthworms burrowing in soil, in the eggs of birds—and in man himself. For these chemicals are now stored in the bodies of the vast majority of human beings, regardless of age. They occur in the mother's milk, and probably in the tissues of the unborn child. . . .

Source: Rachel Carson, *Silent Spring*, Houghton Mifflin, 1962

7 According to Rachel Carson, what is **one** issue that has led to concerns about the environment?   [1]

_____

_____

Document 8a

Millions Join Earth Day Observances Across the Nation

Throngs jamming Fifth Avenue yesterday in response to a call for the regeneration of a polluted environment.

Source: *New York Times,* April 23, 1970 (adapted)

Document 8b

Earth Day, the first mass consideration of the globe's environmental problems, preempted [commanded] the attention and energies of millions of Americans, young and old, across the country yesterday. . . .

Organizers of Earth Day said more than 2,000 colleges, 10,000 grammar and high schools, and citizen groups in 2,000 communities had indicated intentions of participating. . . .

The purpose of the observance was to heighten public awareness of pollution and other ecological problems, which many scientists say urgently require action if the earth is to remain habitable. . . .

Summarizing the implications of the day's activities, Senator Nelson said:

"The question now is whether we are willing to make the commitment for a sustained national drive to solve our environmental problems." . . .

Source: Gladwin Hill, "Activity Ranges From Oratory to Legislation," *New York Times*, April 23, 1970

8 Based on these documents, state ***one*** reason the observance of Earth Day is important to the environmental movement.   [1]

_____

_____

Document 9a

> . . . Earth Day had consequences: it led to the Clean Air Act of 1970, the Clean Water Act of 1972, and the Endangered Species Act of 1973, and to the creation, just eight months after the event, of the Environmental Protection Agency. Throughout the nineteen-seventies, mostly during the Republican Administrations of Richard Nixon and Gerald Ford, Congress passed one environmental bill after another, establishing national controls on air and water pollution. And most of the familiar big green groups are, in their current form, offspring of Earth Day. Dozens of colleges and universities instituted environmental-studies programs, and even many small newspapers created full-time environmental beats. . . .

Source: Nicholas Lemann, "When the Earth Moved: What Happened to the Environmental Movement?"
The New Yorker, April 15, 2013

9*a* According to Nicholas Lemann, what is *one* impact of Earth Day? [1]

_____

_____

Document 9b

Frances Beinecke served as president of the Natural Resources Defense Council [NRDC] from 2006–2014. The Council writes and lobbies for public policy to protect the environment.

My work at NRDC has brought me to the front lines of the climate crisis. I have flown over the massive tar sands strip mines in the boreal forest. I have visited the homes of people coping with frack pads [an area of land used in the fracking process] and wastewater ponds in their backyards. And I have helped my neighbors recover from the devastation of Superstorm Sandy. . . .

Never in my lifetime have the challenges been greater than those we face from climate change. Never have the solutions been more clearly at hand. We know how to defuse the climate threat. We just have to act now. . . .

It's time for us, as Americans, to state as a national goal that we'll hit fast-forward on efforts to clean up our carbon pollution, invest in energy efficiency and shift to renewable power so that we will become a carbon-neutral nation that no longer contributes to climate change. . . .

We have already begun slashing climate change pollution. More than 3.4 million Americans are on the job every day helping to clean up our dirty power plants, get more electricity from the wind and sun, manufacture more hybrid and electric cars, and cut energy waste in our homes, at work and on the road. . . .

The modern environmental movement exists for one purpose: we're here to change the world—to become a place where we care for the natural systems of the Earth as if our very lives depended on them, because they do. That is not yet the world we live in. It is the world we must create.

Source: Frances Beinecke, "The World We Create: My New Book and a Message of Hope for the Planet," *Switchboard: National Resources Defense Council Blog*, October 14, 2014

9*b* According to Frances Beinecke, state *one* reason the environmental movement continues to be important. [1]

Part B: Essay

Directions: Write a well-organized essay that includes an introduction, several paragraphs, and a conclusion. Use evidence from at least *four* documents in the body of the essay. Support your response with relevant facts, examples, and details. Include additional outside information.

Historical Context:

> In the decades following World War II, significant domestic and foreign policy issues led to political and social tensions in the United States. These issues motivated individuals and groups to organize protest movements to bring about change. Protest movements such as the *civil rights movement,* the *anti–Vietnam War movement,* and the *environmental movement* met with varying degrees of success.

Task:

> Using the information from the documents and your knowledge of United States history, write an essay in which you
> Choose *two* protest movements mentioned in the historical context and for *each*
>
> * Describe the historical circumstances surrounding the protest movement
> * Discuss the extent to which the protest movement was successful

Guidelines:

In your essay, be sure to
* Develop all aspects of the task
* Incorporate information from *at least four* documents
* Incorporate relevant outside information
* Support the theme with relevant facts, examples, and details
* Use a logical and clear plan of organization, including an introduction and a conclusion that are beyond a restatement of the theme

Answers
June 2019
United States History and Government

Answer Key

PART I

1. 2	**11.** 4	**21.** 4	**31.** 4	**41.** 4
2. 4	**12.** 3	**22.** 2	**32.** 3	**42.** 2
3. 1	**13.** 2	**23.** 1	**33.** 1	**43.** 3
4. 3	**14.** 4	**24.** 3	**34.** 4	**44.** 1
5. 4	**15.** 4	**25.** 2	**35.** 4	**45.** 3
6. 2	**16.** 1	**26.** 1	**36.** 1	**46.** 2
7. 1	**17.** 1	**27.** 2	**37.** 1	**47.** 1
8. 1	**18.** 3	**28.** 3	**38.** 3	**48.** 2
9. 4	**19.** 2	**29.** 3	**39.** 2	**49.** 2
10. 3	**20.** 2	**30.** 4	**40.** 1	**50.** 3

PART II: Thematic Essay   *See* **Answers Explained** section.

PART III: Document-Based Question   *See* **Answers Explained** section.

Answers Explained

PART I (1–50)

1. **2** In colonial America, the Magna Carta, the English Bill of Rights, and the writings of John Locke contributed to the political ideals and practices of the colonists. All three texts encouraged colonists to challenge the absolute power of the British monarchy. The Magna Carta was a document written by English barons in 1215 to limit the power of the king. The document puts forth the idea that the will of the monarch can be bound by law and by legal procedures; in other words, his power is limited. The English Bill of Rights grew out of a series of events in England in the late 17th century. A crisis had developed involving religion and succession to the throne. Many Protestants were troubled by the possibility that the successors of the Catholic king, James II, would also be Catholic, and that England could become officially Catholic again. Protestant parliamentarians would not stand for this. They rose up in the Glorious Revolution (1688), which empowered Parliament and ended absolute monarchy in England. It also led to the establishment of the English Bill of Rights. The document establishes limits on the powers of the monarch and asserts certain basic rights of Parliament, including having regular meetings, free elections, and freedom of speech in sessions of Parliament. The English Bill of Rights also puts into writing certain individual rights, including the prohibition of cruel and unusual punishment and the right not to be taxed without Parliament's agreement. John Locke's writings were extremely influential on colonial political thought. His work was one of the main intellectual influences in the writing of the Declaration of Independence. He wrote *Two Treatises on Government* in the early 1690s to defend England's Glorious Revolution (1688) and to challenge Thomas Hobbes's defense of an absolutist monarchy. The eloquent preamble of the Declaration of Independence contains key elements of Locke's social contract theory. The theory is based on the idea that people are born with certain basic rights. Governments come into existence to protect these rights. The social contract calls for the people to surrender some of their freedoms to the rules of the government and for the government to protect people's natural rights. Conversely, Locke asserted, if a government violates people's natural rights, the people have the right to abolish it.

WRONG CHOICES EXPLAINED:

(1) The three texts did not contribute to the diversity of religious beliefs among the colonists. Religious diversity existed in colonial America due to the backgrounds of the various groups who immigrated to the colonies. Migrants to

the New World included British men and women from a variety of Protestant sects, such as Anglicans, Puritans, Separatists, and Quakers. Also, French Huguenots (Calvinist Protestants), Jews, and Catholics made their way to the colonies. Enslaved Africans also brought with them a variety of religious beliefs, including Islam and a wide variety of traditional polytheistic belief systems. The concepts of religious toleration and religious freedom developed over time in the colonies due to the diverse nature of colonial society, as well as to the influence of Enlightenment thinkers.

(3) The three texts did not contribute to the economic relationships between the colonists and the mother country. Such economic relationships were shaped by mercantilist principles. There are several important elements of mercantilism. Mercantilism holds that nations increase their power by increasing their share of the world's wealth. A primary means to increasing wealth is for a nation to maintain a favorable balance of trade, with the value of exports exceeding the value of imports. Mercantilist theory suggests that governments should advance these goals by maintaining colonies so as to have a steady and inexpensive source for raw materials. The theory also holds that the colonies should not develop manufacturing but should purchase manufactured goods from the ruling country. Great Britain imposed several navigation laws on the American colonies to make sure the colonies fulfilled their role in the economic relationship.

(4) The three texts did not contribute to the demands of colonists to end the slave trade and the practice of slavery. Most white colonists did not question or challenge the practice of slavery. Colonists who did hold anti-slavery views were influenced by different religious and political traditions.

2. **4** Before 1763, most American colonists settled near the Atlantic Coast or rivers because navigable water offered easier access to trade and employment. Early coastal settlements included Plymouth (1620), Massachusetts Bay Colony (present-day Boston) (1630), Providence (1636), Newport (Rhode Island) (1639), and New Amsterdam (present-day New York) (1624). These settlements were all established on protected harbors at the mouths of rivers. Jamestown (1607) was founded on the James River some 40 miles upriver from the Atlantic Ocean. Connecticut Colony (1636), present-day Hartford, was founded on the Connecticut River, about 40 miles upriver from the Long Island Sound. Such locations allowed for trade with European countries and with the West Indies and Africa. Rivers aided agricultural development through irrigation and transportation of goods. Within a generation, as the flow of English migrants into North America increased, settlements were established inland from these initial coastal and river settlements. The push of settlers into the interior of the continent increased tensions with Native American Indians.

WRONG CHOICES EXPLAINED:

(1) The reason that most American colonists settled near the Atlantic Coast or rivers in the period before 1763 was not that port cities could be more easily defended in times of war. In fact, port cities might be more vulnerable to attack by foreign naval forces. Early colonists were more concerned with conflicts with Native American Indians.

(2) The reason that most American colonists settled near the Atlantic Coast or rivers in the period before 1763 was not that valleys were less fertile. In fact, river valleys are more fertile. Periodic flooding of rivers results in the deposit of nutrient-rich silt on floodplains, producing extremely fertile soil.

(3) The reason that most American colonists settled near the Atlantic Coast or rivers in the period before 1763 was not that English colonists were only allowed to settle in these locations. In 1763, following the French and Indian War, the British did pass an act forbidding colonists from venturing beyond the Appalachian Mountains—the Proclamation Act. The act was intended to reduce tensions between colonists and American Indians, but it resulted in increasing colonial resentment of British policies.

3. **1** One way in which the Declaration of Independence and the original United States Constitution were similar is that both promote the idea of the consent of the governed. The phrase "consent of the governed" refers to the source of the government's power. The Declaration of Independence puts forth the idea that governments derive their "just powers from the consent of the governed." The idea drew inspiration from Enlightenment thinkers, such as John Locke. Its implementation in the newly formed United States represented a radical break with the political arrangements of the day. Most government structures in the 18th century world were based on monarchical power. Many of these monarchs contended that their mandate to rule was granted by "divine right," not the consent of the governed. The Constitution enshrined the concept of the consent of the governed into the legal governing structure of the United States by creating a House of Representatives that is elected by the people. Senators were initially selected by state legislatures, rather than voted on directly by the people. However, it is the people of each state that elect state legislatures, so even the Senate could be said to reflect the consent of the governed.

WRONG CHOICES EXPLAINED:

(2) Neither the Declaration of Independence nor the original United States Constitution promoted the idea of equal rights for women. While neither document explicitly excludes women from political equality, both documents accepted prevailing ideas around male domination in the political realm. The original

Constitution did not prohibit states from excluding women from voting. It was not until ratification of the 19th amendment, in 1920, that the right of women to vote in the United States was enshrined in the Constitution.

(3) Neither the Declaration of Independence nor the original United States Constitution promoted the idea of voting rights for all adult citizens. The declaration does not specifically address the issue of voting rights. The Constitution left voting rules to each state, allowing states to establish property qualifications for voting and to exclude adult citizens from voting because of their race or gender. Property requirements for voting were eliminated by most states by the 1830s. Amendments to the Constitution further broadened the electorate. The 15th amendment (1870) prevented states from denying a citizen the right to vote based on that citizen's race. The 19th amendment (1920) extended the right to vote to women. The 26th amendment (1971) prohibited using age as a reason to deny any citizen the right to vote who are at least 18 years old.

(4) Neither the Declaration of Independence nor the original United States Constitution promoted the idea of judicial review of unjust laws. The declaration does not focus on the specifics of the legal system that would be created in an independent United States. The Constitution established that federal judiciary power shall be vested in a "supreme Court" as well as additional "inferior" courts. The Constitution does not explicitly grant the Supreme Court the power of judicial review. That power—to review laws and determine whether they were constitutional—was explicitly established by the Court in the case of *Marbury* v. *Madison* (1803).

4. **3** The main purpose of the *Federalist Papers* was to urge ratification of the Constitution. The supporters of the Constitution labeled themselves Federalists. Three leading Federalists, Alexander Hamilton, John Jay, and James Madison, wrote a series of articles as the New York convention was debating ratification of the Constitution in 1787 and 1788. The articles were later published in book form—*The Federalist* (in the 20th century, the collection was published as the *Federalist Papers*). This highly influential political tract outlined the failures of the Articles of Confederation and the benefits of a powerful government, with checks and balances. In Federalist Number 10, Madison argued that a complex government, governing a large and diverse population, was the best guarantee of liberty. With such a complex government, no single group could gain control and dominate others. This argument challenged the traditional republican notion that republics must be small in order to be democratic. In Federalist Number 51, he argued for a separation of powers within the government and a system of checks and balances. In that essay, Madison asserted that "ambition must be made to counteract ambition."

WRONG CHOICES EXPLAINED:

(1) The main purpose of the *Federalist Papers* was not to discourage the creation of political parties; the articles were written in support of ratification of the Constitution. The writers saw the development of political parties, or factions, as inevitable. In Federalist Number 10, Madison argues that in a large republic, the effect of factions will be less than it would be in a small republic. In a small republic, one faction could dominate and restrain the liberty of the minority. This would be less likely, he argues, in a large republic.

(2) The main purpose of the *Federalist Papers* was not to support the candidacy of George Washington; the articles were written in support of ratification of the Constitution. Washington did not affiliate with a political party, although his policies and preferences were closer to those of the emerging Federalist Party than those of the Democratic-Republican Party. Washington was the unanimous choice for president of the 69 electors who cast votes in 1788–1789. At the time, electors cast two votes for two different candidates. John Adams received 34 of the second votes cast by electors and became vice-president (other candidates split the remaining second votes).

(4) The main purpose of the *Federalist Papers* was not to advocate independence from Great Britain; the articles were written in support of ratification of the Constitution. The articles were written in 1787 and 1788, over a decade after the United States had declared independence (1776). Great Britain recognized the independence of the United States by signing the Treaty of Paris in 1783.

5. **4** The inclusion of the elastic clause in the Constitution best supports the idea expressed in the quotation. Hamilton is arguing for a flexible document that could meet the needs of a changing society. Many people call the Constitution a living document because it can change—both through the use of the elastic clause and through the amendment clause. The elastic clause stretches the powers of Congress by allowing it to "make all laws necessary and proper" in regard to carrying out its functions. However, the definition of "necessary and proper" soon became a matter of much debate. In 1791, Alexander Hamilton pushed for the creation of a national bank. This national bank would be 20 percent publicly controlled and 80 percent privately controlled. Hamilton thought it was important to have wealthy investors financially and psychologically invested in the new government. Though the power to create a national bank was not granted to Congress in the Constitution, he argued that it was permissible under the elastic clause. Thomas Jefferson argued that the creation of a national bank was not "necessary and proper." Hamilton won this debate, and a national bank was created in 1791. It existed until 1811.

WRONG CHOICES EXPLAINED:

(1) The inclusion of eminent domain in the Constitution does not directly support the idea expressed in the quotation. The quotation focuses on the idea of a changeable Constitution. Eminent domain refers to a specific constitutional principle—that the government may, for a just price, force property owners to sell their property if the government deems that the property will be used for a public purpose. This power is in the fifth amendment of the Constitution.

(2) The inclusion of the electoral college in the Constitution does not directly support the idea expressed in the quotation. The quotation focuses on the idea of a changeable Constitution. The electoral college was established in Article Two of the Constitution, as the basic process for how the president would be elected. Today, after the popular vote for president on Election Day, election boards determine which candidate won in each of the states. Whichever candidate wins the popular vote in a particular state, that candidate receives the electoral votes for that state. (However, in two states, Maine and Nebraska, electoral votes can be divided between candidates.) The number of electors for each state is equal to the number of members of Congress from that state. Bigger states, therefore, get more electors.

(3) The inclusion of separation of powers in the Constitution does not directly support the idea expressed in the quotation. The quotation focuses on the idea of a changeable Constitution. Separation of powers refers to an unchanging, defining feature of the Constitution. Separation of powers describes the basic structure of the government. The framers of the Constitution created a governmental system with three separate branches—the legislative, the executive, and the judicial—each with the ability to check the powers of the other two. The goal was to keep the three branches in balance. The framers were very conscious of the problems of a government with limitless powers. After living under the British monarchy, they came to believe that a powerful government without checks was dangerous to liberty.

6. **2** The main objection to the adoption of the Constitution was based primarily on the belief that individual freedoms could be restricted by a strong central government. Such objections were voiced by a group of opponents—who came to be known as "Antifederalists"—during the debate over ratification of the United States Constitution, which occurred between 1787 and 1789. Antifederalists feared the Constitution would create an omnipotent and unaccountable government. They had vivid memories of the intrusions of the royal British government into their lives, and wanted to have assurances that the people would have basic protections from government abuses. Many Antifederalists agreed to support ratification of the Constitution only after the framers assured them that a bill of

rights would be immediately added to the Constitution. The Bill of Rights, the first ten amendments to the Constitution, was ratified in 1791. The first amendment protects the people from government limitations on freedom of expression and of religion. It also affirms the right of people to protest against government actions. In addition, it also established separation of church and state. The second amendment established the right to "bear arms." The fourth amendment holds that people are to be free from unwarranted searches by government authorities. The fifth and sixth amendments list a variety of protections that people have when they are accused of crimes, such as the right to a "speedy and public trial." The eighth amendment states that the government shall not inflict "cruel and unusual" punishments on people.

WRONG CHOICES EXPLAINED:

(1) Limiting the number of new states that could be admitted to the Union was not a concern of opponents of adopting the Constitution. The Constitution spelled out the process for admitting new states. The Admissions Clause, in Article Four, gives Congress the authority to admit new states. Over time, the Supreme Court has asserted that the Constitution requires all states to be admitted on an equal footing, though this is not specifically spelled out in the Admissions Clause. There is no limit on the number of states admitted.

(3) The impact of a separate judiciary on the effectiveness of the government was not a concern of those opposing the adoption of the Constitution. The Constitution, in Article Three, calls for the establishment of a separate federal judiciary comprised of a Supreme Court and additional "inferior courts," created by Congress.

(4) The enhanced power of the South, stemming from its slave population, was not a concern of opponents of adopting the Constitution. The number of slaves in a particular state did increase that state's representation in the House of Representatives. The Three-fifths Compromise, arrived at during the Constitutional Convention (1787), stipulated that slaves, labeled "other persons" in the Constitution, would be counted as three-fifths of a person in the census. This issue, however, was not a primary concern of those opposed to the Constitution.

7. **1** The use of the electoral college reflects a distrust, among many of the framers of the Constitution, of the average citizen's judgment. Many of the supporters of the Constitution, known as Federalists, voiced their fears of democracy and of the judgment of ordinary people. In a speech to the Constitutional Convention in June 1787, Alexander Hamilton was quoted as saying that within all communities, there are "the few and the many." The first, he said, were the

"rich and the well-born"; the second group was comprised of the "mass of the people." He said that the second group should not be fully trusted with the levers of government, because they "seldom judge or determine right." His solution was to give the wealthy a more prominent voice in the government—"a distinct, permanent share in the Government." The creation of the electoral college demonstrates this concern. It was created as a check on the popular will of the people. It is the electoral college, not the popular vote of the people, that ultimately determines who will be president. Initially, the plan was for electors to be chosen, in a nonpartisan fashion, either by nominating committees or by popular vote. It was expected that these independent-minded men would then choose the most qualified men to be the president. Over time the system become more partisan, driven by voter preference. Today, after the popular vote for president on Election Day, election boards determine which candidate won in each of the states. Whichever candidate wins in a particular state, that candidate gets the electoral votes for that state. (However, in two states, Maine and Nebraska, electoral votes can be divided between candidates.)

WRONG CHOICES EXPLAINED:

(2) The use of the electoral college does not reflect a belief that political parties strengthen the campaign process. The Constitution does not assert that political parties should be part of the electoral college process. It was initially thought that electors would choose a president based on qualifications rather than on party affiliation. Formal political parties developed over time, after the Constitution had been ratified.

(3) The use of the electoral college does not reflect a desire to end property qualifications for voting. The opposite is closer to the truth. The electoral college was intended to put more power in the hands of wealthier men. Property qualifications, which existed in many states when the Constitution was ratified, stipulate that citizens must own a certain amount of property in order to vote. By the end of the 1820s, most states reduced or removed property qualifications for voting so that most free males had the right to vote.

(4) The use of the electoral college does not reflect a commitment to universal suffrage. When the Constitution was ratified, most states limited voting rights to free, white, male property owners. The electoral college, by granting the power to elect the president to a select group of men, did not challenge existing voting restrictions. Over time, the electorate has broadened. By the end of the 1820s, most states had eliminated property qualifications for voting. The Constitution was amended three times to expand voting rights. The 15th amendment (1870) barred discrimination based on race in voting, the 19th amendment (1920) extended the vote to women, and the 26th amendment (1971) lowered the minimum age requirement for voting to 18.

8. **1** The best title for the diagram is "Methods of Amending the Constitution." The diagram shows that either Congress (by two-third majorities in both houses) or a national convention, called by Congress, can propose a constitutional amendment. Then, three-fourths of the states must approve an amendment for it to be ratified. The state-by-state approval process can occur by the consent of the state legislatures or by special state ratifying conventions. The process is difficult, but not insurmountable. Twenty-seven amendments have been added to the Constitution. The amendment process has led to the ending of slavery (13th amendment, 1865), the federal income tax (16th amendment, 1913), women's suffrage (19th amendment, 1920), and an establishment of term limits for the presidency (22nd amendment, 1951).

WRONG CHOICES EXPLAINED:

(2) The title "Procedures of the Executive Branch" would not be appropriate for the diagram. Such a diagram might include the following items: "Nominating department heads and Supreme Court justices," "Signing legislation," and "Carrying out duties as commander-in-chief."

(3) The title "Process of Nominating Presidential Candidates" would not be appropriate for the diagram. Such a diagram might include the following items: "Running in state primary elections," "Having debates among candidates," and "Participating in national nominating conventions."

(4) The title "Admission of New States to the Union" would not be appropriate for the diagram. Such a diagram might include the following items: "The proposed state officially petitioning Congress for statehood," "Both the Senate and the House voting to accept the state," and "The president signing a bill to accept the state."

9. **4** The United States wanted to acquire New Orleans in 1803 in order to secure a port that would improve the transportation of agricultural goods. In the late 1700s and early 1800s, pioneers crossed over the Appalachian Mountains and settled in the Mississippi and Ohio River Valleys and established farms. It was impractical to transport agricultural goods such as wheat and corn by overland routes to the population centers along the Eastern Seaboard. Roads were primitive and railroads had not yet been developed. Therefore, water routes down the Ohio and Mississippi Rivers to New Orleans and beyond became very important for the farmers. However, the United States did not possess New Orleans. Spain controlled it until 1800 and France did after that. The United States got control of it in 1803 as part of the Louisiana Purchase. President Thomas Jefferson overcame any doubts about the constitutionality of a territorial purchase and gave his approval to the purchase of the territory from France for a mere $15 million.

WRONG CHOICES EXPLAINED:

(1) The United States' desire to acquire New Orleans in 1803 was not connected with ending British influence in North America. New Orleans and the entire Louisiana Territory were controlled by France at the time, not by Great Britain.

(2) The United States' desire to acquire New Orleans in 1803 was not connected with promoting the growth of manufacturing in the region. Manufacturing was just in its infancy in the United States in 1803. Further, manufacturing developed in the northeast. The first factory in the United States was built in 1790 in Rhode Island. The Lowell, Massachusetts, textile mills opened in 1823. The region around New Orleans was primarily agricultural.

(3) The United States' desire to acquire New Orleans in 1803 was not connected with establishing a military base to defend against attacks from Mexico. Mexico did not become an independent nation until 1821. Even after independence, Mexico was not seen as a threat to the United States. Later, in the Mexican-American War (1846–1848), the United States proved to be more of a threat to Mexico than Mexico was to the United States.

10. **3** The Supreme Court decision in *Gibbons* v. *Ogden* (1824) is important because it expanded federal control over interstate trade. The Supreme Court affirmed that only the federal government could regulate trade between states. The Court invalidated a monopoly given by the legislature of New York to a ferryboat company to navigate the Hudson River between New York and New Jersey. The Court declared that since the river goes through or between two or more states, it is subject to the interstate commerce clause of the Constitution. Under the leadership of Chief Justice John Marshall (1801–1835), the Supreme Court issued several decisions that established the supremacy of federal laws over state laws. These decisions also included *Fletcher* v. *Peck* (1810), *Dartmouth College* v. *Woodward* (1819), and *McCulloch* v. *Maryland* (1819).

WRONG CHOICES EXPLAINED:

(1) The Supreme Court decision in *Gibbons* v. *Ogden* (1824) did not address the importation of manufactured goods. The Court has never banned the importation of manufactured goods. Earlier, Congress passed the Embargo Act (1807) as a response to the harassment of U.S. shipping by England and France. The act cut off all U.S. trade with any nation. Jefferson thought that this would pressure the belligerent nations to agree to leave U.S. ships alone. However, the main effect of the embargo was to cripple America's mercantile sector. The embargo was meant to avoid warfare, but the United States eventually did go to war with England in 1812. At different points the United States has discouraged the importation of manufactured goods by raising import duties on certain items.

(2) The Supreme Court decision in *Gibbons* v. *Ogden* (1824) did not address state investment in internal improvements. Many states, at the time, did invest money into internal improvements. In 1825, for example, New York completed the Erie Canal, which created an all-water route from New York City to the Midwestern communities around the Great Lakes. This connection facilitated settlement and trade between the Atlantic Coast and the Midwest.

(4) The Supreme Court decision in *Gibbons* v. *Ogden* (1824) did not address taxes on exported goods. The United States does not tax exports. Every country, including the United States, wants to maximize exports; taxes on American exports would make American products less desirable to other countries.

11. **4** Under Chief Justice John Marshall (1801–1835), Supreme Court decisions generally upheld Alexander Hamilton's belief that a loose interpretation of the Constitution could be used to increase federal power. By contrast, believers in a strict interpretation of the Constitution, such as Thomas Jefferson, sought to limit federal power. Hamilton and other believers in a loose interpretation of the Constitution relied on the elastic clause of the Constitution to support their views. The elastic clause is included in Article I, Section 8 of the Constitution. That section lists the specific powers of Congress. Some delegates feared that by listing specific powers, Congress would not be able to exercise additional powers, nor could it address changing circumstances. They therefore pushed for the elastic clause, which stretched the powers of Congress by allowing it to "make all laws necessary and proper" in carrying out its duties. Marshall shared Hamilton's view of a federal government with expansive powers. The decision in *Marbury* v. *Madison*, for example, strengthened the federal judiciary by asserting that the Supreme Court has the power to review laws and determine whether they are consistent with the Constitution. This power of judicial review has been the main function of the Supreme Court since then. In the case of *McCulloch* v. *Maryland*, the Court sided with the Bank of the United States, a federal institution, over the state of Maryland. Maryland had imposed heavy taxes on the local branch of the bank, hoping to tax it out of existence. The Court declared this act unconstitutional. *Gibbons* v. *Ogden* invalidated a monopoly on ferry transportation between New York and New Jersey that had been issued by New York, and asserted that only the federal government could regulate interstate trade.

WRONG CHOICES EXPLAINED:

(1) Alexander Hamilton did not uphold the belief that a national debt would violate the economic principles of the Constitution. Hamilton believed that a national debt, "if it is not excessive, will be to us a national blessing." He believed that if a government took on debt and paid it off in a timely fashion,

then wealthy individuals and institutions would be more likely to invest in the government in the future. As part of his economic program, he argued for increasing the national debt in order to pay off debts carried over from the Revolutionary War (including debts owed by the various states) at full value.

(2) Alexander Hamilton did not uphold the belief that states should have more economic power than the federal government. He believed the opposite. He wanted a strong federal government to guide economic activity. His economic plan called for the creation of a national bank, high federal tariffs on imported manufactured goods, and a federal excise tax on whiskey.

(3) Alexander Hamilton did not uphold the power of Congress should be greater than the power of the president. He promoted the idea of a strong executive. In some ways, Hamilton was enamored by Great Britain's monarchical system. In the end, he accepted the idea of three equal branches, each with the power to check the other two.

12. **3** In the 1855 letter, Abraham Lincoln opposed the Know-Nothing Party because it promoted resentment against minority groups. The Know-Nothing Party (formally known as the American Party) emerged in the 1840s and, by the 1850s, achieved electoral success in several states, especially in the Northeast. The defining issue of the Know-Nothing party was opposition to immigration. The party was the political wing of a growing anti-Catholic, anti-Irish nativist movement that gained traction in the wake of the large-scale Irish immigration of the late 1840s and 1850s. In the letter, Lincoln asserts that followers of the Know-Nothing Party were betraying basic American values. He reminds the recipient of the letter that the United States began by declaring that "all men are created equal." Lincoln wonders whether Americans will still adhere to this assertion. In the future, he predicts that followers of the Know-Nothing Party will try to rewrite the Declaration of Independence so that it reads, "all men are created equal, except negroes, and foreigners, and catholics." When that happens, Lincoln posits that he might want to emigrate to another country.

WRONG CHOICES EXPLAINED:
(1) The Know-Nothing Party did not take a position on imperialism. Imperialism did not become a contentious issue in the United States until the late 1890s. The U.S. engaged in imperialist acts following its victory in the Spanish-American War in 1898. Lincoln's opposition to the Know-Nothing Party was based on its promoting resentment against minority groups, not on foreign policy positions.

(2) The Know-Nothing Party did not favor unrestricted immigration. It wanted to restrict immigration, especially from Ireland. Lincoln's opposition to

the Know-Nothing Party was based on its promoting resentment against minority groups, including recent immigrants.

(4) The Know-Nothing Party did not want equal rights for all people. It promoted nativist and anti-Catholic sentiments. Lincoln's opposition to the Know-Nothing Party was based on its promoting resentment against minority groups.

13. **2** The Supreme Court's decision in *Dred Scott* v. *Sandford* was nullified by the passage of the 13th and 14th amendments. The 1857 case intensified the rift between pro-slavery and anti-slavery Americans and, in many ways, pushed the nation a bit closer to civil war. The case involved the fate of a slave named Dred Scott. Scott was owned by a doctor serving in the United States army. Scott and his wife, along with their owner, lived for a time in the state of Illinois and in the Wisconsin Territories, areas in which slavery had been banned by the Northwest Ordinance. Years after returning to Missouri, Scott sued for his and his wife's freedom on the grounds that they had lived for a time in free areas and that that made them free. The Supreme Court did not find Dred Scott's arguments persuasive. First, the Court ruled that Scott was still a slave and did not even have the right to initiate a lawsuit. That could have been the end of the decision. However, the Court went further. In regard to the issue of free territories, the Supreme Court ruled that Congress had overstepped its bounds in declaring the northern portion of the Louisiana Purchase territory off-limits to slavery. It therefore invalidated the Missouri Compromise of 1820. The Court went even further than that. Not only did Dred Scott not have standing to file suit, the Court declared that no African Americans, not even free men and women, were entitled to citizenship in the United States because they were, according to the Court, "beings of an inferior order." Later, the 13th amendment (1865) ended slavery in the United States, rendering any references to slavery in the Dred Scott decision moot. The 14th amendment (1868) nullified the Court's assertion that African Americans were not entitled to citizenship in the United States. The amendment asserted that all persons born on United States soil were citizens of the United States. It also stated that no person shall be denied "equal protection of the laws."

WRONG CHOICES EXPLAINED:
(1) The Kansas-Nebraska Act did not nullify the Supreme Court's decision in *Dred Scott* v. *Sandford*. The Kansas-Nebraska Act was passed in 1854, three years before the Dred Scott decision. Furthermore, an act of Congress cannot nullify a Supreme Court decision; only the Court or a constitutional amendment can do that. The Kansas-Nebraska Act allowed for the possibility of slavery, under the principle of popular sovereignty, in the territories of Kansas and Nebraska—areas that had been closed to slavery by the Missouri Compromise (1820).

Following passage of the act, violence erupted in "Bleeding Kansas" as pro-slavery and anti-slavery men fought for control of the territory.

(3) The Compromise of 1850 did not nullify the Supreme Court's decision in *Dred Scott* v. *Sandford*. The compromise was reached nine years before the Dred Scott decision. Furthermore, an act of Congress cannot nullify a Supreme Court decision; only the Court or a constitutional amendment can do that. The compromise grew out of the controversy around California's application for statehood as a free state. When Southern senators objected to the admission of an additional free state, Senate negotiators worked out a series of measures that became known as the Compromise of 1850. The most important elements of the compromise were the admittance of California as a free state, which pleased Northern politicians, and a more stringent Fugitive Slave Law, which pleased Southern politicians.

(4) The Reconstruction Act did not nullify the Supreme Court's decision in *Dred Scott* v. *Sandford*. An act of Congress cannot nullify a Supreme Court decision; only the Court or a constitutional amendment can do that. Congress passed the Military Reconstruction Act and three other acts in 1867 in order to reorganize the South (except for Tennessee) as conquered territories. The act divided the South into five military zones. In order to be readmitted, the Southern states had to provide basic rights to African Americans and had to ratify the 14th amendment.

14. **4** The Civil War directly affected the Northern economy by stimulating the growth of factories. The Civil War spurred rapid industrialization of the North. During the Civil War, the Union government required an enormous amount of war materials, from guns and bullets to boots and uniforms. Manufacturers rose to the occasion by rapidly modernizing production. These changes in production sped up the process of industrialization that was in its beginning stages before the war. Key elements of this industrial growth were the development of the railway industry, the use of steam power in factories, the growth of the steel industry, the development of mass production, and the consolidation of big business. Two important changes that occurred as a result of this industrial growth were increased urbanization and the growth of labor unions.

WRONG CHOICES EXPLAINED:
(1) Severe depression was not an impact of the Civil War on the Northern economy. The spending involved in carrying out the Civil War expanded the Northern economy. There was an economic downturn in the decade following the Civil War—the Panic of 1873, which set off an economic depression that lasted from 1873 to 1877. Economic historians attribute the downturn to events

in Europe, speculative investments, inflation, and the demonetization of silver, but not to the Civil War itself. It is one of several economic downturns that have occurred throughout American history.

(2) The destruction of large areas of farmland was not an impact of the Civil War on the Northern economy. The vast majority of fighting in the Civil War took place in the South. The one major battle that took place in the North was the Battle of Gettysburg in Pennsylvania (1863).

(3) The expansion of the canal system was not an impact of the Civil War on the Northern economy. The era of canal building was largely over by the time of the Civil War. After 1830, railroads began to replace canals as a more efficient means of moving goods within the United States.

15. **4** Rapid industrialization during the late 1800s contributed to an increase in immigration to the United States. In response to the demand for labor caused by industrialization, the United States became a major destination for immigrants. During the 1860s, a little over two million new residents entered the United States. That figure jumped to nearly nine million for the first decade of the 20th century. Between 1880 and 1920, an estimated 20 million people, from Russia, Italy, Poland, the Balkan region, and elsewhere, immigrated to the United States. These "new immigrants" settled primarily in the growing industrial cities of the Northeast and the Midwest, such as New York, Philadelphia, Cleveland, and Chicago. Rapid industrialization and immigration led to another important social change— urbanization. Between 1860 and 1900, the number of Americans who lived in cities jumped from 6.2 million to over 30 million, which amounted to a shift in the urban population from 20 percent of the total population to 40 percent.

WRONG CHOICES EXPLAINED:
(1) Rapid industrialization during the late 1800s did not contribute to a decline in the membership of the American Federation of Labor (AFL). The opposite occurred. The AFL was one of several unions that formed and grew after the Civil War to increase the bargaining power of industrial workers as they dealt with owners. Many workers thought they had a better chance to gain concessions from owners if they banded together in unions. The AFL, which included only skilled workers, was born in 1886.

(2) Rapid industrialization during the late 1800s did not contribute to a reduction in government regulation of railroads. The opposite occurred. Several states passed regulatory measures in response to popular pressure. Farmers protested the power, abuses, and rate structures of the major railroad companies. After the Supreme Court ruled in *Wabash* v. *Illinois* (1886) that individual states could not regulate railroads because they crossed state lines, the federal

government created the Interstate Commerce Commission (1887) to regulate railroads. However, the commission was chronically underfunded and was, therefore, ineffective.

(3) Rapid industrialization during the late 1800s did not contribute to a rise in the number of family farms. The opposite occurred. Mechanization and mass-production techniques affected agriculture as much as it affected industry. Expensive, motorized machinery, such as the mechanical reaper and the combine harvester, replaced hand-held tools. Mechanization had both positive and negative effects for American farmers. Mechanization increased overall agricultural production and reduced the man-hours needed for agricultural tasks. At the same time, it worked to undermine small-scale family farms.

16. **1** An important factor that aided the building of the transcontinental railroad was the federal government providing free land to the railroad companies. The completion of the transcontinental railroad at Promontory Summit, Utah, in 1862 was a milestone in the development of a network of railroad lines that connected the far reaches of the country. Railroads sped up the movement of goods and expanded markets. The government encouraged this expansion of the railroad network by giving railroad companies wide swaths of land. These generous land grants totaled more than 180 million acres, an area equal to the size of Texas. The railroad companies built rail lines on this land and also sold land adjacent to the tracks.

WRONG CHOICES EXPLAINED:

(2) Railroads did not establish fair rates for their customers. They were consistently accused of establishing unfair rate structures. Starting in the 1870s, groups that organized to promote the interests of farmers, such as the Grange, became concerned about the power and abuses of large railroad companies. Railroads often overcharged small-scale farmers. The Grange successfully pushed for laws in several states in the 1870s and 1880s to limit abusive practices by railroads.

(3) Congress did not repeal antitrust laws against the railroads. The Sherman Antitrust Act of 1890 was designed to break up trusts. The act had limited success. At first, only a few trusts were challenged. Ironically, the act was used with equal vigor against unions, on the grounds that they were illegal formations that interfered with free trade. In the case of *United States* v. *E.C. Knight Company* (1895), the Supreme Court greatly limited the scope of the act by making a distinction between trade (which would be subject to the act) and manufacturing (which would not).

(4) The Supreme Court did not approve public ownership of the railroad industry; the issue was never brought before the Court. In the United States,

there has been great reluctance to bring any type of economic activity under government ownership. Such moves strike many as steps toward socialism, though many European countries have much greater government involvement in economic activities, including railroads.

17. **1** Big business used strikebreakers and lockouts to limit the power of labor unions. Owners of industrial firms, often labeled "robber barons," could employ a variety of tactics to gain the upper hand in conflicts with labor unions during the late 1800s. One common tactic used by employers was hiring replacement workers, called "scabs" by the union movement, during strikes. Another tactic was locking out workers—preventing them from working and from getting paid. An employer might threaten a lockout to force unionized workers to accept new conditions (such as a pay cut). If the union refused to capitulate, the owner might carry out the threat and lock out the workers. This occurred at the Homestead steel mill in Homestead, Pennsylvania, in 1892. After several wage cuts and disputes with the owners, the union called for a strike. Andrew Carnegie and his plant manager, in an attempt to break the union, shut down the plant and locked out all the workers. The workers responded by declaring a strike. A pitched battle over control of the plant ensued, involving the workers and the community against armed Pinkerton guards and, later, National Guard troops. Ultimately, the union suffered a major defeat, setting back efforts to unionize steelworkers. Employers in the late 1800s also maintained lists of workers who were seen as "troublemakers." These lists would include workers who participated in union activities or who publicly supported political organizations sympathetic to workers. Such blacklists would be distributed among employers, allowing them to deny employment to individuals on the list. Most of the pitched workplace battles of the late 1800s ended in defeat for the workers. Workers saw their position and status erode during this period.

WRONG CHOICES EXPLAINED:
(2) Neither picketing nor walkouts were tactics used by big business in the late 1800s to limit the power of labor unions. Both terms are associated with labor strikes. Striking workers frequently engage in picketing—gathering and marching outside the entrance of their place of employment. The goals of a picket line are both to publicize the cause and to dissuade replacement workers and customers from entering the establishment. A walkout is a spontaneous strike. Normally, strikes are voted on ahead of time by the union; walkouts can occur with little to no advance warning.

(3) Neither collective bargaining nor mediation were tactics used by big business in the late 1800s to limit the power of labor unions. Collective bargaining is the process of a union negotiating on behalf of all the workers in the union.

Instead of each worker bargaining individually with management, unionized workers bargain collectively through their union. Mediation describes efforts by a third party to resolve a labor dispute. The role of the mediator is to listen to the positions of both parties, to make suggestions for a resolution, and to help them reach an agreement satisfactory to both parties. Generally, the results of mediation are not binding. A conflict might end up in arbitration, where the results of the arbitrator are binding on both parties.

(4) Neither wage increase nor shorter hours were tactics used by big business in the late 1800s to limit the power of labor unions. Both are goals of labor unions. A labor strike that resulted in significant wage increases as well as a shorter workday would, almost certainly, represent a victory for the union.

18. **3** The constitutional right that was the central focus in *Plessy* v. *Ferguson* (1896) was equal protection of the law under the 14th amendment. In that case, the Supreme Court ruled that separate rail cars for African Americans were permissible, as long as the facilities for both races were of equal quality. In the case, the Supreme Court decided that racial segregation did not violate the equal protection provision of the 14th amendment. The decision was a setback for those who sought an end to the Jim Crow system of racial segregation in the South. Jim Crow laws were state and local ordinances that first appeared after Reconstruction ended (1877). Typical laws called for separate schools or separate train cars for African Americans. Opponents of racial segregation argued that Jim Crow laws violated the 14th amendment (1868). The amendment, ratified during Reconstruction, states that no person shall be denied "equal protection of the laws." Jim Crow laws, opponents argued, violated the 14th amendment because the laws relegated African Americans to inferior public accommodations and had the effect of making African Americans second-class citizens. However, the Court disagreed. The "separate but equal" doctrine allowed for the continuation of the Jim Crow system until the 1950s and 1960s. The beginning of the end to the system came with the *Brown* v. *Board of Education* decision of 1954.

WRONG CHOICES EXPLAINED:
(1) The constitutional issue of freedom of assembly, as stipulated in the first amendment (1791), was not the focus of *Plessy* v. *Ferguson* (1896). The Supreme Court has generally struck down attempts to limit freedom of assembly. In *Edwards* v. *South Carolina* (1963), for example, the Court overturned the convictions of students arrested for peaceful demonstrations against segregation. The decision stated that the state could not "make criminal the peaceful expression of unpopular views." In *Village of Skokie* v. *National Socialist Party* (1978), the Court ruled that Nazis could not be prohibited from marching peacefully because of the content of their message.

(2) The constitutional issue of due process of the law, as stipulated in the fifth amendment (1791), was not the focus of *Plessy* v. *Ferguson* (1896). The due process clause of the fifth amendment—stating that no one shall "be deprived of life, liberty, or property, without due process of law"—deals with the legal procedures the state must follow in administering justice. The idea of due process is to balance the power of the legal system with the rights of individuals. Supreme Court decisions have interpreted the due process clause in a variety of ways. For example, in the case of *Dred Scott* v. *Sandford* (1857), the Court ruled that prohibiting slavery in U.S. territories would violate the due process clause of the fifth amendment. Other cases, including *Santa Clara County* v. *Southern Pacific Railroad* (1886), have extended due process protections to corporations, based on the theory that they are "legal persons" (establishing "corporate personhood").

(4) The constitutional issue of equal voting rights, as stipulated in the 15th amendment (1870), was not the focus of *Plessy* v. *Ferguson* (1896). In the 19th century the Court narrowed the scope of the 15th amendment. In *United States* v. *Reese* (1876), the Court upheld voting restrictions that were, on the surface, race neutral, but were clearly intended to prevent African Americans from voting. These restrictions included poll taxes, literacy tests, and a grandfather clause. In the 20th century, the Court has interpreted the 15th amendment more broadly. In 1966, the Court ruled, in *Harper* v. *Virginia State Board of Elections*, that state poll taxes violated the fourteenth amendment's equal protection clause.

19. **2** The cartoon is criticizing business consolidation. The specific business being criticized is the Standard Oil Company created by John D. Rockefeller. The cartoonist is depicting the extent of the power Standard Oil exerted in the United States. Standard Oil is represented as an octopus with its tentacles wrapped around the banking and insurance industries, railroads and shipping firms, smaller oil and gas companies, and even a town. The men who established these giant corporate entities were given the nickname "robber barons," implying that they had the power of a medieval baron and the scruples of a common criminal. Giant corporations, such as Standard Oil, are a post–Civil War phenomenon. In the last three decades of the 19th century, corporations came to play a very large role in society. Several of these corporations were able to exercise near-monopoly control of a particular industry. The formation of trusts was seen as harmful to the interests of consumers. Consequently, the government passed the Sherman Antitrust Act. The act had limited success. In the case of *United States* v. *E.C. Knight Company* (1895), the Supreme Court greatly limited the scope of the act by making a distinction between trade (which would be subject to the act) and manufacturing (which would not).

WRONG CHOICES EXPLAINED:

(1) The cartoon is not criticizing environmental degradation. Unregulated industrial growth in the late 19th century took a major toll on the environment. Slowly, reformers pushed for government action. An early champion of preserving wilderness was John Muir. He was one of the founders of the Sierra Club (1892), an organization dedicated to preserving wilderness and to monitoring the federal government's oversight of protected lands. President Theodore Roosevelt (1901–1909) championed the cause of environmental conservation. In pursuit of his conservationist agenda, Roosevelt set aside millions of acres as protected areas. These included six national parks.

(3) The cartoon is not criticizing oil exploration. The cartoon depicts oil wells, but that is in order to show Standard Oil's ruthless crusade to dominate the entire oil processing industry, not to criticize oil exploration. In the 21st century, environmentalists have been critical of government efforts to open protected areas and off-shore sites to oil exploration.

(4) The cartoon is not criticizing federal tax laws. The cartoon does not make any allusions to tax laws. Federal taxes consisted of import duties at the time.

20. **2** One result of the Spanish-American War (1898) was that Puerto Rico became a possession of the United States. The Spanish-American War lasted only several months, but profoundly impacted the direction of the United States. The historical circumstances that led to the war are varied. Many Americans became sympathetic to Cubans who were fighting for independence from Spain. By the 1890s, the conflict became intense with Spanish authorities taking extreme and brutal measures to suppress those seeking independence. Also, some American businessmen were angered by the interruption of the sugar harvest by the fighting between Cuban rebels and Spanish forces. Finally, a United States battleship, the U.S.S. *Maine*, exploded and sunk in the harbor of Havana, Cuba. Many in the United States thought that the destruction of the ship was the work of Spain, especially after American newspapers bluntly accused Spain of the crime, despite the scarcity of evidence. The Spanish-American War was brief. The U.S. declared war on Spain in April; an armistice was signed in August. The United States and Spain negotiated the Treaty of Paris (1898) following the war. In the treaty, Spain agreed to cede Puerto Rico, as well as the Philippines and Guam, to the United States; the United States agreed to pay Spain $20 million for these possessions.

WRONG CHOICES EXPLAINED:

(1) Cuba was not divided into spheres of influence following the Spanish-American War. Cuba, which had been a Spanish possession before the war, became independent following the war, but, in many ways, Cuba became

independent in name only. The United States took steps to ensure that American economic interests would not be challenged by a future Cuban administration. The term "spheres of influence" was applied to China in the late 1800s. By the 1890s, the major European powers had established spheres of influence in China. These nations each declared that they had exclusive trading privileges in their sphere of influence. The Open Door Policy, put forth by the administration of President William McKinley in 1900, asserted that all of China should be open to trade with all nations. The European nations begrudgingly accepted this concept.

(3) The Philippines did not become a Spanish colony following the Spanish-American War. It had been a Spanish colony before the war. The Treaty of Paris transferred possession of the Philippines to the United States. A resistance movement against American control developed in the Philippines and a bloody war, known as the Philippine-American War, ensued. Filipino forces were led by Emilio Aguinaldo. The war cost the American forces 4,000 lives; over 20,000 members of the Filipino resistance died in the conflict, and up to another 100,000 civilians died.

(4) The United States did not lose control of Panama following the Spanish-American War. The United States gained control of the Panama Canal Zone in 1903, five years after the Spanish-American War. Before 1903, Panama was a region of Colombia. American investors had picked the narrow piece of land as an ideal location for a canal. When Colombia refused the United States' offer of $10 million to build a canal, American investors, with the backing of President Theodore Roosevelt and the U.S. military, instigated a "rebellion" in Panama against Colombia. Panama became an independent country and immediately allowed the United States to build and administer a canal. Much later, the United States did agree to give up control of the Panama Canal. President Jimmy Carter negotiated two treaties with Panama in 1977 in which the United States agreed to turn over the Canal Zone to Panama by the end of 1999 (which occurred as agreed upon).

21. **4** The federal actions mentioned in the question—the Chinese Exclusion Act (1882), the Gentlemen's Agreement (1907), and the Emergency Quota Act (1921)—all demonstrate that Americans have favored limiting immigration at different times in the nation's history. Immigration has been a contentious issue throughout American history. The first two items mentioned reflect the strong anti-Asian racism at the time. Racist assumptions held that Asian immigrants would never fully assimilate into the United States. The Gold Rush in California (1848–1855) and the building of the transcontinental railroad attracted many Chinese immigrants to the West. The Chinese Exclusion Act, passed by Congress in 1882, prevented Chinese workers from entering the country. These workers were

generally employed in unskilled positions. It was the only instance of legislation prohibiting a particular nationality from entering the country. In the late 1800s, many Japanese people immigrated to the West Coast of the United States. In California, these Japanese immigrants often suffered discrimination. In the early years of the 20th century, California passed legislation ordering "Orientals" to be segregated from white students in the public school system. When Japan protested, President Theodore Roosevelt and Japanese leaders negotiated a "Gentlemen's Agreement" in which Roosevelt agreed to pressure California to reverse this legislation and Japan agreed to limit the number of emigrants coming into the United States. Later, in the period immediately following World War I, anti-immigrant sentiment, known as nativism, rose steeply. A large wave of immigrants from southern and eastern Europe had arrived in the United States between 1880 and 1920. There are several reasons nativists resented this new wave of immigration. Some nativists focused on the fact that most of the new immigrants were not Protestant, while others objected to the cacophony of languages heard on the streets of New York or Chicago. Some nativists associated the immigrants with either radical movements or drunkenness. Finally, working class people feared that low wage immigrant laborers would take jobs from native-born American workers. This sentiment led to passage of the Emergency Quota Act of 1921. This act greatly reduced the number of immigrants allowed into the United States by establishing quotas for different nations based on the numbers of each national group present in the United States decades earlier. A later act, the National Origins Act (1924), reduced the quotas of different nationalities even further.

WRONG CHOICES EXPLAINED:

(1) The federal actions mentioned in the question—the Chinese Exclusion Act (1882), the Gentlemen's Agreement (1907), and the Emergency Quota Act (1921)—do not demonstrate that Americans have supported the principle of open immigration. Throughout history, many Americans have held a welcoming attitude toward immigrants. Many Americans see the United States as a refuge from oppressive regimes in different parts of the world. In addition, since many Americans are descended from immigrants, they want to give others the same opportunities in the United States that their parents or grandparents were afforded. Also, many Americans have seen immigration as a strong engine for economic growth; immigrants bring their labor power, as well as their purchasing power, to the United States. However, the three items reflect anti-immigrant sentiment.

(2) The federal actions mentioned in the question—the Chinese Exclusion Act (1882), the Gentlemen's Agreement (1907), and the Emergency Quota Act (1921)—do not demonstrate that Americans provided immigrants equal access

to jobs and social programs. Many immigrants have benefited from employment opportunities and social programs in the United States. However, the implementation of the actions in the question reflect moves in the opposite direction. Nativists were determined to deny foreign-born workers better-paying jobs and access to social programs.

(3) The federal actions mentioned in the question—the Chinese Exclusion Act (1882), the Gentlemen's Agreement (1907), and the Emergency Quota Act (1921)—do not demonstrate that Americans forced immigrants to settle in designated areas. This has never been a serious proposal in American history. Immigrants have been denied certain housing opportunities and have gravitated toward certain ethnic enclaves, but there have not been proposals to force immigrants to settle in certain areas of the country. During World War II, President Franklin D. Roosevelt issued Executive Order 9066 (1942), authorizing the government to remove 120,000 Japanese Americans, two-thirds of them citizens, from West Coast states and relocate them to camps throughout the West. In the case of *Korematsu* v. *United States* (1944), the Supreme Court ruled that the relocation was acceptable on the grounds of national security. However, this relocation only lasted for the duration of the war; it was not permanent.

22. **2** In the early 20th century, muckraking authors Upton Sinclair and Ida Tarbell primarily criticized the federal government for ignoring abuses by big government. The term *muckrakers* refers to the crusading journalists and writers of the Progressive Era who exposed wrongdoing by government officials, showed the negative side of industrialization, and let the world see a variety of social ills. Upton Sinclair, for example, wrote a stirring book, *The Jungle* (1906), that exposed conditions in the meatpacking industry at the turn of the 20th century. Though the book is a novel, it was thoroughly researched. The conditions of the meatpacking industry were extremely unsanitary and dangerous. The public uproar that followed publication of the book led Congress to pass two laws in 1906—the Meat Inspection Act and the Pure Food and Drug Act, which established the Food and Drug Administration. Ida M. Tarbell's book, *The History of the Standard Oil Company* (1904), exposed the ruthlessness of John D. Rockefeller's oil company. Her book contributed to the government breakup of the Standard Oil Company in 1911. The push toward increased regulation represented a break with nineteenth-century laissez-faire economic policies. The policy of laissez-faire asserts that government should limit, as much as possible, any interference in the economy. The French phrase *laissez-faire* means "to let alone."

WRONG CHOICES EXPLAINED:

(1) In the early 19th century, neither Upton Sinclair nor Ida Tarbell criticized the government for wasting money on foreign wars. Several authors were critical of American foreign policy in the early 20th century. For example, the author Mark Twain was vice president of the American Anti-Imperialist League from 1901 to the time of his death. In addition, some Progressive reformers were critical of United States' involvement in World War I.

(3) In the early 20th century, neither Upton Sinclair nor Ida Tarbell criticized the government for excessive regulation of the steel industry. In general, muckraking journalists such as Sinclair and Tarbell urged the government to expand its regulatory powers, not reduce them.

(4) In the early 20th century, neither Upton Sinclair nor Ida Tarbell criticized the government for overspending on social welfare programs. Many muckraking journalists and Progressive Era reformers urged the government to create social welfare programs. However, it was not until the New Deal of the 1930s that the government began to play a major role in ensuring the social welfare of vulnerable individuals.

23. **1** During the Progressive Era, voters were given more opportunities to select political party candidates through direct primary elections. Today, primary elections are held by political parties to determine what candidate the party will select to run in the general election. Before direct primary elections, party leaders picked the candidates that would run in the general election. Wisconsin was the first state to adopt a direct primary in 1903. Most other states adopted direct primaries by 1916. Progressive reformers pushed for several reforms that would make the American political system more democratic. For example, they pushed for the 17th amendment (1913), which called for the direct election of senators. Previously, senators were chosen by state legislatures.

WRONG CHOICES EXPLAINED:

(2) The purpose of term limits has been to limit the power of elected officials, not to give voters a greater say in selecting their party's candidates. Some reformers have pushed for term limits for elected officials over the years. Advocates of term limits argue that incumbent candidates have a built-in advantage over challengers; they can use the platform of their office to push for reelection. In addition, these reformers argue that term limits will bring more individuals into public office. Opponents of term limits argue that experienced office holders, such as state legislators or city counselors, might be better able to hold strong executives accountable and create a better sense of balance in government. The Supreme Court ruled in 1995 that states could not impose term

limits on their federal representatives. The 22nd amendment (1951) limited presidential power by allowing the president to serve only two terms.

(3) The purpose of the initiative and the recall has been to give voters more of a voice in the political process, but not to specifically give them a greater say in selecting their party's candidates. The recall would allow the populace to remove unpopular or corrupt elected officials from office before their terms ended. Voters would have to gather a certain number of signatures, and then a special election would be announced. At least nineteen states allow for the recall of state officials. The initiative would enable citizens to introduce a bill to the local or state legislature by petition.

(4) The purpose of public funding of elections has been to remove excessive monetary influence on politicians, not to give voters a greater say in selecting their party's candidates. Publicly funded elections, it is argued, would reduce corruption by funding elections with federal tax dollars. Candidates would not depend on campaign contributions from corporations or wealthy individuals.

24. **3** Theodore Roosevelt's Square Deal and Woodrow Wilson's New Freedom shared the goal of strengthening federal power over large corporations. Both Roosevelt (1901–1909) and Wilson (1913–1921) are considered Progressive presidents. These Progressive Era presidents moved federal policy away from the laissez-faire approach—or hands-off economic matters—that characterized federal policy in the 19th century. Roosevelt saw the concentration of economic power in a few hands as potentially dangerous to the economy as a whole. Using the Sherman Antitrust Act (1890), he made a point of pursuing "bad trusts"—ones that interfered with commerce—but not necessarily the biggest trusts. One of his first targets was the Northern Securities Company, a railroad holding company. His efforts at challenging monopolies earned him the nickname "trust buster." Roosevelt also pushed for important consumer protections in the wake of the publication of *The Jungle*, and stronger measures to protect the environment. Also, Roosevelt pushed for stronger regulation of the powerful railroad industry. Roosevelt strengthened the Interstate Commerce Commission (created in 1887) with the Elkins Act (1903), which targeted the railroad practice of granting rebates to favored customers, and the Hepburn Act (1906), which gave the commission greater latitude to set railroad rates. President Wilson was a strong supporter of small business and took a dim view of the growing power of large corporations. Wilson strengthened the antitrust powers of the federal government with the Clayton Antitrust Act (1914). President Wilson also pushed for the creation of the Federal Trade Commission (1914) to regulate business practices. One of the many regulatory responsibilities of the commission is reducing the power of trusts and guarding against "unfair trade practices."

WRONG CHOICES EXPLAINED:

(1) Neither Theodore Roosevelt's Square Deal nor Woodrow Wilson's New Freedom had the goal of achieving equal rights for minorities. The era of Progressive reform in the first two decades of the 20th century was also a low point in race relations in the United States, as a strong Ku Klux Klan organization, a pervasive Jim Crow system, and increased incidents of lynching characterized American society. Most white Progressive Era reformers, as well as the two Progressive-minded presidents in question, turned a blind eye to the problems of race in the United States. However, African American reformers took the lead in challenging racial discrimination. For instance, Ida B. Wells, an African-American muckraking journalist, challenged the mistreatment of African Americans in the country and exposed the horrors of lynching.

(2) Neither Theodore Roosevelt's Square Deal nor Woodrow Wilson's New Freedom had the goal of protecting the interests of big business. Both reform agendas sought to limit the power of big business by strengthening federal regulatory powers. By contrast, the Republican presidents of the 1920s generally sought to protect the interests of big business. President Calvin Coolidge famously said in 1925, "the chief business of the American people is business."

(4) Neither Theodore Roosevelt's Square Deal nor Woodrow Wilson's New Freedom had the goal of instituting laissez-faire policies. The French phrase *laissez-faire* means "to let alone." It describes a government policy that would take a hands-off approach in regard to economic activities. The Progressive Era presidents in question pursued policies to expand government intervention in economic activities.

25. **2** The Federal Reserve System was created in 1913 to control the money supply. The Federal Reserve Bank, which is part privately controlled and part publicly controlled, was created by legislation in 1913 during the administration of President Woodrow Wilson. One of its main functions is to regulate economic growth by regulating the supply of money. If the economy is sluggish, the Fed will attempt to stimulate economic growth by increasing the money supply; if inflation occurs, the Fed will attempt to slow down economic activity by reducing the money supply. An important mechanism for regulating the money supply is raising or lowering the interest rates at which the Fed loans money to other banks. Other banks follow suit, raising or lowering the interest rates at which they loan money to the public. By lowering interest rates, the Fed stimulates economic activity, making it more attractive for people to borrow money to make major purchases, thus putting more money into circulation.

WRONG CHOICES EXPLAINED:

(1) The Federal Reserve System (1913) was not created to balance the budget. A balanced budget would mean that governmental spending would not surpass its income. Balancing the budget has been a goal of conservative policymakers since the 1980s. Reformers have pushed for an amendment to the Constitution that would require a balanced federal budget. As of 2017, 29 states have submitted requests for a national amendment-proposing convention. Two-thirds, or 34, of the states are required for such a convention to occur.

(3) The Federal Reserve System (1913) was not created to insure savings account deposits. Later, President Franklin D. Roosevelt instituted federal regulation of the banking industry. As part of the New Deal, he pushed for passage of the Glass-Steagall Act (1933), which created the Federal Deposit Insurance Corporation (FDIC). The FDIC insures deposits, so that if a bank does fold, people would not lose their savings.

(4) The Federal Reserve System (1913) was not created to regulate the stock market. Later, President Franklin D. Roosevelt instituted federal regulation of the stock market. As part of the New Deal, he pushed for passage of the Securities and Exchange Commission (1934), which oversees stock market operations by monitoring transactions, licensing brokers, limiting buying on margin, and prohibiting insider trading.

26. **1** The three statements by President Woodrow Wilson demonstrate that during the three years before the United States entered World War I, he gradually changed his foreign policy goals. Wilson initially assumed that the United States could stay neutral in World War I and maintain commercial ties to nations on both sides of the conflict. However, England successfully blockaded U.S. ships from reaching Germany. Out of necessity, U.S. trade shifted to England exclusively. Germany responded by warning that U.S. ships in the waters off of Great Britain would be subject to attack by U-boats, or submarines. The sinking of the British ocean liner *Lusitania* infuriated many Americans (128 Americans were among the dead). Germany, however, wanted to keep the United States out of the war and agreed in the Sussex Pledge (1916) to make no surprise submarine attacks on U.S. ships. The United States took advantage of this pledge and traded extensively with Great Britain. In 1917, Germany rescinded the Sussex Pledge and declared that it would resume unrestricted submarine warfare. When Wilson ran for reelection in 1916, he still maintained an anti-war position, but after reelection, Wilson became increasingly convinced that United States participation in World War I was necessary to make the world "safe for democracy." The United States finally entered the war in 1917.

WRONG CHOICES EXPLAINED:

(2) The three statements by President Woodrow Wilson do not indicate that he eagerly became involved in a war. Initially, Wilson expressed a desire to remain neutral in regard to World War I. It was only over time, and in response to new circumstances, that Wilson changed his foreign policy goals, and urged Congress to issue a declaration of war.

(3) The three statements by President Woodrow Wilson do not indicate that he abused the principle of separation of powers. Wilson followed the procedures outlined in the Constitution in regard to the United States entering a war. He asked Congress for a declaration of war, and Congress voted affirmatively. If he had carried out military actions without congressional approval, this might be seen as an abuse of the principle of separation of powers. During the Vietnam War, Congress became increasingly concerned that President Richard Nixon had abused his power to deploy troops. After the United States withdrew from Vietnam, Congress passed the War Powers Act (1973) as an attempt to check presidential power and strengthen the legislative branch in matters of war.

(4) The three statements by President Woodrow Wilson do not indicate that he was consistent in his policy of strict neutrality. The first statement demonstrates Wilson's desire to stay neutral in regard to World War II. However, the second and third statements indicate that he had changed his foreign policy goals and was ready to intervene in World War I.

27. **2** President Warren Harding's call for a "return to normalcy" meant that the United States should reduce its role in world affairs. The phrase was used by Harding during his presidential campaign of 1920. His call for a "return to normalcy" implied a rejection of the internationalist impulses that propelled the United States into World War I, as well as a rejection of the reformist impulses of the Progressive Era. An important part of this conservative push was isolationism, or retreating from world affairs. Isolationist political leaders were vehemently opposed to United States participation in the League of Nations. Ultimately, in a blow to President Woodrow Wilson, the Senate rejected the Treaty of Versailles, which meant a rejection of United States membership in the league. The League of Nations was dear to Wilson. He included the concept in his Fourteen Points program for the post-war world, and he campaigned vigorously for it in Europe and the United States. Isolationist senators feared that membership in the league might obligate the United States to participate in future wars.

WRONG CHOICES EXPLAINED:

(1) President Warren Harding's call for a "return to normalcy" did not mean that the United States should reduce the number of exports. Policymakers have rarely argued that the United States should limit the number of exports.

When American goods are sold overseas, it benefits the American economy and expands opportunities for American workers. Often, leaders have called for limits on goods imported into the country. Many isolationists in the 1920s argued for higher tariff rates in order to keep imported goods out of the United States.

(3) President Warren Harding's call for a "return to normalcy" did not mean that the United States should expand efforts to end racial segregation. In the first three decades of the 20th century, no president called for an end to racial segregation. Politicians in both major political parties accepted policies that relegated African Americans to a second-class status in the United States.

(4) President Warren Harding's call for a "return to normalcy" did not mean that the United States should support women's suffrage. Harding made his call for a "return to normalcy" the same year that the 19th amendment, which extended the vote to women, was ratified (1920). However, Harding is not voicing support for it. Harding's call for a "return to normalcy" meant a return to traditional values, including a return to traditional ideas around gender.

28. **3** The heading "Causes of the Great Depression" best completes the partial outline. The Great Depression began with the crash of the stock market in 1929. However, the underlying causes of the Great Depression are varied. The first two items in the partial outline, "Overproduction" and "Underconsumption," are two terms describing different aspects of the same phenomenon. In both the industrial sector and the agricultural sector, producers were turning out more and more goods, while consumers were not able to absorb such high levels of production. Mechanization and mass-production techniques boosted production—in both factories and on farms. For much of the 1920s, the public, induced by easy credit and seductive advertising, was able to purchase large quantities of mass produced industrial products. However, consumers, after overspending for several years, could not keep up on paying off their debts. By 1927, consumption slackened, inventories ballooned, and many manufacturing firms began laying off workers. Farmers suffered a similar fate. Farmers had put more acres under cultivation during World War I to meet increased demand for agricultural goods. By the twenties, Europe was back on its feet, yet American farmers did not cut back on production. Overproduction and underconsumption were worsened by the fourth item in the partial outline, "Unequal distribution of wealth." While the wealthiest people saw their fortunes grow even larger in the 1920s, workers saw their wages stagnate. If workers had received higher wages in the 1920s, they might have been able to absorb more of the consumer goods that were piling up in warehouses from 1927 onward. The third item in the partial outline, "Buying on margin," refers to the stock market. Buying stock on margin is the practice of paying only a small portion of the purchase price upfront, with the promise of paying the remainder in the future. This practice worked as long as stock prices

rose, which they did throughout most of the 1920s. By the late 1920s, however, serious investors began to see that stock prices were reaching new heights as the actual earnings of major corporations were declining. This discrepancy between the price per share and the actual earnings of a corporation led investors to begin selling stocks, which stimulated a panic. In October 1929, the stock market crashed, destroying individuals' investments and signaling the beginning of the Great Depression.

WRONG CHOICES EXPLAINED:

(1) The heading "Causes of the Industrial Revolution" would not complete the partial outline in the question. An outline with that heading might include items such as "Abundant natural resources," "Ample labor supply," and "Sufficient amount of investment capital."

(2) The heading "Causes of World War I" would not complete the partial outline in the question. An outline with that heading might include items such as "Rise of nationalism in Europe," "Conflicts over imperialist ambitions," and "The assassination of the heir presumptive of the Austro-Hungarian Empire."

(4) The heading "Causes of World War II" would not complete the partial outline in the question. An outline with that heading might include items such as "The failure of appeasement," "The formation of the Axis Powers," and "The German invasion of Poland."

29. **3** The information provided in the graph supports the conclusion that New Deal programs only partially relieved unemployment. The graph shows that the number of unemployed Americans did go down after President Franklin D. Roosevelt came into office in 1933. After reaching a high of over twelve million in 1933, the number of unemployed hovered between eight and twelve million until 1939. Roosevelt instituted the New Deal to deal with the Great Depression. The administration created a series of public works agencies to address the problem of high unemployment. The Civilian Conservation Corps (1933), for example, provided outdoor jobs for young men. Later, Roosevelt created the Works Progress Administration (1935), one of the largest New Deal programs. The WPA was a vast program of government projects that hired millions of unemployed workers. Individuals hired by the agency, for example, built schools, maintained highways, installed sewer lines, wrote guidebooks, and produced theatrical productions. At its peak in 1938, over three million people worked for the WPA; over 8 million people in total worked for it by the time it was shuttered in 1943. In many ways, it was World War II that ended the Great Depression. The United States began producing military equipment and ammunition when World War II started in 1939. War production spiked after the United States became involved in the war in late 1941.

WRONG CHOICES EXPLAINED:

(1) The information provided in the graph does not support the conclusion that deficit spending ended unemployment. The New Deal did entail deficit spending, when spending outpaces government income. Roosevelt was influenced by the thinking of the economist John Maynard Keynes. Keynes argued that deficit spending by the government was acceptable, and even desirable, as a means of increasing overall demand and stimulating economic activity. However, the graph does not indicate that deficit spending ended unemployment.

(2) The information provided in the graph does not support the conclusion that World War II increased unemployment. The graph ends, in 1939, just as World War II was beginning. If the graph continued throughout the years of World War II (1939–1945), it would show that the number of unemployed Americans dropped to almost zero. Many factories had trouble filling all their slots because war production greatly expanded employment opportunities.

(4) The information provided in the graph does not support the conclusion that unemployment after the New Deal began (1939) was the same as it was before the stock market crash (1929). Before the stock market crash, the number of unemployed Americans was low—less than two million. After the New Deal began, the number of unemployed Americans did not drop below eight million.

30. **4** During the 1930s, poor land management and severe drought conditions across parts of the Midwest resulted in the development of Dust Bowl conditions on the Great Plains. The natural grass cover of the region, which includes parts of Oklahoma and Texas, as well as smaller parts of neighboring states, had been removed in the years leading up to the Dust Bowl, as wheat farmers increased the number of acres under cultivation. With this natural root system gone, the fertile topsoil simply blew away when drought struck from 1934 to 1937. The government, through the Soil Conservation Service, encouraged farmers to replant trees and grass and purchased land to be kept out of cultivation. The Dust Bowl caused the largest migration in American history within a short period of time. During the 1930s, approximately 3.5 million people moved out of the Great Plains states. A major destination for Dust Bowl refugees, often referred to as "Okies" and "Arkies," was California. The Dust Bowl exodus prompted some significant cultural responses, such as the album *Dust Bowl Ballads* by the folk singer Woody Guthrie (1940), which included the songs "I Ain't Got No Home in This World Anymore" and "Blowin' Down This Road." The novel *The Grapes of Wrath* (1939), by John Steinbeck, chronicled the plight of a family of Dust Bowl refugees.

WRONG CHOICES EXPLAINED:

(1) During the 1930s, poor land management and severe drought conditions across parts of the Midwest did not result in the establishment of the United States Department of Agriculture. The Department of Agriculture grew out of the Agricultural Division of the Patent Office, which was established in 1839. Later, in 1849, the office was transferred to the newly formed Department of the Interior. President Abraham Lincoln signed legislation making it an independent agency in 1862. The department was elevated to a Cabinet-level department in 1889.

(2) During the 1930s, poor land management and severe drought conditions across parts of the Midwest did not result in the creation of wheat surpluses. The opposite occurred. Crops were devastated in parts of the Midwest as Dust Bowl conditions led to the fertile topsoil blowing away. Fields lay barren in the 1930s in the areas affected by these conditions.

(3) During the 1930s, poor land management and severe drought conditions across parts of the Midwest did not result in decreased support for conservation. The opposite occurred. The government encouraged conservation through the Soil Conservation Service. This New Deal agency encouraged farmers to replant trees and grass and purchased land to be kept out of cultivation.

31. **4** During the 1930s, United States neutrality legislation was primarily designed to avoid foreign policy mistakes that led to involvement in World War I. Isolationism, which gained strength in the 1920s, continued to hold sway into the 1930s, even as the world was becoming increasingly dangerous with the rise of fascism in Europe and a militaristic government in Japan. In the Neutrality Acts of 1935–1937, Congress made clear that neither the United States government nor private U.S. firms were to trade with belligerent nations. A later Neutrality Act, passed in 1939 as World War II was beginning, allowed the United States to supply the opponents of fascism with materials on a cash-and-carry basis. The cash-and-carry approach allowed the United States to send armaments to Great Britain with the condition that Great Britain pay for the weapons first and transport them in their own ships. The stipulations were intended to avoid American ships being put in the line of fire. The sinking of American merchant ships during the first years of World War I was one of the main factors that convinced many Americans to take action against Germany. As the war progressed, President Franklin Roosevelt pushed for greater American support for the Allied powers. In early 1941, Roosevelt was able to make military supplies more readily available to the Allies with the Lend-Lease Act. This act demonstrated the commitment of the United States to the Allies, but it was not until the attack on Pearl Harbor on December 7, 1941, that the United States formally entered the war.

WRONG CHOICES EXPLAINED:

(1) United States neutrality legislation in the 1930s was not designed to provide military and economic aid to Italy and Japan. Neutrality legislation was designed to keep the United States out of foreign conflicts; providing economic aid to one of the sides would push the United States toward greater involvement. It is true that some advocates of neutrality were sympathetic to fascism. The aviator Charles Lindbergh, for example, and other leading members of the America First Committee were sympathetic to fascism. They called for neutrality, knowing that it was out of the question for the United States to actively support the Axis side in World War II.

(2) United States neutrality legislation in the 1930s was not designed to give the United States time to plan an attack against Germany. The United States was not planning an attack against Germany. It was readying its military for combat, but its main foe for most of World War II was Japan. It was not until D-Day, in June 1944, that the United States launched a major offensive against Germany.

(3) United States neutrality legislation in the 1930s was not designed to protect American lives and property in Latin America. The conflicts of the 1930s, leading toward World War II (1939–1945), occurred in Europe and in Asia, not in Latin America.

32. **3** New Deal supporters would most likely have supported the lyrics of the song. The song is unequivocally pro–New Deal and pro–President Franklin D. Roosevelt. The title of the song, "That's Why We're Voting For Roosevelt," makes clear the lyricist's point of view. The song praises Roosevelt for prioritizing the plight of the "once forgotten man" by getting individuals "back to work" and bringing "prosperity back" to America. The song also praises Roosevelt for challenging the power of the banking industry and of the financial industry. It approves of Roosevelt putting "Wall Street… on the pan"—that is, reining in its power through agencies such as the Securities and Exchange Commission (1934). The line, "Our banks are in the clear," refers to actions Roosevelt took to regulate the banking industry and restore public faith in banks. In 1933, he pushed for passage of the Glass-Steagall Act, which created the Federal Deposit Insurance Corporation (FDIC). The FDIC insures deposits so that if a bank folds, people would not lose their savings. Previously, as rumors swirled about the precariousness of the banking system, thousands of people began withdrawing their money. Such actions often turned rumors into self-fulfilling prophecies. These and other New Deal measures did not end the Great Depression, but they gave many Americans a sense of hope and proved to be very popular with voters. Roosevelt was overwhelmingly reelected in 1936, winning over 60 percent of the vote and carrying all but two states.

WRONG CHOICES EXPLAINED:

(1) Prohibition advocates would not have supported the lyrics of the song, "That's Why We're Voting For Roosevelt." Roosevelt was critical of America's experiment in prohibiting the manufacture, sale, and transportation of "intoxicating beverages." Prohibition began with ratification of the 18th amendment in 1919. Roosevelt had been ambivalent throughout his career about Prohibition. However, by the time he ran for president in 1932, he agreed with most Americans that the experiment was not working. He signed legislation in 1933 allowing for the sale of low-alcohol beer and wine, thought to be nonintoxicating. Later that same year, the 21st amendment, ending Prohibition, was ratified with Roosevelt's support.

(2) Republican Party leaders would not have supported the lyrics of the song, "That's Why We're Voting For Roosevelt." President Franklin D. Roosevelt was a Democrat. His opponent in the 1936 election was Republican Alf Landon. Republican Party leaders would have sung his praises, not Roosevelt's.

(4) Supply-side economists would not have supported the lyrics of the song, "That's Why We're Voting For Roosevelt." Supporters of supply-side economics would have opposed President Franklin D. Roosevelt and the New Deal. Supply-side economics stresses stimulating the supply side of the economy—manufacturers, banks, and insurance corporations. The theory is that if there is growth in the supply side, there will be a general economic revival and the benefits of economic expansion will trickle down to everyone. The presidents of the 1920s, including Herbert Hoover, subscribed to this approach to the economy in the decade before the Great Depression. Roosevelt, on the other hand, supported a demand-side approach, which would emphasize government policies designed to increase workers' wages and benefits, such as welfare and unemployment benefits.

33. **1** According to the song lyrics, people supported Franklin D. Roosevelt primarily because he implemented economic relief and recovery programs. The character in the song had been out of work, but "for now I'm back to work and get my three squares ev'ry day." (The "three squares" refer to three square meals each day.) Roosevelt's New Deal included many relief and recovery programs to help the "forgotten man" get back on his feet. Relief programs, such as the Federal Emergency Relief Agency (1933), provided welfare payments to millions of unemployed Americans. In addition, the New Deal included several public works programs. The Civilian Conservation Corps focused on providing work for young men and the Works Progress Administration created hundreds of public projects. The WPA built schools, installed sewer lines, wrote guidebooks, and produced theatrical productions. Also, the New Deal addressed the welfare of retired

people and people with disabilities by creating the Social Security system in 1935. While this array of programs did not end the Great Depression, Roosevelt was able to convey to the American people that the government was on their side. The New Deal and Roosevelt's assuring tone lessened the fears of many Americans during the Great Depression.

WRONG CHOICES EXPLAINED:

(2) The song lyrics do not imply that Roosevelt's support came from his favoring a national suffrage amendment. Such an amendment was not proposed during Roosevelt's time in office. The 15th amendment (1870) prevented states from denying a citizen the right to vote based on that citizen's race. The 19th amendment (1920) extended the right to vote to women. Later, the 26th amendment (1971) mandated that states lower the minimum voting age to 18 years.

(3) The song lyrics do not imply that Roosevelt's support came from his continuation of Herbert Hoover's economic policies. In fact, Roosevelt broke with Hoover's economic approach to the Great Depression. The song lyrics contrast Hoover's lack of action with the activist approach of the New Deal. President Herbert Hoover (1929–1933) encouraged people affected by the Great Depression to rely on their "rugged individualism," believing that direct relief would make people dependent on the government. Roosevelt's approach was to create programs that were designed to benefit unemployed and poor Americans.

(4) The song lyrics do not imply that Roosevelt's support came from a reduction in federal income taxes. In fact, Roosevelt did not reduce federal taxes. Roosevelt pushed for several increases in tax rates in the 1930s. He hoped to increase revenues in order to fund New Deal programs.

34. **4** The cartoon is critical of President Franklin D. Roosevelt's efforts to increase his power over the Supreme Court. In the cartoon, Roosevelt is depicted as putting his hands in several jars; the jars look like jars of jam, but they are labeled with different sectors of the economy and different branches of the government. The implication is that Roosevelt is overstepping his authority, and that he is "never satisfied" in his drive for power. His next target is labeled "Full control of the Supreme Court." The cartoon is alluding to Roosevelt's "court packing" plan. By 1937, Roosevelt had grown increasingly frustrated with the conservative approach of the Supreme Court. It shot down the National Recovery Act in *Schechter* v. *United States* (1935) and the Agricultural Adjustment Act in *Butler* v. *United States* (1936). In 1937, he announced a plan to increase the number of justices on the Supreme Court to as many as fifteen. He said that some of the older justices had difficulty keeping up with the heavy workload. However, it was

clear that the intent of his "court packing" plan was to create a Supreme Court friendlier to his New Deal programs. The Senate rejected Roosevelt's "court packing" plan in 1937 because the plan would have threatened the principle of checks and balances by making the Supreme Court a rubber stamp for New Deal legislation. Soon, however, openings on the Court allowed Roosevelt to appoint new justices and influence the direction of the Court.

WRONG CHOICES EXPLAINED:

(1) The cartoon is not commenting on President Franklin D. Roosevelt's efforts to force Congress to reduce government waste. Roosevelt appears to be wasting jam in the cartoon, but that is meant to serve as a metaphor for his hunger for power. His desire to get his hands in all the jars is meant to symbolize his attempts to gain greater control over the economy and the government.

(2) The cartoon is not commenting on President Franklin D. Roosevelt's efforts to convince the Supreme Court to pass a constitutional amendment to balance the budget. In fact, the idea of an amendment to balance the budget was not proposed in the 1930s. If it had, Roosevelt would have opposed it. New Deal programs contributed to a deficit in the federal budget, not to a balanced budget. Roosevelt was influenced by the thinking of the economist John Maynard Keynes. Keynes argued that deficit spending by the government was acceptable, and even desirable, as a means of increasing overall demand and stimulating economic activity. Later, Republicans put forth the idea of a balanced budget amendment in the 1980s.

(3) The cartoon is not commenting on President Franklin D. Roosevelt's efforts to reverse the effects of the Great Depression. The cartoon is not depicting the enactment of New Deal programs, which were designed to provide economic relief for individuals, help the economy recover, and reform basic sectors of the economy so that future economic downturns would not be so severe. Rather, the jars in the cartoon represent different sectors of the economy and different branches of government that Roosevelt is attempting to gain control over.

35. **4** The poster indicates that rationing during World War II was a program that applied equally to all Americans. In the first frame of the cartoon, labeled "Without Rationing," a wealthy woman buys a large amount of meat from the butcher, while there is nothing left for the next customer, apparently of more modest means, to purchase. During World War II, a wide variety of goods were diverted to military use—from steel and oil to food products. Consequently, fewer products were available for domestic consumption. The Office of Price Adjustment set up a rationing system in which people could obtain goods needed by the

military only if they had rationing coupons. These goods included butter, meat, shoes, and sugar. The system was designed not only to conserve materials for the military, but also to keep inflation down. During times of war, inflation is a constant threat due to the lack of consumer goods and the additional money that people have in their pockets from all the work available in defense-related industries. Government efforts to control inflation were moderately successful; inflation was about half as much as it was during World War I.

WRONG CHOICES EXPLAINED:

(1) The poster does not indicate that rationing during World War II was a policy to encourage small business owners. Rationing programs applied to large businesses as well as small businesses.

(2) The poster does not indicate that rationing during World War II was a way of assuring that only the wealthy could buy certain products. The poster asserts the opposite—that rationing would be applied equally to all Americans.

(3) The poster does not indicate that rationing during World War II was caused by farm failures during the Great Depression. The poster makes no reference to the causes of shortages during World War II. Most Americans realized that the war effort required a great amount of material goods and that less would be available for civilian use. While it is true that many farms failed during the Great Depression, one of the key problems facing the agricultural sector in the 1920s and 1930s was overproduction and low prices—not underproduction and shortages.

36. **1** A major reason for wartime rationing was ensuring that troops were adequately supplied. During World War II, there were shortages of key items because of the needs of the military. Nearly 18 million men and women served in the United States military during the war. Starting in 1942, the Office of Price Administration began rationing key commodities to civilians, such as gasoline and tires. Next, the government began rationing food—sugar, meat, coffee, lard, butter, and many other items. Families were given ration books and would use ration stamps, along with cash, when they purchased the affected items. In many ways, World War II required the participation of the entire American public, not simply members of the military. These efforts created a sense of unity and common cause in the country.

WRONG CHOICES EXPLAINED:

(2) Restricting lower-priced food imports was not a reason for food rationing during World War II. There were no restrictions imposed on imports during the war, but trade did decline due to the fighting of World War II. Enemy ships routinely sunk merchant ships, making trade difficult.

(3) Providing jobs for the unemployed was not a reason for food rationing during World War II. Unemployment virtually disappeared as the United States began producing armaments for World War II.

(4) Preventing currency deflation was not a reason for food rationing during World War II. The opposite was true. During times of war, inflation often occurs due to the scarcity of consumer items as well as an increase in incomes for workers. Rationing was instituted, in part, to reduce the threat of inflation.

37. **1** The most appropriate heading for the partial outline would be "Issues of Morality during World War II." All the items in the outline refer to controversies during World War II in which Americans took different positions based on their sense of morality. "Treatment of Japanese Americans" (item A) refers the effects of Executive Order 9066 (1942) issued by President Franklin D. Roosevelt during World War II. The order authorized the government to remove 120,000 Japanese Americans, two-thirds of them citizens, from West Coast states and relocate them to camps throughout the West. Most of their property was confiscated by the government. In the case of *Korematsu* v. *United States* (1944), the Supreme Court ruled that the relocation was acceptable on the grounds of national security. "Segregation of African Americans in the armed forces" (item B) refers to the continued practice of maintaining separate units in the military based on race. Despite this, during World War II, African Americans participated in the war effort in unprecedented numbers. Ultimately, around one million African Americans served overseas during World War II. The most famous segregated African-American units were the Tuskegee Airmen and the 761st Tank Battalion. African-American effectiveness on the battlefield encouraged President Truman to later (1948) desegregate the armed services with Executive Order 9981, although he failed to implement it until the Korean War, when the military needed additional personnel. "United States reactions to the Nazi Holocaust" (item C) refers to long debate over whether the United States could have done more to prevent the Holocaust. The Holocaust was the systematic murder of six million European Jews and other "undesirables" by the Nazis. Many have criticized President Roosevelt for refusing to let nearly one thousand Jewish refugees disembark from the German ocean liner *St. Louis* on the eve of World War II. These refugees eventually had to go back to Europe, where most of them died in the Holocaust. Some historians have argued that American planes could have destroyed some of the death camps, such as Auschwitz. The politics, ethics, effectiveness, and logistics of such actions are still being debated. "The Use of the Atomic Bomb" (item D) refers to debates around the decision by the United States to drop the atomic bomb on the Japanese cities of Hiroshima and Nagasaki at the end of World War II in 1945. At the time, the decision to drop the atomic

bomb did not generate much public debate. However, in the decades since the war, some Americans have raised questions about the decision. Critics argue that it was morally wrong for the United States to have targeted civilian populations and that the Japanese were ready to surrender anyway. Many stand by the decision to drop the bomb. The atomic bombing swiftly ended a bloody conflict that consumed 50 million lives. It is not clear that the Japanese were on the verge of surrendering. Some members of the Japanese military argued against surrendering even after the second bomb dropped.

WRONG CHOICES EXPLAINED:

(2) "Domestic policies during World War II" would not be an appropriate heading for the partial outline in the question. Although the first item in the outline, "Treatment of Japanese Americans," would be considered a domestic policy, the others are more clearly military and foreign policy issues. Other domestic policies during World War II include the enactment of wartime rationing, the enforcement of price controls on certain items, and the recruitment of women to work in the defense industry.

(3) "Economic Problems during World War II" would not be an appropriate heading for the partial outline in the question. An outline with that heading might include items such as shortages of certain consumer items and increases in income taxes. Overall, however, World War II proved to provide a boost to the American economy. It was World War II, rather than the New Deal, that ended the Great Depression. Unemployment fell from over 14 percent in 1940 to less than two percent for the last three years of the war—1943 to 1945.

(4) "Reasons for the Success of the Allies during World War II" would not be an appropriate heading for the partial outline in the question. An outline with that heading might include items such as planning and coordination among the "big three" (President Roosevelt, Prime Minister Winston Churchill of the United Kingdom, and Soviet leader Joseph Stalin) and successful mobilization of troops and materials.

38. **3** The best title for the graph for the years 1946 to 1964 is "The Baby Boom Generation." The spike in birthrates from 1946 through the early 1960s produced a baby boom that would have lasting repercussions in American society. The baby boom required states to spend more money on constructing and operating new schools in the 1950s and 1960s. In addition, these young families needed housing. The baby boom contributed to the growth of suburban communities outside of major cities in the 1950s and 1960s. The federal government's Servicemen's Readjustment Act (1944), more commonly known as the GI Bill, provided low interest loans for veterans to purchase homes. Developers often bought large

tracts of land to build hundreds of houses. To save time and money, these developments included many houses that had identical plans. The most famous suburban developer was William Levitt. Levittown, on Long Island, New York, became synonymous with these mass-produced communities.

WRONG CHOICES EXPLAINED:

(1) "The Graying of America" would not be an appropriate title for the graph in the question. A graph with that title would show an increase in the number of people getting to retirement age. This phenomenon is occurring today as the percentage of Americans over the age of sixty-five grows. One reason for the growing percentage of senior citizens is the large number of "baby boomers," born in the period after World War II, reaching retirement age. When such a large percentage of the American public is retired, many people worry that programs extending benefits to the elderly, notably Medicare and Social Security, will be unable to stay financially solvent.

(2) "The Growth of the Middle Class" would not be an appropriate title for the graph in the question. A graph with that title would indicate percentages of Americans at different income levels over time. There was, in fact, a growth in the middle class during the years 1946 to 1964, but this is not indicated in the graph. A number of factors contributed to the rise of the middle class after World War II. The GI Bill (1944), formally known as the Servicemen's Readjustment Act, provided low interest loans for veterans to purchase homes as well as funds for college. The intent of the GI Bill was to help the veterans of World War II adjust to life during peacetime. The program was very successful. It helped millions of veterans advance economically. A college education and home ownership are key components of entrance into the middle class.

(4) "From Suburbs to Cities" would not be an appropriate title for the graph in the question. A graph with that title would indicate the change over time in percentages of Americans living in suburbs and living in cities. Such a graph for the years 1946 to 1964, however, would indicate the opposite trend. Many families left cities and moved to suburbs. Suburbs were built outside of major cities in the years after World War II. Huge numbers of veterans returned from war, quickly married, had children—collectively known as the "baby boom" generation—and looked for affordable housing. The federal government's Servicemen's Readjustment Act (1944), more commonly known as the GI Bill, provided low interest loans for veterans to purchase homes.

39. **2** The immediate cause of the action taken by the United States that is shown in the map was the building of nuclear missile launch sites within range of the United States by the Soviet Union. The action by the United States depicted

in the map was a blockading of Soviet ships, a key move in the Cuban Missile Crisis (1962). The crisis began when an American U-2 spy plane discovered that Cuba was preparing bases for Soviet nuclear missiles to be installed. President Kennedy felt that these missiles, in such close proximity to the United States, amounted to an unacceptable provocation and ordered Soviet Premier Nikita Khrushchev to halt the operation and dismantle the bases. Khrushchev insisted on the right of the Soviet Union to install the missiles. For about a week, the world stood on the brink of nuclear war.

WRONG CHOICES EXPLAINED:

(1) The immediate cause of the Cuban Missile Crisis, which is the subject of the map in the question, was not Cuban refugees lobbying President Dwight Eisenhower to overthrow Fidel Castro. Such lobbying did occur earlier and led to Eisenhower giving the green light to the Bay of Pigs invasion. The administration of President John F. Kennedy implemented the plan to overthrow the Communist government of Castro in 1961. Over one thousand Cubans landed at the Bay of Pigs, but their invasion failed after three days. Though the invasion failed, it heightened Cold War tensions between the United States and the Soviet Union.

(3) The immediate cause of the Cuban Missile Crisis, which is the subject of the map in the question, was not Cuban armed forces closing down United States military bases in the Caribbean. The strength of the Cuban military was dwarfed by the firepower of the United States military. Cuba did not contemplate attempting to close down American bases, nor would such an attempt have been successful. An American naval base, at Guantanamo Bay, was established in Cuba in 1903, and continued to operate after the Cuban Revolution of 1959. It is still in operation despite protests by the Cuban government, which insists that the lease agreement for the base was forced upon Cuba.

(4) The immediate cause of the Cuban Missile Crisis, which is the subject of the map in the question, was not Puerto Rican citizens asking Congress to assist them in repelling Communist advances. Puerto Rico is outside of the blockade area indicated on the map. There was never an attempt by outside Communist forces to "advance" upon Puerto Rico. There is a pro-independence Communist Party within Puerto Rico, but it has a small following.

40. **1** One positive outcome of the situation shown on the map was that the United States and Soviet Union increased communications between the two nations to avoid war. After an American U-2 spy plane discovered that Cuba was preparing bases for Soviet nuclear missiles to be installed, on an island in close proximity to the United States, President John F. Kennedy took several different

actions. Publicly, he ordered a naval blockade of Cuba to prevent Soviet ships from landing at Cuba. Behind the scenes, American and Soviet officials began intense negotiations to avoid World War III. The United States began with the position that the Soviet Union must halt the operation of installing missiles in Cuba and dismantle the bases. Khrushchev insisted on the right of the Soviet Union to install the missiles. Finally, a deal was reached to diffuse the Cuban Missile Crisis. The Soviet Union agreed to abandon its Cuban missile program, and the United States agreed to not invade Cuba without provocation. The United States also quietly agreed to remove missiles from Turkey, which the Soviets argued were as close to the Soviet Union as missiles in Cuba would be to the United States.

WRONG CHOICES EXPLAINED:

(2) An outcome of the Cuban Missile Crisis, which is the subject of the map, was not increased military control by the United States and the Soviet Union over their Latin American colonies. One outcome of the crisis was that the United States agreed to recognize the autonomy of Cuba. The crisis did not lead to any other military engagements in the Americas.

(3) An outcome of the Cuban Missile Crisis, which is the subject of the map, was not cooperative humanitarian efforts in Caribbean nations suffering from natural disasters. There have been cooperative humanitarian efforts to aid Caribbean nations suffering from disasters, but these are unrelated to the Cuban Missile Crisis. Many nations, including the United States, aided Haiti in the aftermath of a powerful earthquake in 2010 that left at least 100,000 people dead. This incident occurred almost two decades after the collapse of the Soviet Union.

(4) An outcome of the Cuban Missile Crisis, which is the subject of the map, was not joint efforts to the end the cruel practices of Cuba's leaders. United States leaders repeatedly called attention to human rights abuses by the Cuban government and organized an embargo against Cuba. However, the Soviet Union denied that such abuses took place, and fully supported the Cuban government from soon after the 1959 Cuban revolution until the collapse of the Soviet Union in 1991.

41. **4** The main reason President John F. Kennedy proposed the establishment of the Peace Corps was to improve conditions in developing nations. In his Inaugural Address in 1961, he implored Americans to be more public-minded and generous with their time and resources—to ask themselves what they could do for their country and for the cause of freedom throughout the world. Toward this end, Kennedy pushed for the creation of the Peace Corps (1961) in order to give support to developing nations in fields such as education, agriculture, and health

care. The program depends on volunteers, often recent college graduates, to work on development projects in poor countries. The Peace Corps reflected a sense of optimism that many saw in the Kennedy administration and in the era of the 1960s. It was also an attempt by the United States, in the midst of a Cold War with the Soviet Union, to shed negative perceptions of its role in foreign countries. The Peace Corps still exists.

WRONG CHOICES EXPLAINED:

(1) President John F. Kennedy's goal in proposing the establishment of the Peace Corps was not to promote trade with Asia. The Peace Corps promotes projects that help communities move to greater self-sufficiency, not greater reliance on goods from the United States.

(2) President John F. Kennedy's goal in proposing the establishment of the Peace Corps was not to combat drug use in American cities. Over the years, officials from all levels of government have taken steps to reduce drug use in American cities, from punitive measures based on strict enforcement of drug possession and dealing laws to expanding the scope of treatment centers for drug addicts. However, these efforts are unrelated to the Peace Corps, which is focused on development projects in other countries.

(3) President John F. Kennedy's goal in proposing the establishment of the Peace Corps was not to gain support from immigrant voters. Immigrant voters are not homogeneous in their voting patterns. Some might support initiatives such as the Peace Corps; others might support programs aimed at helping urban communities in the United States. Naturalized immigrants register to vote with both political parties, but tend to lean Democratic by a factor of two to one.

42. **2** An outcome of the Watergate affair during the administration of President Richard Nixon was that respect for the office of the president declined. The Watergate affair was one of the most serious presidential scandals in American history. The scandal began in June 1972, when five men were caught breaking into the headquarters of the Democratic Party at the Watergate Hotel in Washington, D.C. Persistent reporting by Carl Bernstein and Bob Woodward of the *Washington Post* drew connections between the burglars and Nixon's reelection committee and ultimately the White House. When it became known that Nixon taped conversations in the White House Oval Office, investigators demanded that the tapes be turned over. Nixon argued that executive privilege allowed him to keep the tapes. In *United States* v. *Nixon* (1974), the Supreme Court ordered Nixon to turn over the tapes. Nixon told a press conference in November 1973, "I am not a crook." However, less than a month after the Supreme Court decision in 1974, Nixon resigned. The scandal damaged people's respect for the presidency and led to an erosion in trust of the government.

WRONG CHOICES EXPLAINED:

(1) The Watergate affair during the administration of President Richard Nixon did not lead to an expansion of presidential power. After the scandal began, Congress took action in regard to the president's war-making powers that reduced presidential power. In 1973, it passed the War Powers Act (1973) over President Nixon's veto. The act was passed after the United States had withdrawn from Vietnam. Many congressmen thought the president had abused his power to deploy troops during the Vietnam War. The War Powers Act was an attempt to check presidential power and strengthen the legislative branch in matters of war.

(3) The Watergate affair during the administration of President Richard Nixon did not lead to the Supreme Court clearing President Nixon of charges. In a key case related to the Watergate affair, the Court ruled against Nixon. In *United States* v. *Nixon* (1974), the Supreme Court ordered Nixon to turn over secret tapes that he had made of White House conversations. Less than a month after the Supreme Court decision, Nixon resigned.

(4) The Watergate affair during the administration of President Richard Nixon did not lead Congress to refuse to take action against President Nixon. The opposite occurred. In 1974, the House Judiciary Committee voted in favor of articles of impeachment against President Nixon. Before the question of impeachment could be addressed by the entire House of Representatives, Nixon resigned.

43. **3** The goal of the War Powers Act of 1973 was to limit the president's power to use military force without congressional approval. The act was passed, over President Richard Nixon's veto, soon after the United States withdrew from Vietnam. Many congressmen thought the president had abused his power to deploy troops during the Vietnam War. While it is Congress that has the power to declare war and to allocate money for military actions, presidents have frequently taken military actions unilaterally. It is understandable that presidents would take actions on their own. An attack on the United States would very likely require an immediate and decisive response; there would not be time to wait for Congress to convene and to debate the proper response to such a crisis. However, on different occasions, critics have accused presidents of abusing their power and taking military actions in an arbitrary and misguided manner. The War Powers Act was an attempt to check presidential power and strengthen the legislative branch in matters of war. The act requires the president to report any troop deployments to Congress within 48 hours and thus give Congress the ability to force the withdrawal of U.S. troops after 60 days.

WRONG CHOICES EXPLAINED:

(1) The goal of the War Powers Act of 1973 was not to allow the president to declare war without congressional approval. Congress's power to declare war is enshrined in the Constitution. It would take a constitutional amendment, not an act of Congress, to change that.

(2) The goal of the War Powers Act of 1973 was not to give Congress the sole power to authorize the use of military force. While Congress has the power to formally issue a declaration of war, it is a long accepted practice for the president to order military actions. In many situations, an immediate response is called for. The president would not always have sufficient time to wait for Congress to convene and come to a decision about an appropriate response.

(4) The goal of the War Powers Act of 1973 was not to require a declaration of war for all uses of military force. Situations may arise in which an immediate military response is warranted. If an American base is attacked, for example, the president may call for an immediate counterstrike. Subsequently, Congress would have the option of issuing a formal declaration of war. The act limits the president's power to use military force, but it does not take it away.

44. **1** President George H.W. Bush used the statement in the question to defend taking military action to liberate Kuwait from Iraqi aggression. The United States gets a great deal of its oil from the Middle East, and it has sought to maintain alliances and to prevent any Middle Eastern country from assuming a dominant role in the region. President George H.W. Bush, therefore, became alarmed in 1990 when Iraqi leader Saddam Hussein ordered an Iraqi invasion of Kuwait, another oil-rich Middle Eastern country. In the statement, he expresses a desire to end the crisis peacefully, but states that the United States had exhausted peaceful means of removing Iraqi troops from Kuwait. He described Kuwait, in a different statement, as "small and helpless." President Bush carried out his pledge to defend Kuwaiti autonomy. He organized the Persian Gulf War in 1991. The war accomplished its immediate goal of ousting Iraqi forces from Kuwait. Some criticized President Bush for not attempting to oust Hussein. However, when the United States did topple Hussein as part of Operation Iraqi Freedom (2003), Iraq descended into violence and disorder that led to a longtime United States military presence in that country.

WRONG CHOICES EXPLAINED:

(2) President George H.W. Bush's statement was not meant to defend providing foreign aid to Israel. Israel has been one of the top recipients of foreign aid (including military assistance) since its founding in 1948. This has been true

during Democratic as well as Republican presidential administrations. In 2016, the Obama administration pledged over $38 billion in military aid to Israel over the following decade—the biggest deal of its kind in United States history.

(3) President George H.W. Bush's statement was not meant to defend supporting Egypt against terrorist attacks. Egypt has been an important ally of the United States and one of the largest recipients of foreign aid. In 2017, the United States suspended military aid to Egypt over human rights concerns, but released almost $200 million in 2018 in an effort to strengthen bilateral relations and counterterrorism efforts.

(4) President George H.W. Bush's statement was not meant to defend using United States troops as peacekeepers in Bosnia. The United States did become involved in Bosnia later in the 1990s, as ethnic violence developed in Bosnia after the breakup of Yugoslavia. In 1990, Yugoslavia divided into several smaller nations and a brutal war ensued. Serbian forces clashed with Bosnian Muslims. The United States and other countries decided to take action as reports of Serbian brutality became known. President Bill Clinton brought leaders from Bosnia, Serbia, and Croatia together in 1995 in Ohio. A peace treaty was signed and 20,000 NATO troops were dispatched to enforce it.

45. **3** The cartoon suggests that the middle class is disappearing in the United States. Two factors that have contributed to this problem are consumer debt and nearly stagnant wages. The cartoon depicts the middle class as another extinct species—like ancient ammonites (an extinct marine mollusk) or trilobites (an extinct marine arthropod). Future scientists, the cartoonist imagines, would only find evidence of these extinct species by examining fossilized remains. A variety of political and economic factors can help explain the stagnation of wages for many Americans. From the 1960s onward, the United States has experienced the disappearance of higher-paying manufacturing jobs and the growth of low-wage service-sector jobs. Large numbers of factories have closed in northeastern cities such as New York and Philadelphia, as well as in Midwestern Rust Belt cities such as Pittsburgh, Cleveland, Detroit, and Chicago. Many jobs have been outsourced to countries such as India and China with lower wage scales. Another factor in keeping wages down is the decline of the union movement. As wages have stagnated, consumer debt has mushroomed. Banks and credit card companies have lured people into taking on more debt than they could handle. The most vivid example of this occurred in the early 2000s in regard to the housing market. Banks offered adjustable rate mortgages in which initial low rates would later jump to higher rates. These risky loans were referred to as "subprime mortgages" because they were extended to people whose ability to repay and whose credit rating was less than prime. By 2008, almost 30 percent of mortgages were rated

as "subprime." In 2007 and 2008, the housing bubble burst as housing prices plummeted. Many subprime borrowers found themselves "underwater"—that is, the market value of their homes sank below the amount they owed on their mortgages. In many such situations, individuals could neither sell their homes nor afford to pay their monthly mortgage payments. Their only option was to walk away from their homes and default on their loans, leading to widespread foreclosures.

WRONG CHOICES EXPLAINED:
(1) The problem shown in the cartoon—the disappearance of the middle class—was not caused by lower medical costs and high interest rates. Lower medical costs would help the middle class. Variable-rate loans proved to be problematic for many middle-class people, but high interest rates were not, in and of themselves, a major contributing factor in the decline of the middle class.

(2) The problem shown in the cartoon—the disappearance of the middle class—was not caused by business monopolies and the depletion of natural resources. These two developments are more closely associated with economic problems of the late 1800s. As American industry expanded in the post–Civil War era, powerful monopolies came to dominate several industries. During this era, reformers began to take note of the damage done to natural resources by unregulated industrial growth.

(4) The problem shown in the cartoon—the disappearance of the middle class—was not caused by population migration and the graying of America. There have been major shifts in population in recent decades. The population of the old "Rust Belt" states of the upper Midwest has stagnated as the population of the "Sun Belt" states of the South and the West has grown. In addition, the population of the United States is getting older, or "graying," as the baby boom generation has reached retirement age. However, neither of these two developments are direct causes of the disappearance of the middle class.

46. **2** One way in which the goals of the Know-Nothing Party in the 1850s and the response to the Red Scare of 1919 were similar is that both sought to limit immigration into the United States. The Know-Nothing Party emerged in the wake of large-scale immigration from Ireland in the 1840s and 1850s. The collapse of the potato crop in Ireland had devastating effects on the Irish people. It is estimated that a million Irish starved to death between 1845 and 1850, while another million left for America. Many Americans thought that the new immigrants, who were mostly non-Protestant, lacked the self-control of "proper," middle-class Protestant Americans. For nativists, this lack of self-control was evident in the drinking habits of immigrants. It was in this context that the anti-immigrant and

anti-Catholic Know-Nothing Party emerged. The Know-Nothing Party (formally known as the American Party) was born in 1844 and, by the 1850s, had achieved electoral success in several states, especially in the Northeast. In the 20th century, anti-immigrant sentiment again emerged. In the aftermath of World War I, many Americans were swept up in a crusade against suspected communists, anarchists, labor leaders, and other radicals. This Red Scare contributed to a strong anti-immigrant movement in the 1920s. This movement achieved legislative success with the passage of the Emergency Quota Act (1921) and the National Origins Act (1924), which greatly reduced the number of immigrants allowed into the United States.

WRONG CHOICES EXPLAINED:

(1) Neither the goals of the Know-Nothing Party in the 1850s nor the response to the Red Scare of 1919 called for equal rights for women and African Americans. Anti-immigrant movements frequently have racist undertones. Many nativists base their opposition to immigration on a desire to have a racially "pure" country. In addition, there is often an overlap between nativists and those who call for a return to traditional gender roles. Therefore, these movements are not likely to embrace equal rights for African Americans and women.

(3) Neither the goals of the Know-Nothing Party in the 1850s nor the response to the Red Scare of 1919 supported overseas expansion of the United States. The issue of overseas expansion was not yet part of public debates in the 1850s; it became a contentious issue in the 1890s and 1900s in the wake of the Spanish-American War (1898). In the 1920s, there was an overlap between nativists and isolationists. Therefore, these movements are not likely to support overseas expansion.

(4) Neither the goals of the Know-Nothing Party in the 1850s nor the response to the Red Scare of 1919 attempted to limit the influence of big business on American politics. Some nativists espoused anti-big business politics, asserting that corporations were importing cheap labor into the United States. Others were more pro-business, sharing conservative, laissez-faire views about the role of the government in the economy.

47. **1** The term *containment* best describes United States foreign policy during the Cold War. The United States became increasingly concerned about the growing power of the Soviet Union after World War II and put forth a policy of attempting to prevent the expansion of communism, known as containment. President Harry S. Truman articulated this goal, which has come to be known as the Truman Doctrine, in a speech to Congress in 1947. Truman put the idea of

containment into practice in 1947 by providing $400 million in military aid to Greece and Turkey to prevent those countries from becoming communist. Another example of the containment policy was the Berlin Airlift of 1948. In 1948, before the status of Berlin was settled, the Soviet Union decided it would prevent any food or other supplies from entering the western sector of the city. The goal was for the Soviet Union to block the influence of the United States and its western allies from maintaining its presence in Berlin. Ultimately, the Soviet Union hoped to make all of Berlin part of what would become East Germany. The United States did not stand by idly when it learned of the Berlin blockade. Truman decided to send thousands of planes, filled with supplies, into the western sector of Berlin, in an action known as the Berlin Airlift. The Berlin Airlift prevented the western sector of Berlin from starving and prevented the Soviet Union from taking over the city. The formation of the North Atlantic Treaty Organization (NATO) was also part of the Cold War strategy of containment. NATO was created in 1949 by the United States and its allies to challenge the growing power of the Soviet Union. The members of NATO pledged that they would view an attack on any one member as an attack on all members.

WRONG CHOICES EXPLAINED:

(2) The term *nonalignment* does not accurately describe United States foreign policy during the Cold War. The nonaligned countries during the Cold War period (1945–1991) were those nations that did not ally themselves with either the United States or the Soviet Union. These countries formalized their status with the organization of the Non-Aligned Movement in 1956. The nations who initiated the movement were Yugoslavia, India, Indonesia, Egypt, and Ghana.

(3) The term *Big Stick* does not accurately describe United States foreign policy during the Cold War. The Big Stick Policy is associated with the efforts of President Theodore Roosevelt (1901–1909) for the United States to play a more aggressive role in Latin America. His foreign-policy approach is neatly summed up in his famous adage that the United States should "speak softly, but carry a big stick" when dealing with other nations (Roosevelt borrowed the phrase from an African proverb). The "big stick" implied the threat of military force. He asserted that the "civilized nations" had a duty to police the "backward" countries of the world. This assertion of American might is known as the Roosevelt Corollary to the Monroe Doctrine.

(4) The term *Open Door* does not accurately describe United States foreign policy during the Cold War. The Open Door Policy was put forth by the administration of President William McKinley in 1900 in order to open up China to American trade. In the 1890s, the major European powers had established spheres of influence in China. These nations each declared that they had

exclusive trading privileges in their sphere of influence. The United States asserted that all of China should be open to trade with all nations. The European nations begrudgingly accepted this Open Door concept.

48. **2** The examples in the chart illustrate checks and balances. The chart lists, on the left side, particular actions by different branches of government, and on the right side, reactions taken by another branch of government to limit the power of the first branch. The top pair of entries deals with events during the Reconstruction period, following the Civil War. The action taken by President Andrew Johnson was firing his secretary of war Edwin Stanton (1867), in violation of the Tenure of Office Act. Stanton was the government official in charge of carrying out the government's Reconstruction agenda in the South. Congressional Republicans passed the act in order to protect Stanton, their one ally in the Johnson administration. Johnson proceeded to fire Stanton despite the law, setting off the process that led to his impeachment. The lower two entries deal with events during the Great Depression of the 1930s. The National Industrial Recovery Act (1933) was one of many initiatives, collectively known as the New Deal, that were put forth by the administration of President Franklin D. Roosevelt to address the economic crisis of the 1930s. NIRA called for representatives from labor and competing corporations to draw up a set of codes. These codes were designed to shorten hours for workers, guarantee trade union rights, establish minimum wage levels, regulate the price of certain petroleum products, and promote fair business practices. The idea was that cutthroat competition hurt the economy, pushed workers' wages down, and limited their ability to purchase goods. In the *Schechter* v. *United States* decision (1935), the Court shot down NIRA on the grounds that the president had assumed legislative powers in creating NIRA regulations. It was one of several decisions limiting the powers of the executive branch. Both reactions—Congress's impeachment of Johnson and the Supreme Court's striking down of NIRA—are checks that one branch of government made on another branch. The desired end result of such checking is that all three branches will be in balance. The framers of the Constitution were very conscious of the problems of a government with limitless powers. After living under the British monarchy, they came to believe that a powerful government without checks and balances was dangerous to liberty.

WRONG CHOICES EXPLAINED:
(1) The examples in the chart do not illustrate federalism. Federalism refers to the relationship between the state governments and the national government. In the governing system developed in the Constitution, powers are shared by the national government and the state governments. The goal is that excessive power is not concentrated in either level of government.

ANSWERS June 2019

(3) The examples in the chart do not illustrate states' rights. The concept of states' rights describes the idea that states would retain certain rights even though the national government was supreme. The issue of states' rights became closely identified with the defense of slavery. Defenders of slavery in the South felt that the institution had sufficiently broad support among white Southerners, but they feared that Northern political leaders might use the power of the federal government to limit or abolish slavery. Hence, they firmly embraced the right of states to resist or nullify federal edicts.

(4) The examples in the chart do not illustrate judicial review. Judicial review is the Supreme Court's ability to review laws and determine whether they are consistent with the Constitution. It is not specifically mentioned in the Constitution. It was first exercised by the Supreme Court in the case of *Marbury* v. *Madison* (1803), and has been the main function of the Supreme Court since then.

49. **2** The economic policy that argues that government should limit, as much as possible, any interference in the economy is laissez-faire. The French phrase *laissez-faire* means "to let alone." It describes a government policy that would take a hands-off approach in regard to economic activities. Throughout much of the history of the United States, Americans have been suspicious of government intervention into the economy. The founders of the United States had vivid memories of the overbearing mercantilist policies of Great Britain. With the American economy growing by leaps and bounds in the 19th century, few challenged this doctrine. However, by the 20th century, the country began to face serious economic problems that called into question the laissez-faire doctrine. In the first decades of the 20th century, Progressive reformers called on the government to break up monopolies, regulate the food production industry, help the poor, and create peace between owners and workers. When the Great Depression struck the United States in the 1930s, Franklin D. Roosevelt argued more forcefully that the government must play an activist role. After Roosevelt won the presidential election in 1932, he initiated a sweeping array of programs known as the New Deal. Since the Great Depression, politicians have argued about the nature and degree of government economic intervention in the economy, but few today argue for a complete laissez-faire policy.

WRONG CHOICES EXPLAINED:
(1) Socialism is an economic policy that argues for government ownership of key sectors of the economy. It is the opposite of a laissez-faire approach of nonintervention by the government in the economy.

(3) Mercantilism is an economic policy that argues that the government should play an active role in the economy. A laissez-faire approach, by contrast, argues that the government should play no role in the economy. Mercantilist theory holds that governments should try to increase the wealth of a nation by maintaining colonies so as to have a steady and inexpensive source of raw materials. The theory guided Great Britain in maintaining its American colonies before the American Revolution.

(4) Protectionism is an economic policy that argues that the government should impose tariffs on goods imported into the United States. These tariffs would raise the prices of foreign-made goods and would make American goods comparatively more affordable. The tariffs would, in theory, protect American industry from foreign competition. Protectionism involves government intervention in the economy; laissez-faire implies no government intervention in the economy.

50. **3** W. E. B. Du Bois, Jackie Robinson, and James Meredith are considered pioneers in the area of civil rights. W. E. B. Du Bois was a militant civil rights activist who wrote about the injustices carried out against African Americans in the South. He was one of the founders of the National Association for the Advancement of Colored People (NAACP) in 1909. Du Bois's call for full political equality and civil rights for African Americans was in marked contrast to the more conciliatory approach of Booker T. Washington. Jackie Robinson was the first African American to play major league baseball in the modern era. He began his career with the Brooklyn Dodgers in 1947. Robinson met a great deal of racist anger during his first year in major league baseball. Players on the St. Louis Cardinals threatened to go on strike if Robinson took the field for the Dodgers. In the 1950s, Robinson publicly supported the civil rights movement and urged President Dwight D. Eisenhower to take action to resolve the crisis around the desegregation of public schools in Little Rock, Arkansas, in 1957. James Meredith was the first African American to be admitted to the University of Mississippi in 1962. His admission was met with violent opposition. Riots in the town of Oxford, Mississippi, resulted in the death of two people. All three individuals contributed to the ongoing struggle for civil rights in the United States. The high point for the civil rights movement occurred in the 1950s and 1960s. The civil rights movement gained strength after the Supreme Court, in the case of *Brown* v. *Board of Education of Topeka* (1954), declared that segregation in schools had no place in America. In the years following the *Brown* decision, we see the Montgomery bus boycott in 1955 and 1956, the lunch counter sit-ins in 1960, the Freedom Rides in 1962, and a whole host of other activities. It was in this context that the movement achieved significant victories. The Civil Rights Act of 1964 banned segregation in public facilities and the Voting Rights Act of 1965 removed barriers to African Americans voting.

WRONG CHOICES EXPLAINED:

(1) Neither W. E. B. Du Bois, Jackie Robinson, nor James Meredith are considered pioneers in the area of labor relations. Important figures in the labor movement include Samuel Gompers, one of the founders and the first leader of the American Federation of Labor (AFL) in 1886; Eugene V. Debs, a founder of the American Railway Union (ARU) in 1893 and leader of the Pullman strike of 1894; and John L. Lewis, one of the founders of the Committee for Industrial Organizations (1935) within the AFL.

(2) Neither W. E. B. Du Bois, Jackie Robinson, nor James Meredith are considered pioneers in the area of educational reform. Important figures in the field of educational reform include Horace Mann, who campaigned for free public education from the 1830s to the 1850s and served as a member of the House of Representatives as a Whig (1848–1853), and John Dewey, who critiqued the focus on rote learning rather than critical engagement with the world around the student and founded the experimental Laboratory Schools in Chicago in 1896.

(4) Neither W. E. B. Du Bois, Jackie Robinson, nor James Meredith are considered pioneers in the area of environmental protection. Important figures in the field of environmental protection include John Muir, the preservationist and founder of the Sierra Club (1892), and Rachel Carson, the author of the ground-breaking book, *Silent Spring*, which vividly described the impact of the agricultural chemical DDT on the environment and how modern society was poisoning the Earth.

PART II: THEMATIC ESSAY

Westward Movement of the Frontier

The frontier was, in the 19th century, the unofficial boundary line between settled and unsettled lands. The frontier line shifted farther and farther west as more and more of the United States became settled. The 19th century historian Frederick Jackson Turner argued, in 1893, that the existence of this frontier had been a positive factor in the development of the American character. The experience of living in a frontier situation instilled in the settlers—and their descendants—a sense of egalitarianism, individualism, and freedom. These values, Turner argued, helped create an American identity separate from the more aristocratic and rigid European culture. There are several events in United States history that propelled this westward movement of people. Two significant events were the signing of the Treaty of Paris (1783), ending the American Revolution, and the discovery of gold in California (1848), setting off a frantic Gold Rush. Both of these events had positive and negative effects, both for American settlers and for American Indians.

The Treaty of Paris (1783) opened up the land beyond the Appalachian Mountains to settlement by Americans. Following the American Revolution, thousands of settlers pushed beyond the Appalachian Mountains into the lands along the Ohio River Valley. This was land that the British had tried to close to settlement following the French and Indian War. Great Britain had put forth the Proclamation Act (1763) in an attempt to halt colonists who wanted to settle beyond the mountain range and to prevent future clashes between the colonists and American Indians. With the Treaty of Paris, Great Britain acknowledged the independence of the United States and accepted as its western boundary the Mississippi River, not the Appalachian Mountains. The entire area between the Appalachians and the Mississippi was now under the control of the newly independent United States. No provisions in the treaty recognized the sovereignty of the American Indian nations that lived there and that had been recognized by the British. Of course, the American Indians of this region had not been consulted.

The movement of Americans beyond the Appalachian Mountains following the Treaty of Paris had many positive effects for Americans. Farming thrived in the flat, fertile soil of the Ohio River Valley. The Ohio River and the Mississippi River became busy conduits for trade. The government passed the Harrison Land Law, facilitating the sale of smaller plots of land to settlers. Soon, settlers established the Ohio Territory, and then the Indiana Territory. The opening of this region prompted a series of internal improvements in the early 1800s, including new roads, such as the National Road (also known as the Cumberland Road) from Maryland into the Ohio River Valley, and new canals, most notably the Erie Canal, from the Hudson River in upstate New York to the Great Lakes.

As more Americans began to migrate into the interior of the continent, beyond the Appalachian Mountains, conflicts inevitably ensued with American Indians, especially those in the more northern part of the region—between the Ohio River and the Great Lakes. The government tried to solve the problem by working out the Treaty of Fort Stanwix in 1784. In the treaty, American Indians ceded much of the land in question to the United States. However, this treaty was negotiated with members of the Iroquois Confederacy—a group of American Indian nations that did not, for the most part, occupy the land in question, and whose claims to the land were dubious at best. The main occupants of the region, the Shawnee, the Delaware, and the Miami, were not part of these negotiations and protested bitterly that their land had been ceded without their consent. Subsequently, a series of military conflicts ensued in the 1790s in the region. American troops led by General Arthur St. Clair suffered a massive defeat at the mouth of the Wabash River in 1791. Later, at the Battle of Fallen Timbers (1794), American Indians were soundly defeated by superior American firepower. In the following year, 1795, American Indians gave up claim to most of Ohio in the Treaty of Greenville. The treaty brought only a temporary peace. Within a generation, settlers would push farther into the Ohio and Indiana territories; these incursions would soon create additional conflicts that would not be resolved until the War of 1812.

Later in the 19th century, another historical development—the discovery of gold in California in 1848—led to additional opportunities for Americans and additional conflicts with American Indians. The discovery, and the subsequent Gold Rush, took place within the context of the United States pursuing its "manifest destiny" of expansion across the continent to the Pacific Ocean. This vision of continental domination became a reality with the victory of the United States in the Mexican-American War. Americans had been settling in the Mexican territory of Texas as far back as the 1820s. In 1836, Texans fought for and won independence from Mexico. Texas finally joined the United States as the fifteenth slave state in 1845. Conflict between the United States and Mexico soon ensued. The two countries disagreed over the southern border of Texas. It was at this point, in 1846, that President James K. Polk sent troops into this disputed territory. Skirmishes in the disputed area led to war between Mexico and the United States. The United States won the war, which lasted from 1846 to 1848, and acquired the huge territory that comprised the northern provinces of Mexico, which is known as the Mexican Cession.

An astounding discovery was made in the Mexican Cession territory, just about a week before the Treaty of Guadalupe Hidalgo between the United States and Mexico was signed—gold was found in California at Sutter's Mill in Coloma in January 1848. In March, a month after the United States formally acquired California, word spread far and wide about the existence of gold there. On the positive side, California was quickly settled with thousands of newcomers. A large percentage of the 300,000 people who migrated to California came in 1849—thus their nickname "forty-niners." The Gold Rush drew immigrants from all over—from eastern cities, from Canada, from Europe, from Latin America, and from China. By 1852, 20,000 Chinese immigrants had moved to the United States; by 1860, over 34,000 lived in California alone. California quickly became a thriving, multi-ethnic territory. Most migrants to California did not strike it rich in gold mining, but many thrived by farming in the region's lush valleys. Boomtowns and eventually cities sprouted up, providing additional opportunities for men and women to earn a living.

On the negative side, the rapid settlement of California following the Gold Rush intensified sectional tensions in the United States and pushed the nation closer to civil war. By 1850, California had enough people to form a state. Californians wrote up a constitution to submit to Congress in which slavery would be illegal. Southern senators objected to the admission of an additional free state. Senate negotiators, led by the aging Henry Clay, worked out a series of measures to resolve this extremely contentious problem. These measures became known as the Compromise of 1850. The most important elements of the compromise were the admittance of California as a free state, which pleased Northern politicians, and a more stringent Fugitive Slave Law, which pleased Southern politicians. Ultimately, the Senate "unbundled" the elements of the compromise, so that they were voted on individually. The measures all passed and were signed into law. Many Northerners grew alarmed at the enforcement of the Fugitive Slave Law. Previously, the majority of Northerners could ignore the brutality of the slave system, but following 1850, slave catchers brought the system to the streets of Northern cities. In response, many Northern states passed "personal liberty laws" offering protection to fugitives. Many whites and free African Americans in Northern cities even formed vigilance committees to prevent the slave catchers from carrying out their orders.

Meanwhile, the rapid settlement of California had a devastating impact on American Indians who lived there. Prospectors saw American Indians as impediments to their search for gold, leading to massacres, enslavement, and removal. It is estimated that the Indian population of California dropped from about 150,000 in 1848, on the eve of the Gold Rush, to less than 30,000 by 1860. Disease took the lives of thousands of Indians, but systematic campaigns of extermination by white settlers against the native peoples of California contributed to what many historians label a genocide. White Californians organized paramilitary death squads, with the support of the state government, to kill American Indians. A brutal massacre occurred at Bridge Gulch in 1852, when a group of settlers attacked a band of Wintu Indians in response to the killing of a white settler. The state's first governor, Peter Burnett, saw the massacre of Indians as regrettable but inevitable. In addition, many farmers were eager to exploit the labor of Indians. When the framers of the California constitution prohibited slavery, they had African American slavery in mind, not Indian slavery. Farmers frequently pressed Indians into forced agricultural work. By the 1860s, several Indian groups simply ceased to exist, with their people either killed or dispersed.

The pushing of the frontier farther, and the opening up of new lands to settlement, has profoundly affected the United States. On the one hand, it has provided space for Americans to acquire land, to start over again, and to carve new lives and new communities out of a rugged frontier. On the other hand, the settlement of the West created conflict and suffering. The opening up of new lands intensified sectional conflicts over slavery and contributed to the onset of the Civil War. In addition, the movement of settlers to the West decimated American Indians who were in the path of settlement.

PART III: DOCUMENT-BASED QUESTION

Part A: Short Answer

Document 1a and Document 1b

1 Based on the documents, one form of discrimination that African Americans experienced in the 1960s was segregation in regard to education, housing, and job opportunities.

This answer receives full credit because it states one form of discrimination that African Americans experienced in the 1960s.

Document 2

2 According to Adam Fairclough, one effect of the 1963 demonstrations in Birmingham, Alabama, was that they inspired African Americans in other communities to take action because they saw that if segregation could be successfully challenged in Birmingham, then it was vulnerable throughout the South.

This answer receives full credit because it states one effect of the 1963 demonstrations in Birmingham, Alabama.

Document 3

3a According to President Lyndon B. Johnson, one achievement of the civil rights movement was that it pressured the federal government to pass the Civil Rights Act of 1964.

This answer receives full credit because it states one achievement of the civil rights movement.

3b According to President Lyndon B. Johnson, one remaining goal of the civil rights movement was expanding opportunities so that all Americans can live full and meaningful lives.

This answer receives full credit because it states one remaining goal of the civil rights movement.

Document 4

4(1) According to Toby Goldstein, one reason for the development of the anti–Vietnam War movement was the ever-increasing body count of the war, as more and more American families had to deal with loved ones dying in the war. Another reason for the development of the anti–Vietnam War movement, according to Toby Goldstein, was the dishonest assessment of the war by President Lyndon B. Johnson, who asserted that America could see "light at the end of the tunnel," when in actuality the situation in Vietnam was becoming increasingly grim for American forces.

This answer receives full credit because it states two reasons for the development of the anti–Vietnam War movement.

Document 5

5 According to Nancy Zaroulis and Gerald Sullivan, one reason for protest against the Vietnam War was that many Americans perceived the war to be unconstitutional and illegal because it was an undeclared war.

This answer receives full credit because it states one reason for protest against the Vietnam War.

Document 6

6a According to George C. Herring, one way the anti–Vietnam War movement was not successful was that it did not actually turn large segments of Americans against the war; many Americans became more resentful of the anti-war movement than of the war itself.

This answer receives full credit because it states one way the anti–Vietnam War movement was not successful.

6b According to George C. Herring, one way the anti–Vietnam War movement was successful was that it forced the Johnson administration to act in a more constrained manner and may have prevented Johnson from taking more extreme actions in Vietnam and elsewhere.

This answer receives full credit because it states one way the anti–Vietnam War movement was successful.

Document 7

7 According to Rachel Carson, one issue that has led to concerns about the environment has been the increased exposure to synthetic chemicals that virtually every human being has been subjected to.

This answer receives full credit because it states one issue that has led to concerns about the environment.

Document 8a and Document 8b

8 Based on the documents, one reason the observance of Earth Day is important to the environmental movement is that Earth Day demonstrations captured the attention of millions of ordinary Americans who heard about them in the media or saw the numerous demonstrations in person.

This answer receives full credit because it states one reason the observance of Earth Day is important to the environmental movement.

Document 9a

9a According to Nelson Lemann, one impact of Earth Day is that several key environmental laws were passed, including the Clean Air Act of 1970, the Clean Water Act of 1972, and Endangered Species Act of 1973.

This answer receives full credit because it states one impact of Earth Day.

Document 9b

9b According to Frances Beinecke, one reason the environmental movement continues to be important is that Americans need to be constantly pushed to take immediate action to reduce the causes of climate change before the Earth reaches a tipping point of sustainability.

This answer receives full credit because it states one reason the environmental movement continues to be important.

Part B: Document-Based Essay

In France, during a period of tumultuous protests against the government in 1968, someone wrote on a wall, "Be realistic, demand the impossible." In the decades following World War II, many individuals and groups in America have done just that—they have taken action to change situations that seemed impossible to change. Starting with individuals and small groups, substantial protest movements developed that led to momentous change. Though protest movements didn't accomplish everything they set out to accomplish, they have been remarkable in reforming the United States. One movement for change is the civil rights movement, which challenged systematic racial discrimination and the social assumptions that buttressed that system. Another is the environmental movement, which raised awareness around threats to the planet's ecological balance and today continues to push America to take action on the issue of climate change.

The civil rights movement developed in the context of systematic discrimination, known as the Jim Crow system. After the Civil War, Southern whites created a system of separate facilities for African Americans and white people. Public accommodations—waiting rooms at train stations, water fountains, lunch counters, public schools—had restrictions on African Americans, who either were outright banned or were relegated to separate sections. (Document 1a) African Americans were made to sit toward the back of busses and had to give up their seats as more white passengers boarded. In addition, African Americans were effectively excluded from the political process by a series of carefully tailored voting laws that excluded African Americans without outright stating that African Americans could not vote. (Document 1b) These measures including poll taxes, literacy tests, and grandfather clauses. Without the ability to vote, there was no formal way for African Americans to change the Jim Crow system. This system was the public manifestation of white supremacy—a daily reminder of the second-class status that African Americans were kept in.

The more immediate context of the civil rights movement was World War II. After the war, many African Americans felt a sense of empowerment after having served in the armed forces and were ready to fight for democracy at home. Many veterans had participated in the "Double V" campaign during the war; they wore buttons promoting victory against fascism abroad and victory against racism at home. These veterans, mostly men, as well as organizations of African American women, became increasingly vocal in the late 1940s and early 1950s. Their activism pushed President Harry Truman to integrate the armed forces in 1948 and pushed the Supreme Court, in *Brown* v. *Board of Education* (1954), to abolish "whites only" schools and to order the creation of integrated public schools. Still, the Jim Crow system existed in everyday life for millions of African Americans in the South.

In community after community in the South, African Americans challenged the Jim Crow system. In 1963 activists picked a difficult target—Birmingham, Alabama, a conservative city in the deep South with an entrenched system of segregation. (Document 2) The public safety commissioner of Birmingham, Eugene "Bull" Connor, would not tolerate public demonstrations. He used fire hoses, police dogs, and brutal force to put down the campaign. During the Birmingham campaign, Dr. Martin Luther King Jr. was arrested and wrote his famous "Letter from Birmingham Jail." Connor might not have realized it at the time, but by taking extreme measures against the civil rights movement, he actually helped it. Even if Americans were not so concerned about segregation in the South before, images of police brutality in the media conveyed to Americans that the movement was justified and the authorities were unjust. After several weeks, authorities in Birmingham sat down with activists and negotiated a transition away from the Jim Crow system. Activists throughout the South were heartened; if segregation could be successfully challenged in Birmingham, then it could be brought down anywhere. The actions "exposed the vulnerability" of the entire Jim Crow system, according to historian Adam Fairclough. In the aftermath of the Birmingham campaign, the movement targeted 115 communities with 930 actions. By the end of 1963, over 300 cities agreed to some degree of integration. (Document 2)

The Birmingham campaign and the actions following it in 1963 proved to be a turning point in regard to federal civil rights legislation. In June 1963, the same month that civil rights leader Medgar Evers was murdered in front of his house in Jackson, Mississippi, President John F. Kennedy made a national address in which he called civil rights a "moral issue" and pledged to support civil rights legislation. After Kennedy's assassination in November 1963, President Lyndon Johnson took up the cause of civil rights legislation with vigor, pressuring reluctant Democrats to support the cause. As Johnson said, "the voice of the Negro was the call to action." (Document 3) His efforts helped ensure passage of the 1964 Civil Rights Act, which guaranteed equal access for all Americans to public accommodations. Another section banned discrimination in employment based on race or sex. The following year, Johnson, with equal vigor, pushed for passage of the Voting Rights Act, which outlawed many of the practices that Southern states used to prevent African Americans from voting. It also gave the Justice Department the power to review any new changes to voting rules in Southern states. (Document 3)

Passage of the Civil Rights Act in 1964 and the Voting Rights Act in 1965 were major milestones, but the work of the civil rights movement was not over. As President Johnson said, "freedom is not enough." Persistent patterns of discrimination continue to exist in the United States. The legacy of racism affects the job market and housing patterns. In many ways, African Americans did not have "the same chance as every other American," as President Johnson said in 1965. (Document 3) Equality under the law had been accomplished, but equality of opportunity had not been fully realized. Activists and reformers have continued to push for a more egalitarian society in the decades since the 1960s. In recent years, the Black Lives Matter movement emerged. The phrase "Black lives matter" began to appear in social media in 2013, following the acquittal of George Zimmerman, a neighborhood watch coordinator in Florida who had been accused of shooting and killing Trayvon Martin, an African American teenager. The movement grew to focus on issues of racial profiling, police brutality, and racial and economic inequality.

Another important protest movement that has pressed for change is the environmental movement. The environmental movement developed in the context of nearly a century of industrial growth in the United States. The expansion of industry, accompanied by the extraction of raw materials, the harnessing of fossil fuels, the creation of items that are quickly discarded, and the discharge of pollutants, all took their toll on the environment. Reformers and political leaders around the turn of the 20th century, such as John Muir and Theodore Roosevelt, called attention to the destruction done to natural areas by large-scale mining and logging. Their efforts led to the expansion of the National Park system and the establishment of thousands of acres of protected national forests. However, it is only after World War II that writers and scientists began to note the more systematic damage done to the Earth's ecosystem by various industrial processes. In 1962, Murray Bookchin (writing under the pseudonym Lewis Herber) wrote a groundbreaking book, *Our Synthetic Environment*, warning of the dangers of pesticide use. Later that same year, Rachel Carson published the best-selling book, *Silent Spring*, a detailed description of the harmful effects of toxic chemicals on the environment. She vividly described how synthetic chemicals can be found throughout the environment, even in fish in remote lakes. Most troubling for many readers was the fact that these chemicals were found in humans, even in mothers' milk. She said that the big chemical companies spread false information about their products. The book was especially critical of chemical pesticides such as DDT. (Document 7) Her book shocked many people and was a catalyst for the environmental movement of the 1960s and 1970s.

The environmental protest movement went from consisting of many local efforts to being a national movement in 1970 with the development of Earth Day. Thousands of people, for example, marched down Fifth Avenue in New York City. (Document 8a) In all, demonstrations and other public events occurred at over 2000 colleges and 10,000 schools and in over 2000 communities. (Document 8b) The environmental protest movement became front page news. Earth Day brought people together to protest environmental destruction and inspired others to make a commitment to push for change.

The movement could soon claim some major legislative victories. The administration of President Richard M. Nixon and Congress created the Environmental Protection Agency in 1970 and approved amendments to the 1963 Clean Air Act (also in 1970) that established regulatory and enforcement mechanisms. These amendments first set limits on factory emissions. President Nixon also signed the Clean Water Act of 1972 and the Endangered Species Act to provide the EPA with additional mechanisms to protect the environment. (Document 9a) In addition, many communities across the nation began recycling programs to reduce the amount of garbage and to reuse resources such as aluminum and glass. In the 1970s, many Americans bought smaller, more fuel-efficient cars and were conscious about turning lights off when not in use.

Despite substantial victories, the environmental movement has had only limited success in addressing an even more pressing challenge—climate change. The environmental activist Frances Beinecke has written that, "Never in my lifetime have the challenges been greater" than those posed by climate change. (Document 9b) Since the early 1980s, scientists have become aware of a trend toward warmer global temperatures. Some became convinced that this warming trend was caused by trapped greenhouse gasses, which, in turn, were caused by human activities, primarily the burning of fossil fuels. In the 1990s and 2000s, a virtual consensus emerged in the scientific community around the connection between climate change and the emissions generated by the burning of fossil fuels. Calls were made to limit the human activities linked to climate change. Beinecke praises the movement for raising the issue of climate change and for beginning the work to make the shift toward renewable sources of power. However, she notes, the goal of becoming a "carbon-neutral nation" is still far away. She laments that this is "not yet the world we live in," but asserts that it is the world "we must" create if we hope to avoid the disastrous effects of climate change.

Both the civil rights movement and the environmental movement have played important roles in raising awareness of issues that seemed impossible to tackle. Both movements also contributed to major interim victories. The civil rights movement pushed the government to pass the Civil Rights Act and the Voting Rights Act to end discriminatory government policies. The environmental movement pushed the government to create the Environmental Protection Agency and to pass important protective legislation. However, the work of both protest movements continues. Entrenched patterns of everyday discrimination and white supremacist attitudes continue to exist. Likewise, the industrial production system, as well as everyday practices of millions of Americans, continue to generate the conditions that are worsening climate change. It remains to be seen whether the movements will be able to remake the world in a way where these problems are successfully addressed.

Topic	Question Numbers	*Number of Points
American political history	12, 16, 22, 23, 24, 34, 42, 43, 46	11
Political theory	1, 3	2
Economic theory/policy	14, 19, 25, 28, 29, 45, 49	8
Constitutional principles	4, 5, 6, 7, 8, 10, 11, 13, 18, 48	12
American foreign policy	9, 20, 26, 27, 31, 39, 40, 41, 44, 47	12
American studies—the American people	15, 17, 21, 30, 32, 33, 35, 36, 37, 38, 50	13
Geography	2	1
Skills questions included in the above content areas		
Reading comprehension	5, 12, 21, 26, 32, 33, 44	
Graph/table/diagram interpretation	8, 29, 38, 48	
Cartoon/image interpretation	19, 34, 35, 36, 45	
Map interpretation	39, 40	
Outlining skills	28, 37	

*Note: The 50 questions in Part I are worth a total of 60 percent of the exam. Since each correct answer is worth 60/50 or 1.2 points, totals are shown to the nearest full point in each content category.

PART I

Multiple-Choice Questions by Standard

Standard	Question Numbers
1—United States and New York History	1, 4, 9, 11, 12, 13, 16, 20, 22, 24, 26, 27, 31, 32, 35, 41, 42, 45, 46, 47, 50
2—World History	37, 39, 40, 44
3—Geography	2, 21, 30, 38
4—Economics	14, 15, 17, 19, 25, 28, 29, 33, 36, 49
5—Civics, Citizenship, and Government	3, 5, 6, 7, 8, 10, 18, 23, 34, 43, 48

Parts II and III by Theme and Standard

	Theme	Standards
Thematic Essay	Change; Citizenship; Diversity; Foreign Policy; Government; Immigration and Migration; Technology; Presidential Decisions and Actions	Standards 1, 2, 3, 4, and 5: United States and New York History; World History; Geography; Economics; Civics, Citizenship, and Government
Document-Based Essay	Citizenship; Civic Values; Diversity; Environment; Government; Individuals, Groups, Institutions; Presidential Decisions and Actions; Technology	Standards 1, 2, 3, and 5: United States and New York History; World History; Geography; Civics, Citizenship, and Government

Examination
August 2019
United States History and Government

PART I: MULTIPLE CHOICE

Answer all questions in this part

Directions (1–50): For each statement or question, write in the space provided the *number* of the word or expression that, of those given, best completes the statement or answers the question.

1 Which geographic features contributed to the economic development of the plantation system in the South?

  (1) rocky soil and deep harbors
  (2) short rivers and many waterfalls
  (3) rich soil and warm climate
  (4) high mountains and numerous rivers   1 _____

2 The slogan "no taxation without representation" was first used by Americans to protest Britain's
  (1) policy of salutary neglect
  (2) issuance of the Proclamation of 1763
  (3) passage of the Coercive Acts
  (4) attempts to raise revenue through the Stamp Act   2 _____

3 Weaknesses in the central government under the Articles of Confederation exposed by Shays' Rebellion contributed directly to the

  (1) signing of the Declaration of Independence
  (2) creation of the United States Constitution
  (3) development of a policy of neutrality
  (4) passage of the Northwest Ordinance   3 _____

4 A central issue in the debate between Federalists and Antifederalists over the ratification of the United States Constitution was the

(1) power of judicial review being granted to the judicial branch

(2) threat posed by a strong central government to the rights of citizens

(3) role of the president as commander in chief of the armed forces

(4) danger of unrestricted interstate commerce   4 _____

5 During the 1790s, which factor best explains why the United States was able to stay out of foreign conflicts?

(1) Europe depended on farm products from the United States.

(2) The United States had announced the Monroe Doctrine.

(3) France and Great Britain agreed to end colonialism.

(4) The Atlantic Ocean helped the United States remain isolated from foreign threats.   5 _____

6 Which statement describes an effect of the Louisiana Purchase (1803)?

(1) The size of the United States was doubled.

(2) The boundary with Mexico was finally established.

(3) The Northwest Territory became part of the United States.

(4) The Mississippi River became the western boundary of the United States.   6 _____

7 Many New England citizens opposed United States participation in the War of 1812 because they

(1) feared a Russian invasion in the Northwest

(2) worried that France might try to regain Canada

(3) resented disruption of their trade with England

(4) resisted the extension of slavery into western territories   7 _____

8 The protection against double jeopardy and the right to a speedy
trial are evidence that the United States Constitution supports the
principle of

(1) eminent domain
(2) due process of law
(3) representative democracy
(4) reserved powers   8 _____

9 During the early 1800s, advances in democratic government
included

(1) eliminating property ownership as a voting requirement
(2) ending the role of the electoral college
(3) increasing education and religious requirements for voting
(4) giving states the right to secede from the Union   9 _____

10 One reason abolitionists were unpopular with many Northerners
from the 1830s to 1860 was because the abolitionists

(1) favored the growth of slavery
(2) encouraged the annexation of Texas
(3) advocated views that increased tensions with the South
(4) supported the Fugitive Slave Law   10 _____

11 The Compromise of 1850 was an attempt to resolve issues related to

(1) the protection and spread of slavery
(2) boundary disputes between the United States and Britain over
    the Oregon Country
(3) relations with the Native American Indians of the Great Plains
(4) the role of the federal government in industrial development 11 _____

12 One reason the decision in *Dred Scott* v. *Sandford* (1857) was so
controversial is that it

(1) strengthened the idea of popular sovereignty
(2) gave enslaved persons full citizenship
(3) ruled that Congress had no power to limit slavery in the
    territories
(4) supported Harriet Beecher Stowe's point of view in
    Uncle Tom's Cabin   12 _____

13 When Andrew Carnegie stated, "The man who dies rich, dies disgraced," he was supporting

   (1) consumer credit   (3) Social Darwinism

   (2) charitable giving   (4) antitrust legislation   13 _____

Base your answer to question 14 on the chart below and on your knowledge of social studies.

Buffalo Population: 1800 to 1895

Date	Population
1800	40,000,000
1850	20,000,000
1865	15,000,000
1870	14,000,000
1875	1,000,000
1880	395,000
1885	20,000
1889	1,091
1895	Less than 1,000

Source: U.S. Department of Interior
(adapted)

14 A major impact of the trend shown on the chart was that

   (1) frontier trading posts became more prosperous

   (2) Plains Indians lost their main source of food, shelter, and clothing

   (3) reservations were relocated closer to buffalo migration routes

   (4) white settlers became dependent on buffalo products   14 _____

15 "A government's primary role is to provide a favorable atmosphere for business, including a stable currency, hands-off regulation, and domestic order."

A supporter of this idea would most likely favor
(1) establishing consumer protection laws
(2) securing collective-bargaining rights
(3) levying high taxes on business
(4) following laissez-faire economics   15 _____

Base your answer to question 16 on the photograph below and on your knowledge of social studies.

Source: Solomon Butcher, 1886

16 Which act of Congress most directly contributed to the situation shown in this photo?
(1) the Homestead Act   (3) the purchase of Alaska
(2) the Sherman Antitrust Act   (4) the Interstate Commerce Act   16 _____

Base your answer to question 17 on the passage below and on your knowledge of social studies.

. . . We think the enforced separation of the races, as applied to the internal commerce of the State, neither abridges the privileges or immunities of the colored man, deprives him of his property without due process of law, nor denies him the equal protection of the laws within the meaning of the 14th Amendment . . .

17 Which Supreme Court decision is reflected in this passage?

(1) *Wabash, St. Louis & Pacific R.R.* v. *Illinois* (1886)
(2) *United States* v. *E. C. Knight Co.* (1895)
(3) *In Re Debs* (1895)
(4) *Plessy* v. *Ferguson* (1896)   17 _____

18 In the late 1800s, one reason labor unions struggled to gain support was because

(1) employers could easily replace striking employees
(2) the wages of industrial laborers were high
(3) government-funded public-works jobs were readily available
(4) corporations ended the use of court injunctions   18 _____

19 Which term is most closely associated with the start of the Spanish-American War?

(1) socialism   (3) yellow journalism
(2) populism   (4) isolationism   19 _____

Base your answer to question 20 on the cartoon below and on your knowledge of social studies.

The Appearance of the New Party in the Political Field

Source: W. A. Carson, *Utica Saturday Globe*, 1912 (adapted)

20 What is the main idea of this 1912 cartoon?

(1) The Democratic Party is losing support.
(2) Republicans outnumber Democrats in the United States.
(3) The political process has no room for more than two parties.
(4) A third political party can threaten the two major parties.

20 _____

21 In the late 1800s, the major goal of United States policy in both the annexation of Hawaii and the acquisition of the Philippines was to

(1) obtain coaling stations and seaports for United States ships
(2) expand United States fishing rights in international waters
(3) limit the spread of Japanese influence
(4) protect the area around the Panama Canal   21 _____

22 **"Income Tax Amendment Passes"**
"Congress Enacts Federal Reserve Act"
"Pure Food and Drug Act Passed by Congress"

Which reform movement supported the actions described by these headlines?

(1) Progressive   (3) labor
(2) Prohibition   (4) conservation   22 _____

23 In his war message to Congress, President Woodrow Wilson urged the United States to enter World War I in order to

(1) protect the empires of European countries
(2) create a new world government
(3) make the world safe for democracy
(4) stop a British attack on the United States   23 _____

Base your answer to question 24 on the cartoon below and on your knowledge of social studies.

Step by Step

STRIKES – WALK OUTS

DISORDER – RIOTS

BOLSHEVISM – MURDERS

CHAOS

Source: Sid Greene, *New York Evening Telegram*, 1919
(adapted)

24 What is the cartoonist's point of view in this 1919 cartoon?

(1) Immigrants will easily assimilate into American society.

(2) Industrial production will expand and create more jobs.

(3) Civil liberties will be restricted and ordinary American citizens will be hurt.

(4) The actions of labor unions threaten the American way of life.   24 _____

Base your answer to question 25 on the photograph below and on your knowledge of social studies.

Source: Photo taken in Dayton, Tennessee, 1925;
University of Missouri-Kansas City, School of Law (adapted)

25 This photograph shows one side of the 1920s conflict between

(1) union men and factory owners
(2) science and religion
(3) nativists and immigrants
(4) censorship and free press

25 ____

Base your answer to question 26 on the poem below and on your knowledge of social studies.

I, TOO

I, too, sing America.

I am the darker brother.
They send me to eat in the kitchen
When company comes,
But I laugh,
And eat well,
And grow strong.

Tomorrow,
I'll be at the table
When company comes.
Nobody'll dare
Say to me,
"Eat in the kitchen,"
Then.

Besides,
They'll see how beautiful I am
And be ashamed—

I, too, am America.

—Langston Hughes, "I, Too," 1926

26 During the 1920s, which development was most closely associated with this poem?
  (1) growth of the motion-picture industry
  (2) emergence of an antiwar party
  (3) blossoming of African American culture
  (4) expansion of mass consumption

26 _____

27 In the 1920s, authors such as F. Scott Fitzgerald, Ernest Hemingway, and Sinclair Lewis wrote primarily about

(1) the intolerance of the Ku Klux Klan
(2) post–World War I disillusionment and materialism
(3) the failure of cultural pluralism
(4) the lack of educational opportunities for younger Americans   27 _____

28 The Federal Deposit Insurance Corporation (FDIC) and the Securities and Exchange Commission (SEC) were part of President Franklin D. Roosevelt's efforts to

(1) reduce the power of business monopolies during the Great Depression
(2) give organized labor a stronger voice in politics
(3) reform economic problems that contributed to the Great Depression
(4) bring electricity to rural areas   28 _____

29 President Franklin D. Roosevelt proposed a plan in 1937 to add justices to the Supreme Court primarily because the Court

(1) lacked representation from minority groups
(2) had declared major New Deal laws unconstitutional
(3) had little judicial experience
(4) supported a loose interpretation of the Constitution   29 _____

Base your answers to questions 30 and 31 on the graph below and on your knowledge of social studies.

Unemployment, 1929–1945

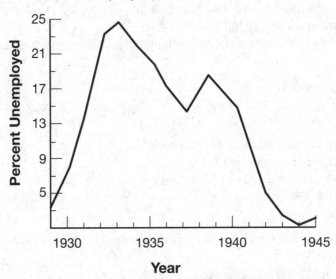

Source: *Historical Statistics of the United States: Colonial Times to 1970*, U.S. Census Bureau, 1975 (adapted)

30 What was the major reason for the change in unemployment shown on the graph between 1933 and 1937?

(1) Banks increased their lending to new businesses, who hired more workers.

(2) The profits of corporations were heavily taxed by the states.

(3) Job opportunities were created by New Deal public-works projects.

(4) The federal government nationalized the transportation and utility industries.   30 _____

31 What was the main cause of the trend in employment shown on the graph between 1942 and 1945?

(1) increased manufacturing to meet the needs of World War II
(2) the success of the Social Security Act
(3) the impact of a high inflation rate
(4) a decline in the number of women in the work force

31 _____

32 The Neutrality Acts (1935–1937) were passed to

(1) support the policy of appeasement
(2) provide troops to halt Italian aggression
(3) increase the profits of United States weapons manufacturers
(4) avoid the actions that led the United States into World War I

32 _____

33 Which government action was a response to the Japanese attack on Pearl Harbor?

(1) drafting all Japanese American men into the United States Army
(2) passing labor laws banning the employment of immigrants
(3) ending all oil sales to Japan
(4) forcing the relocation and internment of Japanese Americans

33 _____

Base your answer to question 34 on the posters below and on your knowledge of social studies.

Source: New York State Works Progress Administration Art Project

Source: Office for Emergency Management

34 Which United States government action was most similar to the goal shown in these World War II posters?

   (1) institution of the draft by the Selective Service Act (1940)

   (2) aid to Russia under the Lend-Lease Act (1941)

   (3) rationing by the Office of Price Administration (1941)

   (4) development of the Manhattan Project (1942)   34 _____

35 The Servicemen's Readjustment Act of 1944 (GI Bill) made a significant impact on post–World War II America because it provided for

(1) aid to veterans for housing and college costs
(2) the rapid demobilization of soldiers
(3) pensions for soldiers from World War I
(4) the establishment of a draft for all males over 18 years of age   35 _____

36 Following World War II, the United States adopted the foreign policy of containment primarily to

(1) return to pre-war isolationism
(2) limit the spread of communism
(3) force European nations to end colonialism
(4) support the work of the World Court   36 _____

37 One important effect of President Eisenhower's proposal for interstate highways was a significant increase in

(1) health-care spending
(2) suburban communities
(3) educational opportunities
(4) sectional differences   37 _____

Base your answer to question 38 on the passage below and on your knowledge of social studies.

The people of the United States share with the people of the Soviet Union their satisfaction for the safe flight of the astronaut in man's first venture into space. We congratulate you and the Soviet scientists and engineers who made this feat possible. It is my sincere desire that in the continuing quest for knowledge of outer space our nations can work together to obtain the greatest benefit to mankind.

—President John F. Kennedy, Telegram to Nikita Khrushchev,
April 12, 1961

38 One way President Kennedy responded to the Soviet action referred to in the telegram was to support

(1) a decrease in the budget for space exploration
(2) an expansion of the Peace Corps to aid impoverished nations
(3) the removal of Soviet troops from East Berlin
(4) the commitment to a Moon landing by the end of the decade   38 _____

39 • Establishing a direct telephone line between Washington and Moscow
 • Negotiating a limited nuclear test-ban treaty
 • Selling surplus wheat to the Soviet Union

These actions by presidents John F. Kennedy and Richard Nixon are examples of their attempts to

(1) meet the Soviet Union's Cold War demands
(2) establish peaceful coexistence with the Soviet Union
(3) support Soviet troops fighting in Afghanistan
(4) weaken the military power of the Soviet Union   39 _____

40 During the 1960s, the escalation of United States involvement in the Vietnam War was based on the belief that

(1) restoring French colonial power was necessary for political stability in Southeast Asia

(2) a strong military presence would limit Japanese trade with Vietnam

(3) a North Vietnamese victory would lead to further losses as predicted by the domino theory

(4) a cease-fire agreement would increase college protests   40 _____

41 What was the major effect of the Civil Rights Act of 1964?

(1) Racial discrimination in public facilities was banned.

(2) Citizenship and voting rights were extended to Native American Indians.

(3) The use of poll taxes and literacy tests for voting were outlawed.

(4) Busing to integrate schools was authorized.   41 _____

42 Which pair of Supreme Court cases upheld the right to counsel for defendants in state criminal cases?

(1) *Mapp* v. *Ohio* (1961) and *Heart of Atlanta Motel* v. *United States* (1964)

(2) *Baker* v. *Carr* (1962) and *Engel* v. *Vitale* (1962)

(3) *Gideon* v. *Wainwright* (1963) and *Miranda* v. *Arizona* (1966)

(4) *Tinker* v. *Des Moines* (1969) and *Roe* v. *Wade* (1973)   42 _____

Base your answer to question 43 on the graph below and on your knowledge of social studies.

Percent of Men and Women in Labor Force: 1950 to 1990

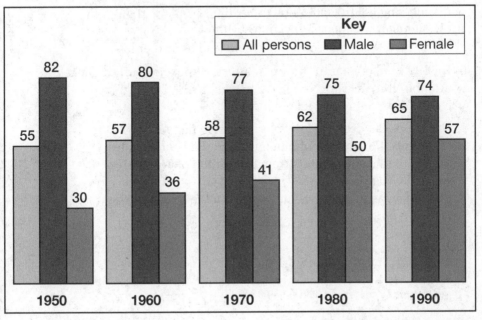

Source: U.S. Census Bureau, 1990 (adapted)

43 Which conclusion is most clearly supported by information in the graph?

   (1) Older Americans remained in the labor force longer in 1990 than in 1950.
   (2) All Americans born during the baby boom after World War II joined the labor force.
   (3) Half as many men were in the labor force in 1990 as compared to 1950.
   (4) In every decade shown, the percentage of women in the labor force grew while the percentage of men in the labor force declined.

43 _____

44 During the Persian Gulf War (1991), the primary aim of the United States was to force Iraq to

(1) withdraw its troops from Kuwait
(2) hold democratic elections
(3) increase the price of its oil exports
(4) submit to weapons inspections by the United Nations   44 _____

45 In 1993, many labor union leaders opposed United States membership in the North American Free Trade Agreement (NAFTA) because they feared it would

(1) cause Americans to lose jobs to foreign nations
(2) reduce the number of immigrants to the United States
(3) result in higher exports from the United States to Mexico and Canada
(4) outlaw wage increases for workers in the United States   45 _____

Base your answer to question 46 on the cartoon below and on your knowledge of social studies.

THE 9-11 HEARINGS...

BLAME

Source: Steve Breen, *San Diego Union-Tribune*, 2004 (adapted)

46 According to the cartoonist, the investigation of intelligence failures related to the 9/11 terrorist attacks resulted in

(1) praise for government efforts to stop intelligence leaks
(2) open immigration from all regions of the world
(3) recommendations to limit dependence on foreign intelligence
(4) various federal agencies attempting to avoid criticism by shifting responsibility

46 _____

47 Between 1881 and 1921, one major cause of the increasing number of immigrants to the United States was the

(1) availability of free land in the Southeast
(2) increased job opportunities in industry
(3) increased need for military personnel
(4) federal aid to pay the housing costs of new arrivals

47 _____

48 Prior to its military involvement in both the War of 1812 and World War I, the United States attempted to maintain a policy of

(1) neutrality   (3) collective security

(2) internationalism   (4) détente   48 _____

49 ". . . We conclude that, in the field of public education, the doctrine of 'separate but equal' has no place. Separate educational facilities are inherently unequal." . . .

These statements were included in which Supreme Court decision?

(1) *Schenck* v. *United States* (1919)

(2) *Korematsu* v. *United States* (1944)

(3) *Brown* v. *Board of Education of Topeka* (1954)

(4) *Vernonia School District* v. *Acton* (1995)   49 _____

50 •   Alien and Sedition Acts of 1798

   •   Espionage Act of 1917

   •   USA Patriot Act of 2001

One common effect of these wartime laws has been to

(1) expand government regulation of the economy

(2) increase the nation's military defenses

(3) promote immigration from neighboring nations

(4) protect national security at the expense of civil liberties   50 _____

In developing your answer to Part II, be sure to keep these general definitions in mind:
  (a) <u>describe</u> means "to illustrate something in words or tell about it"
  (b) <u>discuss</u> means "to make observations about something using facts, reasoning, and argument; to present in some detail"

PART II: THEMATIC ESSAY QUESTION

Directions: Write a well-organized essay that includes an introduction, several paragraphs addressing the task below, and a conclusion.

Theme: Amendments

> The writers of the United States Constitution included an amending process to respond to changing times and unforeseen circumstances. Since the Civil War, important amendments have had an impact on the United States and/or on American society.

Task:

> Select *two* amendments to the United States Constitution *since* the Civil War and for *each*
> • Describe the historical circumstances surrounding the adoption of the amendment
> • Discuss the impact of this amendment on the United States and/or on American society

You may use any constitutional amendment that has been added since the Civil War. Some suggestions you might wish to consider include:

    13th amendment—abolition of slavery (1865)
    15th amendment—African American male suffrage (1870)
    16th amendment—graduated income tax (1913)
    17th amendment—direct election of United States senators (1913)
    18th amendment—Prohibition (1919)
    19th amendment—woman's suffrage (1920)
    26th amendment—18-year-old vote (1971)

You are *not* limited to these suggestions.

Guidelines:

In your essay, be sure to:
- Develop all aspects of the task
- Support the theme with relevant facts, examples, and details
- Use a logical and clear plan of organization, including an introduction and a conclusion that are beyond a restatement of the theme

In developing your answers to Part III, be sure to keep these general definitions in mind:
  (a) <u>describe</u> means "to illustrate something in words or tell about it"
  (b) <u>discuss</u> means "to make observations about something using facts, reasoning, and argument; to present in some detail"

PART III: DOCUMENT-BASED QUESTION

This question is based on the accompanying documents. The question is designed to test your ability to work with historical documents. Some of these documents have been edited for the purposes of this question. As you analyze the documents, take into account the source of each document and any point of view that may be presented in the document. Keep in mind that the language and images used in a document may reflect the historical context of the time in which it was created.

Historical Context:

The president of the United States has been granted power as the commander in chief by the Constitution. Although the president has used his military powers to commit troops overseas, he has also used this power to respond to domestic challenges. These challenges have included *President Grover Cleveland and the Pullman strike, President Herbert Hoover and the Bonus Army,* and *President Harry Truman and segregation in the armed forces.*

Task:

Using the information from the documents and your knowledge of United States history, answer the questions that follow each document in Part A. Your answers to the questions will help you write the Part B essay in which you will be asked to

Select *two* domestic challenges mentioned in the historical context and for *each*

• Describe the historical circumstances that led to the president's action
• Discuss how the president's action influenced the United States and/or American society

Part A: Short-Answer Questions

Directions: Analyze the documents and answer the short-answer questions that follow each document in the space provided.

Document 1

The nation's worst depression of the 19th century began in 1893. In 1894, the worst year of the depression, workers at the Pullman Company went on strike in Chicago.

> . . . The rents Pullman charged were excessive, running about 25 percent higher than in neighboring towns. He sold at ten cents per thousand gallons water that he bought from Chicago at four cents. He forced his tenants to buy their food and other necessities from company stores, where prices far exceeded those of regular outlets. The simmering cauldron of protest boiled over when in 1894 the company cut wages an average of 25 percent, without a comparable cut in rent or in the cost of necessities. Pullman refused to listen to complaints and dismissed from their jobs those who persisted in the outcry. He then closed the plant.
>
> At this juncture [time], the American Railway Union, which had a membership of 150,000, including several thousand Pullman employees, joined the struggle, ordering its members not to handle trains with Pullman cars attached. The strike was quickly turned into a national disruption. Within a month, railroad traffic, particularly in the western states, was almost at a standstill. The beset [besieged] railroad owners hit on the scheme of coupling Pullman cars to trains that carried mail, confident that any interference with the mail was a federal crime. When the strikers still refused to man the trains, the railroads persuaded Attorney General Olney to swear in an army of special deputies—actually in the pay of the railroads—in order to help keep the trains moving.
>
> The leader of the union was Eugene V. Debs, a gentle but dynamic person who had made the interests of workingmen the consuming enthusiasm of his life. He had instructed his members to avoid violence. But it broke out now anyhow between the deputies and the strikers. The railroads in their frustration asked President Cleveland to send federal troops to keep order and to guarantee the safe handling of the mails. . . .

Source: Henry F. Graff, *Grover Cleveland*, Henry Holt and Company, 2002

1*a* According to Henry F. Graff, what was *one* reason Pullman workers went on strike? [1]

_____

_____

b According to Henry F. Graff, what was *one* reason President Grover Cleveland was asked to send federal troops to Chicago? [1]

_____

_____

Document 2a

President Grover Cleveland responded to the strike and to the riots that followed by sending federal troops to Chicago.

> . . . Cleveland also feared the worst, and responded accordingly. Federal troops arrived to quell [stop] the riots, ironically, on July 4. While patriotic citizens set off fireworks, in the city of Chicago they set fires. Thousands of angry protestors lay waste to the city. At the Chicago rail yards more freight trains were flipped over and cars set ablaze. A huge fire that night destroyed the expositions on the grounds of the World's Fair. Chicago degenerated into lawlessness and chaos.
>
> It continued for four days. On July 6, a rail deputy shot two men, inciting the largest riot of all—6,000 rail workers destroyed over $340,000 worth of railroad property on a single day as over 700 railroad cars were torched. The next day, a mob attacked the state militia. The soldiers fired back, killing 4 rioters and wounding 20 others. Reinforcements for the federal troops were called up from surrounding states. No American city had ever experienced such anarchy in peacetime. . . .

Source: Chris Wallace, *Character: Profiles in Presidential Courage*, Rugged Land, 2004

Document 2b

Burning of Six Hundred Freight-Cars on the Panhandle Railroad, South of Fiftieth Street, on the Evening of July 6th.

Source: G. A. Coffin and Charles Mente, *Harper's Weekly*, July 21, 1894

2 Based on these documents, what was *one* effect of President Cleveland's decision to send federal troops to end the Pullman strike? [1]

_____

_____

Document 3

> The Pullman Strike of 1894 was the first national strike in United States history. Before coming to an end, it involved over 150,000 persons and twenty-seven states and territories and would paralyze the nation's railway system. The entire rail labor force of the nation would walk away from their jobs. In supporting the capital side [railroad owners] of this strike President Cleveland for the first time in the Nation's history would send in federal troops, who would fire on and kill United States Citizens, against the wishes of the states. The federal courts of the nation would outlaw striking by the passing of the Omnibus indictment [federal charges against the leaders of the American Railway Union]. This blow to unionized labor would not be struck down until the passing of the Wagner act in 1935. This all began in the little town of Pullman, Illinois, just south of Chicago. . . .

Source: Keith Ladd and Greg Rickman, "The Pullman Strike," kansasheritage.org, 1998 (adapted)

3 According to Keith Ladd and Greg Rickman, what was **one** effect of President Cleveland's decision to support railroad owners during the Pullman strike?   [1]

_____

_____

Document 4a

Veterans' sheds, tents, and shanties sprawled across the Anacostia Flats in Washington, D.C., in 1932.

Source: National Archives (adapted)

Document 4b

Violent clash between police and veterans on the morning of July 28, 1932.

Source: General Douglas MacArthur Foundation

Document 4c

> . . . No "civil commotion" attracted as much attention as the march of the "bonus army." Demanding immediate and full payment of bonuses for their service in World War I, 15,000 to 20,000 unemployed veterans moved on Washington in the spring of 1932. The House passed the bonus bill, but when the Senate voted it down by an overwhelming margin, half the men stayed on; they had no jobs, no homes, no place else to go. Most of them lived in mean shanties on the muddy Anacostia flats, some camped in unused government buildings. General Glassford, the head of the District police, treated the men decently and with discretion, but, as the men stayed on day after day, federal officials panicked. On July 28, 1932, the government decided precipitately [suddenly] to evict bonus marchers from vacant buildings on Pennsylvania Avenue. Two veterans were killed and several District police were injured in a scuffle that followed. President Hoover summoned the U.S. Army to take over. . . .

Source: William E. Leuchtenburg, *The Perils of Prosperity, 1914–1932*, University of Chicago Press, 1993

4*a* Based on these documents, state *one* reason World War I veterans marched on Washington, D.C., in 1932.   [1]

_____

_____

b Based on these documents, state *one* reason President Hoover sent the United States Army to remove the Bonus Marchers.   [1]

_____

_____

Document 5a

Source: *Washington Post*, Friday, July 29, 1932

Document 5b

> . . . A storm of protest followed. Americans who viewed the photographs and read the reports over the next few days found the actions of their government inexcusable. Any remaining faith they still had in Washington was now called into question, especially when Hoover and MacArthur attempted to justify their orders by saying that the marchers were criminals and communists. Far from a revolutionary crowd, the veterans seemed to most people to be little different than the rest of the nation: they had no work and they wanted to feed their families. Squeezed from all directions, the people needed an ally—desperately—and in the Democratic candidate for president in 1932, they finally found one. . . .

Source: Peter Jennings and Todd Brewster, *The Century*, Doubleday, 1998

5 According to these documents, what were *two* reasons many Americans thought the government's action against the veterans was wrong? [2]

(1) _____

_____

(2) _____

_____

Document 6

... American history is punctuated by moments and incidents that become prisms through which larger events are better understood—the Boston Tea Party, Nat Turner's Rebellion, the Alamo, John Brown's Raid. The march of the Bonus Army belongs in such company. But its significance has been obscured [dimmed] by time, even to its direct beneficiaries—the millions of later veterans whose bonus would be the GI Bill and the benefits that have followed to the present day. And, its legacy is everlasting. The First Amendment of the Constitution grants Americans the right "to petition the government for redress of grievances." Millions of Americans have since peacefully marched on Washington in support of various causes, their way paved by the veterans of 1932.

Source: Paul Dickson and Thomas B. Allen, *The Bonus Army: An American Epic*, Walker and Company, 2004

6 According to Paul Dickson and Thomas B. Allen, what was *one* impact of the Bonus Army?   [1]

_____

_____

Document 7a

In 1941, civil rights activist A. Philip Randolph demanded an end to racial segregation in the Armed Forces.

> . . . Roosevelt ignored Randolph's call for a desegregated army. By that time, all branches of the military separated black soldiers into their own units, deployed them on segregated trains, and housed them in old, dilapidated barracks. Most black soldiers served as stewards and cooks or performed menial labor such as maintaining latrines [bathrooms]. As late as 1940, the U.S. armed services included only five black commissioned officers, including Benjamin O. Davis, Sr., the first African-American to reach the rank of general, and Benjamin O. Davis, Jr., the 20th century's first black graduate of West Point. Military leaders routinely denied black soldiers entry into many training classes that would have enabled them to advance in rank. . . .

Source: Mark Bauerlein et al., *Civil Rights Chronicle: The African American Struggle for Freedom*, Legacy, 2003

Document 7b

> . . . Not surprisingly, black organizations pressed hard for equality within the armed services. They viewed the military as a key institution in American life. A direct arm of the government, and a direct expression of the people, it personified the democratic values for which the United States fought. Ending racial discrimination in the armed forces would have a powerful effect on civil society. Moreover, if blacks made an equal contribution to the war effort, their claim to full citizenship would be much stronger. . . .

Source: Adam Fairclough, *Better Day Coming: Blacks and Equality, 1890–2000*, Viking, 2001

7 Based on these documents, what were **two** reasons African American civil rights leaders called for an end to racial segregation in the Armed Forces? [2]

(1) _____

_____

(2) _____

_____

Document 8a

Following World War II, on orders from President Truman, the Army, Navy, and Air Force abolished their traditional Jim Crow units and with very little fanfare integrated themselves. On a recent [September 1963] 3,200-mile tour of the South, we viewed the impressive results.

We saw Negro and white servicemen eating at the same mess-hall tables, drinking at the same on-base bars, playing ball on the same teams. They sleep in the same barracks, share lavatories and showers, borrow money from one another until pay day.

In on-base homes assigned without regard for race, white and Negro families live next door to one another, baby-sit for one another, watch TV together, share backyard barbecues. They swim together in on-base pools, worship together in military chapels. Their children play and squabble happily together on the lawns, attend on-base schools and Sunday schools together. All this has for years been accepted practice on military bases, including many in the Deep South. . . .

Source: Ruth and Edward Brecher, "The Military's Limited War Against Segregation,"
Reporting Civil Rights, The Library of America

Document 8b

Soldiers from the U.S. Army's Integrated Second Infantry Division in Korea

Source: Defense Media Network (adapted)

8 Based on these documents, what were *two* results of President Harry Truman's executive order abolishing segregated "Jim Crow units" in the military? [2]

(1) _____

_____

(2) _____

_____

Document 9

... The military's last all-black unit disbanded in 1954, and the services, with the exception of the navy, which lagged somewhat behind, recruited African Americans for all specialties. Acceptance in the ranks did not, however, mean acceptance in communities adjacent to military installations. While black service personnel had equal access to integrated military family quarters on bases, they faced the same discrimination in housing in local civilian communities that had always existed. . . .

Black military personnel also faced discrimination in furthering their own education. Universities near military installations, especially in the South, refused to accept black students.

Outside the gates of their bases, black military personnel found that civilian communities treated them in the same manner as they did their local minority population. Jim Crow laws, again mostly in the South but to some degree throughout the country, separated black from white in shopping, eating, housing, transportation, and recreational facilities. Frequently these public areas exhibited Whites Only signs, and the towns had police more than willing to enforce these policies. . . .

The arrival of the 1960s brought increased impatience in the black military and civilian communities. Protests continued, with sit-ins the dominant form of nonviolent action as blacks and their supporters challenged local Jim Crow laws restricting their access to eating establishments and other public facilities. . . .

Source: Lt. Colonel (Ret.) Michael Lee Lanning,
The African-American Soldier: From Crispus Attucks to Colin Powell,
Citadel Press, 2004 (adapted)

9 According to Michael Lee Lanning, what was *one* way discrimination against African Americans continued after President Truman's executive order? [1]

_____

_____

Part B: Essay

Directions: Write a well-organized essay that includes an introduction, several paragraphs, and a conclusion. Use evidence from *at least four* documents in your essay. Support your response with relevant facts, examples, and details. Include additional outside information.

Historical Context:

> The president of the United States has been granted power as the commander in chief by the Constitution. Although the president has used his military powers to commit troops overseas, he has also used this power to respond to domestic challenges. These challenges have included **President Grover Cleveland and the Pullman strike, President Herbert Hoover and the Bonus Army,** and **President Harry Truman and segregation in the armed forces.**

Task:

> Using the information from the documents and your knowledge of United States history, write an essay in which you
>
> Select *two* domestic challenges mentioned in the historical context and for *each*
>
> - Describe the historical circumstances that led to the president's action
> - Discuss how the president's action influenced the United States and/or American society

Guidelines:

In your essay, be sure to
- Develop all aspects of the task
- Incorporate information from *at least four* documents
- Incorporate relevant outside information
- Support the theme with relevant facts, examples, and details
- Use a logical and clear plan of organization, including an introduction and a conclusion that are beyond a restatement of the theme

Answers
August 2019
United States History and Government

Answer Key

PART I

1. 3	11. 1	21. 1	31. 1	41. 1
2. 4	12. 3	22. 1	32. 4	42. 3
3. 2	13. 2	23. 3	33. 4	43. 4
4. 2	14. 2	24. 4	34. 3	44. 1
5. 4	15. 4	25. 2	35. 1	45. 1
6. 1	16. 1	26. 3	36. 2	46. 4
7. 3	17. 4	27. 2	37. 2	47. 2
8. 2	18. 1	28. 3	38. 4	48. 1
9. 1	19. 3	29. 2	39. 2	49. 3
10. 3	20. 4	30. 3	40. 3	50. 4

PART II: Thematic Essay   *See* **Answers Explained** section.

PART III: Document-Based Question   *See* **Answers Explained** section.

Answers Explained

PART I (1–50)

1. **3** The presence of rich soil and a warm climate in the South most directly contributed to the economic development of the plantation system. Many colonists from England were drawn to this region in the 1600s and 1700s—first to the colonies around Chesapeake Bay (Virginia and Maryland), and then farther south (the Carolinas and Georgia). The coastal areas of the South are characterized by rich soil and relatively flat land. In addition, the area has a warm climate, with ample rainfall and a long growing season. These qualities made the coastal areas of the South ideal for large-scale tobacco, rice, and indigo plantations. (Cotton did not become a major crop in the United States until the 1790s.) In contrast, the hilly, rocky soil and shorter growing season in the northern colonies proved more suitable for small-scale agriculture and a more mixed economy. The smaller farms of the northern colonies were generally worked by the owner of the property and his family, with, perhaps, more people hired for planting and harvesting. The plantation system of the South, by contrast, was largely worked by slave labor. The first Africans arrived in Virginia in 1619, just twelve years after the arrival of the first English settlers at Jamestown. Slavery became more prominent in colonial America, especially in the southern colonies, as the 17th century progressed.

WRONG CHOICES EXPLAINED:

(1) Rocky soil and deep harbors would not have contributed to the plantation system. These features are more characteristic of New England than of the South. The rocky soil and hilly terrain of New England help explain the persistence of small-scale, single-family farms. Deep harbors lent themselves to the fishing industry, especially cod fishing, which became a key sector of the New England economy. Deep harbors, such as those in Boston, Newport, and New York, also became focal points in the transatlantic trade.

(2) Short rivers and many waterfalls would not have contributed to the plantation system. The abundance of waterfalls in New England contributed to the growth of the factory system in the first half of the 19th century. These factories, mainly textile mills, depended on water power to operate.

(4) High mountains and numerous rivers would not have contributed to the plantation system. While agriculture thrives in areas adjacent to rivers, high mountains inhibit agricultural production. Large-scale farming depends on low-lying flat land.

2. **4** The slogan "no taxation without representation" was first used by Americans to protest Britain's attempts to raise revenue through the Stamp Act. The conflict over the Stamp Act can be traced to the aftermath of the French and Indian War. After that war, which lasted from 1754 to 1763, the British government enacted a series of measures that many colonists found objectionable. These measures included a series of revenue or tax acts that the British imposed, in part to defray the costs of the war. The British believed their victory in the French and Indian War had been especially beneficial to the colonists. In return, the British reasoned it was fair for the colonists to assume some of the costs of the war and of continued protection. The Stamp Act (1765), which imposed a tax on the paper used for various documents in the colonies, provoked the most intense opposition. Many colonists asserted that only representatives elected by them could enact taxes on the colonies. "No taxation without representation" became their rallying cry. The Stamp Act itself was rescinded, but a series of British moves and colonial responses in the coming years worsened the situation.

WRONG CHOICES EXPLAINED:

(1) The slogan "no taxation without representation" was not used by Americans to protest Britain's policy of "salutary neglect." The policy of "salutary neglect" grew out of the difficulty that Britain had in enforcing laws it had enacted to regulate colonial trade. The distance between the North American colonies and Britain made rigid enforcement of British navigation acts impractical. British policymakers saw that the colonies thrived under this "salutary neglect" approach. The policy benefited both the colonies and Great Britain. Great Britain abandoned this policy after the French and Indian War, which ended in 1763. Great Britain wanted the colonies to help pay off the debt from the war and to contribute to colonial defense.

(2) The slogan "no taxation without representation" was not used by Americans to protest Britain's issuance of the Proclamation of 1763. The Proclamation of 1763 established a line along the crest of the Appalachian Mountains. Colonists were forbidden from settling beyond the line. The line was established just after the conclusion of the French and Indian War (1754–1763), which was caused, in part, by colonial expansion into lands beyond the Appalachians. Many colonists protested the Proclamation, but it was not a tax.

(3) The slogan "no taxation without representation" was not used by Americans to protest Britain's passage of the Coercive Acts. Following the Boston Tea Party (1773), the British imposed a series of punitive measures known as the Coercive Acts (1774). These included the Massachusetts Government Act, which brought the governance of Massachusetts under direct British control, and the Administration of Justice Act, which allowed British

authorities to move trials from Massachusetts to Great Britain. Many colonists protested the Coercive Acts, which they labeled the "Intolerable Acts," but the acts did not include new taxes.

3. **2** Weaknesses in the central government under the Articles of Confederation exposed by Shays' Rebellion contributed most directly to the creation of the United States Constitution. The Articles of Confederation, which established governing procedures for the United States during the period 1781–1788, left major powers with the state governments. The framers of this first American government created a "firm league of friendship" among the states, rather than a strong, centralized government. Before 1776 they had lived under a powerful, distant authority and did not want to repeat that experience. Also, many of these early leaders were fiercely loyal to their states and did not want to see state power superseded. Several problems arose during this period, which some historians have labeled the "critical period" (in the sense of a patient being in critical condition). Funding the government proved to be a major problem. As written, the Articles did not give the national government the power to levy taxes. A proposal to alter the document and allow the national government to collect import duties was blocked by Rhode Island and New York—two states with major ports. The event that convinced many Americans that change was needed was Shays' Rebellion (1786–1787). This revolt of Massachusetts farmers who felt cheated by the state's economic policies was eventually put down by state armed forces, but many political leaders came to the conclusion that a stronger national government was necessary. Earlier in 1786, a group of reformers received approval from Congress to meet in Annapolis, Maryland, to discuss possible changes in the Articles of Confederation. A follow-up meeting was scheduled in Philadelphia for May 1787. By the time of the Philadelphia meeting, the delegates, with the news of Shays' Rebellion on their minds, were ready to scrap the entire Articles of Confederation and write something new. The delegates at the Constitutional Convention believed that a strong national government was needed to quickly put down any future disturbances.

WRONG CHOICES EXPLAINED:
(1) Weaknesses in the central government under the Articles of Confederation exposed by Shays' Rebellion did not contribute to the signing of the Declaration of Independence. Shays' Rebellion occurred in 1786 through 1787; the Declaration of Independence was signed a decade earlier, in 1776. The Declaration of Independence grew out of resistance to British rule, not out of frustrations with a limited central government.

(3) Weaknesses in the central government under the Articles of Confederation exposed by Shays' Rebellion did not contribute to the development of a policy of neutrality. Shays' Rebellion was a domestic disturbance, not an international affair. In the 1790s, President George Washington established a policy of neutrality in regard to fighting between Great Britain and the revolutionary government of France. He enunciated this position in the Neutrality Act (1793) and in his Farewell Address (1796), in which he urged the United States to avoid "permanent alliances" with foreign powers. His calls for neutrality have been invoked by isolationists throughout American history, especially preceding the U.S. entrance into both world wars.

(4) Weaknesses in the central government under the Articles of Confederation exposed by Shays' Rebellion did not contribute to passage of the Northwest Ordinance. The Northwest Ordinance (1787) was enacted just a few weeks after Shays' Rebellion was finally put down, but the ordinance does not address questions raised by the rebellion. The Northwest Ordinance spelled out the steps that the old Northwest Territory would have to go through in order to become states. In addition, the Northwest Ordinance banned slavery in the Northwest Territory.

4. **2** A central issue in the debate between Federalists and Antifederalists over the ratification of the Constitution was the threat posed by a strong central government to the rights of citizens. Antifederalists feared the Constitution would create an omnipotent and unaccountable government. They had vivid memories of the intrusions of the royal British government into their lives, and wanted to have assurances that the people would have basic protections from government abuses. Federalists, on the other hand, believed that the Articles of Confederation did not provide the United States with a sufficiently strong central government to meet a series of challenges—including internal rebellion, foreign policy conflicts, and revenue issues. Leading Federalists assured Antifederalists that a bill of rights would be added to the original document if the Antifederalists agreed to support ratification. The Bill of Rights, the first ten amendments to the Constitution, was ratified in 1791. The first amendment protects the people from government limitations on freedom of expression and of religion. In addition, it also established separation of church and state. The second amendment established the right to "bear arms." The fourth amendment holds that people are to be free from unwarranted searches by government authorities. The fifth and sixth amendments list a variety of protections that people have when they are accused of crimes, such as the right to a "speedy and public trial." The eighth amendment states that the government shall not inflict "cruel and unusual" punishments on people.

WRONG CHOICES EXPLAINED:

(1) The granting of the power of judicial review to the judicial branch was not a central issue in the debate between Federalists and Antifederalists over the ratification of the Constitution. In fact, the Constitution does not grant the power of judicial review to the judiciary. This power—to review laws and determine whether they are consistent with the Constitution—developed with the Supreme Court decision in *Marbury* v. *Madison* (1803). The details of the case have to do with the seating of judges that had been appointed during the last days of the John Adams administration. However, the case is important because it established the power of judicial review, which has been the main function of the Supreme Court since then.

(3) The role of the president as commander in chief of the armed forces was not a central issue in the debate between Federalists and Antifederalists over the ratification of the Constitution. Both factions saw the importance of the military being under civilian control. In the period leading up to the American Revolution, many Americans had become concerned that the British military was acting independently of civilian authority. Among the grievances against the king in the Declaration of Independence was that his government had rendered "the military independent of, and superior to, the civil power."

(4) The danger of unrestricted interstate commerce was not a central issue in the debate between Federalists and Antifederalists over the ratification of the Constitution. Commercial activity among the states was not seen as a threat; there was no talk of trying to restrict such trade. However, the power to regulate such trade was a matter of disagreement. The Commerce Clause of the Constitution explicitly grants Congress the power to regulate trade with foreign countries and "among the several States." This clause was an example of the expanded powers of the central government that concerned many Antifederalists.

5. **4** During the 1790s, an important factor as to why the United States was able to stay out of foreign conflicts was that the Atlantic Ocean helped the United States remain isolated from foreign threats. The Atlantic Ocean created distance between the United States and the major world powers—in the 1790s and beyond. This distance allowed the United States to develop independently and to avoid the conflicts that involved European powers. The foreign policy of neutrality is also associated with President George Washington. He issued the 1793 Neutrality Act, and in his Farewell Address (1796) he urged the United States to avoid "permanent alliances" with foreign powers. The context for the development of a neutrality stance in the 1790s was war between the revolutionary governments of France and Great Britain in 1793. Many Americans felt that the

United States had an obligation to help France because France had helped the United States in the Revolutionary War. A treaty between the two countries (1778) committed the United States to help France if it were under attack. Others argued that the United States should stay out. After all, the treaty was made with a French government that no longer existed, and the French Revolution had devolved from a democratic movement into a bloodbath. The latter position won Washington's support. His calls for neutrality have been invoked by isolationists throughout American history, especially preceding the United States entrance into both world wars.

WRONG CHOICES EXPLAINED:

(1) America's avoidance of foreign conflicts in the 1790s cannot be attributed to European dependence on farm products from the United States. At the time, Europe met most of its own food needs. The sale of American export crops to European nations, such as tobacco, declined during the American Revolution and was slow to recover. Cotton did not become a major export crop until the 19th century.

(2) America's avoidance of foreign conflicts in the 1790s cannot be attributed to the Monroe Doctrine. That statement was not issued until 1823. President James Monroe issued the Monroe Doctrine to warn European nations to keep their hands off of the Americas. The European powers honored the Monroe Doctrine, in part, because of the great physical distance between the United States and the European powers.

(3) America's avoidance of foreign conflicts in the 1790s cannot be attributed to France and Great Britain agreeing to end colonialism. In fact, no such agreement was made. Colonialism and imperialism continued well into the 20th century. The era of imperialism finally came to an end because of resistance movements in the nations that were imperialized. The British, for example, were driven out of India in 1947; the French were driven out of Vietnam in 1954 and out of Algeria in 1962.

6. **1** One effect of the Louisiana Purchase (1803) was that it doubled the size of the United States. The territory was long held by France until France ceded it to Spain in 1763 following the French and Indian War. France then regained the territory in 1801. The ambitious French leader Napoleon Bonaparte quickly decided that it was in France's best interest to sell the Louisiana Territory at a reasonable price in order to attain cash to fund war with Great Britain. In 1803, American negotiators agreed to a price of $15 million. President Thomas Jefferson realized that the purchase of such land was not allowed for in the Constitution, but if he waited for a constitutional amendment specifically allowing Congress to

acquire new lands, Napoleon could rescind his offer. So, Jefferson violated his long-held strict constructionist view and quickly presented the offer to Congress, which appropriated the money. The purchase doubled the size of the United States; it added the fertile Great Plains to the United States. This flat area west of the Mississippi would become the most important agricultural region in the United States. Second, the United States gained full control of the port of New Orleans. New Orleans is the outlet of the mighty Mississippi River, which stretches from Minnesota down the spine of the United States. The impact of the Louisiana Purchase on economic growth was remarkable. Between the 1810s and the 1850s, the value of produce from the interior of the United States received at the port of New Orleans increased over tenfold.

WRONG CHOICES EXPLAINED:

(2) The Louisiana Purchase did not establish a boundary with Mexico. Mexico did not gain its independence from Spain until 1821, nearly two decades after the Louisiana Purchase. It was the Treaty of Guadalupe Hidalgo, at the end of the Mexican-American War (1846–1848), and the Gadsden Purchase (1853) that established the boundary between Mexico and the United States.

(3) The Louisiana Purchase did not result in the acquisition of the Northwest Territory. The Northwest Territory was included in the territory of the newly established United States, as stipulated by the Treaty of Paris between Great Britain and the United States in 1783.

(4) The Louisiana Purchase did not establish the Mississippi River as the western boundary of the United States. The Mississippi River was the western boundary of the United States from the moment of its founding, under the Treaty of Paris between Great Britain and the United States in 1783. The purchase of the Louisiana Territory, which included the western banks of the Mississippi River, did give the United States full control of the river, allowing for unfettered navigation of it.

7. **3** Many New England citizens opposed United States participation in the War of 1812 because they resented disruption of their trade with England. The origins of the war can be traced back to ongoing conflicts between Great Britain and France. War between the two nations erupted again in 1803. At first, the United States benefited from trading with both warring partners. Soon, however, both countries tried to block American trade with the other. Great Britain was more aggressive in its efforts to stop American ships. British ships routinely stopped and boarded American ships, often seizing cargo and pressing American seamen into service in the British navy. This practice of impressment affected 6000 American seamen between 1803 and 1812. In 1811, the United States cut off

all trade with Great Britain. At the same time, conflicts with Native American Indians in the interior of the United States worsened tensions between the United States and Great Britain. Some congressmen became convinced that Great Britain was aiding Native American Indian resistance and called for war. The War of 1812 was unpopular among some Americans, especially among New England merchants, who saw their trade with Great Britain disappear. As diplomats were negotiating an end to the war, Federalists from New England convened in Hartford, Connecticut, in December 1814 to express their displeasure with the conflict. Some of the more radical delegates suggested that New England secede from the Union, but this proposal was rejected at the convention. The Hartford Convention did pass a resolution calling for a two-thirds vote in Congress for future declarations of war. The war itself was largely a standoff, with neither side able to achieve a decisive victory. The Treaty of Ghent ended the war where it had begun. The United States and Great Britain agreed to stop fighting and to give back any territory seized in the war. Great Britain agreed to recognize the boundary between the United States and Canada that had been established before the war.

WRONG CHOICES EXPLAINED:
(1) Opposition to the War of 1812 did not involve concerns of a Russian invasion in the Northwest. Russia had made claims to the lands of the Pacific Northwest in the 1700s. However, these claims were tenuous and not supported by settlements. There was never any concern of a Russian invasion. In 1818, the United States and Great Britain established joint ownership of what the United States called the Oregon Country. Later, the boundary between United States and British territories became a source of contention. The Oregon Treaty (1846) partitioned the region along the 49th parallel.

(2) Opposition to the War of 1812 did not involve worries that France might try to regain Canada. France had lost its North American colonial holdings, including the province of Quebec, to the British in 1763, following the French and Indian War. The War of 1812 did not include France, nor did it entail fears of French involvement.

(4) Opposition to the War of 1812 did not involve the question of extending slavery into western territories. A few years later, in 1819, disagreements over the expansion of slavery arose with Missouri's application for statehood. The controversy was temporarily settled with the Missouri Compromise (1820), which allowed for the admission of two new states—Maine as a free state and Missouri as a slave state. It also divided the remaining area of the Louisiana Territory at 36° 30′ north latitude. Above that line, slavery was not permitted (except for in Missouri); below the line, it was permitted.

8. **2** The protection against double jeopardy and the right to a speedy trial are evidence that the United States Constitution supports the principle of due process of law. Both of these elements of due process are found in the Bill of Rights—the first ten amendments to the Constitution. The guarantee against double jeopardy is spelled out in the fifth amendment. The government is given one chance to convict someone of a crime. If the government fails in its case, the defendant does not have to worry about being prosecuted for the same crime again in the future, even if new evidence emerges. Of course, this amendment does not bar a defendant from appealing a guilty verdict to a higher court. The right to a "speedy and public trial" judged by an "impartial jury" is in the sixth amendment. The phrase *due process of law* simply refers to procedures that one goes through after he or she is arrested for committing a crime. These legal procedures, contained in several of the amendments to the Constitution, are intended to protect people's interests and liberties from arbitrary authority and are supposed to be applied equally to all citizens.

WRONG CHOICES EXPLAINED:

(1) The protection against double jeopardy and the right to a speedy trial are not related to the principle of eminent domain. Eminent domain refers to the constitutional principle that the government may, for a just price, force property owners to sell their property if the government deems that the property will be used for a public purpose. This power is in the fifth amendment of the Constitution.

(3) The protection against double jeopardy and the right to a speedy trial are not related to the principle of representative democracy. A representative democracy is a governing system in which citizens vote for representatives to create legislation and to govern on their behalf. It can be differentiated from direct democracy, in which citizens meet face-to-face to make decisions about their communities, as well as from the various forms on undemocratic governments, such as absolute monarchies and dictatorships.

(4) The protection against double jeopardy and the right to a speedy trial are not related to the principle of reserved powers. In the governing system in the United States established by the Constitution, certain powers are given (or delegated) to the national government and certain powers are held onto (or reserved) by the states. Delegated powers include the power to declare war and to issue currency. Reserved powers include the power to establish public education systems and to establish procedures for conducting local elections. Powers held by both the federal and the state governments are called concurrent powers.

9. **1** During the early 1800s, advances in democratic government included eliminating property qualifications as a requirement for voting. In the 1820s, most states reduced or removed property qualifications for voting so that most free males had the right to vote. Previously, voting was frequently restricted to property owners, effectively excluding poor and working-class men from the political process. The election of 1828 is considered by many historians to be the first modern election. First, the electorate was much broader than in previous elections. Consequently, candidates had to campaign more aggressively and tailor their appeal to reach a broader audience. Related to the democratization of the voting process was an increased focus on character and personality.

WRONG CHOICES EXPLAINED:

(2) The development described in this choice—ending the role of the electoral college—has not occurred in United States history. Some argue that ending the role of the electoral college in selecting the president would advance democratic government. However, such a move would require a change to the Constitution, which would require approval of three-fourths of the states. Many smaller and medium-sized states, especially those that are considered swing states, fear that they would be ignored if the electoral college were eliminated.

(3) The development described in this choice—increasing education and religious requirements for voting—has not occurred in United States history. Such a development would not advance democratic government. It would eliminate people from voting rolls. Several states had religious tests for voting in the early decades of the United States. Maryland was the last state to remove such restrictions in 1828.

(4) The development described in this choice—giving states the right to secede—has not occurred in United States history. Such a development might be considered a step toward greater democracy, but that right was never given by the federal government. The United States fought the Civil War (1861–1865) to prevent several states from seceding over the issue of slavery.

10. **3** One reason abolitionists were unpopular with many Northerners from the 1830s to 1860 was because abolitionists advocated views that increased tensions with the South. Some of these anti-abolitionist Northerners might have supported the institution of slavery, some might have been ambivalent, and some might have been uncomfortable with slavery, but they all saw maintaining sectional harmony as more important than challenging slavery. Public opinion in the North became increasingly split on the question of slavery. Anti-slavery sentiment has existed in the North as long as slavery has existed. Most obviously, African Americans—both free and enslaved—opposed the existence of slavery.

Small numbers of white Americans, from the 1600s onward, opposed slavery. Many believers in Enlightenment thought condemned slavery on humanistic grounds, while Quakers and some Evangelical Christians argued that slavery was inconsistent with Christian teachings. During the era of the American Revolution, more white Americans, including some slave holders, began to see slavery as inconsistent with the democratic values of the revolution. Starting in the 1830s, in the wake of the Second Great Awakening, a broader movement for the abolition of slavery began to form. William Lloyd Garrison was a key figure in the movement. He called for the immediate abolition of slavery, in contrast to many other white activists who advocated a more gradual approach to ending slavery. He also asserted that there should be no compensation to slave owners, and that freed slaves were entitled to the same rights as white people. He started a newspaper called *The Liberator* in 1831 to prod the public into challenging the institution of slavery. Starting in the 1840s, the towering figure in the abolitionist movement was Frederick Douglass. Douglass was born into slavery (1818) and escaped to the North in 1838. He had learned to read and write and soon became a powerful speaker in the anti-slavery movement. Douglass remained an important figure before, during, and after the Civil War, until his death in 1895. Harriet Beecher Stowe brought anti-slavery sentiment into the homes of many Northerners with the publication of her best-selling novel, *Uncle Tom's Cabin* (1852). The novel depicted in graphic detail the brutality of slavery. For many Northerners, slavery now had a human face. The novel outraged Southern supporters of slavery, who attempted to ban it.

WRONG CHOICES EXPLAINED:

(1) Abolitionists did not favor the growth of slavery. They took the opposite position; they favored the ending of slavery. Many Southern slaveholders, on the other hand, favored the growth of slavery. Some Northerners took a middle position—they argued that slavery was constitutionally protected in the states where it already existed, but they were opposed to the growth of slavery into new territories and states. This became the position of the newly formed Republican Party, starting in 1854. However, as the Civil War progressed, many Republicans became convinced that slavery needed to come to an end.

(2) Abolitionists did not encourage the annexation of Texas. They took the opposite position; they were opposed to the annexation of Texas. As early as the 1820s, white Americans began moving into the Mexican territory of Texas. In 1835, these Texans rebelled against Mexico. Texans won independence from Mexico, establishing the independent Lone Star Republic in 1836. Most Texans were eager for their Lone Star Republic to join the United States. However, many Northern politicians opposed Texas annexation because they feared that it

would create new tensions around the issue of slavery. Texas was finally annexed in 1845, soon after the victory of the expansionist James K. Polk in the presidential election of 1844.

(4) Abolitionists did not support the Fugitive Slave Act. They took the opposite position; they were opposed to the act. The Fugitive Slave Act mandated that federal and local authorities and individuals cooperate with slave catchers in search of escaped slaves. The United States government passed this stringent Fugitive Slave Act as part of the Compromise of 1850. This compromise evolved following California's application for statehood in 1850. The most important elements of the Compromise of 1850 were the admittance of California as a free state, which pleased Northern politicians, and a more stringent Fugitive Slave Act, which pleased Southern politicians. The act was especially galling to abolitionists in the North; it brought the violence and coercion of Southern slavery to the cities and towns of the North.

11. **1** The Compromise of 1850 was an attempt to resolve issues related to the protection and spread of slavery. The compromise emerged from debates following the Mexican-American War (1846–1848). The United States was victorious in that war. Under the terms of the Treaty of Guadalupe Hidalgo, the United States acquired the Mexican Cession—the huge territory that includes the present-day states of California, Nevada, and Utah, as well as portions of present-day Arizona, New Mexico, Wyoming, and Colorado. The acquisition of new territory brought the question of slavery to the forefront of political debates. Soon after the acquisition of the Mexican Cession, gold was discovered in California (1848). As word spread, thousands of people came to California to try to strike it rich. By 1850, California had enough people to form a state. Californians wrote up a constitution to submit to Congress in which slavery would be illegal. Southern senators objected to the admission of an additional free state. Senate negotiators worked out a series of measures that became known as the Compromise of 1850. The most important elements of the compromise were the admittance of California as a free state, which pleased Northern politicians, and a more stringent Fugitive Slave Law, which pleased Southern politicians. The compromise proved to be a temporary solution to a deeply troubling issue. By the end of the 1850s, the question of slavery so dominated public debates that the country seemed ready to break apart. It did exactly that in the months following the election of Abraham Lincoln in 1860. The secession of most of the slaveholding states led to the Civil War in 1861.

WRONG CHOICES EXPLAINED:

(2) The Compromise of 1850 was not related to boundary disputes between the United States and Great Britain over the Oregon Country. In 1818, the United States and Great Britain established joint ownership of what the

United States called the Oregon Country. Later, the boundary between United States and British territories became a source of contention. In 1846, the administration of President James K. Polk reached a compromise with Great Britain over control of the Oregon Country. The Oregon Treaty (1846) partitioned the region, establishing the border at the 49th parallel. That line is the current boundary between the western United States and Canada.

(3) The Compromise of 1850 was not related to relations with Native American Indians of the Great Plains. The Great Plains is the huge area of relatively flat land between the Mississippi River and the Rocky Mountains. The area was inhabited by the Plains Indians, including the Cheyenne, Comanche, and Sioux nations. The Homestead Act, the mass killing of buffalo, and the completion of the transcontinental railroad contributed to the decline of the Plains Indians. The Plains Indians resisted white encroachment of their lands. The Treaty of Fort Laramie (1868) was an attempt to end the violence, but the treaty soon collapsed. Fighting continued on the Great Plains until the last American Indian resistance was subdued when the military defeated the Sioux at Wounded Knee Creek, South Dakota (1890).

(4) The Compromise of 1850 was not related to the role of the federal government in industrial development. In the 19th century, government policies favored industrial development. For instance, the government encouraged the building of railroads by passing the Pacific [Transcontinental] Railroad Act (1862). The act encouraged the expansion of the railroad network by giving railroad companies wide swaths of federally owned land. Further, Supreme Court decisions favored big business. In *Santa Clara County* v. *Union Pacific Railway* (1886), for example, the Court established the concept of "corporate personhood" and shielded corporations from onerous regulation.

12. **3** One reason the decision in *Dred Scott* v. *Sandford* (1857) was so controversial is that it ruled that Congress had no power to limit slavery in the territories. The decision was a blow to the Republican Party, which sought to use the power of the federal government to prevent the spread of slavery into America's new territories. As part of the decision, the Supreme Court struck down the Missouri Compromise of 1820, which had banned slavery from the northern portion of the Louisiana Purchase territory. The case revolved around Dred Scott, a slave who sued to obtain his freedom on the grounds that he had lived for a time in territories where slavery was banned. The Court ruled that Scott was still a slave and did not even have the right to initiate a lawsuit. The *Dred Scott* decision declared that no African Americans, not even free men and women, were entitled to citizenship in the United States because they were, according to the Court, "beings of an inferior order." The case alarmed African Americans and many white Northerners and is seen as one of the factors that led to the Civil War.

WRONG CHOICES EXPLAINED:

(1) The *Dred Scott* decision did not strengthen the idea of popular sovereignty. The decision did the opposite; it negated the idea of popular sovereignty. The Court affirmed the right of slave owners to take their slaves into the Western territories, thereby undoing the doctrine of popular sovereignty and undermining the platform of the newly created Republican Party.

(2) The *Dred Scott* decision did not give enslaved persons full citizenship. It did the opposite; it negated African-American claims to citizenship. The decision declared that African Americans, even free men and women, were not entitled to citizenship in the United States because they were, according to the Court, "beings of an inferior order."

(4) The *Dred Scott* decision did not support Harriet Beecher Stowe's point of view in *Uncle Tom's Cabin*. It did the opposite; the decision upheld the institution of slavery while the book was critical of it. The best-selling novel, published in 1852, depicted in graphic detail the brutality of slavery. For many Northern readers, slavery now had a human face. The novel outraged Southern supporters of slavery, who attempted to ban it.

13. **2** When Andrew Carnegie stated, "The man who dies rich, dies disgraced," he was supporting charitable giving. Carnegie was encouraging wealthy people to distribute their money to charitable organizations rather than hoarding it until their death. Andrew Carnegie asserted, in an essay entitled "Wealth" (1899), that the wealthy have a duty to live responsible, modest lives and to give back to society. This "gospel of wealth" asserted that wealthy entrepreneurs should distribute their wealth so that it could be put to good use, rather than be frivolously wasted. Carnegie ended up donating the majority of his fortune to charity and public-oriented projects. Carnegie believed in a *laissez-faire* approach to social problems. He did not want the government interfering in the social and economic spheres. That is, in part, why he urged his fellow millionaires to take action on behalf of the community. In this way, the government would not have to.

WRONG CHOICES EXPLAINED:

(1) The quote by Andrew Carnegie does not support consumer credit. Starting in the 1920s, consumers had easier access to credit, enabling them to purchase items that were often beyond their means. This trend led to an increase in consumer debt and is often seen as one of the causes of the Great Depression on the 1920s. Carnegie did not advocate reckless spending; he encouraged people to live within their means.

(3) The quote by Andrew Carnegie does not support Social Darwinism. Social Darwinism was an attempt to apply Charles Darwin's ideas about the natural world to social relations. Social Darwinism was popularized in the United

States by William Graham Sumner. Sumner was attracted to Darwin's ideas about competition and "survival of the fittest." He argued against any attempt at government intervention into the economic and social spheres. Interference, he argued, would hinder the evolution of the human species. This hands-off approach to economic activities is known by the French phrase *laissez-faire*. Social Darwinism appealed to owners of large corporations because it both justified their wealth and power and warned against any type of regulation or reform. While these ideas would appeal to Carnegie, the quote is about charitable giving, not competition in the economic sphere.

(4) The quote by Andrew Carnegie does not support antitrust legislation. Antitrust legislation, such as the Sherman Antitrust Act (1890), was designed to break up trusts. Trusts are combinations of companies established to reduce competition. John D. Rockefeller established the first large trust in the oil processing industry. The formation of trusts in several industries was seen as harmful to the interests of consumers. Consequently, the government passed the Sherman Act. Carnegie was opposed to such legislation.

14. **2** A major impact of the trend shown in the chart was that Plains Indians lost their main source of food, shelter, and clothing. The Plains Indians are the Native American Indian nations, including the Cheyenne, Comanche, and Sioux nations, that lived in the Great Plains region of the United States. The Great Plains is the huge area of relatively flat land between the Mississippi River and the Rocky Mountains. Much of this area has rich soil and a long growing season, making it desirable for white settlers. The government encouraged development of the region by passing the Homestead Act (1862), which provided free land in the region to settlers who were willing to farm it. Hundreds of thousands of people applied for and were granted homesteads. The expansion of railroads into the West, leading to the completion of a transcontinental railroad in 1869, also encouraged white settlement in the Great Plains. The railroads provided an economic lifeline for these new settlers. Freight trains brought crops and cattle from the Great Plains states to cities such as Chicago. This increased economic activity led to Native American Indians being pushed off their land. The railroads also brought sportsmen out west who shot at buffalo herds from their passing train cars. While these buffalo (formally known as American bison) were sport for white travelers, they were a means of sustenance for many Plains Indians. The chart indicates that the buffalo population decreased from approximately 40 million at the turn of the 19th century to less than one thousand by the end of the century. These factors all led to the decline of the Plains Indians. The buffalo, which were threatened with extinction a century ago, have made somewhat of a recovery due to federal protective measures. Currently there are over 30,000 buffalo in North America.

WRONG CHOICES EXPLAINED:

(1) The decline of the buffalo, as indicated on the chart, did not result in frontier trading posts becoming more prosperous. As white settlers became more established in communities in the West, the need for trading posts decreased. Furthermore, the decline of the buffalo was accompanied by a decline in the population of Native American Indians and the virtual destruction of their way of life.

(3) The decline of the buffalo, as indicated on the chart, did not result in reservations being located closer to buffalo migration routes. Federal authorities did not take into consideration the migration patterns of the buffalo when relocating, and often reducing, Native American Indian reservations. In addition, the buffalo were virtually eliminated from the Great Plains.

(4) The decline of the buffalo, as indicated on the chart, did not result in white settlers becoming dependent on buffalo products. The buffalo were killed for sport or were simply massacred. They were not used by white settlers.

15. **4** A supporter of the idea in the quotation would most likely favor following laissez-faire economics. The quotation notes several pro-business government policies, including maintaining a stable currency and domestic order. These are measures designed to create an environment that is more conducive to business investment. It also advocates a "hands-off" policy in regard to regulating business. The speaker would likely be against government actions that regulate minimum wages paid to employees, environmental impacts of industrial processes, or monopolistic practices by large corporations. The policy of laissez-faire asserts that government should limit, as much as possible, any interference in the economy. The French phrase *laissez-faire* means "to let alone." It describes a government policy that would take a hands-off approach in regard to economic activities. Throughout much of the history of the United States, Americans have been suspicious of government intervention into the economy. The founders of the United States had vivid memories of the overbearing mercantilist policies of Great Britain. With the American economy growing by leaps and bounds in the 19th century, the presidents of the late 19th century did not challenge the doctrine of laissez-faire. However, by the 20th century, the country began to face serious economic problems that called into question the laissez-faire doctrine. In the first decades of the 20th century, Progressive reformers called on the government to break up monopolies, regulate the food production industry, help the poor, and create peace between owners and workers. During the Progressive Era of the early 20th century, Presidents Theodore Roosevelt and Woodrow Wilson both took up the call to regulate the economy, to varying degrees.

WRONG CHOICES EXPLAINED:

(1) A supporter of the idea in the quotation would not favor establishing consumer protection laws. Such laws would amount to regulations on business regulations, and the quotation specifically calls for a "hands-off" approach in regard to regulation. In the aftermath of the publication of *The Jungle* (1906), the muckraking novel that exposed conditions in the meatpacking industry, Congress passed the Meat Inspection Act and the Pure Food and Drug Act (both in 1906).

(2) A supporter of the idea in the quotation would not favor securing collective-bargaining rights. Collective bargaining is the process of negotiations between employers and groups of employees, usually through unions. The quotation supports pro-business policies; extending collective-bargaining rights to workers would be seen by business owners as a challenge to their prerogatives and profits. The National Labor Relations Act of 1935 (Wagner Act) guaranteed that workers would have collective-bargaining rights.

(3) A supporter of the idea in the quotation would not favor levying high taxes on business. The quotation reflects a pro-business approach. A supporter of the quotation would probably push for maintaining lower taxes on business, not raising taxes.

16. **1** The passage of the Homestead Act most directly contributed to the situation shown in the photo. The photo depicts a group of people (presumably a family) standing in front of a "soddy"—a rough house built using blocks of sod dug up by homesteaders. Draft horses in the foreground and a cow in the background indicate that this is an agricultural venture. The first-generation pioneers drawn to the Great Plains were nicknamed "sodbusters" because they had to cut through the thick layer of sod to get to the topsoil needed for farming. The Homestead Act (1862) granted people up to 160 acres as an enticement for moving west. The act, along with the completion of the transcontinental railroad (1869), facilitated the movement of settlers and speculators. In the last three decades of the 19th century, millions of native-born whites, immigrants, and African Americans settled on farms west of the Mississippi River. From the last years of the Civil War until the turn of the 20th century, nine new states joined the United States—starting with Nevada (1864) and Nebraska (1867) and ending with Wyoming (1890) and Utah (1896). About a fifth of the farmers who established farms in this era obtained land directly from the government through the Homestead Act and similar federal legislation. Most of the land was purchased either from railroads, which had substantial holdings as a result of land grants from the government, or from speculators who obtained land from unsuccessful homesteaders. As the century progressed, the dream of land ownership proved to

be beyond the means of many people. The family farms of the prairie gave way to large-scale agribusinesses.

WRONG CHOICES EXPLAINED:

(2) The situation shown in the photo—homesteaders living in a "soddy" house on the Great Plains—was not brought about by the passage of the Sherman Antitrust Act. In the late 1800s, critics of corporate power pushed the government to take steps to rein in these massive corporations. The government passed the Sherman Antitrust Act (1890), but it had limited success. In the case of *United States* v. *E.C. Knight Company* (1895), the Supreme Court greatly limited the scope of the act by making a distinction between trade (which would be subject to the act) and manufacturing (which would not). The act had nothing to do with homesteaders moving west.

(3) The situation shown in the photo—homesteaders living in a "soddy" house on the Great Plains—was not brought about by the purchase of Alaska. The purchase of Alaska did lead to more Americans moving there. However, photos of settlers to Alaska might depict them in mining camps or fishing operations; farming was not prevalent among Alaskan settlers due to the short growing season of the region.

(4) The situation shown in the photo—homesteaders living in a "soddy" house on the Great Plains—was not brought about by the Interstate Commerce Act. In the late 1800s, reformers and farmers' organizations took action to check the massive power of railroads to dictate terms of service. Many states passed laws regulating railroad rates and practices. After the Supreme Court ruled in the *Wabash, St. Louis and Pacific Railroad* v. *Illinois* case (1886) that states could not regulate railroads because train service crossed state lines, the federal government created the Interstate Commerce Commission to regulate railroads. The ICC was chronically underfunded and was, therefore, ineffective. The act had nothing to do with homesteaders moving west.

17. **4** The passage is an excerpt from the Supreme Court decision in *Plessy* v. *Ferguson* (1896). The decision was a setback for those who sought an end to the Jim Crow system of racial segregation in the South. Jim Crow laws were state and local ordinances that first appeared after Reconstruction ended (1877). Typical laws called for separate schools or separate train cars for African Americans. Opponents of racial segregation argued that Jim Crow laws violated the 14th amendment (1868). This amendment, ratified during Reconstruction, stated that no person shall be denied "equal protection of the laws." Jim Crow laws, opponents argued, violated the 14th amendment because the laws relegated African Americans to inferior public accommodations and had the effect of making

African Americans second-class citizens. However, the Court disagreed. The decision stated that segregation was acceptable as long as the facilities for both races were of equal quality. This "separate but equal" doctrine allowed for the continuation of the Jim Crow system until the 1950s and 1960s. The beginning of the end to the system came with the *Brown v. Board of Education* decision of 1954.

WRONG CHOICES EXPLAINED:

(1) The passage does not reflect the Supreme Court decision in *Wabash, St. Louis and Pacific Railroad v. Illinois* (1886). That case arose as a result of efforts to regulate railroad rates. Starting in the 1870s, groups to promote the interests of farmers such as the Grange became concerned about the power and abuses of large railroad companies. Railroads often overcharged small-scale farmers. The Grange successfully pushed for laws in several states in the 1870s and 1880s to limit abusive practices by railroads. However, in the *Wabash* case, the Court ruled that Illinois could not regulate railroad rates on rail lines that crossed state boundaries, citing the interstate commerce clause of the Constitution. In response, the federal government created the Interstate Commerce Commission.

(2) The passage does not reflect the Supreme Court decision in *United States v. E.C. Knight Company* (1895). That case arose in the aftermath of the passage of the Sherman Antitrust Act (1890), which made illegal certain business practices that reduced competition. The act was invoked in court, when the government sued the E.C. Knight Company, a key entity in the Sugar Trust that controlled 98 percent of sugar processing in the United States. In the decision, the Court greatly limited the scope of the Sherman Antitrust Act by making a distinction between trade, which would be subject to the act, and manufacturing, which would not.

(3) The passage does not reflect the Supreme Court decision in *In re Debs* (1895). That case arose in the aftermath of the Pullman strike (1894). The Court upheld an injunction issued by the federal government against the strike. The Court ruled, in *In re Debs*, that the government has the right to ensure that interstate commerce is not interrupted and that United States mail is delivered.

18. **1** In the late 1800s, one reason labor unions struggled to gain support was because employers could easily replace striking employees. Owners of industrial firms could employ a variety of tactics to gain the upper hand in conflicts with labor unions during the late 1800s. Without legal protections from the government, striking workers generally were at a marked disadvantage in their struggles against powerful corporations. Employers used replacement workers, called "scabs" by the union movement, during strikes and hired armed guards to prevent

strikers from attempting to block the replacement workers from entering the premises. There was a large pool of potential replacement workers because the United States had become a major destination for immigrants. During the 1860s, a little over two million new residents entered the United States. That figure jumped to nearly nine million for the first decade of the 20th century. In 1886, a strike at the McCormick Reaper Works in Chicago turned violent when unskilled workers at the McCormick works went on strike and their jobs were quickly given to replacement workers. Most of the pitched workplace battles of the late 1800s, such as the Homestead strike of 1892 and the Pullman strike of 1894, ended in defeat for the workers. Workers saw their position and status erode during this period.

WRONG CHOICES EXPLAINED:

(2) In the late 1800s, the failures of the labor movement would not be attributed to high wages for industrial laborers. Wages were not, generally speaking, high. In fact, a major motivation for workers to strike during this period was a desire on the part of the workers for higher wages.

(3) In the late 1800s, the failures of the labor movement would not be attributed to the ready availability of government-funded public-works projects. Local and state governments did initiate and partially fund projects that provided jobs to individuals. In New York City, such projects included the building of Central Park (1857–1876) and of the Brooklyn Bridge (1869–1883). However, it was not until the creation of the New Deal, by President Franklin D. Roosevelt, during the Great Depression of the 1930s that the federal government enacted major public-works projects.

(4) In the late 1800s, the failures of the labor movement would not be attributed to the ending of the use of court injunctions by corporations. The opposite occurred. Corporations requested court injunctions to prevent workers from striking. This occurred during the Pullman strike (1894). The Pullman Company requested and received a federal court injunction against the strike. Subsequently, in *In re Debs*, the Supreme Court upheld the injunction, asserting that the government has the right to ensure that interstate commerce is not interrupted and that United States mail is delivered.

19. **3** The term *yellow journalism* is associated with the start of the Spanish-American War (1898). Yellow journalism refers to the sensationalistic, irresponsible coverage of events in the media. Yellow journalists created support for the Spanish-American War by writing articles about the sinking of the United States battleship *Maine*. In 1898, the *Maine* exploded and sunk in the harbor of Havana, Cuba (which was a colony of Spain). Many in the United States thought that the

destruction of the ship was the work of Spain, especially after American newspapers bluntly accused Spain of the crime, despite the scarcity of evidence. The coverage of the sinking of the *Maine* was one of several causes of the war. An independence movement was trying to break Cuba's ties to Spain. Many Americans wanted the United States to intervene on Cuba's side in this struggle. Some Americans saw parallels between the Cuban struggle for independence from Spain and America's struggle for independence from Great Britain. Also, some American businessmen were angered by the interruption of the sugar harvest by the fighting between Cuban rebels and Spanish forces. American newspapers breathlessly followed events in Cuba, with lurid accounts of Spanish wrongdoing. The Spanish-American War was brief. The U.S. declared war in April; an armistice was signed in August. The United States and Spain negotiated the Treaty of Paris (1898) following the war. In the treaty, Spain agreed to cede the Philippines, Puerto Rico, and Guam to the United States; the United States agreed to pay Spain $20 million for these possessions.

WRONG CHOICES EXPLAINED:

(1) The term *socialism* is not usually associated with the start of the Spanish-American War. The term *socialism* refers to a range of economic and social systems, as well as political ideologies, theories, movements, and parties that seek to establish such systems. Socialist systems are characterized by some form of social ownership of the means of production—either by the government or by the workers themselves, through collective or cooperative ownership. Socialists generally believe in some form of democratic control of the economic sphere. Eugene V. Debs, who had been a leader in the labor movement, was one of the founders of the Socialist Party of America in 1901.

(2) The term *populism* is not usually associated with the start of the Spanish-American War. The term *populism* is associated with the political insurgency by small-scale farmers in the late 1800s. The populists grew angry at the concentration of wealth and power by eastern industrialists. They supported a national income tax so that those with higher incomes would pay more than the poor. They also supported increasing the amount of currency in circulation; farmers supported inflationary policies so that the prices they received for their produce would increase. In common usage, the term *populism* can refer to any political candidate or movement that tries to appeal to ordinary people who feel that their concerns are ignored by established political parties.

(4) The term *isolationism* is not usually associated with the start of the Spanish-American War. The term *isolationism* refers to a policy of neutrality or noninterference in world affairs. Isolationism has been an impulse in U.S. foreign policy for much of its history. President George Washington's farewell

address (1796) urged the United States to avoid "permanent alliances" with European nations. Later, the Monroe Doctrine (1823) urged European nations to stay out of the affairs of the Western Hemisphere and promised that the United States would not involve itself in European affairs. In 1920, the Senate voted to reject U.S. membership in the League of Nations.

20. **4** The main idea of the 1912 cartoon is that a third political party can threaten the two major parties. The cartoon depicts a moose, with the label "Bull Moose" attached to its ear and with eyeglasses suggestive of Theodore Roosevelt, striking fear into an elephant and a donkey—the symbols of the Republican and Democratic Parties. The letters "GOP" on the elephant refer to the nickname of the Republican Party—the Grand Old Party. The cartoon refers to the presidential election of 1912. The Bull Moose Party, formally known as the Progressive Party, was formed to support the independent candidacy of Theodore Roosevelt in 1912. The party formed after a rift had developed between Roosevelt and President William Howard Taft, a fellow Republican who had succeeded him. Roosevelt and his supporters walked out of the Republican Party nominating convention in 1912 after the party nominated Taft to run for reelection. Roosevelt and his loyalists founded the Bull Moose Party. Roosevelt won 4.1 million votes (27 percent) in the 1912 election. As it turned out, it was the Republican Party that had more to fear going into the election than the Democratic Party. Roosevelt divided the vote of the traditional Republican electorate and opened the way for a rare victory for a Democratic presidential candidate—Woodrow Wilson. The party existed until 1916. Third-party candidates—not in one of the two major political parties—have consistently garnered a small percentage of the vote in elections. Elections in the United States are on a "winner takes all" basis. If the United States had a proportional representation system, in which parties received seats in government in proportion to the percentage of the national vote they received, people might be more likely to vote for third-party candidates. But in a "winner takes all" system, people tend to vote for one of the two major political parties.

WRONG CHOICES EXPLAINED:
(1) The cartoon does not suggest that the Democratic Party is losing support. Both parties—the Democratic donkey and the Republican elephant—appear worried about the Bull Moose Party going into the presidential election of 1912. In the end, the Democratic Party benefited from the participation of the Bull Moose Party. The Bull Moose candidate, Theodore Roosevelt, drew support away from his former party, the Republican Party, paving the way for a victory by the Democratic candidate, Woodrow Wilson.

(2) The cartoon does not suggest that Republicans outnumber Democrats in the United States. The cartoon depicts both major parties as worried about the participation of the Bull Moose Party in the election of 1912. It does not suggest that one of the major parties is stronger or weaker than the other.

(3) The cartoon does not suggest that the political system has no room for more than two parties. The cartoon depicts the two major parties—the Democratic donkey and the Republican elephant—as worried about the third-party participation of the Bull Moose Party, but it does not portray this development in a negative way. It seems to suggest that the appearance of a new party is a positive development, shaking up a stagnant political order.

21. **1** In the late 1800s, the major goal of United States policy in both the annexation of Hawaii and the acquisition of the Philippines was to obtain coaling stations and seaports for United States ships. Both actions took place in the context of the United States becoming an imperialist power. Many Americans had long looked to bring Hawaii within the orbit of the United States. American missionaries arrived in Hawaii as early as the 1820s. Later in the century, American businessmen established massive sugar plantations, undermining the local economy. Discord between the American businessmen and the ruler of the island, Queen Liliuokalani, emerged after 1891. The American pineapple grower Sanford Dole urged the United States military to intervene. The American businessmen staged a coup in 1893, deposing Queen Liliuokalani. U.S. forces immediately protected the new provisional government led by Dole. The provisional government hoped for U.S. annexation of the islands, but that did not occur until 1898. The United States acquired the Philippines in the aftermath of the Spanish-American War. In the Treaty of Paris, which ended the war, Spain ceded Puerto Rico, Guam, and the Philippines to the United States. Many Filipino people were not happy to see one imperial power (Spain) replaced by another one (the United States). It took the United States seven years and thousands of casualties to gain control of the Philippines. The idea of establishing coaling stations can be traced to Alfred Thayer Mahan, a retired admiral, who stressed the importance of naval power in achieving and maintaining influence on the world stage. In an 1890 book, he pushed for the United States to develop a strong navy, maintain military bases and coaling stations throughout the world, and administer an overseas empire.

WRONG CHOICES EXPLAINED:

(2) In the late 1800s, the major goal of United States policy in both the annexation of Hawaii and the acquisition of the Philippines was not expanding United States fishing rights in international waters. Fishing rights in international waters has not been the subject of major disputes. International waters,

also known as the high seas, are parts of the oceans that are not under any country's jurisdiction. In these waters, countries have the rights to fishing, navigation, and overflight, as well as conducting scientific research.

(3) In the late 1800s, the major goal of United States policy in both the annexation of Hawaii and the acquisition of the Philippines was not limiting the spread of Japanese influence. The United States did become concerned about the rise of Japanese influence in Asia, but not until the 20th century, especially after Japan's victory in the Russo-Japanese War (1904–1905). The events in the question occurred in the 19th century.

(4) In the late 1800s, the major goal of United States policy in both the annexation of Hawaii and the acquisition of the Philippines was not protecting the area around the Panama Canal. The territories in the question are not in close proximity to the Panama Canal. Furthermore, the Panama Canal was not begun until 1904; it was not completed until 1914. The events in the question occurred in the 19th century.

22. **1** The actions referred to in the three headlines were supported by the Progressive reform movement. Progressivism was an early 20th-century reform movement that promoted government actions to address political, economic, and social problems. Progressivism existed at the grass-roots level as well as in the corridors of power. Two influential presidents, Theodore Roosevelt and Woodrow Wilson, took on the Progressive mantle. The movement claimed many legislative victories, and ultimately influenced both the New Deal and 20th-century liberalism. The three items in the headline reflect the breadth of the movement's concerns. The income tax did not exist in the United States until the 16th amendment was ratified in 1913. This amendment gave the federal government the authority to tax people's incomes. Previously the government gained its revenues almost entirely from import tariffs. A graduated, or progressive, income tax taxes the wealthy at a higher rate than it taxes the poor. The idea is that the wealthy have proportionally more disposable income and are better able to part with a sizable portion of their income. Progressive Era activists believed that such a tax would create a fairer society, especially in light of the disparities of wealth that developed during the Gilded Age of the late 19th century. The Federal Reserve System was created to regulate the money supply. The Federal Reserve Bank, which is in part privately controlled and in part publicly controlled, was created by legislation in 1913 during the administration of President Woodrow Wilson. One of its main functions is to regulate economic growth by regulating the supply of money. If the economy is sluggish, the Fed will attempt to stimulate economic growth by increasing the money supply; if inflation occurs, the Fed will attempt to slow down economic activity

by reducing the money supply. Congress passed the Pure Food and Drug Act, along with the Meat Inspection Act, in 1906, in the aftermath of the publication of the novel *The Jungle* (1906) by Upton Sinclair. Sinclair's novel exposed the underside of the meatpacking industry. The novel follows a Lithuanian immigrant family through the stockyards of Chicago. The novel created a public uproar about the safety of meat, leading Congress to pass the legislation in question.

WRONG CHOICES EXPLAINED:

(2) The actions referred to in the three headlines did not grow out of the concerns of the Prohibition movement. The goal of the Prohibition movement was to ban alcohol from American society. The movement against alcohol consumption was one of the largest movements in United States history, from the early 1800s, until it achieved success with the ratification of the 18th amendment (1919). The amendment, which prohibited the production, sale, and consumption of alcoholic beverages, was repealed in 1933 by the 21st amendment.

(3) The actions referred to in the three headlines did not grow out of the concerns of the labor movement. The goal of the labor movement was to organize workers into unions in order to advance their interests through collective bargaining. A significant early union was the Knights of Labor, founded in 1869. This union welcomed all members, regardless of race, sex, or level of skill. The Knights had a broad agenda that included not only improvements in wages and hours for their workers, but also social reforms such as an end to child labor and better safety rules. A second early union was the American Federation of Labor (1886). The AFL differed from the Knights of Labor in that it included only skilled workers, the "aristocracy of labor."

(4) The actions referred to in the three headlines did not grow out of the concerns of the conservation movement. The conservation movement was concerned with the rapid destruction and disappearance of natural areas in the United States. Logging and mining operations were taking a toll on forested areas starting in the late 1800s. President Theodore Roosevelt (1901–1909) embraced the cause of conservationism. Roosevelt, an avid outdoorsman, set aside millions of acres as protected areas. These included six national parks. Later, the environmental movement of the 1960s and 1970s pushed ecological concerns into public consciousness. The movement was inspired partly by Rachel Carson's book *Silent Spring* (1962), which detailed the harmful effects of toxic chemicals.

23. **3** In his war message to Congress, President Woodrow Wilson urged the United States to enter World War I in order to make the world safe for democracy. When World War I began in 1914, Wilson was opposed to United States participation in it. He initially assumed that the United States could stay neutral in World War I and maintain commercial ties to nations on both sides of the conflict. However, quickly into the war, Britain successfully blockaded American ships from reaching Germany. Out of necessity, United States trade shifted to Britain exclusively. Germany became increasingly belligerent toward the United States as the war progressed. Germany, however, wanted to keep the United States out of the war and agreed in the Sussex Pledge (1916) to make no surprise submarine attacks on U.S. ships. In 1917, Germany rescinded the Sussex Pledge and declared that it would resume unrestricted submarine warfare. Also in 1917, many Americans were angered by an intercepted telegram from German foreign secretary Arthur Zimmerman indicating that Germany would help Mexico regain territory it had lost to the United States in the Mexican-American War (1846–1848) if Mexico joined the war on Germany's side. These factors pushed Wilson toward an interventionist position. He framed American intervention in the altruistic language of fostering democratic practices in the world—that American participation was necessary to make the world "safe for democracy." The United States finally entered the war in 1917.

WRONG CHOICES EXPLAINED:
(1) In his war message to Congress, President Woodrow Wilson's rationale for the United States entrance into World War I was not to protect the empires of European countries. He argued for the opposite. In his Fourteen Points document (1918), he emphasized self-determination for European people—not imperial rule. The document also called for international cooperation, freedom of the seas, removal of barriers to trade, and an international organization to resolve conflicts.

(2) In his war message to Congress, President Woodrow Wilson's rationale for the United States entrance into World War I was not to create a new world government. Later, in his Fourteen Points document (1918), Wilson put forth the idea of a world government. Wilson's idealistic vision for a post-war world included the formation of the League of Nations. Most of the ideas in the Fourteen Points document were rejected by the victorious European powers except for the creation of the League of Nations. Isolationists in the Senate blocked the United States from joining the League.

(4) In his war message to Congress, President Woodrow Wilson's rationale for the United States entrance into World War I was not to stop a British attack on the United States. Though Britain and the United States have had a history of conflict, by the 20th century, the two nations were allies. There was no thought

that Britain would attack the United States. The United States was trading extensively with Britain during the war, much to the consternation of Germany.

24. **4** The cartoonist's point of view is that the actions of labor unions threaten the American way of life. The context of the publication of the cartoon was a massive strike wave by workers and the Red Scare. The cartoon is depicting "Labor" descending down a staircase. The steps in labor's descent are labeled "Strikes—Walkouts," "Disorder—Riots," "Bolshevism—Murder," and "Chaos." After the "Chaos" step, the cartoonist drew a question mark, inviting the viewer to speculate what comes next—perhaps a violent revolution. Organized labor was indeed engaging in a large number of strikes and walkouts in 1919. After World War I, the government disbanded the agencies that were created to control prices and to maintain workplace peace. As wages fell and prices rose, workers across America organized and fought to protect wartime gains. The year 1919 saw the biggest strike wave in American history. There were more than 4500 strikes involving 4 million workers. The biggest strike was the Seattle General Strike in February. In September, more than 340,000 steelworkers went on strike. Late in 1919 and into 1920, the police force in Boston went on strike. Partly in response to this labor militancy, the Red Scare, a crusade against suspected communists, anarchists, labor leaders, and other radicals, emerged. Other factors also contributed to the Red Scare, including the successful Bolshevik revolution in Russia in 1917 and the virulent strain of patriotism unleashed by World War I. The Red Scare was also set in motion by a series of bombs that were detonated in several cities in 1919 and 1920 by radical groups. In January 1920, Attorney General A. Mitchell Palmer began a broad hunt for suspected radicals. Palmer's Justice Department carried out unwarranted raids, known as "Palmer raids," of suspected radicals' homes. While Palmer did not uncover the makings of an uprising, he did end up deporting over 500 noncitizens including the Russian-born anarchist activist Emma Goldman (1919). The cartoon reflects the heightened fears of the era, equating labor strikes with violent revolution.

WRONG CHOICES EXPLAINED:
(1) The cartoon is not suggesting that immigrants assimilate easily into American society. The cartoon does not allude to immigrants, nor to their ability to assimilate. Many of the people who shared the point of view of the cartoonist—that labor strikes were tied to violent revolutionary movements—also held anti-immigrant views. Nativism rose steeply in the years after World War I, leading to the passage of the Emergency Quota Act of 1921 and the National Origins Act of 1924. These acts greatly reduced the number of immigrants allowed into the United States.

(2) The cartoon is not suggesting that industrial production will expand and create more jobs. It is suggesting that striking workers will undermine industrial stability and will lead to economic chaos and violent revolution.

(3) The cartoon is not suggesting that civil liberties will be restricted and ordinary American citizens will be hurt. In fact, the fears that this cartoon is reflecting (and stoking) led to a restriction on civil liberties. The Red Scare, which developed in the context of fears of labor militancy, included a broad hunt for suspected radicals. This hunt included raids of suspected radicals' homes, in violation of the fourth amendment's protection against "unreasonable" searches of people and their "houses, papers, and effects."

25. **2** The photograph shows one side of the 1920s conflict between science and religion. The photograph shows a table organized by the Anti-Evolution League in Dayton, Ohio, during the 1925 trial of John Thomas Scopes. The table is promoting copies of the organization's publication, *The Conflict*, as well as copies of a best-selling book by T.T. Martin, *Hell and the High School*. Martin's book, in vivid language, railed against teachers, "paid by our taxes, who feed our children's minds with the deadly, soul-destroying poison of Evolution." The Scopes trial involved the teaching of evolution in public schools. Scopes, a Tennessee biology teacher, was arrested for violating a state law forbidding the teaching of evolution. The case turned into a national spectacle, with the famous lawyers Clarence Darrow representing Scopes and William Jennings Bryan representing the state. The trial pitted rural, traditional, religious values against science. Though the trial was a local state trial, rather than a Supreme Court case, it garnered headlines across the country. It is one of several important events that highlighted the profound cultural divisions in the 1920s.

WRONG CHOICES EXPLAINED:

(1) The photograph does not show sides in the conflict between union men and factory owners. Such conflicts occurred in large numbers in 1919 and 1920. In 1919, there were more than 4500 strikes involving 4 million workers. Major strikes included the Seattle General Strike, a widespread steelworkers' strike, and a strike by the Boston police.

(3) The photograph does not show sides in the conflict between nativists and immigrants. Such a conflict did occur in the 1920s. Nativism rose steeply in the years after World War I, leading to the passage of the Emergency Quota Act of 1921 and the Immigration Act of 1924. These acts greatly reduced the number of immigrants allowed into the United States.

(4) The photograph does not show sides in the conflict between censorship and the free press. Such a conflict did occur during the Red Scare of 1919 and

1920. The government used World War I–era statutes—the Alien and Espionage Acts (1917 and 1918)—to target publishers of materials that were seen as sympathetic to radical causes.

26. **3** The poem, "I, Too," by Langston Hughes is associated with the blossoming of African-American culture in the 1920s. This cultural movement, known as the Harlem Renaissance, was a literary, artistic, and intellectual movement that celebrated African-American life and forged a new cultural identity among African-American people. The movement was centered in the African-American neighborhood of Harlem in New York City. Langston Hughes was a central figure in the movement. His poems include "Harlem" and "The Negro Speaks of Rivers," as well as "I, Too." "I, Too" notes the exclusion and segregation of African Americans from mainstream institutions in the United States—"They send me to eat in the kitchen," rather than with guests at the dining room table. However, the poem also asserts that in the future such exclusion will be ended—"Tomorrow, I'll be at the table." The poem is an affirmation of strength, determination, and beauty. It also notes the shame that white Americans will feel in the future for creating and benefiting from the system of discrimination they had created. The Harlem Renaissance also included many other influential cultural figures. Duke Ellington, a composer, pianist, and bandleader, was perhaps the most important figure in 20th-century jazz. Some of his most important compositions are "Mood Indigo," "Don't Get Around Much Anymore," and "Take the A Train." Bessie Smith was the most well-known blues and jazz singer of the 1920s. Other contributions to the Harlem Renaissance include the poetry of Claude McKay and Countee Cullen and the jazz music of Louis Armstrong.

WRONG CHOICES EXPLAINED:
(1) The poem is not associated with the growth of the motion-picture industry. The motion-picture industry was growing in prominence in the 1920s. Movie attendance achieved staggering levels. By the end of the decade, three-fourths of the American people (roughly 90 million) were going to the movies every week. The first "talkie," *The Jazz Singer*, came out in 1927. However, the poem does not reference motion pictures.

(2) The poem is not associated with the emergence of an anti-war party. The poem does not refer to war or political parties. During World War I, the Socialist Party (formed in 1901) opposed American participation in the war. Its leader, Eugene V. Debs, ran for president in 1920 from prison, having been convicted of violating the 1917 Espionage Act by speaking out against World War I.

(4) The poem is not associated with the expansion of mass consumption. The poem does not refer to consumer products. The decade of the 1920s is

often noted for the expansion of mass consumption. Mass-production techniques led to greater availability of consumer goods to average families. Cars, radios, toasters, health and beauty aids, and other consumer goods filled showrooms and stores. Easy credit and layaway plans helped move merchandise. The advertising industry expanded to draw more people into the world of mass consumption.

27. **2** In the 1920s, authors such as F. Scott Fitzgerald, Ernest Hemingway, and Sinclair Lewis wrote primarily about post–World War I disillusionment and materialism. The three authors were part of the "Lost Generation" of writers following World War I. Lost Generation writers tended to focus on the materialism and crassness of American society in the 1920s. Lost Generation writers also cast a critical eye at the glorification of war that characterized the World War I era. Hemingway's novel, *A Farewell to Arms* (1929), depicted the cynicism and brutality of World War I. Fitzgerald's novel, *The Great Gatsby* (1925), depicted the carelessness and destructiveness of the very wealthy. Sinclair Lewis wrote a series of novels, including *Main Street* (1920), *Babbitt* (1922), and *Arrowsmith* (1925), satirizing the limited outlook and emptiness of small-town American life.

WRONG CHOICES EXPLAINED:

(1) The authors mentioned in the question did not write about the intolerance of the Ku Klux Klan. The writers of the Lost Generation tended to shy away from issues of race in the United States. African-American writers who were part of the Harlem Renaissance tackled issues of racism and Ku Klux Klan violence head-on. The poetry of Langston Hughes often focused on racism and white supremacy in American society.

(3) The authors mentioned in the question did not write about the failure of cultural pluralism. *Cultural pluralism* is a term used to describe a social order in which smaller ethnic and racial groups participate in the dominant, mainstream society, but still maintain their unique cultural identities. The concept implies acceptance by the broader society of the values and practices of the smaller groups. The idea of cultural pluralism came into widespread usage in the early decades of the 20th century, both as a description of contemporary society and as a societal goal. The idea stood in contrast to the conception of the United States as a "melting pot," in which different ethnic groups lose their unique cultural traits as they assimilate into mainstream culture.

(4) The authors mentioned in the question did not write about the lack of educational opportunities for young Americans. Debates over education policy occurred frequently in the 1920s. In general, educational facilities expanded to accommodate the large numbers of immigrant families that had come into the

United States in the period 1880 to 1920. Many saw public education as a way to assimilate young immigrants into American culture. Conservative reformers in several states attempted to pass laws mandating public education, a move designed to undermine Catholic and other parochial schools. Progressive educators attempted to incorporate the ideas of John Dewey into education by moving away from rote memorization and putting more emphasis on the process of learning and on student participation.

28. **3** The Federal Deposit Insurance Corporation (FDIC) and the Securities and Exchange Commission (SEC) were part of President Franklin D. Roosevelt's efforts to reform economic problems that contributed to the Great Depression. Roosevelt's New Deal agenda included a variety of reforms that were intended to restore people's confidence in the economy. Many people had lost confidence in the banking system and withdrew their money, fearing that their banks might fold. With thousands of people withdrawing their money at the same time, many banks actually did fold, turning their fears into a self-fulfilling prophecy. The Federal Deposit Insurance Corporation, created by the Glass-Steagall Act (1933), insures deposits so that if a bank does fold, people would not lose their savings. Many had also lost confidence in the stock market after the 1929 crash, which was partly caused by unsound practices. The Securities and Exchange Commission was created in 1934 to regulate the stock market and prevent the reckless investment behavior that led to the crash of October 1929. The Securities and Exchange Commission oversees stock market operations by monitoring transactions, licensing brokers, limiting buying on margin, and prohibiting insider trading.

WRONG CHOICES EXPLAINED:

(1) The Federal Deposit Insurance Corporation (FDIC) and the Securities and Exchange Commission (SEC) are not related to efforts to reduce the power of business monopolies during the Great Depression. The power of business monopolies was not seen as a major cause of the Great Depression. Earlier, Roosevelt's distant cousin, President Theodore Roosevelt (1901–1909), was more closely associated with efforts to reduce the power of business monopolies.

(2) The Federal Deposit Insurance Corporation (FDIC) and the Securities and Exchange Commission (SEC) are not related to efforts to give organized labor a stronger voice in politics. Other New Deal initiatives were designed to strengthen organized labor. Notably, the Wagner Act, also known as the National Labor Relations Act, mandated that employers bargain with their unions. It also established the National Labor Relations Board to conduct elections among workers to see if they wanted to be represented by a union. The act also banned certain unfair labor practices.

(4) The Federal Deposit Insurance Corporation (FDIC) and the Securities and Exchange Commission (SEC) are not related to efforts to bring electricity to rural areas. Another New Deal agency, the Tennessee Valley Authority, did that. The TVA was a set a development projects in the Tennessee River area, which includes the states of Kentucky, Virginia, North Carolina, Tennessee, Georgia, Alabama, and Mississippi. The region was especially hard hit by the Great Depression. Even before the depression, poverty was pervasive; most homes in the region were without electricity. The TVA included major infrastructure projects, including electricity-generating dams along the Tennessee River. The strategy was to provide jobs and electricity to people in the region.

29. **2** President Franklin D. Roosevelt proposed a plan in 1937 to add justices to the Supreme Court primarily because the Court had declared major New Deal laws unconstitutional. By 1937, Roosevelt had grown frustrated with the conservative approach of the Supreme Court. It shot down the National Industrial Recovery Act in *Schechter* v. *United States* (1935) and the Agricultural Adjustment Act in *Butler* v. *United States* (1936). In 1937, he announced a plan to increase the number of justices on the Supreme Court to as many as fifteen. He said that some of the older justices had difficulty keeping up with the heavy workload. However, it was clear that he was trying to create a Supreme Court friendlier to his New Deal programs. Congress opposed his "court packing" scheme, and, after much criticism, Roosevelt eventually backed away from it. Soon, however, openings on the Court allowed Roosevelt to appoint new justices and influence the direction of the Court.

WRONG CHOICES EXPLAINED:
(1) President Franklin D. Roosevelt's proposed plan in 1937 to add justices to the Supreme Court was not motivated by the Court lacking representation from minority groups. The Court was all white and male, but Roosevelt was not especially concerned with creating a Supreme Court that reflected the diversity of the United States. He did nominate a Jewish justice—Felix Frankfurter, who replaced another Jewish justice, Benjamin Cardozo (1939). However, the first African-American justice (Thurgood Marshall, 1967), the first female justice (Sandra Day O'Connor, 1981), and the first Latina justice (Sonia Sotomayor, 2009) were all appointed well after Roosevelt's time.
(3) President Franklin D. Roosevelt's proposed plan in 1937 to add justices to the Supreme Court was not motivated by the lack of judicial experience on the Court. Several of the justices had served since the 1910s. In fact, Roosevelt argued the opposite; he argued that several of the judges were too old to keep up with the increased workload. Therefore, he argued, additional justices would

expedite the work of the Court. However, his real motivation was to change the ideological makeup of the Court.

(4) President Franklin D. Roosevelt's proposed plan in 1937 to add justices to the Supreme Court was not motivated by the Court supporting a loose interpretation of the Constitution. The debates between those who favored a loose interpretation of the Constitution and those who favored a strict interpretation date back to the early years of the republic. Thomas Jefferson and Alexander Hamilton disagreed over whether the Constitution allowed for the creation of a national bank. In the 1930s, when the Court struck down key New Deal acts, it was demonstrating a strict interpretation of the Constitution. A loose interpretation might have upheld the agencies in question by invoking the elastic clause, which lets Congress do what it considers "necessary and proper" to carry out its functions.

30. **3** A major reason for the change in unemployment shown on the graph between 1933 and 1937 was that job opportunities were created by New Deal public-works projects. The graph indicates that unemployment dropped during Franklin D. Roosevelt's first term in office from nearly 25 percent in 1933 to just over 14 percent in 1937. Roosevelt won the presidential election in 1932, promising a "new deal" to the American public. Roosevelt promised to take the federal government in a new direction by asserting that it should take some responsibility for the welfare of the people during the economic emergency. His immediate goal was relief for the unemployed through jobs programs. He promised "direct recruitment" of unemployed people to work on public works that would benefit the nation as a whole. The New Deal included jobs programs such as the Civilian Conservation Corps (1933), which focused on young men, and the vast Works Progress Administration (1935), which consisted of a myriad of public projects. The WPA, for example, built schools, installed sewer lines, wrote guidebooks, and produced theatrical productions. Roosevelt's initiatives were unprecedented in their scope and direction. In addition to creating public-works projects, the Roosevelt administration (1933–1945) provided direct relief, or what would be known as welfare today, to millions of families. Also, the New Deal addressed the welfare of retired people and people with disabilities by creating the Social Security system in 1935.

WRONG CHOICES EXPLAINED:

(1) The change in unemployment between 1933 to 1937—a drop from almost 25 percent of the working-age population to just over 14 percent—would not be attributed to banks increasing their lending to new businesses, who then hired additional workers. The banking industry was in crisis during the years in

question and few new businesses were opening in the midst of the worst economic downturn in the nation's history.

(2) The change in unemployment between 1933 to 1937—a drop from almost 25 percent of the working-age population to just over 14 percent—would not be attributed to states heavily taxing corporate profits. Such a move might lead corporations to laying off workers. The public-works projects that did reduce unemployment were funded through federal taxes, as well as deficit spending.

(4) The change in unemployment between 1933 to 1937—a drop from almost 25 percent of the working-age population to just over 14 percent—would not be attributed to the federal government nationalizing the transportation and utility industries. Such a move did not occur. The belief in government ownership of large-scale industry is consistent with socialist ideologies.

31. 1 The main cause of the change in unemployment shown on the graph between 1942 and 1945 was increased manufacturing to meet the needs of World War II. Though the New Deal stabilized the economy, it was really World War II that brought the United States out of the Great Depression. As early as 1939, unemployment in the United States plummeted as factories began the conversion to a wartime economy. The vitality of the wartime economy led to population shifts as people moved to industrial centers. The chart indicated the dramatic drop in the unemployment rate from 1939 until the end of World War II (1945). In 1944, the unemployment rate dropped to close to zero. The government made a concerted effort to recruit people who had not been part of the industrial workforce, including women. Women were needed because factories were working around the clock producing military goods, and much of the male workforce was in the military. Recruiting posters were produced by the government, usually through the Office of War Information, showing women, including the fictional "Rosie the Riveter," in industrial settings. Further, President Franklin D. Roosevelt signed Executive Order 8022 (1941), banning racial discrimination in defense industries. This had the dual effect of helping African Americans emerge from the Great Depression and helping the defense industry meet its wartime needs.

WRONG CHOICES EXPLAINED:

(2) The trend in unemployment between 1942 and 1945—a reduction in the unemployment rate to well below five percent of the workforce—would not be attributed to the success of the Social Security Act. The 1935 act, which created the Social Security system, addressed the welfare of retired people and people with disabilities. It did not create jobs and did not have a direct effect on the unemployment rate.

(3) The trend in unemployment between 1942 and 1945—a reduction in the unemployment rate to well below five percent of the workforce—would not be attributed to the impact of a high inflation rate. During times of war, inflation is a constant threat due to the lack of consumer goods and the additional money that people have in their pockets from defense-related industrial work. However, during World War II, the Office of Price Adjustment (created in 1941) kept inflation in check by imposing price ceilings on most consumer items. Between April 1942 and June 1946, the agency managed to keep the annual rate of inflation rate at around 3.5 percent.

(4) The trend in unemployment between 1942 and 1945—a reduction in the unemployment rate to well below five percent of the workforce—would not be attributed to a decline in the number of women in the workforce. The opposite occurred. The employment needs of the defense industry were so acute that the government made a concerted effort to recruit women to work in the defense industry. The fictional "Rosie the Riveter" character was often featured in this public relations campaign. The World War II recruiting campaign was successful. By 1945, one-third of the workforce was female.

32. **4** The Neutrality Acts (1935–1937) were passed to avoid the actions that led the United States into World War I. For the first three years of World War I, which began in 1914, the United States insisted on its right to trade with belligerent nations while remaining neutral. This insistence on trading with belligerent nations during wartime ultimately contributed to the decision by the United States to enter World War I. German attacks on American ships angered many Americans and pushed President Woodrow Wilson toward a pro-war position. In the Neutrality Acts of 1935–1937, Congress made clear that neither the United States government nor private U.S. firms were to trade with belligerent nations. The acts were an expression of isolationism. President Franklin Roosevelt grew frustrated with these acts because they did not make a distinction between aggressors and victims in the conflicts of the 1930s. A later Neutrality Act (1939) allowed the United States to supply the opponents of fascism with materials on a cash-and-carry basis.

WRONG CHOICES EXPLAINED:

(1) The Neutrality Acts of 1935–1937 were not designed to support the policy of appeasement. Appeasement is the policy of not challenging a rival's moves in order to avoid a direct conflict. This policy was pursued by Great Britain and France toward Germany in the 1930s. The United States was not part of the appeasement policy in the 1930s.

(2) The Neutrality Acts of 1935–1937 were not designed to provide troops to halt Italian aggression. Fascist Italy conquered Ethiopia in 1936. The United States, pursuing a policy of neutrality at the time, did not provide troops to halt Italy.

(3) The Neutrality Acts of 1935–1937 were not designed to increase the profits of weapons manufacturers. Pursuing a policy of neutrality would reduce the need for military preparedness and for additional weaponry. The policy would not, therefore, lead to increased profits for weapons manufacturers. By the 1930s, many Americans became critical of the profits made by weapons manufacturers during World War I. The Senate's Nye committee (1934–1937) uncovered evidence that certain American corporations greatly profited from World War I. Americans wondered if the so-called "merchants of death" had pushed the country into World War I. It was in this atmosphere that the first Neutrality Act was passed (1935).

33. **4** One government action that was taken in response to the Japanese attack on Pearl Harbor was forcing the relocation and internment of Japanese Americans. Emotions ran high following the attack by Japan on Pearl Harbor in 1941. This attack stunned many Americans and made them bitter toward Japan. Many Americans directed their anger at all Japanese people—even ones who had decided to immigrate to the United States. In 1942, President Roosevelt issued Executive Order 9066, authorizing the government to remove 120,000 people, two-thirds of them citizens, from West Coast states and relocate them to camps throughout the West. The order cited the possibility of "espionage" or "sabotage." It asserted that the relocation was necessary for the "successful prosecution" of the war against Japan. Most of their property was confiscated by the government. In the case of *Korematsu* v. *United States* (1944), the Supreme Court ruled that the relocation was acceptable on the grounds of national security. The *Korematsu* decision is one of several rulings by the Supreme Court that have curtailed civil liberties in times of war. Much later, in 1988, the United States government publicly apologized to the surviving victims of the internment and extended $20,000 in reparations to each one.

WRONG CHOICES EXPLAINED:

(1) In responding to the Japanese attack on Pearl Harbor (1941), the government did not draft all Japanese-American men. Some Nisei, American-born children of Japanese immigrants, were drafted over the course of World War II. However, significant numbers of Japanese Americans enlisted to serve. Approximately 33,000 Japanese Americans served in World War II, the vast majority of whom were being kept in internment camps before entering the military.

(2) In responding to the Japanese attack on Pearl Harbor (1941), the government did not pass labor laws banning the employment of immigrants. The defense industry was short of workers during World War II. The government encouraged all Americans—including immigrants, African Americans, and women—to make themselves available for work in the defense industry.

(3) In responding to the Japanese attack on Pearl Harbor (1941), the government did not end all oil sales to Japan. The United States ended oil sales to Japan before the attack on Pearl Harbor. In 1940, the United States, working with its allies, passed the Export Control Act to limit the exportation of important war-related materials, including oil, to Japan. The following year, months before the attack on Pearl Harbor, the United States initiated a complete oil embargo against Japan.

34. **3** The goal shown in the posters—conserving and collecting scrap materials that could be used by the military during World War II—was similar to rationing by the Office of Price Administration. In both cases, the government was attempting to ensure that the military had the materials it needed during World War II. During the war, there were shortages of key items because of the needs of the military. Starting in 1942, the Office of Price Administration began rationing key commodities to civilians, such as gasoline and tires. Next, the government began rationing food—sugar, meat, coffee, lard, butter, and many other items. Families were given ration books and would use ration stamps, along with cash, when they purchased the affected items. The two posters were encouraging Americans to participate in salvaging materials that could be used by the military—metals of various sorts, as well as rubber, rags, paper, and burlap. In many ways, World War II required the participation of the entire American public, not simply members of the military. These efforts created a sense of unity and common cause in the country.

WRONG CHOICES EXPLAINED:

(1) The goal shown in the posters—conserving and collecting scrap materials that could be used by the military during World War II—was not most similar to the institution of the draft by the Selective Service Act (1940). Both initiatives had the overall goal of achieving victory in World War II. However, the goal of the posters was to conserve and collect needed materials, while the purpose of the draft was to ensure that there were enough soldiers to serve in the military. Starting in October 1940, the Selective Service Administration began drafting men into military service by lottery. The Selective Service System ended up providing over 16 million men to the military.

(2) The goal shown in the posters—conserving and collecting scrap materials that could be used by the military during World War II—was not most similar to aid to Russia under the Lend-Lease Act (1941). Both initiatives had the overall goal of achieving victory in World War II. However, the goal of the posters was to conserve and collect needed materials, while the purpose of the Lend-Lease Act was for the United States to extend aid to nations fighting Nazi aggression at the beginning of World War II. The United States ended up supplying the Soviet Union with $11.3 billion worth of war materials.

(4) The goal shown in the posters—conserving and collecting scrap materials that could be used by the military during World War II—was not most similar to the development of the Manhattan Project (1942). Both initiatives had the overall goal of achieving victory in World War II. However, the goal of the posters was to conserve and collect needed materials, while the purpose of the Manhattan Project was to develop the atomic bomb. This secret project, launched in an office building in New York City, involved several sites, but the final assembly of the atomic bomb occurred in Los Alamos, New Mexico. The bomb was ready by July 1945, as the United States was preparing for a final attack on Japan. The United States dropped the atomic bomb on the Japanese city of Hiroshima on August 6, 1945. After the United States dropped a second atomic bomb on the city of Nagasaki, Japan surrendered, ending World War II.

35. **1** The Servicemen's Readjustment Act of 1944 (GI Bill) made a significant impact on post–World War II America because it provided for aid to veterans for housing and college costs. The GI Bill, as the act is more commonly known, provided cash payments for tuition and living expenses to attend college. In addition, the bill provided low-interest loans for veterans to purchase homes as well as to start businesses. The intent of the GI Bill was to help the veterans of World War II adjust to life during peacetime. The program was very successful. It helped millions of veterans advance economically. A college education and home ownership have been seen as key components of entrance into the middle class. The generous benefits extended to World War II veterans can be seen in contrast to the sparse benefits extended to World War I veterans. World War I veterans staged a major protest in 1932, the "Bonus March," to pressure the government to provide them with bonuses that had been promised them.

WRONG CHOICES EXPLAINED:
(2) The Servicemen's Readjustment Act of 1944 (GI Bill) did not provide for the rapid demobilization of soldiers after World War II. The demobilization of over 12 million men and women in the armed forces at the end of World War II was a major logistical challenge. These men and women had to be brought back

to the United States and had to be out-processed at military bases. The process was carried out by the military. The GI Bill was intended to provide aid to veterans once they returned to civilian life.

(3) The Servicemen's Readjustment Act of 1944 (GI Bill) did not provide for pensions for soldiers from World War I. Earlier, in the 1930s, a controversy arose over bonuses promised to World War I veterans. Though the bonuses were not scheduled to be distributed until 1945, a group of unemployed and poor men argued that, because of the Great Depression, they were in a desperate situation and needed their money immediately. In June 1932, a group of World War I veterans, who called themselves the Bonus Expeditionary Force, or Bonus Army, marched into Washington, D.C., to demand that the administration of President Herbert Hoover extend them their bonus—a bonus that they had been promised for their service in the military. About forty thousand people (mostly veterans and their families) set up an encampment in the nation's capital to demand their money. The handling of the Bonus Marchers—which included aggressively dismantling the encampment—seemed to reinforce many people's perception of President Hoover that he did not have the interests of ordinary Americans at heart.

(4) The Servicemen's Readjustment Act of 1944 (GI Bill) did not provide for the establishment of a draft for all males over the age of 18. When World War II began, the draft applied only to men between the ages of 21 and 36. After the United States entered World War II in December 1941, the age range was expanded to cover men between the ages of 18 and 45. Currently, all males, from age 18 through age 25, must be registered with the Selective Service System. Selective Service is waiting for guidance in regard to registering women following a 2019 Supreme Court ruling that declared that an all-male draft registry was unconstitutional.

36. **2** Following World War II, the United States adopted the foreign policy of containment primarily to limit the spread of communism. After the war, the Soviet Union and the United States became rivals in the Cold War. The United States became increasingly concerned about the growing power of the Soviet Union and put forth a policy of attempting to prevent the expansion of communism, known as containment. President Harry S. Truman articulated this goal, which has come to be known as the Truman Doctrine, in a speech to Congress in 1947. Truman put the idea of containment into practice in 1947 by providing $400 million in military aid to Greece and Turkey to prevent those countries from becoming communist. Another example of the containment policy was the Berlin Airlift of 1948. Before the status of Berlin was settled, the Soviet Union decided it would prevent any food or other supplies from entering the western sector of

the city. The goal was for the Soviet Union to block the United States and its western allies from maintaining their presence in Berlin. Ultimately, the Soviet Union hoped to make all of Berlin part of what would become East Germany. The United States did not stand by idly when it learned of the Berlin blockade. President Harry Truman decided to send thousands of planes, filled with supplies, into the western sector of Berlin, in an action known as the Berlin Airlift. The Berlin Airlift prevented the western sector of Berlin from starving and prevented the Soviet Union from taking over the city. The formation of the North Atlantic Treaty Organization (NATO) was also part of the Cold War strategy of containment. NATO was created in 1949 by the United States and its allies to challenge the growing power of the Soviet Union. The members of NATO pledged that they would view an attack on any one member as an attack on all members.

WRONG CHOICES EXPLAINED:

(1) The foreign policy of containment, adopted by the United States following World War II, was not designed to return to pre-war isolationism. The containment policy—working with allies to prevent the spread of communism—involves American engagement in world affairs. Isolationism, on the other hand, entails American withdrawal from world affairs.

(3) The foreign policy of containment, adopted by the United States following World War II, was not designed to force European nations to end colonialism. The United States did not pressure its European allies to withdraw from colonialism after World War II. In many colonies, anti-colonial movements developed after World War II, leading to a broad move away from colonialism. India, for example, gained independence from Great Britain in 1947, and Algeria gained independence from France in 1962. In the second half of the 20th century, the United States itself has sought to withdraw from direct colonial control over other nations. Rather, it has sought to install and cultivate leaders that are generally supportive of United States interests.

(4) The foreign policy of containment, adopted by the United States following World War II, was not designed to support the work of the World Court. The World Court, formally known as the International Court of Justice, was founded in 1945 as the principal judicial organ of the United Nations (which was founded the same year). It continues to exist, and arbitrates international disputes and hears legal issues brought by different UN bodies.

37. **2** One important effect of President Dwight Eisenhower's proposal for interstate highways was a significant increase in suburban communities. The Interstate Highway Act initiated the biggest public-works project in United States

history—a nationwide network of superhighways. The federal government paid 90 percent of the costs of construction, with the states paying the other 10 percent. Between 1956 and 1966, the federal government spent $25 billion to build 40,000 miles of highways. Initiated during the Cold War, the government also saw the act as a defense measure. The highways would allow for quick movement of troops and heavy military equipment. The act was one of a series of developments that made suburbia a viable and desirable option. Housing became affordable in the suburbs. Innovative developers such as William Levitt took large tracts of land outside of major cities and built huge developments of nearly identical, modest houses. He applied the techniques of mass production to these houses, building them rapidly and cheaply. In addition, the government made low-interest loans available to veterans through the GI Bill. Finally, the deterioration of American cities made the suburbs seem more desirable. As older American cities, especially in the Northeast and the upper Midwest, experienced a decline in industrial jobs starting in the 1950s, unemployment, poverty, and crime increased.

WRONG CHOICES EXPLAINED:

(1) President Dwight Eisenhower's proposal for interstate highways did not result in an increase in health care spending. Later, in 1965, the Medicare program was created to provide health care for every American once they reached the age of 65; Medicaid was created that same year to provide health coverage to impoverished Americans. The Patient Protection and Affordable Care Act, passed under President Barack Obama in 2010, overhauled much of the health care industry.

(3) President Dwight Eisenhower's proposal for interstate highways did not result in an increase in educational opportunities. Many new schools opened in the United States in the 1950s. However, this development was primarily a result of the large number of "baby boom" children reaching school age in the 1950s, not a result of the Interstate Highway Act.

(4) President Dwight Eisenhower's proposal for interstate highways did not result in sectional differences. The term *sectional differences* describes the development of regions in the United States with distinct economic and political interests, and even distinct cultural practices. The most important sectional divide in American history has been between the North and the South. In the first half of the 1800s, the practice of slavery persisted and even grew in the South, while it shrank and was eventually eliminated in the North. If anything, the interstate highway system brought the different sections of the country together.

38. **4** One way President John F. Kennedy responded to the action referred to in the telegram was to support the commitment to a Moon landing by the end of the decade. In the telegram, Kennedy is extending his congratulations to the Soviet leader, Premier Nikita Khrushchev, for the Soviet Union sending the first human into outer space. In 1961, Yuri Gagarin, in his capsule Vostok 1, completed one full orbit of Earth. For several years, the Soviet Union had been outpacing the United States in regard to space exploration. In 1957, the Soviet Union launched the unmanned satellite, Sputnik 1, into orbit. The early accomplishments of the Soviet space program were humiliating to the United States. American officials vowed to catch up to and surpass their rival in the Cold War in regard to exploring space. In 1958, Congress created the National Aeronautics and Space Administration (NASA), initiating its space program. In May 1961, a month after Gagarin's mission, Kennedy announced the goal of landing a man on the Moon before the close of the 1960s. This goal was accomplished, as the United States was the first nation to successfully land men on the Moon in 1969.

WRONG CHOICES EXPLAINED:

(1) President John F. Kennedy's response to news that the Soviets had sent a man into orbit was not to decrease the budget for space exploration. The United States saw itself in a bitter rivalry with the Soviet Union. After news of the Soviets sending a man into orbit, the United States put more money into its space program and President Kennedy vowed to land a man on the Moon by the end of the 1960s.

(2) President John F. Kennedy's response to news that the Soviets had sent a man into orbit was not to expand the Peace Corps. The Peace Corps had just been established by Kennedy weeks before Gagarin's mission in 1961. Though both can be understood in the context of the Cold War, the Peace Corps was not a response to the space race. The Peace Corps gives support to developing nations in fields such as education, agriculture, and health care. The program depends on volunteers, often recent college graduates, to work on development projects in poor countries.

(3) President John F. Kennedy's response to news that the Soviets had sent a man into orbit was not to push for the removal of Soviet troops from East Berlin. Kennedy did not make such a push. Throughout the Cold War, the United States maintained troops in West Germany, and the Soviet Union maintained troops in East Germany.

39. **2** The actions listed in the question by presidents John F. Kennedy and Richard Nixon are examples of their attempts to establish peaceful coexistence with the Soviet Union. The United States and the Soviet Union became engaged

in a bitter Cold War after they had been allies in World War II. The Cold War was the period of tensions between the United States and the Soviet Union that lasted from the end of World War II (1945) to the collapse of the Soviet Union (1991). By the 1950s, many Americans had become increasingly fearful of the massive nuclear arsenals that both the United States and the Soviet Union had developed. In the early 1960s, President John F. Kennedy made attempts to ease tensions between the Soviet Union and the United States. The first action, establishing a direct telephone line between the governments of the United States and the Soviet Union, occurred in 1963, several months after the Cuban Missile Crisis brought the two nations to the brink of nuclear war. A "Memorandum of Understanding" was signed by representatives of the United States and the Soviet Union, to create a communications link between the Pentagon and the Kremlin. This hotline was never an actual telephone. The memorandum called for a text-based system. It was originally a teletype machine; later a fax machine (1986); and, finally, a dedicated computer link (2008). The hotline was implemented to forestall crises in the future. The second action, also in 1963, was the negotiating of the Nuclear Test Ban Treaty by the United States, the Soviet Union, and Great Britain (1963). The limited ban on testing nuclear weapons exempted under-ground tests. The third action, carried out by President Richard Nixon in 1972, was the sale of wheat to the Soviet Union. The Soviet Union had generally been producing considerably more wheat than the United States (up to three times as much). However, difficult weather conditions in 1971 and 1972 led to a serious wheat shortfall in the Soviet Union. The agreement Nixon made with the Soviets led to the sale of 10 million tons of wheat. The sale was later criticized because Nixon agreed to sell the wheat at subsidized pricing, costing the United States government $300 million. Further, the sale of such a large quantity of grain con-tributed to a sharp increase in grain prices in the United States. The initiation of surplus wheat sales to the Soviet Union was part of the broader policy of détente— a policy of reducing Cold War tensions and establishing warmer relations between the Soviet Union and the United States. The policy was initiated by President Richard Nixon, who became the first American president to visit Communist China and who held meetings with Soviet leaders in Moscow (both in 1972).

WRONG CHOICES EXPLAINED:
(1) The actions by presidents John F. Kennedy and Richard Nixon described in the question are not attempts to meet the Soviet Union's Cold War demands. The actions represent attempts at coexisting and negotiating with the Soviet Union, not giving in to its demands.
(3) The actions by presidents John F. Kennedy and Richard Nixon described in the question are not attempts to support Soviet troops fighting in Afghanistan. The United States was opposed to Soviet actions in Afghanistan; it

would not have supported Soviet troops. The Soviet Union invaded Afghanistan in 1979. President Jimmy Carter protested this act by suspending grain sales to the Soviet Union and boycotting the 1980 Summer Olympics in Moscow.

(4) The actions by presidents John F. Kennedy and Richard Nixon described in the question are not attempts to weaken the military power of the Soviet Union. The United States had an interest in reducing the military power of the Soviet Union, but the actions in the question involve negotiations and coexistence, not challenging Soviet military power.

40. **3** During the 1960s, the escalation of United States involvement in the Vietnam War was based on a belief that a North Vietnamese victory would lead to further losses as predicted by the domino theory. The domino theory asserts that when a nation become communist, its neighbors will be more likely to become communist. The name of the theory alludes to the game of lining up dominos in a row, so that when the first one is pushed over, the next ones in the row will each in turn be knocked over as well. The theory presumes that communism is imposed on a country from the outside—that it does not develop as a result of internal conditions. United States interest in Vietnam began in the 1950s when it sent military advisors and assistance to the government of South Vietnam after Vietnam was divided in 1954. The United States feared that South Vietnam would become a communist nation as North Vietnam had. The United States became heavily involved in the Vietnam War after Congress gave President Johnson a blank check with the Tonkin Gulf Resolution (1964). Despite the presence of over half a million United States troops and the firepower of the U.S. military, President Lyndon Johnson was not able to declare victory over the communist rebels in South Vietnam. As the war dragged on, and as the United States suffered more casualties, many Americans began to question the wisdom of American policies in Vietnam. United States involvement in Vietnam continued until 1973, when President Richard Nixon withdrew the last American troops. In 1975, the government of South Vietnam became communist.

WRONG CHOICES EXPLAINED:

(1) During the 1960s, the escalation of United States involvement in the Vietnam War was not based on a belief that restoring French colonial power was necessary for political stability in Southeast Asia. The French had been defeated in Vietnam in 1954. France's imperial aspirations had greatly diminished by the 1950s and 1960s as one French colony after another gained independence.

(2) During the 1960s, the escalation of United States involvement in the Vietnam War was not based on a belief that a strong military presence would limit Japanese trade with Vietnam. The United States was allied with Japan in the 1960s. It would not have tried to limit Japanese trade with Vietnam. Earlier, during the lead-up to American involvement in World War II, the United States organized an oil embargo against Japan (1941).

(4) During the 1960s, the escalation of United States involvement in the Vietnam War was not based on a belief that a cease-fire agreement would increase college protests. Protests occurred on college campuses in the 1960s *against* American involvement in Vietnam. Many of the protesters would have welcomed a cease-fire in Vietnam.

41. **1** The major effect of the Civil Rights Act of 1964 was that racial discrimination in public facilities was banned. The passage of the bill was one of the crowning achievements of the civil rights movement of the 1950s and 1960s. Before the passage of the act, a rigid system of segregation of the races, known as the Jim Crow system, dominated Southern life. Jim Crow laws segregated public facilities, such as railroad cars, bathrooms, and schools. These laws, which first appeared in the South after Reconstruction ended (1877), relegated African Americans to a second-class status in the South. Jim Crow laws became more prevalent after 1896 when the Supreme Court, in the case of *Plessy* v. *Ferguson*, accepted segregation as constitutional as long as the facilities for both whites and African Americans were of equal quality. This "separate but equal" rule was the law of the land until the Supreme Court found segregated schools inherently unfair in the *Brown* v. *Board of Education* decision (1954). The Civil Rights Act, signed by President Lyndon Johnson, extended this edict to all public facilities. In addition to ending the segregation of public facilities, the law also put additional powers into the hands of the attorney general to ensure that schools took steps to desegregate. In addition, the law also took measures to ensure that women, as well as African Americans, enjoyed equal treatment in the United States.

WRONG CHOICES EXPLAINED:

(2) The Civil Rights Act of 1964 did not extend citizenship and voting rights to Native American Indians. Earlier, the Indian Citizenship Act (1924) granted citizenship to about 125,000 indigenous peoples of the United States (out of approximately 300,000). By 1948, after some states withdrew the resistance to extending state voting rights, Native American Indians had voting rights throughout the United States.

(3) The Civil Rights Act of 1964 did not outlaw the use of poll taxes and literacy tests for voting. The following year, President Lyndon Johnson signed the Voting Rights Act, which ended these practices. Barriers that had been erected to prevent African Americans from voting were removed by the act. Voting practices on the state level were now subject to the scrutiny of the Department of Justice. African Americans began voting in large numbers; between 1965 and 1977, the number of African Americans elected in Southern states rose from seventy to more than two thousand.

(4) The Civil Rights Act of 1964 did not authorize busing to integrate schools. School busing became a controversial issue in the 1970s. In the years following the Supreme Court decision in *Brown* v. *Board of Education* (1954), which declared racial segregation in public schools to be unconstitutional, many American schools continued to remain largely segregated due to housing patterns. In *Swann* v. *Charlotte-Mecklenburg Board of Education* (1971), the Supreme Court addressed this form of *de facto* segregation and ruled that the federal courts could use busing as a means of desegregating schools.

42. **3** The Supreme Court decisions in *Gideon* v. *Wainwright* (1963) and *Miranda* v. *Arizona* (1966) both upheld the right to counsel for defendants in state criminal cases. The right to have a lawyer in criminal prosecutions is enshrined in the sixth amendment. However, the Constitution does not address how to handle situations in which defendants cannot afford a lawyer or are unaware that they have the right to a lawyer. The Supreme Court addressed the first situation in *Gideon* v. *Wainwright* (1963). Clarence Earl Gideon had been accused of breaking into a poolroom and stealing money from the cash register. The state court rejected his demand for a state-appointed lawyer. After defending himself and being found guilty, he appealed, eventually bringing the case to the Supreme Court. The Court ruled that the states must provide court-appointed lawyers to impoverished defendants. The Court addressed the second situation, in which defendants are unaware that they have the right to a lawyer, in *Miranda* v. *Arizona* (1966). Ernesto Miranda was arrested in 1963 for kidnapping and rape. When police questioned him, he confessed to the crime. He did not know that he had the right to have a lawyer present when he was being questioned, nor that he had the right to remain silent. In this decision, the Court ruled that arrested people must be read basic rights, now known as "Miranda rights," including the right to remain silent and the right to have a lawyer.

WRONG CHOICES EXPLAINED:
(1) Neither *Mapp* v. *Ohio* (1961) nor *Heart of Atlanta Motel* v. *United States* (1964) addressed the issue of the right to counsel for defendants in state criminal cases. In the case of *Mapp* v. *Ohio*, the Supreme Court ruled that evidence

obtained in violation of the fourth amendment protection against "unreasonable searches and seizures" must be excluded from criminal prosecutions in state and federal courts. In the case of *Heart of Atlanta Motel* v. *United States* (1964), the Supreme Court upheld the 1964 Civil Rights Act and asserted that private businesses such as the Heart of Atlanta Motel cannot ban African-American customers.

(2) Neither *Baker* v. *Carr* (1962) nor *Engel* v. *Vitale* (1962) addressed the issue of the right to counsel for defendants in state criminal cases. In the case of *Baker* v. *Carr*, the Supreme Court ruled that states must periodically redraw legislative districts so they have roughly equal numbers of people. In *Engel* v. *Vitale* (1962), the Supreme Court ruled that the Regents' Prayer, a state mandated prayer that was recited by public school children in New York State, was unconstitutional because it violated the doctrine of separation of church and state.

(4) Neither *Tinker* v. *Des Moines* (1969) nor *Roe* v. *Wade* (1973) addressed the issue of the right to counsel for defendants in state criminal cases. In the case of *Tinker* v. *Des Moines*, the Supreme Court ruled that a school board prohibition against students wearing black armbands in protest of the war in Vietnam was unconstitutional. The Court asserted that students in school had the right to free speech, including symbolic speech, as long as their actions did not interfere with the educational process. In *Roe* v. *Wade*, the Supreme Court ruled that states shall not prohibit women from having an abortion during the first two trimesters of pregnancy. Previously the decision had been left to the states, and many states forbade abortions. The Supreme Court reasoned that the Constitution guaranteed people the right to privacy. Abortion, they argued, was a decision that should be left to the woman with the advice of her physician.

43. **4** The graph supports the conclusion that, in every decade shown, the percentage of women in the labor force grew while the percentage of men in the labor force declined. The graph shows that only 30 percent of women in the United States were part of the labor force in 1950. By 1990, the figure rose to 57 percent. In 1950, 82 percent of men were part of the labor force; that figure dropped to 74 percent by 1990. The increase in the percentage of women participating in the labor force is often called the "quiet revolution." There are several reasons for this development. The economy experienced sustained growth in the post–World War II period. As the economy grew in the 1950s and 1960s, the job market expanded, drawing large numbers of women who had previously worked in the home. The number of jobs in fields that were seen as "women's work"—such as secretarial work and teaching—increased dramatically during this period. In addition, in the 1960s the women's liberation movement challenged

traditional gender expectations. Many women felt less pressure to marry at a young age, have children, and work at home. Also, the availability of the birth control pill and of abortions allowed women to have greater control over their reproductive lives. Many women made the decision to focus on a career first, thereby putting off decisions about whether to have children until later.

WRONG CHOICES EXPLAINED:
(1) The graph does not support the conclusion that older Americans remained in the labor force longer in 1990 than in 1950. The graph does not include information about the ages of people in the workforce; it includes information about the percentage of men and women in the labor force—collectively and broken down by gender.

(2) The graph does not support the conclusion that all Americans born during the baby boom after World War II joined the labor force. The graph indicates that in the decades after World War II, participation in the labor force for all men and women ranged between 55 percent and 65 percent. The percentages would be considerably higher if all baby boomers (born between 1945 and 1964) entered the labor force.

(3) The graph does not support the conclusion that half as many men were in the labor force in 1990 as compared to 1950. The graph does not provide absolute numbers; it only provides percentages. The percentage of the total number of men who were in the labor force did fall between 1950 and 1990. In 1950, 82 percent of men were in the labor force; in 1990, that figure was 74 percent. However, the overall number of men in the United States increased between 1950 and 1990, as the overall population increased from 160 million to 258 million. Therefore, the number of men in the labor force increased from 1950 to 1990.

44. **1** During the Persian Gulf War (1991), the primary aim of the United States was to force Iraq to withdraw its troops from Kuwait. The Middle East has loomed large in American foreign policy for decades. The United States has gotten a great deal of its oil from the region, and it has sought to maintain alliances and to prevent any Middle Eastern country from assuming a dominant role in the region. Therefore, President George H.W. Bush became alarmed in 1990 when Iraqi leader Saddam Hussein ordered an Iraqi invasion of Kuwait, another oil-rich Middle Eastern country. He insisted that the United States, with backing from allies and the United Nations, would take action to ensure Kuwaiti independence. President Bush carried out his pledge to defend Kuwaiti autonomy by organizing the Persian Gulf War in 1991. The American military operation in the Persian Gulf War, named "Operation Desert Storm," was successful. Hussein was

quickly forced to withdraw his troops from Kuwait, while the United States suffered relatively few casualties. Some criticized President Bush for not attempting to remove the dictator Saddam Hussein and supporting a transition to a democratic government in the country. However, when President George W. Bush did exactly that a decade later (2003), following the terrorist attacks of 2001, the United States failed to restore stability to Iraq after nearly a decade of military engagement.

WRONG CHOICES EXPLAINED:
(2) During the Persian Gulf War (1991), the primary aim of the United States was not to force Iraq to hold democratic elections; rather, it was to force Iraq to withdraw its troops from Kuwait. Later, in 2003, President George W. Bush attempted to support a transition to a democratic government in Iraq, following the terrorist attacks of 2001. That effort faltered as the United States failed to restore stability to Iraq after nearly a decade of military engagement.

(3) During the Persian Gulf War (1991), the primary aim of the United States was not to force Iraq to increase the price of its oil exports; rather, it was to force Iraq to withdraw its troops from Kuwait. The United States would want Iraqi oil exports to be lower in price, since the U.S. is one of Iraq's customers. Therefore, it would not want to force Iraq to increase the price of its oil exports.

(4) During the Persian Gulf War (1991), the primary aim of the United States was not to force Iraq to submit to weapons inspections by the United Nations; rather, it was to force Iraq to withdraw its troops from Kuwait. Following the war, the United Nations located and destroyed chemical weapons that Iraqi leader Saddam Hussein had developed and used in the 1980s. Iraq was then pressured to agree to United Nations inspectors. The United Nations Special Commission on Iraq (UNSCOM) was established to carry out these inspections. UNSCOM did not find any evidence of the production of weapons of mass destruction. However, in 2001, President George W. Bush insisted that Hussein was developing weapons of mass destruction that could be used against the United States and its allies. The Bush administration used this assertion to justify an invasion of Iraq in 2003. In the aftermath of this invasion, American forces failed to find evidence of such weapons.

45. **1** In 1993, many labor union leaders opposed United States membership in the North American Free Trade Agreement (NAFTA) because they feared it would cause Americans to lose jobs to foreign nations. NAFTA is an international trade agreement that has sought to encourage countries to participate in the global economy by reducing barriers to trade. NAFTA, ratified by Congress in 1993, eliminated all trade barriers and tariffs among the United States, Canada, and Mexico.

NAFTA was the subject of much controversy when it was promoted by President Bill Clinton. Free trade supporters promised global prosperity as more nations participated in the global economy. Opponents worried that nations would no longer be able to implement environmental regulations, ensure workers' rights, or protect fledging industries from foreign competition. Many economists see the push toward free trade agreements as an important factor in the decline of manufacturing jobs in the United States. A study by the Economic Policy Institute asserts that by 2010, the rise in the trade deficit with Mexico since the implementation of NAFTA led to the loss of almost 700,000 American jobs. It estimates that about 60 percent of these jobs were high-paying manufacturing jobs in states like Ohio and Michigan. Supporters of free trade argue that it generates overall economic growth and a more dynamic business sector, which ultimately leads to increases in job creation. Clinton's championing of NAFTA represents a conscious decision by Clinton to try to move the Democratic Party away from its liberal traditions and toward a more centrist approach.

WRONG CHOICES EXPLAINED:

(2) Union leaders did not base their opposition to the North American Free Trade Agreement (1993) on concerns about a reduction in the number of immigrants to the United States. First, NAFTA did not contain provisions related to immigration. Second, labor unions have frequently supported measures that would limit the number of immigrants allowed into the United States in order to protect American jobs from immigrants who might accept work at lower wages.

(3) Union leaders did not base their opposition to the North American Free Trade Agreement (1993) on concerns about increased exports from the United States to Mexico and Canada. The idea of NAFTA was to reduce tariffs and to increase trade among the United States, Mexico, and Canada—with an increase in both imports and exports. Labor unions would not oppose an increase in exports from the United States. An increase in exports would probably entail an increase in manufacturing and an uptick in hiring in the United States for manufacturing jobs.

(4) Union leaders did not base their opposition to the North American Free Trade Agreement (1993) on concerns about the outlawing of wage increases for workers in the United States. NAFTA did not contain provisions that would outlaw wage increases for American workers.

46. **4** According to the cartoonist, the investigation of intelligence failures related to the 9/11 terrorist attacks resulted in various federal agencies attempting to avoid criticism by shifting responsibility. The cartoon is adapting the seal of the United States for satirical purposes. The actual seal depicts a bald eagle with

its two wings jutting out to the left and the right. In the cartoon, the wings are replaced by two hands, with the index finger of each pointed in opposite directions. In the actual seal, the bald eagle is holding a banner containing the nation's traditional motto, *"E pluribus unum."* In the cartoon, the motto is replaced with the word "Blame." The finger-pointing in the cartoon is meant to symbolize different agencies of the government pointing to other agencies in terms of assessing blame for the intelligence failures that occurred before the terrorist attacks on September 11, 2001. On that day, nineteen terrorists working with the al-Qaeda organization hijacked four domestic American airplanes. The idea was to turn the airplanes into missiles that would destroy symbols of American power and wealth. One plane was flown into the Pentagon, inflicting heavy damage, and one plane crashed in a field after the hijackers were overtaken by passengers. The other two airplanes did the most damage, crashing into the two towers of the World Trade Center in New York City. The damage inflicted on each building weakened the structures of each so that both buildings collapsed within two hours. Approximately three thousand people died from the four incidents, with the vast majority of the deaths occurring at the World Trade Center. In 2002, the government established the National Commission on Terrorist Attacks Upon the United States, also known as the 9/11 Commission, to examine the circumstances around the attacks, to assess intelligence lapses that might have occurred, and to make recommendations about steps that could be taken in the future to prevent similar attacks. The commission's final report, issued in July 2004, cited major lapses by both the Central Intelligence Agency and the Federal Bureau of Investigation. The chair of the commission, Thomas Kean, stated that both presidents Bill Clinton and George W. Bush were "not well served" by the nation's intelligence apparatus.

WRONG CHOICES EXPLAINED:

(1) The cartoonist is not asserting that the intelligence failures related to the 9/11 terrorist attacks resulted in praise for government efforts to stop intelligence leaks. The 9/11 Commission report focused on intelligence failures, not on intelligence leaks. The cartoon is not alluding to intelligence leaks.

(2) The cartoonist is not asserting that the intelligence failures related to the 9/11 terrorist attacks resulted in open immigration from all regions of the world. The cartoon is not alluding to immigration policies. Anti-immigrant sentiment increased in the United States in the years after the 9/11 terrorist attacks.

(3) The cartoonist is not asserting that the intelligence failures related to the 9/11 terrorist attacks resulted in recommendations to limit dependence on foreign intelligence. Neither the 9/11 Commission report nor the cartoon alludes to dependence on foreign intelligence. The report calls for greater collaboration between the United States and other countries in regard to intelligence gathering and sharing.

47. **2** Between 1881 and 1921, one major cause of the increasing number of immigrants to the United States was the increased job opportunities in industry. Between 1880 and 1920, an estimated 20 million people, from Russia, Italy, Poland, the Balkan region, and elsewhere, immigrated to the United States, most settling in industrial cities such as New York, Pittsburgh, and Chicago. In the late 1800s, workers were needed as America experienced rapid industrial growth. A variety of factors contributed to a dramatic increase in the industrial production of goods after the Civil War. Technological innovations, greater access to raw materials, new business and financial models, advances in marketing, and a growing labor force all contributed to the development of mass production. During the late 1800s, the era of small, locally oriented businesses began to give way to large corporations and trusts that came to dominate entire industries. The three most important industries of the era were railroads, the steel industry, and the oil industry. As the number of immigrants into the United States increased in the late 1800s and early 1900s, an anti-immigrant, nativist movement gained strength. Some members of the movement expressed prejudice against people who seemed "different." Others did not want immigrant workers to compete with Americans for jobs. Nativists were successful in the 1920s in pushing Congress to restrict immigration. The United States passed the Emergency Quota Act (1921) and the National Origins Act (1924), both of which greatly reduced the number of new immigrants allowed into the United States. These acts set quotas for new immigrants based on nationality. The quotas were in place until the Immigration and Nationality Act of 1965 ended the quota system.

WRONG CHOICES EXPLAINED:

(1) Between 1881 and 1921, the availability of free land in the Southeast was not a cause of the increasing number of immigrants to the United States. Earlier, the Homestead Act (1862) offered free land to people who were willing to settle it, but this applied to sparsely populated lands in the West, not to land in the more populated Southeast.

(3) Between 1881 and 1921, an increased need for military personnel was not a cause of the increasing number of immigrants to the United States. There was a need for military personnel in the United States after it entered World War I in 1917. However, immigration greatly declined during the years of the war. Further, the need for military personnel in a country would not be a positive incentive for people to immigrate to that country.

(4) Between 1881 and 1921, federal aid to pay the housing costs of new arrivals was not a cause of the increasing number of immigrants to the United States. The United States has not implemented such a policy. Earlier, in the mid-19th century, the federal government made free land in the West available to settlers, including immigrants, through the Homestead Act (1862). Later, the federal government

began creating housing projects for low-income families, including immigrant families, through programs such as Title II of the Housing Act of 1949. Furthermore, Section 8 of the Housing Act of 1937 authorizes rental assistance to be paid on behalf of low-income families, including immigrant families.

48. **1** Prior to its military involvement in both the War of 1812 and World War I, the United States attempted to maintain a policy of neutrality. The impulse to maintain neutrality in regard to European conflicts has been strong in United States history. President George Washington is closely identified with the idea of neutrality. In addition to issuing the 1793 Neutrality Act, he urged the United States to avoid "permanent alliances" with foreign powers in his Farewell Address. He did not want the newly independent nation, on precarious footing, to be drawn into the seemingly endless conflicts of Europe. President Thomas Jefferson (1801–1809) attempted to maintain a policy of neutrality in regard to the ongoing conflict between Great Britain and France. He passed the Embargo Act (1807) as a response to the harassment of U.S. shipping by Great Britain and France. Jefferson's act cut off all U.S. trade with any nation. Jefferson thought that this would pressure the belligerent nations to agree to leave U.S. ships alone. However, the main effect of the embargo was to cripple American trade. The embargo was meant to avoid warfare, but the United States eventually did go to war with Great Britain in 1812. A century later, the United States initially assumed that it could stay neutral in World War I (1914–1918) and maintain commercial ties to nations on both sides of the conflict. However, Great Britain successfully blockaded American ships from reaching Germany. Out of necessity, United States trade shifted to Great Britain exclusively. Germany responded by warning the United States that ships in the waters off of England would be subject to attack by U-boats, or submarines. The sinking of the British ocean liner *Lusitania* infuriated many Americans (128 Americans were among the dead). Germany, however, wanted to keep the United States out of the war and agreed in the Sussex Pledge (1916) to make no surprise submarine attacks on American ships. The United States took advantage of this pledge and traded extensively with Great Britain. In 1917, Germany rescinded the Sussex Pledge and declared that it would resume unrestricted submarine warfare; soon after, the United States abandoned its policy of neutrality and declared war on Germany.

WRONG CHOICES EXPLAINED:
    (2) Prior to its military involvement in both the War of 1812 and World War I, the United States did not attempt to maintain a policy of internationalism. Internationalism describes an approach to foreign policy that emphasizes increased political or economic cooperation among nations. For most of its history, the United States avoided such involvement. Since World War II, it has

participated in internationalist organizations, including the United Nations, the World Bank, and the International Monetary Fund. Participation in such organizations has generated debate in the United States. Some argue that United States interests would be better served by scaling back its participation in multilateral agreements. In 2017, for example, President Donald Trump announced his intention to withdraw the United States from the Paris Climate Agreement.

(3) Prior to its military involvement in both the War of 1812 and World War I, the United States did not attempt to maintain a policy of collective security. For most of its history, the United States avoided the alliances and treaty organizations that would constitute collective security. This changed after World War II, when the United States attempted to build a system of alliances in carrying out the Cold War against the Soviet Union and its allies. In 1949, it participated in the formation of the North Atlantic Treaty Organization (NATO).

(4) Prior to its military involvement in both the War of 1812 and World War I, the United States did not attempt to maintain a policy of détente. *Détente* is the French word for loosening and refers to an easing of tensions in the Cold War and a warming of relations between the United States and the Soviet Union. The policy was carried out by President Nixon. In 1972, Nixon became the first United States president to visit Communist China and later that year he held meetings with Soviet leaders in Moscow.

49. **3** The statements in the question were included in the Supreme Court decision in *Brown* v. *Board of Education of Topeka* (1954). This 1954 decision concerned segregated schools. After the Civil War, a rigid Jim Crow system in the Southern states of the United States established separate facilities for African Americans and white people. These included separate waiting rooms at train stations, separate drinking fountains, and separate schools. In many cases, African Americans were simply barred from certain public facilities. This Jim Crow system was challenged in the Supreme Court case *Plessy* v. *Ferguson* (1896), but the Supreme Court ruled that separate facilities were allowable, as long as the facilities for both races were of equal quality. Even though the facilities for African Americans were routinely of inferior quality, this "separate but equal" doctrine was the law of the land until the middle of the 20th century. In the *Brown* case, the Court asserted that segregation in public schools was inherently unfair and detrimental to African-American students.

WRONG CHOICES EXPLAINED:

(1) The statements were not included in the Supreme Court decision in *Schenck* v. *United States* (1919). The decision in *Schenck* v. *United States* upheld the Espionage and Sedition Acts, which were passed during World War I to put limits on public expressions of anti-war sentiment. Charles Schenck and Elizabeth

Baer of the Socialist Party had been arrested for printing and distributing flyers opposing the war and urging young men to resist the draft. The Supreme Court argued that freedom of speech is not absolute and that the government is justified in limiting certain forms of speech during wartime. The Court argued that certain utterances pose a "clear and present danger." By analogy, the Court reasoned that one is not allowed to falsely shout "Fire!" in a crowded theater.

(2) The statements were not included in the Supreme Court decision in *Korematsu* v. *United States* (1944). The decision in *Korematsu* v. *United States* upheld Executive Order 9066 (1942), which had authorized the government to remove over 100,000 Japanese Americans from West Coast states and relocate them to camps in the interior of the United States. The order applied to both *Issei* (Japanese Americans who had emigrated from Japan) and *Nisei* (native-born Japanese Americans). Most of their property was confiscated by the government. In the *Korematsu* case, the Supreme Court ruled that the relocation was acceptable on the grounds of national security.

(4) The statements were not included in the Supreme Court decision in *Vernonia School District* v. *Acton* (1995). The decision in *Vernonia School District* v. *Acton* upheld the random drug testing of students. Opponents challenged random drug testing on the grounds that it amounted to a search without a warrant. The Supreme Court acknowledged that the drug tests amounted to a search, but ruled that a school could conduct them. The Court ruled that school districts have a legitimate interest in preventing teenage drug use.

50. **4** One common effect of the laws listed in the question has been to protect national security at the expense of civil liberties. Debates and conflicts over the proper balance between individual liberty and order have occurred throughout American history. The Alien and Sedition Acts (1798) were passed by a Federalist-dominated Congress in order to limit criticism from the opposition Republican Party during the undeclared Quasi-War with France (1798–1800). The acts were actually comprised of four acts. The Sedition Act made it a crime to defame the president or Congress. The broad wording of the Sedition Act seemed to challenge the free speech guarantees of the recently ratified first amendment. The Espionage Act (1917) was passed soon after the United States entered World War I. This act, along with the Sedition Act (1918), made it a crime to interfere with the draft or with the sales of war bonds, as well as to say anything "disloyal" in regard to the war effort. Charles Schenck and other members of the Socialist Party were arrested in 1918 for printing and distributing flyers opposing the war and urging young men to resist the draft. The case made its way to the Supreme Court after Schenck and fellow Socialist Elizabeth Baer were found guilty in a federal jury trial. The Supreme Court, in *Schenck* v. *United States* (1919), supported the position that during national emergencies, civil liberties may be

limited. The Court argued that freedom of speech is not absolute and that the government is justified in limiting certain forms of speech during wartime and other national emergencies. The Court argued that certain utterances pose a "clear and present danger." By analogy, the Court reasoned that one is not allowed to falsely shout "Fire!" in a crowded theater. The passage of the USA Patriot Act of 2001 occurred in the aftermath of the September 11, 2001 terrorist attacks on the United States. On that day, nineteen terrorists working with the al-Qaeda organization hijacked four domestic American airplanes. One plane was flown into the Pentagon, inflicting heavy damage, and one plane crashed in a field after the hijackers were overtaken by passengers. The other two airplanes did the most damage, crashing into the two towers of the World Trade Center in New York City. Approximately three thousand people died from the four incidents, with the vast majority of the deaths occurring at the World Trade Center. In October 2001, the government passed the USA Patriot Act, giving the government additional powers to carry out surveillance of American citizens. Many argue that the government is using a crisis to circumvent constitutional protections that were intended to be in effect in good times as well as bad. Others contend that the Patriot Act and other such measures have been important in preventing another major terrorist attack.

WRONG CHOICES EXPLAINED:
(1) The wartime laws mentioned in the question did not expand government regulation of the economy. During both world wars, the government created agencies to expand government regulation of the economy. The government sought to ensure a steady flow of materials needed for the war and to prevent inflation from spiraling out of control. During World War I, agencies such as the War Industries Board and the National War Labor Board were created. During World War II, President Franklin D. Roosevelt created the War Production Board, and later the Office of War Mobilization, to oversee the conversion from civilian industry to war production.

(2) The wartime laws mentioned in the question did not increase the nation's military defenses. During times of war, Congress routinely allocates sufficient funds to carry out military operations. During World War II, for example, the government increased income tax rates, sold savings bonds, and borrowed money to meet the enormous monetary requirements of the war.

(3) The wartime laws mentioned in the question did not promote immigration from neighboring nations. During World War II, the administration of Franklin Roosevelt initiated the *bracero* program in 1942 to bring into the United States temporary contract workers from Mexico. The Mexican government pushed the United States to guarantee that these temporary workers

would not be drafted. More than 200,000 Mexicans participated in the program, and it is estimated that at least that number came into the United States as undocumented workers.

PART II: THEMATIC ESSAY

Amendments

The United States Constitution was written to be a living document—that is, the framers wanted the Constitution be a document that could be adapted by future generations to address changing circumstances. This can be seen clearly in the procedure for adopting constitutional amendments. Though the process for amending the Constitution is cumbersome, the document has been amended twenty-seven times, including fifteen times since the end of the Civil War. Two of the post–Civil War amendments address voting. Though the rules around voting are generally left to the states, federal Constitutional amendments have addressed suffrage several times, including with the 15th amendment, barring discrimination in voting based on race, and the 26th amendment, ensuring that all citizens as young as 18 years old could vote. Both of these amendments have profoundly impacted American society.

The immediate circumstances surrounding the adoption of the 15th amendment, which prohibits race-based discrimination in voting, were the tumultuous events of the Civil War and Reconstruction. However, the reasons that the 15th amendment, along with the 13th and 14th amendments, was needed stretch back to the founding of the United States. From its inception, African Americans were thought of as inferior to whites, and were treated as such. The most obvious manifestation of white supremacy was slavery—a system that denied African Americans the most basic of rights. Slaves were denied autonomy over themselves and were excluded from participation in the American democratic system. Even free African Americans were often denied the right to vote.

The more immediate historical circumstances of the 15th amendment grew out of the Civil War. The war ended slavery and the adoption of the 13th amendment (1865) assured that it would not come back, but the future political status of African Americans following the war was unclear. In the immediate aftermath of the war, many members of the old slave-owning class were now back in power in the South. These men tried to replicate the conditions of the old South, including passing a series of restrictive laws known as the Black Codes. Post-war conditions were so similar to pre-war conditions that many Northerners wondered if they had "won the war, but lost the peace." In this atmosphere, a group of Radical Republicans in Congress initiated a more sweeping Reconstruction program, implementing much of it by overriding

President Andrew Johnson's vetoes. Their program included passage of the 14th amendment (1868) to guarantee African Americans citizenship and equal treatment under the law. After passage of the 14th amendment, the Radical Republicans came to see that lasting change could not occur in the South unless African Americans were guaranteed the franchise. This led them to push for adoption of the 15th amendment (1870), which prevented discrimination in voting based on race.

African-American men had, in theory, achieved the right to vote with the ratification of the 15th amendment. During the Reconstruction period, African Americans were able to exercise their right to vote and elected political officials throughout the South. In the 1870s, two African Americans were elected to the United States Senate—Hiram Revels and Blanche K. Bruce—and more than a dozen representatives were elected to the House of Representatives.

After Reconstruction ended, the South figured out ways to limit the impact of the 15th amendment by creating many obstacles to voting for African Americans. Many Southern states had in place literacy tests for voting. Often, local registrars would give African Americans especially difficult passages to read in order to prevent them from registering to vote. In addition, many African Americans in the rural South had limited literacy. Another obstacle to voting was the poll tax. People had to pay a fee to vote. This fee might have been beyond the reach of many African Americans. Finally, white Southerners frequently resorted to violence against those who insisted on their right to vote. Secret societies in the South—notably the Ku Klux Klan—used terror tactics, including lynching, to make African Americans feel insecure about their safety if they ventured to the registrar's office.

Though the amendment was systematically sidestepped for nearly a century, it laid the constitutional framework for a robust defense of voting rights in the 1960s. Following protests by the civil rights movement, the government passed the sweeping Voting Rights Act (1965), which outlawed many of the schemes used by Southern states to violate the intent of the 15th amendment. In addition, the 24th amendment to the Constitution (ratified in 1964) made illegal the use of poll taxes as a condition to vote in federal elections.

Just over a century after the ratification of the 15th amendment, the 26th amendment, which extends voting rights to citizens who are at least 18 years old, was ratified. Several important historical circumstances surround the adoption of the 26th amendment. The tumultuous decade of the 1960s had just ended. This was the decade in which "baby boom" children came of age and took center-stage in the era's dramatic cultural and political developments. On the cultural front, young people developed a vibrant counterculture that questioned the values of their parents' generation. The "hippie" movement became visible in the late 1960s in neighborhoods such as San Francisco's Haight-Ashbury and New York's Greenwich Village. In many ways, this counterculture represented a complete rejection of the materialistic conformity that many young people grew up with in the 1950s.

In regard to politics, it was young people who first questioned the purpose of the armed advisors who were sent to Vietnam in the early 1960s. The United States became heavily involved in the Vietnam War after Congress gave President Lyndon Johnson a blank check with the Gulf of Tonkin Resolution. In August 1964, Johnson announced that American destroyers had been fired upon in the Gulf of Tonkin, off the coast of North Vietnam. The Gulf of Tonkin Resolution can be considered the beginning of the war in Vietnam. Over the next several years, President Johnson escalated American involvement in the Vietnam War. Johnson sent hundreds of thousands of troops to Vietnam, reinstituted the draft, and began aerial bombardment of Vietnam. As the war dragged on, and as the United States suffered more casualties, many young Americans began to protest against American policies in Vietnam. Some thought the war was more of a civil war that the United States should not be part of. In addition, many Americans grew to oppose the war after seeing many unsettling images on television news programs. Families saw American soldiers burn down Vietnamese villages. They saw body bags coming back to the United States. They saw children burned by napalm. Finally, many young men began to oppose the war because they feared they might be drafted. Many of these young men began to see a cruel and unjust irony in United States policies. On the one hand, 18-, 19-, and 20-year-old men could be drafted into the Vietnam War, but on the other hand, these same men could not enter a voting booth to change the political leaders that were carrying out the war.

The call for lowering the voting age intensified as the war continued to drag on despite vocal protests by young people against it. By 1968, Johnson decided that his war policies imperiled his reelection, so he decided to not run for a second term. The following president, Richard Nixon, did not have any more success in moving the United States closer to victory in Vietnam. Congress heeded the call for lowering the voting age by passing the Voting Rights Act amendments of 1970 that mandated that states allow voters as young as 18 to vote. However, later that year, the Supreme Court ruled, in *Oregon v. Mitchell*, that Congress cannot mandate that states lower the voting age for state elections. In 1971, Congress introduced and passed the 26th amendment. Within four months of congressional approval, the amendment was ratified by the requisite number of states (thirty-eight), and became part of the Constitution.

The immediate impact of the 26th amendment has been mixed. In the first presidential election after its ratification, young opponents of the Vietnam War did not seem to have a significant impact on the presidential election. President Richard Nixon soundly defeated George McGovern, an outspoken opponent of the war. In the following decades, youth turnout in presidential elections has fluctuated. In the 1972 election, youth turnout was over 50 percent. It declined in the coming decades, but rose to just under 50 percent in the 2008 presidential election, when Barack Obama was elected. (By comparison, overall voter turnout has generally been in the range of 50 to 58 percent in recent decades.) More broadly, the official inclusion of young people into the body politic of the United States has encouraged young people to become more involved in political activism. Young people were prominent in the movement to divest from businesses involved with the apartheid government of South Africa in the 1980s. Since then, college campuses have been centers of activism around issues such as gun violence, climate change, and justice for the lesbian, gay, bisexual, transgender, and queer community.

The ratification of the 15th amendment in the 19th century and of the 26th amendment in the twentieth illustrate the flexibility of the United States Constitution to adapt to changing circumstances. Both amendments changed basic elements of the American political process by broadening the electorate and influenced American society in profound ways. The two amendments demonstrate the ongoing struggle to make America a more democratic nation and a "more perfect Union."

PART III: DOCUMENT-BASED QUESTION

Part A: Short Answer

Document 1

1a According to Henry F. Graff, one reason Pullman workers went on strike was that the Pullman Company announced wage cuts that averaged 25 percent, but it did not make any reductions in rents in its company-owned housing.

This answer receives full credit because it states one reason Pullman workers went on strike.

1b According to Henry F. Graff, one reason President Grover Cleveland was asked to send federal troops to Chicago was that violence had broken out between striking workers and deputies that were being paid by the Pullman Company.

This answer receives full credit because it states one reason President Grover Cleveland was asked to send federal troops to Chicago.

Document 2a and Document 2b

2 Based on the documents, one effect of President Cleveland's decision to send federal troops to end the Pullman strike was that Chicago was beset by violence and chaos as troops and striking workers engaged in violence that resulted in property destruction and at least four deaths.

This answer receives full credit because it states one effect of President Cleveland's decision to send federal troops to end the Pullman strike.

Document 3

3 According to Keith Lass and Greg Rickman, one effect of President Cleveland's decision to support railroad owners during the Pullman strike was that federal courts issued indictments against the leaders of the strike that dealt a major blow to organized labor that would not be reversed for forty years.

This answer receives full credit because it states one effect of President Cleveland's decision to support railroad owners during the Pullman strike.

Document 4a, Document 4b, and Document 4c

4a Based on the documents, one reason World War I veterans marched on Washington, D.C., in 1932 was to demand the immediate and full payment of bonuses that they had been promised for having served in World War I.

This answer receives full credit because it states one reason World War I veterans marched on Washington, D.C., in 1932.

4b Based on the documents, one reason President Herbert Hoover sent the United States Army to remove the Bonus Marchers was that violence had erupted between the marchers and the local Washington, D.C. police.

This answer receives full credit because it states one reason President Herbert Hoover sent the United States Army to remove the Bonus Marchers.

Document 5a and Document 5b

5(1) Based on the documents, one reason many Americans thought the government's action against the veterans was wrong was that the government used gas bombs and flames, which resulted in at least one death and injuries to at least 60 veterans.

5(2) Based on the documents, another reason many Americans thought the government's action against the veterans was wrong was that the veterans did not seem like a revolutionary mob; rather, they appeared to be like most Americans—out of work, poor, and in need of relief.

These answers receive full credit because they state two reasons many Americans thought the government's action against the veterans was wrong.

Document 6

6 According to Paul Dickson and Thomas B. Allen, one impact of the Bonus March was that it raised the issue of fair treatment of veterans and paved the way for the Serviceman's Readjustment Act (GI Bill) for veterans of World War II.

This answer receives full credit because it states one impact of the Bonus March.

Document 7a and Document 7b

7(1) Based on the documents, one reason African-American civil rights leaders called for an end to racial segregation in the armed forces was that African Americans in the military were primarily relegated to menial jobs and were rarely elevated to officer status.

7(2) Based on the documents, another reason African-American civil rights leaders called for an end to racial segregation in the armed forces was that the military was seen as an expression of the democratic values of the United States and that equal participation in such an institution would constitute a powerful argument for full and fair inclusion in civil society.

These answers receive full credit because they state two reasons African-American civil rights leaders called for an end to racial segregation in the armed forces.

Document 8a and Document 8b

8(1) Based on the documents, one result of President Harry Truman's order abolishing segregated "Jim Crow units" in the military was that African-American and white servicemen lived side-by-side at military bases, eating at the same mess-hall tables, socializing at the same bars, and participating in recreational activities together.

8(2) Based on the documents, another result of President Harry Truman's order abolishing segregated "Jim Crow units" in the military was that African-American and white servicemen fought side-by-side in the Korean War.

These answers receive full credit because they state two results of President Harry Truman's order abolishing segregated "Jim Crow units" in the military.

Document 9

9 According to Michael Lee Lanning, one way discrimination against African Americans continued after President Truman's executive order was

that communities adjacent to army bases frequently continued enforcing Jim Crow segregationist practices in regard to housing and education.

This answer receives full credit because it states one way discrimination against African Americans continued after President Truman's executive order.

Part B: Document-Based Essay

The president of the United States can invoke his powers as commander-in-chief of the armed forces to deploy troops to faraway places—such as Korea, Vietnam, and Afghanistan. However, the president can also use his military powers to respond to challenges closer to home. On several occasions the president has deployed troops to quell disturbances in the United States. Such deployments have often generated controversy, as many Americans have the expectation that the military would be used to deal with foreign threats and that local police and national guard troops (under the control of the nation's governors) would respond to domestic situations. Two dramatic and controversial instances of U.S. troops being used at home were President Grover Cleveland's use of troops during the Pullman strike (1892) and President Herbert Hoover's use of troops during the Bonus Army protests (1932).

The long-term historical circumstances that led to President Cleveland's use of federal troops in the Pullman strike include rapid industrialization in the United States and the rise of the union movement in the late 1800s. After the Civil War, entrepreneurs and innovators developed and adapted techniques to mass produce goods. Using interchangeable parts, steam power, the assembly line, scientific management techniques, and other innovations, American companies transformed the production process. Between 1860 and 1910, the value of products manufactured in the United States went up an astonishing ten times. Also, the number of people employed in industrial processes went up dramatically. However, the benefits of this economic growth were not evenly distributed. While the owners of big industrial firms, often referred to as "robber barons" by their critics, grew wealthy, the typical factory operative struggled to make ends meet. To rectify this situation, workers formed unions to collectively press for higher wages and better working conditions. Many workers thought they had a better chance of gaining concessions from owners if they banded together in unions. Unions made demands for better wages, improved conditions, or shorter hours. They could call a strike if their demands were not met by management. Workers did just that—call a strike—at the Pullman Company in 1894.

The Pullman strike was the immediate historical circumstance surrounding President Cleveland's decision to call out federal troops. The Pullman Company, which built railroad cars, cut wages several times in 1893 and 1894 for a total of approximately 25 percent. (Document 1) These wage cuts occurred during the hard times following the Panic of 1893. The country descended into the worst economic depression up to that point, with 1894 being the worst year of the downturn. (Document 1) The wage cuts were not accompanied by any cuts in rent for the workers. Many of the workers lived in the town of Pullman, built by the Pullman Company in 1880 as a model company town. The housing was better than most working-class housing, but was also approximately 25 percent costlier than housing in neighboring towns. (Document 1) Rents, as well as expenses for supplies from the company store, were taken directly out of the workers' wages.

When workers protested the wage cuts, the Pullman Company closed the plant. (Document 1) Under these circumstances, the workers appealed to the American Railway Union (ARU), led by Eugene V. Debs, to come to their aid. The Pullman strike went from being a local conflict to a national conflict when ARU members across the nation voted to support the strike by refusing to handle trains that contained Pullman cars. Railroad traffic was brought to a standstill. The company then had the idea of coupling each train with at least one car carrying the U.S. mail. In this way, the company could accuse the union of interfering with the delivery of the mail (a federal crime) and could count on the federal government to intervene. (Document 1)

At first, President Cleveland was reluctant to send in troops, but the company pressed the issue by convincing the attorney general to send in special deputies (paid for by the company). Violence ensued between the deputies and the strikers. At this point, the company successfully pushed Cleveland to send troops. (Document 1) The presence of troops worsened an already tense situation. The troops were greeted with four days of rioting. Seven hundred railroad cars were burned, the grounds of the recently closed Chicago's World's Fair were destroyed, several strikers were shot, and chaos ensued. (Documents 2a and 2b) Eventually, twenty-five strikers would be killed in the violence surrounding the Pullman strike.

President Cleveland's actions influenced events in the short term and in the long term. In the short term, the presence of the troops ended the strike in a bitter defeat for the union. The Supreme Court declared Cleveland's actions legal and justified in its decision in *In re Debs* (1895). In the long term, Cleveland's actions influenced American society by dealing a major blow to organized labor. It became clear that, when push came to shove, the federal government would come down firmly on "the capital side," even when it meant

U.S. troops firing upon and killing U.S. citizens. Furthermore, the courts took the lead of the president. Federal courts issued a sweeping indictment against the ARU and the leaders of the strike. (Document 3) The case went to the Supreme Court, which declared Cleveland's actions legal and justified in its decision in *In re Debs* (1895). The setback suffered by the labor movement in the aftermath of Cleveland's actions would be felt for another four decades. It would not be until the New Deal, according to historians Keith Ladd and Greg Rickman, that the labor movement would recover from the events around the Pullman strike. In 1935, President Franklin D. Roosevelt signed the Wagner Act, which strengthened unions by mandating that employers bargain with their unions. (Document 3) The act also established the National Labor Relations Board to conduct elections among workers to see if they wanted to be represented by a union. The act also banned certain unfair labor practices.

During the Great Depression, which lasted from 1929 to the beginning of World War II, the military was again called upon to deal with a domestic situation. President Herbert Hoover called on U.S. troops to disperse the Bonus March protestors who had set up an encampment in the nation's capital. The long-term historical circumstance of the actions in Washington, D.C., was the Great Depression. Starting in 1929, the economy began a descent into the worst economic crisis of the nation's history, surpassing the downturn following the Panic of 1892. Between 1929 and 1933, wages fell by 60 percent and unemployment tripled to over 12 million. With no safety net in place, families were forced out of their homes. Most cities had makeshift communities of shacks known derisively as "Hoovervilles." People picked through garbage cans for food and formed long lines at soup kitchens. People who had managed to save some money in the 1920s frequently lost their savings when banks failed.

The Great Depression was the backdrop to the more immediate circumstance surrounding the Bonus March—the demands of a group of veterans from World War I for promised bonuses following their military service. (Document 4c) Though the bonuses were not to be distributed until 1945, these men were in a desperate situation and wanted their money immediately. The House of Representatives was supportive of their demands. It voted to take up a bill to allow for the immediate payment of the veterans' bonuses, and it was all set to pass such a bill. However, the marchers had fewer friends in the Senate, which rejected the measure. (Document 4c) The president indicated that he would veto such a bill if it came before him. The press was also hostile to the Bonus Marchers.

The Bonus Marchers set up an encampment on the Anacostia Flats in Washington, D.C., and were allowed to maintain their encampment for several weeks. (Document 4a) But, by the end of July, President Hoover had had enough, especially after violence occurred between the protesters and the local police. (Document 4b) He informed the secretary of war that he wanted the encampment "evicted." The *Washington Post* reported that the army moved in on the Bonus Army using tear gas and force. Very quickly, one marcher was killed and sixty were injured as the army "routed" the Bonus Army and burned their shacks. (Document 5a) The secretary of war ordered General Douglas MacArthur to carry out the evacuation of the Bonus Marchers' camp. (Document 5b)

The immediate influence of Hoover's actions against the Bonus Marchers was that it damaged his reputation. The image of current members of the military taking up arms against former members of the military angered many Americans. Hoover was held responsible for the violence against the Bonus Marchers. The handling of the Bonus Marchers seemed to reinforce many people's perception of President Hoover that he did not have the interests of ordinary Americans at heart. The American people "needed an ally," according to historians Peter Jennings and Todd Brewster, and Hoover was not that person. Hoover's handling of the Bonus Marchers was one of the key factors that led to his losing the election of 1932 to Franklin D. Roosevelt. (Document 5b)

In the long run, the outcome of the Bonus March incident influenced the way American society treated its veterans. After seeing the veterans of World War I treated in a shabby manner, many Americans were resolved to not make the same error in regard to the veterans of World War II. In 1944, Congress passed the GI Bill, formally known as the Servicemen's Readjustment Act, to provide low-interest loans for veterans to purchase homes as well as funds to attend college. The intent of the GI Bill was to help the veterans of World War II adjust to life during peacetime. The program was very successful. Over the decades, it has helped millions of veterans advance economically. (Document 6)

Hoover's handling of the Bonus March was a setback for the veterans involved, but the episode established a pattern of people descending on Washington, D.C., to make their voices heard and to demand change. Historians Paul Dickson and Thomas B. Allen note that "millions of Americans" have followed in the footsteps of the Bonus March. (Document 6) In many ways, the same is true of the Pullman strike. Though the handling of it by President Cleveland dealt a setback to the cause of workers' rights, the strike would inspire other workers in the 20th century to take similar actions. By the 1930s, workers won the right to organize a union and to collectively bargain with their employers.

In both episodes—federal troops suppressing the Pullman strike and federal troops ousting the Bonus Marchers—ideas that were initially dismissed by government officials and much of the public as radical or impractical were later embraced by American society as the fair and decent thing to do. The Pullman strikers' insistence that workers be allowed to engage in collective bargaining and the Bonus Marchers' demand that the government provide veterans with funds to readjust to civilian life were violently rejected at first by the actions of federal troops, but in the ensuing decades came to be seen as commonplace provisions.

Topic	Question Numbers	*Number of Points
American political history	9, 11, 20, 22, 29, 34, 46, 50	10
Economic theory/policy	2, 13, 15, 28, 30, 31	7
Constitutional principles	3, 4, 8, 12, 17, 42, 49	8
American foreign policy	5, 7, 19, 21, 23, 32, 33, 36, 38, 39, 40, 44, 45, 48	17
American studies—the American people	10, 14, 16, 18, 24, 25, 35, 37, 41, 43, 47	13
Social/cultural developments	26, 27	2
Geography	1, 6	2
Skills questions included in the above content areas		
Reading comprehension	15, 17, 22, 26, 38, 39, 49, 50	
Graph/chart/table interpretation	14, 30, 31, 43	
Cartoon/image interpretation	16, 20, 24, 25, 34, 46	

*Note: The 50 questions in Part I are worth a total of 60 percent of the exam. Since each correct answer is worth 60/50 or 1.2 points, totals are shown to the nearest full point in each content category.

PART I

Multiple-Choice Questions by Standard

Standard	Question Numbers
1—United States and New York History	3, 5, 7, 10, 11, 13, 16, 19, 21, 22, 23, 25, 26, 27, 31, 32, 33, 40, 41, 46, 48
2—World History	36, 38, 39, 44
3—Geography	1, 6, 37, 47
4—Economics	14, 15, 18, 24, 28, 30, 34, 35, 43, 45
5—Civics, Citizenship, and Government	2, 4, 8, 9, 12, 17, 20, 29, 42, 49, 50

Parts II and III by Theme and Standard

	Theme	Standards
Thematic Essay	Change; Citizenship; Civic Values; Constitutional Principles; Diversity; Government; Individuals, Groups, Institutions; Reform Movements	Standards 1, 4, and 5: United States and New York History; Economics; Civics, Citizenship, and Government
Document-Based Essay	Citizenship; Civic Values; Constitutional Principles; Diversity; Government; Individuals, Groups, Institutions; Presidential Decisions and Actions	Standards 1, 4, and 5: United States and New York History; Economics; Civics, Citizenship, and Government